Theologians
of the Baptist Tradition

Theologians
of the Baptist Tradition

Timothy George and
David S. Dockery, Editors

BROADMAN
&HOLMAN
PUBLISHERS

NASHVILLE, TENNESSEE

0–8054–1772–9

Published by Broadman & Holman Publishers, Nashville, Tennessee

Dewey Decimal Classification: 230
Subject Heading: BAPTIST THEOLOGIANS

Unless otherwise noted, Scripture quotations are from the Holy Bible, New International Version, © copyright 1973, 1978, 1984.

Library of Congress Cataloging-in-Publication Data
Theologians of the Baptist tradition / Timothy George and David S.
   Dockery, editors.—Rev. ed.
    p. cm.
   Rev. ed. of: Baptist theologians. c1990.
   Includes bibliographical references.
   ISBN 0–8054–1772–9
   1. Baptists—Doctrines—History. 2. Theologians. I. George,
Timothy. II. Dockery, David S. III. Baptist theologians.
   BX6331.2 .B29 2001
   230'.6'0922—dc21
                                    2001025126
1 2 3 4 5 6 7 8 9 10 05 04 03 02 01

in piam memoriam

Bessie Jane Hamel
(1892–1968)
and
Pansye Pierson Dockery
(1925–1999)

Contents

Contributors

Timothy George is the Founding Dean of Beeson Divinity School of Samford University and Senior Editor of *Christianity Today*. He holds degrees from the University of Tennessee at Chattanooga (A.B.), Harvard Divinity School (M.Div.), and Harvard University (Th.D.). A prolific author, he has written and edited numerous articles and books, including *John Robinson and the English Separatist Tradition; Theology of the Reformers; Faithful Witness: The Life and Mission of William Carey; Amazing Grace: God's Initiative, Our Response;* and the New American Commentary volume on *Galatians*. He is a member of the Board of Trustees of Wheaton College and also serves on the Boards of Prison Fellowship Ministries, The Center for Catholic and Evangelical Theology, and *Books and Culture: A Christian Review*. He also chairs the theological education commission of the Baptist World Alliance. He and his wife Denise have two teenage children, Christian and Alyce.

R. Phillip Roberts is President of Midwestern Baptist Theological Seminary in Kansas City, Missouri. A native of Ohio, he holds degrees from Georgetown College (B.A.), Southern Baptist Theological Seminary (M.Div.), and the Free University of Amsterdam (Ph.D.). Dr. Roberts is well-known as an evangelist, pastor, and theological educator. In addition to his service as a professor in two SBC seminaries, he has held academic and church leadership roles in England, Belgium, Germany, Romania, and Russia. A prolific author, he has written numerous articles and books, including *Continuity and Change: London Calvinistic Baptists and the Evangelical Revival,* and *Mormonism Unmasked*.

Mark E. Dever is Pastor of Capitol Hill Baptist Church in Washington, D.C. A native of Kentucky, he holds degrees from Duke University (B.A.), Gordon-Conwell Theological Seminary (M.Div.), Southern Baptist Theological Seminary (Th.M.), and Cambridge University (Ph.D.). A popular speaker and writer, Dever has been a visiting professor at Samford University's Beeson Divinity School and Southern Seminary in Louisville. His writings include *Nine Marks of a Healthy Church,* and *Richard Sibbes: Puritanism and Calvinism in Late Elizabethan and Early Stuart England*. In addition to his pastoral responsibilities, Dever serves as Senior Fellow for the Center for Church Reform in Washington.

David S. Dockery is President of Union University in Jackson, Tennessee. A native of Alabama, he holds degrees from the University of Alabama at Birmingham (B.S.), Grace Theological Seminary (M.Div.), Southwestern Baptist Theological Seminary (M.Div.), Texas Christian University (M.A.), and the University of Texas-Arlington (Ph.D.). He is a member of numerous professional associations, including the Society of Biblical Literature, the Institute for Biblical Research, and the Evangelical Theological Society. In addition to coediting *Baptist Theologians,* he has written and edited many other publications, including *People of God: Essays on the Believers' Church; Holman Bible Handbook; Foundations for Biblical Interpretation; Southern Baptists and American Evangelicals; The Challenge of Postmodernism: An Evangelical Engagement and Christian Scripture: An Evangelical Perspective on Inspiration, Authority and Interpretation.* He is also a contributing editor for *Christianity Today* and Associate General Editor of the New American Commentary.

Lewis A. Drummond is the Billy Graham Professor of Evangelism at Beeson Divinity School of Samford University. A native of Dixon, Illinois, he holds degrees from Samford University (A.B.), Southwestern Baptist Theological Seminary (B.D., Th.M.), and the University of London (Ph.D.). A renowned evangelist and theological educator, Dr. Drummond is a former President of Southeastern Baptist Theological Seminary. He is the author of twenty-two books, including *The Word of the Cross: A Contemporary Theology of Evangelism; Eight Keys to Biblical Revival; The Awakening That Must Come; Life Can Be Real;* and biographical studies of Charles G. Finney, Charles H. Spurgeon, Bertha Smith, Henry Drummond, and (with Betty Drummond) *Women of Awakenings.* He has served as President of the Academy of Professors of Evangelism and is a member of the Evangelical Philosophical Society and the Royal Institute of Philosophy.

Greg Alan Thornbury is Associate Professor of Christian Studies at Union University in Jackson, Tennessee, where he also serves as Director of the Center for Christian Leadership. A native of Pennsylvania, he holds degrees from Messiah College (B.A.), and Southern Baptist Theological Seminary (M.Div., Ph.D.). He has contributed articles on hermeneutics and Baptist historiography to the *Southern Baptist Journal of Theology* and is coeditor (with Paul R. House) of *Who Will Be Saved?* He is a member of the Evangelical Theological Society and a Fellow of the Center for Church Reform in Washington, D.C.

James Spivey is Associate Professor of Church History at Southwestern Baptist Theological Seminary. A native of Alabama, he holds degrees from Auburn University (B.A.), Southwestern Baptist Theological Seminary (M.Div.), and Oxford University (D.Phil.). In addition to serving as a pastor and professor, Spivey has had a distinguished career as a chaplain in the armed forces. He has contributed articles and essays in various publications, including *Dictionary of Christianity in America* and *Biblical Hermeneutics: A Comprehensive Introduction to Biblical Interpretation.*

Fisher Humphreys is Professor of Divinity at Beeson Divinity School of Samford University. A native of Mississippi, he holds degrees from Mississippi College (B.A.), Loyola University (M.A.), Oxford University (M.Litt.), and New Orleans Baptist Theological Seminary (M.Div.; Th.D.). A prolific author, Humphreys has contributed many articles and reviews to various journals and has written eight books, including *The Heart of Prayer, The Nature of God, Thinking about God, Southern Baptist Heritage, The Death of Christ,* and *The Way We Were.* He is also the editor of *Nineteenth Century Evangelical Theology.* A popular teacher and speaker, Humphreys has also served as Distinguished Visiting Professor at the University of Alabama at Birmingham.

James Leo Garrett Jr. is Distinguished Professor of Theology Emeritus at Southwestern Baptist Theological Seminary. A native of Waco, Texas, he holds degrees from Baylor University (B.A.), Southwestern Baptist Theological Seminary (B.D., Th.D.), Princeton Theological Seminary (Th.M.), and Harvard University (Ph.D.). A renowned Baptist theologian and churchman, Garrett has been a leader in numerous academic and ecumenical initiatives, including service as Chair of the Division of Study and Research of the Baptist World Alliance. He has written and edited thirteen books, including *Baptist Church Discipline, The Concept of the Believers' Church, We Baptists,* and a two-volume *Systematic Theology.* He holds membership in several professional societies, including the Conference on Faith and History, the Southern Baptist Historical Society, and the American Society of Church History.

Paige Patterson is President of Southeastern Baptist Theological Seminary in Wake Forest, North Carolina, and past President of the Southern Baptist Convention. A native of Fort Worth, Texas, he holds degrees from Hardin-Simmons University (B.A.), and New Orleans Baptist Theological Seminary (Th.M., Th.D.). He has written numerous articles and books, including *Living in Hope of Eternal Life* and *Heaven* (with W. A. Criswell). Patterson has served as a Trustee of the SBC's International Mission Board and holds membership in several professional associations, including the American Academy of Religion and the Evangelical Theological Society.

Robert B. Sloan Jr. is President of Baylor University. A native Texan, he holds degrees from Baylor University (B.A.), Princeton Theological Seminary (M.Div.), and the University of Basel, Switzerland (Th.D.). A well-known New Testament scholar, Sloan is a member of the Society of Biblical Literature, the Institute for Biblical Research, the National Association of Baptist Professors of Religion and Studiorum Novi

Nestamenti Societas. He is the author of two books, *Discovering I Corinthians* and *The Favorable Year of the Lord* and has edited and contributed to many scholarly journals and publications. Before assuming the presidency of Baylor, Sloan served as Founding Dean of George W. Truett Theological Seminary.

R. Albert Mohler Jr. is President of the Southern Baptist Theological Seminary in Louisville, Kentucky. A native of Florida, he holds degrees from Samford University (B.A.) and Southern Seminary (M.Div., Ph.D.). He serves as Editor-in-Chief of the *Southern Baptist Journal of Theology* and has edited and contributed chapters to several books, including *The Coming Evangelical Crisis, Here We Stand: A Call from Confessing Evangelicals,* and *The Gods of the Age and the God of the Ages: Essays by Carl F. H. Henry.* A well-known columnist and commentator, Mohler contributes regularly to Religion News Service and *World* magazine.

Paul A. Basden is Pastor of Brookwood Baptist Church in Birmingham, Alabama. A native of Dallas, Texas, he holds degrees from Baylor University (B.A.), and Southwestern Baptist Theological Seminary (M.Div., Ph.D.). He has edited (with David S. Dockery) *The People of God: Essays on the Believers' Church* and *Has Our Theology Changed? Southern Baptists Thoughts Since 1845.* He has also written *The Worship Maze.* Dr. Basden regularly serves as an adjunctive professor at Beeson Divinity School of Samford University.

Bradley G. Green is Assistant Professor of Christian Studies at Union University in Jackson, Tennessee. He holds degrees from Northeast Louisiana University (B.A.), Southern Baptist Theological Seminary (M.Div.), Southwestern Baptist Theological Seminary (Th.M.), and Baylor University (Ph.D.). He is a contributor to the volume *New Testament Interpretation* and is currently working on a study of Augustine and the Trinity.

Preface

"WHOEVER WRITES A BOOK SEEMS BY CUSTOM OBLIGED TO WRITE A PREFACE to it; wherein it is expected, he should show the motive which induced him to write the same." So declared Thomas Crosby in 1738 in the opening lines of his four-volume study of *The History of the English Baptist*s.

We can trace the origin and motive of this book to a cemetery. One summer afternoon in 1987, the two of us walked together through Cave Hill Cemetery in Louisville, Kentucky, where several of the theologians featured in this volume lie buried. We discussed the debt each of us felt to the rich theological legacy of these and other great saints of God. We lamented the fact that so many Baptist giants of days gone by were either no longer remembered at all or, at best, relegated to the realm of affectionate obscurity. We determined to collect a volume of essays we hoped would serve as a resource for pastors, students, and teachers, an introduction to the life and thought of some of the most notable shapers of Baptist theology.

When we mentioned to a colleague that we were considering bringing out a book on Baptist theologians, he replied with something of a smirk, "Well, that shouldn't take you very long. It will surely be a slender volume!" As a matter of fact, the predecessor to this book, published in 1990, contained thirty-five chapters and more than seven hundred pages. One reviewer commented: "*Baptist Theologians* demonstrates forcefully that, while there may never have existed a single 'Baptist mind,' there certainly have existed many outstanding Baptist minds. Baptists should read it to gain a better sense of who they are, others to discover an underappreciated contribution to Christianity's theological heritage." We know that many people did read the book and found it helpful in just this way. It has been adopted as a textbook in college and seminary classes and is still frequently cited as a standard reference work in the field. Now, ten years later, we are pleased to offer this new, updated, and substantially reshaped edition, now titled *Theologians of the Baptist Tradition*.

Before explaining the new arrangement of this volume, we should say a word about the differing contexts of these two editions. In 1990 the Southern Baptist Convention was embroiled in a major theological brouhaha known to many of its participants simply as "the Controversy." This major church struggle sent shock waves not only throughout America's largest Protestant denomination but also within the wider Baptist and evangelical family. We have both published our own perspectives on the Controversy elsewhere and shall not repeat those ideas here. Suffice it to say that it was our original hope that *Baptist Theologians* might contribute to the healing and renewal of the denomination we love and to which we belong.

During the past ten years, we have been involved in various conversations, study projects, and face-to-face encounters aimed at seeking a principled reconciliation. We remain convinced that the SBC needed a serious redirection toward its biblical and evangelical roots, and we are grateful that this has happened in some measure. But we also believe that how we act and relate to one another within the body of Christ is no less important than the theology we profess and the beliefs we champion. Indeed, they are inextricably linked, for true revival and spiritual awakening will only come in the context of repentance, humility, and forgiveness. We still hope for what we called in the preface to the first edition "the miracle of dialogue— not a raucous shouting at one another, nor a snide whispering behind each other's backs, but a genuine listening and learning in the context of humane inquiry and disciplined thought." Though the Controversy is receding into history, as well it should, we still sense the urgent need for the kind of substantive historical and theological engagement that has always been central to the cultivation of a vibrant Christian orthodoxy. As the essays in this volume show, this has been a distinctive mark of the Baptist tradition at its best.

Most, though not all, of the theologians surveyed in this volume have lived and worked within the context of the Southern Baptist Convention. Every one of them has been a formative shaper of that tradition. We are well aware that the word *Baptist* is not exhausted by the SBC. There are some forty-five million Baptists around the globe related to the Baptist World Alliance and countless other independent congregations and baptistic movements unaffiliated with official denominational structures. A very different volume of essays could, and we think should, be gathered profiling Baptist theologians from Europe, Latin America, Africa, Asia, and Australia. We think it is important for Southern Baptists to see themselves and their theological heritage in the context of this wider Baptist fellowship and the world Christian movement. Even in North America, the makeup of the predominately white SBC is progressively changing with the influx of African-American and other ethnic congregations. Southern Baptist theology in the future will be greatly enriched by these new faces and new voices. In this volume, however, we focus on those theologians whose writings and witness have decisively shaped the Southern Baptist theological tradition as it is today. Even so, for lack of space we have had to omit many worthy representatives, including a sizeable number who were included in the first edition.

The essays in this volume also raise another question: What is the future of Baptist theology in an increasingly postdenominational world? Do the Baptists have anything to say that no one else can say? A growing number of Baptist congregations in North America no longer use the label Baptist in presenting themselves to their communities. Some younger Baptist theologians are enamored with postmodernism and its tendency in some forms to blur not only historic Baptist distinctives but even the foundational truths of the Christian faith itself. As the studies of Robert Wuthnow and others have shown, a major realignment has taken place on the North American religious landscape so that many Christians, liberals and evangelicals alike, now share deeper affinities with like-minded believers outside their own denomination than with those within who wear the same label but march to a different drummer. Two examples of this phenomenon from recent SBC history are illuminating. In 1994 the SBC commended a Roman Catholic nun, Mother Teresa, for her stirring rebuke of (Southern Baptist!) President Bill Clinton and voted to include the text of her speech on the sanctity of human life in its official record. And in 1998 the closing message at the SBC annual meeting was delivered by Dr. James Dobson, a Nazarene. Neither of these events would have been conceivable thirty years ago, much less during the era in which most of the figures surveyed in this volume lived and wrote.

We ourselves are committed to a healthy ecumenism that seeks to foster mutual understanding without compromising biblical truth. We think it is a good thing for Southern Baptists to make common cause with other Bible-believing Christians for the furtherance of the gospel through joint efforts in missions, evangelism, and moral witness in the public square. But we have not given up on the Baptist tradition. Indeed, we believe that Baptists can make a stronger contribution to the wider Christian movement by being more fully aware and anchored in their own heritage, including the rich legacy of Baptist theology and piety discussed in this book.

In the first and final chapters of the volume we have set forth our own personal perspectives on the course and future of Baptist theology. Otherwise we have allowed the essays to stand as submitted by our various contributors in hopes that the diversity of theologians considered and interpretations given might stimulate further research and dialogue. Throughout we have been guided by the conviction that seeing how others before us have articulated the Baptist vision will better enable us to formulate a proper theology for our own turbulent times.

Perhaps a word of explanation is in order as to why we have chosen to focus on these particular theologians out of many others who could have been chosen, including some who were treated in our first edition. Early Baptists were legally excluded from the English universities and were slow in developing their own theological academies, the first arising from a fund for ministerial education established at Bristol in 1679. Theology in that age tended to be written by pastors who, if lacking in formal training, were far from unlearned. That epoch of Baptist theology is represented in this volume by John Gill and Andrew Fuller, arguably the two most influential Baptist theologians before the twentieth century. The writings of both Gill and Fuller were reprinted and carefully studied by their fellow Baptists across the Atlantic, and their ideas framed many of the debates carried on in the New World. Both John L. Dagg and James P. Boyce wrote systematic theologies that were used as textbooks in Baptist colleges and seminaries. Boyce reflects the Calvinistic theology of his Princeton mentor, Charles Hodge, while Dagg, equally Reformed in his convictions, writes in a more pastoral tone with an emphasis in the direction of practical application.

In the late-nineteenth century Charles Haddon Spurgeon was a Baptist colossus whose sermons and ministry at the famous Metropolitan Tabernacle in London made a great impact around the world. Spurgeon's "all-round ministry" was matched by his balanced theology that emphasized both God's sovereignty in salvation and human responsibility. Near the end of his life, he became embroiled in the famous Downgrade Controversy, warning his fellow Baptists against the corrosive influence of destructive biblical criticism. At Spurgeon's death in 1892, B. H. Carroll paid the following tribute: "He combined the preaching power of Jonathan Edwards and Whitfield with the organizing power of Wesley, and the energy, fire, and courage of Luther. In answer to the question: 'How do you account for Spurgeon?' The answer is the monosyllable: 'God.'"

John A. Broadus and his son-in-law, A. T. Robertson, together taught for seventy-five uninterrupted years at The Southern Baptist Theological Seminary in Louisville. Broadus was the greater preacher and Robertson the greater New Testament scholar, although both were passionately committed to serious study of the Scriptures and faithful proclamation of God's Word. Both were also denominational statesmen and molders of a scholarly conservative consensus that prevailed through the early decades of the twentieth century. B. H. Carroll, the Texas Ranger turned seminary founder, was in many ways a stark contrast to the erudite Broadus. Yet perhaps no Baptist leader since Oncken in Germany has had such a dominating influence on a given region as Carroll had in Texas and the Southwest. Some of his eschatological ideas have fallen out of favor with later generations, but his unflappable commitment to the truthfulness of Scripture and his passion for evangelism have left an indelible mark on the Southern Baptist soul.

Augustus H. Strong and E. Y. Mullins were the two premier Baptist theologians of the early twentieth century. Both wrote systematic theologies and both served long tenures as presidents of influential Baptist seminaries. Both were also deeply learned and widely read in the literature of the day, including developments in science and philosophy. Perhaps the term "progressive conservatism" best summarizes their approach to Baptist theology. Both Strong and Mullins died in the 1920s just as the Fundamentalist-Modernist Controversy was reaching its zenith. After Strong's death, Northern Baptists suffered several major splits and a sharp loss of membership and influence in the culture. Under Mullins's leadership, Baptists in the South published their first denomination-wide confession of faith in 1925 and united around the themes of missions and evangelism. Some of the issues, however, which were latent in the Mullins's era surfaced again among Southern Baptists in the latter third of the twentieth century. In the meantime, Mullins's constructive theology was carried forward by W .T. Conner, who had studied both with Strong at Rochester and Mullins at Louisville. Conner interacted with trends in Roman Catholic thought as well as the theology of Karl Barth, but he is best remembered as an exemplary teacher of his own conservative biblical theology.

Herschel H. Hobbs and W. A. Criswell were lifelong friends from their student days together in Louisville. Like Gill, Fuller, and Spurgeon, these two great leaders were pastor-theologians. While Criswell is sometimes portrayed as the "godfather" of the conservative resurgence in the SBC, both he and Hobbs consistently advocated biblical inerrancy and warned against dangerous deviations from historic Baptist beliefs. In his later years, Hobbs sought to be a reconciler among the various factions in the SBC. Criswell's persistent advocacy of dispensationalist premillennialism has helped to make it the most popular eschatological view among Southern Baptists today.

The 1990 edition of *Baptist Theologians* included chapters on Eric Rust, Dale Moody, Clark H. Pinnock, and Frank Stagg, all brilliant thinkers who have contributed significantly to Baptist theologizing during the latter half of the twentieth century. Pinnock is the most interesting of this group because of the radical shifts in his theology over the years. Moody and Rust were both constructive thinkers and controversial figures in their day, introducing Southern Baptists to new and challenging patterns of thought from England and the Continent. However, in this edition we have chosen Frank Stagg to represent what might be called the progressivist wing of Southern Baptist theology. A biblical scholar rather than a systematic theologian, Stagg championed racial reconciliation and equality for women in ministry, while some of his other ideas pushed beyond the bounds of what most Baptists regarded as historic Christian orthodoxy.

Carl F. H. Henry, James Leo Garrett, and Millard Erickson all represent the confluence of Southern Baptist and evangelical theologies in the latter decades of the twentieth century. Henry was a member of the original faculty at Fuller Theological Seminary and the founding editor of *Christianity Today*. Yet he had been a Baptist since his conversion to Christ in early adulthood. His six-volume *God, Revelation and Authority* remains the most sustained theological epistemology by any American evangelical theologian. Garrett's two-volume *Systematic Theology* carries the subtitle *Biblical, Historical, and Evangelical*. It is a masterful compendium of historical theology that interacts with the entire history of doctrine. Garrett is also important for his participation in the joint project *Are Southern Baptists "Evangelicals"?* While others demurred, Garrett answered affirmatively, demonstrating important historical connections between Southern Baptists and the wider evangelical community. Millard Erickson is one of the most prolific evangelical theologians of the late-twentieth century. His many writings cover a wide range of theological themes. His recent interactions with "left-wing evangelicals" and "postmodern evangelicals" show his desire to stay in touch with current trends and emerging issues in theology. Erickson is also important as a bridging figure among various constituencies. Longtime dean at Bethel Seminary in St. Paul, Minnesota, an institution affiliated with the Baptist General Conference, Erickson has taught in recent years at Southwestern Baptist Theological Seminary and at Baylor University's Truett Theological Seminary. His gentle spirit and scholarly wisdom have enabled him to transcend barriers and contribute to evangelical dialogues from several Baptist bases.

This book is dedicated *in piam memorian* to two women who will never be written about in any theological handbook: Pansye Pierson Dockery (David's mother) and Bessie Jane Hamel (Timothy's grandmother). One was largely self-educated; the other could barely read. But they taught us many precious things without the knowledge of which all our subsequent theological training would have been useless: that God is good, that the Bible is true, that Jesus saves, and that love casts out all fear. They also took us to church and taught us to cherish the Baptist tradition. They were our Lois and Eunice, and we remember them with affection and esteem.

David S. Dockery
Timothy George

1

The Future of Baptist Theology

By Timothy George

SEVERAL YEARS AGO WILL D. CAMPBELL PUBLISHED A FASCINATING NOVEL entitled *The Glad River*. The chief character is a man named Doops Momber. Actually his real name was Claudy Momber, but everybody called him Doops because Claudy sounded too much like a girl's name. He grew up among the Baptists of Mississippi, attended the revivals, the hayrides, and the Sunday school wiener roasts, but somehow he never got baptized. Later, when he was inducted into the army, his sergeant asked, "You a Protestant or a Catholic?" Doops did not answer for a moment. Then he said, "I guess I'm neither. I'm neither Catholic nor Protestant. I never joined. But all my people are Baptist." "But there's a P on your dog tag. Why not a C?" "They asked me what I was and I told them the same thing I told you. And the guy stamped a P on it." "Why do you suppose they did that?" the sergeant asked. "Well," said Doops, "I guess in America you have to be something."[1]

The confusion Doops encountered about his own religious identity is symptomatic of many other Baptist Christians who, unlike Doops, have indeed taken the plunge but who, no more than he, have any solid understanding about what that means in a postdenominational age of generic religion and dog-tags Christianity. In the first edition of *Baptist Theologians*, I wrote an opening essay entitled "The Renewal of Baptist Theology," which began with the following lamentation.

> There is a crisis in Baptist life today that cannot be resolved by bigger budgets, better programs, or more sophisticated systems of data processing and mass communication. It is a crisis of identity rooted in a fundamental theological failure of nerve. The two major diseases of the contemporary church are spiritual amnesia (we have forgotten who we are) and ecclesiastical myopia (whoever we are, we are glad we are not like "them"). While these maladies are not unique to the people of God called Baptists, they are perhaps most glaringly present among us.[2]

1

This article is a sequel to that earlier essay. First of all, I want to point out some of the difficulties in speaking about the theological identity of Baptists. Then, in the heart of the paper, I will present a mosaic for the renewal of Baptist theology by identifying five major components for such an agenda.

Diversity and Adversity

The first problem in sorting out the theological identity of Baptists is the sheer diversity of the movement. From the beginning of the Baptist experiment in seventeenth-century England, General (Arminian) and Particular (Calvinistic) Baptists developed diverse, even mutually incompatible, paradigms for what it meant to be a Baptist. The Particulars, who were better educated, better organized, and more successful than the Generals, forged alliances with other mainstream Dissenting bodies, denying that they were in any way guilty of "those heterodoxies and fundamental errors" that had been unfairly attributed to them.[3] The Generals, on the other hand, were drawn into the orbit of that "swarm of sectaries and schismatics," as John Taylor put it, which included Levellers, Ranters, Seekers, Quakers, and, at the very far end of the Puritan movement, the mysterious Family of Love. It was, as Christopher Hill has called it, a world turned upside down. An anonymous rhymester may well have had the General Baptists in mind when he penned these lines in 1641: "When women preach and cobblers pray, the fiends in hell make holiday."[4]

The diversification of the Baptist tradition that began in England was accelerated in America where the great fact of national life was the frontier—a seemingly endless expanse of space that offered limitless opportunities for escaping the past. "If you and yours don't agree with me and mine, you can pack your Scofield Bibles in your hip pocket and start your own church!" And so they did. And the line stretches from Roger Williams, who left Massachusetts to practice soul-liberty in Rhode Island, to Brigham Young, who carried the Mormons to Utah, to Jim Jones in California and David Koresh in Waco. The frontier was always there.

As for the Baptists, one only has to skim through Mead's *Handbook of Denominations* to appreciate the bewildering variety. Among many others, there are American Baptists, Southern Baptists, National Baptists, United Baptists, Conservative Baptists, General Association of Regular Baptists (GARB), Free Will Baptists, Landmark Baptists, Duck River and Kindred Associations of Baptists, Six-Principle Baptists, Primitive Baptists, Seventh-Day Baptists, Two-Seed-in-the-Spirit Predestinarian Baptists, and the National Baptist Evangelical Life and Soul-Saving Assembly of the USA, Inc.! That's a lot of Baptists! How do you talk about theological identity amidst that kind of variety?

There's a second factor we also need to consider—not only *diversity* within the tradition but *adversity* from the environing culture. While Baptists in America, especially in the South, have long been accustomed to the accoutrements of an established religion, they began as a small, persecuted sect. Long after the 1689 Act of Toleration granted statutory freedom of worship, Baptists, along with other Nonconformists in England, suffered harassment, discrimination, and ridicule. One critic labelled them as "miscreants begat in rebellion, born in sedition, and nursed in faction."[5] The struggles for religious liberty continued for Baptists in America where Obadiah Holmes was publicly beaten on the streets of Danvers, Massachusetts, and John Leland was clapped up in a Virginia jail.

An example of the low esteem in which Baptist folk were held in the early nineteenth century was recorded by David Benedict, who traveled by horseback through all seventeen states of the new nation collecting historical information and impressions about the Baptists. One person, "a very honest and candid old lady," gave Benedict the following impression she had formed of the Baptists:

> There was a company of them in the back part of our town, and an outlandish set of people they certainly were. . . . You could hardly find one among them but what was deformed in some way or other. Some of them were hair-lipped, others were bleary-eyed, or hump-backed, or bow-legged, or clump-footed; hardly any of them looked like other people. But they were all strong for plunging, and let their poor ignorant children run wild, and never had the seal of the covenant put on them.[6]

Despite diversity within and adversity without, by the mid-nineteenth century Baptists in America had developed a remarkable unity of purpose and vision, a theological consensus that even cut across the seismic fault line produced by slavery and the Civil War. Thus in 1861, Francis Wayland, a Northern Baptist, could write:

> I do not believe that any denomination of Christians exists, which, for so long a period as the Baptist, have maintained so invariably the truth of their early confessions. . . . The theological tenets of the Baptists, both in England and America, may be briefly stated as follows: they are emphatically the doctrines of the Reformation, and they have been held with singular unanimity and consistency.[7]

Thus despite countless splits and some doctrinal defections (e.g., the lapse of certain Baptists into universalism), there emerged among Baptists in the late-nineteenth, early-twentieth century America what might be called an orthodox Baptist consensus, represented in the North by Augustus H. Strong, in the South by E. Y. Mullins.

One knew instinctively when the bounds of this consensus had been transgressed. Thus in the controversy surrounding the forced departure of Crawford Howell Toy from Southern Seminary in 1879, both Toy himself and the colleagues who bid him a tearful adieu were all aware, as Toy himself put it, that he "no longer stood where most of his brethren did."[8]

Erosion of Theological Consensus

The history of the Baptist movement in the twentieth century could be largely written as the story of the erosion of that theological consensus that obtained in most places until the Fundamentalist-Modernist disputes. In the face of the pressures of this era, the Baptist apologetic made a twofold response, neither of which was really adequate to deal with the challenge at hand. The first response was an appeal to "Baptist distinctives." In part this effort was fueled by old-fashioned denominational braggadocio, as seen in the book *Baptist Why and Why Not* published by the SBC's Baptist Sunday School Board in 1900. Chapter titles include: "Why Baptist and Not Methodist," "Why Baptist and Not Episcopalian," "Why Immersion and Not Sprinkling," "Why Close Communion and Not Open Communion," etc.[9]

Further emphasis on Baptist distinctives such as the separation of church and state, the nonsacramental character of the ordinances, and the noncreedal character of our confessions appeared as a litany of negative constraints, rather than the positive exposition of an essential doctrinal core. Indeed, for some Baptists these so-called distinctives, often interpreted in an attenuated, reductionistic form, became the essence of the Baptist tradition itself.

This consensus was further eroded by what may be called the privatization of Baptist theology. Historically Baptist life was shaped by strong communitarian features. The congregation was not merely an aggregate of like-minded individuals, but rather a body of baptized believers gathered in solemn *covenant* with one another and the Lord. Nor were Baptists doctrinal anarchists who boasted of their "right" to believe in anything they wanted to. Instead of flaunting their Christian freedom in this way, Baptists used it to produce and publish *confessions* of faith both as a means of declaring their own faith to the world and of guarding the theological integrity of their own fellowship.[10] Nor did Baptists want their young children "to think for themselves," as the liberal cliché has it, but instead to be thoroughly grounded in the faith once for all delivered to the saints. Thus they developed Baptist *catechisms* and used them in both home and church to instruct their children in the rudiments of Christian theology.

The communitarian character of Baptist life, exemplified by covenants, confessions, and catechisms, was undermined by the privatization of

Baptist theology and the rising tide of modern rugged individualism that swept through American culture in the early twentieth century. It should be noted that this movement influenced Baptists at both ends of the religious spectrum. Liberal Baptists followed the theological trajectory of Schleiermacher and Ritschl into revisionist models of theology that denied, in some cases, the most fundamental truths of the gospel.[11] At the other extreme, anti-intellectual pietism and emotion-laden revivalism pitted theology against piety, soul religion against a reflective faith, thus producing a split between sound doctrine and holy living. Although Billy Sunday belonged to another denomination, many Baptists could resonate with his assertion that he did not know any more about theology than a jackrabbit knew about Ping-Pong!

What are the benchmarks for shaping Baptist theological identity in the new world of the third millennium? Rather than put forth subtle speculations or a new methodology, I propose that we look again at five classic principles drawn from the wider Baptist heritage. These five affirmations form a cluster of convictions that have seen us through turbulent storms in the past. They are worthy anchors for us to cast into the sea of postmodernity as we seek not merely to weather the storm but to sail with confidence into the future God has prepared for us.

Identity Markers

1. *Orthodox Convictions.* In 1994 the Southern Baptist Convention unanimously adopted a resolution acknowledging that "Southern Baptists have historically confessed with all true Christians everywhere belief in the Triune God, Father, Son, and Holy Spirit, the full deity and perfect humanity of Jesus Christ, His virgin birth, His sinless life, His substitutionary atonement for sins, His resurrection from the dead, His exaltation to the right hand of God, and His triumphal return; and we recognize that born again believers in the Lord Jesus Christ may be found in all Christian denominations." The recognition of common Christian convictions shared by Baptists and other believers has led the Baptist World Alliance to sponsor interconfessional discussions and dialogues with both Roman Catholics and Protestants of several denominational traditions.

Baptists are orthodox Christians who stand in continuity with the dogmatic consensus of the early church on matters such as the scope of Holy Scripture (canon), the doctrine of God (Trinity), and the person and work of Jesus Christ (Christology). Leon McBeth is correct when he observes that Baptists have "often used confessions not to proclaim 'Baptist distinctives' but instead to show how similar Baptists were to other orthodox Christians."[12] Thus the "Orthodox Confession" of 1678 incorporated (article 38) the Apostles', Nicene, and Athanasian creeds, declaring that all three "ought thoroughly to be received, and believed. For we believe, that they may be proved, by most undoubted authority of Holy Scripture and are necessary to be understood of all Christians."[13] Reflecting this same impulse, the Baptists who gathered in London for the inaugural meeting of the Baptist World Alliance in 1905 stood in that assembly and recited in unison the Apostles' Creed.

Fundamentalism arose in the early part of this century as a protest against the concessions and denials of liberal theologians on cardinal tenets such as the virgin birth of Christ, the inerrancy of the Bible, and penal substitutionary atonement. This was a valid and necessary protest, and we should be grateful for those worthy forebearers who stood with courage and conviction on these matters. However, the problem with fundamentalism as a theological movement was its tendency toward reductionism—not what it affirmed, but what it left out. In recent years the inspiration and authority of the Bible have again assumed a major role in Baptist polemics, especially within the Southern Baptist Convention. From the drafting of the *Baptist Faith and Message* in 1963 through the adoption of the *Presidential Theological Study Committee Report* in 1994, Southern Baptists have repeatedly affirmed their confidence in the inerrancy or total truthfulness of Holy Scripture. As the latter report declares, "What the Bible says, God says; what the Bible says happened, really happened; every miracle, every event, in every book of the Old and New Testaments is altogether true and trustworthy."

In more recent years, however, the SBC has found it necessary to address other pressing doctrinal issues such as the being of God and the importance of using biblical language to address him (over against certain models of contemporary feminism), and the belief in Jesus Christ as sole and sufficient Savior (over against universalism and soteriological pluralism). Within the Baptist General Conference, divine omniscience has been debated as certain theologians have denied God's absolute knowledge of the future. All Baptists need to cultivate a holistic orthodoxy, based on a high view of the Scriptures and congruent with the trinitarian and Christological consensus of the early church. Only in this way will we avoid the dangers of rigid reductionism on the one hand and liberal revisionism on the other.

2. *Evangelical Heritage.* Baptists are evangelical Christians who affirm with Martin Luther and John Calvin both the formal and material principles of the Reformation: Scripture alone and justification by faith alone. In setting forth these twin peaks of evangelical faith, the Reformers were not introducing new doctrines or novel ideas. They argued like this: If the doctrine of the Trinity really presents us with the true God of creation and redemption; if Jesus Christ really is what we confess him to be, that is, God from God, Light from Light, very God from very God; and if original sin

is as pervasive and debilitating as we believe it to be, then the doctrine of justification by faith alone is the only faithful interpretation of the New Testament promise of forgiveness, pardon, and new life in Christ. While not agreeing with everything Luther or Calvin taught, Baptists claim the heritage of the Reformation as their own. We gladly identify ourselves with other evangelical believers who are "not ashamed of the gospel of Christ for it is the power of God unto salvation for all who believe" (Rom. 1:16).

The word *evangelical* has a myriad of other meanings as well, and Baptists in North America can rightly claim at least two of these. First, we are heirs of the Evangelical Awakening that swept across the eighteenth century, producing Pietism in Germany, Methodism in England, and the First Great Awakening in the American colonies. Many features of Baptist life resonate deeply with this mighty moving of the Spirit of God. Our evangelistic witness and missionary vision, our historic emphasis on disciplined church life and godly living, our commitment to a regenerate church membership and Spirit-filled worship, our refusal to divorce the personal and social dimensions of the gospel.

More recently, the word *evangelical* has been associated with the postfundamentalist resurgence among Bible-believing Christians in North America. Significantly, the two most formative shapers of this movement are both (Southern) Baptists: Billy Graham and Carl F. H. Henry. Far more important than wearing the "evangelical" label is the substance of the word in the three senses outlined here. Baptists of North America can and should rightly lay claim to the doctrinal legacy of the Reformation, the missionary and evangelistic impulse of the Great Awakening, and a transdenominational fellowship of Bible-believing Christians with whom we share a common commitment to the Word of God and the task of world evangelization.

3. *Reformed Perspective.* Despite a persistent Arminian strain within Baptist life, for much of our history most Baptists adhered faithfully to the doctrines of grace as set forth in Pauline-Augustinian-Reformed theology. David Benedict, following his extensive tour of Baptist churches throughout America in the early nineteenth century, gave the following summary of the Baptist theology he encountered: "Take this denomination at large, I believe the following will be found a pretty correct statement of their views of doctrine. They hold that man in his natural condition is entirely depraved and sinful; but unless he is born again—changed by grace—or made alive unto God—he cannot be fitted for the communion of saints on earth, nor the enjoyment of God in heaven; that where God hath begun a good work, he will carry it on to the end; that there is an election of grace—an effectual calling, etc. and that the *happiness* of the righteous and the misery of the wicked will both be eternal."[4]

When in 1856 James Petigru Boyce set forth his plan for the first Baptist theological seminary in the South, he warned against the twin errors of Campbellism and Arminianism, the distinctive principles of which "have been ingrafted upon many of our churches: and even some of our ministry have not hesitated publicly to avow them."[15]

As late as 1905, F. H. Kerfoot, Boyce's successor as professor of systematic theology at Southern Seminary, could still say, "Nearly all Baptists believe what are usually termed the 'doctrines of grace.'"[16] E. Y. Mullins, who disliked the labels "Calvinist" and "Arminian," sought to transcend the controversy altogether. While retaining most of the content of traditional Calvinist soteriology, he gave it a new casting by restating it in terms of his distinctive theology of experience. A. H. Strong played a similar role among Northern Baptists during this same era.

For some the evangelical Calvinism of earlier Baptist generations has been eclipsed by a truncated hyper-Calvinism with its antimissionary, antievangelistic emphases. Many other factors have also contributed to the blurring of this part of the Reformation heritage that has shaped Baptist identity: the routinization of revivalism, the growth of pragmatism as a denominational strategy, an attenuated doctrine of the Holy Spirit, and a general theological laxity that has resulted in doctrinal apathy. While seeking to restate traditional themes in fresh, contemporary ways, Baptists would do well to connect again with the ideas that inform the theology of such great heroes of the past as John Bunyan, Roger Williams, Andrew Fuller, Adoniram Judson, Luther Rice, and Charles Haddon Spurgeon.

I rejoice in the growing awareness of Reformed theology among many Baptists today. I know of nothing that has happened in the history of salvation since the days of Fuller, Carey, and Spurgeon that would make their understanding of God's grace obsolete in the modern world. To the contrary, a renewed commitment to the sovereignty of God in salvation, worship that centers on the glory of God rather than the entertainment of the audience, and a perspective on history and culture that sees Jesus Christ as Lord of time and eternity—all of this can only result in the building up of the body of Christ. At the same time, it is imperative for Reformed Baptists to guard against the real dangers of hyper-Calvinism, which emphasizes divine sovereignty to the exclusion of human responsibility and which denies that the offer of the gospel is to be extended to all peoples everywhere. We must learn to live in gracious equipoise with some of our brothers and sisters who may not ring all five bells quite the way we do! In this regard we do well to heed the following statement by the great missionary statesman Luther Rice: "How absurd it is, therefore, to contend against the doctrine of election, or decrees, or divine sovereignty. Let us not, however, become bitter against those who view this matter in a different light, nor treat them in a supercilious manner; rather let us be gentle towards all men. For who has made us to differ from what we once were? Who has removed the scales from our eyes?"[17]

4. *Baptist Distinctives*. While Baptists owe much to the great doctrinal legacy of the mainline reformers, our ecclesiology most closely approximates the Anabaptist ideal in its emphasis on the church as an intentional community composed of regenerated and baptized believers who are bound to one another and their Lord by a solemn covenant. One of the most important contributions that Baptists have made to the wider life of the church is the recovery of the early church practice of baptism as an adult rite of initiation signifying a committed participation in the life, death, and resurrection of Jesus Christ. In many contemporary Baptist settings, however, baptism is in danger of being divorced from the context of a decisive life commitment. This unfortunate development is reflected both in the liturgical placement of baptism in the worship service—often tacked on at the end as a kind of afterthought—and also in the proper age and preparation of baptismal candidates. This situation muffles the historic Baptist protest against infant baptism, a protest that insisted on the intrinsic connection between biblical baptism and repentance and faith.[18]

We must also guard against a minimalist understanding of the Lord's Supper, which reduces this vital ordinance to an empty ritual detached from the spiritual life of believers. Several years ago I experienced a powerful service of the Lord's Supper at the First Baptist Church of Dallas, Texas. During a Sunday morning service that great congregation was asked to kneel and prayerfully receive the elements while the meaning of the ordinance was carefully explained from the Scriptures. In this kind of setting the experience of worship is a transforming encounter with the living Christ. We need not fall prey to the lure of sacramentalism or the false doctrine of transubstantiation to reclaim the historic Baptist understanding of the Lord's Supper that has nowhere been better described than in the *Second London Confession* of 1689: "Worthy receivers, outwardly partaking of the visible elements in this ordinance, do then also inwardly by faith, really and indeed, yet not carnally and corporally, but spiritually receive, and feed upon Christ crucified and all the benefits of his death: the Body and Blood of Christ, being then not corporally, or carnally, but spiritually present to the faith of believers, in that ordinance, as the elements themselves are to the outward senses."

5. *Confessional Context*. As Baptists seek to be faithful shapers of the future under the lordship of Jesus Christ, we would do well to remember and reclaim the confessional character of our common Christian commitment. Baptists are not a creedal people, for we regard no humanly devised statement as equal to the Bible. Nor do we believe that the state has any authority to impose religious beliefs on its subjects. However, Baptists have historically approved and circulated confessions of faith for a threefold

purpose: as an expression of our religious liberty, as a statement of our theological convictions, and as a witness of the truths we hold in sacred trust. Our confessions are always accountable to Holy Scripture and revisable in the light of that divine revelation. Just as a confession declares what we believe, so a church covenant is concerned with how we live. It sets forth in practical terms the ideal of the Christian life: a living faith working by love leading to holiness. The congregation's covenant also outlines that process of mutual admonition and responsibility through which fellow believers engage to "watch over" one another through encouragement, correction, and prayer.

Finally, catechesis is concerned with passing on the faith intact to the rising generation. This responsibility is jointly shared by parents and pastors. May God give us again Baptist families and Baptist churches who will take seriously the awesome responsibility of indoctrinating our children in the things of God.

Conclusion

In his *Commentary on Daniel* (9:25), John Calvin compared the work of God among his ancient people with the challenge of his own day. "God still wishes in these days to build his spiritual temple amidst the anxieties of the times. The faithful must still hold the trowel in one hand and the sword in the other, because the building of the church must still be combined with many struggles." That struggle continues today, not against enemies of flesh and blood but against principalities and powers, against lethargy and laziness, against defection and darkness on every hand. Yet God does continue to build his church amidst the anxieties of the times. For nearly four centuries he has blessed and used the people of God called Baptists in ways that future historians will record as remarkable beyond belief. As we remember and give thanks for the mighty acts of God in days gone by, let us press forward in the earnest expectation that the Lord "hath yet more truth and light to break forth out of his Holy Word." Above all, let us never forget that it is "not by might, nor by power, but by my Spirit, saith the Lord."

2
John Gill

By Timothy George

Biography

SHORTLY AFTER THE DEATH OF JOHN GILL IN 1771, AUGUSTUS TOPLADY, famed as the author of the hymn "Rock of Ages," gave the following estimate of the legacy of his deceased friend: "While true religion and sound learning have a single friend remaining in the British Empire, the works and name of GILL will be precious and revered."[1] Toplady's sentiment was echoed by Christian leaders on both sides of the Atlantic who mourned the

11

loss of the greatest Baptist theologian of the eighteenth century. One admirer expressed his grief in verse:

> What doleful tidings strike my list'ning ear,
>   or wound the tender feelings of my heart?
> Must the bright star forever disappear?
>   Must the great Man, the learned Gill depart?
> Zion may mourn, for grief becomes her well.
>   To lose the man whose Heav'n instructed pen
> Taught knowledge clearly, while before him fell
>   Gigantic errors of deluded men.[2]

John Gill was the first Baptist to develop a complete systematic theology and also the first Baptist to write a verse-by-verse commentary on the entire Bible. An indefatigable scholar and writer, "Dr. Voluminous," as he was affectionately called, published more than ten thousand pages during his lifetime, more than many ordinary mortals are able to read over a similar span. Undoubtedly the leading light among the Calvinistic Baptists of his day, Gill influenced an entire generation of younger ministers through his remarkable preaching and pastoral labors, which he discharged faithfully in the same congregation for nearly fifty-two years![3]

Despite these accomplishments, it has not fallen the lot of Gill to be remembered by future generations "as one of the Fathers of the Church," as an early-nineteenth-century historian thought he might.[4] When he is mentioned in standard denominational histories, he is invariably caricatured as the bogeyman of hyper-Calvinism, a dour pedant whose "high and dry" theology single-handedly doused the flames of revival among English Baptists, spawning instead "a spiritual dry-rot" among churches within that fellowship.[5]

We can discern at least three reasons for the prevailing negative assessment of Gill and his legacy. First, like most polemical theologians, Gill was more interested in defending "the cause of God and truth," to quote the title of one of his best-known writings, than in winning friends or influencing people. He attracted ardent adversaries as well as admiring disciples. On one occasion the famous Welsh evangelist Christmas Evans remarked to the English preacher Robert Hall, "How I wish, Mr. Hall, that Dr. Gill's works had been written in Welsh."

"I wish they had, sir," replied Hall. "I wish they had, with all my heart, for then I should never have read them. They are a continent of mud, sir."[6]

Second, just as the disciples of John Calvin transmuted as well as transmitted the legacy of the great Genevan reformer, so the "Gillites" carried certain positions of their mentor to extremes he would not, or at least did not, himself embrace. Later historians tended to interpret Gill, and his significance for Baptist history, exclusively through the lenses of the Gillite-

Fullerite dispute rather than in terms of the issues of his own day. Inevitably, such faulty methodology resulted in a distorted image.

Third, whether or not one *should* interpret Gill as a hyper-Calvinist, he was such an effective proponent of the doctrines of grace that this dimension of his theological work has tended to overshadow the many other important doctrinal concerns that occupied his prodigious mind and pen. A more balanced presentation of his life and work is long overdue.

John Gill was born at Kettering, Northamptonshire, on November 23, 1697. He was the son of Edward and Elizabeth Gill.[7] His father, who made his living in the woolen trade, was known as a man of "grace, piety, and holy conversation." He later became a deacon in the Particular Baptist congregation at Kettering. Young Gill was an ardent student, mastering the rudiments of Latin and Greek before he was forced to withdraw from the local grammar school at the age of eleven due to the schoolmaster's insistence that all his pupils, including those from dissenting families, attend daily prayer services in the neighboring parish church. Thereafter, Gill continued his studies on his own, becoming almost a fixture among the shelves of the local bookstore. John Rippon reports that when the residents of Kettering wanted to speak of anything as certain they would say, "It is as sure as that John Gill is in the bookseller's shop."[8] By the age of ten Gill had read through the entire Greek New Testament. Thereafter, he taught himself Hebrew with the aid of a secondhand grammar and lexicon he had acquired.

When he was about twelve years old, Gill heard a sermon by William Wallis, the founding pastor of the Baptist church his family attended, on the text, "And the LORD God called unto Adam, and said unto him, Where art thou?" (Gen. 3:9 KJV). Through this message he was made aware of his need for Christ and, being under conviction, was drawn to the Lord, finding "a comfortable hope and faith of interest in Him, from several exceeding great and precious promises, powerfully applied to his soul."[9] Gill postponed baptism until he was nearly nineteen years old, partly because of the propriety of making such a profession at a more tender age, but also because he sensed that his church was overeager to thrust him into the ministry before he was ready for this step. On November 1, 1716, he was immersed in a river near Kettering and, on the following Sunday, was received into the fellowship of his home church, partaking for the first time of the Lord's Supper.

Almost immediately Gill began to exercise his gifts as a preacher and expositor of the Scriptures. With the blessing of his fellow church members, he moved to the village of Higham Ferrers, where he boarded with the local minister, John Davis, and assisted as a pastoral intern in the congregation. Here he met Elizabeth Megus, whom he married in 1718 and who shared the labors of his ministry for more than forty-six years. They had three children who survived infancy, one of whom, Elizabeth, died at age twelve.

Following a brief stint back in Kettering as assistant minister in his home church, Gill was invited to London to preach in view of a call as pastor of the church meeting at Goat Yard, Horsleydown, in Southwark. This congregation, located about a mile from London Bridge, was one of the leading Particular Baptist churches of the metropolis, having been founded by the venerable Benjamin Keach in 1672 and served by his son-in-law, Benjamin Stinton. Gill was perhaps brought to the attention of this church through John Noble, a London pastor who had been impressed with his young friend's pulpit work in Northamptonshire. Noble had nominated him for a grant from the Particular Baptist Fund, a scholarship for young ministers jointly sponsored by several Calvinistic Baptist churches in the city.

Gill's call to the Horsleydown church has all the drama of an ecclesiastical soap opera. On September 13, 1719, a majority of the congregation voted to invite Gill to become their pastor. This decision was strongly contested by the minority who protested that, contrary to the custom of the church, women members had been allowed to vote and that this irregularity had tilted the decision in favor of Gill. For a while the anti-Gill faction secured control of the meetinghouse and excluded their opponents, who were forced to conduct their worship services in a neighboring schoolhouse. When the lease on the Goat Yard property expired, the pro-Gill group negotiated its renewal and thus reclaimed the original building for their use, the others removing themselves to a new meetinghouse at Unicorn Yard. Meanwhile, Gill united with the church that had called him as pastor. His former congregation in Kettering granted a letter of dismissal, commending John Gill as a "Dear Brother" and one who "hath walked in all good conscience and holy conversation amongst us."[10]

B. R. White has summarized well the dilemma that Gill faced at this critical juncture of his ministry: "Gill's own stand was the key to the situation: if he remained firm long enough he could hope to live down the initial opposition; if he faltered, his own future as a minister in London was in grave doubt. Whilst there can be no doubt that his firmness stemmed from his own certainty that this was God's will for him the prospect was one before which most men of his age would have quailed."[11]

In fact, Gill appeared undaunted as he set his face toward London to assume his first "full-time" pastoral charge. Perhaps we have a clue to Gill's overwhelming personality in the remark of Robert Morgan, one of the members who had voted against calling a pastor so young and untested: "Mr. Gill might become a useful man, if it should please God to keep him humble."[12]

On March 22, 1720, Gill was formally installed as pastor of the Horsleydown church in a public service of ordination. Following a time of psalm-singing and prayer, the presiding minister, John Skepp of Cripplegate, posed the standard questions concerning Gill's call by the church and his acceptance of this work. Gill's friend, John Noble, then led the congregation to reaffirm its choice of Gill as pastor by solemnly lifting up their hands. Then turning to Gill, he said: "If you as in the presence of God do heartily accept this solemn call of this church to the pastoral office, signify the same to this church now by a free and solemn declaration."[13] Thomas Crosby, one of the deacons, reported that Gill did so, committing himself to take God's Word for his rule, God's Spirit for his guide, God's promises for his support, and Christ's fullness for the supply of all his wants. Gill then received the laying on of hands, and following the ordination of several deacons, the service concluded with the singing of Psalm 133 and an apostolic benediction by the newly inducted pastor.

Having survived a church split and the boycott of his ordination by certain key pastors (only ten ministers participated in the event), Gill had surmounted the first major challenge to his full acceptance by the London Baptist community. Other tests would follow, including a second splintering off of other leading church members and a bout with the fever that left the young pastor physically depleted.[14] Gradually, however, Gill was emerging as a force to be reckoned with among the religious leaders of the day. In 1724 he became a manager of the Particular Baptist Fund. The same year he began his phenomenal writing career, breaking into print with a funeral sermon he preached for one of his deacons. Other books and pamphlets followed, including a sermon entitled "The Urim and Thummin found with Christ" (based on Deut. 33:8); his *Exposition of the Song of Solomon* (1728); and a defense of baptism by immersion, written at the request of Northamptonshire Baptists to refute the arguments of an Independent pastor, Matthias Maurice, who had attacked the Baptist practice of this ordinance. Gill's treatise on baptism circulated widely among Baptists in America as well as in England and helped gain his reputation as a spokesman for the Baptist interest on both sides of the Atlantic. Charles Haddon Spurgeon, who was an ardent admirer of Gill and yet critical of him at points, looked back on Gill's early labors in London and remarked: "Little did the friends dream what sort of man they had chosen to be their teacher, but had they known it, they would have rejoiced that a man of such vast erudition, such indefatigable industry, such sound judgment and such sterling honesty had come among them."[15]

By 1729 Gill's popularity had reached beyond the Baptist community to the other dissenting denominations as well. In that year a circle of his friends from various London churches formed a society to sponsor a weekly lecture by Gill to be delivered each Wednesday evening at Great

Eastcheap. For some twenty-seven years Gill spoke from this forum to eager audiences who regarded their speaker as not only one of the great living preachers of the day but also as the seminal theologian for Calvinistic dissent. Many of Gill's major writings, including his treatises on the Trinity and justification, his classic defense of Calvinistic soteriology, *The Cause of God and Truth,* and several of his commentaries on both the Old and New Testaments, were originally presented at the Great Eastcheap lectures.

Gill took a special delight in the study of Hebrew and amassed a considerable library in rabbinics and Oriental languages. He applied this expertise to the study of the New Testament, recognizing that it was written by men, all of whom had been Jews. Gill's biblical studies are interlaced with references to the Mishnah, the Talmud, and ancient Jewish commentaries. In 1748 Marichal College of the University of Aberdeen conferred on Gill the degree Doctor of Divinity in recognition of his outstanding work in this field, which was truly a remarkable accolade for a self-taught Baptist preacher! When the deacons of his church congratulated him on receiving this prestigious award, he thanked them and then added, "I neither thought it, nor bought it, nor sought it."[16]

A hundred years after his death, William Cathcart made the following evaluation of Gill's scholarly reputation: "It is within bounds to say that no man in the eighteenth century was so well versed in the literature and customs of the ancient Jews as John Gill. He has sometimes been called the Doctor John Lightfoot of the Baptists. This compliment, in the estimation of some persons, flatters Doctor Lightfoot more than Doctor Gill."[17]

Although Gill is frequently portrayed as a stern logician who artificially conformed the truth of theology to the rigors of a preconceived system, it is important to recognize that he was a careful exegete of Holy Scripture who wrote a massive commentary on every book, chapter, and verse in the Bible. His *Exposition of the New Testament,* completed in 1748, filled three hefty volumes, while his *Exposition of the Old Testament,* which kept him busy until 1766, was a six-volume project. Only after he had worked his way through the valleys and peaks of scriptural revelation did he attempt a systematic gleaning of doctrinal truth. In 1769 he published in two volumes *A Body of Doctrinal Divinity.* Rippon wrote of this, Gill's *magnum opus:* "Here is the Doctor's whole creed. Here his very heart appears, while he states, maintains, and defends the Truth as it is in Jesus." Divided into seven books, this compendium of Christian theology took up, in order, the being and attributes of God; the internal acts of God (i.e., the eternal decrees); the external acts of God (creation, providence, permission of the Fall); the acts of God's grace in time; the person, work, and offices of Christ; the blessings of grace in the elect; and the final state of man. Gill was well aware that "systematical divinity," as he called it, had fallen onto hard times in his day. "Formulas and articles of faith, creeds, confessions, catechisms, and summaries of divine truths, are greatly decried in our age." Gill asked, "Why should divinity, the most noble science, be without a system?" He defined the task of theology as gathering out of Scripture the principles of evangelical truth and arranging them in an orderly method to show their connection, harmony, and agreement. In pursuing this task, Gill saw himself in continuity with the great tradition of historic Christianity beginning with the Apostles' Creed and including the major Fathers, schoolmen, and reformers, many of whom had produced "bodies or systems of divinity," that proved "very serviceable to lead men into the knowledge of evangelical doctrine, and confirm them in it."[18]

Throughout his long career, Gill sought to apply the doctrines he believed and proclaimed to the practical issues of the Christian life. "Doctrine and practice should go together," he said. "In order both to know and do the will of God, instruction in doctrine and practice is necessary; and the one being first taught will lead on to the other."[19] In this spirit Gill published *A Body of Practical Divinity* in 1770 to complement his earlier summary of Christian theology. A volume of over five hundred pages, this book reflected a series of sermons Gill had preached to his congregation dealing with such themes as public worship, church membership, baptism and the Lord's Supper, family responsibilities, and so forth. A visitor was asked what he thought of the message that day. "Why," said he, "if I had not been told it was the great Dr. Gill who preached, I should have said that I had heard an Arminian!"[20] Although Gill was justly revered as a "distinguished patron of the doctrines of grace," as his biographer aptly put it, he was nonetheless a champion of "practical experimental godliness." In the best tradition of Reformed theology, he emphasized the cementing bond between what Calvin called the twofold grace *(duplicem gratiam)* of justification and sanctification, that is, the connection between the free imputation of Christ's righteousness and actual holiness of life.[21]

In 1757 Gill's congregation moved from their location at Horsleydown to a new meetinghouse in Carter Lane. Gill used this occasion to review his ministry and reaffirm his commitment as a preacher of God's Word. "What doctrines may be taught in this place, after I am gone, is not for me to know; but, as for my own part, I am at a point; I am determined, and have been long ago, what to make the subject of my ministry. It is now upwards of forty years since I entered into the arduous work; and the first sermon I have preached was from these words of the apostle, 'For I am determined not to know any thing among you, save Jesus Christ, and him crucified'; and, through the grace of God, I have been enabled, in some good measure, to abide by the same resolution hitherto, as many of you here are my witnesses; and I hope, through divine assistance, I ever shall, as long as I am in this tabernacle and engaged in such a work."[22]

Gill was an energetic preacher who sometimes went through three or four handkerchiefs in a single sermon. A contemporary witness declared that he was "blessed with ready utterance and with great volubility of speech. . . . With what gravity and majesty had he used to stand and feed the Church of God! How did his listening audiences hang as it were upon his lips, while evangelical truths did sweetly drop from his mellifluous tongue."[23] If this reads like the assessment of an uncritical admirer, it is well to remember that Gill every Sunday was not everyone's cup of tea. One old man in his congregation frequently responded to his pastor's exertions by asking in a cynical tone, "Is that preaching?"

Gill suffered such abuse with good humor for a while, but one day exploded in anger against his detractor. With the full strength of his voice, he pointed toward the pulpit and said, "Go up and do better—Go up and do better!"[24]

This last anecdote, taken from Rippon's biography, shows us a very human Gill who was not above losing his temper or venting his anger. Samuel Stennett, who delivered the eulogy at Gill's funeral, recalled this aspect of his friend's personality, along with his capacity for self-judgment and forgiveness. "And though he knew how with a spirit to resent an injury, he knew how also with becoming meekness to endure and forgive it. His warmth might indeed on some occasions exceed, yet he had prudence and resolution to check it; and failed not afterwards like a good man as he was, to feel great pain on account of it."[25]

John Wesley, who crossed polemical swords with Gill, referred to him as "a positive man" who "fights for his opinions through thick and thin." Doubtless, Gill was the kind of man who engendered feelings of love and loyalty, as well as dislike and contempt, from those who encountered the force of his strong personality. When, as an old man, he thought he had outlived his usefulness to his congregation and offered to resign, his church members sent him the following letter: "Another grievous circumstance is, which if the Church is willing, you seem inclined to resign your office as Pastor. This expression is extremely alarming to us, and is what can by no means find a place in our thoughts, it being our fixed desire and continual prayer, which you may live and die in that endeared relation. We say with united voice, 'How can a father give up his children, or affectionate children their father?' Dear sir, we beseech you not to cast us off, but bear us upon your heart and spiritual affections all your days and let us be remembered to God through your prayers, and who knows but the Lord may visit us again and make us break forth on the right hand and on the left?"[26]

Following a prolonged illness, Gill died on October 14, 1771. Shortly before his demise, Gill had penned some "Dying Thoughts" on the importance of a godly preparation for death, which he defined as "the time of the Lord's in-gathering of his people to himself; then it is he who comes into his garden, and gathers his lilies, and this and the other flower, to put into his bosom."[27] To his nephew and namesake, John Gill of Saint Albans, he declared that his hope was not based on any services he had been permitted to perform for the good of the church, but rather upon "my interest in the Persons of the Trinity, the free grace of God, and the blessings of grace streaming to me through the blood and righteousness of Christ." Thus, as Samuel Stennett put it, "Sinking under the gradual decay of nature, he gently fell asleep in Jesus, in the 74th year of his age."[28] There was great mourning throughout the land, especially among Baptists who had lost one of their brightest lights, and a general recognition by all Christians that "a great man is fallen in Israel."

Exposition

John Gill belonged to that period of English Nonconformity that has been characterized as the "Old Dissent."[29] This term is used in contrast to the "New Dissent," which was the result of the evangelical revival led by John and Charles Wesley, George Whitefield, and, among Baptists, Dan Taylor and Andrew Fuller. Following the English Civil War in the seventeenth century, those Christians who refused to attend the Church of England, or conform to its legally imposed pattern of worship, were severely persecuted by the established authorities. Both John Bunyan and Benjamin Keach were imprisoned on account of their religious convictions.

The Glorious Revolution of 1688, which brought William III and his wife Mary to the throne, restored statutory freedom of worship to the dissenters and ushered in a long period of toleration and decline. Although many Anglicans still showed "an implacable hatred to the Nonconformists," they were permitted to convene national assemblies, erect stately meetinghouses, publish confessions of faith, establish their own theological academies, and sustain a public presence in the community.[30] As a recent historian has put it, for the most, dissenters "were now able to go about their daily business without fear of the informer, the constable, and the magistrate."[31]

Unfortunately, however, material prosperity and spiritual vitality did not go hand in hand. If the blood of the martyrs was the seed of the church, then toleration bred moral apathy, doctrinal laxity, and general unconcern. At the height of his career in 1750, Gill reviewed the religious torpor that had beset all of the dissenting denominations, but especially his own Baptist fellowship. "Of late years, there has been a very visible decline; and a night is coming on, which we are entered into; the shadows of evening are stretching out apace upon us, and the signs of eventide are very manifest. A sleepy form of spirit has seized us; both ministers and churches are asleep; and being so, the enemy is busy in sowing the tares of error and heresies, and which will grow up and spread more and more."[32]

Historian Carl L. Becker has described the Augustan Age in which Gill flourished in the following way: "What we have to realize is that in those years God was on trial."[33] In 1696 the publication of John Toland's *Christianity Not Mysterious* marked the rise of Deism with its belief that natural religion alone, apart from the special revelation of the Christian faith, was quite sufficient. Various strands of "rational theology" had led many thinkers to question the most basic presuppositions of historic Christian orthodoxy such as the doctrines of God and Christ inherent in the Nicene and Athanasian creeds. By the mid-eighteenth century the General Baptists and the Presbyterians had succumbed almost entirely to Unitarianism while many others, both inside the established church and among the dissenters, found the supernatural dimension of Christianity increasingly an embarrassment. John Gill believed that there was an intrinsic connection between the doctrinal erosion he observed and the spiritual decay he lamented in the life of the church. Like Athanasius in the fourth century, and Luther and Calvin during the Reformation, Gill dared to say no to those forms of teaching that, if carried out consistently, would have threatened the truth of divine revelation itself. In so doing, he helped to preserve the theological integrity of the Particular Baptists and thus, indirectly, prepared them to receive the awakening that came once he was gone.

Holy Scripture

In 1729 Gill led his congregation to renew its church covenant and to include a confession of faith to which each person would give assent before being admitted to church membership. The first article of this confession presented a succinct statement of the common Baptist understanding of the Bible. "We believe that the Scriptures of the Old and New Testament are the word of God, and the only rule of faith and practice."[34] While this brief affirmation suffers by comparison with the extensive article on Scripture that is found in the 1689 Second London Confession, one should not take this as a weakened view of the Bible on Gill's part. Although Gill does allow for a measure of divine revelation imparted through nature and reason, these channels are utterly insufficient, for "the light of nature leaves man entirely without the knowledge of the way of salvation by the Son of God."[35] This predicament has occurred because the rupture of the fall left humankind groping helplessly in the dark apart from God's gracious revelation of himself in the history of salvation and the inscripturation of revelation.

The first two chapters in book 1 of Gill's *Body of Doctrinal Divinity* deal with the being of God and Holy Scripture. After defining the scope of Scripture to coincide with those books that have been received by the church as canonical (excluding the Apocrypha and other "spurious writings"), Gill expounds in turn the authority, perfection, and perspicuity of the Bible.

Gill asserts without equivocation the divine inspiration and total truthfulness of God's written Word. To be sure, he does not spend much time trying to explain precisely *how* the Scriptures were inspired. However, he clearly affirms the divine origin of the Bible; the biblical authors were "under the impulse and direction of God in all they wrote." Nor did this divine impulsion obliterate their role as instruments in the process of inspiration. Gill, ever a careful student of the Bible, recognized the various genres of literature and differences of style among the different strata of Scripture. Like Calvin, Gill appealed to the principle of accommodation to account for such phenomena. God simply adapted himself "to the style such persons were wont to use, and that was natural to them, and agreeable to their genius and circumstances."[36] In this way, Gill affirms the humanity of the biblical writers without sacrificing the divine character of the biblical text. Indeed, far from proposing a so-called "mechanical dictation" theory of inspiration, Gill allows for a kind of source theory of composition, claiming that Moses and other writers of Scripture may well have made use of "diaries, annals and journals of their own and former times."[37] However, the final product included precisely what God intended for it to contain, even to the very words that God was pleased to employ in disclosing his holy oracles.

Although Gill lived prior to the frontal assault against the integrity of Scripture by rationalistic critics of the last two centuries, he anticipated many of the arguments used by later theologians in their defense of the doctrine of biblical inerrancy. Since the Scriptures are given by God, a perfect Being, they can contain nothing of "ignorance, error, or imperfection." As God's work in creation, providence, and redemption is perfect, so is his work in providing the Scriptures to his people. Of course, Gill fully supported the discipline of textual criticism and made important contributions to it himself. Only the "original exemplars" in the original languages could be regarded as free from every error of transmission, translation, and so forth. Gill also saw the perfection of the Bible displayed in the way it contained a refutation for every heresy and false doctrine that had arisen in the history of the church, as well as a corrective word for every sin that could be committed.

In contending for the perspicuity of the Bible, Gill harked back to a cardinal tenet—the Reformation principle of *sola Scriptura,* the "clarity and certainty of the Word of God," as Zwingli's famous treatise of 1523 put it. Gill admitted that not all Scriptures were equally plain: He quoted Gregory the Great as saying that the Bible is like a great river in which a lamb may walk, and an elephant swim, at different places. Moreover, he also discerned the principle of progressive revelation—"the light of the Scriptures has been a growing one; it was but dim under the dispensation of the law of Moses; it became more clear through the writings of the prophets; but most clear under the gospel dispensation."[38] Still, not everyone who read or studied the Bible could necessarily understand it. It is "a sealed book, which neither learned nor unlearned men can understand and interpret without the Spirit of God."[39] Gill's emphasis on the internal witness of the Holy Spirit saved him from the error of biblical rationalism and from an overreliance on the kind of evidentialist arguments that characterized Protestant apologetics during the Age of Reason.

Gill believed that Scripture was its own best interpreter, and he appealed to the infallibility of the Bible against two opposing errors. On the one hand, he rejected the Roman Catholic attempt to subordinate the Scriptures to the church. Neither the church nor its pastors, neither councils, nor popes, may sit in judgment on the Word of God. On the other hand, Gill dismissed at once the claims of those "enthusiastic persons" (perhaps Quakers?) who were so enamoured of the Spirit that they saw little need for the written Word. He did acknowledge a legitimate private interpretation of the Bible ("that every Christian may make, according to his ability and light") as well as a duly ordered public one (the preaching of the Word). In both cases, however, both are subject to, and to be determined by, the Scripture itself, which is the only certain and infallible rule of faith and practice.

Trinity

When the General Baptist churches of the Midlands published their "Orthodox Creed" in 1678, they included the Apostles', Nicene, and Athanasian creeds that, they declared, "ought thoroughly to be received, and believed: and used both to edify believers and to prevent heresy in doctrine and practice."[40] In the preface to this document they went so far as to assert that "the denying of baptism is a less evil than to deny the Divinity or Humanity of Christ."[41] Such concerns were well placed, for in the decades that followed serious divisions arose among General Baptists concerning both the person of Christ and the doctrine of the Trinity. The sources of such deviant Christology and anti-Trinitarianism were complex and soon spread to other dissenting denominations. In the year of John Gill's disputed call to the pastorate of the Horsleydown congregation, a major dispute arose among the Presbyterian, Congregationalist, and General and Particular Baptist ministers of London concerning their subscription to a Trinitarian affirmation. Significantly, all but two of the Particular Baptists present at this conference, held at Salters' Hall, willingly signed this confessional statement, while only one of the General Baptists did so. Raymond Brown has aptly described the sequence of events that ensued: "Resistance to subscription became the prelude to heterodoxy. People who refused to sign the articles came eventually to deny them and those General Baptists who were theologically uncertain ultimately became committed Unitarians."[42]

While few Particular Baptist churches became Unitarian, Gill was well aware of the dangers that confronted all orthodox Christians on these cardinal tenets of the faith. It was this concern that prompted him to publish his *Treatise on the Defense of the Trinity* in 1731, issue a second edition virtually unchanged in 1752, and incorporate much of the same material in his *Body of Doctrinal Divinity* in 1769. Gill vigorously defended the attention he paid to this doctrine by showing how vital it was to every aspect of the Christian life. "The doctrine of the Trinity is often represented as a speculative point, of no great moment whether it is believed or no, too mysterious and curious to be pried into, and that it had better be left alone than meddled with; but, alas! it enters into the whole of our salvation, and all the parts of it; into all the doctrines of the gospel, and into the experience of the saints."[43]

Gill proceeds to show how all three Persons of the one Triune God are involved in all the works of creation, providence, and redemption. He points out that in the economy of salvation election is usually ascribed in Scripture to the Father, redemption to the Son, and sanctification to the Holy Spirit. Yet the plurality in the Godhead must never be set over against the primal unity that is implied in the very existence of God as a necessary Being, all-sufficient, omnipotent, and supreme in all perfections. In discussing the particularizing characteristics of the divine Persons, Gill follows the distinctions set forth by the Cappadocian Fathers of the fourth century: The Father is *begetting,* the Son *begotten,* and the Holy Spirit *breathed.* Gill echoes Augustine and the Western Church generally in affirming the dual procession of the Holy Spirit: He proceeds from the Father and the Son. Gill also returns to the patristic notion that the personal relations within God are a necessary reflection of the nature of God. "As he is the best, the greatest and most perfect of Beings, his happiness in himself must be the most perfect and complete; now happiness lies not in solitude, but in society; hence the three personal distinctions in Deity, seem necessary to perfect happiness, which lies in that glorious, inconceivable, and inexpressible communion the three Persons have with one another; and that arises from the incomprehensible in-being and unspeakable nearness they have to each other."[44]

Gill interpreted modern anti-Trinitarianism as a revival of the "old stale error" of Sabellianism and Arianism. He was alarmed that "some who profess evangelical doctrines have embraced it, or are nibbling at it."[45] In defending classical Trinitarian orthodoxy, he was required, as Calvin before him had done, to move beyond the strict use of biblical language for the sake of biblical truth. An earlier meeting of the General Assembly of the General Baptists had decided that the controversy "respecting the Trinity and the Christ of God" should be voiced "in Scripture words and terms and in no other terms."[46] Gill saw this principle as unduly restrictive and intentionally deceptive. Rather than reflecting a true reverence for the biblical text, it frequently camouflaged doctrinal deviance. He contended that "words and phrases though not literally expressed in scripture, yet if what is meant by them is to be found there, they may be lawfully made use of."[47] While Gill, in good Baptist fashion, could acclaim the Bible only, and not confessions, catechisms, or articles of faith, as the proper standard of orthodoxy, he nonetheless showed remarkable respect for the doctrinal consensus of the early Fathers and was most reluctant "to oppose a doctrine the church of God has always held, and especially being what the Scriptures abundantly bear testimony unto."[48] In this sense he was a true catholic theologian.

Sovereign Grace

John Gill was a leading exponent of the Calvinistic doctrines of grace that had characterized Particular Baptist churches since their emergence in the late 1630s. The substance of these doctrines was summarized at the Dutch Reformed Synod of Dort (1618–19) in five major assertions: (1) the decrees of election and reprobation are absolute and unconditional; (2) the scope of the atonement is restricted to the elect although the death of Christ is sufficient to expiate the sins of the whole world; (3) because of the fall human beings are totally incapable of any saving good apart from the regenerating work of the Holy Spirit; (4) God's call is effectual and hence his grace cannot be ultimately thwarted by human resistance; (5) those whom God calls and regenerates he also keeps so that they do not totally nor finally fall from faith and grace.[49] These teachings were repeated in the Westminster Confession (1647), the official creed of English Presbyterianism; the Savoy Declaration (1658) of the English Congregationalists, and in the First (1644) and Second (1677/1689) London Confessions of the Particular Baptists. Gill was heir to this theological tradition, which in his day had come increasingly under attack from Deists and Unitarians on the left and from evangelical Arminians such as the General Baptist leader Thomas Grantham, who blasted the "cruel and soul-devouring doctrines of Calvinism," and the great Puritan divine Richard Baxter, who proposed a mediating compromise between the two camps.

Gill, like Augustine and Calvin, was drawn into predestinarian polemics when challenged by opposing views that seemed to disparage the grace of God and his sovereignty in salvation. It was Toplady's judgment that no one since Augustine himself had written so extensively or so persuasively in defense of the doctrines of grace as Gill. After reading Gill's reply to Wesley's attack on the doctrine of perseverance, his Anglican friend wrote: "Between morning and afternoon service, read through Dr. Gill's excellent and nervous tract on Predestination, against Wesley. How sweet is that blessed and glorious doctrine to the soul, when it is received through the channel of inward experience! I believe it may be said of my learned friend, as it was of the Duke of Marlborough, that he never fought a battle which he did not win."[50]

Gill's major defense of the Calvinistic doctrines, *The Cause of God and Truth,* was published in four parts between 1735 and 1738. This work, originally delivered as lectures in Gill's Great Eastcheap series, was intended as a definitive reply to Daniel Whitby's *Discourses on the Five Points,* which many considered an unanswerable attack on "the Calvinistical System." The Gill-Whitby exchange surely deserves a place among the classic debates on the doctrine of election. The first two parts of *The Cause* consist of detailed considerations of the scriptural passages, pro and con, which are alleged against the doctrines of grace. Part 3 examines the philosophical arguments for these views and refutes the charge of Stoic fatalism against them. Gill was greatly concerned to vindicate the basic tenets of Calvinism on rational grounds, believing that "they are no more disagreeable to right reason than to divine revelation."[51] Here, perhaps, we see most clearly Gill's indebtedness to the broader intellectual environment of Protestant Scholasticism in its desire to correlate philosophy and dogmatics, that is, to express and formulate the faith in terms compatible with the leading systems of rational inquiry. Gill followed the Protestant dogmatician Herman Witsius (1636–1708), whose writings he often quoted and helped to edit. Part 4 of *The Cause* is a masterful excursus into patristic literature intended to show that, far from being a novel teaching, the doctrines related to predestination were supported by "the whole stream of antiquity."[52]

The kernel of Gill's predestinarian theology was present in the articles of faith that he led his congregation to incorporate into their church covenant in 1729.

> We believe, that before the world began, God did elect a certain number of men unto everlasting Salvation whom he did predestinate to the adoption of children by Jesus of his own free grace and according to the good pleasure of his will, and that in pursuance of this gratious design, he did contrive and make a covenant of grace and peace with his Son Jesus Christ, on ye behalf of those persons, wherein a Saviour was appointed, and all spritual blessings provided for them; as also that their persons with all their grace and glory, were put into ye hands of Christ, and made his care and charge. . . . We believe, yet that Eternal Redemption that Christ has obtained by the shedding of his blood, is special and particular . . . that the Justification of God's

Elect, is only by the righteousness of Christ imputed to them, without yet consideration of any works of righteousness done by them . . . yet the work of regeneration, conversion, sanctification, and faith is not an act of man's free will and power, but of the mighty, efficacious and irresistible grace of God . . . that all those who are chosen by the father, redeemed by the son and sanctified by the spirit shall certainly and finally persevere, so yet none of 'em shall ever perish, but shall have everlasting life.[53]

While this is certainly a *strict* Calvinist statement, it hardly merits the pejorative label, hyper-Calvinist. Bunyan and Keach before him, and Fuller and Spurgeon after him, could have embraced without reservation Gill's congregational confession, which, in reality, was merely an abstract of the 1689 Second London Confession. Why, then, has Gill been portrayed as the paradigm of hyper-Calvinism?

Richard Condon has written that "a nuance in an ideological difference is a wide chasm."[54] On three distinct issues Gill's writings were taken to lend support to extreme views that appeared to undermine the necessity of conversion, the moral requirements of the Christian life, and the evangelistic mission of the church. It can be shown that Gill never intended for his ideas to have such questionable consequences. Nor was he himself guilty of pressing the logic (or illogic?) of his position to such nonevangelical conclusions. It is another question, however, of whether he sufficiently anticipated or guarded against such misinterpretations.

Gill's doctrine of *eternal justification* was a stumbling block to many who could not square it with the necessity of conversion as a personal experience of grace. In his *Body of Doctrinal Divinity,* Gill considers justification under two distinct rubrics. In book 2, chapter 5, he treats justification as one of the "eternal and immanent acts in God"; in book 6, chapter 8, he deals with the same topic "as it terminates in the conscience of a believer."[55] This distinction was not original with Gill but followed the pattern of covenant theology expounded by earlier Reformed theologians such as Witsius, Macovius, and Ames, who had distinguished active justification, God's eternal act based on his sovereign goodwill, and passive justification, the personal application of the former to the elect believer within space and time. Gill defended this teaching, stressing the priority of justification over faith. Faith, he said, is the effect, not the cause of our justification: "The reason why we are justified is not because we have faith, but the reason why we have faith is because we are justified."[56] To those who objected that no one could be justified before he or she existed, Gill replied that while no one *actually* existed before conception and birth, the elect did enjoy a *representative* existence in their Mediator, Jesus Christ, who, as the eternal Son of God, participated in the decree of election that He would fulfill on their behalf in the course of the history of salvation.

Clearly, Gill did not intend to exalt so highly the initiative of God in salvation that he preempted the requirements of repentance, faith, and conversion. Yet the doctrine of eternal justification was a perilous teaching, insofar as it encouraged sinners to think of themselves as actually justified regardless of their personal response to Christ and the gospel. Doubtless, for this reason the framers of the Second London Confession (echoing the Westminster divines) had declared that although "God did from all eternity decree to justify all the Elect . . . nevertheless they are not justified personally, until the Holy Spirit, doth in due time actually apply Christ unto them."[57] Happily, on this controverted issue most Particular Baptists followed the fathers of the Second London Confession rather than John Gill.

Closely related to the fear that Gill's theology of grace might disrupt the morphology of conversion was the frequently articulated concern that it would also lead to antinomianism. *Antinomianism* is the view that, since Christ both bore the penalty of sin and fulfilled the law, those under grace are not required to obey the moral law. Although Gill did republish the works of Tobias Crisp and John Skepp, two earlier theologians whose writings were considered a haven for antinomian interpretations, he strenuously resisted the temptation to make light of the importance of good works in the life of a Christian. "I *abhor* the thought of setting the law of God aside as the rule of walk and conversation; and constantly affirm . . . that all who believe in Christ for righteousness should be careful to maintain good works, for necessary uses."[58] Anyone who has examined Gill's *Body of Practical Divinity* or looked at his sermons on "The Law Established by the Gospel" (1756) and "The Law in the Hand of Christ" (1761) will know how spurious is the charge of antinomianism against him. As John Rippon expressed it, "His preaching was as pointed on the *agenda* as on the *credenda* of the Christian system." Just as Christ was crucified between two thieves, continued Rippon, so Gill was pilloried between two robbers—Arminianism, which robs God of his grace, and antinomianism, which robs him of his glory.[59] Gill could not be an Arminian, for he maintained the five distinguishing doctrines that they denied, nor could he be an antinomian, because he denied the axiom that they affirmed, namely, that the moral law did not apply to believers as their rule of conduct.

The third issue on which Gill's hyper-Calvinist reputation is based was his presumed refusal to preach the gospel promiscuously to the lost. This controversy went back to a book published by the Congregationalist minister Joseph Hussey entitled *God's Operations of Grace but No Offers of His Grace* (1707). Hussey declared that anyone who claimed to believe in God's election and yet offered Christ to all was only a "half-hearted Calvinist." Peter Toon has traced the birth of hyper-Calvinism to Hussey and his writings.[60] It is true that Gill regarded Hussey, along with Tobias Crisp, as "men of great piety and learning, of long standing and much usefulness in the Church of Christ."[61] And Gill, like Hussey, believed that the word *offer* could be misleading when applied to the presentation of the gospel to the lost. Just as we might object to an evangelist who loosely talks about his (as opposed to God's) saving of souls, Gill maintained that, in a proper sense, only the Holy Spirit could truly "offer" Christ and salvation to sinners. Hussey's writings formed the backdrop for the controversy over the "Modern Question," so called from the title of a pamphlet published in 1737 by Matthias Maurice, against whom Gill had earlier written on the topic of infant baptism. In *A Modern Question Modestly Answer'd,* Maurice raised the question of whether it was "the duty of poor unconverted sinners, who hear the gospel preached or published, to believe in Jesus Christ."[62] Those who answered this question in the negative (i.e., the true hyper-Calvinists) saw little need for the promiscuous preaching of the gospel, since it was obviously useless to exhort unconverted sinners to do what they neither *could* do, nor indeed had any obligation to do! There is no doubt that such views gained currency among Particular Baptists in the late eighteenth century and consequently, as Spurgeon put it, "chilled many churches to their very soul," leading them "to omit the free invitations of the gospel, and to deny that it is the duty of sinners to believe in Jesus."[63] It was precisely against such theology that Andrew Fuller reacted in his epochal *The Gospel Worthy of All Acceptation* (1785).

In light of the later Gillite-Fullerite debate and in view of the fact that many exponents of what Joseph Ivimey called the "non-invitation, non-application scheme" appealed to his writings, many historians have traced the source of such "false Calvinism" (Fuller's phrase) to Gill himself. However, a close reading of his sermons and doctrinal treatises will show this to be a hasty judgment that may need to be reconsidered. For example, Tom Nettles has shown that Gill's interpretation of the words of Jesus, "Come unto me" (Matt. 11:28), differ markedly from that of Hussey. The latter understood these words to refer to the literal "coming on their feet to Christ" of the Jews in ancient Palestine. Gill's exposition extends their meaning greatly. "Those who come to Christ aright, come as sinners, to a full, suitable, able, and willing Saviour; venture their souls upon him, and trust in him for righteousness, life, and salvation, which they are encouraged to do, by this kind of invitation, which shows his willingness to save, and his readiness to give relief to distressed minds."[64]

Gill persistently encouraged young ministers to "preach the gospel of salvation to all men, and declare, that whosoever believes shall be saved: for this they are commissioned to do."[65] At the ordination service of a certain John Davis, Gill delivered the following charge: "Souls sensible to sin and danger, and who are crying out, What shall we do to be saved? you are to observe, and point out Christ the tree of live to them; and say, as some of the cherubs did to one in such circumstances, Believe on the Lord Jesus Christ and thou shalt be saved, Acts XVI:31. Your work is to lead men, under a sense of sin and guilt, to the blood of Christ, shed for many for the remission of sin, and in this name you are to preach the forgiveness to them."[66]

On another occasion, he declared that if a minister fails to exhort sinners to repent and believe in Christ, "their blood will be required at his hands. . . . What can, or does, more strongly engage ministers to take heed to themselves than this? That they may be useful in the conversion and so in the salvation of precious and immortal souls, which are of more worth than the world."[67] We may justly conclude that while Gill believed in harmony with the wider Augustinian tradition, which God, to the praise of his glory, had chosen from eternity to save a certain number of persons from the lost race of humanity, he disparaged neither the means God had ordained to effect the conversion of the elect nor the evangelical mandate to proclaim the good news of God's gracious provision to all the lost.

Recent research has shown that it is inaccurate to lump together indiscriminately Crisp, Hussey, Skepp, Brine, and Gill.[68] Each of these theologians presented a nuanced discussion of the doctrines of grace with distinctive corollaries and diverging consequences. On the "Modern Question," Fuller himself acknowledged that "Dr. Gill took no active part in the controversy. . . . It cannot be denied that, when engaged in other controversies, he frequently argues in a manner favorable to our side; and his writings contain various concessions on this subject that, if any one else had made them, would not be much to the satisfaction of our opposing brethren."[69]

Still, we cannot quite exonerate Gill of all responsibility in the fostering of an atmosphere in which the forthright promulgation of the missionary mandate of the church was seen to be a threat to, rather than an extension of, the gospel of grace. What Fuller said of Hussey could also be applied to Gill: he was of "that warm turn of mind which frequently misleads even the greatest of men, especially in defending a favorite sentimental."[70] True, Gill did not go so far as the real hyper-Calvinists; but he was so preoccupied in defending the gospel from dangers on the left that he did little to stay the erosion on his right.

Evaluation

The visitor to modern London can find the stately tomb of John Gill in the famous Nonconformist cemetery at Bunhill Fields, which is across from the house on City Road where John Wesley, who died twenty years later, spent the last years of his life. It is ironic that these two great leaders, paradigms of the Old and the New Dissent, should thus find themselves in such close proximity at the end of their earthly walks. Gill lies buried among other notables of the dissenting tradition, including John Bunyan, John Owen, George Foxe, Isaac Watts, and his successor and biographer, John Rippon. On his tomb is a Latin inscription describing Gill, among other things, as "a sincere disciple of Jesus, an excellent preacher of the gospel, a courageous defender of the Christian faith." At his death the church he had served for so long voted to raise a mortgage and go into debt in order to pay for a portrait of their beloved pastor, from which small prints were provided for every member of the congregation.[71] John Fellows summed up Gill's life in the following couplet from an elegy he published shortly after the death of his friend:

> Zion was his delight; his whole design
> Was to adorn the church, and make her shine.[72]

Gill's influence within the Baptist tradition remained strong for many years after his death. His books were required reading for many young ministerial students whose mentors preferred Gill's hefty tomes to "the frothy and flimsy productions of the present day," as one of them put it.[73] Gill's courage in resisting laxity and error inspired Spurgeon during the Downgrade Controversy as he sought to stave off "the boiling mudshowers of modern heresy" that were beginning to descend on Baptist life in his day. "My eminent predecessor, Dr. Gill, was told by a certain member of his congregation who ought to have known better, that, if he published his book, *The Cause of God and Truth,* he would lose some of his best friends, and that his income would fall off. The doctor said, 'I can afford to be poor, but I cannot afford to injure my conscience,' and he has left his mantle as well as his chair in our vestry."[74]

At the same time, Spurgeon could be critical of Gill's lack of zeal in pursuing an aggressive evangelistic strategy. His own ministry embodies the best of both Gill and Fuller: a concern for doctrinal integrity on the essentials of the faith and an unswerving commitment to the evangelistic and missionary purpose of the church.

The theology of grace in Christian history oscillates between the poles of divine sovereignty and human responsibility. Both are biblical and evangelical truths that must be held in tension if the gospel is to be proclaimed in its purity and urgency. If Gill erred in overstressing God's initiative in salvation, it was because he believed this foundational fact was being undermined by the inroads of Deism, rationalism, and the misdirected message of Arminianism. His theology was a corrective to these trends that, if left unchecked, might well have so eviscerated the Particular Baptists (as they did in fact the Generals) that there would have been little, if anything, to awaken when revival did come.

The vital springs of piety that nourished Gill's life and thought are sometimes obscured by the abstract form his theology assumed. Yet Luther's dictum that it is "not speculating but rather living, dying and being damned" that make one a theologian applies to Gill as well. As Gill's twelve-year-old daughter Elizabeth lay dying, he hovered over her bed and tried to calm her fears about not being yet baptized. He listened as she confessed great affection for the Savior. "She would sometimes say within herself, *I love him, me thinks, I could hug him in my arms."*

"My dear," he asked, "can you say, Christ died for you?"

"Yes," she replied, "Christ died for me."

"Nay," he later recalled, "one time she said she thought she even saw Christ."

At her funeral service Gill related the testimony of his daughter's assurance in Christ and preached a powerful sermon on the hope of the resurrection. He spoke to himself as well as to the gathered mourners when he observed: "So hard a thing is it for us to keep the doctrines of the gospel always in view; and harder still to make sure of them, and live up to them, when we most want them."[75] Precisely in the midst of such trials Gill found himself sustained by the God of grace, the grace he had proclaimed to others, the grace he had defended at length against its detractors, the grace that overcomes every obstacle in life and in death.

Along with Gill's piety it is also easy to miss his humility. He sometimes sounds, as Castellio said of Calvin, that he has just returned from conversing with the angels! Yet in the end Gill knew, as all true theologians must, that all of our efforts to describe God's glory and power, his majesty and mercy, fall far short of their ineffable object. Unlike Augustine, Gill never wrote a volume of retractions. But the proviso that governed his massive theological output is the confession that should be in the heart of every person who dares to speak, with reverence and fidelity, for the living God:

If I have written anything contrary to the divine perfections, or what may reflect any dishonor on the dear name of Jesus, or be any way injurious to the truth as it is in him, or be detrimental to the intent of pure and undefiled religion, I do most humbly intreat forgiveness at the hands of God.[76]

Bibliography

Works by Gill

The Cause of God and Truth. Grand Rapids: Baker, 1980 [reprint of the 1855 London edition].

A Collection of Sermons and Tracts. Streamwood, Ill.: Primitive Baptist Library, 1981 [reprint of the 1814 London edition].

A Complete Body of Doctrinal and Practical Divinity. Paris, Ark.: Baptist Standard Bearer, 1984 [reprint of the 1839 London edition].

The Dissenter's Reasons for Separating from the Church of England. London: n.p., 1753.

A Dissertation Concerning the Antiquity of the Hebrew Language. London: n.p., 1767.

The Doctrine of Grace Cleared from the Charge of Licentiousness. London: n.p., 1751.

The Doctrine of Predestination Stated. London: n.p., 1752.

The Faithful Minister of Christ Crowned. London: n.p., 1767.

The Form of Sound Words Held Fast. London: n.p., 1766.

Gill's Commentaries (6 vols.) Grand Rapids: Baker Book House, 1980 [reprint of the 1852–1854 London edition].

The Law Established by the Gospel. London: n.p., 1756.

The Quiet and Easy Passage of Christ's Purchased People. London: n.p., 1763.

A Sermon on the Death of Elizabeth Gill. London: n.p., 1738.

Treatise on the Doctrine of the Trinity. London: n.p., 1752.

The Work of a Gospel Minister Recommended to Consideration. London: n.p., 1763.

Works about Gill

Brantley, W. T. "Gill and Fuller." *Columbian Star and Christian Index* 2 (16 Jan. 1830): 39–40.

Brown, Raymond. *The English Baptists of the Eighteenth Century.* London: Baptist Historical Society, 1986.

Bush, L. Russ and Thomas J. Nettles. *Baptists and the Bible,* 2d. ed. Nashville: Broadman & Holman, 1999.

Cathcart, William. "John Gill." *The Baptist Encyclopedia* I (1881): 452–54.

Clipsham, E. R. "Andrew Fuller and Fullerism: A Study in Evangelical Calvinism." *Baptist Quarterly* 20 (1965): 99–114.

Daniel, Curt. "Hyper-Calvinism and John Gill." Ph.D. dissertation, Edinburgh University, 1983.

Ella, George M. *John Gill and the Cause of God and Truth.* Eggleston, England: Go Publications, 1995.

————. *John Gill and Justification from Eternity: A Tercentenary Appreciation.* Eggleston: Go Publications, 1998.

Haykin, Michael A. G. *The Life and Thought of John Gill (1697–1771): A Tercentennial Appreciation.* Studies in the History of Christian Thought, Vol. 77. Leiden: E. J. Brill, 1997.

————. "'Resisting Evil': Civil Retaliation, Non-Resistance, and the Interpretation of Matthew 5:39a Among Eighteenth-Century Calvinistic Baptists," *Baptist Quarterly* 36 (Jan. 1996): 212–27.

Nettles, Thomas J. *By His Grace and for His Glory.* Grand Rapids: Baker, 1986.

Newport, Kenneth G. C. "Revelation 13 and the Papal Antichrist in Eighteenth-Century England: A Study in New Testament Eisegesis," *Bulletin of the John Rylands University Library of Manchester* 79 (Spring 1997): 143–60.

Nuttall, G. F. "Northamptonshire and the Modern Question." *Journal of Theological Studies* 16 (1965).

Price, Seymour. "Dr. Gill's Confession of 1729." *Baptist Quarterly* 4 (1928–29).

Rippon, John. *A Brief Memoir . . . of the late Rev John Gill.* London: n.p., 1838.

Robison, O. C. "The Legacy of John Gill." *Baptist Quarterly* 24 (1971): 111–25.

Sell, Alan R. F. *The Great Debate: Calvinism, Arminianism and Salvation.* Grand Rapids: Baker Book House, 1983.

Seymour, R. E. "John Gill—Baptist Theologian." Ph.D. dissertation, Edinburgh University, 1954.

Stennett, Samuel. *The Victorious Christian Receiving the Crown.* London: n.p., 1771.

Toon, Peter. *The Emergence of Hyper-Calvinism in English Nonconformity, 1689–1765.* London: Olive Tree, 1967.

Warren, Edward. *Dr. Gill's Exposition of Such Parts of the New Testament as Refer to the Ordinance of Believers' Baptism: With a Few Observations.* London: Houlston & Stoneman, 1850.

Watts, Michael. *The Dissenters.* Oxford: Clarendon Press, 1978.

Wallin, Benjamin. *The Address at the Interment of Gill. Sacred Remains.* London: n.p., 1852.

Wesley, John. *An Answer to All That the Revd. Dr. Gill Has Printed on the Final Perseverance of the Saints.* London: J. Robinson and T. James, 1754.

White, B. R. "John Gill in London, 1719–1729: A Biographical Fragment." *Baptist Quarterly* 22 (1967): 72–91.

3
Andrew Fuller

By Phil Roberts

Lowly his birth,
And though his manners rough—his aspect stern—
Th' observing eye must soon a DIAMOND discern![1]

THUS THE ODE "CARMEN FLEBILE" DESCRIBED THE ROOTS AND CHARACTER of
Andrew Fuller, the man who exercised the single greatest theological influence on English Particular Baptists in their pilgrimage to becoming a missionary people.

Fuller was born on February 5, 1754, in Wicken, Cambridgeshire, England. His father was a yeoman farmer, and both parents, from dissenting stock, were Baptists. Fuller was born when England was on the verge of becoming a vast world empire. He would live through the American conflict and the French would be the constant enemy of England throughout his life. The rise of Napoleon, whose final defeat at Waterloo came the month after Fuller's death, caused evangelicals to believe the dictator might be the beast of Revelation. A greater measure of prosperity and a slightly increasing life span were concomitants of the burgeoning agricultural revolution. Increasing world trade had introduced tea drinking, among other customs, into the average Englishman's life.

Philosophically and religiously, matters were fluid. Orthodoxy was being challenged by rationalism and empiricism. Many churchmen had tired of the religious wars and controversies of the 1600s. Arianism, Socinianism, and Unitarianism became respectively and increasingly popular and forceful as the century progressed. On the other hand, much of Anglicanism initially, and then after 1750 Orthodox Dissent itself, had been revived by the Methodist Revival under the influence of its leaders, the Calvinist George Whitefield (1714–70) and the Arminian John Wesley (1703–91).

In 1754 the Particular Baptists were as yet mostly untouched by the revival. They were generally strict Dissenters, closed communionists, and many of them were hyper or "high Calvinists." The appellation *hyper* or *high* meant that they were not merely Calvinists of the "five-point" variety, but that for them evangelism in an open and indiscriminate manner did a disservice to God's sovereignty. Baptists generally viewed themselves as the final outgrowth of the Reformation, the *ecclesia semper reformanda,* the manifestation of congregations ordered and governed only by the New Testament. They had yet to embrace the missionary mandate that would be an essential element of their character in the nineteenth century.

Andrew Fuller was reared in a high Calvinistic context. He wrote that as a youth the preaching of his pastor "was not adapted to awaken my conscience" and seldom did he say anything to unbelievers.[2] Consequently his conversion was a protracted, troubled affair and mirrored the questions he would later forcefully address: May one apply directly to Christ for salvation without any certainty that he or she is elect? Should everyone be exhorted to believe in Christ?

A "warrant" or evidence of election was necessary, Fuller had been led to believe, before one could have confidence that God would accept any person for salvation. On one occasion, preservation from a dangerous situation ignited his hope that he might be a "favourite of heaven."[3] The habit of "lying, cursing and swearing," however, often left him in despair.[4]

Fuller's reading encouraged him to continue to seek Christ. John Bunyan's *The Pilgrim's Progress,* among other works, spoke to him about Christ's sufficiency to save, but he was still not convinced "that any poor sinner had a warrant to believe in Christ."[6] Concern came and went, but he found no encouragement to trust Christ from his parents, church, or pastor. He was "like a man drowning, looking every way for help."[7]

Finally, the Bible was to provide the answer he needed. He read Job's resolution, "Though he slay me, yet will I trust in him." He read of Esther, who entered the king's presence *"contrary to the law."* "Like her," he wrote, "I seemed reduced to extremities, impelled . . . to run all hazards, even though I should perish in the attempt."[8] Biblical proof texts and a fear of damnation drove Fuller to believe. He came to the point of complete trust—"I must—I will trust . . . my sinful . . . soul in his hands. In this way I continued above an hour, weeping and supplicating mercy for the Saviour's sake; . . . my guilt and fears were gradually . . . removed."[9]

In 1770 he was baptized and became a member of the Baptist church in Soham. He was made its pastor in May 1775 but still continued for several years in high Calvinism, not daring to "address an invitation to the unconverted to come to Jesus."[10] By 1781, however, having studied his Bible carefully, reread Bunyan, and made acquaintance with pastors John Sutcliff of Olney and Robert Hall of Arnesby, who in turn introduced him to the writings of Jonathan Edwards and other New England divines, Fuller changed his position. In that year he wrote a work advocating indiscriminate gospel preaching. Four years later he published it as *The Gospel of Christ Worthy of All Acceptation: or The Obligations of Men Fully to Credit, and Cordially to Approve, Whatever God Makes Known. Wherein is Considered the Nature of Faith in Christ, and the Duty of Those Where the Gospel Comes in That Matter.* In eighteenth-century style, its title described the contents and almost rivaled them in length. Although Fuller would write other pieces (the Sprinkle edition of his *Works* covers 2,419 pages), some dealing with the same issue, none would be so important as *The Gospel Worthy.*

Both high Calvinists and Arminians attacked this first piece. Other treatises, however, followed. They included *The Calvinistic and Socinian Systems Compared* (1793), *Socinianism Indefensible* (1797), *The Gospel Its Own Witness* (1799), *Letters to Mr. Vidler on the Doctrine of Universal Salvation* (1802), *Strictures on Sandemanianism* (1810), as well as a second edition of *The Gospel Worthy* (1801). In addition to these major pieces, he wrote and published numerous sermons, tracts, letters, and book reviews appearing in, among others, both the *Baptist* and *Evangelical* magazines.

Fuller's concern for evangelism and world missions went beyond theory because the work of his life was the organization, management, and support of the Baptist Missionary Society (hereafter the BMS).[11] Much of his missiological-soteriological thought and theology was worked out in the matrix of sending and supporting missionaries. Fuller attended the organizational meeting of the missionary society on October 2, 1792, and was elected its first secretary. He retained that position until his death and worked tirelessly on its behalf in fund-raising, promotion, and defense in the face of occasional political opposition.

Throughout his life, Fuller remained a pastor, serving two congregations—the church at Soham from 1775 to 1782 and one in Kettering from 1782 to his death.

The Kettering church never exceeded 150 members, although up to a thousand people attended worship in the last decade of Fuller's life.[12] While not a particularly eloquent or exciting preacher (one friend said his "voice was heavy" and his speech was "deformed by colloquialisms") seemingly no one in his preaching had "greater warmth" or more "holy zeal" than Fuller.[13] As an evangelist he was always desirous to practice what he preached, being often "occupied in village preaching" (i.e., evangelistic itinerations).[14] His gospel preaching was punctuated and concluded with forceful evangelistic appeals, if not in a twentieth-century altar-call style, at least with a personal exhortation to belief and trust in Christ.[15]

In recognition of his theological contribution, even though he mastered no biblical languages, Princeton University, then the College of New Jersey, awarded him the D.D. in 1798, and Yale University followed with the same honor in 1805. He refused the Princeton degree, feeling himself intellectually inadequate for it, but accepted Yale's, sensing the same inadequacy, while never using the title.[16] Having earlier contracted an "affection of the lungs," Andrew Fuller died of tuberculosis on May 7, 1815. The assurance of salvation remained with him to the end. "I can go into eternity with composure," he wrote shortly before his death—"Come, Lord Jesus."[17]

Exposition

> Unmov'd by clamor, unseduc'd to wrong
> Fuller the truth maintain'd;
> Resolv'd, in consciousness of right, to stand—
> By fear and lure ungain'd!
>
> ("Carmen Flebile")

As was the case with every Baptist theologian of his day and earlier, Fuller developed his theology as an active pastor. His published work was the result of his preaching and counseling and was often shaped by the questions of his own as well as his congregation's experience. Additionally, due to his unusual intellectual curiosity, his commitment to Scripture and particularly its application to evangelism, and given the unknowns of his character, Fuller's theology work was primarily polemical. He was not a systematizer like John Gill but more a "Valiant-for-Truth." Controversy seemed to fuel his theological production even though he often tired of it and was quite interested in systematic theology.[18] This was true of his first major work *The Gospel of Christ Worthy of All Acceptation* (hereafter the *GWAA*) and much of that which was to follow.

Although having mainly sprung from English Congregationalism and with a debated measure of influence among Baptists, eighteenth-century high Calvinism had a pervasive influence on Fuller's life. Through the work of John Gill (1703–71), a London Baptist pastor, and perhaps more especially that of his neighbor John Brine (1703–65), the particularly important high-Calvinistic doctrine of eternal justification (the view that the elect were justified from eternity even before their conversion) was often used to justify excluding open invitations to believe the gospel. The high Calvinists believed that only people who evidenced signs of election, or a "warrant to believe," should be exhorted to put their faith and trust in Christ.

On the other hand, many English Particular Baptists were by the last quarter of the 1700s greatly under the theological influence of the evangelical Calvinism of the Methodist Revival. English Baptist Calvinism then was not a monolithic system with all of its emphases originating from John Calvin. Fuller's conversion to active and open evangelism was aided by the influence of his contemporaries—Robert Hall, John Ryland Jr., William Carey, and John Sutcliff—who had read the works of Jonathan Edwards and who admired the zeal of George Whitefield. Hall's father, in fact, Robert Hall Sr. published in 1781 *Help to Zion's Travellers,* a sermon advocating general evangelism. He had also advised Fuller to read Edwards. Fuller's first full treatise, the *GWAA,* brought together the best of the ideas of evangelical Calvinism and served as its definitive apologetic in its conflict with its hypercounterpart. The work served to justify identifying evangelical Calvinism in Baptist and Congregational ranks as "Fullerism."

The *GWAA* was issued in Northampton in 1785 and was comprised of 196 pages. It included an introductory first part with "the subject stated, defined and explained" with an "introduction on the importance of the subject."[19] For our purposes, part 2 is more important, because there Fuller lists six arguments, backed and supported primarily by biblical proof texts, to encourage open evangelism. They are: (1) Faith in Christ is commanded in the Bible of unconverted sinners; (2) Every person is bound to approve of what God reveals; (3) The gospel, even as a message of grace, requires obedience; (4) Lack of faith in Christ is sin; (5) God will punish unbelief; and (6) As other spiritual dispositions and exercises such as forgiveness, charity, and the like are required by biblical demands, so is faith a duty. He then answers objections, makes certain inferences from his propositions, and clarifies that he is not intending "to vindicate all the language that has been addressed" to the unconverted nor "all the principles" of those who do. Finally, he spends eleven pages clarifying the moral inability argument he adopted from Jonathan Edwards's *Treatise on the Freedom of the Will*. Simply put, it states that human unwillingness to believe stems from a perverted moral nature and not from any physical or natural incapacity, as high Calvinists often argued.

The *GWAA* touched off significant debate within Baptist ranks on both sides of the question. While his arguments may appear to be obvious to a twentieth-first-century observer, they, in fact, were directed straight at the logic of high Calvinism. William Button, pastor of Dean Street London, was the first who sought to refute it with *Remarks on a Treatise Entitled, The Gospel Worthy*. Button relied on a classically eighteenth-century high-Calvinistic line of argument: (1) Saving faith is of a unique and supernatural character and is distinct from general faith in God. It is that "which none ever had, or was . . . possible to have" except the elect. (2) Man does not have the natural or moral capacity for such faith (making exception with Fuller and Edward's inability argument). (3) God never requires what man cannot do in and of himself. The conclusion, in Button's opinion, is that faith should not be demanded of any person except the elect.[20]

Fuller was well aware of these arguments, having grown up with them and having addressed them in the *GWAA*. However, he replied to Button in 1787 with *A Defense of a Treatise Entitled, the GWAA*. Therein he reasserted that the theories of high Calvinism have been "assumed instead of being proved."[21] He sought then to demonstrate not only the rationale of a free offer of the gospel but its biblical nature as opposed to its opponents' conjectures. Then he questioned Button's failure, as well as that of other high Calvinists, to exegete clearly biblical passages encouraging universal faith and obedience. "I ask . . . in what manner do Mr. B.'s sentiments lead him to EXPOUND SCRIPTURE? How has he expounded the second psalm and the sixth of Jeremiah? What has he made these passages to require more than external obedience?"[22]

This feature of the warfare between the two views carried over to the next year (1788) when another London Baptist pastor, John Martin, published *Thoughts on the Duty of Man Relative to Faith in Jesus Christ*. As a high Calvinist, he also attacked Fuller's arguments that in Scripture faith is commanded of unregenerated sinners and that every person is bound to receive what God reveals. He reworded but used Button's same arguments and logic with little appeal to Scripture.

Fuller responded with *Remarks on Mr. Martin's Publications*. He answered him tersely in only forty pages, perhaps revealing his impatience with the reiteration of old arguments. Fuller asserted that his views were reflective of contemporary Baptist leaders. He also restated his main position that Scripture calls all persons indiscriminately to faith in Christ, and therefore, they are obliged to respond. Martin answered in 1789 with part 2 of

Thoughts on the Duty of Man. In it he repeated previous arguments, but by this time Fuller had lost interest in the debate and did not reply. His reticence did not deter Martin who produced a third part to which, once again, Fuller did not respond.

The Button and Martin writings revealed that among English Particular Baptists high Calvinism was not dead but had stagnated by the late 1780s, seemingly due to its inability to convince people that it was biblically justifiable. Fuller, confessedly a former high Calvinist, as well as other Baptists, had become disenchanted with the lack of adequate scriptural exegesis on the part of their stricter Calvinistic brethren.

Additionally, Fuller was challenged by Daniel Taylor (1738–1816) and Archibald McLean of Scotland (1753–1812). Taylor released his piece pseudonymously—"Philanthropos," or "lover of all men" under the title *Observations on the Rev. Andrew Fuller's Late Pamphlet Entitled the GWAA.* As the founder of the evangelical Arminian Baptist group, the "New Connexion" of General Baptists, he had no argument with Fuller's general thesis that faith is the duty of all. He did disagree with Fuller's Calvinism. Taylor maintained that if God has "determined not to save" everyone, "why should they seek after salvation?"[23] And he, ironically in agreement with the high Calvinists, argued that it is not morally justifiable that God should punish people for what the evangelical Calvinists themselves admit they are not able to do without the renewing power of the Holy Spirit (i.e., to believe in Christ).[24] Taylor continued that God, in universally offering salvation to all people, removed their inability to believe, implying that their inability was due only to their ignorance of the truth.

Fuller responded with his *A Defense of a Treatise Entitled the Gospel of Christ . . . With a Reply to Mr. Buttons Remarks and the Observations of Philanthropos* (1787). He argued that Taylor had failed to recognize the thorough perversity of sin in corrupting the will to believe. Grace alone can overcome that, Fuller maintained. According to Taylor, as Fuller saw it, God offers not grace to sinners but a natural ability to believe. Fuller wrote that natural ability already belongs to sinners in their rational faculties, in the fact that there are not natural impediments in the way of their belief, and because God has clearly manifested his love to them in the giving of his Son.[25] Also Fuller argued that Taylor ignored biblical texts which proved, in his view, that God assures the salvation of the elect in the giving of Jesus Christ. Given the moral inability of sinners, which could only be overcome by grace, it seemed absurd to him that people would be exhorted to believe unless the salvation of those who believed were guaranteed.[26]

Fuller's concern then was with the maintenance of what he believed to be a clear scriptural principle—the election of God's people, one which also supported his Calvinism. Taylor responded twice to Fuller, although the latter seemingly ignored Taylor's further argumentation, perhaps due to what he considered more pressing concerns.

Archibald McLean of the Sandemanians, a Scottish Baptist element which argued that saving faith is the simple intellectual acceptance of the revelation of the gospel, challenged Fuller that making faith anything more (i.e., trust and continuation in obedience—according to Fuller) hampered free invitations to belief. It seemed to him that it was asking people to seek a "warrant" for faith, something Fuller had struggled with in his own conversion, rather than to view faith as the simple intellectual acceptance of Christ's saving work. Fuller, however, chose to stick with his definition of faith that went beyond the intellectual and included at its root trust and reliance on Christ. Given the nature of faith and the depravity of man, Fuller maintained that conviction and regeneration must precede and accompany faith. McLean agreed with the primacy of regeneration but continued to reject Fuller's view of faith. Notably, neither Taylor nor McLean argued with Fuller on the principle of calling all, indiscriminately, to faith in Christ.

The issue of regeneration surfaced again in the course of Fuller's writings before 1800. In 1796, Abraham Booth (1734–1806), a London Baptist pastor at Prescott Street, former General Baptist and now Particular Baptist, published *Glad Tidings to Perishing Sinners or, The Genuine Gospel a Complete Warrant for the Ungodly to Believe in Jesus*. His purpose was to argue in support of the free invitation of the gospel and to defend the doctrine of justification by faith alone, which he felt was threatened by an emphasis on regeneration as anterior to saving faith, a view synonymous with classic Calvinism. Regeneration was being made a prerequisite for indiscriminate evangelism, he felt, and possibly limited its universality. "The genuine gospel" he argued "is a complete warrant . . . to believe in Jesus; and that no degree of holiness, (i.e., regeneration), is necessary for that purpose."[27] Specifically, he was remonstrating against Fuller's the *GWAA* wherein Fuller had argued for the primacy of regeneration, or efficacious conviction, before repentance and public faith.

Booth was answered directly by Thomas Scott (1747–1821), evangelical vicar of Olney, in his *Warrant and Nature of Faith Considered* (1718), in which he supported the necessity of regeneration for belief. Consequently Booth, in 1800, revised and reissued *Glad Tidings*, in which he lengthened his argument by thirty-four pages. Therein he accused Fuller's position of promulgating preparationism and hindering the gospel's free call. Ironically, Fuller as the champion of evangelical Calvinism was now being charged with hindering the gospel. Fuller reviewed Booth's new edition but saved the weight of his argument for a second edition of the *GWAA* in 1801.

In the 1801 edition, Fuller added an appendix "on the question whether the existence of a holy disposition of heart be necessary to believing." Its arguments were aimed straight at Archibald McLean as well as Abraham Booth. Cogently, Fuller presented the case that true belief foregoes "all claim and expectation of favour on the ground of our own deservings" and that "the only hope which remains for us is in the free mercy of God through Jesus Christ." He expressed surprise that anyone would believe that a faith "which implies contrition" should be supposed to oppose the true gospel.[28] While Fuller could hold the tension of his beliefs between the mandate to evangelize everyone and the primacy of regeneration in the *ordo salutis*, McLean and Booth felt they could not. They also sensed that Fuller's views might hamper evangelism. Interestingly, the Fuller-Booth, McLean, and Taylor controversies demonstrated the triumph of evangelical Calvinism because the issue was no longer a question of whether to offer the gospel but was an attempt to remove all hindrances to such ministry.

In a later shorter work "The Nature of Regeneration," Fuller was reticent on the *modus* of the Holy Spirit's operation in regeneration but not its nature.[29] Sin is so terrible in the extent and nature of its influence—exercised primarily on the heart and character—and is total in its ability to destroy proper spiritual judgment. Therefore, regeneration (i.e., conviction and the renewal of the heart) is and must remain absolutely primary in God's order of salvation.

It must be emphasized then that not only was Fuller concerned with high Calvinism and its deadening influence on missions but also with intellectual believism, easy believism, or, in eighteenth-century nomenclature, Sandemanianism. The flowering of his work in this area was his 1810 publication of *Strictures on Sandemanianism, In Twelve Letters to a Friend*. He dealt in greater detail with the necessity of "regeneration" for belief, of the deceptive nature of unbelief, of the shallowness of "mere acceptance of Gospel facts" as being the "faith of devils," of the nature of justification resting in our union and identity with Christ—the fruit of faith—and not the reward of it, and of the danger of allowing the primacy of regeneration, as he saw it, to deter or restrict evangelism.[30]

For the twentieth-century evangelical, the regeneration debate seemingly falls into two parts with a "split decision" going to Andrew Fuller. Abraham Booth's argument raises the important question of nomenclature. Part of Booth's concern, it seems, focuses on whether it is proper to employ the term *regenerate* except for persons who have already put their faith in Jesus Christ. Does it not create confusion to do otherwise? In addition, Fuller's clear stance for the necessity of genuine conviction and the efficacious work of the Holy Spirit in conversion reminds us of the spiritual nature of salvation. True belief is the fruit of not mere persuasion but genuine regeneration. He held this belief in tension with the indelible command of

Scripture for believers to evangelize in a positive and forceful manner—"calling all men everywhere to repent."

The important note regarding Fuller's Calvinistic soteriology was its intensely practical and evangelical nature based upon biblical exegesis. For instance, when discussing the issue of election, he was desirous to have it understood practically. It was to be applied "to declare the source of salvation to be mere grace . . . to cut off all hopes of acceptance with God by works of any kind"; to account for the unbelief of the greater part of the Jewish nation, "without excusing them in it"—in regards to Romans 9; and "to show the certain success of Christ's undertaking as it were in defiance of unbelievers."[31]

His soteriology was intensely evangelical and evangelistic—desiring always to support the *missio Dei*. He summarized it in seven points: (1) "There is no way of obtaining eternal life but by Jesus Christ"; (2) "They that enjoy eternal life must come to Christ for it"; (3) "It is the revealed will of Christ that everyone who hears the gospel should come to him for life"; (4) "The depravity of human nature is such that no man, of his own accord, will come to Christ for life"; (5) "The degree of this depravity is such that, . . . men cannot come to Christ for life"; (6) "A conviction of the righteous of God's government, of the . . . goodness of his law . . . our lost condition by nature . . . is necessary in order to our coming to Christ"; and (7) "There is absolute necessity of a special Divine agency in order to our coming to Christ."[32] The first three points establish Fuller clearly as evangelical, and they also motivated him to be evangelistic. The next four place him firmly in the Calvinistic camp. His avoidance of excessive Calvinistic jargon and high-Calvinistic convictions, however, makes him less than extreme. Point six sets him in opposition to antinomianism.

Fuller's uncompromising advocacy of the exclusiveness of salvation through Christ alone led him into controversy with the universalist William Vidler (1758–1816). Vidler was a former Particular Baptist who had been attracted to universalism by what he felt to be the harshness of the evangelical doctrine of eternal punishment. He joined a small, but growing, number of universalist congregations in the last quarter of the eighteenth century.[33]

Vidler published *God's Love to His Creatures Asserted and Vindicated* in 1799. It was released partly in response to a series of published letters by Fuller to Vidler that appeared in the *Evangelical Magazine* and the *Universalist's Miscellany*, beginning in 1795. The twelve letters were collected and published in 1802 under the title *Letters to Mr. Vidler, on the Doctrine of Universal Salvation*. They represent clear evangelical argument on the issue.

In response to Vidler's view that damnation calls into question both God's mercy and justice, Fuller maintained that universalism obscures and distorts the meaning of the cross. In Vidler's view, cleansing came through temporary punishment for sin in perdition. This concept of cleansing undermined the suffering of Christ's atoning death.[34] Universalism also encouraged unbelievers to continue in their sin, believing that punishment is not eternal. More importantly, perhaps, Fuller spent most of his time exposing Vidler's exegetical and philological weaknesses. In much the caustic style of the period, he surmised, "I never recollect to have seen so much violence done to the word of God in so small a compass. According to your scheme, all things work together for good to them that love not God, as well as to them that love him."[35] Fuller's own exegesis reveals expert and insightful handling of Scripture.

Vidler counterattacked in his *Letters to Mr. Fuller on the Universal Restoration* (1803). Fuller did not respond. These pieces, as well as his well-known polemics against Deism and Socinianism, clearly established Fuller as an important apologist not just for Calvinism, which later in his life bore proportionately much less of his attention, but for the gospel in broader and more evangelical terms.[36]

Abraham Booth, however, felt that by 1801 Fuller had slipped his Calvinistic moorings. With the release that year of a new edition of the *GWAA*, Fuller had seemingly adopted a less strict view of particular redemption than evidenced in the first edition. In the period between the two editions, Fuller had read extensively many of the New England divines and had corresponded with several of them—Jonathan Edwards the younger, Joseph Bellamy, Samuel Hopkins, and Timothy Dwight. Their view of the atonement tended to reflect the thought of Hugo Grotius, a sixteenth-century Dutch divine who had postulated the moral-government view of the cross. This theory stressed God's position as "moral governor of the universe" and not so much as offended Deity, and emphasized his love for order, peace, and forgiveness rather than on his wrath against individual sin. This view tended toward a more general and a less-personalized soteriology.[37]

The New England position militated against that propounded by Tobias Crisp, John Gill, and other high Calvinists, which asserted that Christ had the actual sin of the elect imputed to Him on the cross and that he suffered retribution proportionately to the amount of their sin.[38] In the 1801 version of the *GWAA*, Fuller strongly suggested that that interpretation might support a restricted offer of the gospel: "If the atonement of Christ were considered as the literal payment of a debt . . . it might be inconsistent with indefinite invitations . . . if the atonement of Christ proceed on the principle . . . of moral justice . . . no such inconsistency can justly be ascribed to it."[39]

Fuller was apparently wrong if he thought that Booth's soteriology would significantly hamper Booth's evangelism, while Booth charged Fuller with denying "that Christ died as a substitute," a serious accusation against a self-confessed strict Calvinist.[40] Subsequent publication demonstrates that Fuller rejected any merely symbolic view of the atonement; he countered that Christ suffered indeed as a substitute for sinners while not being made a "sinner" or being made culpable of their sins, a direction in which high Calvinism and antinomianism tended. Additionally, he adopted, if not wholly at least partially, some New England thought in arguing that the atonement was the "great end of moral government" and was in itself "not a pecuniary, but a moral ransom."[41] In so doing, however, it is clear that his goal was to protect the free offer of the gospel while upholding the uniqueness and substitutionary nature of Christ's death on the cross.

Although Fuller was principally concerned with soteriological issues, as has been noted, other issues occupied his thinking as well. He believed firmly in congregational church order and strict discipline and oversight of members in both morals and doctrine; he argued vehemently for believers' baptism as well as for closed communion. Momentum for a relaxation of communion practice to admit nonbaptized members increased by the close of the eighteenth century, but Fuller maintained that to do so was an inversion of the New Testament order of baptism first and then the Lord's Supper. His publication of *The Discipline of the Primitive Churches Illustrated and Enforced* in 1799 made his position clear.[42] Through his influence, as well, missionaries with the BMS were required to practice strict or closed communion.

In his final work before his death, he delved into a new area of theological discourse—eschatology. As late as 1799 he wrote to William Carey—"I have never been deeply versed in prophecies."[43] But he gave himself more completely to its study over the next fifteen years and published *Expository Discourses on the Apocalypse* in 1815. Therein he revealed his adherence to "Latter-Day-Glory" postmillennialism. He had accepted the popular contemporary view first widely promulgated by Jonathan Edwards, and held by Carey as well, that the eighteenth-century revivals and awakenings, the subsequent reformation of society, the rise of missionary activity, and the general revitalization of the church were the prolegomena to Christ's reign upon the earth to be expressed through the conquest of the church. He accepted a historicist view of the Apocalypse, believing along with Edwards that history was then in the period of the sixth vial (cf. Rev. 16:12–16), the period of the overthrow of the temporal power of Antichrist and the introduction to the final vial when God's truth and morality will exercise "its spiritual dominion, or the hold which it has on the minds of men."[44] His eschatology, however unpopular it might be at present, was nonetheless his because he believed it was the accurate biblical position which in turn went the furthest to encourage the evangelization of the world.

Evaluation

What conclusions may be drawn from the theology of Andrew Fuller? First, it is clear that his main work and contribution was soteriological, with emphases on its practical application for evangelism and missions. While some thinkers would tend to lead us to believe that Fuller combated Calvinism generally, it must be noted that his concern was to oppose high Calvinism and to promote a thoroughly evangelistic and evangelical form of that theology.

In so doing, Fuller manifested a willingness to deal with the intricate issues of conversion and salvation that today are often treated glibly and superficially. The two enemies in the camp, so to speak, of evangelical Calvinism were in his view an antimissionary, unbalanced hyper-Calvinism and a mechanical, rationalistic Sandemanianism. In taking the stand that he did, he demonstrated the value of a thoughtful, biblical theology of conversion as an incentive for evangelism and as a check to mental assent alone as being synonymous with genuine repentance and faith.

For most of the nineteenth century, evangelical Calvinism would typify the theological position of the vast majority of English and American Baptists, including those who would constitute the Southern Baptist Convention (1845). Andrew Fuller's work, particularly the *Gospel Worthy of All Acceptation,* made perhaps the most notable contribution toward providing a missionary theology and incentive for world evangelism in the midst of a people both Calvinistic and church oriented. He helped to link the earlier Baptists, whose chief concern was the establishment of ideal New Testament congregations, with those in the nineteenth century driven to make the gospel known worldwide. His contribution helped to guarantee that many of the leading Baptists of the 1800s would typify fervent evangelism and world missions. Charles Spurgeon and J. P. Boyce would be fervent evangelical Calvinists rather than stricter and more scholastic Calvinists typical of Fuller's predecessors at Kettering and London pastors like John Gill and John Brine.

Notably as well, Fuller built his theology on scriptural grounds. It was the Bible and mainly the Bible that proved decisive in his conversion. While friends and other theologians, especially Jonathan Edwards, encouraged him toward an evangelical-evangelistic Calvinism, their influence, it seems, was measured only insofar as Fuller felt them to be faithful to Scripture itself. He wrote several short apologies on the necessity of revelation for divine truth and on the Bible as being the written revelation of God passed on to men, the only source of complete and reliable theology. While eschewing mechanical dictation, he affirmed that, at the least, biblical inspiration meant for him "a Divine superintendence, preserving him [the biblical writer] from error, and from other defects and faults, to which ordinary historians are subject."[45] His faithfulness to Scripture kept him firmly in the Baptist tradition and contributed to the continuum of Baptist concern with biblical theology.

Additionally, his concern for truth and his view that the preservation of theological and biblical veracity was vital to evangelical missions led him to the conviction that controversy should not be eschewed but initiated if the truth was in danger of dilution or perversion. He wrote, "If you love Christ, you will root up those principles which degrade his dignity and set aside his atonement."[46] Without his courage and doctrinal integrity in the face of what he considered to be theological aberrations, the Baptist mission movement might have been stillborn. Theological truth is often preserved and balance achieved only in the crucible of conflict and controversy, a lesson Fuller believed and which many timid Christians today should well learn. He believed, additionally, that confessions and creeds were useful to protect doctrinal integrity. While all truth was in Scripture, he argued that it was not wrong "for a number of individuals, who agree in their judgments [on biblical doctrines], to express that agreement in explicit terms, and consider themselves as bound to walk by the same rule."[47] For him the truth was the fuel and one's personal relationship to God through Christ the flame of the fire of vital biblical Christianity.

For Fuller correct doctrine and theology were not the niceties of the faith but indispensable building blocks of the kingdom of God. In his understanding that meant a Chalcedonian Christology, evangelical Calvinism, and a Baptist church order. Each of these was to be expressed with Christian love and applied practically to world evangelization and mission.

Bibliography

Works by Fuller

An Account of the Particular Baptist Society (used for propagating the gospel among the heathen). 1792.

An Address to the Baptist Churches of the Northamptonshire Association. Northampton: n.p., 1818.

The Admission of Unbaptized Persons to the Lord's Supper, Inconsistent with the New Testament, A Letter, published by Dr. W. Newman. London: n.p., 1815.

Antinomianism Contrasted with the Religion Taught and Exemplified in the Holy Scriptures. 2d ed. Bristol: n.p., 1817.

An Apology for the Late Christian Mission to India. New York: American Tract Society, 1854.

The Backslider; or, an Enquiry into the Nature, Symptoms, and Effects of Religious Declension, with the Means of Recovery. Philadelphia: American Baptist Publication Society, 1856.

"The Blessedness of the Dead Who Die in the Lord" (funeral sermon for Beeby Wallis). London: n.p., 1792.

Calvinistic and Socinian Systems Compared. Philadelphia: 1796.

Christian Patriotism. A Discourse. Demstable: n.p., 1803.

A Collection of Sermons and Tractates, 2 vols. 1784–1817, London, n.d.

A Collection of Tracts and Sermons, 2 vols. Clipstone: n.p., 1801.

The Complete Works of Andrew Fuller. London: n.p., 1841.

The Complete Works of Andrew Fuller, 3 vols. Sprinkle edition with preface by Dr. Tom Nettles, Harrisonburg, Virginia, 1988.

The Complete Works of Andrew Fuller, 8 vols. London: n.p., 1824.

The Complete Works of the Rev. Andrew Fuller, 5 vols. With a memoir of his life by Andrew G. Fuller. 3 vols. Philadelphia: n.p., 1852.

A Defence of a Treatise Entitled the Gospel of Christ Worthy of All Acceptation. With a reply to Mr. Button's Remarks and the observations of Philanthropos. Philadelphia: n.p., 1810.

"Dialogues, Letters and Essays on Various Subjects." Hartford: n.p., 1820.

The Discipline of the Primitive Churches Illustrated and Enforced. New York: n.p., 1825.

The Christian Doctrine of Rewards. Boston: n.p., 1802.

An Essay on Truth. Boston: n.p., 1806.

"The Excellence and Utility of the Grace of Hope" (circular letter of the Northamptonshire Association). Northampton: n.p., 1782.

Expository Discourses on the Apocalypse. Kettering: n.p., 1815.

Expository Discourses on the Book of Genesis. London: n.p., 1836.

Expository Remarks on the Discipline of the Primitive Church. Providence: n.p., 1820.

God's Approbation of Our Labours Necessary to the Hope of Success. Boston: n.p., 1802.

The Gospel of Christ Worthy of All Acceptation. Boston: n.p., 1846.

The Gospel its own Witness. Philadelphia: n.p., 1803.

The Great Question Answered. London: n.p., 1803.

The Harmony of Scripture. London: n.p., 1817.

Hints to Ministers and Churches. London: n.p., 1826.

The Importance of a Deep and Intimate Knowledge of Divine Truth. London: n.p., 1796.

"An Inquiry into the Nature, Symptoms, and Effects of Religions Declension, with the Means of Recovery" (circular letter). Philadelphia: n.p., 1832.

Jesus the True Messiah. London: n.p, 1811.

"Joy in God" (circular letter). Northampton: n.p., 1793.

Letters to Mr. Vidler on the Doctrine of Universal Salvation. Ohio: n.p., 1832.

Memoirs of Pearce. 4th ed. London: n.p., 1816.

Miscellaneous Pieces on Various Religious Subjects. London: n.p., 1826.

Missionary Correspondence: Extracts of Letters from Samuel Pearce and John Thornas. London: n.p., 1814.

"Moral and Positive Obedience" (circular letter). Spalding: n.p., 1807.

A Narrative of Facts relative to a late occurrence in the Country of Cambridge, in Answer to a Statement contained in a Unitarian Publication called "The Monthly Repository." London: n. p., 1810.

The Nature and Importance of Walking by Faith. Boston: n.p., 1802.

"Open Communion Unscriptural: A Letter to the Rev. William Ward." London: n.p., 1824.

"Oration Delivered at the Funeral of the Rev. Robert Hall, Sr." London: n.p., 1791.

"The Pastor's Address to His Christian Hearers, Entreating Their Assistance in Promoting the Interest of Christ." Leicester: n.p., 1806.

"The Perniscious Influence of Delay in religious Concerns" (a sermon at Clipstone). Clipstone: n.p., 1791.

The Practical Uses of Christian Baptism. Montpelier, Vt.: n.p., 1814.

The Principal Works and Remains of the Rev. Andrew Fuller (with a New Memoir by His Son the Rev. Andrew G. Fuller). London: n.p., 1864.

"The Principles and Prospects of a Servant of Christ" (a sermon preached at the funeral of the Rev. John Sutcliff). Kettering: n.p., 1814.

The Reality and Efficacy of Divine Grace; by Agnostos. London: n.p., n.d.

"On Religious Declension: as an Inquiry into Its Nature, Symptoms, and Effects, With the Means of Recovery." London: n.p., n.d.

Remarks on Mr. Martin's Publication entitled "Thoughts on the Duty of Man relative to Faith in Jesus Christ." London: n.p., 1789.

Remarks on the state of Baptist churches in Ireland after his trip in 1804. London: n.p., 1804.

Salvation Through a Mediator Consistent with Sober Reason. London: n.p., n.d.

"A Sermon Delivered at the Ordination of Thomas Morgan." Birmingham, n.p., 1802.

"The Situation of the Widows and Orphans of Christian Ministers" (circular letter). Northampton: n.p., 1815.

Socinianism Indefensible on the Ground of its Moral Tendency. London: n.p., 1797.

A Statement of the Committee of Shacklewell. 1807.

Strictures on Sandemanianism. New York: n. p., 1812.

"The Substance of Two Discourses Delivered at the Settlement of the Rev. Robert Fawkner at Thorn in Bedfordshire." London: n.p., 1787.

"Substance of the Charge Delivered to the Missionaries at the Parting Meeting at Leicester." Clipstone: n.p., 1793.

Summary of the Principal Evidences for the Truth, and Divine Origin of the Christian Revelation. New York: n.p., 1801.

"Thoughts on Open Communion in a Letter from the late Rev. Andrew Fuller to the Rev. William Ward." London: n.p., 1817.

"A Vindication of Protestant Dissent" (from the charges of the Rev. Thomas Robinson) Vicar of St. Mary's. Leicester: n.p., 1804.

Fuller, Andrew, and Sutcliff, John. "Two Discourses delivered at a Meeting of Ministers at Clipstone" (27 April 1791). London: n.p., 1791.

Works about Fuller

Anonymous. "Carmen Flebile: Or, An Ode, to the Memory of the Late Andrew Fuller." London: n.p., 1815.

Clipsham, E. P. "Andrew Fuller and Fullerism: a Study in Evangelical Calvinism," *The Baptist Quarterly*, vol. 20, 1963–64.

———. "Andrew Fuller's Doctrine of Salvation," B.D. thesis, Oxford University, 1971.

Duncan, Pope A., Sr. "The influence of Andrew Fuller on Calvinism," Th.D. thesis, The Southern Baptist Theological Seminary, 1917.

Eddins, John W., Jr. "Andrew Fuller's Theology of Grace," Th.D. thesis, The Southern Baptist Theological Seminary, 1957.

Ella, George M. *Law and Gospel in the Theology of Andrew Fuller*. Eggleston, Co. Durham, England: Go Publications, 1996.

Fuller, Andrew G. *Andrew Fuller*, London: n.p., 1882.

———. *The Complete Works of the Rev. Andrew Fuller in one volume: with a Memoir of His Life*. London: n.p., 1841. This memoir also appears in the third and fifth volume edition of Fuller's *Works*.

Fuller, T. E. *A Memoir of the Life and Writings of Andrew Fuller*. London: n.p., 1863.

Haykin, Michael A.G. *One Heart and One Soul: John Sutcliff of Olney, His Friends and His Times*. Darlington, England: Evangelical Press, 1994.

———. "'Resisting Evil': Civil Retaliation, Non-Resistance, and the Interpretation of Matthew 5:39a Among Eighteenth-Century Calvinistic Baptists," *Baptist Quarterly* 36 (Jan. 1996), p. 212–27.

———. "A Socinian and Calvinistic Compared: Joseph Priestley and Andrew Fuller on the Propriety of Prayer to Christ," *Dutch Review of Church History*. 73, no 2 (1993), p. 178–98.

———. "'The Oracles of God': Andrew Fuller and the Scriptures," *Churchman*. 103 no 1 (1989), p. 60–76.

Ivimey, Joseph. *The Perpetual Intercession of Christ for His Church; A Source of Consolation Under The Loss of Useful Ministers. A Sermon To The Memory of the late Rev. Andrew Fuller*. London: n. p., 1815.

Keown, Harlice E. "The Preaching of Andrew Fuller," Th.M. thesis, The Southern Baptist Theological Seminary, 1957.

Kirkby, A. H. "Andrew Fuller—Evangelical Calvinist," *Baptist Quarterly* 15 (1953–54).

———. "The Theology of Andrew Fuller and Its Relation to Calvinism," Ph.D. thesis, University of Edinburgh, 1956.

Laws, Gilbert. *Andrew Fuller, Pastor, Theologian, Ropeholder*. London: n.p., 1942.

McKibbens, Thomas R. "Disseminating Biblical Doctrine Through Preaching," *Baptist History and Heritage* 19 (1984), p. 42–52.

Morris, J. W. *Memoirs of the Life and Writings of the Rev Andrew Fuller*. London: n.p., 1826.

Nelson, Thomas. *The Gospel Its Own Witness, with a Life of the Author*. Edinburgh: n.p., 1830.

Newman, William. *Reflections on the Fall of a Great Man. A Sermon Occasioned by the Death of the Rev Andrew Fuller.* London: n.p., 1815.

Nuttall, Geoffrey F. "'The State of Religion in Northamptonshire' (1793) by Andrew Fuller," *Baptist Quarterly* 29 No 4 (Oct. 1981), p. 177–179.

Ryland, John. *The Work of Faith, the Labour of Love, and the Patience of Hope, illustrated; in the Life and Death of the Rev. Andrew Fuller.* London: n.p., 1818.

South, Thomas J. "The Response of Andrew Fuller to the Sandemanian View of Saving Faith," Th.D. thesis, Mid-America Baptist Theological Seminary, 1993.

Young, Doyle L. "Andrew Fuller and the Modern Missions Movement," *Baptist History and Heritage* 17 (1982), p. 17–27.

4
John L. Dagg

By Mark E. Dever

Biography

JOHN LEADLEY DAGG (1794–1884) WAS THE FIRST SOUTHERN BAPTIST systematic theologian to be read widely by Southern Baptists. He exercised a long, prominent, and influential ministry as pastor, administrator, and teacher in Virginia, Pennsylvania, Alabama, and Georgia. Over one hundred years after his birth, his *Manual of Theology* was still frequently cited and used in colleges and theological seminaries. Now more than two hundred years after his birth, this comparatively unknown theologian's *Manual of Theology* and *Church Order* is again in print. In 1903 E. Y. Mullins wrote that Dagg "was one of the most conspicuous figures among the Baptists of the South during the nineteenth century. . . . His work on theology has exerted a widespread and powerful influence throughout the South as well as elsewhere. Truly his was a life rich in influence for good and these influences continue in power to the present hour."[1] Who was this man? What did he teach?

John L. Dagg was born on February 14, 1794, in Middleburg, Virginia.[2] Dagg's boyhood was largely uneventful. His formal education was scant. Religion was not a large part of the Dagg household during his earliest years. Although his mother was raised as a Presbyterian, neither of his parents claimed to be converted until Dagg's early teenage years. He recounts his own conversion as having occurred in 1809.

Once converted, Dagg undertook a study of the highly controversial doctrine of infant baptism. Surrounded by Presbyterian literature and friends, Dagg thought it his duty to investigate the claims of infant baptism. Coming to baptistic conclusions, Dagg was baptized into the Ebeneezer Baptist Church by William Fristoe in the spring of 1812. After a few years studying medicine, Dagg was ordained to the ministry in November 1817. He spent the next eight years in his native northern Virginia pastoring several smaller churches. A preacher of some ability, Dagg received calls to large, city churches.[3] He declined these calls, however, and continued serving the small churches.

The second chapter of Dagg's ministry began in January 1825, when he accepted the call to the fashionable Fifth Baptist Church of Philadelphia. This young congregation already boasted a sanctuary that could seat 1,300—the largest Baptist sanctuary in Philadelphia. During this time his involvement in larger denominational concerns naturally increased.[4] He was an ardent spokesman for missions work, whether in western Pennsylvania or among the Cherokees in Georgia. Dagg's successful pastorate in Philadelphia ended due to the failure of his voice in 1834. Wanting to retain his services in the area, the Baptists of the Philadelphia Association approached him about serving as president and professor of theology at a new school (the Haddington Institute) they desired to open. Dagg accepted the position and served there until 1836, when the school was dissolved.

Dagg spent the next eight years of his life in Tuscaloosa, Alabama, as president of the Alabama Female Athenaeum. He continued to be active in Baptist life, serving on many committees and as an officer of the Alabama Baptist Convention. He was not, however, able to attend national meetings easily due to his poor health and the difficulties of the journey.

Dagg left Tuscaloosa on January 29, 1844, to journey to Mercer University in Penfield, Georgia, where he had been called as president and professor of theology. Dagg went with high hopes that Mercer would become the "Theological Seminary for the Southern States."[5] As president (1844–54), Dagg labored to build the theological department of Mercer. By the early 1850s, it was perhaps the most celebrated theological school in the South.[6] As a professor (1844–55), he was held in high regard by his peers. Mercer enjoyed great prosperity during his presidency, with student enrollment, value of property, and endowment growing severalfold.[7] During his successful tenure at Mercer, Dagg was called upon for larger denominational service.[8] In 1856 he retired from teaching theology at Mercer.

Dagg continued to live in Georgia for the next fifteen years. During the first years of his retirement he wrote his four larger books. The first and most celebrated was his *Manual of Theology*, published in 1857.[9] Then followed his *Treatise on Church Order* (1858), *Elements of Moral Science* (1859), and *Evidences of Christianity* (not published until 1869). During this time, his infirmities greatly increased. In 1870 Dagg moved with his daughter, Mrs. Henry Rugeley, to Lowndesboro for a few months, then to Hayneville, Alabama (near Montgomery), where he remained until his death on June 11, 1884, at the age of ninety.

Dagg attended the 1869 meeting of the Southern Baptist Convention in Macon, Georgia. Then seventy-five years old, Dagg's only involvement was to lead in the devotional exercises on the first morning of the Convention. While Dagg was never able to attend another Convention meeting, it is clear that his influence on the body endured. Through his long years of outstanding service in Virginia, Pennsylvania, Alabama, and Georgia, Dagg had developed many close relationships with the religious leaders of the day. His service at Mercer was well known and greatly appreciated. His writings served to keep his thoughts before the minds of thousands of his fellow ministers. In 1879 during the meeting of the Southern Baptist Convention in Atlanta, W. H. Whitsitt moved that "a catechism . . . containing the substance of the Christian religion" be drawn up by the "venerable" J. L. Dagg. The resolution passed unanimously.[10] Such was the respect and influence of John Leadley Dagg.[11]

Exposition

John L. Dagg's *Manual of Theology* reveals a theology both simple and profound. In the *Manual* itself, Dagg neither quoted nor mentioned any authors, other than the Author of Holy Scripture. "It has been my aim to lead the mind of the reader directly to the sources of religious knowledge, and incite him to investigate them for himself, without respect to human authority."[12] Dagg presented theology as always an expression of piety, a loving heart desiring to know more of its Beloved. To search out the nature of God, his will, and his works, was an obligation for every sincere believer. Theology was not the task of the theologian any more than it was the task of the pastor, the deacon, or the church member. "The study of religious truth ought to be undertaken and prosecuted from a sense of duty, and with a view of the improvement of the heart. When learned, it ought not to be laid on the shelf, as an object of speculation; but it should be deposited deep in the heart, where its sanctifying power ought to be felt. To study theology, for the purpose of gratifying curiosity, or preparing for a profession, is an abuse and profanation of what ought to be regarded as most holy. To learn things pertaining to God, merely for the sake of amusement, or secular advantage, or to gratify the mere love of knowledge, is to treat the Most High with contempt."[13]

Sanctification and edification rather than mere illumination were the ends of all proper theology. Knowledge of God was presented as the vehicle that the Holy Spirit used to bring one to know God, and to be completely transformed by him. Dagg, therefore, introduced each of the eight "books" of his *Manual of Theology* with a section on the duty arising from the doctrine discussed within the book. Knowledge, for Dagg, clearly involved responsibility.

God

How do we know about God in order to know him personally? Dagg presented four valid means of religious knowledge—personal moral and religious feelings, the moral and religious feelings of society, the natural world, and divine revelation. The first three of these, Dagg wrote, led to "Natural Religion," which taught the "fundamental truths on which all religion is based . . . ." Among these fundamentals, Dagg included knowledge of the existence of God, that this God is to be worshiped, that the soul is immortal, some basic morality, and that all people are ultimately accountable for their actions. Yet none of this was saving knowledge of God. For that, we are specifically given the unique divine revelation of the Bible, the written word—"the perfect source of religious knowledge, and the infallible standard of religious truth."[14]

After exhorting his readers to the love of God, Dagg set out the doctrine of God in traditional terms. The existence of God is "demonstrated" by our own moral nature, the existence of the world, and the common consent of mankind to this fact. Yet ultimately, the existence and character of God can only be established beyond doubt by God's revelation of himself in the Bible.

What do we learn about God from divine revelation? From Scripture we learn that there is but one God. This God is a spirit who is everywhere, eternal, and who knows all things. He is free, all-powerful, infinitely benevolent, always truthful, perfectly just, immaculately holy, and infinitely wise. As was typical of Protestant thought into the nineteenth century, Dagg held that "holiness" was the essence of God's character, comprising in itself all the other characteristics of God. These attributes were to be seen as a unified whole, together reflecting the nature of God.

God is not a static, unmoved mover but is an active God. God has a plan for the world and actively pursues that plan to the delight of all true believers. In discussing the will of God, Dagg distinguished between the will of "command" and the will of "purpose." By the former Dagg intended simply that which God commands us to do. This will is that which he would require of us; it is our duty revealed in his statutes and judgments, revealed most clearly in the Bible. God's will of "purpose" is his free, self-conscious determination of what he in fact does.

The fact that God has so determined his actions should not be taken as destroying the free agency of humans. Though he overrules all things, God is not to be charged with the authorship of sin. Dagg distinguished the authorship of sin from the permission of sin. The first is clearly denied in Scripture (1 John 1:5; James 1:13,17); the second is clearly affirmed (Acts 14:16). This distinction, helpful as it has been in Christian theology, leaves much unanswered. Dagg recognized this in his treatment of the vexed question of the reprobate. Here, Dagg exhorted his readers simply to trust God and to know that the author of justice can never himself be unjust. Dagg explained, "If right principles prevailed in our hearts, we would not presume to dictate to the Infinitely Wise, nor find fault with his plans, but wait with pleasure on the development of his will: and when we cannot see the wisdom and goodness of his works, we should, in the simplicity of faith, rest assured that his plan, when fully unfolded, will be found most righteous and most wise."[15]

What has God in fact willed? Dagg answered this with the traditional distinction of God's acts of creation and providence. Creation was God's action of creating all things out of nothing. His works of providence include his continual preservation of all things by his power and his control of their changes, of nature, of the moral sense of humanity, and ultimately of human actions. God has providentially predestined all things. His design is, at points, mysterious (as in its provision for sin in the world) but is, nevertheless, certain. In this mystery human philosophy must always show its inadequacy for the task of theology.

Humanity

And what of humanity? The fact that God has called all to repent (Matt. 3:2; Acts 17:30) is evidence of the present sinful state of humanity. Originally, man and woman were created holy. Humans are not sinful by creation but only by the great perversion—the Fall. Dagg taught that a literal, historical Adam and Eve had been created as the first humans by God and that they personally had violated their obligations of obedience to God.[16] This single act of disobedience plunged their entire offspring—the human race—into a state of alienation from God. By the act of one, all became transgressors of the covenant of God.

In recounting his conversion, Dagg wrote, "I saw clearly its [sin's] tendency to dethrone God, and felt that by this tendency its guilt was to be estimated."[17] Dagg believed that this was the experience of all humanity. Adam and Eve had acted as holy representatives for all of their progeny; therefore, their depravity entailed our own. Through them human nature became sinful. This total depravity did not mean that there are no "amiable affections" in the heart of the fallen person. Rather, it meant that "the love of God dethroned from the heart, and therefore the grand principle of morality is wanting, and no true morality exists. A total absence of that by which the actions should be controlled and directed, is total depravity."[18]

Love of self replaced the love of God. The corruption and guilt of this ruling love of self came to all of Adam's descendants by their federal, moral, and natural unions with Adam. The federal union was that by which God constituted Adam the representative of all of his descendants. The moral union is the actual sin that all humans, Adam and his descendants, willingly commit. The natural union is the fact of the physical descent of all humans from Adam. Dagg was unclear about exactly how this sinful nature was transmitted, but he asserted that it was clear that it was transmitted. Depravity entails the corruption of the image of God in humanity—conscience, actions, and even our mental capacities. It does not, however, entail the loss of the human will. Yet since a person's will always follows his own nature (that is now sinful) the person will inevitably will to sin. All humans are, therefore, condemned, helpless, and—apart from the intervention of God's Holy Spirit—spiritually dead.[19]

Christ

The necessity of this intervention of the Holy Spirit leads into Dagg's treatment of Christ. The object of our belief—Christ—must be understood to be both a man and God. Following Anselm (though without mentioning him) Dagg argued that God had to become man in order for him to be a suitable sacrifice for those whose places he would assume. And yet the man Christ Jesus is also presented in Scripture as God (John 1:1, 14; 20:28; Acts 20:28; Rom. 9:5; Heb. 1:8; 1 John 1:3; Rev. 19:13). Names of God, attributes of God, works of God, Old Testament references to God, and worship of God are all ascribed to Jesus Christ in the New Testament. Without referring to Chalcedon, or using all of its language, Dagg taught Chalcedonian orthodoxy. The union of the divine and human natures in Jesus Christ was without confusion or dissolution.

Dagg clearly affirmed the preexistence of Christ, his incarnation, and his resurrection, ascension, and intercession. He used the traditional tripartite distinction of the three offices of Christ—prophet, priest, and king. As a prophet, Jesus Christ revealed God to humans. As a priest, he made "an efficacious sacrifice for the sins of his people, and intercedes for them at the right hand of God, and blesses them with all spiritual blessings."[20] Finally, as king, Christ has authority over all for the glory of God and for the good of his people. Dagg treated the office of priest most extensively. Dagg taught that Christ's sacrifice effected atonement between helpless sinners and God. Christ died as a substitute for those who had incurred God's wrath, thereby reconciling sinners and God. He rejected any idea of the cross as simply a stirring example. That Christ's death was actually an atoning sacrifice for our sins was, he wrote, the doctrine that was "essential to Christianity."[21] "It was not Christ transfigured on Mount Tabor; not Christ stilling the tempest, and raising the dead; not Christ rising triumphantly from the grave, and ascending gloriously, amidst shouts of attendant angels, to his throne in the highest heavens: but Christ on the cross, expiring in darkness and woe, which the first preachers of the Gospel delighted to exhibit to the faith of their hearers. This was their Gospel; its centre, and its glory."[22]

Holy Spirit

Dagg's briefest "book" in his *Manual of Theology* was reserved for the Holy Spirit. This brevity is not evidence of a low, or undeveloped pneumatology, but rather of an entire theology done "in tandem" with the Holy Spirit. Each doctrine is treated as a sanctifying tool of the Holy Spirit. Therefore, much of the work of the Spirit is discussed in other places throughout his *Manual of Theology*. Dagg taught that Christians are utterly dependent for their spiritual lives upon a Person, distinct from the Father and the Son—the Holy Spirit. This third Person of the Trinity is no mere force, or influence, but clearly a Person. And this Person is clearly God. In the formula for baptism, and in the Great Commission, the Holy Spirit is named along with the Father and the Son as God. The Holy Spirit is legitimately worshiped (1 Cor. 6:19) and can be sinned against (Acts 5:3–4). Furthermore, passages in the Old Testament applied to God are clearly applied in the New Testament to the Holy Spirit (Exod. 17:7; cf. Heb 3:9; Isa. 6:8; cf. Acts 28:25; Jer. 31:31–34; cf. Heb. 10:15–17). The Holy Spirit is eternal, omnipresent, omniscient. He created, performs miracles, and raised Christ from the dead. In short, the Holy Spirit is God. His work among Christians is to set us apart as God's special people and to comfort us. He has become our Emmanuel.

Salvation

Divine grace is very important in Dagg's theology. As a Baptist Dagg stood in the Reformed tradition of earlier Baptist theologians such as John Bunyan, Benjamin Keach, John Gill, Andrew Fuller, and Isaac Backus. Dagg's theology emphasized God's grace and the human response of gratitude. One could almost say that for Dagg all of theology was a study in the grace of God. It is not surprising, therefore, to find his treatment of the doctrine of the Trinity in his book on "Divine Grace." "The doctrine of a threefold distinction in the Godhead, belongs especially to the economy of grace . . . ."[23] This is so because Dagg combined an orthodox, Nicene treatment of the Trinity (affirming that Father, Son, and Holy Spirit, are three Persons in one divine essence) with the expressions of Covenant theology. This theology originated among the Reformers and was most clearly developed in the late-fifteenth and sixteenth centuries. Covenant theology taught that before the foundations of the world, the three divine Persons of the Trinity had determined to cooperate in salvation according to an eternal, pretemporal, intra-Trinitarian covenant. Dagg, too, taught that this was the framework upon which the entire story of redemption was to be understood.[24]

"The salvation of men is entirely of divine grace."[25] Each aspect of our salvation—our pardon, justification, adoption, regeneration, sanctification, final perseverance, and ultimate perfection—is accomplished only by the grace of God. This is consistent with Dagg's teaching of the helplessness of depraved humanity. That salvation is due completely to the grace of God is seen most clearly in Christ's bearing our burden of sin for us. Only his blood could effectually remove our sins. Apart from his action, no one could be saved. His righteousness is imputed to those for whom he died. Believers obtain this benefit from Christ by means of their consensual, spiritual, and federal unions with Christ (paralleling humanity's three unions with Adam). The consensual union is that union of Christ and the believer by that Christ consents to be the believer's substitute, and the believer consents to be found in Christ. The spiritual union is that union of the spirit by which the believer's spirit is reborn by the Spirit of God. The federal union is that union by which the believer is incorporated into the covenant of grace, now taking Christ as his legal representative before God. By these unions with Christ, believers are justified before God. Adoption is accomplished, whereby God's love and discipline are freely given to the believer. Regeneration is made possible only through God's gift of faith.[26] Sanctification, too, is primarily the work of the Spirit of God. Perseverance of the regenerate is certain, by God's grace. Rejecting the doctrine of final perseverance placed the hope of salvation on human effort, not on the purpose and grace of God. From the work of election to glorification, Dagg resisted any notion that would transfer salvation from the responsibility of God to the responsibility of man.

This insistence on the priority of God in salvation arose, in part, from Dagg's understanding of the Scripture's teaching on election, particular redemption, and effectual calling. In these doctrines the consistent, cooperative activities of Father, Son, and Holy Spirit could be seen, each working for the salvation of a great multitude of humanity. Before the foundations of the world, the Father elected some. Since the salvation of any was purely a matter of grace, exceeding mere human justice or desert, the charge of injustice could not meaningfully be hurled at God in any of his saving actions. Dagg asserted an uncompromising eternal election by God as the basis of salvation. "All who will finally be saved, were chosen to salvation by God the Father, before the foundation of the world, and given to Jesus Christ in the covenant of grace."[27] This election is taught in Scripture and is mandated by the fact that God will certainly distinguish between the righteous and the unrighteous at the day of judgment. If it is right for him to so distinguish in judgment, then it was right for such to be his purpose from all eternity. Dagg specifically rejected the Arminian interpretation (although not by name) that God's election was based upon his foreknowledge of the faith and obedience of some. He insisted that God by his mere grace chose some from among all of those who were under just condemnation and elected them to be the objects of his mercy.

Dagg defined the practical implications of this doctrine. Instead of making human effort useless, election produces that ultimate trust in and dependence upon God that is most needful for us to continue living as believers. Instead of undermining morality and creating antinomianism, it encourages believers to live holy and obedient lives, knowing that the Scriptures teach that such lives are evidences of God's election. Rather than suggesting that God is unjust, it shows him to be at once truly sovereign and just yet also merciful and gracious. Rather than proving God to be a "respecter of persons," it demonstrates that those regenerated are not so blessed because of any superiority within themselves but simply by God's grace. Rather than rendering a "promiscuous" preaching of the gospel to all "insincere," such an understanding of the doctrine of election underscores the faithfulness of God to all, whether in judgment of their sins or in gracious salvation to those who respond in trust to him through the gospel message. Rather than diminishing the extent of God's love, it leaves the ultimate extent unchanged from the Arminian perspective yet increases its depth and height (i.e., from eternity to eternity). Rather than presenting God as a despotic tyrant because of his reprobation of a part of the human race to misery, God is shown to be just yet gracious (cf. Matt. 20:13–15). And finally, rather than being the doctrine of those who assume that they are among the chosen, this doctrine is the teaching of Scripture, creating not pride and self-satisfaction among those who receive it but humility and a recognition of their utter dependence upon God. God's favor can never be earned—not even by the believer's acceptance of the doctrine of election.[28]

The doctrine of particular redemption clearly followed from this doctrine of election. Those whom the Father elected, the Son redeemed. Jesus had a particular people in view when he laid down his life. Just as the Father's election was particular, not extending to every individual, so the Son died to redeem not every individual, but a particular people. The cross was not a divine gamble, but a divine triumph. This is consistent, Dagg insisted, with the idea of the existence of hell. For should any suffer in hell if Christ has already suffered for them? Would not this be unjust? And yet if Christ died as a substitute for all, surely none could be sent to suffer again for those same sins for which Christ has already suffered. Dagg maintained that the intent of the atonement was clearly that the elect should be redeemed. To object either that the death of Christ must have been infinitely valuable, or that He had to suffer a specific additional amount for each one of those who respond to the gospel was to go beyond the testimony of Scripture. Simple faith would dictate that Christ's death was of appropriate value for the end He intended for it. To say that it was more than that, or to try to evaluate it more specifically, is unwarranted by God's self-revelation in Scripture. All the Scripture clearly teaches is that "the Son of God gave his life to redeem those who were given to him by the Father in the covenant of grace."[29]

The Holy Spirit's part in this covenant of redemption was to call effectually to repentance and belief all whom the Father had elected and for whom Christ had died. While all who hear the gospel are called externally, only those who have felt the distinguishing grace of God, the internal grace, have that external call made effectual. This effectual calling of the sinner by the Holy Spirit always results in regeneration. Again, God is the author of salvation. All are under the just condemnation of God for their willful rebellion, and yet God—Father, Son, and Holy Spirit—has acted to bring some graciously to new life to the praise of his glory. Such action by such a God toward such creatures is entirely beyond explanation apart from his supreme love to us in Christ.

Eschatology

What was to be the end of this grand drama of redemption? Dagg answered that for the soul and the body, and for the righteous and the wicked, the ends will be different. For the soul, Dagg taught that there was immortality. God created each soul immortal. This was not so because philosophically it must be so, but because biblically God had revealed that it was so (2 Cor. 5:8; Luke 23:43; John 14:3). For the body, the Scriptures taught that the bodies of all who die "will be raised from the dead, and reunited to their spirits, for the judgment of the great day."[30]

Finally, there is to be a future day of judgment in which Christ will judge all people according to their works. This day of judgment will be at Christ's second advent. Dagg did not clearly state his position on the Second Coming of Christ along the division common today (premillennial, postmillennial, or amillennial). What was important to him was the certainty and the outcome of that event. The certainty of it was clear from Scripture—Christ would bodily return in power and great glory to judge the living and the dead. The outcome of that event was twofold. For the righteous, the outcome will be heaven and perpetual happiness in the presence and enjoyment of God. While much is untold in Scripture, it is certain that there will be the best possible society, the most delightful employment, the absence of all unhappiness and the presence of all true enjoyment. For the wicked, hell is their eternal destination. There they "will suffer everlasting punishment for their sins."[31] Wherever and whenever hell may literally be, Scripture clearly teaches that this is to be the nature of it. This misery is not for the sake of purification, so that all may ultimately be restored to God, nor is it ultimately annihilating. God's justice demands that each person is considered a moral agent, bound to love and obey him, and that those who do not do so are justly guilty, and liable to, and even require punishment. This, Dagg taught, in no way mars God's benevolence to humanity; rather, it ensures the existence of true morality in the world.

The Church

That doctrine which is most distinctive of Baptists, and yet which has been the most disputed within Baptist groups is certainly the doctrine of the church. Questions of structure, forms of worship, the nature of the church (local and/or universal) and, of course, baptism have repeatedly divided and defined Baptist groups. In the middle of the nineteenth century the American frontier was the arena of Alexander Campbell and J. R. Graves. Denominational strife and pride were unusually prominent. It is not surprising, therefore, that John L. Dagg would choose to write a separate book, almost equal in length to his *Manual of Theology*, which dealt solely with ecclesiology. This reflected not only Dagg's historical situation but also his commitment to the reality and importance of obedience to Christ in all that is revealed. Dagg concluded his introduction to *A Treatise on Church Order* by writing that

> Church order and the ceremonials of religion are less important
> than a new heart; and in the view of some, any laborious inves-
> tigation of questions respecting them may appear to be needless
> and unprofitable. But we know, from the Holy Scriptures,
> which Christ gave commands on these subjects, and we cannot
> refuse to obey. Love prompts our obedience; and love prompts

also the search that may be necessary to ascertain his will. Let us, therefore, prosecute the investigations that are before us, with a fervent prayer, that the Holy Spirit, who guides into all truth, may assist us to learn the will of him whom we supremely love and adore.[32]

Dagg taught that a Christian church is "an assembly of believers in Christ, organized into a body, according to the Holy Scriptures, for the worship and service of God."[33] Unlike the "Landmarkists" of his day, Dagg used *church* to refer to local assemblies of Christians, regardless of denominational distinctives. The members of a church are only those who profess saving trust in Christ. (Dagg recognized that this was not equivalent to saying that only the elect are members of the local church, but it was denying, among other things, the practice of infant membership.)[34] This church was by definition an organized assembly. It was also a distinct, independent assembly, the New Testament having nowhere taught that one church was to be supervised by any organization or individual outside of the local church. The guiding rule for contemporary churches must always be the practice of the New Testament church. While not implying that "every minute particular in the doings of a church" is regulated by following New Testament practice, in major matters the New Testament is meant as the church's pattern.[35] Thus, baptism is still a prerequisite for church membership because it was so in the New Testament church.

Dagg also taught that the word *church* was used in the New Testament to refer to a universal company of all of those who are saved by Christ. This position was stringently criticized in the new teachings of the "Landmarkists." Yet Dagg specifically defended this doctrine against the Landmarkers, even quoting from their own popular writings.[36] Dagg did not, however, equate the local-universal dichotomy with the visible-invisible dichotomy. He insisted that any who were to be truly considered members of either the local or universal church must be visible to the world. "Notwithstanding the errors that human judgment may commit in individual cases, it still remains true, that the light of piety is visible."[37] Nor did he equate the universal church with any organization. The church universal was united not by organization, but by its spiritual nature. It will be culminated at the end of the world and will continue eternally. The word *church* in Dagg's thought "applies to a local church, because the members of it actually assemble; and it applies to the church universal, because the members of it will actually assemble in the presence, and for the everlasting worship of God."[38]

Baptism was one of the earliest doctrines with which Dagg wrestled. His early struggle left him with clear opinions on almost every conceivable aspect of the doctrine and practice of baptism. Baptism with water was certainly an ordinance for the church until the kingdom of God should be consummated by the return of Christ. The Christian is not merely to seek a "spiritual" baptism but is obligated to seek water baptism by the command of Christ and the apostles. It may not be set aside as a matter of indifference to the modern Christian. Dagg went to great lengths to demonstrate that the only proper understanding of baptism, is, by the very nature of the word, "to immerse."[39] This is proved by the use of the Greek word, and by the symbolic purpose of the act of baptism in Scripture. To read *baptizo* any other way, is to deny the clear results of etymological, historical, and scriptural research. The only proper subjects of this baptism are those who repent of their sins and trust in Christ for salvation. "Baptism was designed to be the ceremony of Christian profession" with none but baptized persons properly being able to be admitted to membership in the church.[40] To forego this would be to allow clear disobedience to the Christ one claims to follow.

It is not surprising, therefore, to find that Dagg adamantly opposed infant membership in the church. By this, Dagg did not mean to suggest that children were not to be admitted to the church. Anyone, adult or child, who gave credible profession of faith and was baptized was to be admitted to the church. Infants, however, incapable of faith and with only the claim of the faith of their parents, were not proper candidates for membership. "As the covenant of circumcision in its literal sense, admitted none into the covenant seed but literal descendants of Abraham; so in the allegorical sense, none are included in the spiritual seed but true believers."[41] Therefore, infant baptism was wrong. The fact that those dying in infancy may, in fact, be saved by the grace of God, is no argument for the unbiblical practice of infant baptism. Infant baptism is nowhere commanded in the New Testament. Those who were baptized in the New Testament were disciples, which infants cannot be. The analogy of baptism to circumcision in the Scriptures is an analogy made with the circumcision of the heart (conversion) and not with the circumcision of the flesh. Indeed, Dagg argued, infant baptism is not heard of earlier than the close of the second century.

If Dagg gave a somewhat unconventional answer to the question, "Who may be baptized?" he did not give such an unconventional answer to the question, "Who may baptize?" Admitting that his conclusion here was reached by a more subtle series of reasonings from Scripture and history, he suggested that "the authority to administer baptism is conferred in the ordinary course of the ministerial succession, when an individual, called by the Holy Spirit to the ministry of the word, is publicly set apart to this service."[42] Again arguing against the Landmarkers, Dagg insisted that unbaptized ministers be recognized as true, if erring, ministers, and treated with respect. George Whitefield, Jonathan Edwards, Samuel Davies, and Edward Payson are all examples heralded by Dagg of men who were indisputably used of God as ministers of the gospel, even if they were in error on the matter of baptism. Baptists must know and proclaim the truth of baptism, yet realize that this is not the essence of Christianity. To make this error is to fall into a new type of "popery."

> It is our duty, while rendering punctilious obedience to all the commands of God, to regard the forms and ceremonies of religion as of far less importance than its moral truths and precepts. . . . Because we differ from other professors of religion in our faith and practice respecting the externals of religion, we are under a constant temptation to make too much account of these external peculiarities. Against this temptation we should ever struggle. If we magnify ceremony unduly, we abandon our principles, and cease to fulfill the mission to which the Head of the church has assigned us.[43]

The distinctives of our denomination must never be confused with the essentials of our faith.

Like baptism, communion is to be observed by the church until the end of the world because it was so instituted by Christ. While denying the automatic efficacy of the rite of communion, Dagg saw a fuller significance in communion than many Baptists have allowed. This Supper is to be understood as a memorial of Christ, "a representation that the communicant receives spiritual nourishment from him, and a token of fellowship among the communicants."[44] This Supper is to be celebrated in local churches by baptized members of any recognized churches there present. Dagg defended the position known as "strict communion." That is, while welcoming Christians of any denomination to the table, Dagg would deny the table to any who had not been immersed as believers. He denied, however, that paedobaptist brethren should feel disowned by this restriction: ". . . there are surely many modes of testifying and cherishing the warmest affection toward erring brethren, without participating in their errors. We may be ready, in obedience to Christ, to lay down our lives for our brethren— though we may choose to die, rather than, in false tenderness to them, violate the least of his commandments."[45]

The rest of Roman Catholicism's "seven sacraments," and the foot washing some fellow Baptists considered as an ordinance, Dagg specifically rejected. Only baptism and the Lord's Supper were ordered by Christ to be perpetually observed in his church.

Dagg dealt briefly with the rest of the external matters of the church. Public worship should be held on Sunday, the Christian sabbath. The church's regular meeting should be characterized by "prayers, songs of praise, and the reading and expounding of God's word."[46] Prescribed forms of prayers are objectionable, yet the use of hymnbooks is not. Those ministering the Word should be those who have been specifically called by

God to do so. They should be set apart specifically for the work of the preaching of the Word. Although the apostolic ministry has ceased, God has continued to give his church ministers and missionaries to spread the gospel. Dagg taught that the prophetic gift, too, had ceased, and that this was simply one more attestation of the sufficiency of the revelation of Scripture. The one called to the ministry should especially study the Scripture, and should have his call corroborated by the larger body of Christ in his church; because, "every man who believes alone, that he is called of God to the ministry, has reason to apprehend that he is under a delusion. If he finds that those who give proof that they honor God and love the souls of men, do not discover his ministerial qualifications, he has reason to suspect that they do not exist."[47] Deacons, too, are to be recognized by the local church, as necessity demands. Ordination is appropriate, but not obligatory (not being ordered in Scripture). From among these ministers of the Word, the church is to choose bishops, or pastors, for their local congregation. Such deacons and bishops (pastors) are the only offices mandated for the local church in Scripture. Members should labor carefully for the edification of all their brothers and sisters in Christ through punctual and regular attendance of preaching, Bible study, religious reading and discussions, good works, and prayer meetings. Excommunication, too, should be used by the local church as a tool for the sanctification of the body of Christ.

Evaluation

To evaluate the theology of John L. Dagg, one must first recall his purpose in his theological writings. His *Manual of Theology* and all of his expressly theological writings were "designed for the use of those who have not time and opportunity to study larger works on theology. In preparing it, my aim has been to present the system of Christian doctrine with plainness and brevity; and to demonstrate, at every point, its truth, and its tendency to sanctify the heart. Men who have inclination and talent for deep research, will prefer more elaborate discussions; but if the novice in religion shall be assisted in determining what is truth, and what the proper use to be made of it, the chief end for which I have written will have been attained."[48]

Thus Dagg makes no attempt to reproduce Gill's massive *Body of Divinity*, a work influential in his own theological formation. Dagg's *Manual of Theology* can only imperfectly be compared to Boyce's *Abstract of Systematic Theology* (a text of Boyce's lecture notes, in which discussion of historical theological debates is given prominence). Dagg's approach could better be compared with J. M. Pendleton's *Christian Doctrine* or E. Y. Mullins's *The Christian Religion in Its Doctrinal Expression*. Neither of these later volumes was renowned for its complex discussion of classical theological problems. Rather they, like Dagg's *Manual of Theology*, served as simple expositions of Christian truth from a Baptist perspective. And, it may be noted, their very simplicity has given them much of the wide influence they have known in the denomination's thought and practice.

Yet Dagg's *Manual of Theology* was not only simple and therefore accessible (like the written theologies of Pendleton and Mullins). It was written specifically as an exercise in theological edification. "It has been no part of my design, to lead the humble inquirer into the thorny region of polemic theology. To avoid everything that has been a subject of controversy, was impossible, for every part of divine truth has been assailed. But it has been my plan to pursue our course of investigation, affected as little as possible by the strife of religious disputants, and to know no controversy, but with the unbelief of our own hearts."[49]

As part of this plan, Dagg decided to appeal to no authority but Scripture itself. Therefore, while Dagg goes into careful exegeses of passages, and at points deals extensively with the original languages, he nowhere expressly engages in the historical debates that have done much to shape contemporary Christian theology. Nicea and the Reformation, the Council of Trent, and the Westminster Assembly nowhere appear by name in his theology, though many of his expressions and arguments are formed by the discussions that took place in these contexts. Dagg has, as it were, recreated many of the debates of the history of Christian theology (he was certainly not ignorant of them), yet in the context of simple, apparently contemporary discussions about the Scriptures. This has the advantage of recreating in the reader that which was always the fundamental theological issue for Dagg—"What sayeth the Scripture?" Yet it must also be said that however helpful this may be for the layperson, it is not an adequate introduction to the theological science for the student of theology. Ideally the student should be supplied not only with Dagg's reading of the text and the problems but also with exact historical theological definitions and disputes and the circumstances in which they arose.

This is not to say that Dagg's theological method was wrong. His attempt to be ultimately dependent upon Scripture alone is laudable. That should be the goal of every biblical theologian. Too, his concern for the sanctification of the heart via theological inquiry is very fitting (and, it must be added, is sadly lacking today, especially amidst much contemporary unbelieving "theology"). Dagg's concern for the knowing of God that permeates his discussion of the knowledge of God is searching and singularly appropriate. To combine this zeal for remembering the presence of God throughout the discussion of God, with a careful notation of histories of the discussions would be an admirable goal for any written theology.

Dagg's chief concern may well be said to be the holiness of God—not simply God's moral rectitude, but his God-ness. All of his attributes are thereby seen to be a unity in the divine character, not separable units. Everything is to be done to the glory of God. Everything is to be known to the glory of God. Everything is to the glory of God. Thus we are to search after, love, obey, believe, and thank God. The introductory sections in his *Manual of Theology* are the practical summary of Dagg's theology. This is also the basis for Dagg's discussion of that thorniest of theological issues— theodicy. God is, by his nature, to be trusted. He may be misunderstood by us in what he does or allows, but he cannot be declared wrong. Ultimately, Dagg would answer with the apostle Paul, "Who are you, a man, to answer back to God?" (Rom. 9:20).

To some, Dagg's devotional manner may seem to be in striking dissonance with his uncompromisingly Reformed presentation of God; yet it could be argued that these two are perfectly complementary—a "high" view of God, matched by a strong devotion to him. This God was not to be condemned so much for the problem of evil as praised for the unmerited love that he shows in Christ. Election shows God not to be a despotic tyrant, but a determined lover. Morally, humanity stands rightfully condemned by its choice of disobedience. The only justice to be demanded is humanity's condemnation. God's love, shown to us in Christ, is a matter for tremendous praise exactly because God was not obligated to treat us so.

In all of this Dagg could well be a teacher to contemporary Christianity in the English-speaking world. To both Arminian evangelicals and many more "progressive" theologians, Dagg might well ask uncomfortable questions: How can one assert biblically that God champions the greatest good of each person at all times regardless of their actions? Such an idea surely would be popular, but how does it conform to the more uncomfortable realities of the biblical text and of the real world? Here Dagg's theology, antiquated as it may seem to some by its style and its substance, may address some basic difficulties that the modern, egalitarian person has in comprehending and "allowing" there to be an absolutely sovereign, righteous, loving, and self-existent God.

It is, however, exactly at this point that we should also note Dagg's ethical teachings—the source of his infamy in some circles today. Dagg's *Elements of Moral Science* (1859) was the last major defense of slavery published in book form. While Dagg's ethics deserve a more extensive treatment, such must be left to the reader through perusing the work for oneself. Dagg asserted that the moral quality of an act lay in the intention behind it. He also taught that there should be no equality of rights apart from equality of condition.[50] Social rights were always unequal in society (as in the recognition of private property, or of the rights of parents over children). It was proper of the government to restrict the liberties of some more than the liberties of others if it were intended for their own good. Also, Dagg defended slavery as an institution condoned and not condemned in Scripture. Finally, Dagg argued pragmatically that while slavery had many grievous evils, God, by his overruling providence, had actually prospered the Africans through it.

The sources of Dagg's conservatism in social issues are matters of speculation. Some have attributed his satisfaction with the status quo to his Calvinism, perhaps thinking that Dagg assumed that all about him was the perfect will of God.[51] While his Calvinistic theology could be an indirect source, filtering through attitudes or priorities, it certainly would not be a direct source of his social conservatism. Dagg himself was painfully aware of the fallenness and imperfection of the present world. Too, he was active for change in other social affairs. He was an early leader among Baptists in issues of temperance, education, and dealing with the problems of the native Americans.

Dagg clearly conceded that slavery as it was practiced was accompanied by great evil. Yet he reacted against the calls for radical change in the culture that he had known for half a century. There was certainly ample material in Scripture from which to draw a defense of slavery, if that were one's intent. Many of his more educated contemporaries (R. L. Dabney, J. H. Thornwell) had long before taken up a defense of slavery. Dagg reacted with a natural and lamentable defensiveness when the faults of his own culture (clear to us) were presented to the nation. The fact that these faults were presented most loudly and dramatically by those who were most opposed to slavery simply made it all the easier to caricature his cultural assailants. Too, the Baptists (and Methodists) had become established in the South and evident spiritual good had been accomplished among the slaves. Often, it must have seemed, the Northern rationalists and liberals would not admit this, and therefore perhaps evidenced their widely differing values from the more orthodox, scriptural concerns of the South. At this point Dagg's culture molded his Christianity in a most perverse direction.

Dagg's chief theological distinction among Baptists was his clear maintenance of what had been Baptist orthodoxy in the South—Calvinism—and his clear rebuttal of what was replacing it as Baptist orthodoxy on the frontier—Landmarkism. The Landmarkism of J. R. Graves, A. C. Dayton, and J. M. Pendleton was a theology that accepted Calvinism yet deemphasized it. The Baptists of the seventeenth, eighteenth, and nineteenth centuries whose theologies were distinctively Calvinistic were often those who stressed their essential unity with other evangelical Protestants. The central doctrines of God, humanity, Christ, and grace were those around which groups formed, by which they were defined, and over which they divided. By the middle of the nineteenth century, the emphasis on the American frontier was increasingly shifting from those central issues that united evangelical Christians to those issues that distinguished one body of Christians from another. Landmarkism was the dominant form that this emphasis took among Baptists. Dagg was courageous, courteous, and uncompromising in his defense of an earlier version of baptistic Christianity—uncompromisingly Baptist but clearly fundamentally Christian—over against the unwarranted claims of the Landmarkists. Dagg rightly taught that God had owned the ministry of those who were in error in varying ways, including in their doctrine of baptism. Dagg rightly taught that *church* was used in the Scriptures in a local and universal sense, and that it could rightly be used even of those local assemblies that misunderstood baptism. In all of this Dagg was writing "against the stream" but did so in such a clearly orthodox fashion that even the Landmark champion J. M. Pendleton would later commend Dagg's *Manual of Theology* and *Church Order* and use it as a text at Union University in Tennessee.

In conclusion, it would be fair to say that Dagg makes no distinctive contributions to those engaged in the theological task today. His expositions of doctrine were typical of historic Christian positions formulated initially by others. However much it may be felt that the biblical orthodoxy of Dagg's theology must be recovered today, if theology is to avoid suicide and to express the true gospel of Christ, it must be admitted that, in most ways, it is better learned from others with more searching presentations of Scripture, doctrine, history and reason.[52] Dagg's writings are inadequate for use as the theology text in a modern seminary. Having said that, it must be stated that if Dagg is not a particularly notable doctor in the content of theology, he is almost unsurpassed among Baptists as a doctor in the purpose of theology. Dagg would teach that if the pursuit of theology is to be legitimate, its purpose must be clear. To pursue knowledge of the biblical God can only properly be done by seeking to know the biblical God. To be captivated by the knowledge of God is idolatrous unless one is captivated by God himself. That Dagg was so captivated is clear; that he may so teach us is his enduring contribution.

Bibliography

Works by Dagg

Autobiography of Rev. John L. Dagg, D.D. Rome, Ga.: F. Shanklin, Printer, 1886.

"Effectual Calling." *The Christian Index,* 31 (11 May 1863): 1.

The Elements of Moral Science. New York: Sheldon and Co., 1859.

The Evidences of Christianity. Macon, Ga.: J. W. Burke and Co., 1869.

"The Fallen State of Man." *The Christian Index,* 32 (20 March 1863): 1.

A Manual of Theology. Charleston: Southern Baptist Publication Society, 1857.

A Treatise on Church Order. Charleston: Southern Baptist Publication Society, 1858.

Works about Dagg

Blackaby, Melvin Duane. "The Nature of the Church and Its Relationship to the Kingdom of God in Baptist Theology: John Leadley Dagg, Benjamin Harvey Carroll, and Dale Moody," Ph.D. dissertation, Southwestern Baptist Theological Seminary, 1997.

Brantley, W. T., Sr. "The Doctrines of Grace." *The Columbian Star,* 1 (8 Aug. 1829): 91.

Cline, C. W. "Some Baptist Systematic Theologians." *Review and Expositor,* 20 (1923): 311–16.

Cuttino, Thomas E. "A Study of the Theological Works of John Leadley Dagg." Th.M. thesis, The Southern Baptist Theological Seminary, 1954.

Dever, Mark E. "Representative Aspects of the Theologies of John L. Dagg and James P. Boyce: Reformed Theology and Southern Baptists." Th.M. thesis, The Southern Baptist Theological Seminary, 1987.

———. ed., *Baptist Polity.* Washington: Center for Church Reform, 2000.

Gardner, Robert G. "The Alabama Female Athenaeum and John Leadley Dagg in Alabama." *The Alabama Baptist Historian,* 5 (July 1969): 3–32.

———. "The Bible . . . A Revelation from God, Supplying the Defects of Natural Religion." *Foundations,* 4 (July 1961): 241–58.

———. "John Leadley Dagg." *Review and Expositor,* 54 (April 1957): 246–63.

———. "John Leadley Dagg in Georgia." *Baptist History and Heritage,* 3 (Jan. 1968): 43–50.

———. "John Leadley Dagg, National Leader." *The Quarterly Review,* 33 (April–June 1973): 48–53.

———. "John Leadley Dagg: Pioneer American Baptist Theologian." Ph.D. dissertation, Duke University, 1957.

———. "Men under the Dominion of the Lower Propensities." *The Chronicle,* 20 (July 1957): 115–30.

———. "A Tenth-Hour Apology for Slavery." *The Journal of Southern History,* 26 (Aug. 1960): 352–67.

Holifield, E. Brooks. *The Gentleman Theologians.* Durham, N.C.: Duke University Press, 1978.

Humphreys, Fisher, ed. *Nineteenth Century Evangelical Theology.* Nashville: Broadman Press, 1983.

Kutilek, Doug. "The Text and Translation of the Bible: Nineteenth Century American Baptist Views," Th.M. thesis, Central Baptist Theological Seminary, 1998.

Loftis, John. "Factors in Southern Baptist Identity as Reflected by Ministerial Role Models, 1750–1925." Ph.D. dissertation, The Southern Baptist Theological Seminary, 1987.

Lumpkin, William L. *Baptist Foundations in the South.* Nashville: Broadman Press, 1961.

Mallary, C. D. Review of A *Manual of Theology,* by John L. Dagg. *The Christian Index,* 36 (14 Oct. 1857): 162–63.

Matheson, Mark. "Religious Knowledge in the Theologies of John Leadley Dagg and James Petigru Boyce: With Special Reference to the Influence of Common Sense Realism." Ph.D. dissertation, Southwestern Baptist Theological Seminary, 1984.

Moody, Dwight A. "Doctrines of Inspiration in the Southern Baptist Theological Tradition." Ph.D. dissertation, The Southern Baptist Theological Seminary, 1982.

Mueller, William A. "Southern Baptists and Theology." *The Theological Educator,* 1 (Oct. 1970): 49–62.

Nettles, Thomas J. *By His Grace and for His Glory.* Grand Rapids: Baker Book House, 1986.

Patterson, L. Paige. "An Evaluation of the Soteriological Thought of John Leadley Dagg."

Pendleton, J. M. *Christian Doctrines: A Compendium of Theology.* Philadelphia: American Baptist Publication Society, 1878.

Phillips, Charles D. "The Southern Baptist View of the Church: As Reflected in the Thought of J. L. Dagg, E. C. Dargan, and H. E. Dana." Th.M. thesis, The Southern Baptist Theological Seminary, 1957.

Reviews of *A Manual of Theology,* by John L. Dagg, in *The Baptist Family Magazine,* 1 (Oct. 1857): 310; *The Commission,* 2 (Jan. 1858): 223; *Mississippi Baptist,* 1 (8 Oct. 1857): 2; *The Southern Baptist,* 12 (29 Sept. 1857): 2; and *Western Recorder,* 24 (7 Oct. 1857): 154.

Sands, William. Review of *A Manual of Theology,* by John L. Dagg. *The Religious Herald,* 26 (1 Oct. 1857): 2.

Straton, Hillyer Hawthorne. "John Leadley Dagg." M.A. thesis, Mercer University, 1926.

5

James Petigru Boyce

By Timothy George

Biography

JAMES PETIGRU BOYCE WAS BORN ON JANUARY 11, 1827, IN Charleston, South Carolina.[1] Charleston, a city of some thirty thousand, was a flourishing center of commerce and culture where two ideals of civilization converged: the Cavalier and the Puritan. The spirit of the jolly Cavalier, brought from France and England, exemplified in fox-hunting parsons and state-sponsored Anglicanism, resulted in a culture of civility and urbanity that left its mark on young Boyce. His father, Ker Boyce, was one of the wealthiest men in South Carolina. Being a banker and business magnate, he desired his precocious son to follow in his steps. Like the father of Martin Luther centuries before, Boyce's father wanted his son to study law and was bitterly disappointed when he opted for the ministry instead. One of his father's business partners, upon hearing that "Jimmy Boyce" meant to be a preacher, said: "Well, well, why don't he follow some useful occupation?"[2] Although he was to pursue a different path, Boyce did inherit his father's penchant for business success. His life's work, the founding of the first theological seminary among Baptists in the South, would not have been possible without his extraordinary acumen in business and financial affairs.

The Cavalier culture was also reflected in Boyce's marked concern about manners. At the seminary, Boyce taught the students not only about the doctrine of justification and the eternal decrees of God but also how to eat properly with a fork and knife, how to help a lady into her seat, how to stand in a pulpit, how to dress correctly for class, and how to make pastoral visits with propriety and discretion. It is not surprising that Boyce appears on Brooks Holifield's list of "gentlemen theologians" who had a decisive effect on Southern culture in the nineteenth century.[3]

However, it was not the Cavalier but rather the Puritan ideal that was to shape Boyce's destiny. His mother, Amanda Jane Caroline Johnston, descended from strict Presbyterian stock. She had been converted under the ministry of Basil Manly Sr., who came to be pastor of the First Baptist Church of Charleston in 1826. Early in his life, Boyce came under the tutelage of this great Baptist leader, who was both an able exponent of Calvinistic theology and one of the first proponents of a common theological seminary for Southern Baptists. He was later to serve as chairman of the first board of trustees of Southern Seminary. At his funeral service in 1868 Boyce recalled the formative influence Manly Sr. had exerted in his young life.

> After a lapse of more than thirty years I can yet feel the weight of his hand, resting in gentleness and love upon my head. I can recall the words of fatherly tenderness, with which he sought to guide my childish steps. I can see his beloved form in the study, in the house on King Street. I can again behold him in our own family circle. . . . I can call to mind his conversations with my mother, to whose salvation had been blessed a sermon preached on the Sunday after the death of one of his children on the text, "If I be bereaved of my children, I am bereaved." And once more come to me the words of sympathy that he spake while he wept with her family over her dead body, and ministered to them as it was laid in the grave.[4]

From his mother and from his pastor Boyce gained a sense of the transcendent. He became attuned to the life of the spirit and the life of the mind. His "barrel-shaped" figure, as one of his contemporaries described it, prevented him from engaging in the popular schoolboy sports, such as baseball or shinny. More often, he was sequestered in a corner reading a book. Throughout his entire life, he was an omnivorous reader and a bibliophile without peer.

After studying for two years at the College of Charleston, Boyce moved to Providence, Rhode Island, where he enrolled at Brown University, the first college founded by Baptists in America. Here he came under the influence of Francis Wayland, renowned Baptist statesman and educator and one of the formative leaders of the Triennial Convention. Wayland required his students to memorize a given lesson in advance and stand to recite it when called upon in class. Boyce later used this method of teaching by "recitation" in his own courses at Southern Seminary.

It was also under the influence of Francis Wayland that Boyce was converted to Christ. The Second Great Awakening had begun with a powerful revival at Yale College under Timothy Dwight. A similar outpouring of the Spirit occurred at Brown when Boyce was a student there. Dr. Wayland prayed for the students who had never professed faith in Christ and preached in chapel on the importance of spiritual welfare as well as intellectual advance. When Boyce returned to Charleston for spring break in 1846, he was under deep conviction. Despite his wealthy status, his promising future, his polish, and education, Broadus says "he felt himself a ruined sinner and . . . had to look to the merits of Christ alone for salvation."[5] He was saved and baptized during a protracted meeting conducted by Richard Fuller. Boyce returned to Brown a changed man. He became greatly concerned for his fellow classmates who were as yet unconverted. He began to pray for them and to share the gospel with them. "Two or three," he wrote home, "who had been brought up on the doctrines of Universalism [came] to look to Jesus as the author and finisher of our faith." Again, he wrote, "May God make me instrumental in his hands in the salvation of many!"[6] From his conversion in 1845 until his death in 1888, Boyce lost neither his devotion to God nor his dedication to disciplined study that was for him an expression of devotion to God.

Boyce received his formal theological training at Princeton Theological Seminary, where he studied from 1849 to 1851 under Archibald Alexander, his son Addison Alexander, and—above all—Charles Hodge, whose three-volume *Systematic Theology* would later serve as a model for Boyce's own *Abstract of Systematic Theology*. By the mid-nineteenth century, Princeton had become the theological center of Calvinist orthodoxy in America, and Boyce drank deeply from the wells of his great Reformed teachers. At Princeton, Boyce was exposed to the classic writings of Reformed

Scholasticism, including the *Institutio theologiae elencticae* by Francis Turretin, Calvin's successor as city pastor and theologian in Geneva. Boyce later adopted this book as a required text in his course on "Latin theology" at Southern Seminary, where it influenced an entire generation of Southern Baptist ministers. Boyce also thought highly of the Scottish Presbyterian John Dick, whose *Lectures on Theology* he used repeatedly as a text in his systematic theology classes. Despite the formative role his Princeton experience had on his theological development, one should not think that Boyce was somehow seduced by an influence alien to his indigenous Baptist background. W. O. Carver, whose own theology was of a different bent than that of Boyce, put it succinctly: "I think that it was under Hodge's teaching that he formulated his theological views but these views did not differ from the theological atmosphere in which he had grown up."[7] Princeton provided Boyce with a systematic framework in which to cast the Calvinist theology he had imbibed from Basil Manly Sr. and his other Charleston pastors.[8]

After completing his work at Princeton, Boyce served for two years as pastor of the First Baptist Church of Columbia, South Carolina. At his ordination council, Dr. Thomas Curtis asked Boyce whether he proposed to make a lifelong matter of preaching. "Yes," he replied, "provided I do not become a professor of theology."[9] In 1855 Boyce was elected to teach theology at Furman University. In July 1856 he delivered his inaugural address, entitled "Three Changes in Theological Institutions." By all accounts, this was a virtuoso performance, the more remarkable when one considers that it was delivered by a young man only twenty-nine-years old. A. M. Poindexter, secretary of the Southern Baptist Foreign Mission Board, declared Boyce's address to be "the ablest thing of the kind he had ever heard."[10] "Three Changes" was a virtual manifesto for a common theological seminary for Baptists in the South. Boyce suggested three ideals that such a school should embody. The first was *openness,* a seminary for everybody called by God regardless of academic background or social status. This was unheard of in the nineteenth century, when it was universally agreed that a thorough grounding in the classical disciplines was an essential prerequisite for theological education. Boyce had two concerns in proposing this change. First, he knew that most Baptist preachers did not have, and many could not acquire, the advantages of a classical education, yet they and the churches they served would be enhanced by their exposure to theological study. He also hoped that the experience of students from diverse backgrounds mingling together in a common community of learning and piety would engender mutual respect and lessen the jealousies and resentments that frequently flared up among Baptist pastors.

His second ideal was equally important—*excellence.* Boyce was intent upon establishing an advanced program of theological study which in its academic rigor would be on a par with the kind of instruction offered at Princeton, Andover, Harvard, Yale, or anywhere else in the world. He envisioned, as he put it, "a band of scholars," trained for original research and committed to accurate scholarship, which would go out from the seminary to contribute significantly to the theological life of the church by their teaching and writing as well as by their preaching and witness in the world.

The third ideal was *confessional identity.* Boyce proposed that the seminary be established on a set of doctrinal principles that would provide consistency and direction for the future. This, too, was a radical step in the context of nineteenth-century Baptist life. Newton Theological Institute, the first seminary founded by Baptists in America, had no such confessional guidelines. Nor, indeed, did the Southern Baptist Convention, organized in 1845. However, Boyce firmly believed that it was necessary to protect the seminary from doctrinal erosion. From his student days in New England, Boyce was aware of the recent currents in theology: Unitarianism, Transcendentalism, the New Divinity. In particular, he spoke against the "blasphemous doctrines" of Theodore Parker, who had denied that Christianity was based on a special revelation of God. At the same time he was concerned about populist theologies in the South, and warned against the "twin errors of Campbellism and Arminianism."[11]

In setting forth the rationale for Southern Baptists' first theological seminary, Boyce insisted that each professor subscribe to a set of doctrinal principles. Moreover, he declared, "his agreement with the standard should be exact. His declaration of it should be based upon no mental reservation, upon no private understanding with those who immediately invest him into office."[12] Boyce was well aware that there were those who felt that such a policy of strict subscription was a violation of academic freedom and liberty of conscience, but he urged its adoption nonetheless:

> You will infringe the rights of no man, and you will secure the
> rights of those who have established here an instrumentality for
> the production of a sound ministry. It is no hardship to those
> who teach here, to be called upon to sign the declaration of their
> principles, for there are fields of usefulness open elsewhere to
> every man, and none need accept your call who can not conscientiously sign your formulary.[13]

Boyce related the reluctance of some Baptists to adopt a specific doctrinal standard to the influence of Alexander Campbell, whose slogan of "no creed but the Bible" had lured many Baptists away from their traditional confessional moorings.[14] Campbell had decried the use of confessions as an infringement upon the rights of conscience. Boyce, however, in a brilliant rebuttal, traced the history of confessional statements from New Testament times down to his own day. He showed that Baptists in particular had been prolific in promulgating confessions, both as public declarations of their own faith and as a means of testing the true faith in others. Following these guidelines, Basil Manly Jr. drafted an Abstract of Principles that were incorporated into the Fundamental Laws of Southern Seminary. Since the founding of Southern Seminary in 1859 every professor who has served on the faculty of that institution has signed this original document, pledging thereby to teach "in accordance with and not contrary to" its provisions.[15] The Abstract of Principles was intentionally modeled on the Philadelphia Confession of Faith, which was based on the Second London Confession, which, in turn, was a Baptist adaptation of the Westminster Confession. Robert Lynn has said of the ideal of confessional identity that, while it has sometimes been a point of controversy, it has also provided "a thread of continuity which links past, present and future."[16]

Boyce's hopes for the seminary soon fell victim to the convulsions of the American Civil War. In 1862 the seminary disbanded. Although Boyce had been a vocal opponent of secession, both he and his colleague John A. Broadus ministered as chaplains among the Confederate troops. During this time, Boyce also served in the South Carolina state legislature. He so distinguished himself in that body that he was urged on all sides to give himself entirely to political life. On December 5, 1862, Broadus discouraged his friend from following such an alluring career:

> You have doubtless been told already that such capacities for
> public usefulness ought to be permanently devoted to the public
> good, and all that. My dear fellow, don't listen to it. Your mis-
> sion is to bring theological science into practical relation to this
> busy world, and if God spares your life and grants the country
> peace, this seminary which was founded by your labors shall yet
> shine in conspicuous usefulness.[17]

Broadus's advice prevailed, and after the war, the four original founders of the seminary—Boyce, Broadus, Manly, and William Williams—gathered at the Boyce home in Greenville, South Carolina. They joined in prayer and a deep seeking of the will of God. At the end of the day Broadus said, "Suppose we quietly agree that the seminary may die, but we will die first."[18] All heads were silently bowed, and the matter was decided.

Boyce not only conceived and birthed the seminary but also nurtured it and kept it alive when for good reason nearly everyone else expected it to die. Time and again he gave generously out of his own dwindling estate to help needy students through another semester or to pay the salaries of the other professors. Once when the Southern Baptist Convention met in Nashville, Boyce was pleading so earnestly on behalf of the seminary that he actually burst into tears and began to weep profusely. "I would not beg for myself, or for my family like this, but for our beloved Seminary I am willing to beg." Boyce was repeatedly offered the presidency of railroads and banks and great universities, including Brown and Mercer. He declined them all to stay at Southern Seminary and fulfill his life's work.

In the summer of 1888, with his health failing, Boyce sailed for Europe in what would be his first and last trip abroad. He died in Southern France in December 1888. Had he lived two more weeks, he would have been sixty-two years old. His body was brought back to Louisville where, on a snowy January day, he was buried in Cave Hill Cemetery. Soon thereafter an impressive monument was erected over his grave, which bears this inscription: "James P. Boyce, to whom, under God, the Seminary owes its existence." At the funeral, John A. Broadus, his closest friend and fellow laborer in the founding of the Seminary, gave the following eulogy:

> Oh Brother beloved, true yokefellow through years of toil, best
> and dearest friend, sweet shall be thy memory 'til we meet again!
> And may there be those always ready, as the years come and go,
> to carry on, with widening reach and heightened power, the work
> we sought to do, and did begin![19]

Exposition

Boyce served for thirty years as a professor of systematic and polemical theology. It was one of the great regrets of his life that due to the burdens of his office he was never able to give himself fully to the discipline he loved so dearly. Yet his theology had a profound and long-lasting influence on Southern Baptists. E. Y. Mullins, whose theology of experience led to a different paradigm, nonetheless had great respect for Boyce as a theologian and continued to use his *Abstract of Systematic Theology* as a required text for the first seventeen years of his own teaching career at Southern Seminary. In reviewing the central themes in Boyce's theology, we shall focus on his treatment of the doctrines of grace and his views on the authority of Scripture.

The Doctrines of Grace

Boyce defined *theology* as "the science which treats of God." His *Abstract* is a true *the*-ology in terms of its emphasis on the doctrine of God. The first sixteen chapters deal with the being, attributes, and decrees of God. The meatiest sections of the book deal with the various "moments" in the *ordo salutis:* the Fall, atonement, election, calling, regeneration, repentance, faith, and so forth. On all disputed points of soteriology, Boyce took pains to present opposing views with fairness, but in the end he invariably came down as a consistent, if somewhat benignant, Calvinist. E. E. Folk, one of his former students, once remarked:

"Although the young men were generally rank Arminians when they came to the Seminary, few went through the course [in systematic theology] under him without being converted to his strong Calvinistic views."[20]

The Calvinist cast of Boyce's theology derived from his conviction that "a crisis in Baptist theology" was fast approaching. This crisis could only be avoided, he believed, by returning "to the doctrine which formerly distinguished us."[21] In his inaugural address at Furman, he had lamented the fact that the principles of Arminianism "have been engrafted upon many of our churches; and even some of our ministry have not hesitated publicly to avow them."[22] In the first decade of the nineteenth century the Baptist historian David Benedict made an extensive tour of Baptist churches throughout America. He gave the following summary of the Baptist theology he encountered:

> Take this denomination at large, I believe the following will be found a pretty correct statement of their views of doctrine. They hold that man in his natural condition is entirely depraved and sinful; that unless he is born again—changed by grace—or made alive unto God—he cannot be fitted for the communion of saints on earth, nor the enjoyment of God in Heaven; that where God hath begun a good work, he will carry it on to the end; that there is an election of grace—an effectual calling, etc. and that the happiness of the righteous and the misery of the wicked will both be eternal.[23]

Despite a persistent Arminian strain within Baptist life, for most of their history most Baptists have adhered faithfully to the doctrines of grace as set forth by the mainline reformers. For example, the Philadelphia Confession of Faith, first published in 1742, was adopted verbatim by the Charleston Association, whence it exercised a profound influence on Baptist life in the South.[24] Boyce emphasized the sovereignty of God and the gratuity of salvation as a corrective to what he perceived as a growing laxity about these vital themes.

In his *Abstract* Boyce clearly affirmed all five "points" of doctrine set forth in the famous Canons of the Synod of Dort (1618–19). In keeping with the Reformed tradition, Boyce asserted the federal headship of Adam and the totality of depravity that had passed to all his descendants. The inheritance of a fallen, sinful nature entailed not only corruption but also condemnation. In his *Catechism* Boyce asked: "What evil effects followed the sin of Adam?" "He, with all his posterity, became corrupt and sinful, and fell under the condemnation of the law of God."[25] Boyce did not believe that all people were equally sinful, nor that the image of God had been totally effaced by the Fall. However, he did stress the "total" incapacity of fallen human beings to contribute anything toward their salvation apart from the interposition of divine grace.[26]

Boyce's complete definition of *election,* with manifold qualifications to prevent misunderstanding, presents a strong predestinarian doctrine of salvation.

> God (who and not man is the one who chooses or elects), of his own purpose (in accordance with his will, and not from any obligation to man, nor because of any will of man), has from Eternity (the period of God's action, not in time in which man acts), determined to save (not has actually saved, but simply determined to do so), and to save (not to confer gospel or church privileges upon), a definite number of mankind (not the whole or a part of the race, nor of a nation, nor of a church, nor of a class, as of believers or the pious; but individuals), not for or because of any merit or work of theirs, not of any value of him of them (not for their good works, nor their holiness, nor excellence, nor their faith, nor their spiritual sanctification, although the choice is to a salvation attained through faith and sanctification; nor their value to him, though their salvation tends greatly to the manifested glory of his grace); but of his own good pleasure (simply because he was pleased so to choose).[27]

Central to Boyce's soteriology was the doctrine of atonement. Through his sufferings and death, Christ "incurred the penalty of the sins of those whose substitute he was, so that he made a real satisfaction to the justice of God for the law which they had broken. On this account, God now pardons all their sins, and being fully reconciled to them, his electing love flows out freely towards them."[28] While teaching particular redemption, Boyce, like Calvin, could say that Christ's death was sufficient for all, but efficient only for the elect. The salvation of the believer is due to the overcoming grace of God, displayed in the elect through the regenerating power of the Holy Spirit, who enables them to persevere in faith and holiness unto the end.

Boyce was well aware that there were some who emphasized the sovereignty of God to the exclusion of human responsibility. In the nineteenth century a powerful hyper-Calvinist movement arose among Baptists in the South. Known variously as Primitive or Hardshell Baptists, these groups opposed organized missionary work, evangelism, Sunday schools, and, especially, theological seminaries. Boyce had no truck with this perspective. His zeal for preaching the gospel began in his student days and continued throughout his life. He had a great burden for missions and organized a monthly Missionary Day at Southern Seminary, a tradition that continued until the 1960s. When D. L. Moody brought his evangelistic campaign to

Louisville in 1888, Boyce permitted him to erect his five-thousand-seat tabernacle on seminary property, while seminary professors and students served as counselors in the inquiry room.[29] For Boyce the doctrines of grace were not inhibiting but rather motivating factors in the witness of the church. They underscored the fact that while we are called to be colaborers with God, all of the glory belongs to him alone.

A final word should be said about Boyce's Calvinism: While he was a doughty defender of a high-predestinarian theology, he was tolerant of other evangelical Christians who disagreed with his precise formulations of the doctrines of grace. He recognized that the shape of one's theology was largely a matter of emphasis and that the differences between a Wesley and a Whitefield, for example, "are not due to any contrariety of teaching the word of God, but to human failure to emphasize correctly."[30] Doubtless he would have agreed with the following statement of the great missionary statesman Luther Rice:

> How absurd it is, therefore, to contend against the doctrine of election, or decrees, or divine sovereignty. Let us not, however, become bitter against those who view this matter in a different light, nor treat them in a supercilious manner; rather let us be gentle towards all men. For who has made us to differ from what we once were? Who has removed the scales from our eyes?[31]

The Authority of Scripture

In his inaugural address of 1856, Boyce signaled the vital role a reverent approach to the study of the Bible would play in the seminary he envisioned.

> It has been felt as a sore evil, that we have been dependent in great part upon the criticism of Germany for all the more learned investigations in biblical criticism and exegesis, and that . . . we have been compelled to depend upon works in which much of error has been mingled with truth, owing to the defective standpoint occupied by their authors.[32]

The heavy emphasis placed on biblical studies in the seminary curriculum, including a strong commitment to both biblical languages, assured a tradition of disciplined scholars committed to the centrality of Holy Scripture in theological education. Broadus's *Commentary on Matthew* (1886), A. T. Robertson's *Grammar of the Greek New Testament in the Light of Historical Research* (1914), and John R. Sampey's work as chairman of the Old Testament section of the American Standard Bible Revision Committee (1930–38) are evidence of the scholarly erudition and biblical emphasis that established the reputation of Southern Seminary as a leading center of evangelical biblical scholarship.[33]

Boyce clearly expressed his own views concerning the inspiration and authority of the Bible. In the preface to his *Abstract of Systematic Theology*, he declared his belief in the "perfect inspiration and absolute authority of the divine revelation" which alone among the world's literature is untainted with "the liability to error that arises from human imperfection."[34] In his *Brief Catechism of Bible Doctrine*, Boyce devised the following questions and answers:

> Q: How came [the Bible] to be written?
> A: God inspired holy men to write it.
> Q: Did they write it exactly as God wished?
> A: Yes; as much as if he had written every word himself.
> Q: Ought it, therefore, to be believed and obeyed?
> A: Yes; as much as though God had spoken directly to us.[35]

Boyce devotes little attention to the doctrine of Scripture in his *Abstract* because this theological topic was covered in the course on Biblical Introduction. However, he does refer to the Bible as "infallible" and divinely secured "from all possibility of error."[36] His hearty endorsement of the explicitly inerrantist views of his colleague Basil Manly Jr. (whose *The Bible Doctrine of Inspiration Explained and Vindicated* [1888] was written at Boyce's behest) confirms the recent conclusion of Dwight Moody that Boyce "favored a conservative doctrine of the inspiration of Scriptures, generally known as the plenary verbal theory, which produces an inerrant manuscript containing infallible truth."[37]

For all that, however, Boyce was neither impervious to the difficult questions raised by the critical study of the Bible nor indifferent to scholarly efforts to face such problems fearlessly and honestly. For example, he freely admits that the Scriptures use the language of appearance and observation to describe natural events, just as even today, long after Copernicus, we still speak of the sun as "rising" or "setting." Had the Bible been written originally in the language of true science, "age after age would have rejected it as false."[38] While Boyce was well aware of incipient theories of evolution, and even admitted the possibility of a pre-Adamite race, he strongly maintained the unity of the "race of men now existing," and traced their origin to the special creation of Adam and Eve as recorded in the opening chapters of Genesis.[39] The universal sinfulness of human beings, together with the New Testament analogy of Christ to Adam, requires such an affirmation that is, after all, the clear and obvious meaning of the scriptural text.

It is sometimes claimed that Boyce, with his Princeton background, held to a stricter doctrine of inerrancy than his great colleague Broadus, who was trained at the University of Virginia. There is no evidence, however, to support this supposition. Both Boyce and Broadus published catechisms that were intended to be taught and memorized by new converts. If anything, Broadus's interrogations on Scripture are more comprehensive and precise than those of Boyce. For example, in a section of "Advanced Questions" Broadus presents the following concerns:

> Did the inspired writers receive everything by direct revelation? The inspired writers learned many things by observation or inquiry, but they were preserved by the Holy Spirit from error, whether in learning or in writing these things.
>
> What if inspired writers sometimes appear to disagree in their statements? Most cases of apparent disagreement in the inspired writings have been explained, and we may be sure that all could be explained if we had fuller information.
>
> Has it been proven that the inspired writers stated anything as true that was not true? No; there is no proof that the inspired writers made any mistake of any kind.[40]

W. H. Whitsitt once described Boyce and Broadus as Southern Baptists' great pair of twins, on the order of Luther and Melanchthon or Calvin and Beza.[41] Doubtless, both were equally committed to the Bible as the unique source of religious authority, just as they were united in guarding the seminary they had cofounded against an erosion of this commitment.

One of the most painful episodes in Boyce's life was the controversy over Crawford H. Toy, who had joined the faculty of Southern Seminary in 1869. At that time, Toy's commitment to the total truthfulness of Holy Scripture was explicitly stated in his impressive inaugural address: "The Bible, its real assertions being known, is in every iota of its substance absolutely and infallibly true."[42] Over the years, however, Toy gradually moved away from this position as he came more and more under the influence of Darwinian evolutionism and the theory of Pentateuchal criticism advanced by the German scholars Kuenen and Wellhausen. Enamored by the heady theories of "progressive" scholarship, Toy came to deny that many of the events recorded in the Old Testament had actually occurred. Moreover, he also questioned the Christological implications of many messianic prophecies, including Genesis 49:10, which the New Testament (Rev. 5:5) specifically applies to Christ. In 1876 Boyce wrote Toy a "gentle remonstrance and earnest entreaty" concerning his views on inspiration.[43] During the 1878–79 academic year, Toy's teaching became a matter of concern to the seminary trustees, chaired at that time by the venerable Baptist leader J. B. Jeter. Boyce requested Toy to refrain from espousing his radical critical views in the classroom. The latter agreed, but found that he could not do so. In the spring of 1879 Toy, under considerable pressure, tendered his resignation, acknowledging that it had "become apparent to me that my views of inspiration differ considerably from those of the body of my brethren."[44]

Broadus spoke for Boyce, the faculty, and the trustees (with the exception of two dissenting members) when he characterized the painful necessity of Toy's removal from the seminary community: "Duty to the founders of the institution and to all who had given money for its support and endowment, duty to the Baptist churches from whom its students must come, required [Boyce] to see to it that such teaching should not continue." Boyce took no joy in the departure of Toy. In a poignant scene at the railway station, Boyce embraced Toy and, lifting his right arm, exclaimed: "Oh, Toy, I would freely give that arm to be cut off if you could be where you were five years ago, and stay there."[45] Toy subsequently became a professor at Harvard University, where he affiliated with the Unitarian church and embraced even more radically critical views on the inspiration and authority of the Bible.[46]

Doubtless, the departure of Toy contributed to the conservative reputation that Southern Seminary enjoyed within the denomination and beyond. Once on a trip for the seminary, Boyce heard about certain students from Crozier Theological School who were trying to dissuade young preachers from coming to Southern because of the "antediluvian theology taught at Louisville." To which Boyce replied, "If my theology were not older than the days of Noah, it wouldn't be worth teaching!"[47]

On October 1, 1888, just two months before he died, Boyce wrote to his colleague, Basil Manly Jr. With an eye to the Toy controversy. which was just beginning to subside, he said:

> I greatly rejoice in the certain triumph of the truth. I feel that nothing but our own folly can prevent the success of the seminary. If we keep things orthodox and correct within and avoid injudicious compromises while we patiently submit and laboriously labor, we shall find continuous blessing. So much do I feel this that I look back on my life's work without any apprehension of future disaster.[48]

Evaluation

The legacy of James Petigru Boyce, like that of his younger contemporary, B. H. Carroll, is incarnated in the seminary he founded and into which he unstintingly poured his life. In Baptist history, Boyce stands as a link between an earlier generation of theological giants, the Gills, Fullers, and Furmans, and newer voices who sought to restate Baptist orthodoxy in a "world come of age," the Strongs, Mullinses, and Conners of the early-twentieth century. As we have seen, Boyce was both a strict (though not hyper-) Calvinist and a biblical inerrantist. It would be a mistake, however, to interpret him as a protofundamentalist, at least in the more recent, pejorative sense that label has assumed. If by *fundamentalist* we mean narrow-minded, mean-spirited, obscurantist, sectarian, then Boyce was no fundamentalist. His training at Brown and Princeton, his wide reading and extensive contacts all contributed to a broad and sympathetic spirit. In what may be his finest piece of theological reflection, Boyce wrote an extensive essay on "The Doctrine of the Suffering of Christ," which was published in England in *The Baptist Quarterly* in 1870. As his apology for entering into this well-worn topic, he wrote:

> It is manifestly important . . . that . . . definitions of doctrine should frequently be restated and re-examined. . . . It is well that they should be tested in the crucible of every age and every mind, that if there be any error it may be detected and the correction applied.[49]

These are not the words of a rigid ideologue, locked in a closed system. Boyce believed in an error-free Bible, but he did not presume an unrevisable theology. For this reason, the task of theology is a never-finished one in the life of the church.

One of the major functions of the theologian is to help the church distinguish between evangelical essentials and matters of tolerable diversity in the realm of doctrine. Boyce faced this issue squarely when he established strict confessional guidelines for the seminary faculty. While the Abstract of Principles was intended to be "a complete exhibition of the fundamental doctrines of grace, so that in no essential particular should they speak dubiously," they were at the same time loudly silent on some specific points of Calvinistic doctrine that had been spelled out plainly in the Philadelphia Confession of Faith. Thus nothing was included about the scope of the atonement or the doctrine of reprobation. As promulgated, the articles of faith represented a consensus of what Boyce called "the common heritage of the whole denomination."[50] This later became a matter of controversy not with reference to the strong Calvinism of the articles, but rather in connection with their laxity on points of Landmarkist ecclesiology. Although Boyce himself did not approve of the practice of "alien immersion," he defended his colleague William Williams, who had been criticized for holding this view. Within his own faculty, then, Boyce was forced to make a distinction between doctrinal views that—however much he might personally disagree with them—were acceptable within the commonly agreed upon confessional standard, and others that clearly undermined confidence in the essential evangelical commitment of the school. Thus he protected Williams against the Landmarkers, while he urged, with gentle firmness, the resignation of Toy.[51]

Boyce's theology has been characterized as a form of scholastic rationalism, philosophically derived from Scottish common-sense realism, and issuing in authoritarianism and even anthropocentrism.[52] Doubtless, Boyce borrowed much, both methodologically and substantially, from his Princeton mentors. He valued highly the role of reason and allowed for a robust natural theology. He was saved from the extreme dangers of this tendency, however, by his recognition that human fallenness encompassed the mind as well as the will and by his refusal to follow a speculative trajectory in theology. We might well wish that Boyce had studied Calvin more closely than Turretin, and that he had emphasized the internal witness of the Holy Spirit as strongly as the objective content of revelation. However, in an age seduced by uncritical subjectivism and relativist moralism, Boyce stood as an uncompromising witness on behalf of the living God who speaks and acts and redeems. Far from countenancing a human-centered approach in theology, Boyce was consumed with the vision of the greatness, majesty, and grace of the Sovereign God, the Lord of heaven and earth. David M. Ramsay recalled the following incident about "Jim Peter," as the students fondly called Boyce.

> One Sunday at the seminary dinner, a bunch of students came in from church saying,
> "We heard the greatest sermon of our lives today."
> "Who preached it?"
> "Jim Peter."
> "What was his text."
> "God"
> "What was his theme?"
> "God."
> "What were the divisions of the discourse?"
> "God"
> That was the man.[53]

Boyce still stands as an important model for the theological revitalization of the Baptist tradition. He calls us back to a vision of the true and living God, the God who meets us in judgment and mercy, the God whose favor we can never merit, but who in his sheer grace has called us to himself, through a baby in a manger, and a man on a cross.

Bibliography

Works by Boyce

Abstract of Systematic Theology. Philadelphia: American Baptist Publication Society, 1887.

A Brief Catechism of Bible Doctrine. Rev. ed. Louisville: Coperton and Cotes, 1878.

"The Doctrine of the Suffering Christ." *The Baptist Quarterly* 4 (1870): 385–411.

"The Good Cause." *Louisville Courier Journal* 3 (September 1877). Introductory lecture given at the opening of The Southern Baptist Theological Seminary.

Life and Death the Christian's Portion. New York: Sheldon & Co., 1869.

Sermon Manuscripts of James Petigru Boyce. The Southern Baptist Theological Seminary Library, Louisville.

Three Changes in Theological Institutions: An Inaugural Address Delivered before the Board of Trustees of the Furman University: Greenville, S.C.: C. J. Elford, 1856.

The Uses and Doctrine of the Sanctuary. Columbia, S.C.: Robert M. Stokes, 1859.

Works about Boyce

Broadus, John A. *Memoir of James Petigru Boyce.* New York: A. C. Armstrong, 1893.

Cody, Z. T. "James Petigru Boyce." *Review and Expositor* 24 (1927): 145–66.

Dever, Mark Edward. "Representative Aspects of the Theologies of John L. Dagg and James P. Boyce: Reformed Theology and Southern Baptists," Th.M. thesis, The Southern Baptist Theological Seminary, 1987.

Draughon, Walter D. "A Critical Evaluation of the Diminishing Influence of Calvinism on the Doctrine of Atonement in Representative Southern Baptist Theologians James Petigru Boyce, Edgar Young Mullins, Walter Thomas Conner, and Dale Moody," Ph.D. dissertation, Southwestern Baptist Theological Seminary, 1987.

George, Timothy. *James Petigru Boyce: Selected Writings.* Nashville: Broadman Press, 1989.

———. Review of *Abstract of Systematic Theology* by James Petigru Boyce, *Review and Expositor* 81 (1984): 461–64.

———. "Systematic Theology at Southern Seminary." *Review and Expositor* 82 (1985): 31–47.

Hinson, E. Glenn. "Between Two Worlds: Southern Seminary, Southern Baptists, and American Theological Education." *Baptist History and Heritage* 20 (April 1985): 28–35.

Honeycutt, Roy Lee. "Heritage Creating Hope: The Pilgrimage of The Southern Baptist Theological Seminary." *Review and Expositor* 81 (1984): 367–91.

Kutilek, Doug. "The Text and Translation of the Bible: Nineteenth Century American Baptist Views," Th.M. Thesis, Central Baptist Theological Seminary, 1998.

Matheson, Mark Edward. "Religious Knowledge in the Theologies of John Leadley Dagg and James Petigru Boyce; with Special Reference to the Influence of Common Sense Realism," Ph.D. dissertation, Southwestern Baptist Theological Seminary, 1984.

Mohler, R. Albert, Jr. "Don't Just Do Something; Stand There! Southern Seminary and the Abstract of Principles," A Convocation Address Delivered by R. Albert Mohler Jr., 31 August 1993, The Southern Baptist Theological Seminary, 1993.

Mueller, William A. *A History of Southern Baptist Theological Seminary.* Nashville: Broadman Press, 1959.

Nettles, Thomas J. *By His Grace and for His Glory: A Historical, Theological, and Practical Study of the Doctrines of Grace in Baptist Life.* Grand Rapids, Mich.: Baker Book House, 1986.

Ramsay, David Marshall. "James Petigru Boyce, God's Gentleman." *Review and Expositor* 21 (1924): 129–45.

Sampey, John R. *Southern Baptist Theological Seminary: The First Thirty Years, 1859–1889.* Baltimore: Wharton, Barron & Co., 1890.

Walker, Douglas Clyde. "The Doctrine of Salvation in the Thought of James Petigru Boyce, Edgar Young Mullins, and Dale Moody," Ph.D. dissertation, The Southern Baptist Theological Seminary, 1986.

6
The Broadus-Robertson Tradition
By David S. Dockery

ONE OF THE MOST INFLUENTIAL STREAMS OF THOUGHT IMPACTING AND influencing Baptist theology for the last 140 years developed from the life and work of John A. Broadus and his son-in-law, A. T. Robertson. From these two giants, brilliant in every way and mighty in the Scriptures, came a devotion to biblical exegesis, expositional preaching, and church-focused theology. Throughout the twentieth century this tradition shaped seminary and college classrooms in Baptist life but moreover influenced hundreds of pulpits across the land. To the contributions of these two giants we now turn our attention.

Life and Work
John Albert Broadus (1827–1895)

John Albert Broadus was born January 24, 1827 in Culpepper County, Virginia. When he died on March 16, 1895, he was regarded as one of North America's most capable Christian scholars of the nineteenth century and certainly one of the world's greatest preachers. Almost three decades after Broadus's death, his greatest student, A. T. Robertson reflected:

> The world has never seemed the same to me since Broadus passed on. For ten years I was enthralled by the witchery of his matchless personality. For three years I was his student. For seven years I was his assistant and colleague and for part of the last year an inmate of his home. It was my sacred and sad privilege to see the passing of this prince in Israel. No man has ever stirred my nature as Broadus did in the classroom and in the pulpit. It has been my fortune to hear Beecher and Phillips Brooks, Maclaren, Joseph Parker and Spurgeon, John Hall and Moody, John Clifford and David Lloyd George. At his best and in a congenial atmosphere Broadus was the equal of any man that I have ever heard.[1]

It comes as little surprise then, that Robertson's first major publication was a tribute to the mentor whom he so greatly loved. *The Life and Letters of John A. Broadus* was first published in 1901. Robertson's esteem for the late Broadus and enthusiasm for the work were reflected in the length of the original manuscript. Robertson's original proposal was over one thousand pages in length! His high personal regard and appreciation for Broadus were clearly demonstrated in the content of *Life and Letters*. Evidence for this can be seen in Robertson's conclusion that his friend and mentor was "one of the finest fruits of modern Christianity."[2]

The Early Years

The Broadus family was of Welsh extraction (the name was formerly spelled Broadhurst) and had long been rooted in the soil of the Old Dominion. They were a farming family, but several of Broadus's ancestors had devoted time to teaching, and several had become ministers of the gospel, some of them having attained great distinction and power. The family had deep spiritual roots and were almost unanimously members of the country Baptist churches of Virginia.

His father, Major Edmund Broadus, was a man of high character, ability, and independence of judgment that expressed itself in a variety of ways. Not only was he a farmer and major in the Culpepper County militia; Broadus was also a miller, a teacher, a leader of the Whig party of the state, and a member of the Virginia legislature for eighteen years. He was gifted with strong common sense and keen insight into the character and motives of people. Above all he was a deeply spiritual man, an ardent Baptist, and a strong leader in his church and local association. His life and work demonstrated it was indeed possible to be invested in the public square of his day as an active Christian.

The significant accomplishments of John A. Broadus can in many ways be traced to the marvelous model and paternal love and wisdom provided by his father. The presence of social, political, and religious leaders in the Broadus home greatly influenced John. Major Broadus had offered much support to Thomas Jefferson in the development of the University of Virginia, with which his famous son was to be so long and so intimately associated. Broadus's mother was a woman of godly character and a competence that admirably prepared her to be the wife of her notable husband and the mother of her remarkable children.

John Broadus was educated in the private subscription schools of Culpepper County. His schooling was completed at the Black Hill Boarding School under the capable tutelage of his uncle, Albert G. Simms. Young John went from this classroom well prepared for his formative years at the University of Virginia.

While he was still at his uncle's school, a lengthy revival meeting was conducted at the Mt. Poney Church by Rev. Charles Lewis and Rev. Barnett Grimsley. Broadus was converted at this revival. While under conviction and feeling unable to take hold of the promises of God, a friend quoted to him from John's Gospel: "All that the Father giveth me shall come to me; and him that cometh to me I will in no wise cast out" (John 6:37). His friend inquired, "Can you take hold of this, John?" Somehow the work of the Spirit dawned in his life by the use of this passage and the gift of regeneration came to young Broadus at that moment. His close friend, James G. Field, wrote:

> I knew him quite intimately from 1842 to 1847. We were youths of about the same age, he going to school to his uncle, Albert G. Simms, and I living in the store of Thomas Hill & Son, at Culpepper. Our fathers had been opposing candidates for the legislature. In May, 1843, at a protracted meeting conducted by Elder Charles Lewis with the Mt. Poney Church, at Culpepper, we both professed conversion . . . and were baptized by Rev. Cumberland George . . . He did not remain in the Mt. Poney

Church very long, but took his letter and joined New Salem, the church where his father and family had their membership.[3]

University of Virginia Years

Following the advice of his teachers and pastors, Broadus began the study of Greek when he entered the University of Virginia in 1846. This eager and dedicated student was endowed with great and rich gifts of mind as well as heart, which he never allowed to substitute for intense and persistent study. Broadus was a toiler, the apostle of hard work throughout life, which he had learned in the farm country of Virginia. It was said of Broadus later in his life that if genius is the ability and willingness to do hard work he was a genius. This diligent work ethic followed him all his days. Professor F. H. Smith of the University of Virginia observed that while a student at the University Broadus "cultivated a great power of application and grew to have a great ability to work, and was not ashamed that others should know it." Professor Smith continued, "The wonderful result of this steady, methodical industry was that in later years he could do unheard of things in the briefest time. His disciplined faculties were so under his will that the result, while natural, was surprising."[4]

While at the University of Virginia he continued to mature in his Christian faith. For Broadus conversion was closely related to the call to service, which meant he was involved in seeking to bring others to Christian belief. This practice had begun a few months after his conversion and continued throughout his lifetime. Robertson relates an early evangelistic effort that Broadus frequently shared with his students in later days:

> In a meeting a few months after John's conversion, the preacher urged all Christians at the close of the service to move about and talk to the unconverted. John looked anxiously around to see if there was anybody present he could talk to about his soul's salvation. He had never done anything of the kind before. Finally he saw a man . . . named Sandy. He thought he might venture to speak to him . . . and Sandy was converted.[5]

After Broadus went away to school he would often return home where he would be met by Sandy who would run across the street to meet him and say: "Howdy, John! thankee, John. Howdy, John, thankee, John." In later years as Broadus would retell the story he would add: "And if I ever reach the heavenly home and walk the golden streets, I know the first person to meet me will be Sandy, coming and saying again: 'Howdy, John! thankee, John.'"[6]

Another formative event characterizing the university years is noteworthy. In a note to a fellow student he once wrote this line in Greek: *hen se hysterei* (one thing thou lackest). This simultaneous compliment and delicate admonition bore fruit in the conversion of Broadus's fellow student. Broadus frequently looked for these ordinary contacts and relationships in life to communicate the truths of the gospel.

These events and others like them provided the context that confirmed his call to ministry. It was not unexpected that a Broadus should consider ministry as a possible life work. His uncle was a notable preacher who took special interest in his gifted nephew. Many other members of the Broadus family (sometimes spelled Broaddus, as well as Broadhurst) had been ministers.

Broadus had manifested serious interest in Christian service since the time of his conversion. He regularly attended church services on Sunday as well as Wednesday and Saturday. His work in the Sunday school encouraged him to think that he was called to preach. He struggled with the call to preach, thinking he was not qualified because he could not speak well in public. But in 1846, the same year he entered the university, Broadus surrendered to the ministry; never again for one moment did he think of wavering.

The years at the University of Virginia had a profound influence on Broadus. Particularly was he influenced by two professors: Gessner Harrison, professor of Greek, and W. H. McGuffey, professor of moral philosophy. Though he initially struggled with the high demands of the University of Virginia curriculum, he was regarded as the leading scholar of the institution by the time he was graduated with the A.M. degree in 1850. Following graduation he set for himself a broad self-study course in Old and New Testament, church history, and theology. On August 12 of that same year he was ordained to the full work of the ministry in the New Salem Church that he had joined soon after his conversion. If all of this were not enough for one year, he also (in 1850) married the daughter of Gessner Harrison, his great teacher, professor, and friend.

Numerous opportunities for teaching and preaching came to him. Such invitations followed him the rest of his life. It is doubtful if any Baptist anywhere during that period of time had more invitations both by churches and institutions of higher education than Broadus. Yet he held few positions over his lifetime. His first pastorate began in September 1851 at Charlottesville, Virginia, which enabled him simultaneously to accept the invitation from his *alma mater* to serve as assistant professor of Latin and Greek. Thus he was able at once to combine his dual loves of preaching and teaching.

Broadus served the church for eight years. After two years in the classroom, the University prevailed upon him to become their chaplain. During this time there was much discussion, especially in the South Carolina area, concerning the need for a Southern Baptist seminary.

The Southern Baptist Theological Seminary Years

Broadus himself had not attended a seminary. His university education provided him an outstanding background in the classical languages and philosophy, but his theological preparation, like so many other Baptist preachers in the South, came about through self-study. The freestanding theological seminary was a distinctively American idea, and was by this time becoming recognized in the American educational system. Newton Theological Institute had been in operation in the North since 1825, but there was no Baptist seminary in the South. The vision for this seminary largely came through the work of James Petigru Boyce. While Boyce is generally credited with the founding of The Southern Baptist Theological Seminary, he could not have built such an institution without Basil Manly Jr. and especially John A. Broadus. In 1856 Broadus was appointed by the Southern Baptist Convention to serve on a feasibility study committee to prepare a plan for the new seminary. This work was the introduction for Broadus of what was to be his life's work. When Broadus and Manly were asked to join the original seminary faculty, both responded reciprocally to each other, "I'll go if you will go." Still Broadus wrestled with leaving the Charlottesville pastorate and his beloved Virginia homeland. When the time came for him to respond to the invitation from the seminary, he could not for a year tear himself away from his first love; and when he did decide to go to the new seminary in Greenville, South Carolina, it brought great sorrow both to him and to the church.

Even though Manly and Boyce had been educated in northern seminaries, it was Broadus, the one who had not attended seminary, who was given the assignment to organize the plan of instruction. Not surprisingly the new proposal was based largely on a University of Virginia model, one based upon the English Bible, with freedom for the students in their selection of course work. It was a creative proposal that was fifty years ahead of other advances in theological education in North America. The plan emphasized scholarship for the able students with something worthwhile for all. The seminary opened its doors in Greenville, South Carolina in 1859 with twenty-six students. During the Civil War years, however, the new institution was forced to suspend its course of study.[7]

At the request of Stonewall Jackson, Broadus was asked to become a preacher to the Army of Northern Virginia. Writing to an associate of Broadus, J. William Jones, Jackson said of Broadus, "Write to him by all means and beg him to come. Tell him that he never had a better opportunity for preaching the gospel than he would have right now in these camps."[8] During the years of the Civil War, Broadus became a chaplain in Lee's army.

The seminary reopened following the war in the fall of 1865. At this time Broadus began his famous commentary on *The Gospel of Matthew* in the American Commentary. He labored for twenty years on the project that was ultimately published in 1886. When the seminary began classes after the Civil War, Broadus had only one student in his homiletics class, and this student was blind. Therefore Broadus taught him by lectures that were later published in 1870. For decades it was the most widely used book on homiletics in the world. This volume, *On the Preparation and Delivery of Sermons*, is still employed today in some settings. Without question it was Broadus's most famous work. The publication of the volume evidenced God's providential oversight. Here was a book that came about through lectures to one blind student in a small, at that time almost anonymous, institution in Greenville, South Carolina.

In this influential volume Broadus fleshed out the ideals of preaching he had formed over the past two decades. These ideas had been shaped by his study of the great masters of the art of preaching throughout the history of the church. By the time of the book's publication Broadus was already known all over the country as a preacher of rare ability and power. The book expressed what Broadus preached about preaching.[10]

When the seminary faced seemingly insurmountable financial obstacles in the mid-1870s, a decision was made to move the institution to Louisville, Kentucky. Broadus, too, moved to Louisville, his home until his death in 1895. The move was successful largely due to Boyce's courageous vision and Broadus's unrelenting will and their common trust in God. Broadus challenged his colleagues not to give up their efforts in behalf of the struggling seminary, uttering his famous words, "The seminary may die, but let us die first."

Although Broadus was offered pastorates in several prominent churches as well as the presidency of Brown University and Crozer Theological Seminary, all of which offered significantly greater salaries, he chose to remain in his faculty position at the seminary. In 1889, Broadus was elected president of The Southern Baptist Theological Seminary following the death of James P. Boyce. In the same year Broadus was invited to deliver the prestigious Lyman Beecher lectures on preaching at Yale University. Unfortunately, the lectures were never written down, and their contents can only be reconstructed from newspaper articles from *The Examiner* and *The Christian Inquirer*. Broadus never took notes with him into the pulpit and did not like for his messages to be transcribed.[11]

Broadus's fame and influence continued to spread. He delivered prestigious lectureships around the country, including a presentation on "Textual Criticism of the New Testament" at Newton and on "Jesus of Nazareth" at Johns Hopkins University.

The added responsibility of presidential leadership and the death of Boyce had a considerable impact on Broadus. A. T. Robertson observed that after 1889 Broadus never regained the buoyancy of life he had once had. In his final year as president, Broadus's health continued to grow weaker. Yet his standing as a national Baptist leader continued to build the seminary both financially and in terms of national and international recognition. The great Baptist leader, preacher, and scholar died on March 16, 1895. On that day, the *Louisville Courier-Journal* reported, "There is no man in the United States whose passing would cause more widespread sorrow than that of Doctor Broadus."[12]

Broadus had no greater impact than his influence on his prize student and son-in-law, A. T. Robertson. A special bond was formed between them, especially during Robertson's years on the Southern faculty. Robertson affectionately called Broadus his "truest earthly friend." Broadus thought of Robertson as his greatest discovery and modeled for the young professor two disciplines for which Robertson became equally, if not more, famous: New Testament interpretation and preaching. It was the model of Broadus's approach to the New Testament which later bore fruit in the method of interpretation used by Robertson in his mammoth *Greek Grammar*.

Broadus modeled for Robertson an interpretive method that took into account the recent developments in critical scholarship while still remaining true to the authority of Holy Scripture. Robertson's intimate acquaintance with Broadus's work, as seen in the critical textual notes he contributed to Broadus's *Harmony of the Gospels*, reveals his continuity with, and addition to, the Broadus legacy. One of the finest compliments Robertson ever received was from J. H. Farmer, of McMaster University, who observed, "Professor Robertson has worthily maintained the Broadus tradition."[13] Robertson"s Greek grammar and *Word Pictures* clearly reflect the impact of Broadus upon the prolific professor.[14]

Archibald Thomas Robertson (1863–1934)

Archibald Thomas Robertson taught at The Southern Baptist Theological Seminary for forty-six years (1888–1934). Robertson, who was born on November 6, 1863, to John and Ella Martin Robertson in Chatham, Virginia, was the greatest biblical scholar in the history of the Southern Baptist Convention. He died on Monday evening, September 24, 1934, at six o'clock at his home on Rainbow Drive near the seminary campus. Characteristically, Dr. Robertson at his death was writing another book on the New Testament for Harper & Brothers.[15]

Robertson began a teaching career at Southern Seminary in 1888, which did not end until his. His role as professor impacted the lives of hundreds, multiplying his scholarship and ministry through Baptist pulpits around the country and even around the world. Without question Robertson's teaching ministry was characterized by excellence and demanding rigor. Yet it was his writing career, which extended even to the day of his death, that set Robertson apart as the greatest biblical scholar in Baptist history.

Both his teaching and writing ministry can only be understood and interpreted in light of Robertson's genuine evangelical piety and churchmanship. A churchman of the highest order, Robertson's scholarly pursuits were always in the service of the church, primarily for the preacher. He thought of himself first and foremost as a preacher. When asked which of the three kinds of service was the highest, preaching, teaching, or writing, Robertson replied: "Preaching! Yes, preaching is the greatest work in the world. The element in the other two that makes them worthwhile is the preaching that they contain."[16]

The Early Years

In 1875, the Robertson family moved from Virginia to Cool Spring, North Carolina, when young Archibald was twelve years old. For the next four years Robertson attended Boone Preparatory School, Statesville, North Carolina. From 1879 to 1885 he attended Wake Forest College, combining some high school subjects with the college core curriculum to earn the M.A. degree.

The Robertson family had little money. In fact, they, like other farmers, struggled desperately to make ends meet during the 1870s and 1880s. Yet it was during this time that young Archie used to say, "I learned to work, to work hard, and to keep on working."[17]

When the Robertsons arrived in their new North Carolina town, there was no Baptist church. For three Sundays of the month they attended the Presbyterian church, and the other Sunday they attended Baptist services at the courthouse conducted by Rev. J. B. Boone. Pastor Boone was strongly attracted to the Robertson family. He sensed the interest that young Archie had in spiritual matters. Boone became a veritable Paul to this young Timothy. As the area grew and more Baptists came into the area, a church was formed. Baptisms were held in a pond at the edge of town, the first in the history of that strong Presbyterian center. Archie heard a neighbor say that she had seen the likes of a baptism before, but her husband had never seen the like, so she was going to let him go.

In March 1876, during a revival meeting led by Rev. F. M. Jordan, Archie "felt a change of heart." He was baptized along with his brother Eugene and two older sisters. Baptism by immersion was so new and strange that Archie was mocked by his Presbyterian playmates when he was baptized.

Mr. Boone prepared the equivalent of a college preparatory curriculum for young people not able to attend school. The plan focused on Archie Robertson, who was given free tuition. Archie began his studies in 1878 with courses in Latin, arithmetic, geography, and grammar. The school desk always had to be set aside when plowing and farm duties took priority. Boone's plan enabled Robertson to fulfill his educational longing and his passionate desire to prepare to serve the Lord. Archie's older brother, Martin, made great personal sacrifices that allowed Archie to pursue work with Boone, as well as eventual studies at Wake Forest College.

On his sixteenth birthday, November 6, 1879, Archie enrolled at Wake Forest, having borrowed ten dollars from a friend to purchase the train ticket. He arrived with two dollars in his pocket. Though he entered two months late in November 1879 instead of September 1, he caught up with his classmates through his diligent effort. One of his former fellow-students made this illuminating observation that Archie, though arriving late that first year, soon led his class in Greek because of his "meticulous observation and a marvelous memory." These same great gifts served him well throughout his years of brilliant scholarship.

When Robertson entered Wake Forest, he had a serious impediment in his speech. He spent many hours alone, reading aloud and reciting choice selections of literature, which he memorized for that purpose. He enrolled in a special course to help eliminate this self-conscious problem. Eventually by learning to breathe differently, the matter was corrected. He later joined and participated in the Evzelian Literary Society to improve both his reasoning and speaking abilities. Robertson's mentors at Wake Forest included William Louis Poteat (languages), Charles Elisha Taylor (Latin), and William B. Royal (Greek). Robertson placed first or second in his class in French, Latin, and Greek, making grades of 95 to 100 in every course. He was coeditor of the renowned college paper, *The Wake Forest Student*, called by *The Cleveland New Era* "the best college magazine published in this country."[18]

Surprising as it may seem, it was in Greek, not French or Latin, where Robertson won the second-place medal. What was then a keen disappointment became the motivating force for him in later years to excel in New Testament scholarship. His second-place finish was used as a stepping stone to higher achievement in forthcoming years. His six years at Wake Forest may well have been the most important of his entire career.

Robertson entered Wake Forest poorly prepared at the age of sixteen. He graduated in June 1885 as an accomplished student and budding scholar. Though offered a professorship at his alma mater, Robertson turned his efforts toward his calling to preach and headed for further training at The Southern Baptist Theological Seminary in Louisville, Kentucky.

The Southern Seminary Years

At age sixteen Robertson was licensed to preach. During that same year he preached his first sermon in a Black church in North Carolina. His journey to Southern Seminary was the next step on his lifelong pursuit of the "call to preach."

The seminary had been in its new home city eight years when Archibald T. Robertson entered as a new student in 1885. As yet, the struggling institution had no home of its own. The Waverly Hotel served as dormitory, while the lecture rooms were up two flights of steps in the library hall on Fourth Avenue, an arrangement that continued until 1888.

Robertson worked hard his first two years taking senior Greek, textual criticism, and patristic Greek, all courses normally taken in one's final year. He also found numerous opportunities to preach both in Louisville during the school session, as well as back in the mountains of North Carolina during the vacation periods. He also served the homeless in a downtown mission called the California Mission.

During the early days of the 1888 school year, D. L. Moody held a six-week campaign in Louisville. Robertson wrote in his diary of an encouraging opportunity he had in soul-winning. It was his privilege to lead a self-identified universalist from West Virginia to the Lord. Robertson was spiritually moved by that experience and the powerful preaching of Moody. Though Robertson was concerned about Moody's poor grammar and use of the English language, he nevertheless observed that: "He [Moody] has a grip on the Bible, human nature, and God." He commented that Moody's exposition of the Holy Spirit was "the most enrapturing and heaven-inspired discourse" he had ever heard.[19]

As he neared the end of his student days, he recalled that on his fifteenth birthday his mother told him that she would still be prouder of him after fifteen more years. Yet he wondered whether the Lord would fulfill his mother's prophecy. The answer came on April 7, 1888, when the faculty invited Robertson to become an assistant to John A. Broadus in Greek and homiletics. With this invitation Robertson's life course was set: he was to be a man of the Book and a teacher of preachers rather than a pastor. So it was that Archie Robertson, the student, found himself at age twenty-five at his desk, addressed as Professor Robertson, and affectionately as "Doctor Bob." His career as professor began October 1, 1888, and continued for the next forty-six years.

He joined the esteemed faculty of what was becoming the most significant seminary in the land. Those men with whom he had studied—Broadus, James P. Boyce, William Whitsett, Basil Manley Jr.—now became his colleagues. Upon joining the faculty, John R. Sampey observed that Robertson was clearly the foremost student of his period in the seminary. As he began his new work, the young professor remarked: "I am sure I do not know how to teach, but I am equally determined, by the grace of God to learn how."[20] Nothing Robertson ever penned opened up for us his person as these words that described his humility, his determination, and his dependence on the grace of God.

It was certainly the grace and providence of God that gave Robertson the opportunity to spend the first year of his professorate at the house of Southern Seminary's founding president, James P. Boyce. Unfortunately, Boyce would pass away by the end of the year. Still, the opportunity to spend his first year as a faculty member living with Boyce, and Boyce's successor in the department of theology, F. H. Kerfoot, instilled within Robertson a love for the seminary where he would spend the rest of his academic career. Not unlike Boyce, Robertson threw himself wholeheartedly into every enterprise in which he was involved. In addition to his duties as a seminary professor, Robertson also became pastor of the Newcastle Baptist Church in Newcastle, Kentucky. His eagerness to fulfill the role of both teacher and preacher, however, soon placed Robertson's well-being in jeopardy. The aggressive schedule of preaching and teaching eventually caught up with the young professor and threw him into states of deep melancholy.[21] Realizing his limitations, Robertson gave up his pastoral work at Newcastle. Nevertheless, Robertson saw his whole life as service to his God, stating, "After all, what is a man's life worth if it be not given to God, and his kindred and mankind?"[22]

There was no doubt that Robertson, however, was on the rise as an academician. The surrounding faculty admired his ability and motivation. Although already an original thinker and scholar, Robertson himself would have pointed to those same faculty members as the formative influences on his illustrative career. A.T. Robertson was gaining a solid reputation as a New Testament scholar in the already substantive Southern Seminary tradition. In particular, Robertson formed a special relationship with the famous Southern Baptist New Testament scholar, preacher, and cofounder of Southern Seminary, John A. Broadus, whom, as we have noted, he affectionately called his "truest earthly friend." Later, Broadus's daughter Ella would become his beloved wife, and so Robertson truly became regarded as part of the Broadus family. Broadus himself thought of Robertson as his greatest discovery, and modeled for the young professor two disciplines for which Robertson later became famous: New Testament interpretation and preaching. It was the model of Broadus's approach to the New Testament which later bore fruit in the interpretative method of Robertson in his mammoth Greek grammar. Broadus modeled for Robertson an interpretive method that took into account the recent developments in critical scholarship while still remaining true to the authority of Holy Scripture. Robertson's intimate acquaintance with Broadus's work, as seen in the critical textual notes he contributed to Broadus's *Harmony of the Gospels*, reveals his continuity with, and addition to, the Broadus legacy. One of the highest compliments Robertson ever received was from J. H. Farmer, of

McMaster University, who observed, "Professor Robertson has worthily maintained the Broadus tradition."[23] Robertson's Greek grammar and *Word Pictures* clearly reflect the imprint of Broadus upon the young professor.

Robertson, however, was not one merely to be a student of the masters; he became a master himself. He would become regarded as the greatest New Testament scholar to ever teach at Southern Seminary, and one of the greatest in the history of New Testament interpretation. Robertson's ardent dedication to study continually sharpened his keen mind, and he could always be found at his desk, between classes, poring over his latest writing projects and research. Roberston's output of scholarly writings was exceptional. Edgar McKnight has observed that between the years 1914 and the year of his death in 1934, there were only two years in which Robertson did not have volumes published.[24] In addition, his scholarly contributions transcended his primary field of expertise in New Testament and included works of theology, preaching, history, and denominational analysis. Robertson also became a frequent contributor to numerous Baptist state papers in the South, the Seminary's *Review and Expositor,* as well as Northern Baptist periodicals such as *The Baptist* and *The Watchman Examiner.* In all of these, Robertson dealt faithfully with the weighty, fundamental theological issues confronting Baptists at the dawn of the twentieth century. While Robertson never penned a major work in theology, he nevertheless addressed the major theological issue of the day consistent with historic orthodoxy.

Robertson also carefully blended level-headed, genuine scholarship with a passion for the seminary classroom. Students found his courses extremely demanding but never boring. His keen wit and dry humor were among the most notable aspects of his teaching style, and the daily recitations he required in class always kept his students awake. William Mueller recounts a situation in which a student sought to come to blows with Robertson over something the professor had said in class and asked "Doctor Bob" to take off his coat and defend himself. Robertson wisely replied, "All right, all right, but let us first kneel down and pray!"[25] Even in the most difficult situations, Robertson was there, pointing his students to Christ.

The professor also played a critical role during one of the most turbulent times in the history of Southern Baptists' mother seminary: The Whitsitt controversy. Along with his fellow faculty, Robertson stood behind the president, William Whitsitt, in the heated theological and historical debate over Landmarkism. Robertson realized that Whitsitt's historical investigations and evaluations of Baptist successionism were not unfaithful to sound Baptist theology and a proud heritage. Robertson and his fellow faculty prided themselves on the "theological soundness" of Southern Seminary and urged caution in dealing with the issue at hand.[26] Their concern primarily was for a "faithful preaching of a pure gospel," coupled with sound scholarship.[27]

Robertson cared deeply for his students and the seminary and the high calling of training ministers for the gospel ministry. Perhaps the greatest testament to this fact is that Robertson was teaching on the day on which he grew gravely ill, was taken home, and later died of a severe stroke. One student remarked that even before his death, students began to develop a historical consciousness concerning the import of their professor's work in the field of New Testament interpretation.[28] In spite of his established international reputation as a well-published scholar and theologian, the end of A. T. Robertson's life found him where he was preeminently dedicated and well remembered: the halls and classrooms of Southern Seminary.

Mighty in the Scriptures: Their Theological Influence

John Broadus: Exegesis, Exposition, and Pastoral Theology

John Broadus, together with James P. Boyce and Basil Manly Jr., shaped the Southern Baptist theological tradition. The combination of the names of *Broad*us and *Man*ly were joined together to provide the name for the book publishing arm of the Baptist Sunday School Board: Broad(us) Man(ly) Press. Their theological commitments can best be seen in The Abstract of Principles (1859), which from the founding of the seminary has served as the guiding confession of faith.

The theological tradition reflected in the *Abstract* is in line with historic orthodoxy at every point. The soteriology can be called moderately Calvinistic and the ecclesiology baptistic. Broadus's work was carried forth in a manner faithful to this tradition.

Many things shape a successful scholar-theologian. Obviously Broadus was blessed by divine enablement and multigiftedness. On the human level such a person is a complex force. The natural endowment must be there to begin with, and there must be tireless energy and much preparation. Many persons are gifted but are neither successful as scholars or preachers. Broadus excelled because of his strong work ethic, the focus of his work, the subject matter explored, the drive for excellence, and his rigorous pursuit to handle accurately the material.

His first major work was *On the Preparation and Delivery of Sermons* (1870). Broadus was not the first to address the subject of preaching, but the incredible success of the book can be traced to Broadus's marvelous ability to communicate complex material in a popular way. He presented similar material in a more challenging and scholarly treatise in the publication of his five lectures on *The History of Preaching* given at Newton in 1876.

The volume that best exemplifies his first-rate scholarship was his twenty-year effort on the *Gospel of Matthew*. While not as well known as *On the Preparation and Delivery of Sermons*, this volume in the *American Commentary* is generally considered the greatest of all his works. Just as there were significant volumes on preaching prior to Broadus's 1870 publication, so there were hundreds of works on the Gospel of Matthew prior to the work by Broadus. Yet for over a century it has clearly remained the most important published volume in the American Commentary series, and one of the truly scholarly volumes on the first gospel.

Three other works on the Gospels are worthy of note. Shortly after the publication of the Matthew commentary, he penned a brief work on *Jesus of Nazareth*, which was the revision of lectures given at Johns Hopkins. In 1893 he completed the famous *A Harmony of the Gospels*, which had several revisions and editions over the years by A. T. Robertson. His *Commentary on the Gospel of Mark* was published posthumously in 1905.

He contemplated several other works on New Testament themes, which were never published. When the issue concerning biblical authority and the use of historical criticism became a major issue on the Southern Seminary campus in 1879, Broadus addressed the subject by defending the full truthfulness of the Bible in *Three Questions as to the Bible* (1883) and the *Paramount and Permanent Authority of the Bible* (1887).

Following the death of his beloved colaborer, Broadus authored *The Memoirs of James P. Boyce*, published in 1893. With every publication Broadus sought to do good, to edify his readers, to expand their knowledge, and to build up the church of Jesus Christ. The sentence that concludes the preface to *The History of Preaching* may be taken as the motto and prayer of all his writings: "God grant that the little volume may be of some real use!" Each work reflects his commitment to careful scholarship, industrious research, accuracy of knowledge, and conscientious thought in his communication. Whatever he did was worth, in his favorite phrase, "working at." His works have retained their place over the years because his work was not the effusions of mere ambition to be a published author.

Those who heard him said he was even a better preacher than writer. Here he combined his scholarly commitment to New Testament exegesis, evident in his commentaries, with his masterful understanding of the art and history of preaching. The skillful, yet simple, touch of a master was evident by all who heard him proclaim the message of God's Word. At this point it will be helpful to examine Broadus's views on biblical inspiration and his approach to biblical interpretation.

To have an accurate understanding of Broadus's exegetical method and his important and distinctive contributions to biblical exposition in the evangelical tradition, we need to examine his view on the inspiration of the Bible. The issue had become a major issue on the campus of Southern

Seminary in the 1870s and 1880s as the faculty attempted to respond to their departed colleague, C. H. Toy, who resigned over his acceptance of historical-critical conclusions. The major treatise was produced by Basil Manly Jr. titled *The Bible Doctrine of Inspiration* (1888). The key to understanding Manly and Broadus is to recognize their common opposition and response to Toy. Both disagreed with Toy's doctrine of Scripture and its practical implications.[29] Manly affirmed plenary inspiration and carefully refuted any theory of mechanical dictation. Broadus also refuted any theory of mechanical dictation, but was cautious in theorizing as to verbal inspiration.[30] Both clearly affirmed every aspect of Scripture as infallible truth and divine authority. In *Three Questions as to the Bible*, he answered "completely" to the question, "To what extent ought we regard the sacred writings of the Old and New Testaments as inspired?" His work *The Paramount and Permanent Authority of the Bible* took seriously the human authorship of the Bible as well as its divine origin. He contended for the complete truthfulness of Holy Scripture in a manner reflective of other great Christian leaders of the nineteenth century like Boyce, Manly, J. L. Dagg, and Alvah Hovey, yet with an independence and creativity characteristic of all of his work.[31] Perhaps most telling are words expressed to a group of young seminarians in a New Testament class he addressed for the last time a few days before his death. He communicated his earnest desire for them was that they be "mighty in the Scriptures."[32]

Broadus attributed the doctrinal unity among Baptists and other evangelicals during the nineteenth century to their emphasis on the authority of the Bible in matters of faith and practice.[33] In *The Paramount and Permanent Authority of the Bible*, he wrote: "Now, I address myself to people who believe that the Bible is the Word of God; not merely that it contains the Word of God, which wise persons may disentangle from other things in the book, but that it is the Word of God." He continues: "It is entirely possible that we may have no creed or system of theology, no professors or even preachers, nor even newspaper writers, nor writers of tracts, that can always interpret the Bible with infallible success. But our persuasion is that the real meaning of the Bible is true."[34]

These statements reflect an explicit affirmation from Broadus that the Bible, apart from human interpretation, has objective meaning and value.

While Broadus was at the forefront of American biblical scholarship in the nineteenth century and was a pacesetter in certain areas, it is interesting to hear him say that with all the progress of the nineteenth century, "It does not follow that this century is superior to all previous centuries in thinking, for in some respects our age has not time to be wiser."[35] Thus we see that his careful and wise scholarship remained faithful to the authority of Holy Scripture as the only and sufficient revelation of God. As such he stated that "a 'progressive orthodoxy' that forsakes or adds to the teaching of Christ becomes heterodoxy."[36] His words for his time are equally applicable for contemporary readers in his discussion about current archeological, philosophical, and scientific debates. "The great principle, in all such inquiries," he claimed, "is that while it is lawful to reinvestigate the Scripture in the light of current opinion and feeling, it is not lawful to put anything as authority above God's Word."[37]

Broadus unhesitatingly defended the trustworthiness and authority of the Bible, but was cautious in asserting a definition of inspiration. In *Three Questions as to the Bible*, he wrote, "But whatever these (biblical) writers meant to say, or whatever we learn from subsequent revelation that God meant to say through their words, though not by themselves fully understood, that we hold to be true, thoroughly true, not only in substance but in statement."[38] In conclusion, Broadus summarized, "even today I know of no discrepancies in the Bible which impair its credibility."[39] These foundational commitments served to undergird his painstaking and even-handed exegesis that characterized his lifework.

In the preface to his *Commentary on the Gospel of Matthew*, Broadus thoroughly discussed textual matters, various viewpoints, evaluations, comparisons, and conclusions. For example he observed: "The general contributions to textual criticism made by Westcott and Hort are invaluable, and most of their judgments as to particular passages seem to me correct. But in a number of cases I have felt bound to dissent, and to give the reasons as fully and strongly as the character and limits of this work allowed."[40]

The commentary offered insights on Greek grammar and syntax, with copious footnotes. Yet the direct word-by-word, phrase-by-phrase exposition makes the work useful for the Sunday school teacher, as well as pastors and scholars.

Broadus did not sidestep the tough questions impacting the veracity and accuracy of the biblical text. He addressed seeming contradictions and errors simply and directly, reflecting his convictional trust in the Bible's truthfulness.[41] After wrestling to determine the historical meaning of the text, Broadus practiced the steps outlined in *Three Questions* with his "homiletical and practical" comments, wedding exacting exegesis with solid application. By focusing on the practical aspects as well, Broadus brilliantly combined his two specialties, showing that biblical interpretation and theology must ultimately be done in the service of the church.

His theological conclusions throughout the commentary evidence his Reformed convictions, reflecting the Philadelphia/Charleston confessional traditions that gave birth to Southern Seminary. For example, he contended for the virgin birth (see 1:21), affirmed that Jesus claimed that he was the Messiah (see 13:10–17), and expounded the need for divine initiative for God to make himself known to depraved men and women (see 22:14).

Overall, Broadus's work on Matthew is a model commentary, and in many ways ushered in a new era of commentary writing within evangelical scholarship.[42] Significant advances included the incorporation of historical, textual, and grammatical research that was being advocated during his lifetime. He demonstrated an awareness and conservative openness to European critical scholarship, but he was not willing to subject Holy Scripture unreservedly to the antisupernatural biases of much of the German critical approaches. His work included grammatical, exegetical, theological, and practical comments, thus making it valuable to a very wide readership.

His commentary work was not the only place Broadus made original contributions. In the *Harmony of the Gospels*, Robertson comments:

> Dr. Broadus was the first one to depart from the traditional
> division of the ministry of Christ by the Passovers rather than the
> natural unfolding of the ministry itself . . . Dr. Broadus's work is
> the ripe fruit of a lifetime of rich study and reflection by one of
> the rarest teachers of the New Testament that any age or country
> has ever seen.[43]

Broadus's firm theological foundation and level-headed explorations allowed him to employ the best of European critical scholarship without embracing the conclusions. His openness has been misinterpreted by some. For example, Finke and Starke claim that "Broadus was extremely impressed with the application of critical methods to biblical studies that was going on in European universities, especially in Germany."[44]

Yet the comments from J. M. Carter's notes on Broadus's lectures on New Testament Introduction are informative.[45] While Broadus was certainly open to new advances, his interpretive method could not be considered progressive. He rejected notions that the Gospel of John was in conflict with the other Gospels, despite recent critical objections. He clearly held to a Johannine authorship of the Fourth Gospel. Throughout his lectures on the four Gospels he affirmed the supernatural origin of the Gospels and the author's eyewitness accounts.

A. T. Robertson: Theologian and Statesman

Robertson's work and influence were not limited to the confines of the seminary life and the academic enterprise. Robertson gave himself to the larger work of Baptist denominational life, and especially the concerns of Baptists around the world. It was Robertson who originally suggested the concept for what would later become the Baptist World Congress. In 1905, a year after his suggestion in *The Baptist Argus*, the Baptist World Alliance convened in London, a meeting in which Robertson took part. In addition, he contributed to the life and thought of the Southern Baptist Convention, and especially its churches. Robertson had a passion for the centrality of preaching in the church and could regularly be found in pulpits throughout Kentucky preaching on weekends and ministering the Word. Robertson wanted to model for his students a careful, expositional approach to preaching the Bible. Like Broadus, he wanted his students to be "mighty in the Scriptures." On one occasion Robertson wryly observed, "The greatest proof that the Bible is inspired is that it has withstood so much bad preaching." Roberston's biographer, Everett Gill, recounts that when interpreting the Scripture passage, 'a savor of life unto life or of death unto death,' the professor asserted, "Preaching . . . is the most dangerous thing in the world."[46] Above all, Robertson's life and ministry had the edification and growth of the church of Jesus Christ in mind. He once remarked to his students, "God pity the poor preacher who has to hunt for something to preach—and the people who have to listen." The wise scholar had a heartbeat for God's people. As William Mueller has observed: "The great New Testament scholar seemed happiest when he stood before a congregation pointing men and women to the Lord Jesus Christ as their only Master and Savior."[47]

Roberston's influence was also felt throughout the North during the contentious Fundamentalist-Modernist debates in the Northern Baptist Convention. It was not uncommon for the reader of such papers as the *Watchman-Examiner* and *The Baptist* to find articles and essays with Robertson defending the supernatural nature of the Christian truth claim and supporting the affirmation of the "fundamentals" of Christianity. Much like his colleague, President E. Y. Mullins, Robertson was a man in demand, one to whose opinion Baptists would pay heed. Robertson proved to be a steady voice in unsteady times, a trustworthy scholar for all Baptists, both North and South.

As a theologian, Robertson did not hesitate to state his convictions. Robertson's confidence in the historical reliability and complete truthfulness of Scripture can be clearly seen in Robertson's view of biblical inspiration. While Robertson certainly believed that Christian scholars should avail themselves of the most accurate historical data and interpretation, he simultaneously believed that all such human speculations must fall under the authority of the divine disclosure of the Scriptures. Robertson declared concerning the historical reliability of the Gospel of Luke in reference to the divinity and virgin birth of Jesus:

> It remains that the whole truth about Jesus lies in the interpretation given by Luke in the opening chapters of his gospel. The view of Luke the physician holds the field today in the full glare of modern science and historical research.[48]

Thus, Robertson was convinced of the veracity of Scripture in light of the findings of modern historical methodology. As such, he was willing to use the best possible historical tools and research in demonstrating the full truthfulness of the Scriptures. Robertson felt that the tools of critical methodology, if cautiously used in reverence for the authority of Scripture, could aid the interpreter in understanding the biblical text. Consequently, Robertson's openness to the proper use of critical tools in interpreting Scriptures should not be viewed as an antithetical position to that of Robertson's forebearers such as John A. Broadus and Basil Manly Jr. but rather as a contemporary exposition of that same tradition.

As such, Robertson became a standard in Southern Baptist circles by which New Testament scholarship and biblical fidelity would later be judged. Upon the occasion of his death, one of his students remarked that if all the buildings of the seminary were blown down and Professor Robertson alone were left standing "the seminary would have been more real than it was with him gone."[49] He was part of the impetus which brought Southern Baptist life and scholarship to the forefront of the theological world. In many ways, Robertson's reputation has yet to be paralleled. His legacy to his colleagues, students, and Southern Seminary was, in the words of his successor Hershey Davis, "inestimable."

Epochs in the Life of Jesus shows us a fundamental concern of Robertson's: expounding and retelling the stories of the New Testament. In the light of the work of liberal scholars, like Albert Schweitzer, who were seeking to give their position on the historical Jesus, Robertson saw the need to write his own biography of the life of Christ. In place of Schweitzer's assertion that the titles of Jesus are mere "historical parables," Robertson clearly confesses him as the Messiah, the Son of God. In place of the confused identity with which "The Quest for the Historical Jesus" had sought to depict Jesus, Robertson reveals the unified witness of the Gospel material: that Jesus is in fact Lord and Savior. In *The Christ of the Logia*, we see evidence of Robertson's careful mixture of both a conservative approach to biblical exegesis—using critical method and a reverence and commitment to the Scripture's confession of the person and work of Christ. Robertson clearly confessed the unity of the Synoptic Gospels' witness to Jesus as both Savior and Lord.

In the article, "The Bible as Authority," Robertson asserted that the Bible is actually the Word of God, and "since there is no ultimate authority in the spiritual realm outside of God," the Bible has the authority to command obedience, action, and belief. In this essay, Christ is revealed as the interpretive principle for all of Scripture. Robertson concluded that critical study of the Bible must be supplemented by the guidance of the Holy Spirit in its interpretation, stating, "The Bible must be studied by the scientific historical method, but also with an enlightened soul in touch with the Spirit of God." What is more, Robertson affirmed the historic Baptist principle that Scripture must be interpreted in light of Scripture, and that the Bible can be plainly understood, on its own terms, and in its own words. The Bible, he felt, has stood against so much criticism, unbelief, and misinterpretation, so as to demonstrate through those facts alone that it must be the Word of God.

His work, "The Relative Authority of Scripture and Reason," was originally an address delivered before the tenth meeting of the Baptist Congress in May 1892. For several days, Robertson had listened to theologians such as William Newton Clarke stand before the assembly and cast aspersions upon the infallibility and nature of the Bible. Robertson was so disappointed with the tone and spirit of some of the speakers from the platform that he decided to answer their toughest questions, and advance a few theses of his own, which resulted in one of the greatest treasures of the Robertson literary corpus. Here is Robertson at his best: thinking on his feet, responding to critics, and defending the faith. In a similar vein, he addressed the issue of the validity and importance of the supernatural conception of Jesus Christ in "Is The Virgin Birth Still Credible Today?" Robertson's answer to that question is a resounding yes as it appeared during the height of the Fundamentalist–Modernist controversy among Northern Baptists in the early 1920s. But Robertson's approach is not an uncritical literalism which hides away when the facts are presented. Rather, it embraces all of the truth God has shown us in the natural order as but further evidence of his powerful ability to accomplish his providential purposes. As such, Robertson declared with his Baptist predecessors that the Scripture "has God for its author, salvation for its end, and truth, without any mixture of error for its matter."

Robertson converted his mastery of Greek into theological applications for the believer in "The Greek Article and the Deity of Christ," and "Grammar and Preaching." In the former, Robertson refutes the questionable exegesis which has supplied false evidence for all those who seek to deny the deity of Jesus Christ by claiming a loophole in the grammatical construct of the first chapter of the Gospel of John. In "Grammar and Preaching" Robertson again weds the practicality of knowledge of Greek grammar with sound exegetical preaching that is faithful to the text as God's Word.

Conclusion

John A. Broadus and A. T. Robertson unhesitatingly affirmed and faithfully expounded what can be called Baptist distinctives. Robertson was once reported to have said, "Give a man an open Bible, an open mind, a conscience in good working order, and he will have a hard time to keep from being a Baptist." This commitment was carried forward in the lives and labors of both Robertson and Broadus.

Robertson was honored to carry forth the Broadus tradition, which today we may call the Broadus-Robertson tradition. They faithfully taught the Bible in the spirit and conviction of the Baptist heritage, while advancing Baptist scholarship into the twentieth century, and placing it on a solid, but contemporary footing. We now have the privilege and responsibility to carry forth this tradition in a faithful way into the twenty-first century, a generation that will handle accurately the Word of God (2 Tim. 2:15).

The legacy of their work is not only in their writings, but in the lives of those whom they taught, best exemplified in pulpit giants like H. H. Hobbs and W. A. Criswell. Their commitment to exegetical theology, however, was simultaneously a strength and a weakness. They upheld the authority of Scripture, but both were cautious at best in developing a systematic approach to theology. This approach advanced biblical theology but failed to advance a coherent Baptist theology. In a similar way that E. Y. Mullins's theology developed and reshaped the consistent Calvinism of J. P. Boyce, so Broadus to some degree and Robertson even more so moved to a more synergistic soteriology.

The strengths of the Broadus-Robertson tradition focused on New Testament theology and preaching. They stood faithfully on the truthfulness of Holy Scripture. Their works on the Gospels stand to this day as standard-bearers. They recognized the pitfalls in harmonizing the Gospels if by doing so the unique emphasis of each Gospel would be lost. They warned that the Gospels are not a mere mass to be artificially reconstructed, for each Gospel is a living and independent whole. Yet they saw the value of providing an overall look at the life of Christ as a way to reconcile apparent discrepancies in the Gospels.

In conclusion, we must recognize in their works the pervasive tone of solemn reverence for Scripture and an abiding and deep spirituality. Their thoroughgoing scholarship and devotional spirit is a worthy model of imitation for Baptists in the twenty-first century. John A. Broadus and A. T. Robertson practiced what they taught their students, for indeed they were men "mighty in the Scriptures."[50]

Bibliography

Major Works by Broadus

On the Preparation and Delivery of Sermons. 1870; San Francisco: Harper Row, 1979.

Three Questions as to the Bible. Philadelphia: American Baptist Publication Society, 1883.

Commentary on the Gospel of Matthew. Philadelphia: American Baptist Publication Society, 1886.

The Paramount and Permanent Authority of the Bible. Philadelphia: American
   Baptist Publication Society, 1887.
Memoir of James P. Boyce. Philadelphia: American Baptist Publication Society,
   1893.
A Harmony of the Gospels. New York: Doran, 1893.
Commentary on the Gospel of Mark. Philadelphia: American Baptist Publication
   Society, 1905.

Selected Works about Broadus

Cox, James W. "*On the Preparation and Delivery of Sermons*: A Book Review."
   Review and Expositor 81 (1984), 464–66.
———. "The Pulpit and Southern." *Review and Expositor* 82 (1985), 77–78.
DeRemer, Bernard R. "The Life of John Albert Broadus." *Christianity Today,* 13
   April 1962, 22–23.
Dockery, David. S. "John A. Broadus" in *Bible Interpreters of the Twentieth
   Century: A Selection of Evangelical Voices,* ed. Walter A. Elwell. Grand Rapids:
   Baker, 1999.
Jones, J. Estill. "The New Testament and Southern." *Review and Expositor* 82
   (1985), 21–22.
McGlothlin, W. J. "John Albert Broadus." *Review and Expositor* 27 (1930),
   141–68.
Mohler, R. Albert. "Classic Texts Deserve Valued Spot in the Preacher's Bookshelf."
   Preaching, March-April, 1989, 33–34.
Mueller, William. *A History of The Southern Baptist Theological Seminary.*
   Nashville: Broadman, 1959.
Reagles, Steve. "The Century after the 1889 Yale Lectures: A Reflection on
   Broadus's Homiletical Thought." *Preaching,* November-December 1989, 32–36.
Robertson, A. T. "Broadus as Scholar and Preacher." *The Minister and His Greek
   New Testament.* 1923; Nashville: Broadman, 1977.
———. *Life and Letters of John A. Broadus.* Philadelphia: American Baptist
   Publication Society, 1901.
Whitsett, W. H. "John Albert Broadus." *Review and Expositor* 4 (1907), 339–51.

Selected Works about Robertson

Dockery, David S., compiler. *The Best of A. T. Robertson.* Nashville: Broadman &
   Holman, 1996.
Gill, Everett. *A. T. Robertson: A Biography.* New York: Macmillan, 1943.
Leavell, Frank H. "Archibald Thomas Robertson: An Interview for Students." *The
   Baptist Student.* X (May, 1932), 3–4.
McKnight, Edgar. "A Baptist Scholar." Founder's Day Address. The Southern
   Baptist Theological Seminary. 4 February 1986.

Selected Works by Robertson

A Grammar of the Greek New Testament in the Light of Historical Research. New
York and London: Hodder & Stoughton, 1914. Pages xl–1360. Second edition
in 1915 (New York: George H. Doran Co.). Third edition thoroughly revised
and much enlarged in 1919. Pages lxxxvi–1454. Fourth edition in 1923.

A Harmony of the Gospels for Students of the Life of Christ. New York and
London. 1922. Pages xl–305. Second edition in 1923 (San Francisco: Harper).

A Short Grammar of the Greek New Testament. New York and London: A. C.
Armstrong and Sons, 1908. Pages xxx–240. Sixth edition in 1923. Four transla-
tions have appeared:

> *Beknopte Grammatica op Het Grieksche Nieuwe Testament.* By
> Prof. F. W. Grosheide. Kampen, 1912.
> *Breve Grammatica del Nuovo Testamento Greco.* By Prof. G.
> Bonaccorst. Florence, 1910.
> *Grammaire du Grec du Nouveau Testament.* Traduite sur la seconde
> edition par Prof. E. Montet. Paris, 1911.
> *Kurzgefasste Grammatik des Neutestamentlichen Griechisch.*
> Deutsche Ausgabe von Hermann Stocks. Leipzig, 1911.

"Critical Notes" for Broadus's *Harmony of the Gospels for Students of the Life of
Christ.* Pages 232–64. New York, 1892 (reprinted by George H. Doran Co.,
1922). A dozen editions. This collaboration with John A. Broadus was the first
piece of scholarly literary work undertaken.

Epochs in the Life of Jesus. New York and London: C. Scribner's Sons, 1907.

Epochs in the Life of Paul. New York and London: C. Scribner's Sons, 1909.

Epochs in the Life of Simon Peter. Nashville: Broadman Press, 1974.

Introduction to the Textual Criticism of the New Testament. New York: Doran,
1925.

Keywords in the Teaching of Jesus. Philadelphia: American Baptist Publication
Society, 1906.

Life and Letters of John A. Broadus. Philadelphia: American Baptist Publication
Society, 1901.

Luke the Historian in the Light of Research. New York and Edinburgh: C. Scribner's
Sons, 1920.

New Testament and Greek Syllabus. Louisville, 1900.

Paul and the Intellectuals: The Epistle to the Colossians. Revised and edited by N. C.
Strickland. Nashville: Broadman Press, 1959.

Practical and Social Aspects of Christianity: The Wisdom of James. New York and
London, 1915. Third edition in 1923: *Studies in the Epistle of James.* Edited by
H. F. Peacock. Nashville: Broadman Press, 1959.

Some Minor Characters in the New Testament. Nashville: Sunday School Board of
the Southern Baptist Convention, 1928.

Studies in Mark's Gospel. New York and London: Macmillan, 1919.

Studies in the New Testament. Nashville and New York: Revell, 1915.

Syllabus for New Testament Study. A guide for lessons in the classroom. Louisville,
1901.

The Christ of the Logia. Nashville: Sunday School Board of the Southern Baptist
Convention, 1924.

The Glory of the Ministry: Paul's Exultation in Preaching (2 Corinthians 2:12 to 6:10). New York and Chicago: Fleming H. Revell Co., 1911.

The Minister and His Greek New Testament. New York and London: George H. Doran Co., 1923.

The Pharisees and Jesus. The Stone (Princeton) Lectures for 1915–16. New York and London: Duckworth, 1920.

The Teaching of Jesus Concerning God the Father. The Teaching of Jesus Series. New York: American Tract Society, 1904.

Types of Preachers in the New Testament. New York and London: George H. Doran, 1922.

Word Pictures in the New Testament. Nashville: Broadman, 1930.

Professor Robertson was also a frequent contributor to many of the leading theological journals, American and foreign, among which may be noted:

The Expositor (London)
The Contemporary Review
The Expository Times
The Homiletic Review
The Biblical Review
The Expositor (Cleveland)
The Review and Expositor
The Methodist Review

He also contributed articles to:

Hastings' Dictionary of Christ and the Gospels
Hastings' Dictionary of the Apostolic Age
Orr's International Standard Bible Encyclopaedia
The Cross Reference Bible
The System Bible Study

7
Charles Haddon Spurgeon

By Lewis A. Drummond

DURING CHARLES HADDON SPURGEON'S THIRTY-SEVEN-YEAR MINISTRY AT THE
New Park Street Baptist Church in London, fourteen thousand members
joined the congregation, making this the largest Protestant church in the
world. Over three hundred million copies of his sermons and books have
been sold. He is probably the most-read minister of all time. At any rate,
there are still today more of Spurgeon's books in print than of any other
English author. He is even being reprinted in an updated English style.

He was not only a great preacher and pastor; he was a remarkable thinker and writer.

Why this unusual popularity? Many ministers have been prolific. Why did people around the world seem to hang on his ministry—verbal and written—during his lifetime and even today?

Answers to these questions are varied and complex. Yet certainly the theological and spiritual matrix of Spurgeon's life constitutes a major factor in the tremendous impact of his life. And what was the matrix of his work? The answer is plain: Puritanism. The London pulpiteer was an avowed and proud nineteenth-century Puritan of the Reformed tradition. William Gladstone, the "Grand Old Man" of British politics, called Spurgeon, "The Last of the Puritans." Whether the prime minister was correct in the chronology of this statement or not, the moniker stuck, and it provides insight into Spurgeon's approach as a theologian and preacher. This chapter argues that the Puritan legacy is evident throughout his entire ministry. Further, and not incidentally, it may provide something of an insight to the development of an effective ministry in any age.

Biography

Spurgeon testifies to the Puritan legacy and its influence in his entire service to Christ. On June 19, 1834, when the cries of Thomas and Eliza Spurgeon's firstborn were heard, little did the young couple realize what destiny had in store for their newborn son. That he should be a pastor perhaps would have been expected; Thomas served as a Congregational pastor, as did the baby's paternal grandfather, James.

Due to rather stringent economic conditions, at eighteen months of age Charles was sent to live with his grandparents in Stanbourne, Essex. There his "Aunt Anne," the spinster daughter of the grandparents, doted on him, perhaps spoiling him a bit. At the age of six, little Charles happened one day into an old musty room in the manse at Stanbourne. The single window had been sealed off many years earlier because of the illogical window tax. Properties were taxed by the number of windows in the home. The room exuded the odor of old leather-bound volumes. Most six-year-olds would have made a hasty exit, but Charles thought he had discovered a gold mine! There were old, well-worn Puritan theological folios. He could already read well and loved books. Delving into his newfound treasure, he picked up a copy of Bunyan's *The Pilgrim's Progress*. It fascinated him, and he read it more than one hundred times in his lifetime. It became something of the pattern of his own pilgrimage.

A few years later Charles returned to his parents' home in Colchester. His education was somewhat above average for a boy of his time, and he became what we would call a "bookish" boy. Young Charles always seemed rather awkward physically, sports hardly being his forte; but he became an avid reader and student. A fair portion of his reading centered in Puritan theological works even at that early age. Further, his father and grandfather, being evangelical Congregationalists, were Reformed in their understanding and approach to Christian doctrine. They fulfilled to the letter the model set up by Richard Baxter in *The Reformed Pastor.* Such was the atmosphere in which Charles's early spiritual experiences took place.

In this setting, it becomes understandable why by the age of fifteen, Charles sank deeply under conviction of sin and desperately sought salvation. His conversion story, which he loved to tell, is typical of the Puritan approach. It culminated one Sunday morning in January 1850.

The snow was pelting down as the swordlike wind howling off the frigid North Sea cut him to the bone. Trudging with head down into the gale, young Charles tried vainly to ignore the miserable weather. He stopped, shivered, and looked down the swirling white street. At that moment he remembered his mother had told him about a Primitive Methodist chapel on old Artillery Street. "I'll go there," he reasoned, "it's right near, and the church where I intended to go is still a long way off."

Charles had determined he would attend every church in his hometown of Colchester, a small community some fifty miles northwest of London. He had to find *the answer.* Of course, it was not unusual for a young man to go to church in 1850; the Victorians were notoriously religious. As one historian put it, "No one will ever understand Victorian England who does not appreciate that among the highly civilized . . . it was one of the most religious that the world has ever known." *The answer* Charles sought centered in Christ. But seek as he would, salvation's peace eluded him. He had struggled long, just like Bunyan's Pilgrim, but he kept seeking forgiveness and relief. His Puritan upbringing had given birth to guilt, remorse, and misery in his very soul.

So to church after church in Colchester Charles went, hoping the burden on his back would fall away "at yonder wicket gate," as did Pilgrim's. Down Artillery Street he trudged, thinking he might find his *answer* there.

When Charles timidly entered the little church building, not more than fifteen people had assembled. He quietly slipped in and sat down about five or six pews from the rear, on the preacher's right, somewhat hidden under the small gallery. With head bowed—not because of the miserable weather now, but because of the miserable storm in his soul—he hardly looked up as the service progressed.

Charles previously nursed a few misgivings about worshiping in a Primitive Methodist church. That group had a reputation for splitting one's eardrums with their vociferous singing. Most people called them the "Ranters." But Charles was hardly aware, he felt so terrible. He did notice, nonetheless, that the pastor had not arrived when the service began. So a simple man, as Charles viewed him, took charge of the worship. It all proved quite different for the young seeker with his Puritan-Congregational background; he felt very much alone. The sermon began as the Primitive preacher took his text: "Look unto me, and be ye saved, all the ends of the earth." He appeared to Charles more primitive than just in name; the preacher did not even pronounce the words correctly. Charles remembered the old preacher's actual words:

> My dear friends this is a simple text indeed. It says, Look. Now lookin' don't take a deal of pains. It ain't lifting your foot or your finger. It is just "look." Well, a man needn't get to college to learn to look. You may be the biggest fool and yet you can look. A man needn't be worth a thousand pounds a year to be able to look. Anyone can look: even a child can look. But then the text says, "Look unto me" . . . many of ye are lookin' to yourselves, but it's no use lookin' there. You'll never find any comfort in yourselves. Some look to God the Father. No, look to him by and by. Jesus Christ says, "Look unto me." Some of ye say, "We must wait for the Spirit's workin'." You have no business with that just now. Look unto *Christ*. The text says, "Look unto me."

Charles went on in his description of the dramatic moment:

> Whether he, the old Essex preacher, had reached the end of his tether having spun out about ten minutes or whether he was lifted out of himself and spoke words given to him at that moment, he fixed his eyes on the "stranger," [young Charles], easily distinguished amidst the company, and said, "Young man, you look very miserable." I was miserable. It was a blow struck right home, and although the young man had never had such a personal word from the pulpit before, he was too much in earnest to resent it. He continued, "You always will be miserable—miserable in life and miserable in death if you don't obey my text; but if you obey now, this moment you will be saved." Then lifting up his hands he shouted, as only a Primitive Methodist of Essex could, "Young man, look to Jesus Christ! Look! Look! Look! You have nothing to do but to look and live." I had been waiting to do fifty things, but when I heard the word Look, I could have almost looked my eyes away . . . I could have risen that instant and sung with the most enthusiastic of them of the precious blood of Christ, and the simple faith that looks alone to him. I thought I could dance all the way home. I could understand what John Bunyan meant when he declared he wanted to tell the cows on the plowed land all about his conversion. He was too full to hold. He must tell somebody. At such a time, clang went every

harp in heaven. . . . Between half past ten, when I entered the
chapel, and half past twelve, when I returned home, what a
change had taken place in me.[1]

The answer came. Charles Haddon Spurgeon had been graciously
saved. In that little Primitive Methodist chapel, under the preaching of an
unlettered man, a pilgrimage of ministry began, the universality of which no
one there on that miserable Sunday could have imagined.

Spurgeon soon became convinced he should be baptized by immersion,
leaving his Congregational background, at least on that point. When he announced this decision to his mother, she said, "Charles, I have often prayed
for your conversion, but *not* that you would become a Baptist." Charles
replied, "That shows, dear mother, that God has done exceeding abundantly above all you asked or thought." After baptism in the River Lark, he
joined the St. Andrews Baptist Church in Cambridge, where he was attending school. He remained a Baptist throughout his days.

Four years later at age nineteen, Charles Spurgeon received a call to become pastor of the historic and prestigious New Park Street Baptist Church
in Southwark, South London. John Rippon, Benjamin Keach, and theologian John Gill had been illustrious predecessors at the church. When Charles
was only five years old, Richard Knill prophesied that he would become a
preacher. The well-known prophecy had come to pass. Yet nineteen seemed
a very young age to begin a ministry in great London. But he had already
served for two years as pastor of the Waterbeach Baptist Church in
Cambridgeshire—and that with unusual success. Moreover, his theology
had become quite well fixed. He said he learned all this theology from an
old maidservant in Cambridge. That was probably an exaggeration. Still, he
felt himself rooted in the doctrine of Puritan Calvinism, even though he was
saved in an Arminian Methodist setting. From that Reformed theological
stance Spurgeon never departed in any measurable degree, as his preaching
demonstrates. Some have argued he would have been a broader man theologically had he been formally educated in the theological disciplines. (All
know he never attended a theological school.) Yet that is doubtful.
Spurgeon, strong willed and strong minded, had Puritan Calvinism deeply
ingrained in the very fabric of his personhood. As Kruppa put it,
"Intellectually, he remained captive to the evangelical Calvinism of his
youth."[2] The Downgrade Controversy, the theological battle of his last years
that caused him to leave the Baptist Union, supports such a contention.

So the "boy preacher of the Fens" (the "Fens" being Essex and parts of
Cambridgeshire) began his London ministry of nearly four decades. His
first sermon at the New Park Street Baptist Church was heard by a mere
eighty people. In six months, two thousand were being crammed into the
old church building while one thousand a Sunday were turned away, unable
to get in. Soon the Metropolitan Tabernacle was constructed, and he

preached to six thousand every Lord's Day. And although Spurgeon died at the relatively young age of fifty-seven, the world has rarely seen a more productive ministry. Along with thousands of common folks, notables came to hear his magnificent oratory—Prime Minister Gladstone, missionary David Livingstone, philanthropist Lord Shaftesbury, and even Queen Victoria in disguise. He started over twenty different social and evangelistic ministries through the Tabernacle. Two hundred new churches emerged from the ministry. To this day, the Pastor's College trains men and women for service. The Stockwell Orphanage also continues. Above all, the personal appeal of Spurgeon's writing converts and blesses many to the present hour. And permeating it all: the Puritan legacy. If Spurgeon were not "the Last of the Puritans," he certainly was one of the best.

Exposition

Puritan Theology

Charles Haddon Spurgeon exercised a tremendously effective, widespread pastoral and evangelistic ministry because he saw himself as just that: a pastor-evangelist. Moreover, Spurgeon obviously held strong theological convictions. This is clear to everyone who knows his writings. Understanding that doctrinal base becomes essential in the attempt to grasp the insight that explains Spurgeon's powerful ministry.

Spurgeon, as seen, stood as an avowed Calvinist, not a "high Calvinist," but he certainly held tenaciously to the basic position of the Geneva Reformer. Spurgeon said concerning the influence of his Puritan Calvinistic grandfather: "I sometimes feel the shadow of his broad brim (Puritan hat) come over my spirit." He confessed, "I have been charged with being a mere echo of the Puritans, but I had rather be the echo of truth than the voice of falsehood." What did all that mean for Spurgeon?

If any theme of traditional Calvinism emerged as central in Spurgeon's Puritan theology, it would be contained in the Calvinistic phrase "free grace." Spurgeon said concerning free grace, "What an abyss is the grace of God! Who can measure its breadth? Who can fathom its depth? Like all the rest of the divine attributes, it is infinite."[3] Spurgeon saw grace as ingredient to the very nature of God. The bestowal of grace was purposed in the heart and mind of God long before our Lord ever freely poured it out on the sinner.

Moreover, Spurgeon stressed that this grace of God is *free*. It cannot be purchased, earned, or acquired by any human effort. He believed people are dead in trespasses and sin and therefore totally incapable of doing anything to please God or ever being worthy of grace. In other words, grace is bestowed by the *sovereignty of God*. That is to say, God freely grants his grace upon whom he pleases when and how he alone pleases. And on whom is that grace bestowed? Spurgeon made it very clear: the *elect* become the ones who receive free grace. He gave no room for any Pelagianism.

The doctrine of election in Spurgeon's theology, as implied, revolves around the concept that God in his sovereignty, according to his own purpose of total grace, has foreknown and elected to salvation a certain number of individuals. This election took place before the foundation of the world. God calls those elected through the Holy Spirit and brings them to Christ for salvation. This number was given to Christ, who stood for them and died and paid their sin debt. They are the predestined ones.

For Spurgeon election and predestination meant virtually the same thing. Still, he did make a subtle distinction. He said:

> In one sense election is the result of a previous predestination,
> that is, during the past ages of eternity, before the creation of the
> world, and prior to human history the triune Godhead deter-
> mined and designed a plan of redemption in which fallen
> mankind would be raised to a higher position than that which
> Adam had attained before he fell into sin.[4]

Furthermore, God calls the elect with an effectual call; those whom God calls to Christ always respond. Moreover, Spurgeon forthrightly preached this doctrine. He did not downplay the idea, thinking it would offend people. Taking 2 Thessalonians 2:13 as his text, he said:

> By the word "calling" in Scripture, we understand two things—
> one, the "general call," which in the preaching of the gospel is
> given to every creature under heaven; the second call is the special
> call—which we call the effectual call, whereby God secretly, in the
> use of means, by the irresistible power of his Holy Spirit, calls out
> of mankind a certain number whom he himself hath before
> elected, calling them from their sins to become righteous, from
> their death in trespass and sins to become living spiritual men, and
> from their worldly pursuits to become the lovers of Jesus Christ.

Although Spurgeon felt that these concepts should be clearly preached, he did warn preachers to handle them with prudence and care. The preaching of these ideas was to bring praise, reverence, adoration, and glory to the sovereign God. And when one receives the call and is saved, that is exactly what happens: God is magnified. After all, Spurgeon would argue, the angels rejoice over just one sinner who repents.

Despite his consistent Calvinism, however, Spurgeon never slipped into a "hyper" supralapsarian stance in his Reformed Puritan views. Most of Spurgeon's contemporaries realized this. For example, *The World Newspaper* on September 18, 1818, reported: "Mr. Spurgeon is *nominally* a Calvinist." Actually, some churches would not have him in their pulpit because his Calvinism was not "high" enough. Others, of course, rejected him because he stood a far distance from Arminianism. Probably, Spurgeon saw himself in the tradition of John Calvin himself, primarily a biblical exegete. He was not a systematic theologian of the later Reformed school as were Theodore Beza, William Perkins, and John Gill, his predecessor in London. It was their systematizing of Calvin that precipitated what came to be called *high* Calvinism. But Spurgeon walked the razor's edge. He firmly believed in divine election and predestination. He was convinced the Bible taught it, so he preached it. At the same time he tenaciously held to the necessity of human response—and human responsibility to respond. He firmly believed that people must repent and believe. The Bible teaches that too, he argued. He said:

> Saving repentance is an evangelical grace, whereby a person, being led by the Holy Spirit made sensible of the manifold evils of his sin, doth, by faith in Christ, humble himself for it with godly sorrow, detestation of it, and self-abhorrency, praying for pardon and strength of grace, with a purpose and endeavor, by supplies of the Spirit, to walk before God unto all well-pleasing in all things.

Further, Spurgeon believed faith was the other necessary side of repentance. He stated: "True faith is reliance. It does not merely mean to believe, but to trust, to confide in, to commit to, entrust with, and so forth; and the marrow of the meaning of faith is confidence in, reliance upon."

Saving faith thus brings one, in Spurgeon's words, into an "immediate relation to Christ, accepting, receiving, and resting upon him alone for justification, sanctification, and eternal life, by virtue of the covenant of grace." This act of faith humans are *required* to do. Perhaps Spurgeon's own dramatic, "Arminian-style" conversion contributed to that insistence, as well as his commitment to the biblical call to repentance and faith.

Yet it is only correct to say Spurgeon believed that no person could exercise repentance and faith apart from the inner work of the Holy Spirit. Those graces cannot be worked up by mere human generation. Faith must always be seen as a gift of God. But he constantly called people to repentance and faith. Thus, he kept the tension between the two concepts of predestination and human responsibility and walked the paradoxical razor's edge in his preaching. Perhaps that is why he prayed in the Metropolitan Tabernacle, "Lord, call out your elect, and then elect some more." Well known is his pungent retort to a person who asked him how he reconciled the ideas: "I do not try to reconcile friends."

Christology

Spurgeon saw the reception of God's marvelous free grace as possible because of the all-sufficiency of Jesus Christ and his work on the cross. Concerning Christ's person, Spurgeon said:

> Oh marvelous sight! . . . a Child of a virgin, what a mixture!
> There is the finite and the infinite, there is the mortal and the im-
> mortal, corruption and incorruption, the manhood and the
> Godhead, time married to eternity, God linked with a creature . . .
> He who fastened the pillars of the universe, and riveted the nails
> of creation, hanging on a mortal breast, depending on a creature
> for nourishment.

Spurgeon was happy with the Chalcedonian formulation of Christology.

Further, the purpose of the good news of Christ's coming centered in his substitutionary atoning passion. He said in a sermon: "There is no preaching the gospel if the atonement is left out. No matter how well we speak of Jesus as a pattern, we have done nothing unless we point him out as the substitute and sin-bearer." The passion of Christ *always* took center stage in the preaching of Spurgeon. He said, "I take my text and make a bee-line to the cross." Because Christ suffered *vicariously,* he saw in that act the penalty of sin paid. Spurgeon found himself absolutely committed to the substitutionary view of the atonement. Actually, this became one of the prime issues in the Downgrade Controversy for which Spurgeon put his entire ministry on the line. *Substitution* and *satisfaction* became key words for the preacher.

Human Depravity

This emphasis in Spurgeon's theology grew out of his deep conviction concerning human need. He saw the human race as ruined and totally depraved because of sin (that is, human rebellion to God's control of life). He took the Fall very seriously indeed. In Spurgeon's view, in the original act of rebellion against God, Adam as humanity's federal representative brought the judgment of God upon the whole human race and upon the entire earth. That opened the race to sin. He said:

> There is much to sadden us in a view of the ruins of our
> race. . . . When we behold the ruins of that godly structure which
> God has piled, that creature, matchless in symmetry, second only
> to angelic intellect, that mighty being, man, when we behold how
> he is "fallen, fallen, fallen, from his high estate," (he) lies in a
> mass of destruction. . . . The fall of Adam was our fall; we fell in
> and with him; we were equal sufferers. It is the ruin of our own
> house that we lament.[5]

Spurgeon believed firmly that the Fall precipitated the "total depravity" of all. As a result of Adam's sin, all are born with an innate tendency to sin. This does not mean that men and women are mere depraved beasts or utterly corrupt in all their ways. It means that the original sin of Adam is imputed to all his descendants, affecting them with rebellion in every part of their mind, soul, and body. The Anglican Shorter Catechism, which Spurgeon accepted, states:

> The sinfulness of that estate whereinto man fell, consists in, the guilt of Adam's first sin, the want of original righteousness, and the corruption of his whole nature, which is commonly called original sin; together with all actual transgressions which proceed from it.

Salvation

At the point of sin, the power of salvation precipitates a radical transformation. Spurgeon viewed salvation in a very broad sense. Salvation gives more to the believer than mere deliverance from the guilt and condemnation of sin. It encompasses sanctification, preservation, and glorification—the kingdom of God no less. These blessings take place through the power of the Triune God: Father, Son, and Holy Spirit. Thus there comes about a total transformation of the Christian into a holy being and a partaker with Christ of the heavenly glory. And in that transformation, one rests secure.

It must be granted nothing "new" can be found in Spurgeon's theology; it stands as an echo of mainline Puritanism. But it served him well, and when it all came together in his preaching, one can understand why he was utterly committed to evangelism and urgent in presenting the gospel of free grace to all. Although it had been said of some, "They lost their evangelism, because they failed to prevent their theology from slipping away," Spurgeon could never be accused of failure on that score. He really believed, as all the Calvinistic Puritans before him, that everyone needed Christ and he was absolutely convinced the Lord Jesus Christ stood as sufficient for all the elect. That constitutes the core of his theology.

Puritan Evangelism

Spurgeon's ministry grew out of his basic theology. For Spurgeon, theology was a "theology of the road" (that is, it must "work" in practical ministry), and that related dramatically to his evangelism. As a result, Spurgeon will always stand as the "Prince of Preachers." The fact is, he not only served as a great pastoral preacher; he was an extremely effective evangelist as well. That is true not only as a pastor-evangelist but, as an itinerant proclaimer of the gospel. Every week, as schedule and health permitted, he traveled about, preaching what we today would probably call evangelistic rallies. The impact he made in that arena stands as a story in itself. Untold numbers were converted in that setting. His approach can be exemplified in his warm relationship to D. L. Moody and the British crusades. He would often invite such evangelists to his own pulpit. Ira D. Sankey actually sang at Spurgeon's funeral in 1892.

Spurgeon said about evangelistic preaching and its impact, "The revealed Word awakened me; but it was the preached Word that saved me; and I must ever attach peculiar value to the hearing of the truth." With this conviction it becomes understandable why he would then state, "I now think I am bound never to preach a sermon without preaching to sinners. I do think that a minister who can preach a sermon without addressing sinners does not know how to preach." He always saw the pulpit as his primary evangelistic tool. He went so far as to say in *The Sportman* in September 1890, "The ordinary sermon should *always* be evangelistic." And that evangelistic ministry emerged from his strong theological understanding.

Strange perhaps is the fact that Spurgeon was not particularly warm to planned, protracted series of evangelistic services in his own church, though he did affirm Moody and others and did use some such methods at times on a limited scale. He feared the "low" after the "high" of a crusade in his church. Yet he could say, "I am not very scrupulous about the means I use for doing good. I would preach standing on my head, if I thought I could convert your souls." The romance of his effective preaching at the Metropolitan Tabernacle and his itinerant ministry serves as ample evidence of his effectiveness in pulpit evangelism. His pungent evangelistic preaching to the common people possessed a power seldom seen in London. He baptized over ten thousand new converts in the Tabernacle.

As pointed out, Spurgeon's theological understanding and faithful preaching of the gospel undergirded his evangelism. But there were two other vital factors at work—one obvious, the other not quite so well known.

The obvious element, together with his preaching of Christ, centered in his fervent heart and burden for people. No one is useful in ministry until there is a burning compassion to reach people for Christ. Spurgeon had that spirit; hear him in *The Word and Work,* February 1891: "When a dog is not noticed, he doesn't like it. But when a dog is after a fox, he does not care whether he is noticed or not. If a minister is *seeking for souls,* he will not think of himself." Perhaps that accounts for a significant measure of Spurgeon's success.

Spurgeon's Puritan legacy is also important in explaining his contagious influence. Puritanism, because of its Calvinistic theology, constantly affirmed the absolute necessity of God's sovereign act in effecting personal redemption. Therefore, Spurgeon exemplified a constant seeking for the moving of the Holy Spirit to come upon the preaching of the Word to bring people to Christ. He constantly sought a reviving, an awakening, an out-pouring of power. Simply put, he fervently prayed for revival. Spurgeon's pneumatology moved him in that basic direction.

In seeking the "outpouring" of power, he was not disappointed. Revival came to the New Park Street Baptist Church almost simultaneously with his arrival in London. Actually, Spurgeon became something of a har-binger of the so-called Prayer Revival of 1858 that finally reached Britain by 1860 after its inception in America.

Few biographers, it seems, have realized this Puritan revival principle in the early ministry of Charles Haddon Spurgeon. So often his success is ex-plained merely on the grounds that he was a great preacher and social worker. Great preaching and service alone cannot explain such a phenom-enal ministry. Recognizing this, Spurgeon said, "The times of refreshing from the presence of the Lord have at last dawned upon our land. Everywhere there are signs of aroused activity and increased earnestness. A spirit of prayer is visiting our churches, and its path are dropping fatness. The first breath of the rushing mighty wind is already discerned, while on rising evangelists the tongues of fire have evidently descended."

An awakening of such magnitude as the 1858 Prayer Revival always encompasses vast areas. The spirit of prayer had moved across the Atlantic from America and initially touched Ireland. In 1858 the Presbyterian Church of Ireland dispatched observers to the United States to investigate the prayer revival that had now engulfed the entire nation. They returned home thrilled. Soon Belfast, Dublin, Cork, and all the countryside fell under the impact of the prayer revival. The nation was on its knees.

As the continuing news and thrilling stories of the American awaken-ing spread through the British Isles, Scotland soon became aroused. Prayer meetings sprang up in Glasgow, Edinburgh, and in many of the cities and towns of the country. By 1859 the United Presbyterian Church reported that one-fourth of its members regularly attended a prayer meeting for spir-itual awakening.

Wales also came under the power of God—almost simultaneously with Ireland. Before long Wales caught on fire with awakening power.

Finally, England began to be warmed by the conflagration. A united prayer meeting was held in the Throne Room of the Cosby Hall, London, in 1859. Soon attendance reached one hundred at the noon hour service. By the end of the year, twenty-four daily and sixty weekly prayer meetings were being held in the London area. In a matter of days, the number grew to 120; then it exploded all over the land.

In 1860 the Fortune, the Garrick, and Sadler Wells theaters opened their doors for Sunday evangelistic services. Even Saint Paul's and Westminster Cathedrals conducted special revival services. In Dorset, people were flocking to hear Evan Hopkins of later Keswick Convention notoriety. Charles Finney, the great American revivalist, was preaching with great effect in Bolton. William and Catherine Booth of Salvation Army fame ministered with fresh power. Oxford and Cambridge Universities commenced special prayer meetings. All England, it seemed, was looking up in prayer. As can be imagined, the awakening had its critics. Members of the secular press raised their voices in chorus to negate the positive impact of the movement. But historians now realize the awakening left a legacy of blessing extending even to this day. During the revival one million new members entered the churches of Britain. The Salvation Army, the Children's Special Service Mission, the China Inland Mission, and a host of new institutions were founded. As Spurgeon put it:

> It were well . . . that the Divine life would break forth everywhere—in the parlor, the workshop, counting house, the market and streets. We are far too ready to confine it to the channel of Sunday services and religious meetings; it deserves a broader floodway and must have it if we are to see gladder times. It must burst out upon men who do not care for it, and invade chambers where it will be regarded as an intrusion; it must be seen by wayfaring men streaming down the places of traffic and concourse, *hindering the progress of sinful trades,* and surrounding all, whether they will or no. Would to God that religion were more vital and forceful among us, so as to create *a powerful public opinion on behalf of truth, justice and holiness.* . . . A life which would *purify the age.* It is much to be desired that the Christian church may yet have *more power and influence* all over the world for *righteousness . . . social reform and moral progress.*

That is how Spurgeon understood revival, and that is what Britain was experiencing by 1860. Actually, the Prayer Revival became one of the last great spiritual awakenings to sweep all of Great Britain.

But notice, Spurgeon had been in the grip of real revival at the New Park Street Baptist Church for several years before the British Prayer Revival of 1860. That is vital to an understanding of the Spurgeon phenomenon. In 1860 Spurgeon said, "For six years the dew has never ceased to fall, and the rain has never been held. At this time the converts are more numerous than hither-to-fore, and the zeal of the church groweth exceedingly."

The foundation for the fresh move of the Holy Spirit in revival at New Park Street had been laid by the faithful praying members of the church. Spurgeon described those early days:

> When I came to New Park Street Church, it was but a mere handful of people to whom I first preached, yet I could never forget how earnestly they prayed. Sometimes they seemed to plead as though they could really see the Angel of the Covenant present

with them, and as if they must have a blessing from him. More than once we were all so awe-struck with the solemnity of the meeting that we sat silent for some moments while the Lord's Power appeared to overshadow us; and all I could do on such occasions was to pronounce the benediction, and say "Dear friends, we have had the Spirit of God here very manifestly tonight; let us go home and take care not to lose his gracious influence." Then down came the blessings; the house was filled with hearers, and many souls were saved.

Spurgeon knew that revival explained his outstanding ministry, and he deeply desired it for all of England. The awakening deepened, and for three years one thousand people were turned away every Sunday from the ten-thousand-seat capacity Surrey Gardens Music Hall, where Spurgeon preached before the construction of the Tabernacle.

Some quite amazing occurrences took place in those revival days. For example, one Sunday in the Music Hall a man sat listening intently to Spurgeon preach. In his sermon Spurgeon said, "There is a man sitting here, who is a shoemaker; he keeps his shop open on Sundays, and it was open last Sunday morning; he took in nine pence and there was a four pence profit; he sold his soul to Satan for four pence." The man listening so intently felt cut to the heart. He actually was a shoemaker, and he had kept his shop open the previous Sunday and had taken in nine pence, and he did make a profit of four pence. He trusted Christ immediately. Dozens were saved in similar dramatic circumstances and joined the great Baptist church. The simple statistics of conversions during those years were phenomenal.

What rested back of this profound spiritual awakening? What did Spurgeon get hold of that precipitated revival even before the emergence of the general awakening of 1860? If revival stands as one of the key answers to Spurgeon's staggering evangelistic success, why did it happen to him at that time? Three factors seem dominant. The primary foundation stone, as already implied, rested on the sacrificial, fervent prayers of the New Park Street people. Young Spurgeon inherited that blessed gift. Moreover, that spirit of prayer continued through the years into the decades of the great Metropolitan Tabernacle ministry. Often repeated is the well-known anecdote of Charles Haddon Spurgeon taking visitors through the Metropolitan Tabernacle and showing them the prayer room in the basement and remarking, "Here is our power house." Genuine spiritual awakening is always spawned in prayer.

Spurgeon expressed another central feature in the revival:

> Sound doctrine and loving invitation make a good basis of material, which, when modeled by the hand of prayer and faith, will form sermons of far more value in the saving of souls than

the most philosophic essays prepared elaborately, and delivered with eloquence and propriety.

The revival had its birth and was carried on in the context of "sound doctrine" (that is, good theology, presented with "loving invitation"). Biblical theology presented in love cannot be divorced from revival. The great Puritan-pietistic movement that engulfed Britain and the continent beginning in the last decades of the sixteenth century has spawned many awakenings. No doubt one of the prime reasons for the spiritual impact of that powerful thrust centered in its insistence that orthodox, biblical theology and preaching must be at the core of one's ministry.

That theological approach made "the Last of the Puritans" critical of any sort of humanism that downplayed the sovereignty of God. He would have been appalled at what goes under the name of evangelism and ministry in some circles today. There often seems little doctrine and theology in it. Human, psychological persuasion appears to be the central motif. Like his Puritan models, Spurgeon believed a lasting revival is born only through the power and sovereignty of God accompanied by prayer and the plain declaration of the essential truths of orthodox evangelical theology. That meant for Spurgeon a sound Christology, a clear-cut grasp of the *kerygma* (gospel proclamation), a theology that emanates in godliness, all based on the infallible Scriptures. Thus he filled his sermons with rich biblical, theological truths that some modern evangelists consider too "heavy" for the light-hearted crowd in today's world.

So through prayer, sound theology, and the preaching of Christ with loving invitation the revival flamed to life. The spiritual atmosphere of London crackled with excitement as hundreds of thousands thronged to hear the young man of God.

In that general setting, the fires of effective ministry burned in Spurgeon's heart. Moreover, his methods of ministry were used with integrity. For example, there was no superficial taking in of members in the Tabernacle. Every one of the converts was personally counseled by a team of spiritually perceptive laypersons. Their report was given to the church in business session. The candidates for baptism then at times appeared before the congregation to give a personal testimony to demonstrate "the evidence of a work of grace in their lives," as they expressed it. Then they were approved for baptism and church membership. And if they did not persevere, they were excommunicated. The church enforced redemptive discipline.

Much of this effective ministry took place in an urban setting among common working people. The church in Britain has always tended to be a middle-class institution, often leaving the urban masses largely untouched. Spurgeon broke that spiritual syndrome. Even though he possessed a brilliant mind and developed a quite involved Reformed theology, he spoke the language of the working class. He identified with them in their South London crush. His social ministries touched them where they hurt. His unconventionality in the pulpit communicated to them. He broke through their prejudices against the middle-upper-class mentality of the established church. Somehow they knew he loved them, and they responded—a lesson we desperately need to learn today.

What made Spurgeon that sort of a minister? Much of the answer is found in his spirituality and personal devotion to Jesus Christ as well as his theological acumen.

Puritan Spirituality

Once again, Spurgeon's spirituality reflects his Puritan theological orientation. This stands essentially true, in the first place, because of the London preacher's concept of the guide to life in the Spirit that for him was always the Bible, the Holy Scriptures. His spirituality was essentially a biblical spirituality that rested on his Calvinistic theology. Spurgeon could not be numbered among the mystics. But he did not come over as a biblical legalist. It would be best to say that the source of Spurgeon's spirituality rested objectively in the Bible, and experientially in the Christ of the Bible. Thus he combined the objective Scriptures with the existential experience of the living Christ as the sole source of true spirituality. This principle meant several things for Spurgeon.

First of all, spirituality demanded Bible study. In Spurgeon's early days as a new Christian, he developed a keen discernment concerning scriptural exegesis and its relation to spiritual life. He grasped that principle the very next Sunday after his conversion. He tells the story:

> I went to that same chapel, as it was very natural that I
> should, but I never went afterwards, and for this reason, that during my first week as a Christian, the new life that was in me had been compelled to fight for its existence. And the conflict with the old nature had been vigorously carried on. Now, I knew this fight within to be a special token of the indwelling grace within my soul. But in that same chapel, I heard a sermon on the text "Oh wretched man that I am, who shall deliver me from the body of this death?" And the preacher declared that Paul was not a Christian when he had that experience. Babe as I was, I knew better than to believe so absurd a statement. What but divine grace could produce such a sighing and crying after deliverance from indwelling sin? I felt that a person who could talk such nonsense knew little of the life of a true believer. He may be a good exhorter to sinners, but he cannot feed believers.

Spurgeon always rejected the antinomian belief in perfectionism. But the point is this: It is really quite remarkable that a young man of fifteen had grasped those biblical issues, had thought them through, and had arrived at his own understanding and interpretation of who is the "wretched man" of Romans 7. Moreover, he had enough knowledge of the Scriptures to discern what at least he felt fit him best as a young believer. He said, "When I was but a child, I could have discussed many a knotty problem of controversial theology."

For Spurgeon, the Bible imparts life. But the principle goes beyond just knowing the words of the Bible; rather, one must be filled with the message of the Scriptures so that one can say with Jeremiah, "Thy words were found, and I did eat them; and [they became] unto me the joy and rejoicing of [my] heart." Spurgeon said:

> There is a style of majesty about God's Word, and with this majesty a vividness never found elsewhere. No other writing has within it a heavenly life that works miracles and even imparts life to its reader. It's a living and incorruptible seed. It moves, it stirs itself, it lives, it communes with living men as the living Word. Solomon says concerning it, "It shall talk with thee." You need not bring life to Scripture. You should draw life from Scripture.

Typical of his biblical understanding, Spurgeon couched his spirituality in most personal terms. As implied, the principle of personal application of the Scriptures to life was vital to the Puritan Reformed view of spirituality. Spurgeon readily agreed. He recalled a story that illustrates this point.

> I remember once feeling many questions as to whether I was a child of God or not. I went into a little chapel and I heard a good man preach. He was a simple working man and I heard him preach and I made my handkerchief wet with my tears as I heard him talk about Christ. When I was preaching the same things to others, I was wondering whether this truth was mine. But while I was hearing it for myself, I knew it was mine, for my very soul lived upon it. I went to that good man and I thanked him for the sermon. He asked me who I was. When I told him, he turned all manner of colors. "Why," he said, "Sir, that was your own sermon." I said yes, I knew it was. And it was good of the Lord to feed me with the food I had prepared for others.

Spurgeon maintained that if the Bible is to make an effective impact in human life and experience, listening quietly and sensitively and prayerfully to its message becomes a necessary spiritual discipline. As Raymond Brown points out:

In this manner, as in so much else, he was essentially in the tradition of the Reformed as well as Puritan spirituality. The concept of meditation was of immense importance in Luther and in Calvin. Luther used to say that there were three things that make a preacher, meditation, prayer and suffering. John Calvin often spoke of the importance time and again, especially in his commentaries, of meditation, giving yourself quietly to its message. And I would not judge you when I say to my fellow preachers and say it with great love, it's so important for us.

This applies to the preacher, for the danger of becoming too technical in the study of the Bible always lurks about. Having the responsibility of facing the congregation on the next Lord's Day, Spurgeon said:

> The Spirit has taught us in meditation to ponder its message, to put aside, if we will, the responsibility of preparing the message we've got to give. Just trust God for that. But first, meditate on it, quietly ponder it, let it sink deep into our souls. Have you not often been surprised and overcome with delight as Holy Scripture is opened up as if the gates of the Golden City have been set back for you to enter? A few minutes silent openness of soul before the Lord has brought us more treasure of truth than hours of learned research.

But, Spurgeon argued, it must always be kept foremost in mind that the Bible—unique, inspired, and reliable—is always meant to point its readers to Christ. Spurgeon was not guilty of bibliolatry. The ultimate source of all rich spirituality rests in the Living Word to whom the written Word points. And wisely, Spurgeon refused to separate, or confuse, the two. Without the Bible, he argued, Christ might be but the projection of one's own intangible dreams, the product even, of one's imagination. One can build up a portrait of Jesus by taking selected passages of Scripture and proclaim a Christ that suits one's prejudices. A rich Christology must be found in a balanced study of *all* the Scriptures. Spurgeon loved to exalt the biblical Christ, but the Bible is not Jesus. Spurgeon's spirituality was drawn not only from the pages of Scripture, but from the presence of Jesus himself.

Spurgeon obviously took his cue from the Puritans and their theological understandings on these points. In the introduction to his book *The Saint and His Saviour,* which expounds more fully his spirituality than almost any other, he quotes the Puritan Richard Sibbes, who declares that the special work of the preacher is to lay open Christ, to hold up the tapestry and unfold the mysteries of Christ himself.

Thus, the Bible and the living Christ became the source of Spurgeon's spirituality. Yet a catholicity in his approach can be found. Spurgeon contended that many forms emerge in which Christ and his gospel may be conveyed and experienced. In *The Saint and His Saviour,* he said:

> He who dares to prescribe one uniform standard of experience for the children of God, is either grievously ignorant or hopelessly full of self-esteem. Uniformity is not God's rule to spirituality. In grace as well as in providence, He delights to display the most charming variety.

Spurgeon saw a rich variety of experience in spirituality. His preaching clearly demonstrates the principle. In his sermons he quotes from Justin Martyr, Tertullian, Origen, the school of Alexandria, and Gregory of Nazianzus. The great Augustine, Gregory the Great, and Bernard of Clairvaux are cited, along with John Bunyan, George Foxe, the Quakers, Richard Baxter, John Owen, John Howe, Joseph Alleine, and Benjamin Keach. We are not surprised to hear him quote from his favorite preacher, George Whitefield. Those other leaders in the evangelical revival, Roland Hill, Jonathan Edwards, David Brainerd, John Gill, Andrew Fuller, and John Newton, all receive mention in his sermons. He even quotes F. W. Faber, one of the Tractarians in the Anglo-Catholic school. And all of that is just a small sample of the balanced catholicity of Spurgeon's search for spirituality.

At the same time there was nothing unreal or "other worldly" about Spurgeon's spirituality; he did not retreat from life's harsh realities. His spirituality dealt with life's extremities. In his lovely *Pictures from Pilgrim's Progress* he wrote:

> If you will help others out of the slough of despond, you must have a bending back. You cannot draw them out if you stand bold upright. You must go right down to where the poor creatures are sinking in the mire. They're almost gone. The mud and the slime are well nigh over their heads so you must roll up your sleeves and go to work with a will, if you mean to rescue them. Learn to stoop.

A bubbly, effervescent, unreal spirituality did not appeal to the preacher. He preached against any spirituality that insisted on the novel, the dramatic, or spectacular. Spurgeon's realism taught him, "Grace grows best in the winter." In a sermon on Hebrews 12, he stated, "Nobody ever grew holy without consenting, desiring, agonizing to be holy. Sin will grow without sowing, but holiness needs cultivation. Follow it, it will not run after you." In that he reflected his innate Puritanism; spirituality comes about as the result of realistic biblical discipline.

Spurgeon's Confidence in and Use of the Bible

If one seeks a summary of Spurgeon's tremendous power in ministry and the essence of his theology, one must obviously look to his confidence in and use of the Bible. This has been made amply clear: Spurgeon had great gifts. He had a photographic mind, a beautiful voice, a natural eloquence, a dramatic flair, and a great heart. His social sensitivity was outstanding. These factors all made a positive contribution to his effectiveness. But above all, his handling of the Word of God in the power of the Spirit stands as the real source of his effectiveness. And again, the Reformed theological legacy shines forth in unmistakable bold relief.

In *The Greatest Fight in the World*, Spurgeon said:

> After preaching the Gospel for forty years, and after printing the sermons that I have preached for more than six and thirty years reaching now to the number of 2,200 in weekly succession, I think I'm fairly entitled to speak about the fullness and richness of the Bible as a preacher's book. Brethren, it is inexhaustible. No question about its freshness will arise if we keep closely to the text of the Sacred Volume. There can be no difficulties as to finding themes totally distinct from those we've handled before. The variety is as infinite as the fullness. A long life will only suffice us to skirt the shores of this great continent of light. In the forty years of my own ministry, I've only touched the hem of the garment of Divine Truth. But oh, what virtue has flowed out of it. The Word is like its author, infinite, immeasurable, without end. If you were to be ordained to be a preacher throughout eternity, you would have before you a theme equal to everlasting demands. Our Bible will suffice for ages to come for new themes every morning and for fresh songs and discourses, world without end.

Spurgeon admitted his utter reliance on the Scripture for his theology and his sermons. As one put it, "He knew only two subjects really well—the text of the English Bible and the writings of the Puritan divines . . . He measured everything he read against the yardstick of a verbally inspired Bible."

Moreover, Spurgeon was a "defender of the biblical, evangelical faith." He filled the role of "Mr. Valiant for Truth" in Bunyan's *The Pilgrim's Progress*. Unaffected by any pressure from any source, he once said, "I will never modify a doctrine I believe to please any man that walks upon earth." But he rarely launched a frontal assault upon the philosophy of a purely rational, empirical, epistemological hermeneutic, trying to prove, for example, that every jot and tittle of Genesis 1–11 was literally true with no figurative language, or to disprove the Bible on these rational grounds. Moreover, he rejected the challenge of naturalistic science and history to the veracity of Scripture. He would point out that the very nature of the empirical, scientific method is merely a project of a hypothesis. He put all his trust in what he considered the unchanging, immutable truth of the Bible as he grasped it and understood it on good hermeneutical grounds. Thus, he left his critics, at least as he saw it, with the sinking ship of experiment. He stated: "Is the thing called 'science' infallible? The history of ignorance which calls itself 'philosophy' is absolutely identical with the history of fools, except where it diverges into madness." Such a statement seems rather dogmatic today; yet in Spurgeon's time the scientists and naturalistic critics were as dogmatic in their negative assertions about the Bible as he was in his attack on their presupposition.

What then constitutes the one infallible rule of truth? Where can "reality" be found? The answer is obvious—the Holy Scriptures. Spurgeon was unwilling to make the slightest concession on any point which challenged this view of the Bible as the plenary, verbally inspired Word of God. He believed in the all-or-nothing fallacy (that is, either everything was inspired or nothing was). He stated, "If the book of Genesis be an allegory, the Bible is an allegory all through. . . . We will never attempt to save half the truth by casting any part of it away. . . . We will stand by it all or have none of it. We will have a whole Bible or no Bible." He asked, "If this book be not infallible, where shall we find infallibility and unless we have infallibility somewhere, faith is impossible."

During the last years of Spurgeon's ministry, these issues came to a head in the famous Downgrade Controversy. Believing that the Baptist Union harbored ministers whose doctrinal views placed them outside the pale of evangelical Christianity, Spurgeon published a series of articles lamenting the "downgrade" the church had slipped on and calling for the adoption of a clear theological standard. In the end Spurgeon refused to name those he suspected of heresy because their names had been given to him in confidentiality. In 1887 Spurgeon withdrew from the Baptist Union rather than countenance what he called "wretched indifferentism" and doctrinal deviation. In the following year the Union passed a censure against Spurgeon, and he left the Union. Although he might have formed a new denomination of disaffected Baptists, he urged others not to follow him out of the Union. Noteworthy is the fact that he joined the Surrey-Middlesex Baptist Association. He did not become an "independent" Baptist. He had strong ecclesiastical convictions.

Not only did the Puritan legacy impact Spurgeon's theology as to the nature of the Bible; it largely determined his use of it in preaching. He learned from the Puritans the lesson of concise organization and structured subdivision of a text. For example, the following introduction to one of his sermons presents an example of the typical Puritan approach to the use of the Bible in preaching. Spurgeon stated:

The narrative before us seems to me to suggest three points, and these three points each of them triplets. I shall notice in this narrative, first, *the three stages of faith;* in the second place, *the three diseases to which faith is subject;* and in the third place to ask *three questions about your faith.*

Through this analytical, Aristotelian approach, Spurgeon attempted to make each of his sermons simple enough for a child to understand. And he usually succeeded.

He never tried to please "rationalistic" theologians and modern higher critics. Consequently, they were frequently appalled by his explication of texts. Horton Davies contended, "His exegesis could be capricious, idiosyncratic, and even grotesque." Whether this is true or not, we would probably all agree today that he tended to play too much upon the meanings of words in the English text without a thorough grounding in the original language of the text, a common practice of Victorian preachers.

Because of the Victorian concern for the words of the text, Spurgeon became what today we would call a "textual preacher." Rarely did he take a text and not turn it, digest it, and give it every twist possible. As a consequence, at times he no doubt did too much with a verse. Still the people heard the Word, and in that they reveled and grew in the faith.

Evaluation

The question is constantly raised: Would Spurgeon with his Calvinistic theology be effective in today's urban, secular world? The religious Victorian age is past, to be sure, and he was a man of that century. Yet Spurgeon would have been most effective in any era—and for the very reasons he was effective over a century ago. Why do I say that? First, because he was culturally a man of his day, he knew how to communicate to it. Second, he had a firm grasp on the essential gospel. His biblical theology held him in good stead. This is perennially important—and relevant. Third, he was a man of God with a contagious spirituality. People always respond to that in a minister. And he ministered to people in their *real needs.* Finally, he faithfully believed in and preached the "whole counsel of God"—the Holy Scriptures. And he did it all in an innovative fashion that ministered to people where they were in life. That sort of ministry is always alive, relevant, and responded to in any age. So "the Last of the Puritans" made his contribution; and the legacy lingers on.

Bibliography

Works by Spurgeon

All of Grace: An Earnest Word with Those Who Are Seeking Salvation by the Lord Jesus Christ. London: Passmore and Alabaster, 1892.

Autobiography, rev. ed. 2 vols. Edinburgh: Banner of Truth Trust, 1962, 1973.

C. H. Spurgeon's Prayers. With an Introduction by Dinsdale T. Young. London: Passmore and Alabaster, 1905.

The Cheque Book of the Bank of Faith. London: Passmore & Alabaster, 1888.

Commenting and Commentaries: Two Lectures Addressed to the Students of the Pastors' College, Metropolitan Tabernacle, Together with a Catalogue of Biblical Commentaries and Expositions. London: Passmore & Alabaster, 1876.

John Ploughman's Pictures: or More of His Plain Talk for Plain People. London: Passmore & Alabaster, 1880.

Lectures to My Students: A Selection from Addresses Delivered to the Students of the Pastors' College, Metropolitan Tabernacle. London: Passmore & Alabaster, 1890.

The Metropolitan Tabernacle Pulpit, 57 vols. London: Passmore & Alabaster, 1861–1917.

Morning by Morning: or, Daily Readings for the Family or the Closet. London: Passmore and Alabaster, n.d.

Morning by Morning. Grand Rapids: Baker Book House, 1975.

The New Park Street Pulpit, 6 vols. London: Passmore and Alabaster, 1855–60.

The Soul-Winner; or, How to Lead Sinners to the Saviour. London: Passmore & Alabaster, 1895.

The Treasury of David: Containing an Original Exposition of the Book of Psalms; A Collection of Illustrative Extracts from the Whole Range of Literature; A Series of Homiletical Hints upon Almost Every Verse; and Lists of Writers upon Each Psalm, 7 vols. London: Passmore and Alabaster.

Works about Spurgeon

Bacon, Ernest W. *Spurgeon: Heir of the Puritans*. London: George Allen & Unwin, 1967.

Briggs, John H. Y. "Charles Haddon Spurgeon and the Baptist Denomination." *Baptist Quarterly* 31 (January 1986), 218–40.

Dallimore, Arnold A. *Spurgeon: A New Biography*. Edinburgh: Banner of Truth Trust, 1985.

Davies, Horton. "Expository Preaching: Charles Haddon Spurgeon." *Foundations* 6 (1963): 14–25.

Day, Richard Ellsworth. *The Shadow of the Broad Brim: The Life Story of Charles Haddon Spurgeon: Heir of the Puritans*. Philadelphia: Judson Press, 1934.

Drummond, Lewis A. *Spurgeon, Prince of Preachers*. Grand Rapids: Kregel Publications, 1992.

Duke, David N. "Asking the Right Questions about War: A Lesson from C. H. Spurgeon," *Evangelical Quarterly* 61 (1989): 71–80.

————. "Charles Haddon Spurgeon: Social Concern Exceeding an Individualistic, Self-Help Ideology [1857-92]," *Baptist History and Heritage* 22 (1987): 47–56.

Ferguson, Duncan S. "The Bible and Protestant Orthodoxy: The Hermeneutics of Charles Spurgeon." *Journal of the Evangelical Theological Society* 25 (1982): 455–66.

Fullerton, W. Y. *C. H. Spurgeon: A Biography.* London: Williams and Norgate, 1920.

George, Timothy, ed. *A Marvelous Ministry: How the All-Round Ministry of C. H. Spurgeon Speaks to Us Today.* Ligonier, Pa.: Soli Deo Gloria Publications, 1993.

Haykin, Michael A. G. "'Where the Spirit of God Is, There Is Power': An Introduction to Spurgeon's Teaching on the Holy Spirit." *Churchman* 106 (1992): 197–208.

Hopkins, Mark. "The Down Grade Controversy: New Evidence [S. H. Booth correspondence]," *Baptist Quarterly* 35 (1994): 262–78.

Hopkins, Mark T. E. "Spurgeon's Opponents in the Downgrade Controversy," *Baptist Quarterly* 32 (1988): 274–94.

Lorimer, George C. *Charles Haddon Spurgeon: The Puritan Preacher in the Nineteenth Century.* Boston: James H. Earle, 1892.

Maroney, Nina Reid. "Spurgeon and British Evangelical Theological Education," in *Theological Education in the Evangelical Tradition.* Grand Rapids: Baker Books, 1996.

Mohler, R. Albert, Jr. "A Bee-Line to the Cross: The Preaching of Charles H. Spurgeon." *Preaching* 8 (Nov./Dec 1992): 25–26, 28–30.

Murray, Iain H. *The Forgotten Spurgeon.* 2d ed. Edinburgh: Banner of Truth Trust, 1973.

————. *Spurgeon vs. Hyper-Calvinism: The Battle for Gospel Preaching.* Carlisle, Pa.: Banner of Truth Trust, 1995.

Nicholls, Michael. "Charles Haddon Spurgeon, 1834–1892: Church Planter," in *Mission to the World.* Didcot, England: Baptist Historical Society, 1991.

Nicholls, Michael K. "Mission Yesterday and Today: Charles Haddon Spurgeon 1834–1892," *Baptist Review of Theology/La Revue Baptiste de Theologie* 2 (Spring 1992): 37–49.

Payne, Ernest A. "The Down Grade Controversy: A Postscript." *Baptist Quarterly* 28 (1979): 146–58.

Skinner, Craig. "The Preaching of Charles Haddon Spurgeon." *Baptist History and Heritage* 19 (1984): 16–26.

Smith, David S. "Luther and Spurgeon: Purposeful Preachers," *Concordia Journal* 22 (Jan. 1996), 35–44.

Swanson, Dennis M. "The Millennial Position of Spurgeon." *Master's Seminary Journal* 7 (1996): 183–212.

Sweatman, Kent Ellis. "The Doctrines of Calvinism in the Preaching of Charles Haddon Spurgeon." Ph.D. dissertation, Southwestern Baptist Theological Seminary, 1998.

Travis, William G. "Urban Pilgrims and Pioneers: Charles H. Spurgeon and the Poor," *Urban Mission* 10 (Spring 1992): 29–36.

Walker, Michael. "Charles Haddon Spurgeon (1834–1892) and John Clifford (1836–1923) on the Lord's Supper," *American Baptist Quarterly* 7 (June 1988): 128–50.

8

Augustus Hopkins Strong

By Gregory Alan Thornbury

IN THE ARCHIVES OF THE COLGATE-ROCHESTER DIVINITY SCHOOL IN
Rochester, New York, lies a fascinating photograph of the faculty of the
Rochester Theological Seminary. The photograph, taken in 1907, provides
a helpful window into the complex and often perplexing life of Augustus
Hopkins Strong (1836–1921), one of the most influential Baptist theolo-
gians of the twentieth century. At the center of the picture sits Augustus
Hopkins Strong, the venerable president of Rochester Theological

Seminary. Surrounding Strong are his faculty colleagues, men he personally chose to teach at Northern Baptists' most prestigious seminary. To Strong's right stands Cornelius Woelfkin, who taught preaching at Rochester for twelve years. Woelfkin, a one-time president of the American Baptist Foreign Mission Society and pastor of the Fifth Avenue (later Park Avenue) Baptist Church, played an important role in the development of the Fundamentalist-Modernist Controversy.[1] An avowed modernist, Woelfkin helped block a fundamentalist victory at the Northern Baptist Convention in 1922 by arguing against the adoption of the New Hampshire Confession of Faith as a doctrinal standard for denominational mission boards and agencies.

To Strong's left stands Walter Rauschenbusch, the well-known father of the social gospel movement. Rauschenbusch, who had been chided as a seminary student by the staunchly orthodox Strong for agreeing with Horace Bushnell's theory of the atonement, held a prominent place on Rochester's faculty during Strong's presidency.[2] Rauschenbusch, who dedicated his *Theology for the Social Gospel* to Strong, considered Strong his mentor and enjoyed Strong's faithful support despite his often controversial theological and political positions.

The photograph of the Rochester faculty in 1907 offers a metaphor for Strong's life and ministry. Strong was a theological conservative surrounded and deeply affected by the pervasive and encroaching advance of modernity. Although Strong considered himself a defender of theological orthodoxy, he hired modernists to teach on his faculty. While he eschewed the skepticism of the Enlightenment, he immersed himself in the intellectual currents of modernity. Although Strong lauded Rauschenbusch in his efforts for social reform on behalf of the poor, he moved in elite social circles among the wealthy and powerful and typified the sensibilities of the Gilded Age. John D. Rockefeller counted Strong among his closest associates. Echoing a sentiment worthy of Russell H. Conwell, Strong once candidly admitted, "I was originally intended for a millionaire. I have a taste for splendor. Largeness pleases me."[3] Augustus Hopkins Strong embodied significant and profound contradictions.

Strong's life and theological contribution cast a long shadow over twentieth-century Baptist theology. For forty years many of the most influential and educated Baptist ministers of the North sat in Strong's classrooms at Rochester and learned their theology from him. Several of Strong's students, such as George B. Foster, Walter Rauschenbusch, Albert Henry Newman, H. B. Hackett, and Strong's own son, Charles Augustus Strong, became famous thinkers in their own right. Strong's encyclopedic *Systematic Theology* went through eight editions, remained a frequently used seminary textbook until very recent times, and is still in print. Even during his own lifetime, conflicting opinions about Strong's theological legacy emerged. E. Y. Mullins, president of the Southern Baptist Theological Seminary in Louisville, Kentucky, commended Strong's attempt to make use of recent philosophical discoveries without succumbing to their dangers.[4] Conversely, the historian J. L. Neve accused Strong of advocating "the liberalizing and humanizing process in theology."[5] Strong continues to play an important role in the definition of evangelical theology. Clark Pinnock has recently elicited Strong's support in his advocacy of soteriological inclusivism.[6] As Strong's grandson and Yale professor Richard Sewall once wrote: "He was august—no one was ever better named."[7]

Biography

Born in Rochester, New York on August 3, 1836, to Alvah Strong and Catherine Hopkins, Augustus Hopkins Strong enjoyed his early life in a Christian home. Strong's father, Alvah, owned and operated the city's local newspaper, the *Rochester Democrat,* and held a prominent place in Rochester society. Subsequent to a dramatic personal encounter with Charles Grandison Finney after an evangelistic crusade, Alvah converted to Christianity in 1830, and joined the local Baptist church, where he remained an officer and active member.[8] Later he acted as treasurer for the fledging seminary at Rochester, and his son Augustus, who had completed his high school course at fifteen but was too young to enter college, helped him manage the seminary's finances. "I little thought as I paid the beneficiaries their appropriations," Augustus reflected, "that the time would come when I should myself be the president of the institution and teach theology to the sons of the very students to whom I then gave aid."[9]

Augustus entered Yale in 1854 without having made a profession of personal faith in Christ. At Yale, Strong studied with scholars of the generation subsequent to the New Divinity School. Two of his teachers, Noah Porter and George Park Fisher, exerted a special influence on Strong. Porter, the president of Yale, studied under Nathaniel W. Taylor and taught his students philosophy and ethics with a warm evangelical piety. Porter particularly encouraged students entering the Christian ministry. Fisher, also a disciple of Taylor and Edwards Amasa Park, was more progressive in his theological perspective, advocating historical-critical methods in biblical interpretation. Like most American undergraduate institutions of the time, original thinking was not required of students. Strong later expressed some disappointment that critical thinking and discussion were not encouraged in the classical curriculum of Yale. From very early in his academic career, Strong's interests were epistemological.

In April 1856, following in his father's footsteps, Strong attended a revival held by Charles Finney. Although Strong later pointed to the meeting as the place of his conversion to Christianity, he suggested a slightly more nuanced chronology in his theology primer for laypersons, *What Shall I Believe?* Strong wrote:

> During a college vacation, at my own home, I found myself at a revival meeting under the eagle eye of Charles G. Finney, the evangelist. He seemed to speak directly to me, when he said: "If there is any one here who sees that he ought to forsake his sins and to serve God, let him rise and go into the inquiry room, and someone will tell him what to do." So I arose and went out. A minister of the Gospel met me, and asked me if I would begin from that hour to serve God, looking to him to show me the way. After much hesitation, I told him that I would, and I went home in the dark, thinking all the way that I was very foolish, yet determined to begin a new life from that day. I began to read my Bible. I began to pray. But though I sought God, I did not find him until, some weeks after returning to college, bowed down with a new sense of sin and need, I read the verse in 2 Cor. 6:17, 18, "Wherefore come ye out from among them and be ye separate, saith the Lord, and touch not the unclean thing, and I will receive you, and ye shall be my sons and daughters, saith the Lord Almighty." Then I said to myself, "That is I: God is my Father and friend!" And for the first time in my life I felt that there was a tie that bound me to God.[10]

Following what Strong referred to as his "Arminian or Pelagian conversion," he continued to struggle spiritually. Part of this was due to the fact that Strong felt as though his conversion had been made in a theological vacuum. He lamented that, "It was indeed a very unintelligent conversion. I do not remember that I had any thought of the Lord Jesus Christ as the way to God or as the sacrifice for sin; much less did I regard myself as having come to any definite relationship or union of fellowship with him. Nor did I think of the Holy Spirit as in any way influencing me, nor or myself as dependent upon the Holy Spirit for wisdom or renewal."[11] Only after a near-fatal climbing accident did Strong recognize God's providential hand upon his life. Strong resolved to commit his life to God in the service of the ministry.

After the completion of his studies at Yale in 1857, Strong enrolled at Rochester Theological Seminary. Although Strong had not yet committed himself denominationally, he "felt it safer" to prepare himself theologically at a Baptist institution. The most attractive feature of going to Rochester, Strong admitted, was the opportunity to study theology with Ezekiel Gilman Robinson. Robinson taught theology and homiletics at Rochester Seminary from 1853 to 1872, and from 1872 to 1889 served as president of Brown University. A student of Francis Wayland, Robinson earned a reputation as one of the most formidable Baptist theologians in the North during the mid-nineteenth century.[12] Strong enjoyed the contrast in pedagogy between Yale and Rochester. Robinson's teaching style was more dynamic and engaging than the cold, classical recitations in which he participated at Yale. Robinson's lectures took the form of theological argumentation, and this enraptured the youthful Strong. Unlike his undergraduate teachers, Robinson, said Strong, "taught us how to think."[13] Consequently, Strong learned much of his theological method from Robinson and greatly revered him throughout his life. Although Strong felt as though he later rid himself of some of the epistemological problems he saw present in Robinson's theology, he never fully escaped his influence.

During his seminary days Strong began his ministry somewhat inauspiciously, preaching to youth in a dilapidated schoolhouse at a local Sunday school at "The Rapids" near Rochester. He described his congregation as "a forlorn set of children and a rude set of young people . . . unwashed, low, and often bad."[14] Despite the difficulties Strong persevered and witnessed many of the young people become "soundly converted" who "grew up to be teachers of others."[15] The experience helped Strong formulate a theologically well-rounded message of evangelism. "I had learned at my conversion the guilt and helplessness of sin. My subsequent instability had taught me that only God can regenerate. Now I learned the lesson that no man had a right to believe in God as a savior except on the ground of the sacrificial death of Jesus. And the way of it was this: the more thoughtful inquirers in my meetings were troubled about the way of salvation. It was not enough to tell them that God would forgive them; they needed to see *how* God could be just and yet justify."[16] By Strong's own admission he learned nearly as much during his first little pastorate as he did in seminary. If Strong was theologically uninformed when he entered Rochester, he left devoutly orthodox, holding Calvinistic perspectives on God, sin, and the nature of salvation. Strong continued to excel in his studies at Rochester, graduated after two years, and left the United States to see the world.

Upon his return from extensive world travel, Strong commenced the search for a pastorate. Strong faced disappointment when First Baptist, New York, failed to call him as pastor. He had always fancied himself a big-city pastor. Immediately following on the heels of that blow, Strong accepted a call to a small Baptist church in Haverhill, Massachusetts, a rural town with about ten thousand inhabitants. During that time Strong encountered relational discouragement as well when his fiancée, Julia Finney, the daughter of Charles Finney, broke off their engagement. Strong once again found himself at the point of despair. But while at Haverhill, he married Hattie Savage of Rochester, who proved to be an excellent companion for him. Ironically, both his first church and romance with Finney had ended in frustration. Soon things would change for the better for Strong.

After doing pulpit supply for North Baptist Church in Chicago, Strong received a call to the pastorate of the First Baptist Church of Cleveland, Ohio. Although he appreciated the little church of his first pastorate, Strong hastily prepared to leave Haverhill: he resigned on Thursday, packed on Saturday, and said good-bye on Sunday. Strong finally achieved what he hoped for, a prominent Baptist church in one of the great cities in the North. The congregation met Strong's preaching with favor, and soon six to seven hundred people regularly attended Sunday services. During his pastorate Strong preached substantive, doctrinal sermons. His own outline of systematic theology dictated his lectionary. Strong wanted his congregation to be theologically grounded. "So we went over the doctrines of the existence of God, the Trinity, inspiration, sin, the person of Christ, the atonement, and all the major truths of theology."[17] Strong's stay in Cleveland developed into a time for rapid intellectual growth. While at Haverhill Strong had discarded all of his books except a few commentaries and exegetical tools. Now in the more cosmopolitan environment of Cleveland, Strong read extensively in the areas of science, philosophy, history, and theology.

As Strong's intellectual and literary achievements grew, a conflict arose in his mind between his studies and his pastoral duties.[18] By this time Strong's reputation and influence had grown to the point that he assumed the role of a Baptist statesman at large. In 1869, Strong preached before the Judson Missionary Society at Brown University, and at the next commencement exercises Brown awarded Strong an honorary doctor of divinity degree. This was the first of many such honors for Strong. He subsequently received honorary degrees from Yale, Princeton, Bucknell, and the University of Rochester.

In 1871, Ezekiel Gilman Robinson left the presidency at Rochester Seminary to assume the helm of Brown University. When the trustees of the seminary offered Strong the chair of theology at Rochester, he accepted upon the condition that he also become president. Strong firmly believed that he needed to "have affairs in his own hands" to work effectively.[19] The trustees granted the request, and Strong presided over his own *alma mater* for the next forty years.

Strong became the personal embodiment of Rochester Theological Seminary until his retirement in 1911. Under his leadership the seminary continued to gain prominence among institutions of its kind. Strong's vision for theological education placed emphasis on the importance of the advance of the gospel in the world and the production of competent, well-equipped ministers. "The training of the ministry," Strong observed at the dedication of Rockefeller Hall in 1880, "implies conviction that the work of preaching Christ and the wide range of his truth as it is made known in the Scriptures, demands an intellectual and religious preparation beyond that of any mere human calling."[20] This training, he continued, "since it has to do with men's souls and of God's kingdom, should be the most ample and complete that our wisdom can devise and that is warranted by the means Providence has placed at our disposal."[21] Strong also enacted curricular reforms at the seminary to help ensure that graduates from Rochester Seminary would be fit for the churches. Strong argued:

> I admit that not every young man who proposes to enter a theological seminary is a fit object of these of gifts of the churches. . . . For this reason I would have the curriculum a rigorous one—so rigorous that nothing but industry and self-denying devotion to study can enable the pupil successfully to accomplish its requirements. I would set the standard so high that neither an incompetent nor indolent man should be able to complete the course, and this intellectual test I would apply without fear or favor. We want not so much numbers, as quality, in the ministry—men disciplined, alert, energetic; and the Theological Seminary is the very place where these qualities should be encouraged and trained.[22]

The seminary greatly benefited from Strong's leadership. His faculty appointments continued to distinguish Rochester Seminary as a premier theological institution. In addition, Strong served as a unifying influence amid the usual internal faculty struggles. The seminary's endowment increased tenfold, and the physical plant grew during his tenure thanks in part to wealthy patrons whose friendships he cultivated. The most famous of these was John D. Rockefeller, with whom Strong traveled extensively. The close friendship between the Strong and Rockefeller families resulted in Strong's son Charles' marriage to Rockefeller's daughter Bessie. The friendship between Strong and Rockefeller began to unravel when Strong repeatedly exhorted Rockefeller to fund a Baptist university in New York City. Strong, who also chaired the board of trustees at Vassar College, envisioned himself as the new University's president and leader. Rockefeller negatively reacted to being told what to do with his money and resented Strong's warnings regarding the responsibility of wealth. In his biography of Rockefeller, Ron Chernow paints an unflattering picture of Strong in which the Baptist theologian pestered Rockefeller regarding the endowment of a Baptist university in New York. Chernow details how Thomas W. Goodspeed and William Rainey Harper upstaged Strong's "blunderbuss approach" and won Rockefeller's support for the new University of Chicago.[23]

Strong suffered several other bitter disappointments later in life. His brilliant son Charles, who shared the Walker Fellowship at Harvard with

George Santanyana, repudiated the Christian faith. Strong felt responsible. In the final years of his life, Strong also lamented the liberal drift within his own seminary and his own denomination.[24] In *A Tour of the Missions* Strong decried the deleterious effects of modern criticism on theology both in the denomination and on the mission field.[25] Strong's pointed words came as a surprise to some observers. Many persons perceived Strong as being supportive of the modernist trend among Northern Baptists and pointed to his faculty appointments at Rochester Seminary as proof. Walter Rauschenbusch once stated that he accepted the invitation to teach at Rochester Seminary partly because he approved of "President Strong's apparent shift in a liberal direction."[26]

When the debate over whether Northern Baptists should adopt a confession of faith erupted in the 1920s, Strong cast his vote of support for the fundamentalists. Only four months before his death, Strong wrote in the *Watchman Examiner*:

> I wish now therefore to set myself . . . squarely on the side of those who demand that our Baptist institutions should be true to the faith once for all delivered to the saints, and that no one who is unable or unwilling to confess that faith, should have a place in the government or in the instructions of those institutions. . . . And let us inaugurate this change by the adoption of a "confession of faith" that makes it clear that we are not only Christians but Baptists. To justify that evasion of the plea that Baptist liberty permits doubt of Christ's virgin birth and substitutionary atonement is to grant to professed Baptists the right to undermine our Baptist foundations, and ultimately destroy the Baptist denomination itself.[27]

Privately Strong feared his imprecations had been too late in coming. He died in November 1921.

Exposition

Much like the events in his life, paradox and change distinguish Strong's theology. Throughout his long career Strong produced an impressive amount of theological material. The most accessible form of Strong's theology is found in the successive editions of his *Systematic Theology*.[28] The written record of Strong's theological pilgrimage reveals a man who seriously engaged modern thought and sought to provide a thoughtful Christian response to contemporary challenges to the Christian faith. Strong contended that Christians need not be theological and cultural Luddites. He once exhorted his students:

> Without openness of mind you will see little that is new, and when you do see it you will be prejudiced against it. You will

regard all science and philosophy and literature and art as anti-Christian, and your narrowness will prevent the acceptance of Christianity by those whom you would most desire to influence. Theology will be to you a book closed and sealed, a series of dead formulas without power to move you or to move others. I urge you to a better mood than this. When the new challenges your attention, I would have you to ask, not "What is there here that I can contradict and oppose?" but rather "What is there here that I can accept and utilize?" I would have you ready to recognize and welcome truth, from whatsoever source it comes.[29]

Strong put into practice his own advice. He drank deeply from the wells of modernity and heavily incorporated the rationalistic and empiricist traditions of the Enlightenment into his theological method. As a result, appropriating Strong's theology is both a simple and complex task, and one can read his work on several different levels. On the first level Strong's theology identified him as a conservative, orthodox theologian, truly a "fundamentalist" in the early twentieth-century sense of the word. Strong defended such traditional doctrines as the deity of Christ, the virgin birth, the supernatural reality of the biblical miracles, substitutionary atonement, and the inspiration and authority of the Bible. On the second level Strong maintained considerable continuity with the Reformed theological tradition. Strong held to a high view of God's sovereignty, imputation and original sin, unconditional election, a particular application of the atonement, and the efficacy of grace. On the third and perhaps most profound level, Strong's theology was thoroughly modern. Strong sought a rapprochement between classical theology and the challenges he saw posed to it by philosophical and scientific discourse. Consequently, for example, Strong accepted theistic evolution as the most plausible explanation of human origins, modified his view of biblical inspiration, and altered his doctrine of God to allow for a more immanent understanding of the deity. Strong thus constructed a deeply apologetic theology and argued that the survival of Christianity depended on it. "Christianity," he warned, "must appropriate and disseminate all knowledge, or she must confess that she is the child of ignorance and fanaticism. She must conquer all good learning, or she must herself be conquered."[30]

Like his southern counterpart E. Y. Mullins, Strong has been claimed by both liberals and conservatives as one of their own. Strong's life and theology invite such contradictions, and such debates are likely to continue. But to understand Strong and his theology, one must realize that his thought took shape during a time of profound change in the history of western thought. Darwinian evolution and Kantian philosophy among other influences combined irrevocably to shape the landscape of late nineteenth- and early twentieth-century thought. The triumph of the scientific spirit, wedded to an implicit confidence in the inevitability of human progress, produced the distinctive ethos historians have called "the Gilded Age." Grant Wacker, a leading interpreter of Strong, argued that the emergence of "historical consciousness" in nineteenth-century social sciences is the key to understanding the changing nature of Strong's life and thought. While historical consciousness (i.e. "the assumption that all knowledge, including all forms of religious knowledge, is fashioned wholly from the materials of human history") certainly impacted Strong, it does not fully explain the epistemological and doctrinal development which took place in his thought.[31] Strong's theology succumbed not so much from forces external to his theological tradition but from pressures within. The post-Reformation philosophical tradition which theological conservatives had come to rely upon contained internal conflicts which resulted in an unraveling of their dependence on divine revelation as the central epistemological axiom for theology.

Theological Method

Augustus Hopkins Strong stands in a long line of conservative Protestant theologians in the Reformed tradition whose theologies were profoundly impacted by what George Marsden has called "unquestionably *the* American philosophy," the philosophy of Scottish Common Sense Realism.[32] The Scottish Common Sense school of philosophy, founded by Thomas Reid and disseminated among nineteenth-century American clergy, developed a dualist epistemology with seemingly antithetical poles: intuitionism and empiricism. Common Sense epistemology pursued a methodology in which its claims to self-evident truth conflicted with its evidentialism. The application of Reid's philosophy did not end with a refutation of Locke, Berkeley, and Hume and their "theory of ideas." Reid wedded his epistemology to a theological method. Reid's attempt to ground a fully orbed natural theology in self-evident principles created a confused epistemological identity. On the one hand Reid wanted to demonstrate that Common Sense principles were indeed intuitive; on the other hand, following Descartes' project, he sought to prove the existence of God and his attributes and other theological categories by the use of reason in his *Lectures on Natural Theology.*[33]

A few modern interpreters of Reid have noted the internal tension between intuitionism and empiricism which this approach elicited in Common Sense thought. William Eakin, an authority on Reid, observed that "Reid rejects his own argument that a self-evident belief cannot be proven true by attempting 'proofs' of first principles."[34] Reid encountered similar difficulty establishing a natural theology based on Common Sense principles. Reason and revelation are presented as complementary paths to knowledge in Reid's theological method, but their content is unclear. Nevertheless, in the prosecution of Reid's argument, reason, and "natural religion" gain the higher honor, since, Reid argues, it is reason that judges revelation. Revelation establishes or confirms what we already know to be true in nature. Reid remarked, "'Tis by reason that we must judge whether Revelation be really so; 'tis by reason that we must judge of what is revealed."[35]

Reid never resolved this uneasy alliance of intuition and evidence, revelation and reason, natural theology and special revelation. As a result, it produced in the heirs of his thought a similarly conflicted epistemology—one they neither could solve. In particular, the theologians who followed Common Sense Realism found themselves in the awkward position of trying to fit Common Sense categories into their theological systems. Like Reid, they produced theologies with an unstable epistemology. This instability fostered an environment in which theological systems built upon the Scottish philosophy became susceptible to significant epistemological changes, changes which sought to soften Reid's unresolved tensions. Augustus Hopkins Strong is an example of a theologian who appropriated the Scottish philosophy's severe epistemological tensions.

Strong began his journey toward becoming the greatest Baptist theologian of the Gilded Age under the tutelage of the venerable Ezekiel Gilman Robinson. Robinson not only served as Strong's theology professor but also acted as a mentor for Strong during his days as a seminarian. Strong heard a classical presentation of the Scottish Common Sense philosophy in his classroom experiences with Robinson. Robinson learned Common Sense from his teacher Francis Wayland, who wrote a popular nineteenth-century philosophical text which repristinated Thomas Reid's system. Strong spoke of Robinson with considerable reverence and viewed him as a unique thinker, who constantly improved upon the content of the theological discipline which he taught. "His dictations in theology had the forms of Old Princeton," he remembered, "but these were merely tentative—he himself was criticizing and inquiring and gradually working his way out from these forms into a realistic system more true to the facts and to Scripture."[36]

The perspective of Common Sense Realism pervaded Robinson's classroom and, on Strong's account, naturally impacted an entire generation of Northern Baptist preachers. Robinson's epistemology relied heavily on the work of Sir William Hamilton, a follower of Thomas Reid who added Kantian elements to Common Sense Realism. Strong imbibed the philosophy of his mentor: "Under Dr. Robinson all my ideas with regard to metaphysics were changed. I began to see that it alone dealt with realities, that, in fact, one could have no firm footing in any other department of knowledge unless he had reached a good metaphysical foundation. I was stimulated to read Sir William Hamilton."[37] Strong explained the influence which Robinson's position had upon him. "As Dr. Robinson himself was a convert to the doctrine of relativity propounded by Kant and taken up by Hamilton and Mansel, I naturally regarded this as the ultimate philosophy, and for many years it shaped my theological thinking."[38] Although Strong later claimed that his *Systematic Theology* was constructed without reference to Robinson's *Christian Theology*, he later admitted his intellectual debt to Robinson.

> I am humbled to find how much of my own thinking that I thought original has been an unconscious reproduction of his own. Words and phrases which I must have heard from him in the class-room thirty-five years ago, and which have come to be a part of my mental furniture, I now recognize as not my own but his. And the ruling idea of his system,—that stands out as the ruling idea of mine; I did not know until now that I owed it almost wholly to him.[39]

Indeed, early on Strong proved to be a faithful expositor of the Scottish philosophy, as is evidenced in his lectures "Science and Religion" (1867), "Philosophy and Religion" (1868), and his *Lectures on Theology* (1876).[40] Like Robinson, Strong mixed intuitionism and empiricism and filled his arguments with appeals to *a priori* "first truths" and scientific induction. Strong struggled to combine the two elements and often exhibited frustration with his own epistemological system. The best example of the presence of Common Sense's conflicted epistemology in Strong's thought can be found in his early treatment of the existence of God. On the one hand Strong considered knowledge of God's existence to be self-evident. Referring to God's existence, he declared, "A knowledge, thus fundamental, necessary, and universal, we call an intuitive knowledge. Of this sort we consider the knowledge of God's existence. We hold God's existence to be a first truth, like the knowledge of our own personal existence, or the belief in causality." Strong concludes, "Therefore . . . all men have at the very basis of their being, and as the deepest principle of all their thinking, a knowledge of the existence of God, as a Power upon which they are dependent."[41] Yet only several lines later, Strong stands his previous statement on its head claiming knowledge of God's existence "is a knowledge which logically precedes all observation and all reasoning—yet only reflection upon the phenomena of nature occasions its rise in consciousness." He thus concludes, "A first truth is a knowledge . . . developed upon sense-perception and reflection."[42]

According to Common Sense thinking, a scientific foundation was essential to metaphysics. Therefore, in this understanding, philosophical method provided the bridge across which religion could arrive at scientific credibility. For Strong only a foundationalist approach to theology fitted the need of the hour. Thus, as Strong remarked, "Religion, as a scientific system, rests upon the basis of philosophy. The inevitable tendency of the mind to form to itself a definite and connected scheme of knowledge impels it . . . to search for the foundations of those beliefs." Strong continued, "And philosophy is the science of foundations. It busies itself with the examination of the grounds of faith. It seeks to determine whether religion has a safe basis and support in the facts of consciousness." Strong finished with a remarkable conclusion: "There is still another service which philosophy renders to religion, namely, that of defining and correlating the great primary conceptions of revelation."[43]

While Strong developed a doctrine of special revelation which supplements that found in nature, his philosophical priorities mitigated against it. Like Robinson, Strong introduced the concept of scriptural revelation without providing a sustained argument concerning its nature and purpose. Simply put, in the main, Strong's epistemology emphasized philosophical categories over scriptural revelation. His theory of knowledge was not so much rooted in revelation as it was in philosophical proofs. At the same time, however, Strong clearly recognized the indispensability of biblical revelation to the Christian truth claim. Thus, as Carl F. H. Henry rightly observes, "Strong, like Robinson before him, fluctuated in an appeal to philosophical and revelational considerations."[44]

For an heir of Common Sense philosophy like Strong, epistemological conflicts were commonplace. But Strong increasingly tired of trying to defend the conflicted epistemological front of his Scottish Realism. Still there was too much at stake for Strong to abandon completely the claims to truth emanating from the intuitionistic structures of consciousness and the rapidly expanding scientific consensus of modernity. In fact, the evolutionary nature of the physical universe was so important for Strong he could no longer justify the old Scottish distinctions between the human consciousness (mind) and external reality (matter). Strong proposed an answer by combining the Personalism of Boston University's Borden Parker Bowne, Edgar Brightman, and the German idealist Hermann Lotze with the monism which was in vogue in the contemporary scientific understanding.[45] The result Strong called "ethical monism," which he introduced in his pivotal work *Christ and Creation and Ethical Monism*. Strong provided the following definition of ethical monism in his *Systematic Theology*.

> *Ethical Monism:* Universe = Finite, partial, graded manifestation of the divine life; Matter being God's self limitation under the law of necessity, Humanity being God's self-limitation under the law of freedom, Incarnation and Atonement being God's self limitation under the law of grace. Metaphysical monism, or the doctrine of Substance, Principle, or Ground of

Being, is consistent with Psychological Dualism, or the doctrine that the soul is personally distinct from matter on the one hand and from God on the other.[46]

In the opening pages of the final edition of his systematic theology, Strong stressed the importance of his new discovery: "That Christ is the one and only Revealer of God, in nature, in humanity, in history, in science, in Scripture, is in my judgment the key to theology. This view implies a monistic and idealistic conception of the world, together with an evolutionary idea as to its progress."[47] Christological monism made the person of Christ the epistemological cohesive which binds matter and mind together. Because this is true, Strong argued, the universe is not a cold, mechanistic place. Rather, through Christ, it is the expression of God's person and character. While he thoroughly rejected pantheism (hence his "psychological dualism"), Strong taught that Christ is the common substance which unifies reality and bridges the divide between the spiritual and material world. Christ, Strong emphasized, "is all in all," and "the principle of cohesion, attraction, interaction, not only in the physical universe, but in the intellectual and moral universe as well."[48] Strong believed his theological discovery arose from Scripture and cited passages such as Colossians 1:16–17 ("in him all things hold together") and John 1:3 ("through him all things were made") as evidence.

Ethical monism, Strong thought, eliminated the problems created by Kant's phenomenal-noumenal distinction by offering the person of Christ as the mediating factor between the spiritual and material worlds. Strong lauded ethical monism's "ability to solve the problems of existence in a more complete and satisfactory way than that of the old dualistic theory."[49] For Strong, monism explained how the self-evident truth claims of intuition and the evidential proofs of science could be harmonized. He believed that the person of Christ interpenetrated both mind and nature and thus made religious knowledge possible. Few interpreters of Strong have seen the epistemological epiphany in monism which he did because they fail to understand Strong's methodology as a reaction to the challenges presented by Common Sense's dualism. While a critical reading finds Strong's monism shackled with essentially the same problems he had forsaken in Scottish Realism (viz. the conflict between intuitionism and empiricism), Strong claimed a profound feeling of release due to his new epistemological axiom. Regarding the philosophical dualism taught to him by Robinson, Strong confessed:

It took me more than a quarter of a century to see my way out of it. When I discovered that in knowing the phenomena we also know the thing in itself and that, instead of seeking to know the reality apart from the phenomena, we should be content to know the reality in and through the phenomena, it was a wonderful relief to me. Then I saw that God is not concealed by his manifestations but that in his manifestations we know him. But in those days, all this was hid from me, and in some respects my philosophy became a fetter to me.[50]

Strong hoped that his christological reading of monism, which he saw as the prevailing philosophy of the age, would set Christianity on a firm and scientifically credible foundation for the future. Both liberals and conservatives expressed deep reservations about Strong's new conclusions. Liberal reviewers complained that Strong did not emphasize immanentism enough. Despite his denials conservatives still suspected Strong of pantheism. In addition to this, others held deep reservations regarding Strong's definition of miracles as occurring within the laws of nature.[51] Stalwarts such as Casper Wistar Hodge, the defender of Old School Calvinism, thought Strong too closely identified God with the world and distrusted his embrace of modernity.[52] Strong's dream of the sweeping tide of monism never materialized.

Strong's acceptance of a profoundly empirical approach to theological method, in both its Common Sense and Idealist forms, produced repercussions throughout his doctrinal system. Several of Strong's doctrines received sufficiently unique expression in his system to warrant more detailed discussion.

The Doctrine of Creation

Strong's acceptance of theistic evolution remains the most well-known aspect of his theology. Not well-known, however, is that Strong's positive reaction to the scientific accuracy of Darwinian evolution took place long before Strong's adoption of monism. In an address given before the Literary Societies at Colby University in 1878 entitled "The Philosophy of Evolution," Strong critiqued the views of Herbert Spencer, an English philosopher and editor of *The Economist* who advocated positivism. Although Strong eschewed Spencer for his atheistic naturalism, he made clear that he agreed with Spencer on the basic mechanism of evolution. "We are ourselves evolutionists then," Strong affirmed, "within certain limits, and we accept a large portion of Mr. Spencer's work. We gratefully appropriate whatever science can prove. . . . So, the day is past, in our judgment, when thoughtful men can believe that there was a creative fiat of God at the introduction of every variety of vegetable and animal life. God may work by means, and a law of variation and of natural selection may have been and probably was the method in which his great design in the vast majority of living forms was carried out."[53]

When Strong later accepted ethical monism as his guiding principle, he finally found a hermeneutic which could more consistently incorporate the scientific consensus regarding evolution. "Christ," Strong averred, "is the principle of evolution . . . Darwin was able to assign no reason why the development of living forms should be upward rather than downward, toward the cosmos rather than toward chaos. . . . If Darwin had recognized Christ as the omnipresent life and law of the world, he would not have been obliged to pass his hands across his face in despair of comprehending the marks of wisdom in the universe."[54] On this basis, Strong saw the impetus for a total reconstrual of the doctrine of creation.

> The law of the Spirit of life in Christ Jesus frees us from the law of sin and death, and a new and holy evolution begins, the power and principle of which is the Son of God. Why should we regret the publication and acceptance of the doctrine of evolution, if it reveals to us the method of Christ's working in both nature and grace? . . . Nature reveals a present God, and evolution is the common method of his working. It is from this point of view that we explain the imperfections of the natural world. These are partial and elementary lessons in God's great scheme of instruction, to be understood only in their connection with the whole. The plan of God is a plan of growth—not first the spiritual and then the natural, but first the natural and then the spiritual.[55]

Strong reconceived his doctrine of God so as to ensure God's participation within the natural world order. The progression of Strong's argument in the preceding paragraph simply follows his epistemological commitments: God's method of working begins with nature and then proceeds to the spiritual. Evolution served as the perfect vehicle for Strong's empirically bound theology. Although he never wavered in advocating God's ultimate transcendence and distinction from the world, his theological progression generally follows the *analogia entis*. In both the cases of God and man, Strong begins with nature and the structures of consciousness, and then charts a path to revelation, which, in turn, sheds light upon the processes of nature.

The Doctrines of Humanity and Imputation of Sin

As we have seen, Strong held that the origin of the cosmos occurred within the evolutionary process with the superintending hand of Providence guiding the development. But man, as the pinnacle of God's creation, exhibited "radical differences" from the rest of the created order, namely, that he had a soul, mind, and will. While Strong conceded that human beings possessed a "brute ancestry" from the apes, he nonetheless proposed a direct intervention by God when man was first created. In other words, God directly created man's soul and his *homo sapiens* body. Strong thus qualified his evolutionary account of human origins: "First, that the laws which have been followed in man's origin are only the methods of God and proofs of his creatorship; secondly, that man, when he appears on the scene, is no longer brute, but a self conscious and free determining being, made in the image of God his Creator and capable of free moral decision between good and evil." Strong added that "the fact that God used preexisting material does not prevent his authorship of the result. . . . We assert that though man came *through* the brute, he did not come *from* the brute. He came from God, whose immanent life he reveals, whose image he reflects in a finished moral personality. Because God succeeded, a fall was possible."[56] Strong realized that this qualification was necessary if he was to preserve the doctrines of original righteousness, the Fall, and the moral accountability of humanity before God.

Although Strong in the main remained a Calvinist throughout his life, several features of the Protestant Scholastic and Old School Calvinist theology bothered him. One of them was federal theology and its account of the doctrine of imputation. Like Ezekiel Gilman Robinson before him, Strong came to reject federal theology. Since Strong preferred neither the Old School nor the New School accounts of the doctrine of imputation, as a creative theologian Strong formed one of his own, drawn from his principle of ethical monism and union with Christ. For Strong, "*three imputations* are declared in Scripture as essential to evangelical doctrine. They are, first, the imputation of Adam's sin to the whole human race; secondly, the imputation of all human sin to Christ; and, thirdly, the imputation of Christ's merits and righteousness to the believer."[57] For Strong, federal theology was "a legal fiction . . . which seemed to involve God in a merely forensic process, to make [God] a God of expedients, to reduce divine justice to book-keeping."[58] Strong held to federal theology until, through personal experience, he understood the importance of the believer's personal union with Christ, Strong's most beloved doctrine. After this, Strong recounted, "My federalism was succeeded by *realistic theology. Imputation is grounded in union,* not union in imputation. Because I am one with Christ, and Christ's life has become my life, God can attribute to me whatever Christ is, and whatever Christ has done. The relation is *biological,* rather than forensic."[59] Strong's defense of an Augustinian understanding of natural headship identified him as the most famous advocate of that position in the modern period.

The Doctrine of Inspiration

Perhaps the most significant development which took place in Strong's theology occurred in his view of inspiration and biblical inerrancy. Throughout his career Strong continued to soften his position on inspiration to allow for the discoveries of biblical criticism and scientific discovery. Strong's changing position on the nature and extent of inspiration may be seen as a gradual outworking of his overarching theological method which, as I have argued, placed empirical categories above revelatory ones. In his early work, particularly in *Lectures on Theology* (1876) and his article on "The Method of Inspiration" in *The Examiner* (1880), Strong affirmed a dynamic view of inspiration as opposed to other theories such as intuition, illumination, and dictation. Strong defined his dynamic view of inspiration as "neither natural, partial, nor mechanical, but supernatural, plenary and dynamical."[60] Regarding the method of inspiration, Strong proposed a kind of negative version of plenary inspiration.

> Thought is possible without words and in the order of nature precedes words. The Scripture writers appear to have been so influenced by the Holy Spirit that they perceived and felt even the new truths they were to publish, as discoveries of their own minds, and were left to the action of their own minds, in the expression of these truths, with the single exception that they were supernaturally held back from the selection of wrong words, and when needful were provided with the right ones. Inspiration is therefore verbal as to its result, but not verbal as to its method.[61]

During his early period, before the emergence of ethical monism in his thought, Strong repeatedly denied the existence of any errors in Scripture, whether scientific or historical. Strong observed that Scripture's "absolute freedom from all proved historical error . . . render[s] it impossible for the reader to avoid the conclusion that over the whole process of composition a wisdom higher than this world, even the wisdom of the Holy Spirit, must have presided."[62] In his article on the "Method of Inspiration," Strong maintained that in Scripture, "error is excluded," "God secured the sacred writers from errors," and that inspiration "is always guarding against from error in the final elaboration."[63] Although Strong appeared to be advocating an approach very close to inerrancy, his understanding of inspiration, following his empirical method, allowed for the possibility of errors in the text of Scripture, if science or criticism could find them. Throughout the various stages of his career, Strong repeatedly maintained that as long as the religious, moral, and salvific meanings were preserved, even the presence of historical or scientific error would not disprove biblical inspiration.[64]

While he continued to stand by his statements regarding scriptural accuracy, Strong showed signs of permissiveness with regard to the importance of an inerrant Bible. Strong refused to make the doctrine of biblical inerrancy an issue of importance. "I am not willing," Strong averred in *Christ in Creation*, "to stake the Christian faith upon the correctness of even the original autographs of Scripture in matters so unessential," as errors of science or history.[65] In an unpublished address given in 1893, Strong exhibited a remarkable candor on the issues of inspiration and inerrancy. Strong began his address by affirming modern theology's tendency "to emphasize less the authority of Scripture and to emphasize more the authority of Christ."[66] Further, Strong underscored that "inspiration only vouches for the divine selection of the passage and the putting of it into permanent and written form as valuable for the moral and religious instruction of mankind."[67] Strong continued, "How much imperfection may there be in Scripture? Just as much as is consistent with its teaching all needed moral and religious truth. The human element may extend to slight errors that do not affect the moral and religious teaching, and the facts that are themselves doctrines such as incarnation and resurrection."[68] Strong went on to suggest possible errors such as whether there were "one or two blind men," in the parables in the Gospels. Strong also hinted that Job may be literary rather than historical narrative. Summing up his position, Strong argued, "The principle . . . is that of sufficiency, not perfection—sufficiency for practical ends, not conformity to ideal standards."[69]

Strong's radical Christocentrism, the programmatic principle worked out in *Christ in Creation*, eliminated the need for a high view of inspiration. Strong thought a high view of Christ ameliorated the need for a high view of Scripture. "Scripture," Strong posited in his *Systematic Theology*, "is an imperfect mirror of Christ. It is defective, yet it reflects him and leads to him. Authority resides not in it, but in him."[70] Such difficult statements on Scripture led to profound misunderstandings of Strong's position on biblical inspiration. By stating that Scripture was "an imperfect mirror of Christ," Strong did not mean what later evangelicals referred to as God's condescension in language. Strong intended to say that the doctrinal and ethical teaching remains the issue of primary importance. Despite his concern over encroaching liberalism in his day, Strong never saw the correlation between biblical perfection and doctrinal accuracy. Nevertheless, Strong continued to pursue his emphasis on empirical categories, even when it appeared to undermine his own doctrinal superstructure. As Strong forthrightly stated, "We are content to let science and criticism tell us what inspiration is."[71]

Salvation and Union with Christ

Redemption, according to Strong, consists in a series of sacrifices and self-limitations on God's part in order for him to identify with and provide atonement for fallen humanity. The cosmic Christ, the principle of creation for Strong, is God condescending to participate in the affairs of the universe and in the lives of human beings. According to Strong, Christ permeates "every atom of the universe" and shares a "natural union with all of humanity."[72] Despite this identification humanity continues to resist God's presence in the world through Christ. God overcomes the sinner by giving of himself, who is Christ, and thus offers the believer a share in the very life of God through the work of Christ's atonement on the cross. In love God also takes from the sinner his or her sin, guilt, and penalty. Strong thus defines salvation as "giving and taking on the part of God, and also giving and taking on the part of the believer."[73] Because of Christ's monistic presence in the world, Strong argued, a reconciliation and atonement with the world and sinners must be made. Strong saw this logical progression as the greatest defense of substitutionary atonement. Strong concluded, "If criticis had only seen the Atonement as a fact of life, all their objections to vicarious atonement, as a matter of book-keeeping, would have vanished. If Christ is our life, if all we have and are is derived from him, and if he is God manifest in the flesh, but essentially independent of space and time, then the atonement is a *biological necessity.*"[74]

Strong's explanation of the believer's union with Christ stands as his most moving and practical doctrine. Citing texts such as Colossians 1:27 ("Christ in you, the hope of glory"), Strong posited that the life of Christ "subjugates and penetrates" the life of the believer. Drawing upon Paul's statement in Galatians 2:20, "It is no longer I who live, but Christ who lives in me," Strong contends that the life of the believer becomes inextricably bound up in the life of Christ. This "vital union" results in a life filled with love, holiness, faith, and good works. Further, the union is mystical, "not in the sense of being unintelligible to the Christian or beyond the reach of his experience, but only in the sense of *surpassing in its intimacy and value any other union of souls that we know.*"[75]

The doctrine of cosmic union with Christ produced some unorthodox turns in his overall soteriology. The close identification which Strong made between Christ and all of humanity (even unbelievers) led Strong to suggest the possibility of implicit faith in Christ on the basis of general revelation. Strong stated in his *Systematic Theology,* "Since Christ is the Word of God and the Truth of God, he may be received even by those who have not heard of his manifestation in the flesh. . . . We have, therefore, the hope that even among the heathen there may be some, like Socrates, who, under the guidance of the Holy Spirit working through the nature and conscience, have found the way to life and salvation."[76] Strong's acceptance of soteriological inclusivism has received recent attention from Millard Erickson who cites Strong as an early example of the evangelical drift on the doctrine of salvation.[77] As mentioned earlier in this article, Clark Pinnock, a current advocate of inclusivism, has cited Strong's position as evidence that the doctrine of "implicit faith" found support from a number of respected theologians throughout the history of the evangelical tradition.

Evaluation

Augustus Hopkins Strong commends himself to historians of Baptist theology by virtue of his colorful biography, substantive theology, and compelling interaction with the modern mind. Strong continues to fascinate us because he grappled with many of the same relational, philosophical, and theological struggles modern persons face. Strong was, in many ways, a brave figure. Unintimidated by the rapidly changing world around him, Strong sought to answer the questions that perplex modern Christians most: How do the claims of faith relate to the claims of science? How should I relate to persons with whom I deeply disagree? What are the essential doctrines of the Christian faith? How may I have a more vital relationship with God? Strong faced these questions squarely and offered specific proposals on each. He spoke both to the philosopher and the average layperson and sought to provide leadership for Baptists in a time of considerable uncertainty.

As a theologian, Strong towers above his peers in the history of Baptist theology. Strong produced an influential *Systematic Theology* which remains unrivaled in Baptist history in its terms of depth, scope, and consideration of issues. While others offered smaller, less technical compendiums of Christian doctrine, Strong gave Baptists a work of serious substance. Although his contemporaries, both liberal and conservative, frequently disagreed with his doctrinal positions, they respected Strong. At over one thousand pages of very fine print and detailed theological interpretation, Strong's *Systematic Theology* still awaits a worthy Baptist competitor. As Carl Henry once stated, "Among Northern Baptists, no theological treatise has been more influential."[78]

But if Strong's theological contribution was a brave one, it was a tragic one as well. As we have seen, Strong worried at the end of his life about the growing tide of liberalism all around him. Strong desperately wanted to maintain his orthodox theological conclusions but undergirded it with a thoroughly modern epistemological superstructure. I have argued throughout this essay that Strong pursued a methodological course which produced unorthodox conclusions in what was, on the whole, an orthodox theology. Strong's inherited philosophical tradition of Common Sense Realism, long the darling of conservative Protestant thinkers, emphasized the intuitive powers of the human mind and the empirical verification of truth, and predisposed Strong to value claims to evidence as the greatest good in theological consideration. I then showed how Strong took the next logical step, the conflation of mind and matter, by developing his doctrine of ethical monism which placed God and his work within the world of empirical scrutiny. Strong's epistemology thus affected subsequent doctrines which followed in his theology. In the doctrine of creation, Strong rejected fiat creationism in favor of theistic evolution. In the doctrine of imputation, Strong preferred biological realism. With regard to Scripture, Strong allowed science and criticism to modify his definition of biblical inspiration. In the doctrine of salvation, Strong proposed a "biological necessity" for the atonement and held that general revelation could lead a person who had never heard the gospel to implicit faith in Christ.

Strong developed a natural theology that mitigated against the doctrine of revelation as the driving force in theological expression. Strong did not see the doctrinal sliding scale which resulted from his concessions to a system which rooted itself in natural theology. Once a preference for human intuition, reason, and empirical ability achieves a place of primacy in one's theological method, doctrinal definition will follow (often slavishly) current ideological, philosophical, and scientific trends. Essentially Strong's epistemology showed little difference from that of theological modernists of his own time such as George B. Foster, William Newton Clarke, Walter Rauschenbusch, and Shailer Mathews, two of whom were students who sat in Strong's classrooms at Rochester. Strong, who repudiated liberal theology, shared much common philosophical, if not theological, ground with his modernist counterparts. Consequently, Strong wished to affirm conservative theological conclusions that were not supported by his own epistemology.

What lessons may we learn from Augustus Hopkins Strong? Strong teaches theologians of all persuasions the powerful lesson of the overwhelming influence of methodology on theology. The subtle but inevitable shaping forces of tradition, culture, and other persons with whom we are in conversation all combine to shape our theological conclusions. We must constantly examine ourselves and our theology, in light of Scripture, to look for signs of unfaithfulness. Despite his shortcomings, Strong wanted to be theologically faithful and could say with confidence at the end of his life, "I have not apostatized from the faith." May the same be said of each of us.

Bibliography

Works by Strong

American Poets and Their Theology. Philadelphia: Griffith and Rowland Press, 1916.

[Annual Alumni Dinner Address (title varies)]. *Rochester Theological Seminary Record.* 1 (1906)–7 (1912).

Address at the Dedication of Rockefeller Hall, May 19, 1880. Rochester, N.Y.: Press of E. R. Andrews, 1880.

"Address before the Minister's Conference. Rochester, Oct. 2, 1893, Rockefeller Hall." Rochester, N.Y.: Strong Manuscript Collection, American Baptist Historical Society.

Appreciation [of William Rainey Harper]. *Biblical World* 27 (1916): 235–36.

Autobiography of Augustus Hopkins Strong. Philadelphia: Judson Press, 1981.

Christ in Creation and Ethical Monism. Philadelphia: The Roger Williams Press, 1899.

"Confessions of Our Faith." *The Watchman-Examiner* 9 (July 7, 1921): 910.

Ethical Monism in Two Series of Three Articles Each; and Christ in Creation. Examiner, 1896.

"Ezekiel Gilman Robinson as a Theologian." *Ezekiel Gilman Robinson; An Autobiography with a Supplement.* Boston: Silver, Burdett and Company, 1896.

Lectures on Theology. Rochester: Press of E. R. Andrews, 1876.

"Man a Living Soul." *Rochester Theological Seminary Record* 7 (May 1912): 12–16.

"The Miracle at Cana. With an Attempt at a Philosophy of Miracles," Delivered at the Second Conference, held at Mathewson Street Methodist Episcopal Church, 11 November 1903. n.p., n.d. Rochester, N.Y.: The American Baptist Historical Society.

"Miracles as Attesting a Divine Revelation." *Baptist Quarterly Review* Vol. 1, no. 2 (April): 274–304.

Miscellanies. 2 vols. Philadelphia: The Griffith & Rowland Press, 1912.

"Modifications in the Theological Curriculum." *American Journal of Theology* 3 (1899): 326–30.

"My Views on the Universe in General." *Baptist.* 1920, 625–26.

One Hundred Chapel-Talks to Theological Students Together with Two Autobiographical Addresses. Philadelphia: Griffith and Rowland Press, 1913.

Philosophy and Religion. 2d ed. New York: Griffith and Rowland Press, 1888.

Popular Lectures on the Books of the New Testament. Philadelphia: Griffith and Rowland Press, 1914.

Systematic Theology: A Compendium and Commonplace Book Designed for the Use of Theological Students. Rochester, N.Y.: Press of E. R. Andrews, 1886.

Systematic Theology. 8th ed., rev. and enl. Philadelphia: Griffith and Rowland Press, 1907–09. Reprint (3 vols. in 1). Old Tappan, N.J.: Fleming H. Revell, 1970.

A Tour of the Missions: Observations and Conclusions. Philadelphia: Griffith and Rowland Press, 1918.

The Uncertainty of Life: A Sermon Preached in the First Baptist Church, Cleveland {Ohio}, January 28, 1866, n.p., n.d.

Union with Christ; A Chapter of Systematic Theology. Philadelphia: American Baptist Publication Society, 1913.

What Shall I Believe? A Primer of Christian Theology. Grand Rapids: F. H. Revell, 1922.

Works about Strong

Allen, Arthur Lynn. "A Comparative Study of the Person of Christ in Selected Baptist Theologians: Augustus H. Strong, William N. Clarke, Edgar Y. Mullins, and Walter T. Conner." Ph.D. diss., New Orleans Baptist Theological Seminary, 1979.

Barbour, Clarence. "President-Emeritus Augustus Hopkins Strong. An Appreciation," *Watchman Examiner,* 1921, 1649–50.

Brown, William Adams. "Recent Treatises on Systematic Theology." *American Journal of Theology* 12 (1908): 150–55.

Henry, Carl F. H. *Personal Idealism and Strong's Theology.* Wheaton, Ill.: Van Kampen Press, 1951.

Johnson, John W. "Prerequisites to an Understanding of the Theology of Augustus Hopkins Strong." *The Review and Expositor.* Vol. 19, No. 3 (July 1922): 333–41.

Langford, S. Fraser. "The Gospel of Augustus Hopkins Strong and Walter Rauschenbusch." *Chronicle.* Vol. 14, no. 1. January 1951.

Loewen, Howard J. "Augustus H. Strong: Baptist Theologian for the Mennonite Brethren." *Mennonites and Baptists.* Winnipeg, Man.: Kindred Pr, 1993.,193–210, 252–58.

Lewis, Frank Grant. "The Presidency of Dr. Augustus Hopkins Strong, 1872–1912." Rochester Theological Seminary Anniversary Volume *The Record.* May 1925.

Newman, Albert Henry. "Strong's Systematic Theology." *Baptist Review and Expositor* 2 (Jan. 1905): 41–66.

Sebastian, David F. "The Doctrine of Atonement in the Theology of Augustus Hopkins Strong." Th.M. thesis, Princeton Theological Seminary, 1952.

Strong, John H. "Augustus Hopkins Strong, 1836–1921," Rochester Historical Society Publication, 235–61.

Wacker, Grant. *Augustus Hopkins Strong and the Dilemma of Historical Consciousness.* Macon, Ga.: Mercer University Press, 1985.

Witheridge, David E. "The Proposed 'Rockefeller University' of Augustus H. Strong; A Chapter in the Founding of the University of Chicago." M.A. thesis, University of Chicago, 1948.

Contributor's Note: The above bibliography is intended to be a representative, not exhaustive, bibliography of primary and secondary works on Augustus Hopkins Strong.

9

Benajah Harvey Carroll

By James Spivey

Biography

BENAJAH HARVEY CARROLL, THE SEVENTH OF THIRTEEN CHILDREN, was born December 27, 1843, near Carrollton in Carroll County, Mississippi. His parents, Benajah and Mary Eliza (Mallad), raised twelve children to maturity and adopted twelve more on the meager income of a bivocational Baptist minister-farmer.[1] When Harvey was seven, his family moved to Drew County, Arkansas, and he began school in Monticello.

Though from a truly devout family, he felt strangely alienated from religion. At thirteen he was "converted" and baptized at a revival meeting, but realizing that this had been merely a catechetical exercise, he remained an avowed "infidel."[2] He imbibed Rousseau, Paine, Hume, and Voltaire, yet he also read the Bible several times and studied the great Christian theologians. He was no atheist, pantheist, or materialist; evolutionism he disregarded as "a godless, materialistic anti-climax of philosophy."[3] He explained "My infidelity related to the Bible and its manifest doctrines. I doubted that it was God's book. . . . I doubted miracles. I doubted the divinity of Jesus of Nazareth. . . . I doubted his vicarious expiation. . . . I doubted any real power and vitality in the Christian religion."[4]

In December 1858, the Carrolls moved west. Riding the family mule, Harvey led the way and scouted the entire journey to Burleson County, Texas. At sixteen, after just six months of school in Caldwell, he entered old Baylor University at Independence as a junior. There he became a renowned debater aspiring to a legal career, but the war interrupted those plans—permanently.

Carroll debated persuasively against secession, but eventually his Southern loyalty caused him to enlist. In April 1861, only weeks before graduation,[5] he volunteered for McCullough's Rangers, the first regiment mustered into Confederate service. Soon double tragedy struck. In November, Harvey was summoned from the Texas frontier to visit his dying father. While on emergency leave, he fell in love with a fifteen-year-old Caldwell girl, and they were married December 13, 1861. However, she refused to return to West Texas with him, and during the next two years she made clear she had never loved him. The fact that a jury granted him a divorce because of her infidelity was no consolation to Harvey.[6] After this and his father's death, he lamented, "It blasted every hope and left me in Egyptian darkness. The battle of life was lost. In seeking the field of war, I sought death. . . . I had my church connection dissolved, and turned utterly away from every semblance of Bible belief. In the hour of my darkness I turned unreservedly to infidelity."[7]

Immediately, he enlisted in the Seventeenth Texas Infantry Regiment which was deploying to Arkansas and Louisiana. Carroll threw himself into the heat of every battle. At the battle of Mansfield (April 8, 1864), a huge "Minnie ball" grazed his femoral artery, and for weeks his life "hung upon a very brittle thread."[8] For him the war was over. While convalescing in Burleson County, he opened a school at Yellow Prairie and then moved it to Caldwell.[9]

In 1865, Reconstruction austerity crippled the skeptic with debt, and his confidence in secular philosophy evaporated on the blistering, drought-ridden Texas plains. As he desperately searched Scripture, Ecclesiastes and Job gripped him with "unearthly power": "and like Job, regarding God as my adversary, I cried out for a revelation."[10] Though he had vowed never again to enter church, that autumn his mother persuaded him to attend a Methodist camp meeting. The sermon left Carroll cold, but the closing appeal burned through his soul. The minister's exhortation "to make a practical, experiential test" of Christianity and his unique translation of John 7:17 opened Harvey's eyes: "The knowledge as to whether doctrine was of God depended not upon external action and not upon exact conformity with God's will, but upon the internal disposition—'whosoever willeth or wishes to do God's will.'"[11]

He mentally committed himself to the "experiment," but his heart still hesitated. After the meeting Carroll was overcome by a vision which accompanied his recollection of Jesus' invitation in Matthew 11:28. That evening Carroll became convinced that God was calling him to preach.[12] A few days later he was baptized by his former Baylor schoolmate, W. W. "Spurgeon" Harris, in Caldwell.[13] Dove Baptist Church confirmed Carroll's call by licensing and ordaining him in 1866.[14]

Soon Harvey began to court seventeen-year-old Ellen Virginia Bell, whose family had moved from Starkville, Mississippi. On December 28, 1866, Carroll's college president and friend, R. C. Burleson, married them at the Caldwell church. Still burdened with debt, during the next three years Carroll barely provided for his growing family[15] as a schoolteacher, supply preacher, itinerant evangelist, and part-time pastor of Post Oaks Church in Burleson County. Finally, after a failed farming venture, he determined to make it as a full-time minister. In the fall of 1869, he was called as pastor of New Hope Baptist Church at Goat Neck, McLennan County. His reputation as a preacher spread rapidly. Early in 1870, he agreed to preach twice monthly at nearby First Baptist Church of Waco in the absence of the interim pastor, Dr. Burleson. After a year that church called him as pastor, and he served there for twenty-eight years.

That year Orceneth Fisher, a highly reputed Methodist polemicist, was baiting Baptists from the pulpit of Fifth Street Methodist Church in Waco. Not to be intimidated, in April Carroll defeated Fisher at a well-publicized debate in Davilla. The *Texas Baptist Herald* printed accounts of this debate for the next eighteen months and made the young Waco pastor an instant Texas Baptist hero. Carroll gained notoriety throughout the Southern Baptist Convention.[16]

His growing reputation never equaled the man himself. He became one of those truly larger than life personalities who capture the attention of even casual observers. Strikingly handsome with his Moses-like beard, he was physically impressive. Standing six feet and four inches tall and weighing 250 pounds, his bearing was always erect and stately. His strong voice and persuasive oratorical style personified self-assurance. According to W. W. Barnes, he "considered himself as much the agent of God as did any of the Biblical characters, with his abilities directed by a conscious knowledge of the mind of God and led by the Spirit he was irresistible. He had much of the mystic in his conscious contact with the Divine."[17]

Above all B. H. Carroll was a great preacher and pastor. Comparing him with Chrysostom, George W. Truett described his former pastor as "the greatest preacher our State has ever known."[18] J. B. Cranfill claimed that his oratorical style equaled that of such giants as John Broadus, Henry Ward Beecher, William Jennings Bryan, and Woodrow Wilson.[19] But his real strengths were his practical teaching style and his biblical exposition.[20] His preaching influenced two generations of Baylor ministerial students, provided material for eighteen volumes of sermons, and laid the foundation for his exegetical summa, *An Interpretation of the English Bible*. Each week many pastors eagerly awaited the delivery of their Baptist newspapers in order to glean from his latest published sermons.

Carroll did the entire work of a pastor: he indoctrinated, oversaw discipline, and managed all special collections. He conducted his own annual revival meetings, and with great results: the 1893 meeting resulted in hundreds joining the Waco church and the spreading of revival to every church in the city.[21] In an age when most Baptists disregarded organization, he efficiently marshaled church resources. First Baptist became a great church-planting institution. At one time it provided half of the salaries of the Waco Association missionaries and one-third of all home, state, and foreign mission contributions in Texas. During his tenure the church added 2,325 members and became one of the largest in the state.[22] J. M. Dawson, a successor, attested to his indelible influence: "B. H. Carroll's pastoral work abides. . . . I have found his deep, abiding footprints everywhere about here. He hovers like a great, benign, inspiring spirit over us all."[23]

Carroll's ministry extended also to the social needs of Waco and Texas. During 1885–86, he led the McLennan County antiliquor forces to victory in a local option election. The following year he organized the state prohibition effort. During these campaigns he was a daunting opponent in debates against U.S. Senators Roger Q. Mills and Richard Coke and Governor L. S. Ross.[24] In 1894, he led the Waco ministers in opposing the Sunday opening of the Cotton Palace.[25] Neither pleas of economic necessity from his own members, nor Burleson's opposition,[26] nor personal threats could force his retreat.[27] He was ever a champion of civic righteousness. So powerful was his influence that one of his members, Governor Pat Neff, declared that Carroll lived vicariously in the governor's office during Neff's term.[28]

L. R. Scarborough's reference to Carroll as a "kingdom builder"[29] appropriately describes his denominational work. He served as chairman of several Waco Association committees and boards, the most important being his presidency of the mission board (1874–88 and 1889–92). For most of 1871–85, he was elected vice president of the Baptist General Association of Texas under Burleson's presidency. As chairman of a BGA special committee (1883), Carroll began consolidating Texas Baptist work. During the next three years he influenced Texas Baptists to form the Baptist General Convention of Texas (BGCT) and to unify their newspapers, Sunday School conventions, women's work, and their two largest universities.[30] In 1894, when the Texas mission board was disintegrating financially, Carroll took a three-month furlough, and, with George Truett's aid, raised over $7,000 to keep the board solvent.[31]

A conspicuous figure in Southern Baptist life, for thirty years Carroll preached at almost every annual meeting, and in 1878 he delivered the Convention sermon. Besides his extensive committee work, he was the Texas member of the Foreign Mission Board for years and a trustee of the Southern Baptist Theological Seminary (1894–1911). Denominational leaders relied on his advice at almost every critical juncture: hence, John R. Sampey's comment to him, "You are now—since Broadus is gone—our natural leader in the Southern Convention."[32] He convinced Texas Baptists to align with the Southern Home Mission Board (HMB) rather than with the Northern Home Mission Society, which promised greater financial aid. In 1888, his Convention address at Richmond persuaded messengers to give the HMB their vote of full confidence instead of dismantling it. Two years later at Fort Worth, his oratorical skills helped J. M. Frost convince the Convention to establish its own Sunday School Board. Likewise, in Chattanooga (1906), he turned the tide in favor of establishing a Department of Evangelism in the Home Mission Board.[33]

Carroll's strong denominational position often led him into troubled waters. The evangelist Matthew T. Martin, whose theology already had been challenged in the *Texas Baptist and Herald* (1884), joined Carroll's church in 1886 and used it as his base of operations. In 1889, when it became apparent that his teachings were truly heterodox and that he presented a threat to Texas Baptists, Carroll used his influence to lift Martin's credentials and temporarily to disfellowship the Marlin Church when it restored his ordination.[34]

Next came the Landmark attacks on Texas missions. From the moment T. P. Crawford launched his independent Gospel Mission Movement (1892), Carroll recognized its subversiveness. He used his furlough (1894) to rally statewide support behind the Foreign Mission Board, and Crawford's momentum in Texas stalled.[35] That year Samuel Hayden, editor of the *Texas Baptist and Herald* began attacking the state mission board. His subsequent confrontation with Carroll resulted in Hayden's expulsion from the BGCT (1897) and the formation of a rival organization, the Baptist Missionary Association (1900). Unfortunately, Carroll's close friend R. C. Burleson supported Hayden.[36]

Another controversy focused on William H. Whitsitt, professor of church history and president of Southern Seminary. Landmark sentiments were kindled against him in 1895 when he suggested his theory that American and English Baptists had not immersed prior to 1641. Though he disagreed with Whitsitt's "literary and historic criticism,"[37] Carroll avoided open confrontation until, as a trustee, he was pressured by his Texas constituency to take action. Advising restraint, he recommended that the trustees judiciously investigate the case at the Wilmington Convention (1897). When they glossed over the matter at that meeting, he believed his only alternative was to "go public" with the facts and to encourage renewed public discussion of the issue. From then he became identified as a leader of the anti-Whitsitt party which brought about the professor's resignation in 1898.[38]

Carroll said that his role in denominational controversy served one purpose: to promote unity. Facing Hayden in 1896, he exhorted Texas Baptists to affirm the purposes of their convention: harmony of feeling, concert of action, and a system of operative measures to promote missions.[39] He saw the real issue in the Whitsitt dispute as the threat of "breaking up of Southern unity, and the quite possible dismemberment of the convention."[40]

Carroll's most influential legacy was his gift of theological education. Though he never attended a seminary, he was a profound student of theology. A voracious reader, he read about three hundred pages a day for over fifty years.[41] He did not have a photographic memory, but he could remember virtually every pertinent fact he had ever read and was able to cite its reference with phenomenal accuracy. J. B. Gambrell described him as having "the most capacious mind I have met in my life. . . . He was an intellectual Colossus."[42] This was confirmed by his honorary degrees: M.A. from Baylor University, D.D. from the University of Tennessee, and LL.D. from Keatchie College, Louisiana.[43]

From his first days in Waco, he helped to educate other Baptist ministers. In 1871, he accepted the chairmanship of the General Association Committee for Schools and Education and began raising $30,000 for the endowment of Waco University.[44] Possibly as early as 1872, he assisted President Burleson in teaching ministerial students. They gathered in his study where he tutored them in the English Bible, J. M. Pendleton's *Church Manual,* and Robert's *Rules of Order.* Eventually this developed into a well-rounded theological course of the university curriculum.[45]

When Baylor University at Waco was chartered, Carroll was elected president of the trustees—a position he held for over twenty years (1887–1907). In 1891, he enlisted the help of George Truett to liquidate Baylor's debt. Within two years they raised the required $90,000, enabling the university to expand. When a Bible Department was formed (1894) and

Carroll was appointed to the Chair of Exegesis and Systematic Theology, he was in the unique position of working for the institution he governed. He also continued as pastor of First Baptist Church until shortly after his wife's death (1897). Just over a year later, his brother James prevailed upon him to resign the pastorate and to head the Texas Baptist Education Commission.[46] While in that office (1899–1902), he became the dean of the Bible Department and married one of his former parishioners, Hallie Harrison, the daughter of General Tom Harrison.[47]

Carroll's crowning achievement for theological education grew out of a vision he had in 1905 while traveling by train in the Panhandle of Texas. Believing Christ had commissioned him to establish a theological seminary in the Southwest, he immediately began to raise funds. In August he obtained the Baylor trustees' approval to constitute Baylor Theological Seminary and to start classes that fall. The faculty consisted of Carroll, A. H. Newman, L. W. Doolan, C. B. Williams, and Calvin Goodspeed. The state convention at San Antonio (1907) voted to separate the seminary from Baylor University, and it was chartered as Southwestern Baptist Theological Seminary in Waco on May 14, 1908. That year Carroll created the first Chair of Evangelism in any seminary. The "Chair of Fire," as he called it,[48]was filled by L. R. Scarborough. Finally, the seminary moved to Fort Worth, which had raised $100,000 for its support and provided a suitable site just south of the city: with a faculty of seven and 126 students, Carroll's dream was fulfilled when the doors of the new campus opened on Monday, October 3, 1910.[49]

B. H. Carroll died November 11, 1914, and was buried in Oakwood Cemetery, Waco, Texas. His deathbed commission to his successor, Scarborough, provides a succinct commentary on Carroll's theology:

> Lee, keep the Seminary lashed to the cross. If heresy ever
> comes in the teaching, take it to the faculty. If they will not hear
> you and take prompt action, take it to the trustees of the
> Seminary. If they will not hear you, take it to the Convention
> that appoints the Board of Trustees, and if they will not hear
> you, take it to the great common people of our churches. You
> will not fail to get a hearing then.[50]

Exposition

Carroll's concern for doctrinal purity was a driving force in his three ministerial roles. At the First Baptist Church of Waco, he used scriptural exposition to develop a biblical and pastoral theology. As a denominational leader, he employed sermons, editorials, addresses, debates, and private correspondence to propagate a biblical and confessional theology. Also employing a biblical and confessional approach in his teaching role, he used expository lectures, confessions, catechisms, and manuals as his instruments. He was essentially an expositor and polemicist with a biblical-pastoral theology who made little attempt to systematize doctrine. This exposition reconstructs Carroll's theology from his sermons, lectures, and addresses. For a more comprehensive view, it must be read in context with the New Hampshire Confession (revised 1853), which Carroll regularly employed.[51]

Revelation

Carroll acknowledged the traditional categories of general and special revelation. The first, the "revelation of wrath," was of two types: the influence of nature reveals God's providence, and intuitive light makes one cognizant of moral responsibility to God. Three forms comprise special revelation: unwritten, direct communication from God antedating Scripture; God's written Word; and the living Word, Jesus Christ. Though he called these "revelation from God," he also considered general revelation to be of divine origin.[52]

As a young skeptic, far from affirming scriptural authority, Carroll claimed to have detected almost one thousand apparent discrepancies in the Bible. But after conversion and diligent study, he resolved all except six "contradictions," which he attributed to his own limited comprehension of God's truth, not to any scriptural fallibility.[53] He held a high view of divine inspiration: God's infallible[54] and inerrant word[55] does not just contain the word of God; it *is* God's very word.[56] He taught verbal, plenary inspiration: every word, not just the idea, is inspired—even down to the vowel points![57] This applies to the whole Bible: it is not inspired just in certain spots,[58] nor are certain passages less inspired than others. Yet Carroll did not agree with some in his day who said that the entire text should be interpreted literally and that every passage was equally important. Though he conceded that only the originals were inspired, he believed that God had preserved the Bible "in a way that no other book has been preserved."[59]

He said Scripture has two purposes: to reveal salvation and to show Christians how to live.[60] Primacy must be given to the New Testament as the "Law of Christianity," which is God's fulfilled revelation. So Carroll refused to use the Old Testament as a model for Christian ethics or institutions.[61] He affirmed the perspicuity of Scripture: the unfettered, open Book is sufficiently clear to instruct all believers. Thus, he exhorted students, "The Book is open—who of you will read it?"[62] Carroll stood on four hermeneutical principles: (1) Since "the Bible is its own interpreter," view difficult passages in conformity with less ambiguous Scriptures; (2) appropriate biblical truths with faith and obedience in order to fulfill their practical purposes; (3) assurance of right interpretation comes through a maturing relationship with the Lord; (4) reverently appeal to the Holy

Spirit for right understanding and application. While asserting that spiritually illuminated individuals should be able to interpret Scripture correctly and make competent decisions, he rejected exclusive, private interpretation.[63] Nor was Carroll a pure biblicist. For the sake of identity, unity, and doctrinal strength, he encouraged the use of covenants and confessions.[64]

The True God

The primary antecedent for all theology and morality is the fact that "God is."[65] Carroll explains this in Trinitarian terms. God is revealed in "three subsistencies," the essence (nature) of which is eternally immanent. This unified Godhead is "the key to every doctrine in the Bible." The distinction in the Trinity is between the persons, who, though equal in divine perfection, have different offices. Regarding office and personal relationships, the Holy Spirit is subordinate to the Son, as the Son is to the Father. He affirmed the "filioque clause" as the true relation of the Holy Spirit to the Father and the Son.[66] The Trinitarian idea is objective truth which is best appropriated by faith in Scripture: rationalistic, psychological explanations by themselves, being too subjective, inevitably yield erroneous doctrine.[67]

Regarding creation, Carroll affirmed that the Trinity made the universe from nothing. Though this was not done in a literal week, each day of creative activity was twenty-four hours long.[68] He accepted Archbishop Ussher's dating of the start of the human race at 4004 B.C. He opposed Darwinian evolutionism, but he accepted development within the species as biblical.[69]

Carroll described God's providence as his "direction, control and issue of all the events in the physical and moral universe." It goes beyond foreknowledge; God guides everything in order to accomplish his purpose without impinging on the freedom of moral creatures. Whatever God wills is best, for that will is an extension of himself, who is the ultimate good.[70] He manifests this will in four ways: through preventive, permissive, directive, and determinative providence. Able to prevent evil, sometimes he permits it by withholding his preventive force. He directs/diverts evil actions, so as to frustrate sinners' intentions; and he determines boundaries which evil cannot transcend.[71] In all cases God's will is never frustrated.[72] For each person he has a plan, and one's vision of this provides motivation for right action.[73] Man's response to divine providence should be humble, penitent prayer, whereby he discovers God's will on the "zig-zag" road leading to "his destiny on earth and in Heaven."[74]

Concerning the Son, Carroll disagreed with his friend W. C. Buck. Both maintained that the seed of life, as well as sin, comes from the male, not the female. They also agreed that Jesus, being of the Holy Spirit, did not inherit Adam's sin. However, while this led Buck to affirm the Apollinarian idea that Christ did not have a human soul, Carroll followed Broadus's lead in rejecting that heresy. Yet this does not square with his traducianist anthropology, discussed below.[75] Unlike William Shedd, who distinguished Christ's humanity from his divinity by saying that the Logos exercised limited influence on his body and soul, Carroll argued that the Spirit controlled Jesus' entire being.[76] He emphasized the atonement to such a degree that he ascribed a fourth role to Christ: to prophet, priest, and king he added the "sacrifice."[77]

Carroll described the Holy Spirit's coming in two ways. First, at Pentecost, the Spirit came to "occupy" the existing church and to "accredit" it through miraculous signs. That "baptism of the Spirit" was for the whole church, not just individuals; it was for a limited time, though the "graces" of faith, hope, and love continued. Second, the Paraclete, or the "other Jesus" involved in every phase of salvation, came as the "vicar of Christ" with absolute sovereignty over his kingdom. Thus, Carroll exhorted Christians individually to receive the Holy Spirit: not as part of "regenerating grace," this is "a blessing of God entirely distinct from and subsequent to . . . repentance and . . . faith."[78]

Anthropology

Repudiating Darwinianism as a heathen doctrine, Carroll described its Christian advocates as "neither fish not fowl, neither pig not puppy."[79] Scriptural creationism and Darwin were irreconcilable: "There is no ground of compromise. . . . The variance is radical, fundamental and vital. Both cannot be true and a mixture is less desirable than either."[80] Christian evolutionists such as Henry Ward Beecher reversed Scripture by saying the higher that man ascends, the more he needs God. Carroll said man needs salvation precisely because he has fallen away from God.[81]

The unity of humanity undergirds the plan of redemption: since all have descended from Adam, for whose descendants the gospel was sent, then to all the gospel must be proclaimed.[82] Rejecting the hyper-Calvinism of Daniel Parker, Carroll argued that the human race had not been divided into the "two seeds" of Eve. Parker's idea opposed Carroll's belief that Adam, not Eve, was ultimately culpable in the Fall. Also, "two-seedism" undercut the plan of redemption by withholding the gospel from the non-elect.[83]

Carroll said that Adam was created physically mortal but with a provision for eliminating mortality "by continually eating of the tree of life."[84] Man is not a trichotomy. He is body (outer man) and soul (inner man): a dichotomous, yet unified, being. Carroll used the term "spirit," only to distinguish the higher (inner) from the lower (outer, body/soul) nature—thus he is still a dichotomy.[85]

Carroll believed the Fall was a historic event through which Adam became totally depraved; he lost the moral image of God but kept a deathless spirit.[86] Adam, the federal head, has conveyed "original sin" to all persons, who inherit their souls (traducianism) from male issuance, not from female conception. Carroll said that Christ, who had a human soul, did not inherit a depraved nature from an earthly father.[87] But the obvious problem remains unresolved: if the human soul is inherited through the male line, where did Christ get his human soul?

In one sense, Carroll noted, human sin is corporate. Angels are the only beings who sin only individually (i.e., apart from the federal head). Man's sin is also intensely personal, and individuals will be held accountable for their own actions.[88] Still, original sin alone is sufficient to condemn if Christ's grace is not operative; hence, dying infants must be, and by God's grace will be, regenerated.[89] With original sin comes the condemnation of death; with actual sin comes the condemnation of guilt.[90]

Satan is a personal being who, though limited in power, is incomparably stronger than man.[91] His motive for tempting Adam and Eve, Carroll reasoned, was to destroy the new race which had been created to have dominion over the angels.[92] Regarding adversity, Carroll said that temptation comes from Satan, while trials come from God, but often it is difficult to differentiate the two.[93]

Soteriology

Carroll distinguished between the legal (external) and the spiritual (internal) requirements for salvation. He used two formulas to explain this. First, the legal need is fulfilled by redemption, which is two-sided: having (1) made atonement, Christ (2) offers justification. Justification outwardly provides remission of sins; it inwardly expiates guilt. Second, the spiritual need, encompassing regeneration and sanctification, is fulfilled when divine grace evokes human response. The legal and the spiritual requirements meet with the intersection of divine remission and human trust.

Four elements comprise Carroll's soteriological scheme: redemption, atonement, justification, and adoption. Redemption, the buying back of the sinner, is achieved through the atonement and is applied through regeneration. In redemption the legal and the spiritual operations of salvation meet.[94] Christ's atonement was sacrificial, voluntary, vicarious, penal, and satisfactory.[95] It occurred in two stages. Christ paid an expiatory sacrifice to purge sin and to conquer Satan,[96] then He made propitiation before the Father, who reconciled sinners to himself through the Son's blood.[97] The external application of the atonement is justification. The moment a sinner believes in Christ, he is instantly pronounced just by the Father and his sins are remitted; this is forensic justification.[98] The proclamatory imputation of Christ's righteousness does not mean the sinner is "made" personally righteous; that is done in the spiritual operation of salvation.[99] Carroll distinguished between expiation and justification. Apparently opposing antinomianism, he emphasized that sin also must be *actually* remitted: the cross made the provision, but the fact is not accomplished until the individual believes.[100] He distinguished between justification and pardon: "Justification comes from God's justice; pardon comes from his mercy." Justification is accomplished by payment of the debt, but the debt is still owed to the payee. Pardon results when the payee cancels the debt.[101] Justification, being irrevocable,[102] lays the foundation for adoption. Entry into God's family comes only with belief, but God had foreordained it in eternity.[103]

The spiritual fruit of salvation comes by regeneration and sanctification. Regeneration involves both human and divine action. God acts in two stages: He gives a "holy disposition" to the mind and then purges the defilement.[104] Cleansing begins at the point of belief, when remittance of sin, the legal product of justification, is applied. Cleansing continues throughout life. Preparatory to this, the "holy disposition" comes through divine conviction and prevenient grace. Man, formerly passive, awakens and responds; conviction brings contrition, and grace brings action. The order of action is prayer, repentance, confession, conversion, and faith. As God's grace meets man's response, new birth occurs.[105] This is not a multistage regeneration. Against M. T. Martin, Carroll strongly repudiated regeneration as a "two-stage" process.[106] Instead, it is a single process which allows an "appreciable time element between the several exercises."[107]

Each human "exercise" is a response to divine prompting. Contrition, the response to conviction, is godly sorrow which is the point of no return: once the sinner experiences this, God's irresistible grace will draw him to faith.[108] Repentance is the "change of mind toward God on account of sin."[109] Carroll realized that "conversion" is popularly equated with completed regeneration (i.e., to be "saved"). However, he defined it as "right about face," an action which *precedes* faith. Faith, which means "receiving and relying on Him," is the culminating human response in regeneration. Here justification and regeneration, legal and spiritual salvation, intersect.[110]

Sanctification is the other spiritual part of salvation. Regarding it as inseparable from regeneration,[111] Carroll repudiated John Wesley's idea of "second blessing."[112] Going beyond imputed righteousness, sanctification is the process of making the believer *personally* holy. It begins with regeneration and continues until death.[113] Here the contrast between the legal and spiritual aspects of salvation is sharp. Justification is the forensic pronouncement by the Father which is done in heaven and certified on earth. Sanctification is the Holy Spirit making the believer actually holy; it is done on earth and certified in heaven. Justification is instantaneous and external. Sanctification is progressive and internal.[114]

Ecclesiology

Carroll rejected any concept of a universal church, whether visible or invisible. The church is neither parochial nor a denominational composite of local bodies. He defined it as the spiritual, visible, local assembly of believers who are called out of their homes to organize an autonomous, non-hierarchical, democratic body. Members are admitted through baptism and upon their confession, which give evidence of regeneration.[115] The church is not the kingdom of God. The kingdom is more comprehensive, and the church is an institution within the kingdom.[116] The purpose of the church is to fulfill Christ's mandates. Therefore, as the executive branch of his kingdom, it is first a missionary organization.[117] As the judicial arm, it maintains spiritual discipline.[118] This current, particular church is different from the "glory church," which will become a reality only when all the redeemed have been glorified.[119]

The two ordinances are the ceremonial aspects of salvation: baptism symbolizes regeneration; the Lord's Supper represents sanctification.[120] For baptism to be valid, four requirements must be met: (1) the proper authority, the church, administers it; (2) the proper subject is the penitent believer; (3) the proper act is immersion; and (4) the proper design is symbolic, with no trace of baptismal regeneration. Salvation precedes baptism, not vice versa. Though time may be allowed between the two events for catechizing, baptism is still a prerequisite for communion. Allowing no "alien baptism," Carroll accepted only members baptized in a Baptist church.[121] At the Lord's Supper he emphasized commemoration more than fellowship. Yet he practiced "close communion," even to the point of forbidding communicants to sit with nonparticipants during the ceremony. Unlike Landmarkers, Carroll allowed Baptists from other churches to commune in Waco.[122]

The pastor and the deacons are the ordained officers of the church. Other unordained officers such as the clerk and the sexton may be employed. The deacons are not a ministerial order, a board of directors, a disciplinary body, or a pulpit committee. Their purpose is to assist the chief officer, the pastor, so that he has more time for ministerial functions. The deaconess is also a legitimate office, but she is not to be ordained; neither is a woman to be a pastor, to pray in open assembly, or to teach in a position of authority over men.[123]

Under Christ as its head, the church is an autocracy. Its human government is a pure democracy, with all members being equal and sharing in autonomous rule. However, this does not mean the church can do anything it desires with majority approval. Inasmuch as it is still subject to the law of Christ, Carroll agreed with J. R. Graves: "Principles, not majorities, constitute a church."[124]

Much of Carroll's ecclesiology resembled Landmarkism. He praised J. M. Pendleton, J. R. Graves, and A. C. Dayton as "the great Baptist trio of the South," and he used Pendleton's *Church Manual* as his text for ecclesiology lectures.[125] Carroll's definition of the church as a particular assembly and his rejection of the universal church are Landmark tenets. Though admitting it was impossible to verify, he believed in a succession of true churches since the apostolic era. He suggested these were Baptist churches and that John was the "first Baptist."[126] However, his disagreement with Whitsitt was not prompted by a strong advocacy of successionism. Furthermore, Carroll staunchly opposed Landmarkers like Crawford and Hayden because they threatened Baptist solidarity and the viability of organized missions. Certain of his practices opposed Landmarkism. He encouraged associational discipline and cooperation. His "close communion" was less restrictive, and he refused to equate the local churches with the kingdom of God.

Eschatology[127]

Carroll greatly emphasized this doctrine, especially the millennium. What seemed insignificant to others, he described as fundamental to all interpretation. He was a postmillennialist who said his position, being found in virtually every major Christian creed, represented the majority of Christendom. Though he respected certain premillennialists such as C. H. Spurgeon, D. L. Moody, A. J. Gordon, and J. R. Graves, he described their eschatology as dogmatic, complicated, stereotypical, and shallow. On the other hand he opposed radical critics intent on minimizing the supernatural, prophetic element in the Book of Revelation. By his silence on the subject, Carroll disregarded amillennialism altogether.[128]

Carroll described postmillennialism as being remarkably simple. In heaven Christ reigns over his mediatorial kingdom and intercedes as High Priest. His vicar, the Holy Spirit, applies salvation through preaching of the gospel by the churches. In the future the millennium will be ushered in by the triumph of the gospel: Satan will be bound; the Jews will be converted in a day; a mighty outpouring of the Spirit will occur; and there will be universal peace and prosperity. This will conclude with the loosing of Satan, who, as the Antichrist will oppress Christians briefly. Then Christ will return victoriously with one general resurrection of the just and the unjust; judgment, with degrees of reward and punishment pronounced from the great white throne; and the purging of wickedness from the world by a baptism of fire. Finally, the saints will inherit the new earth, and Christ will return the kingdom to the Father.[129] This scheme undergirds Carroll's soteriology and ecclesiology. Progressive sanctification points to the consummation of the kingdom.[130] Societal transformation and the reign of peace depend on the church fulfilling its missionary purpose—preaching the gospel.[131] He said premillennialism practically relegated the gospel to failure and undercut the motivation for missions.[132] Conversely, he criticized postmillennialists who deemphasized the Parousia. He avoided this error by teaching the "personal, real, visible, audible, palpable, tangible coming of the Lord Jesus Christ."[133]

Evaluation

"President Carroll, Bible in hand, standardized orthodoxy in Texas. He rallied the hosts of Baptists to the vital, ruling doctrines of the Holy Scriptures."[134] Thus J. B. Gambrell identified a common thread in Carroll's roles as pastor, denominational leader, and Christian educator. In each area he championed Christian truth and Baptist unity, faith, and practice. Like Irenaeus he was a pastor-polemicist who developed a strong, biblical theology to defeat heresy and schism. His doctrine of revelation developed in reaction to Christian modernists.[135] He developed soteriological responses to Martinism, the Methodist "second blessing," and Campbellite views on regeneration.[136] The antimissionism of Campbell and Daniel Parker evoked strong ecclesiological statements from Carroll,[137] as did the Whitsitt, Hayden, and Crawford controversies. Christian Science doctrine was targeted in his writings on pneumatology,[138] and his entire hermeneutical scheme was at variance with that of the premillennialists.[139]

Carroll's theology was influenced most by other conservative Baptists, especially Boyce, Strong, Spurgeon, and Broadus, whose catechism he recommended highly.[140] To say that he was a conservative evangelical is not adequate. Though the term was not yet in vogue, he could be described as a "Fundamentalist." His doctrine agreed with the basic tenets of *The Fundamentals* (1910–15), and he thoroughly disdained modernists as "cuckoos of infidelity." This antipathy was directed against Northern liberals when he encouraged a group of fundamentalist Illinois Baptists to seek admission to the SBC (1910). Led by Landmarker, W. P. Throgmorton, they had intended to align with Ben Bogard, a sympathizer with Carroll's nemesis, Samuel Hayden. In spite of strong resistance from some Southern Baptists, they were admitted partly because of Carroll's support.[141] The influence of Graves, Pendleton, and Dayton still embraced Carroll. Of "Landmarkish" convictions he imbibed their ultraconservatism and much of their ecclesiology, but he could never abide their fissiparous spirit, especially regarding missions.

Carroll was a Calvinist in line with the moderate tone of the New Hampshire Confession. He said man, as totally depraved, has lost God's moral image but retains a "deathless spirit."[142] He held a supralapsarian view of single election: from eternity God unconditionally elected some for salvation. The nonelect were not chosen for reprobation; they simply have not been given grace sufficient for salvation. The human race was never divided into two irrevocably predetermined lots.[143] On limited atonement Carroll was not rigid: Christ's death is certainly effective for the elect, and though he died for all, everyone will not be saved.[144] He made allowance for those who had not heard the gospel by stating that at the final judgment, "each man is judged according to his light, privileges, opportunities, and environment . . . [and] one's attitude toward Christ in his gospel, his cause and his people."[145] The irresistibility of God's grace operates from the moment of contrition to bring the sinner to salvation.[146] Believers will surely persevere, and though assurance is not required for salvation, it is ascertainable.[147] This scheme eschewed any hint of antinomianism or hyper-Calvinism.[148]

J. W. Crowder described Carroll's written works as "a fine, juicy, comprehensive, Systematic Theology."[149] But Carroll systematized very little. Of the works published during his lifetime, all except two are on miscellaneous topics. Only *Baptists and their Doctrines* and *The Bible Doctrine of Repentance* resemble systematic studies. The nearest Carroll's work came to being "systematized" was through the editing of Crowder and J. B. Cranfill. They published 248 sermons by subject in eighteen volumes: these contain the essence of Carroll's pastoral theology. Their publication of his exegetical lectures in *An Interpretation of the English Bible* made his biblical theology available. Most of the truly systematic work is contained in the typewritten manuscripts edited by Crowder. These reveal that Carroll's main theological interests were ecclesiology, soteriology, eschatology, and revelation.

Carroll's great strength as a theologian was his conviction that "doctrine must be so received by faith and assimilated by obedience as to become experimental knowledge. 'Whosoever willeth to do the will of God shall know of the doctrine whether it be of God.'" This was the Methodist revivalist's text from thirty-seven years before. Since that time Carroll had remained true to "experiential" religion and had urged his church members to do the same:

> Hence the prayer that the eyes of their understanding might
> be open to see the fullness [of God], their faith increased to grasp
> and appropriate it, their graces enlarged to corresponding
> strength to stand and work in that fullness. So fulfilled they real-
> ize in *experience* the fact that the Holy Spirit in all the fullness of
> God had already entered this particular body of Christ, and was
> only waiting to be recognized.[150]

W. T. Conner said the two ideals that controlled Carroll's life were "an authoritative Bible and the reality of Christian experience."[151] This completes the picture. For Carroll theology was a practical tool for edifying and equipping the church. His basis was the Bible, which shows, "first, how to be saved, and second, what saved people should believe and do."[152] From it he formulated a biblical-pastoral theology of practical value which called the church to evangelism and ethical responsibility.

Bibliography

Works by Carroll

Ambitious Dreams of Youth. Compiled by J. W. Crowder and edited by J. B. Cranfill. Dallas: Helms Printing Co., 1939.

Baptists and Their Doctrines. Compiled by J. B. Cranfill. New York: Fleming H. Revell Co., 1913. New edition compiled by Timothy George. Library of Baptist Classics. Nashville: Broadman and Holman, 1995.

The Bible Doctrine of Repentance. Louisville: Baptist Book Concern, 1897.

Christ and His Church. Compiled by J. W. Crowder and edited by J. B. Cranfill. Dallas: Helms Printing Co., 1940.

Christian Education and Some Social Problems, Sermons. Compiled and edited by J. W. Crowder. Ft. Worth: n.p., 1948.

Christ's Marching Orders. Compiled by J. W. Crowder and edited by J. B. Cranfill. Dallas: Helms Printing Co., 1941.

The Day of the Lord. Compiled by J. W. Crowder and edited by J. B. Cranfill. Nashville: Broadman Press, 1936.

Evangelistic Sermons. Compiled by J. B. Cranfill. New York: Fleming H. Revell Co., 1913.

The Faith that Saves. Compiled by J. W. Crowder and edited by J. B. Cranfill. Dallas: Helms Printing Co., 1939.

The Holy Spirit. Compiled by J. W. Crowder and edited by J. B. Cranfill. Grand Rapids, Mich.: Zondervan Publishing House, 1939.

Inspiration of the Bible. Compiled and edited by J. B. Cranfill. New York: Fleming H. Revell Co., 1930.

An Interpretation of the English Bible. 17 vols. Edited by J. B. Cranfill and J. W. Crowder. New York: Fleming H. Revell; Nashville: Broadman Press, 1913–48.

Jesus the Christ. Compiled by J. W. Crowder and edited by J. B. Cranfill. Nashville: Baird-Ward Press, 1937.

Messages on Prayer. Compiled by J. W. Crowder and edited by J. B. Cranfill. Nashville: Broadman Press, 1942.

Patriotism and Prohibition. Compiled and edited J. W. Crowder. Ft. Worth: n.p., 1952.

The Providence of God. Compiled by J. W. Crowder and edited by J. B. Cranfill. Dallas: Helms Printing Co., 1940.

Revival Messages. Compiled by J. W. Crowder and edited by J. B. Cranfill. Grand Rapids, Mich.: Zondervan Publishing House, 1939.

The River of Life and Other Sermons. Compiled and edited by J. B. Cranfill. Nashville: The Sunday School Board of the S.B.C., 1928.

Saved to Serve. Compiled by J. W. Crowder and edited by J. B. Cranfill. Dallas: Helms Printing Co., 1941.

Sermons and Life Sketch of B. H. Carroll. Compiled by J. B. Cranfill. Philadelphia: American Baptist Publication Society, 1893.

Studies in Genesis. Nashville: Broadman Press, 1937.

Studies in Romans. Nashville: The Sunday School Board of the S.B.C., 1935.

Studies in Romans, Ephesians, and Colossians. B. H. Carroll and E. Y. Mullins. Nashville: Broadman Press, 1936.

The Supper and Suffering of Our Lord. Compiled and edited by J. W. Crowder. Ft. Worth: n.p., 1947.

The Ten Commandments. Nashville: Broadman Press, 1938.

The Way of the Cross. Compiled by J. W. Crowder, edited by J. B. Cranfill. Dallas: Helms Printing Co., 1941.

Works about Carroll

Baker, Robert A. Tell the Generations Following. A History of Southwestern Baptist Theological Seminary, 1908–1983. Nashville: Broadman Press, 1983.

Cates, J. Dee. "B. H. Carroll: The Man and His Ethics." Th.D. diss., Southwestern Baptist Theological Seminary, 1962.

Cogburn, Keith Lynn. "B. H. Carroll and Controversy: A Study of His Leadership among Texas Baptists, 1871–1899." M.A. thesis, Baylor University, 1983.

Crowder, J. W., comp. and ed. *Dr. B. H. Carroll, the Colossus of Baptist History.* Fort Worth: By the editor, 1946.

Lefever, Alan J. Fighting the Good Fight: The Life and Work of Benajah Harvey Carroll. Austin, Tx.: Eakin Press, 1994.

Ray, Jeff. B. H. Carroll. Nashville: The Sunday School Board of the S.B.C., 1927.

Robinson, Robert Jackson. "The Homiletical Method of Benajah Harvey Carroll." Th.D. diss., Southwestern Baptist Theological Seminary, 1956.

Segler, Franklin M. "B.H. Carroll: Model for Ministers," Southwestern Journal of Theology. 25 No 2 (Spring 1983), 4–23.

Stewart, Wilson Lannin. "Ecclesia: The Motif of B. H. Carroll's Theology." Th.D. diss., Southwestern Baptist Theological Seminary, 1959.

Watson, Tom L. "The Eschatology of B. H. Carroll." M.Th. thesis, Southwestern Baptist Theological Seminary, 1960.

10
Edgar Young Mullins

By Fisher Humphreys

Biography

EDGAR YOUNG MULLINS WAS BORN IN FRANKLIN COUNTY, MISSISSIPPI, on January 5, 1860.[1] He was the fourth child and the first son of Seth Granberry Mullins and Cornelia Mullins. The senior Mullins was a farmer, a teacher, and a Baptist minister; he and his wife dedicated their newborn son to the Christian ministry, a commitment about which the son was told for the first time on his thirty-fifth birthday, after he had served as a minister for ten years.[2]

Shortly after General William T. Sherman's siege of nearby Vicksburg in 1863, S. G. Mullins moved his family to Copiah County in Mississippi, which was less directly affected by the war.[3] In 1869, the family moved to Corsicana, Texas, a frontier town, where Reverend Mullins established a school and a church, now the First Baptist Church of Corsicana.[4] He was a graduate of Mississippi College, and he encouraged his children to go to college. Edgar, at age fifteen, took a responsible position as a telegrapher for the Associated Press to contribute to the college expenses of his older sisters.[5] He was a member of the first class to enter Texas A & M in 1876, and he completed his basic college work there in 1879, continuing his work as a telegrapher during his college years.

E. Y. Mullins was preparing for a career in law. He had not yet made a profession of faith in Christ. He was converted at a revival meeting in Dallas and was baptized by his father in Corsicana at the age of twenty. He soon felt called to the Christian ministry, and he entered the Southern Baptist Theological Seminary in Louisville, Kentucky, in 1881. The trauma of the war, the fact that he had a strong family life, the quasimilitary discipline of Texas A & M, and his years of working as a telegrapher combined to give Mullins a maturity beyond his years. He was elected by the student body to act as manager of the dormitory, Waverly Hall, a position he held until he completed the full course of work and graduated in 1885.

Mullins had intended to become a missionary, but his doctor advised against it. After graduation he accepted the position of pastor of the Harrodsburg Baptist Church in Harrodsburg, Kentucky. In 1886, he married Isla May Hawley. Mrs. Mullins later described her husband's appearance at this time as follows: "a slender, graceful figure of six feet, two inches, very erect . . . an abundant shock of very dark hair . . . a beard of soft fineness which was then attractive and added much to his look of maturity."[6] The Mullinses eventually had two children, both sons, both of whom died young.

In 1888, Mullins went to Baltimore as pastor of the Lee Street Baptist Church, where he remained for seven years. He resigned from that position and worked for a few months for the Foreign Mission Board of the Southern Baptist Convention in Richmond, Virginia. In 1895, he accepted the pastorate of the Baptist church in Newton Centre, Massachusetts, adjacent to Boston. Movement between churches affiliated with the Baptist conventions of the North and South was not as rare then as it later became.

In 1899, Mullins became president of the Southern Baptist Theological Seminary in Louisville. He held this position until his death in 1928. He was also professor of theology during this entire period. During his presidency the seminary experienced dramatic growth in its endowments and in the size of its faculty and student body. It moved from a downtown location to a fifty-eight-acre campus known as "The Beeches." The seminary also began publication of *The Review and Expositor* under Mullins's leadership, and Mullins contributed many articles and reviews to it over the years.

From his position as president of the seminary, Mullins exerted great influence on Baptist and public life. William E. Ellis says that Mullins acted as a kind of liaison between Baptists of the North and South. He also bridged other gaps. For example, he was asked by the organizers of the Federal Council of Churches to help bring the Southern Baptist Convention into the new organization.[7] In 1904, the Southern Baptist Convention rejected an invitation to join the Council and enthusiastically accepted an invitation to participate in the nascent Baptist World Alliance.[8] Following World War I, Mullins and other leaders went to Europe to bring Baptists there greetings from the Southern Baptist Convention and to arrange for help for European Baptists who were suffering from the war and its aftermath. Mullins was president of the Southern Baptist Convention from 1921 to 1924 and president of the Baptist World Alliance from 1923 to 1928.[9] In 1923, the city of Louisville proclaimed an "E. Y. Mullins Day." The extent of Mullins's influence in Baptist life and public life may be gauged by reviewing the outpouring of appreciation for him when he died in 1928.[10] W. O. Carver described him as "the best known Baptist in the world" and said that he was "unsurpassed in influence for good by any man in his denomination."[11]

Exposition

Theological Issues

The three decades during which Mullins exercised great influence in Baptist life were turbulent ones. Mullins responded to a series of three theological issues which were polarizing Baptists.

First, the school to which he came as president in 1899 was of "a tenacious theological type,"[12] because of the Calvinism of its founder, James P. Boyce. Mullins continued to use Boyce's *Abstract of Systematic Theology* (1887) as a textbook in his theology classes for several years. But he also used other books, and his own book, *The Christian Religion in Its Doctrinal Expression*, became the textbook after its publication in 1917.[13] In the preface to *The Christian Religion in Its Doctrinal Expression,* a book dedicated to the memory of Boyce, Mullins positioned himself as follows:

> For example, Arminianism overlooked certain essential truths about God in its strong championship of human freedom. As against it, Calvinism ran to extremes in some of its

conclusions in its very earnest desire to safeguard the truth of God's sovereignty. We are learning to discard both names and to adhere more closely to the Scriptures, while retaining the truth in both systems.[14]

Mullins consciously adopted a moderate position toward the Calvinist-Arminian polarity and also toward other polarities. He wrote:

As usual the extreme parties are doing most of the harm. On one side is the ultra-conservative, the man of the hammer and anvil method, who relies chiefly upon denunciation of opponents, and who cannot tolerate discussion on a fraternal basis; on the other is the ultra-progressive whose lofty contempt of the "traditionalist" shuts him out from the ranks of sane scholarship and wise leadership. The really safe leaders of thought, however, are between these extremes.[15]

Mullins's consciously adopted moderation has been noticed by those who study him,[16] and it has been variously evaluated. Russell H. Dilday Jr. praises Mullins for it and sees it as a good pattern for leaders today.[17] William E. Ellis seems to feel that, in the end, it was a position which was defeated.

After 1925 he lost ground not only among his coreligionists but with other theists as well. Assailed on the right by fundamentalists within his own denomination and abandoned on the left by modernists who no longer had much patience with moderate evangelicals, Mullins was tormented by a loss of prestige and position in his last years.[18]

Mullins's moderation did not prevail on every issue, but his moderate Calvinism did, in fact, prevail in Southern Baptist life.

A second theological issue which Mullins faced was the Landmark Baptist interpretation of Baptist history. Landmark Baptists believed that local congregations of baptized believers are the only ecclesiastical organizations which are authorized by the New Testament. They further held that a succession of such congregations has existed from the first century to Baptists today, a line which includes Montanists, Donatists, Waldenses, and others. William Heth Whitsitt, a church historian and Mullins's immediate predecessor as president of the Southern Baptist Theological Seminary, had written a book entitled *A Question in Baptist History* (1896) in which he said that believer's baptism by immersion cannot be shown on historical grounds to have existed prior to the seventeenth century in England.[19] Landmark Baptists' dismay at Whitsitt's conclusions led the trustees of the seminary to accept his resignation in 1899.

Mullins's handling of the Landmark concerns was conciliatory and diplomatic. He could refer to the same line of tradition that the Landmark Baptists did,[20] but "ultimately he rested the issue with historical scholarship."[21] Perhaps most interesting of all, he wrote little about the doctrine of the church himself. For example, he did not include a chapter on the church in his systematic theology, *The Christian Religion in Its Doctrinal Expression.* He wrote: "Our present purpose does not contemplate a discussion of either church or kingdom in any of the controverted aspects of these great themes."[22] The basic reason seems to have been that the curriculum at the seminary was arranged so that systematic theology was a separate course from pastoral work, and ecclesiology was included with the latter.[23] This arrangement had been inherited by seminaries such as Princeton and Union in New York, from the German theological encyclopedia in which theological education comprised four parts: biblical, historical, theological, and practical.[24] When Mullins began to teach theology in 1899, the ecclesiology-pastoral work course was being taught by Edwin C. Dargan, who used as a textbook his own book, *Ecclesiology: A Study of the Church* (1897).

The third theological polarity which Mullins faced was the Fundamentalist-Modernist controversy. This controversy centered around a cluster of issues involving the implications of the critical study of history for the history reported in the Bible, of the natural sciences for the miracles reported in the Bible, and of evolution for the creation stories recorded in the Bible. One or more of these questions was on the theological agenda throughout the three decades of Mullins's teaching career. In each case, what was threatened was the Bible and the church's understanding of it; and in each case the threat came from the critical consciousness which had arisen in the Western world in the seventeenth century (science) and in the eighteenth century (history). As he did with Calvinism, once again he took a moderate stance; he adopted a position that resisted naturalistic reductions of Christian faith and the obscurantist rejection of the legitimate claims of history or science.

These polarities were all imposed on Mullins by circumstances in his denomination and world. They do not necessarily represent his own deepest concerns. To those concerns, and to the theology which he constructed, we now turn.

Writings

The faculty of the Southern Baptist Theological Seminary wrote a memorial of Mullins shortly after his death. In it they listed six of his books, with the comment: "These are not all of the books he wrote, but they show the ripeness and profoundness of scholarship that signalized his intellectual life."[25] The six are: *Why Is Christianity True?* (1905), *The Axioms of*

Religion (1908), *Baptist Beliefs* (1912), *Freedom and Authority in Religion* (1913), *The Christian Religion in Its Doctrinal Expression* (1917), and *Christianity at the Cross Roads* (1924).

Why Is Christianity True? would today be called Christian apologetics. Written in four parts, it is a cumulative case for the truth of Christian faith and beliefs. First, Mullins demonstrates the superiority of theism as an explanatory hypothesis for our universe to five alternative hypotheses: pantheism, idealism, materialism, agnosticism, and evolution. Next, Mullins presents Christ as the essence of Christianity and says that the Bible portrays Christ as a divine Savior as well as a great Teacher and that he rose from the dead. Third, Mullins argues that the Christian experience of regeneration, including the moral transformation of life, verifies this New Testament portrait. Finally, Mullins argues "pragmatically" that Christianity has proved itself to be powerful and true through nineteen centuries of history. He also touches briefly on two other religions, Islam and Buddhism, finding that they both contain some truth but also they both are very inferior to Christianity.

Many of Mullins's great concerns are evident in this early book. He is an apologist who defends what will later be called "mere Christianity" or "plain Christianity" or "basic Christianity," against unbelief and disbelief on its left and other religions on its right.[26] He insists that science and religion are separate disciplines using separate methods to deal with separate facts. Christian experience is indispensable not only for Christian theology but also for Christian faith. While Mullins benefited greatly from the studies of religious experience by William James and others, and from the importance given to experience in the theology of F. D. E. Schleiermacher, his own mind turned naturally and consistently to the experience of conversion as preached and emphasized in churches influenced by revivalism. Mullins assumed that persons and personal life are appropriate and adequate categories for speaking of God and of human beings. Mullins was eloquent about Christian missions and evangelism, seeing their successes as indications of the truthfulness of their message, and he was optimistic about their future.

It is interesting to compare *Why Is Christianity True?* to a recent work of Christian apologetics, *On Being a Christian,* by the Roman Catholic Hans Küng. Both make Christ the center of Christianity, and both say that its truthfulness stands or falls with Christ. Both respond to unbelief on the left and to other religions on the right. Both accept a critical reading of the Gospels, though Küng is more explicit about this than Mullins. Neither feels that the traditional arguments for God's existence are compelling, but both think those arguments make a contribution. Mullins is more emphatic about the historicity of Jesus' resurrection than Küng, but both treat it as indispensable for both understanding and trusting him. Mullins issues a call to conversion, to be followed by discipleship; Küng issues a call to a radically human life in the church.

Mullins's second great book, *The Axioms of Religion*, is subtitled *A New Interpretation of the Baptist Faith*. It probably has done more than any other single volume to define Baptists in the twentieth century. Mullins says that the most distinctive and important of all Baptist beliefs is the belief in "soul competency," that is, in the freedom, ability, and responsibility of each person to respond to God for herself or himself. From this simple, universal "mother principle,"[27] Mullins derived six propositions, which are, he argued, axiomatic, that is, self-evidently true to all who accept Christianity and even to many who do not.

The theological axiom is that "the holy and loving God has a right to be sovereign." Mullins understands God as a sovereign Father rather than as sovereign omnipotence.[28] God asserts his sovereignty over human beings by personal and moral influences. "His sovereignty is holy and it is loving; it respects human freedom."[29]

The religious axiom is that all persons have an equal right to direct access to God.[30] Mullins wrote, "It is a species of spiritual tyranny for men to interpose the church itself, its ordinances, or ceremonies, or its formal creeds, between the human soul and Christ."[31] Mullins acknowledged that this axiom was not applicable to ancient Israel and that it was lost by the church when infant baptism and the Constantinian settlement were accepted, but he insisted that it is the clear teaching of the New Testament.

The ecclesiastical axiom is that "all believers have a right to equal privileges in the church."[32] Mullins believed that democracy is the only church polity which is really true to this axiom. "No other polity leaves the soul free."[33] The autonomy of local congregations is not threatened by the existence of Baptist agencies or conventions, for these have no authority over local congregations.[34]

The moral axiom is that "to be responsible the soul must be free."[35] This axiom is the basis of all ethics, and it is the antithesis of all forms of determinism.

The religio-civic axiom is "a free church in a free state."[36] "When Roger Williams founded the commonwealth of Rhode Island, a new era in man's spiritual history began."[37] By their adherence to the separation of church and state, and their refusal to be content with mere toleration, Baptists "made a real contribution to the world's civilization."[38] But "there will, of course, remain a borderline where it will not always be clear how to discriminate and apply the principle correctly."[39]

The social axiom is, "You shall love your neighbor as yourself."[40] Christianity has emphasized two correlative truths: every individual has worth, and every human being is a social being. Social progress is the product of individual regeneration. The imitation of Christ does not link

Christians to a single reform movement, but it does compel them to work for the welfare of all persons.[41] "The best service which Christianity can render to society is to produce righteousness in individual character and at the same time set the man free as an agent of righteousness in society at large."[42]

Mullins presents three chapters in which he applies the axioms to three sets of concerns. First, he says that the best denominational structure is that which respects the autonomy of churches, even though it may be frustrating when the churches do not cooperate as fully as they might. Second, he argues that the movement for church union—which will later be called the ecumenical movement—can proceed properly only if it accepts congregational polity; every effort to create church union along hierarchical lines must be resisted in the name of freedom.[43] Third, Mullins responds to critics who wish to be Christians without any commitment to institutional churches. They fail to take account either of the authority of Christ or of the realities of Christian history, both of which indicate the need for institutional churches, baptism, and the Lord's Supper.

Mullins discusses the Baptist contribution to American civilization (it is the ideal of liberty) and also argues that the axioms are of incalculable value if the human race is to continue to make progress. In every area of human endeavor—the educational, the scientific, the philosophical, the political—progress will occur in direct proportion to the implementation of the truths of these axioms. "The axioms of religion derived from the gospel of Jesus Christ are fitted to lead the progressive civilization of the race."[44]

In some ways *The Axioms of Religion* bears the marks of its time. Many writers today would shy away from employing a vocabulary of "rights." Others might observe that Mullins asserted rather than demonstrated that individuals are really free. A historian might resist the assumption that authentic Christianity is always individualistic. Mullins's optimism about the future seems too facile.

And yet many of Mullins's ideas made an impact on religion in America. Church and state are still separate. Many denominations emphasize the importance of a personal conversion experience. Historian Martin E. Marty has written of the "Baptistification" of American life, so Mullins's optimism was not totally unrealistic.[45] *The Axioms of Religion* may have been the most original book Mullins wrote. It was a very American book and a very Baptist book, and it went to the heart of Mullins's religious and theological concerns.

In *The Axioms of Religion* Mullins articulated for thoughtful readers the hidden assumptions underlying Baptist life; in *Baptist Beliefs* he interpreted for the general reader the beliefs which Baptists regularly confess. His method was to comment on the "excellent Baptist creeds" which are "now in existence in common use among us."[46] The topics with which

Mullins dealt, and the sequence of the topics, reflect the New Hampshire Declaration, to which Mullins added comments on five topics—the kingdom of God, liberty of conscience, missions, education, and social service. Twelve years after the publication of this book, Mullins would become chairman of a committee to draw up a confession of faith for the Southern Baptist Convention; the committee began, as Mullins did, with the New Hampshire Declaration, and added to it articles on the same five topics Mullins had discussed along with articles on peace and war, cooperation, and stewardship.[47] In both these sets of additions, Mullins's theological and ecclesiastical concerns are evident.

Baptist Beliefs is folk theology at its best. It is readable. It addresses the real concerns of ordinary Christians. It explains but is not condescending. It argues but is not adversarial. It is coherent but not rationalistic. In some ways, what is most interesting is what is omitted; the emphasis on personal experience which characterizes *The Christian Religion in Its Doctrinal Expression* five years later is barely evident here, presumably because Mullins recognized that that emphasis was his own rather than characteristic of the Baptist confessions of which he was providing a fresh statement.

Freedom and Authority in Religion is unique among Mullins's books in that it has a single thesis, namely, that Jesus Christ is the religious authority for Christians and that he exercises his authority in such a way as to give Christians freedom rather than deprive them of it. The book might have been shorter than it is, but Mullins returns in it to themes in his earlier books. He also in this book carries on a sustained dialogue with many of his contemporary theologians.

The argument runs as follows. First, ours is an age which longs for freedom, which it understands as living and thinking without deference to any external authority. Second, Jesus claimed to be a unique and indispensable religious authority. Third, science is competent to deal with physical realities but not with spiritual realities such as the soul, freedom, immorality, and God; only religion is competent to deal with these. "Religion begins, therefore, exactly where science ends."[48] Fourth, philosophy, the quest for understanding which arose long after religion—the quest for redemption—produces an unsettled state of mind which is inadequate for religion.

Next Mullins begins his constructive work. Fifth, religious truth is assimilated through experience; it is a special form of personal knowledge which is arrived at by living as much as by thinking. It does not contradict logic or science, but it goes beyond them, to a direct encounter of the human will with the living God. Sixth, in every sphere of life, authority inevitably develops as truth is discovered and expressed. Seventh, religion is a universal human activity consisting of knowing about a supernatural personal spirit, and seeking a relationship with that spirit, and seeking deliverance from the human predicament. Christianity teaches that God takes the initiative in establishing the relationship and providing the deliverance. "God's revelation to us does mean that our experience religiously assimilates revealed truth and it becomes valid for us not as propositions imposed by sheer divine authority, but is recognized by us as the answer to our deepest needs and congruous with our highest aspirations."[49] Eighth, religious knowledge is given, not by inference, but empirically, that is, in the Christian experience of redemption. It is personal knowledge, that is, knowledge in terms of persons and personal relationships, not in terms of physical cause and effect. It is not subjective knowledge, for it is knowledge of an "object" outside oneself acting upon oneself. It is moral and spiritual knowledge, but it is just as cognitive as any other form of knowledge.

Ninth, "now we shall find, paradoxical as it may seem, that Jesus Christ while retaining the principle of authority combines it with the perfect ideal of human freedom. Christianity is as truly the religion of freedom as it is the religion of authority."[50] God is the supreme authority in religion; Jesus is the true revelation of God, and therefore the seat of religious authority. The New Testament and the Christian experience of redemption converge to affirm Jesus as the seat of religious authority. By putting us in touch with God, and providing redemption, Jesus gives us freedom. Christ gives his revelations to us in such a way that they become discoveries of truth by us. He exerts his authority over us precisely by making us free and by allowing us to accept it freely. His authority is the authority of a friendship.

Finally, Mullins turns his attention to the place of the Bible in Christianity. The Bible is "the literary expression of living experience in the religious life, the spontaneous and free output of that experience under the guidance of God's Spirit, (so that) it is precisely adapted to reproduce that experience in man to-day."[51] It is in that sense the final authority in religion, and this is perfectly consistent with Jesus Christ as the seat of authority in religion, because the Bible is the inspired interpretation of Christ which creates the possibility of his life being experienced by people today. "Christ as the Revealer of God and Redeemer of man is the seat of authority in religion and above and underneath and before the Bible. But the Bible is the authoritative literature which leads us to Christ."[52] It does this without coercion, and so it is an authority which respects human freedom and creates it, just as Christ does.

The Christian Religion in Its Doctrinal Expression is Mullins's largest and most constructive book. The first thing that strikes the reader of this systematic theology is the unusual title, and the second thing is the unusual sequence of topics. The title alerts us not to confuse the Christian religion—"religion" is a positive term for Mullins—with theology. The sequence of topics alerts us that Mullins will resist any effort to tear theology away from its roots in authentic religious life. The chapter titles are:

1. Religion and Theology
2. The Knowledge of God
3. Preliminary Study of Christian Experience
4. Christian and Other Forms of Knowledge
5. Revelation
6. The Supreme Revelation: Jesus Christ
7. The Deity of Jesus Christ
8. The Holy Spirit and the Trinity
9. The God of Our Lord Jesus Christ
10. Creation
11. Providence
12. Sin
13. The Living Word of Christ
14. Election: God's Initiative in Salvation
15. The Beginning of the Christian Life
16. The Continuance of the Christian Life
17. Last Things

The first four chapters would, in Germany, be called "prolegomena," and the unusual thing about them is the emphasis on Christian experience. Mullins deals with Christian experience as prolegomena and then returns to it later in chapters 7, 15, and 16. The chapter on the Spirit and the Trinity seems contrived, since Mullins does not integrate it into the Christian experience; this is surely a missed opportunity. To speak of God only after speaking of Jesus is not really true either to experience or to chronology; we do, after all, have some knowledge of God before Christ. Five chapters intervene between Christ's person and work, and should not the emphasis on Christian experience lead one to deal first with Christ's work and then with his person?

We shall look briefly at what Mullins does in each chapter.

First, he distinguishes religion from theology and attempts to justify his emphasis on Christian experience. He thinks the latter is intellectually justifiable, and it also prevents us from thinking of Christianity in exclusively intellectual terms. He defends the autonomy of religious experience; it is an experience that should not be reduced to other terms, and it puts us in touch with realities we cannot know in any other way. He carefully defends his emphasis on experience from the charge that it is a capitulation to subjectivism. Christianity, he says, "has to do with two great groups of facts: the facts of experience and the facts of the historical revelation of God through Christ."[53] Christian experience is made possible because God has graciously revealed himself in a historical person, Jesus Christ. Christian theology is real knowledge, which uses appropriate methods to deal with its particular subject matter, God. The highest qualification for the study of theology is to be a person of religious faith. Scholarly and intuitive gifts are also helpful, as are moral qualities such as humility.

In the second chapter Mullins defines religion and examines the sources of religious knowledge. Religious knowledge may be inferred from nature or man, or from the religious conscience, or learned from comparative religions, or accepted on the authority of the church or the Bible. But the supreme source of religious knowledge is the revelation of God given in Jesus Christ. Jesus was a historical person, and the New Testament tells what he was like, but he also transcends history and is active in human experience. We know God supremely through Christ, and we know Christ through the New Testament and through our experience of him.

In chapter 3, Mullins lays down several general assumptions to prepare for his argument from experience. In his analysis of Christian experience, he says that God initiates or makes contact with man at the point of sin and elicits a free response. This is possible because man is personal. God acts upon both the unconscious and conscious mind of man. Christian doctrine arises out of Christian experience; it is an experiential knowledge but is none the less rational for that. It is knowledge with certainty; you cannot doubt what you learn from experience.

Chapter 4 traces the relationship of Christian knowledge to the knowledge of the physical sciences, of the psychology of religion, of ethics, of comparative religion, and of philosophy. Science and religion are separate spheres of knowledge and cannot conflict. The psychology of religion, as expressed by William James, for example, suggests the working of God in religious experience. The kingdom of God is, in fact, the highest expression known to us of the ethical ideal, and ethics finds its securest ground in God. Other religions are not wholly false, but they are moving upward toward an ideal which is already found in Christian religion. Philosophy is a quest for the true worldview, which is natural for mankind, but it often arrives at false conclusions because it adopts too narrow a view of reality. False worldviews include agnosticism, materialism, and idealism, but personalism is much nearer the truth. Christian theism takes up where personalism leaves off. The traditional arguments for God's existence are less convincing to Christians than their knowledge of God from the revelation given in Christ, but they are welcomed as supplementary confirmations with cumulative force. The arguments help us to infer that God is, while an experience gives us a direct knowledge that God is. Mullins resists the charge of subjectivism with this argument:

> The charge of subjectivism may be brought by any objector
> to any conclusion in any sphere. All the data which we handle in
> our reasonings must pass through the human mold. Our intellect
> impresses its forms upon all facts, just as a dipper shapes the
> water it takes out of the bucket. But all truth becomes truth only

on the supposition that our reason gives us reliable information. The fact that reason is satisfied and a religious need is met surely cannot be justly held to discredit it. It is rather the strongest of proofs that it is true. And when a form of experience like the Christian's, which belongs to a great order of experience running through nearly two thousand years, and embracing millions of other Christians, and which can be scientifically analyzed and explained—when such an experience is under consideration the charge of subjectivism loses all its force. If the experience were merely individual and exceptional there would be some point in the objection. But not otherwise.[54]

Chapter 5 begins by affirming that all religions consider revelation to be indispensable. The Christian claim that revelation was given in a Person, Jesus Christ, is unique. The Christian revelation "is primarily a revelation of God himself rather than of truths about God," "revelation is primarily salvation," and "revelation is 'acquaintance with' and not mere 'knowledge about' God."[55] "God's revelations can only become revelations when they become our discoveries."[56]

The Bible is the record of God's revelation. The biblical revelation is historical, experiential, morally transforming, progressive, purposive, congruous with life, and supernatural; it is also sufficient, certain, and authoritative for religion.

Jesus Christ is God's supreme revelation. We know him through the New Testament; we also experience his redeeming work in our lives. The deity of Christ is an essential article of Christian faith. Jesus reveals God as personal, and as loving, and he reveals the purpose of God in creation and the worthwhileness of human existence. Many efforts have been made to say how Christ can be both divine and human; we need to stress that he was one Person before we attempt to explain the two natures. Christ existed as God's Son before his birth, and he accepted self-imposed limitations in order to be a human being. The acceptance of those limitations is a great revelation of the self-sacrificing love of God. Jesus grew, as all human beings do; he grew intellectually and morally and in his consciousness that he was the Messiah. Mullins rejects the idea that Christ was merely human, or that he was merely filled with God's presence, or that he preexisted only ideally. He rejects William Sanday's proposal that Christ's consciousness was human and his unconsciousness divine as well as Albrecht Ritschl's suggestion that Christ has for us the value of God.

The Holy Spirit is a personal being distinct from Christ and the Father, who "makes the historical revelation in and through Christ morally and spiritually effective in the life of believers."[57] The one God is, both immanently and economically, Father, Son, and Holy Spirit.

The God of our Lord Jesus Christ is the supreme personal Spirit, perfect in all his attributes, the source, support, and end of the universe, who guides it according to the wise, righteous, loving purpose revealed in Christ, and who indwells in all things by his Spirit seeking to transform them and to create his kingdom. God is not immune to suffering. God's sovereignty is not that of an absolute and arbitrary Oriental monarch but of a wise and loving heavenly Father.

God created all that exists. His purpose is to make "a spiritual kingdom of free persons living together in eternal bonds of righteous love."[58] He is carrying out that purpose in his developing universe. Man is God's crowning work of creation; man is both physical and spiritual and bears the divine image.

God preserves his creation, that is, sustains its existence; and he rules providentially over it, that is, directs it toward the fulfillment of his purpose. His providence extends to individuals as well as to humankind as a whole. Sometimes he uses miracles—which are restorations rather than violations—to carry out his purpose. He answers the prayers of his children. It is presumptuous of human beings to assume that they are the only personal creatures made by God; angels are real enough, though we know little about them.

God made men to be free; men freely chose to disobey God. In that choice is the origin of sin. Sin is universal, and each sinner is guilty and condemned for his or her sins.

Christ died for the sins of the world. The Bible provides numerous interpretations of that unique event. Although God's love and justice are never in conflict, the necessity of Christ's death is located in the moral nature of God as well as of man. Christ identified himself fully with human beings and so experienced God's wrath against sin—not an angry passion or vindictiveness but the suffering and death which are the consequences of human sinning. "God of course did not really forsake Christ, but in his death there was, in some real sense, beyond our power to fathom, a clouding of his consciousness of God. He entered the region and shadow of death for human sin."[59] In so doing, he broke the reign of the principle of sin and death over human beings. In a profoundly personal and moral way, Christ became not only the head and representative of the human race but also its substitute. He died for all, not only for the elect.

Election is the sovereign initiative which God takes toward man in order to carry out his eternal purpose. If God did not take this initiative, no one could ever be saved. Election does not eliminate human freedom but acts by inviting, persuading, and appealing.

The Holy Spirit reveals Christ and his salvation to men. He alerts men to their sin and calls them to repentance and to faith. Faith is knowledge of the gospel plus assent to the gospel plus a decision to trust Christ as

Savior. The initial trust becomes a permanent attitude. Regeneration is the new life given at the moment of conversion. Justification is the legal acquittal of sinners by which God delivers them from condemnation and restores them to his favor. Adoption is God's taking sinners into his family. Regeneration, conversion, justification, and adoption are different expressions of a single great reality, which may be summarized as union with Christ.

God's purpose is to produce a community of holy men and women, and this means they must first be placed in a new relationship with God, and then a new character must be produced in them. Sanctification is God's inner transformation of sinners into persons of Christian character. It is both a gift and a task for the Christian, who must strive for it with the help of God. Christians reject antinomianism and perfectionism. Left to themselves Christians would be in danger of falling from grace, so God preserves them in their salvation; they must cooperate with him in every way they can, and this includes taking seriously the biblical warnings against apostasy. His preservation is not mechanical: "The personal God deals with personal man in a free personal manner."[60]

Eschatology is the attempt to describe the final carrying out of God's eternal purpose and is an essential part of Christian theology. Following the death of the body, Christians enter a temporary intermediate state—not to be confused with purgatory or with soul-sleep—to await their resurrection and the final judgment, when they will enter heaven and receive their rewards. The end of history will occur when Christ returns personally to the earth. The millennium has been given too much prominence in recent theology, and none of the millennial views is fully satisfactory; what matters is the Second Coming of Christ and the resurrection of the body, which must not be confused with the immortality of the soul. Heaven and hell are real, and denials of the latter are to be resisted. God cannot make men who freely choose to be bad, to be happy. "Christians to-day with practical unanimity hold that infants dying in infancy are saved. This means about one-third of the human race."[61]

Mullins's last book, *Christianity at the Cross Roads,* was published when Mullins was sixty-four years old and in poor health. The crossroads of the title was the Fundamentalist-Modernist controversy which was then at fever pitch in the churches.

In a chapter entitled "The Modern Spirit," Mullins criticizes modernity's lack of respect for the past, its one-sidedness, its loss of the sense of mystery, and its excessive simplification of reality.

In the chapter "Fundamental Issues," Mullins says that the issue is not between two forms of evangelical Christianity, or between science and religion, or between doctrine and culture. The issue concerns facts—the facts of Jesus Christ and of the supernatural in his life. It is about the rights of religion to deal with its facts. It is about what will really bring salvation to humankind.

"The Rights of Religion" include the right to reject the reductionism which eliminates the supernatural. It also includes the right to allow religious knowledge to be known religiously, by those with a personal relationship with God. Scientists as such are not equipped to evaluate religion, nor are religious persons as such qualified to evaluate science.

"Reducing Christianity: Modern Science" continues this line of thinking and includes a paragraph which represents Mullins's position on evolution clearly. Mullins is describing an evangelical thinker:

> He is perfectly willing to admit that God made the world gradually through long eras of time, that there is progress and growth in the universe, that the world is dynamic with a great divine purpose which is moving towards a shining goal. Moreover he refuses to dogmatize in the scientific realm. He holds himself open to the acceptance of any established fact of science. He insists at the same time that science should practice the same modesty that it enjoins upon others. Let it assert only when the evidence warrants it.[62]

This chapter is a sustained polemic against the modernistic reduction of Christianity by the elimination of the supernatural in the name of science. The argument continues in chapter 5. Mullins writes:

> Religious experience knows more than biological science has discovered. It knows that a universe flattened down to the level of the law of continuity does not represent all the reality that is. It knows that any system which flattens out the personality of God and man to that biological level is contrary to the best attested items of our spiritual experience.[63]

Mullins says that the religion of biological science, represented by men such as E. G. Conklin, has collapsed because its god is not transcendent and personal, it does not see people as immaterial souls, and it restricts human hope to social progress. This religion is so empty that it attracts few followers, but, says Mullins, some are attempting to work out a compromise between it and Christianity. "The Compromise" (ch. 6) has a personal God, but Jesus is only a great teacher, not a redeemer, and the supernatural elements in the New Testament are rejected. The compromise position is mere theism, and it is always being pulled forward toward Christianity and backward toward naturalism and must always fight for its life. "One is constantly surprised at the narrowness of vision, lack of sympathy and spiritual insight, and especially the lack of courage on the part of modern biologists who insist upon a thorough-going naturalism."[64]

Mullins next turns his attention to the reduction of Christianity by modern philosophy. Philosophy seeks to understand many ultimate problems on principles of rationality; religion seeks a relationship between God and man upon principles of personality.

> Christianity is primarily not a philosophy of the universe. It is a religion. It is not founded upon metaphysics. Like all things known to us, there is an implied philosophy. There is a certain view of God and nature and man and the world in the background of our faith. But Christianity is a historical religion, and a religion of experience. It is grounded in facts. The Christian world-view rests upon these facts.[65]

Philosophy cannot prescribe what religion ought to be or to teach.

Then Mullins turns to the reduction of Christianity by means of historical criticism. The best way to study the New Testament is with "a sound historical criticism, combined with spiritual appreciation of its contents."[66] Historical criticism goes wrong when it eliminates some of the evidence—such as Jesus' miracles—or when it accepts one kind of evidence as if it were all there is, as when, for example, Harnack portrays Jesus as if he were only a teacher of morals or Schweitzer portrays Jesus as if he were only an apocalyptic prophet.

The last form of reductionism to which Mullins responds is "the latest theory," namely, the effort to account for Christianity by setting it in the context of other religions in the first century. Mullins welcomes the method of comparative religion, and he believes we have benefited from some of its conclusions. For example, Paul used terms found in mystery religions; but then, missionaries today also use terms taken from a non-Christian vocabulary. But the claim of, for example, Alfred Loisy, that Jesus was regarded by the church as a Savior-God only because the church was made up of people familiar with the mystery religions is exaggerated and highly improbable; in fact, it is not even certain that the mystery religions existed as early as the first century.

The final four chapters of the book are Mullins's constructive work. They deal with "the irreducible Christ" and Christian experience, the New Testament, the spiritual life of the world, and Christian history, respectively. He summarized his view in these words:

> Christianity is at the cross roads. We face a great issue. The alternatives are clear. On the one hand we may listen to the voice of the New Testament, of a sound criticism, of a sound historical method, to the voice of a regenerating and redeeming Christian experience, to the voice of history during two thousand years and thus retain all the great elements in our historical faith. On the

other hand we may listen to alien voices, that of physical science, philosophic speculation, subjective criticism, and comparative religion and thus reduce Christianity to the dimensions of an ethical movement or philosophic cult.[67]

In his earlier books Mullins positioned himself carefully in a middle, moderate position, between the extremes. No doubt he thought of himself in a similar position in this book, between the extremes of fundamentalism and modernism. But the book itself is a sustained polemic against naturalism on his left, and against the versions of Christianity called modernism and liberalism which he regards as the thin edge of the naturalist wedge entering the church's life. For whatever reason, Mullins is here more than in any other of his books, the conservative defender of traditional views.

Evaluation

One of America's most widely read literary critics has appraised Mullins's importance in the following way:

> Edgar Young Mullins I would nominate as the Calvin or Luther or Wesley of the Southern Baptists, but only in the belated American sense, because Mullins was not the founder of the Southern Baptists but their re-founder, the definer of their creedless faith. An endlessly subtle and original religious thinker, Mullins is the most neglected of major American theologians. Pragmatically he is more important than Jonathan Edwards, Horace Bushnell, and the Niebuhrs, because Mullins reformulated (perhaps even first formulated) the faith of a major American denomination.

Perhaps Harold Bloom was engaging in hyperbole in this estimate, but he was right to call attention to the fact that it would be unwise to evaluate Mullins as a theologian without taking into account the fact that he was an enormously influential leader of Southern Baptists. Still, he was a theologian, and it is his theological work that will be evaluated here.

Mullins's greatest theological achievement may have been to guide Baptists, especially Southern Baptists, away from some of the more extreme expressions of Calvinism and Landmarkism. He was not able to do the same with fundamentalism. He established moderation as a virtue in theological work for many Southern Baptists. He helped many to move in their understanding of science and religion beyond the warfare stage to a separate-spheres understanding. He was not able to negotiate a similar movement regarding evolution in particular. He demonstrated the importance of the categories of persons, personal life, freedom, and Christian experience, for theological work by Baptists.

Mullins's theology could have been more balanced. He enthusiastically unpacked the meaning of his Protestant heritage, his revivalist heritage, and his distinctively Baptist heritage. But he seemed to think that the universal Christian heritage needed little or no exposition, only a strong defense. For example, the most universal, most distinctively Christian understanding of God is the Trinitarian. So far as I can tell, Mullins devotes, out of the two thousand pages in his six major books, only nine pages to this great teaching. This is unbalanced.

Mullins was wise to insist that Christianity is about persons—about a personal God in interpersonal relationships with human persons. Mullins saw that science and philosophy threatened the personal categories, but he did not seem to notice the greater threat of the psychology of the unconscious to persons.

Nor did he deal successfully with the social experience of Christianity. He formally assented to the importance of Christian community, but his mind turned instinctively and inevitably to the private experiences of conversion and moral transformation. He was intoxicated by personal freedom, even by personal rights—a category which owes more to the Enlightenment than to the New Testament—even to the loss of the indispensability of society and social relationships for personal life.[68]

His utilization of the category of experience was excellent. He successfully shielded himself from charges of subjectivism. The form of experience to which he referred was almost always that of conversion followed by moral transformation. This experience yields a knowledge—a certain knowledge—available in no other way. However, Mullins does not seem to have noticed the implications of the fact that that particular form of religious experience is widespread, in part, because it is carefully fostered in the revivalist tradition. Christian experience is possible because Christ acts in people's lives; the conversionist structure of experience is possible because it is managed by a church committed to it.

Mullins was a responsible, careful theologian; he read widely; he thought carefully; he was constructive; he spoke to the concerns of his time; he was not rationalistic, narrow, vague, or overly defensive; he was a great Baptist theologian.

Bibliography

Works by Mullins

The Axioms of Religion. Philadelphia: American Baptist Publication Society, 1908.

The Axioms of Religion. R. Albert Mohler Jr., compiler, ed. Timothy George. Library of Baptist Classics. Nashville: Broadman & Holman Publishers, 1997.

Baptist Beliefs. Louisville: Baptist World Publishing Co., 1912.

The Christian Religion in Its Doctrinal Expression. Philadelphia: Roger Williams Press, 1917.

Christianity at the Cross Roads. Nashville: Sunday School Board of the Southern Baptist Convention, 1924.

Freedom and Authority in Religion. Philadelphia: The Griffith & Rowland Press, 1913.

The Life in Christ. New York: Fleming H. Revell Co., 1917. A collection of sermons, one of which was also included in *The Fundamentals.*

Spiritualism—a Delusion. Nashville: Sunday School Board of the Southern Baptist Convention, 1920.

Studies in Ephesians and Colossians. Nashville: Sunday School Board of the Southern Baptist Convention, 1913.

Talks on Soul Winning. Nashville: Sunday School Board of the Southern Baptist Convention, 1920.

Why Is Christianity True? Philadelphia: The Judson Press, 1905; originally published by Christian Culture Press, Chicago.

Works about Mullins

Bloom, Harold. *The American Religion.* New York: Simon & Schuster, 1992.

Carrell, William D. M. "Edgar Young Mullins and the Competency of the Soul in Religion," Ph.D. dissertation, Baylor University, 1993.

Carver, W. O. "Edgar Young Mullins—Leader and Builder," *The Review and Expositor* (April 1929).

Dilday, Russell H., Jr. "E. Y. Mullins: The Bible's Authority Is a Living Transforming Reality." *The Unfettered Word.* Edited by Robison B. James. Waco: Word Books, 1987.

Dobbins, Gaines S. "Edgar Young Mullins." *Encyclopedia of Southern Baptists* II. Nashville: Broadman Press, 1958.

Ellis, William E. *A Man of Books and a Man of the People.* Macon: Mercer University Press, 1985.

The Faculty of the Southern Baptist Theological Seminary. *Edgar Young Mullins: A Study in Christian Character.* Louisville: n.p., n.d.

Fletcher, Jesse C. "Shapers of the Southern Baptist Spirit." *Baptist History and Heritage* 30 (July 1995), 6–15.

Hardenbergh, Jane Slaughter. "E. Y. Mullins: Man of Vision." *American Baptist Quarterly* 11 (Spring 1992), 246–58.

Lee, Won Kee. "The Organic Correlation between the Historical Revelation of God and the Believer's Historic Christian Experience in Edgar Young Mullins' Experiential Theology," Ph.D. dissertation, Trinity Evangelical Divinity School, 1994.

Maddux, H. Clark. "Edgar Young Mullins and Evangelical Developments in the Southern Baptist Convention." *Baptist History and Heritage* 33 (Spring 1998), 62–73.

Mohler, R. Albert Jr. "Introduction." E. Y. Mullins, *The Axioms of Religion,* ed. Timothy George. Library of Baptist Classics. Nashville: Broadman & Holman Publishers, 1997, 1–32.

Mullins, Isla May. *Edgar Young Mullins: An Intimate Biography.* Nashville: Sunday School Board of the Southern Baptist Convention, 1929.

————. "Dr. Mullins as a Student." *The Review and Expositor* (April 1929).

Scaer, David P. "Edgar Young Mullins." *Handbook of Evangelical Theologians,* ed. Walter Elwell. Grand Rapids, Mich.: Baker Books, 1993.

Stubblefield, Jerry M. "The Ecumenical Impact of E. Y. Mullins." *Journal of Ecumenical Studies* (Spring 1980).

Thomas, Bill Clark. "Edgar Young Mullins: A Baptist Exponent of Theological Restatement." Ph.D. dissertation, The Southern Baptist Theological Seminary, 1963.

"E. Y. Mullins." *The Southern Baptist Journal of Theology* 3 (Winter 2000).

"The Mullins Legacy." *Review and Expositor* 96, No. 1 (Winter 1999).

11
Walter Thomas Conner

By James Leo Garrett Jr.

Biography[1]

Birth and Boyhood

WALTER THOMAS, THE SECOND SON OF PHILIP ORLANDER CONNER (1846–1896) and Frances Jane Monk Conner (? –1904), was born on January 19, 1877,[2] at Center, now called Rowell,[3] in Cleveland County,

Arkansas. Orlander Conner had been born near Pontotoc, Mississippi, and three of his four brothers had died in the Confederate cause. He, his son born to his deceased first wife, and his second wife had moved from Mississippi to Center, twenty-five miles south of Pine Bluff.[4] After Walter's birth, Orlander bought on credit and moved to an eighty-acre farm on the road from Pine Bluff to Warren and near the present village of Rye.[5] In 1889, Orlander Conner moved his family to Kingsland, Arkansas, where he was employed in a sawmill.[6] Commenting in later years on his childhood, Walter T. Conner stated, "I was brought up in the dire poverty of the South after the Civil War."[7] His early education consisted of attending "ungraded country schools on an average of three or four months a year and some years practically none."[8]

In November 1892, when Walter was fifteen, Orlander Conner again moved his family, this time a far greater distance. The new home was to be a farm in West Texas, some eight miles southwest of Abilene in Taylor County, in a community then called Tebo but now known as Tye.[9]

Conversion, Call to the Ministry, and Early Preaching

The beginnings of the Christian motivation, which was to dominate the life and ministry of W. T. Conner, are recorded in his own words: "My earliest religious impressions go back to the [Enon] church where my parents and grandparents belonged in Cleveland County, Arkansas."[10] On one occasion in that church Walter was inclined to make a profession of faith in response to a gospel appeal, but his older brother caught his coat and held him back.[11] In the Kingsland community the Conner family was "not convenient to a Baptist church and . . . attended a country Methodist church." Walter Conner recalled his experience at about age fourteen of being in a Methodist service in which the young preacher had made "an intense and protracted appeal" for non-Christians to evidence some interest in becoming Christians, and he resisted that appeal.[12]

After the move to Texas, young Conner discovered that Baptist and Methodist preachers "were still talking about the cross and the love of God." His conversion occurred in the summer of 1894 when he was seventeen.

> I was converted in an old-time, horrah, Methodist meeting. . . . My conviction of sin gradually deepened until it became a very definite and heavy load. . . . I became deeply enough interested to begin to go forward for prayer and thus seek for help. . . . A number of people talked to me at what was then known as the mourner's bench but none of them seemed to give me any very definite help. . . . Finally, my load became so heavy, not knowing what else to do, I gave up. The expression "gave up" expresses my experience better than any other that I can think of. When I gave up, my burden was removed but I did not have any ecstatic

joy or feel like shouting or anything of the kind. I simply felt that
my burden was gone and I hardly knew what had happened. . . .
Finally . . . it came to me that I was saved by putting my trust in
Christ and not by any particular type of feeling that I had had.[13]

Both Conner's life and theology were grounded upon an abiding confidence in the validity of evangelical Christian conversion. He was baptized
by W. M. Reynolds[14] and received into the fellowship of Harmony Baptist
Church at Caps, Texas.[15]

According to Conner, his impression of a call to preach the gospel went
"back to the time when I was a small boy, and became a definite conviction soon after I was converted."[16] In the small library in the Conner home
there were books of a doctrinal nature. He participated in a young men's
prayer meeting in the Caps community, from which came at least half a
dozen Baptist and Methodist preachers. In a country debating society
Conner learned to speak in public.[17] J. M. Reynolds, brother of W. M.
Reynolds, while preaching in evangelistic services at Caps in the summer of
1895, interrogated young Conner as to his conviction of a divine call to
preach. When Conner answered affirmatively, Reynolds encouraged the
church to license Conner, and the church did so.[18] Conner's first sermon
was on the text, "Wist ye not that I must be about my Father's business?"[19]
Through J. M. Reynolds's assistance Conner soon had preaching appointments in nearby Baptist churches.[20]

Conner's first pastorate was at Tuscola, Texas, during 1898–99.[21] In
October 1899, the church at Caps ordained him,[22] and he served that
church as pastor during 1899–1900. During 1903–04, Conner was resident
pastor of Baptist churches in south Texas at Eagle Lake half-time and at
Rock Island and East Bernard quarter time,[23] having been recommended
by B. H. Carroll.[24] Later, for a period ending in 1908, Conner was pastor
of the Baptist churches at Blum and Rio Vista in Johnson County, south of
Fort Worth.

Academic and Theological Education

Conner's determination to pursue an education which would equip
him for his lifework may be seen in events which covered nearly two
decades. His struggles for an education were made more difficult by the
death of his father in 1896. During 1896–1898, he was enrolled intermit-
tently as a student at Simmons College (now Hardin-Simmons University)
in Abilene, Texas. After borrowing money, he entered Baylor University,
Waco, in the fall of 1898, but after one term had to withdraw in order to
pay his debts. He returned to Baylor in the fall of 1901 but withdrew in
January 1903, this time to make it possible for his brother John to continue
as a student at Baylor.[25] Early in his Baylor days, W. T. Conner came to the
conviction that he should be a foreign missionary; this conviction was due

to a large extent to the influence of Professor John S. Tanner, whose missionary zeal led to the founding of an organization of students committed to foreign missionary service.[26]

In the fall of 1904, Conner again enrolled in Baylor and continued until he graduated with the B.A. degree in 1906.[27] Also in the 1906 Baylor graduating class was Miss Blanche Ethel Horne of Albany, Texas,[28] who became on June 4, 1907, Mrs. W. T. Conner. Both husband and wife, the latter a capable student of Latin and Greek, taught Latin at Baylor University during 1907–1908.

Conner continued his studies at the Baylor Theological Seminary, which had received full seminary status in 1905 under the mentorship of its dean, B. H. Carroll. Its faculty included Albert Henry Newman, Charles B. Williams, Calvin Goodspeed, and L. W. Doolan.[29] In 1908, Conner received a Th.B. degree from the seminary, which in March had been chartered as Southwestern Baptist Theological Seminary, and an M.A. degree from Baylor University.[30]

During 1906–1908, B. H. Carroll indicated to W. T. Conner that he "would be offered the position of teacher of theology in the seminary" if he "would make proper preparation." The original suggestion concerning Conner seems to have come from A. H. Newman. Conner went, therefore, to Rochester Theological Seminary, Rochester, New York, for two years of study with the understanding that he would return to teach theology at Southwestern.[31] He was graduated from Rochester in the spring of 1909, "no degree being given then on graduation." At the suggestion of Professor Walter Rauschenbusch, he wrote a fellowship thesis on "Theodore Parker's Theological System." After one more year of study at Rochester on the fellowship, he received in 1910 the B.D. degree.[32] His teachers at Rochester included Rauschenbusch, A. H. Strong, William A. Stevens, and H. C. Mabie.[33] Conner studied for two weeks in the summer of 1910 under George B. Foster at the University of Chicago before returning to Texas.[34] In September he assumed his duties as a professor at Southwestern Seminary, which was in process of moving from Waco to Seminary Hill, Texas, now within the corporate limits of Fort Worth. Conner had been elected to succeed Calvin Goodspeed, whose title had been "professor of systematic theology, apologetics, polemics, and ecclesiology."[35]

During 1914, Conner was given a leave of absence for graduate study at the Southern Baptist Theological Seminary, Louisville, Kentucky. There he pursued a major in theology under Edgar Young Mullins and minors in philosophy of religion and psychology of religion under William O. Carver and B. H. Dement, respectively. In May 1916, Conner received the Th.D. degree, having written a thesis on "Pragmatism and Theology."[36] In the summer of 1920, he studied at the University of Chicago for six weeks, and during the same summer Baylor University conferred on him the honorary

D.D. degree.[37] Later, when Southern Baptist Theological Seminary granted the Ph.D. degree instead of the Th.D. degree, it gave to its alumni who held the latter degree the privilege of writing an additional thesis on the basis of which the Ph.D. degree would be conferred. Conner wrote another thesis on "The Idea of the Incarnation in the Gospel of John" and received the degree in March 1931.[38]

Professorship and Related Activities

Conner's teaching career at Southwestern extended from September 1910 to May 1949, when a stroke compelled his retirement from active service. From 1910 to 1913, he was "acting professor" and from 1913 to 1949, professor. During certain periods of his career, it became necessary for Conner to assume the teaching of courses other than systematic theology, chiefly because of changes in personnel in the seminary faculty; these other disciplines included English New Testament (1921–22), biblical theology (1923–25), and Greek New Testament exegesis (1939–44).[39]

From 1910 until 1917, the Southwestern professor used as a text in his basic systematic theology course A. H. Strong's *Systematic Theology.* From about 1918 until 1922, he used *The Christian Religion in Its Doctrinal Expression* by E. Y. Mullins. In 1922, Conner began to use his own notes in mimeographed form and in 1926 shifted to his book, *A System of Christian Doctrine.* In later years he required the reading of his *Revelation and God* and *The Gospel of Redemption.*[40]

Conner's classroom technique enabled him to hold the attention of his students. A native Irish wit, a keen sense of the proper use of anecdote, and his concern that theological concepts should be applied were combined to create an interesting classroom lecture.[41]

Conner was pastor of Baptist churches at Godley and Handley, Texas, and was the first pastor of the Seminary Hill Baptist Church, now the Gambrell Street Baptist Church of Fort Worth. Supply or interim pastorates were numerous. He often lectured at Bible conferences and summer assemblies and sometimes addressed Baptist conventions and preached in evangelistic meetings. Although Conner did not enter foreign mission service, he and Mrs. Conner had a distinctive Christian ministry among the Chinese in Fort Worth. A continuing interest in world missions characterized his entire career, and the Foreign Mission Board of the Southern Baptist Convention "relied upon" his counsel concerning candidates for appointment.[42]

In 1928, Conner addressed the fourth world congress of the Baptist World Alliance in Toronto on theological education.[43] He was an active member of the Southwestern Society of Biblical Study and Research, serving as chairman of its council in 1933 and 1942 and as president in 1941.[44] The

Fort Worth professor delivered in 1946 the Wilkinson Lectures at Northern Baptist Theological Seminary, Chicago, on Johannine theology.[45]

Years of financial stringency both before and during the Great Depression were very difficult for Conner and his colleagues at Southwestern, especially since Conner's six children, all of whom became college graduates, were enrolled in college between 1925 and 1940. Conner also had several illnesses, including three cases of pneumonia.[46] He declined a professorship in philosophy at Baylor University in 1926 and the presidency of Kansas City Baptist Theological Seminary in 1937.[47] In his later years Conner's recommendation of young men for the Southwestern faculty was tantamount to their election.

Conner died on May 26, 1952, and was buried in Mount Olivet Cemetery, Fort Worth.[48]

Exposition

Investigation into the sources of and the influences upon Conner's theology, made more difficult by his practice of providing limited documentation of such, has been undertaken elsewhere[49] by the author and can only be summarized here. Probable sources or influences include the Baylor faculty,[50] the Rochester faculty,[51] the Louisville faculty,[52] the Chicago faculty,[53] Baptist denominationalism,[54] the Southwestern faculty and Fort Worth,[55] British evangelicals,[56] Baptists in the United States,[57] other American theologians,[58] American philosophers,[59] other British theologians,[60] Continental European theologians,[61] and classical theologians.[62]

Conner's work in New Testament theology came to fruition in *The Faith of the New Testament* (1940). Following the pattern laid down by George Barker Stevens[63] and Henry Clay Sheldon,[64] Conner organized his book according to the principal types of New Testament literature: Synoptic, Jewish Christian, Pauline, and Johannine. Conner recognized both unity and variety of teaching in the New Testament. In this volume he emphasizes Jesus' wilderness temptations, explains his teaching about the kingdom of God and about prayer, reckons the Epistle to the Hebrews to be of Alexandrian method, and explicates Paul on the universality of sin and John on "eternal life."[65]

Conner also engaged in polemics and apologetics. His earliest major effort came in his short monographs providing a theological refutation of the teachings of Christian Science[66] and of what we now call Jehovah's Witnesses.[67] Beginning with his Rochester thesis on Theodore Parker and continuing in his books, he offered criticisms of Unitarianism. In various books and articles the Southwestern theologian refuted teachings of Baptist antimissions ("Hardshellism"), pedobaptism, the theology of Thomas and Alexander Campbell, theological modernism and liberalism, dispensational premillennialism, the theology of Karl Barth, Roman Catholic theology, Holiness and Pentecostal movements, and anti-Christian philosophies (materialism, pantheism, agnosticism, and anti-Christian theism).[68]

"It has come to pass again that men are not ashamed to be known as theologians." Those words Conner wrote in the preface to *The Gospel of Redemption* (1945),[69] as he noted that the "science of religion" was no longer prevailing. The rise of biblical theology and the renascence of systematic theology even affected Conner, who had never winced at being a theologian. His *The Gospel of Redemption,* a revision of the second half of *A System of Christian Doctrine* (1924), showed the impact of biblical theology to a degree not found in *Revelation and God* (1936), a revision of the first half of the same book.

Conner began his systematic exposition of Christian doctrine with the doctrine of revelation rather than with the doctrine of God. He paid particular attention to the human capability to receive divine revelation. Human beings by creation have the capacity to know God and a craving to worship and trust God, and despite their sin they are valuable in God's sight. Conner drew upon personalism rather than biblical theology to provide the characteristics of human beings as spiritual persons: intelligence, rational affection, free will, and conscience. In 1924, Conner treated the revelation of God in Christ prior to discussion of Old Testament revelation and revelation through nature, but in 1936, revelation through nature preceded biblical revelation. Conner stressed "man's religious consciousness" and restated the classic arguments for God's existence. Without specifying such, Conner basically agreed with the position of John Calvin and Emil Brunner that general revelation is not salvific but the basis for human accountability and preparatory for the revelation in Jesus Christ. Conner clearly differentiated revelation and the Bible, which is the product and record of unique and historic divine revelation and a book of religion. Following Strong, he did not attempt to espouse a specific theory as to the process of divine inspiration of the Bible, and following Mullins, he utilized the concept of progressive revelation. The Bible's "central interest" is redemption, and its unity is found in Jesus Christ. Conner was accustomed to reply to a student who would ask, "But doesn't the Bible mean what it *says?*" by saying, "No. It means what it *means.*"[70] Revelation in Christ, which is "final" or ultimate, involves Jesus' own consciousness of God, his teaching about God the Father, his own character and life, his claims relative to his unique relationship with the Father, and his redemptive work. Paralleling the objective revelation in Christ is the subjective revelation through the Holy Spirit, and faith is the "venture" and "vision" necessary for receiving God's self-disclosure. For Conner "the authority of the Bible is the authority of Christ" so that there are not dual authorities.[71]

The doctrine of God in the inclusive sense meant for Conner the person of Jesus Christ, the nature and relations of God the Father, the Holy Spirit, and the Trinity. In Conner's books the person of Christ was always treated prior to the doctrine of God, probably because Christ was seen as the Revealer of God and so that the doctrine of God would "square with the character, work, and teachings of Christ."[72] For Conner the "person" of Christ embraced not only the interrelation of humanity and deity in him but also the virgin birth, sinlessness, miracles, and resurrection of Jesus. Conner was more emphatic than Mullins on the humanity of Jesus, and, unlike Strong and Mullins, related Jesus' sinlessness to his humanity.[73] Affirming both virgin birth and resurrection, both preexistence and ascension, Conner found Jesus' favorite self-designation to be "Son of man." The deity of Christ received detailed treatment, and the Incarnation was identified as a "mystery." Various kenotic theories were rejected, but a basic condescension or self-emptying was retained. Conner acknowledged that the application of personhood to God is analogical. What some theologians described as the "natural attributes" of God he treated as "the absoluteness" of God or his "infinity." From it can be inferred God's self-existence, unity, and supremacy. God is related to space/time in terms of omnipresence, eternity, and immensity. As omniscient God can foresee acts that are also free acts. The moral attributes for Conner were chiefly holiness, or transcendence, righteousness, and love. Conner taught both creation and sustenance, both natural law and miracle. The Holy Spirit is God's power at work in the world. The Fort Worth theologian became less certain that in the Old Testament the Spirit of God is hypostatically distinct from God but was sure that in the New Testament such distinction is clear. The Spirit enabled Jesus in his ministry, was bestowed at Pentecost, is to enable Christians, and gives charismata for the edification of the church. Conner deplored various modern substitutes for the working of the Holy Spirit. He did not find full-blown Trinitarian teaching in the Old Testament but was led by the deity of Jesus and the personhood of the Holy Spirit to mainstream immanental Trinitarianism in which ancient heresies are avoided and the term *person* is used advisedly.[74]

Conner saw sin as a religious conception and as the result of the temptation of the personal Satan. He clearly rejected idealism's tendency to explain sin as being due to bodily appetites or man's possession of a physical body—or an evolutionary animal hangover—and naturalism's tendency to explain sin as due to human creaturely finitude. Instead, the nature of sin centers in willful rebellion and unbelief. For Conner there are degrees of guilt. Departing from Calvin's concept of depravity as hereditary corruption, he taught depravity as the inevitability of sinning. Conner refused to accept either the Augustinian or the federal theories as to "original sin" as human sharing in Adamic guilt and shifted the focus from Romans

5:12–21 to Romans 1:18–3:20. For him a historical Adam was no problem, but human beings, while perversely affected by the sin of Adam and Eve, are guilty only for their own sin. Conner developed the concept that suffering or natural evil could have been the "anticipative consequence" of sin. Sin separates the sinner from God, alienates him from his fellow humans, and destroys the true self; sin issues in death.[75]

Redemption, a major theme in Conner's theology, includes election, the work of Christ, becoming a Christian, the Christian life, the church, and last things. Election for Conner was definable in terms of God's purpose, not God's decrees. It embraces both the totality of God's people and individuals and is the unfolding of God's plan. But it is not the self-election of believers by repentance and faith or merely God's foreknowing who would repent and believe. God is responsible for faith but not for unbelief. Hence Conner has been classified under "modified Calvinistic predestination."[76] On the doctrine of the saving work of Christ, Conner shifted from his earlier commitment to a moderate form of the penal substitutionary theory in *A System of Christian Doctrine* (1924) and *Gospel Doctrines* (1925) to his later embracing of the Christ as victor theory in *The Gospel of Redemption* (1945) and *The Cross in the New Testament* (1954).[77] He favored the term *the cross* rather than the term *atonement*. Christ's saving work must embrace his life and his resurrection as well as his death and cannot be separated from the person of Christ. Conner explored and criticized the Anselmic (satisfaction), the Grotian (governmental), the Abelardian (moral influence), the Socinian (example), the "commercial" or quantitatively penal, and A. H. Strong's eternal atonement theories.[78]

Rather than follow the classical Protestant pattern of justification, sanctification, and glorification, Conner gave attention to the various New Testament terms used to describe one's becoming a Christian, although "salvation" (past, present, future) was used comprehensively. He successively expounded union with Christ, forgiveness, justification, reconciliation, adoption, new life, and sanctification. Conner was critical of the forensic doctrine of justification ("declared righteous") issuing from the Reformation and argued for a vital doctrine ("made righteous") which was devoid of Roman Catholic works-righteousness and closely joined to regeneration.[79] On sanctification Conner moved away from Protestant orthodoxy by insisting that the term had initial, continuing, and consummative uses, not merely the continuing. Identifying repentance and faith as "conditions of salvation," in 1924 Conner placed them prior to the discussion of the aforementioned terms and in 1945 after such discussion. The final rubric under becoming a Christian was assurance. The Christian life was interpreted under four themes: providence, prayer, perseverance, and growth. Objections to providence, including that arising from suffering, are answered, and a special providence affirmed. Prayer "is communion of the soul with God"; Conner noted its various moods and answered objections to prayer. Conner's doctrine of stewardship, including his objection to "storehouse tithing," was expressed in various articles. On perseverance Conner clearly remained a Calvinist with no disposition to allow apostasy, but his careful definition of perseverance has led to his being identified as a "modified Calvinist."[80] He advocated Christian growth but rejected perfectionism.[81]

Moving beyond Baptist Landmarkism, Conner found the term *church* to be used in the New Testament in a universal as well as local sense. The church as the body of Christ is primarily fellowship rather than organization. Conner favored democratic polity, basing it on the principles of New Testament Christianity rather than on proof-texts. In 1925, he stressed edification, evangelization, benevolence, and moral dynamism as the mission of the church, whereas in 1945, he contended that "the first business" of a church is worship. Emphatic about a divine call to preach, he reckoned baptism and the Lord's Supper to be pictorial and symbolic, rejected pedobaptism and "alien immersion," and held to close communion. Conner treated last things under the title "The Consummation of Salvation: The Coming of the Kingdom of God." Recognizing that there were unique difficulties vis-à-vis eschatology, he set forth a fivefold interpretation of the kingdom of God: universal sovereignty, the theocracy of Israel, the spiritual rule founded by Jesus, "a progressive power in the world," and the consummated or eternal kingship. In 1924, Conner taught one general resurrection of all humans at the time of the second coming of Jesus, whereas in 1945 he, following T. P. Stafford, inclined toward the view that resurrection bodies are received at death and resurrection itself will accompany the Second Coming. In 1924, Conner inclined toward postmillennialism, but in 1945, he identified himself generally with amillennialism. The final judgment will reveal human character, assign destinies, and vindicate God's dealings with humanity. Conner affirmed heaven and hell, rejecting restorationism and annihilationism.[82]

Evaluation

The theology of W. T. Conner has numerous elements of *strength* that can be recognized five decades after his work ended. For him Christian theology was to be closely related to Christian experience and the church and hence was not to be primarily speculative. Conner's writing style, marked by simplicity and an Anglo-Saxon vocabulary, made his teachings available to pastors and laypeople.[83] Conner gave emphasis to the doctrine of revelation when it was receiving much attention from Protestant theologians. His anti-Barthian espousal of general revelation and his teaching of the finality in Christ are seen as strengths by this author. The attributes of God are to be interpreted so as to attain to the moral self-consistency of God, and the doctrine of God should be framed in the light of Jesus Christ. Conner was increasingly concerned with the doctrine of the Holy Spirit, especially the Spirit's work. Man is not worthy of salvation yet is worth saving. Man is personally responsible for sin, and hence Conner had no tolerance for theories of imputation of Adamic guilt. Late in life Conner made a major shift from penal substitution to Christ as victor. His departure from Protestant orthodoxy concerning sanctification is probably more persuasive than his departure concerning justification. Providence, for Conner, meant Romans 8:28–29. Moreover, the kingdom of God should be so interpreted as to be consistent with the mission of Jesus himself.[84]

Weaknesses in the theology of Conner are also identifiable. Certain major topics treated by other theologians during the nineteenth and twentieth centuries were bypassed or treated only slightly by Conner; for example, theories concerning the divine inspiration of the Bible, the biblical doctrine of the image of God in man, and the relation of the doctrine of the creation of man to evolutionary science. Sometimes the readers of Conner's books may be inclined to want to press questions upon him. Have you mistakenly fused general revelation and theistic arguments for God's existence? Are there no clearer conclusions to be drawn concerning Chalcedonian Christology and kenoticism? Is not the Trinity more important for other doctrines and for one's total theology than you have specified? Have not your objection to "alien immersion" and your defense of close communion become anachronistic among Southern Baptists? A Southern Presbyterian criticized *The Gospel of Redemption* for its lack of "a sense of dialectic" and for its failure to "grapple seriously" with great contemporary issues confronting church and society.[85] Those who would identify Conner as a fundamentalist will fall short of proving their case, and those who would interpret him as a full-blown Synod of Dort Calvinist must face the fact that he clearly taught only two (election and perseverance) of the "five points."[86]

The *classification* of Conner as a theologian is a difficult task. Clearly he was a Southern Baptist theologian. Aspects of his theology agreed with classical Christian orthodoxy and with Protestant teachings, but he deviated at key points from Protestant orthodoxy. Philosophers of religion may classify him under "traditional supernaturalism."[87] Perhaps he can best be identified with conservative or constructive evangelicalism.

Conner's *influence* was almost exclusively limited to Southern Baptists, although some of his books were translated into Spanish, Portuguese, and Chinese. Nearly four decades of students were shaped in his classroom, and his books were widely circulated until the 1960s. In the 1980s and 1990s, his theological work has been found to be relevant to the problems confronting Southern Baptists and a field for intensive research.

Bibliography

Works by Conner

Books
Christian Doctrine. Nashville: Broadman Press, 1937.
The Christ We Need. Grand Rapids: Zondervan, 1938.
The Cross in the New Testament. Edited by Jesse J. Northcutt. Nashville: Broadman Press, 1954.
The Epistles of John: Their Meaning and Message. New York: Fleming H. Revell Co., 1929.
The Faith of the New Testament. Nashville: Broadman Press, 1940.
Gospel Doctrines. Nashville: Sunday School Board of the Southern Baptist Convention, 1925.
The Gospel of Redemption. Nashville: Broadman Press, 1945.
Personal Christianity. Grand Rapids: Zondervan, 1937.
The Resurrection of Jesus. Nashville: Sunday School Board of the Southern Baptist Convention, 1926.
Revelation and God: An Introduction to Christian Doctrine. Nashville: Broadman Press, 1936.
A System of Christian Doctrine. Nashville: Sunday School Board of the Southern Baptist Convention, 1924.
The Teachings of Mrs. Eddy. Nashville: Broadman Press, 1926.
The Teachings of "Pastor" Russell. Nashville: Sunday School Board of the Southern Baptist Convention, 1926.
What Is a Saint? Nashville: Broadman Press, 1948.
The Work of the Holy Spirit. Nashville: Broadman Press, 1949.

Contributions to Monographs
"Theological Education," *Fourth Baptist World Congress: Record of Proceedings,* 286–91. Edited by W. T. Whitley. London: Kingsgate Press, 1928.
"Infant Baptism." *Re-thinking Baptist Doctrines,* 61–80. Edited by Victor I. Masters. Louisville: *Western Recorder,* 1937.
"Autobiographical Sketch" and "The Place of Prayer in the Christian Life." *Southwestern Men and Messages,* 41–43, 44–51. Edited by J. M. Price. Kansas City, Kan.: Central Seminary Press, 1948.

Unpublished Theses
"The Idea of the Incarnation in the Gospel of John." Unpublished Ph.D. thesis, Southern Baptist Theological Seminary, Louisville, Kentucky, 1931. 150 pp.
"Pragmatism and Theology." Unpublished Th.D. thesis, Southern Baptist Theological Seminary, Louisville, Kentucky, 1916. 77 pp.
"Theodore Parker's Theological System." Thesis offered for fellowship, Rochester Theological Seminary, Rochester, New York, 1909. 33 pp.

Selected Journal Articles

"The Call to the Work of the Ministry." *Southwestern Journal of Theology* o.s. 3 (July 1919): 48–56.

"Christ's Death and Our Redemption." *Southwestern Journal of Theology* o.s. 7 (October 1923): 58–67.

"Eddyism vs. Christianity." *Southwestern Journal of Theology* o.s. 6 (October 1922): 3–13.

"The Essentials of Christian Union." *Southwestern Journal of Theology* o.s. 7 (April 1923): 47–55.

"The Formal Factor in Christianity." *Review and Expositor* 13 (January 1916): 38–52.

"The Fundamental Baptist Principle." *Southwestern Journal of Theology* o.s. 1 (April 1917): 26–29.

"The Glorified Christ." *Southwestern Journal of Theology* o.s. 5 (January 1921): 56–66.

"God's Purpose and Providence." *Southwestern Journal of Theology* o.s. 7 (January 1923): 36–49.

"Human Nature in the Light of the Incarnation." *Southwestern Journal of Theology* o.s. 1 (October 1917): 72–82.

"The Importance of Ecclesiology to Baptists." *Review and Expositor* 37 (January 1940): 13–22.

"Is Christian Science Christian?" *Southwestern Journal of Theology* o.s. 2 (April 1918): 47–53.

"Is Paul's Doctrine of Justification Forensic?" *Review and Expositor* 40 (January 1943): 48–53.

"Jesus and the Gospel." *Southwestern Journal of Theology* o.s. 8 (January 1924): 11–20.

"The Nature of the Authority of the Bible." *Southwestern Journal of Theology* o.s. 2 (October 1918): 11–17.

"The Relation of the Work of the Holy Spirit to the Person and Work of Jesus Christ." *Southwestern Journal of Theology* o.s. 4 (January 1920): 26–33.

"The Significance of Baptism." *Southwestern Journal of Theology* o.s. 4 (April 1920): 49–60.

"Theology, a Practical Discipline." *Review and Expositor* 41 (October 1944): 350–60.

"Theories of Atonement." *Review and Expositor* 24 (July 1927): 301–11.

"Three Theories of Atonement." *Review and Expositor* 43 (July 1946): 275–90.

"Three Types of Teaching in the New Testament on the Meaning of the Death of Christ." *Review and Expositor* 43 (April 1946): 150–66.

"The Throne and the Lamb." *Review and Expositor* 39 (April 1942): 206–12.

Works about Conner

Allen, Arthur Lynn. "A Comparative Study of the Person of Christ in Selected Baptist Theologians: Augustus H. Strong, William N. Clarke, Edgar Y. Mullins, and Walter T. Conner." Th.D. diss., New Orleans Baptist Theological Seminary, 1979.

Basden, Paul Abbott. "Theologies of Predestination in the Southern Baptist Tradition: A Critical Evaluation." Ph.D. diss., Southwestern Baptist Theological Seminary, 1986.

Carroll, Raymond Evans. "Dimensions of Individualism in Southern Baptist Thought." Th.D. dissertation., New Orleans Baptist Theological Seminary, 1995.

Draughon, Walter D., III. "A Critical Evaluation of the Diminishing Influence of Calvinism on the Doctrine of Atonement in Representative Southern Baptist Theologians: James Petigru Boyce, Edgar Young Mullins, Walter Thomas Conner, and Dale Moody." Ph.D. diss., Southwestern Baptist Theological Seminary, 1987.

Garrett, James Leo, Jr. "The Bible at Southwestern Seminary During Its Formative Years: A Study of H. E. Dana and W. T. Conner." *Baptist History and Heritage* 21 (October 1986): 29–43.

———. "Conner, Walter Thomas." *Encyclopedia of Religion in the South*. Ed. Samuel S. Hill. Macon, Ga.: Mercer University Press, 1984.

———. "Conner, Walter Thomas." *Encyclopedia of Southern Baptists*. Vol. 1. Nashville: Broadman Press, 1958.

———. "The Theology of Walter Thomas Conner." Th.D. diss., Southwestern Baptist Theological Seminary, 1954.

———. "W. T. Conner: Contemporary Theologian." *Southwestern Journal of Theology* n.s. 25 (Spring 1983): 43–60.

Gray, Elmer Leslie. "The Ultimate Purpose of God." Th.D. diss., Southwestern Baptist Theological Seminary, 1951.

Hunt, William Boyd. "Southern Baptists and Systematic Theology." *Southwestern Journal of Theology* n.s. 1 (April 1959): 43–49.

Hurst, Clyde J. "The Problem of Religious Knowledge in the Theology of Edgar Young Mullins and Walter Thomas Conner." *Review and Expositor* 52 (April 1955): 166–82.

McClendon, James William. *Pacemakers of Christian Thought*. Nashville: Broadman Press, 1962.

Moody, Dwight Allan. "Doctrines of Inspiration in the Southern Baptist Theological Tradition." Ph.D. diss., The Southern Baptist Theological Seminary, 1982.

Morgan, Darold H. "Traditional Supernaturalism and the Problem of Evil." Th.D. diss., Southwestern Baptist Theological Seminary, 1953.

Newman, Stewart Albert. W. T. *Conner: Theologian of the Southwest*. Nashville: Broadman Press, 1964.

Northcutt, Jesse James. "Walter Thomas Conner: Theologian of Southwestern." *Southwestern Journal of Theology* n.s. 9 (Fall 1966): 81–89.

Parks, Robert Keith. "A Biblical Evaluation of the Doctrine of Justification in Recent American Baptist Theology: With Special Reference to A. H. Strong, E. Y. Mullins, and W. T. Conner." Th.D. diss., Southwestern Baptist Theological Seminary, 1954.

Youngblood, Clark Richard. "The Question of Apostasy in Southern Baptist Thought since 1900: A Critical Evaluation." Ph.D. diss., The Southern Baptist Theological Seminary, 1979.

12

Herschel H. Hobbs

By David S. Dockery

Biography

HERSCHEL H. HOBBS, BY ANY ACCOUNT, WAS ONE OF THE MOST INFLUENTIAL and shaping leaders in Southern Baptist life in the twentieth century. His role as chairman of the 1963 "Baptist Faith and Message" Committee, coupled with his tireless efforts to formulate and articulate Southern Baptist doctrine and distinctives for almost four decades, have cemented his position in history. Hobbs, as preacher, author, denominational statesman, and pastor-theologian, has often been called "Mr. Southern Baptist." By examining only his early years, few would have predicted the influence he later would have on Baptist life. Hobbs stepped onto the Southern Baptist stage under the guidance of and with the obvious blessings of God's providential hand, for he had no family tradition of church leadership, denominational involvement, serious biblical exposition, or theological reflection on which to build.

The Early Years

Hobbs was born on October 24, 1907, in the rural community of Marble Valley in Coosa County, Alabama. Born to Elbert Oscar and Emma Octavia Whatley Hobbs, Herschel was the sixth child and first son in the family. His father died of malaria when Herschel was two.

Hobbs's mother was a Baptist, and his father had been a member of the Church of Christ, though he had led the singing at the local Methodist church. The first church Herschel remembered attending was the Blue Springs Methodist Church. At five years of age, he was asked what he wanted to do when he grew up. Hobbs responded, "I'm going to be a Methodist preacher like Brother Smith." Later in his life he would recall, "I have always felt that even at a tender age God had planted in my mind that I was to be a preacher."[1] After his father's death, his mother took her children to the local Baptist church, which according to Hobbs was the primary reason he grew up a Baptist.

Hobbs made a public profession of faith in Jesus Christ when he was eleven years old during a revival service in the Enon Baptist Church in Chilton County, Alabama. The revival preacher was Reverend Ernest Davis, a ministerial student at Howard College (later called Samford University), who baptized Herschel in Montevallo Creek. The words he spoke on that occasion serve as a foreshadowing of Hobbs's strong emphasis on religious experience: "Back there I felt bad; I came, and now I feel good."[2]

In the spring of 1920, his mother sold the family farm and moved her family to Birmingham, Alabama, in order to provide better educational opportunities for her children. Hobbs graduated from Phillips High School in Birmingham in 1926. At this stage of life, Hobbs had learned the value of hard work through various jobs and family responsibilities but had yet to develop a commitment to serious study and academic excellence.[3]

The Hobbs family moved to a suburb on the west side of Birmingham, called Ensley, where they joined the Ensley Baptist Church. Here Herschel met Frances Jackson, the daughter of a bivocational preacher who soon thereafter would become his wife. Herschel and Frances were married at 8:30 A.M. on Sunday morning, April 10, 1927, in a simple wedding in the parlor of her home. For their honeymoon they went to Sunday school and church and B.Y.P.U. and church that night. Six weeks later Frances graduated from high school under her maiden name.[4]

Preparation for Ministry

Shortly after they were married, Hobbs publicly made a commitment to full-time vocational ministry—and as he put it, "I have never turned back!"[5] Upon telling Frances's family about his commitment, his mother-in-law responded: "Well, if you are going to preach, you and 'Sis' (Frances) are going to Howard College. . . . We don't want a 'jack-leg' preacher in the family."[6] Hobbs recalled his first sermon, titled "God's Universal Call to Humanity" from John 1:39, "Come and see." Hobbs, adapting the words of R. G. Lee, said, "I had a text and topic large enough to support a skyscraper. And I built a chicken coop on top of it."[7]

Herschel and Frances entered Howard College in 1930, where he graduated two and one-half years later. With a special decision from the president, he was allowed to graduate early. They then moved to Louisville, Kentucky, where Herschel enrolled in the Th.M. program at the Southern Baptist Theological Seminary.[8] He studied New Testament under W. Hersey Davis and A. T. Robertson for his Th.M., and went on to complete his Ph.D. under Davis, writing his dissertation on the issue of "Does the Author of the Fourth Gospel Consciously Supplement the Synoptic Gospels?"[9] The large influence and long shadow of Davis and Robertson would manifest itself in Hobbs's preaching and particularly his writing over the next sixty years.

Although Hobbs did not have the privilege to study with E. Y. Mullins (1860–1928), his theology was significantly shaped by Mullins's work, *The Christian Religion in Its Doctrinal Expression.* Hobbs claimed to have virtually memorized this important book and was convinced that Mullins was the premier Baptist theologian of all time. Hobbs reflected: "Though I never got to sit at his [Mullins's] feet, I have lived with his books to the point that I feel that I did know him."[10] Hobbs largely formed his understanding of Baptist distinctives from Mullins's work, *The Axioms of Religion,* which Hobbs revised and republished in 1978.[11]

Pastor and Denominational Leader

During his seminary days Hobbs pastored churches in Indiana and Kentucky. After graduation he served key churches in Louisiana and Alabama, including the Dauphin Way Baptist Church in Mobile, but it was not until he came to First Baptist Church, Oklahoma City, in 1949, that he began to play an unparalleled role in Southern Baptist life. He served on numerous boards[12] and held offices in state conventions, the Southern Baptist Convention, and the Baptist World Alliance, for which he served as vice president from 1965 to 1970. A few of his board memberships included New Orleans Seminary, Oklahoma Baptist University, Foreign Mission Board, and the Executive Committee of the SBC. He served as president of the SBC Pastors' Conference and the Baptist General Convention of Oklahoma. Through these roles and his eighteen years of preaching on *The Baptist Hour,* a weekly radio program produced by the Radio and Television Commission of the SBC, Hobbs became one of a handful of major denominational spokespersons for Southern Baptists.[13]

Hobbs's most prominent denominational service occurred when he served as president of the Southern Baptist Convention (1961–1963). During this time he chaired the committee that revised "The Baptist Faith and Message," which was adopted by the Convention in 1963. Reflecting on the importance of this unique role, Hobbs stated:

> What do I consider my most abiding service for the Kingdom of God? I would like to think that all I have said and done was to this end. But if I should have to choose, I would say: as a pastor-preacher, writer, radio preacher, and Chairman of the Committee which drew up the 1963 revised statement of "the Baptist Faith and Message," perhaps Convention-wide, the last will have the most lasting effect.[14]

His service outside of Baptist life was limited, though he served as a member of the board of trustees of *Christianity Today* for several years. He retired from the pastorate of First Baptist Church, Oklahoma City, in 1972 at the age of 65.[15] Still he continued to serve Southern Baptists for the next two decades before his death in the fall of 1995.

Prolific Author

Through the years Hobbs developed a prolific writing ministry. In 1951, Hobbs published his first book. Forty-four years later Hobbs had penned about 150 different works for laypersons and pastors alike. He has written more books than anyone else in Southern Baptist history and more materials for the Sunday School Board (now LifeWay) than anyone else. In addition he has authored innumerable articles for state papers and other periodicals. More than one hundred of these books were Bible study guides for Sunday school teachers called *Studying Adult Life and Work Lessons,* which he published quarterly from 1968 to 1993. More than forty of these books focused on Baptist doctrine, Baptist heritage, or biblical commentary/exposition, particularly on New Testament books. He wrote commentaries on Genesis, the four Gospels, Revelation, and almost all of the Pauline Epistles.

Hobbs was often asked, "How do you find time to write as much as you do?" "My reply," he said, "is manifold":

I have had a sympathetic wife who did not begrudge me the time, an understanding church, and a staff that has taken much of the load of details off me. And for most of these years, I have had my study in my home. In that way I do much of my writing at night. For instance, if Frances was doing something that did not involve me, I would go into my study and write. I would not leave her to go to the church to do it. Since Frances' death I find relief from loneliness by staying busy. And writing has been my way of studying. Writing for publication makes me study more carefully. The product may not be worth publishing, but I try. All in all, I have written for seven publishers, the reason being that I have written books faster than any one publisher would want to publish books by the same author. I am grateful to each one of them.[16]

While his books also included pastoral and evangelistic works, in addition to the biblical commentaries and teaching guides, the rest of this chapter will focus on Hobbs's exposition of Baptist doctrine. His most important doctrinal contributions included: *Who Is This?* (1952); *Fundamentals of Our Faith* (1960); *What Baptists Believe* (1964); *The Life and Times of Jesus* (1966); *The Holy Spirit* (1967); *The Baptist Faith and Message* (1971); *The Cosmic Drama* (1971); *A Layman's Handbook of Christian Doctrine* (1974); *The Axioms of Religion* (revised 1978); *You Are Chosen: The Priesthood of All Believers* (1990); and "People of the Book: The Baptist Doctrine of the Holy Scripture" published posthumously in *Baptists Why and Why Not Revisited* (1997).

Exposition

Baptist historian Walter B. Shurden described Herschel Hobbs as one of the most influential Southern Baptist theologians of the twentieth century. Along with E. Y. Mullins, Shurden named Hobbs as one of two Southern Baptist leaders primarily responsible for the formulation and articulation of Southern Baptist distinctives. He expanded this observation, saying:

Mullins served as Southern Baptists' theologian in the first half of this century and Hobbs in the latter half. Both were inspiring preachers, concerned denominational statesmen and strong advocates of Southern Baptist doctrines. Mullins was responsible for Southern Baptists' first confession of faith in 1925 and Hobbs for the confession of 1963. Moreover, Mullins wrote and Hobbs revised the classic statement of Southern Baptist distinctives, a little book entitled *The Axioms of Religion*. When, therefore, Southern Baptists want to know "historic" Southern

Baptist distinctives, they must return to the writings of these revered leaders. Mullins and Hobbs handled the Word of God reverently, and obediently, seeking to make sure that Baptist distinctives came from the Bible and not from culture. They also knew Baptist history and affirmed those Baptist doctrines which were in the mainstream of Baptist thought.[17]

Hobbs, like his friend W. A. Criswell, developed his theological works out of messages delivered to his congregation. In that sense Hobbs's theology is Baptist theology at its best, theology developed out of the church for the church. The writings represent Hobbs's efforts to set forth his understanding of Baptist beliefs. For Hobbs, theology is the reasonable study of God. It is trying, by use of God's Word, to learn more about who God is, his will, way, and work. Theology is not the province of preachers; it belongs to all believers. It is something to be believed, practiced, and taught.[18]

Hobbs sought to present Baptist doctrine to a wider readership in order for men and women to grow in their faith (2 Tim. 2:15) and to be able to defend their faith (1 Pet. 3:15).[19] In general Hobbs's theology represents the historic teaching of the church through the centuries based on what the Bible says.[20] Hobbs was convinced that the Bible is the inspired Word of God and that all theology should be derived from it.[21] In his examination prior to his ordination, one pastor asked the young Hobbs, "Does the Bible *contain* the Word of God or *is* the Bible the Word of God?" Hobbs said, "Frankly, I had never even thought about it . . . but I soon learned and still believe that the Bible *is* the Word of God."[22] Hobbs was aware of issues in historical theology and the role of tradition in Baptist life. He used reason appropriately and, like Mullins before him, put great emphasis on personal experience as a confirming aspect of theology. But without question or apology, the Bible served as the primary source for Hobbs's theological constructions. Hobbs's books on the *Fundamentals of Our Faith* and *What Baptists Believe* contain careful explications of the doctrine of Scripture and demonstrate that the Bible is the source for Hobbs's understanding of God, Jesus Christ, the Holy Spirit, salvation, the church, last things, and other doctrinal teachings.

While Hobbs looked to an authoritative and inspired Bible as the source of his theology and while he had a great appreciation for our Baptist heritage, he nevertheless was hesitant to acknowledge the place of doctrinal confessions as normative for the Christian community. His emphasis on individualism and the competency of the soul in each believer moved him to a false dichotomy between a "living faith" and a "confessional or creedal faith." In the preamble to the 1963 Baptist Faith and Message, Hobbs claimed that the confession has "no authority over the conscience." While no Baptist would want to put any confession on the same level with Scripture or confuse a confession about Jesus with a dynamic trust in Jesus, to say that the confession has no authority is certainly an overstatement. The confession is a secondary or tertiary source of authority, not a primary one. Nevertheless, confessions have historically been understood to have a normative place for believers. James Leo Garrett's comments at this point are most helpful:

> Herschel Harold Hobbs has declared that Southern Baptists "have a living faith rather than a creedal one." The present author [Garrett] would contend that the statement poses an improper antithesis. The opposite of a living faith is a dead faith. The opposite of a creedal or confessional faith is a vague or contentless or undefined faith. Admittedly confessions of faith may be differentiated from creeds, and the danger of a decadent faith must be clearly recognized, but our Christian faith should be both living and confessional! One can no more eat choice beef from a boneless cow and one can no more work safely in a skyscraper that has no structural steel than one can practice and communicate the Christian religion without basic Christian affirmations or doctrines.[23]

Let us now turn our attention to Hobbs's exposition and explication of key theological issues.

The Doctrine of Scripture

Baptists have been called a people of the Book. "The Baptist Faith and Message" begins its statements on the Scriptures by avowing that "the Holy Bible was written by men divinely inspired and is the record of God's revelation of Himself to man."[24] Thus Hobbs believed that the Bible is the inspired written record of God's revelation to men. He maintained that God is not discovered but is manifest to humanity through God's own self-disclosure. God's self-revelation in his written Word is more clear than any other source of revelation.[25]

Throughout his life and ministry, Hobbs affirmed the inspiration of the Bible. In 1971, he identified four theories describing how God inspired the Scriptures: (1) the intuition theory, (2) the illumination theory, (3) the dictation theory, and (4) the dynamic theory.[26] Hobbs noted that the first two of these theories hold that only portions of the Bible are inspired and thus should be rejected. One or the other of the last two theories, maintained Hobbs, is held by the vast majority of Southern Baptists. Hobbs, at that time, supported the dynamic theory, meaning that the Holy Spirit inspired the thoughts rather than the exact words to express the biblical truth.

In 1971, Hobbs did not mention the plenary view; but in one of the last pieces he penned, an article titled "The People of the Book," he alluded to the fact that Basil Manly Jr., in his classic work of inspiration, espoused plenary inspiration. In this same article Hobbs suggested that both the plenary view and the dynamic view see the Bible as the inspired Word of God.[27]

Hobbs was clear that the Bible is an inspired, divine-human book. He unhesitatingly affirmed that "the Bible is historically accurate" and "scientifically correct." The Bible is not a textbook in science, he said, "but when it speaks in that realm, it speaks truth."[28] Thus Hobbs maintained, like his mentor, A. T. Robertson, that the Bible is inerrant in the original manuscripts. He insightfully noted that:

> To use the word infallible weakens the statement [on
> Scripture]. Some dictionaries give two meanings of infallible:
> without error; and anything that does what it is supposed to do.
> You may have a dull knife with gaps in the blade. But if you use
> it only to cut string, and it does, in that sense, it is infallible, even
> though it is full of flaws. In that sense, the Bible could be full of
> errors. But if it is to lead people to salvation in Christ, and if it
> does, it is infallible. No, the stronger word is **inerrant**.[29]

Certainly Hobbs was a thoroughgoing biblicist since the early days of his ordination examination. However, with his huge influence over Southern Baptists, one has to wonder if the controversy over Scripture, which took place in the last decades of the twentieth century, would have taken a different road if Hobbs had emphasized in a more pronounced way his own commitment to biblical inerrancy.[30] Hobbs clearly confessed the full inspiration, authority, truthfulness, and inerrancy of the Bible as the position of Southern Baptists at the conclusion of the twentieth century.[31]

In what may have been Hobbs's final words from his powerful pen, he raised these questions: "Are you willing to place your trust in something that is in a constant state of flux? Or will you place it in the Bible, God's solid rock of revealed truth? Your answer bears eternal consequences."[32]

God and Creation

The foundational supposition that God exists is practically universal, according to Hobbs. In *Fundamentals of Our Faith,* he wrote:

> The Bible does not argue the existence of God; it only de-
> clares his will and purpose. With only one statement the Bible
> dismisses the atheist: "The fool hath said in his heart, There is no
> God" (Ps. 53:1). . . . Anyone, like the Psalmist, can look about
> him and see even in nature the evidence of God's existence and
> work (Ps. 19:1).[33]

Consistent with theologians throughout history, Hobbs maintained that God is infinite and thus impossible to define. Following Mullins, Hobbs offered this description (not definition) of God:

God is the supreme personal Spirit; perfect in all his attributes; who is the source, support, and end of the universe; who
guides it according to the wise, righteous, and loving purpose revealed in Jesus Christ; who indwells in all things by his Holy
Spirit, seeking ever to transform them according to his own will
and bring them to the goal of his kingdom.[34]

Similarly Hobbs followed Mullins's understanding and description of
the attributes of God with seven natural and four moral attributes.[35]
Hobbs emphasized the personal nature of God, affirming there is one God
and three persons: Father, Son, and Spirit, all equal in essence and power.
Hobbs was unhesitatingly Trinitarian, but his explanation had modalistic
tendencies emphasizing three manifestations of God over the classic onto-
logical understanding of the Trinity.[36] Certainly the doctrine of the Trinity
is incomprehensible. It is truth for the heart. The fact that it cannot be completely explained is something that should not surprise us. A God who is
understood completely is no God. No one could have imagined this doctrine; such a truth had to be revealed. As the church fathers affirmed, the
Trinity is divinely revealed, not humanly constructed.

Hobbs affirmed God as Creator (Gen. 1:1). He was noncommittal as
to the length of days in Genesis 1, but he believed that science and the
Scriptures could be harmonized.[37]

Jesus Christ

Hobbs's theology was Christocentric in the best sense of that term. He
believed that Jesus Christ is the key to humanity's knowledge of God and
history.[38] Hobbs saw Christ throughout Holy Scripture:

The Old Testament sounds the messianic hope. The Gospels
record Christ's incarnation; Acts relates his continuing work
through the Holy Spirit; the Epistles interpret his person and
work; Revelation proclaims his final triumph and glory.[39]

The addition of the phrase, "The criterion by which the Bible is to be
interpreted is Jesus Christ" to the 1963 "Baptist Faith and Message" reflects Hobbs's belief that "as an individual reads the Bible, it is essential
that he keeps in mind that Christ is central."[40]

Hobbs's Christology was a reflection of classic Chalcedonian orthodoxy. He affirmed the preexistence of Christ as the eternal second person of
the Godhead.[41] He contended that Jesus Christ is God of very God, the center of the universe.[42] Similarly he maintained that the eternal *Logos,* who is
God himself, took on human form to identify fully with and fully reveal
God to humanity. Indeed he is the God-man. Thus he affirmed the self-
emptying of Christ, his virgin birth, and his divine and human natures.[43]

Hobbs taught that Jesus Christ was prophet, priest, and king. He revealed God perfectly to humanity, was the perfect sacrifice for sins, and reigns over the kingdom of God. Hobbs was at his best in describing the work of Jesus Christ in behalf of sinners. Only through the death of Jesus Christ on the cross could the righteousness and holiness of God be satisfied. He explained that:

> By the death of the Son of God, and by nothing less, could a just God become justifier of sinful man. In the councils of eternity, then the Lamb of God was slain from before the foundation of the world. The cross, thus, was the enactment in time of that which already had been accomplished in eternity.[44]

Hobbs believed that Christ's death was a sufficient and substitutionary atonement, redeeming humans from the penalty of sin and reconciling them to God—doing for them what they could in no way do for themselves.[45]

Hobbs took seriously the challenges to the belief in a bodily resurrection. But he carefully countered each challenge and defended the bodily resurrection of Jesus Christ with biblical and historical evidence, concluding that it "is one of the best authenticated events in all of history."[46] He emphasized that the resurrection demonstrated the complete deity of Jesus Christ while giving hope to believers regarding their future resurrection with Christ. The ascension, exaltation, and return of Christ point to Christ's ultimate victory over sin, death, and Satan.[47]

Holy Spirit and Christian Life

The Holy Spirit is the "Spirit of God" and the "Spirit of Christ." As God is a person, so is the Holy Spirit a person. He possesses all the attributes of God and all elements of personality. With these broad comments Hobbs described the Holy Spirit, the third person of the Trinity. In the commentary on *The Baptist Faith and Message,* he identified four specific aspects of the work of the Holy Spirit, which are summarized below:

1. The Holy Spirit revealed God's will to men. This is related to the Scriptures themselves. The Spirit inspired chosen ones to write Scripture and illumines our minds to understand it.
2. The second aspect of the Spirit's work is enabling the disciples to understand and communicate the full significance of Jesus' redemptive work.
3. The third element is the Spirit's work with lost people. The Holy Spirit convicts them of their sin, shows them the righteousness God demands, and reveals to them the judgment to come for those who reject Christ. The Spirit enables lost sinners to turn to Christ in faith, sealing and sanctifying them as God's possession.
4. The Spirit then dwells in believers, taking up his abode in their lives. In this way he also dwells in the churches. He indwells believers and fills them for service. The presence of the Spirit in one's life is evidence of

regeneration, not of a second blessing or even of sanctification. The fruit of the Spirit is manifest in godly virtues not ecstatic demonstrations. The Holy Spirit does not reveal himself; he reveals God in Christ.[48]

Hobbs's treatment of the Christian life is underdeveloped. This is reflected in the revised statement on sanctification in the 1963 "Baptist Faith and Message." The 1925 statement was more expanded. Hobbs wrote the section in the 1963 statement himself. The 1925 statement called sanctification a process. Hobbs disagreed, choosing to emphasize sanctification as "an instantaneous experience whereby the regenerated one is set apart to God's service. Thereafter, he should grow, develop, and serve in the state of sanctification."[49] Sanctification, then, is a work of the Holy Spirit which fits believers for God's use. Believers grow and develop, not unto sanctification, but within the state of sanctification.[50]

Salvation

Steve Gaines has observed that the doctrine of salvation was "at the heart of Hobbs's 'Baptist Hour' preaching."[51] For Hobbs, God's redemptive purpose in Christ is the Bible's theme from beginning to end. Jesus Christ is "the Lamb slain from the foundation of the world" (Rev. 13:8). He taught that from before the foundation of the world forgiveness was in God's heart before sin was in man's.[52] A look at the historical context in which Hobbs developed this doctrine will be helpful.

The first one hundred years of Southern Baptist life witnessed a soteriological understanding largely within a Calvinistic framework. From the early years of J. P. Boyce (1827–88) to the death of W. T. Conner (1877–1952), Southern Baptists saw the diminishing influence of Calvinism. The strict Calvinism of Boyce shifted to a growing consensus that emerged around the moderate (modified) Calvinism of Mullins and Conner. Led by the thought of Herschel Hobbs, Southern Baptists in the middle and latter years of the twentieth century moved toward a modified Arminian understanding of salvation.[53] Hobbs embraced the Arminian understanding of predestination and foreknowledge. He believed that God affirmed every free human choice in such a way that the choices are not predetermined.[54]

Hobbs believed in human sinfulness but not in total depravity, as understood by Boyce, Mullins, or Conner. For the 1925 "Baptist Faith and Message" confessed that Adam's "posterity inherit a nature corrupt and in bondage to sin." Hobbs's language in 1963 said that Adam's "posterity inherit a nature and an environment inclined toward sin."

He rejected the idea that God's election is based on his choice of some. Instead he maintained that God chose to limit his sovereignty so that men and women could either accept or reject God's salvific offer in Christ.[55]

Hobbs believed that election referred to God's plan of salvation designed for all people. All who responded positively by faith are thus elect. So God elected that all who are "in Christ" will be saved. God's sovereignty has set the condition, but human free will determines the result.[56]

Hobbs rejected unconditional election and irresistible grace, both of which had been affirmed by Boyce. Mullins and Conner had revised the understanding of irresistible grace, but Hobbs rejected both. His work was more in line with the General Baptists of the seventeenth century than with either Boyce, Mullins, or Conner. He believed in a general atonement and a universal call to salvation, believing that "God's purpose in election is to save not a few but as many as possible."[57] Any limitation in God's plan comes not from God but from human choice.

Yet Hobbs parted company with Arminians at the point of perseverance or eternal security. "The thundering answer of Scripture," he proclaimed to the question as to whether a Christian "once saved" can "ever be lost again" was "No!"[58] Hobbs emphasized the perseverance passages in Scripture and generally ignored or reinterpreted the so-called warning passages. For example, instead of reading the warning passages in the Book of Hebrews as real warnings to genuine Christians, Hobbs suggested that the texts refer to Christians who are "faced with the peril of an arrested Christian growth by which they are in peril of falling short of their ultimate destiny in Christian behavior and service."[59] Hobbs's emphasis on "once saved, always saved" is one of his great legacies in Southern Baptist life.

Hobbs, who believed that salvation is by grace through faith, defined *faith* as "believing what is written about Christ, trusting in him and his work for salvation, and committing one's self to him."[60] He believed that faith resulted in conversion and regeneration, bringing about a new life and turning from the old life of rebellion against God to one of love of and service for God.[61]

Salvation, for Hobbs, has three aspects as articulated in the 1963 "Baptist Faith and Message": regeneration, sanctification, and glorification. Hobbs wrote:

> Regeneration is the salvation of the soul; sanctification is the Christian life; glorification is the heavenly state. In regeneration one is saved from the penalty of sin; in sanctification one is saved from the power of sin; in glorification one is saved from the presence of sin. In this threefold sense it is proper to say, "I am saved; I am being saved; I will be saved."[62]

Hobbs's strong emphasis on individual experience[63] in salvation caused him to downplay the legal and objective aspects of justification and adoption and the corporate aspects of union with Christ. Hobbs tended to ignore the important distinctions between regeneration and adoption, blurring them together in an unhelpful manner.[64] Sanctification means to be set apart by God for service in God's kingdom throughout life.[65] Glorification is the ultimate aspect of salvation experienced in heaven when one is saved completely for all eternity. Thus salvation is permanent, eternal, and cannot be lost.

The Church

Hobbs understood that the church in the New Testament never refers to organized Christianity or to a group of churches. It denotes either a local body of baptized believers or includes all the redeemed through the ages. The emphasis among Baptists is on the local church.[66] The 1963 "Baptist Faith and Message" says "the New Testament speaks also of the church as the body of Christ which includes all of the redeemed of all the ages." This addition served as a significant development to Landmarkism's theology of the church as only the local church.

Expecting this phrase to be challenged on the floor of the 1963 convention, Albert McClellan provided Hobbs with pages he had cut out of leading books on Baptist theology, including the first page of J. M. Pendleton's *Church Manual.* When asked about the phrase, "The redeemed of all ages," Hobbs quoted Pendleton, saying, "The word *ekklesia* is sometimes used in the New Testament to refer to the redeemed in aggregate."[67] The article on the church was then received with near unanimity.

Perhaps because Mullins, his theological model, did not expound a doctrine of the church in his volume *The Christian Doctrine in Its Doctrinal Expression* or perhaps because of his own emphasis on the individual aspect of the Christian faith, Hobbs gave little attention to the corporate nature of the church.

In his two works that constructed aspects of a Baptist theology of the church, *The Axioms of Religion* (1978) and *You Are Chosen: The Priesthood of All Believers* (1990), Hobbs suggested that the distinctives of Baptist life are not the doctrine of salvation, a regenerate church membership, believers' baptism, the Lord's Supper, or church-state matters—as important as these are (and all affirmed by Hobbs)—but the competency of the soul and the priesthood of every believer.

According to Hobbs, "the priesthood of the believer" entails both privileges ("direct access to God," "confession of our sins directly to God," and "the right to reach and interpret the Scriptures as led by the Holy Spirit") and responsibilities (holiness, love, Bible study, witness) and implies or is related to the doctrine of salvation, the Holy Spirit, ministry, the church, and religious liberty.[68] Hobbs missed the corporate nature of the priesthood in the New Testament and thus de-emphasized the corporate aspect of the church and worship. The church for Hobbs was a fellowship of individual believers gathered together for service, evangelism, and missions. Baptist churches, he claimed, are autonomous fellowships who exercise their independence through voluntary cooperation.[69] It could reasonably be said that Hobbs had a more fully developed doctrine of the Southern Baptist Convention, its structure, organization, purpose, and mission than of the local or universal church.

Last Things

Hobbs affirmed that the last judgment determines the final state of those who appear before the judgment seat. Their final state is either one of everlasting misery and separation from God or one of eternal blessedness. In the final state the wicked are consigned to the place of condemnation, the eternal lake of fire (Rev. 20:14–15). The abode of believers will be heaven, a place prepared by Christ (John 14:2). Heaven is not merely spiritual but is the establishment of the new heavens and new earth (Rev. 21–22). Hobbs maintained that all believers will share in "the blessed hope and the glorious appearing of the great God and our Savior Jesus Christ" (Tit. 2:13). His doctrine of Christ's return moved from a premillennial viewpoint without a program in his early years to what he viewed as an exegetically informed amillennialism.[70]

The eschatology of key Baptist leaders in the nineteenth century tended to be predominantly postmillennial. At the end of the twentieth century, the large majority of Southern Baptist leaders could be characterized as premillennial.[71] But the early and middle years of the twentieth century were generally championed by amillennialists. Mullins, Conner, Ray Summers, as well as Hobbs, and several others articulated an amillennial eschatology. Hobbs taught that Christ's return would be certain, imminent, sudden, universal, and victorious. Needless to say, his amillennialist position had great influence across Southern Baptist life.

Conclusion

Herschel Hobbs was indeed "one of a kind."[72] His abilities as preacher, teacher, author, denominational statesman, and pastor-theologian put him in unique company, perhaps only equaled in his widespread influence by his longtime friend W. A. Criswell. His great sense of humor, his ability to weave a story, and his powerful gifts as a communicator served him well in every situation. His role in shaping the Southern Baptist Convention, his boardsmanship and statesmanship, were unsurpassed. His role as mediator and his conciliatory style were used to forge a broad consensus (what historian Bill Leonard called the "Grand Compromise") that carried Southern Baptists through the 1960s and 1970s and was used to hold divergent groups together through the 1980s and into the 1990s.

His leadership style and pastoral emphasis were reflected in his theology as well. Hobbs was a thoroughgoing biblicist, a well-educated and capable biblical interpreter, and a theologian for the church. He saw his role as one to interpret scholars and theologians to pastors and laity and also to interpret pastors and laity to theologians and scholars. It would be fair to say that Hobbs, a progressive conservative by his own identification,[73] was a centrist, but one with courage and by conviction. Hobbs believed that 90 percent of Southern Baptists could be classified as centrists with 5 percent to the right and 5 percent to the left.[74] The consensus, with its broad center, broke down in the last two decades of the twentieth century. It came apart because the "centrists" would not take seriously the conservatives' concerns about the creeping liberalism in Southern Baptist life, for in Hobbs's own words, "we failed to heed the protests."[75]

When concerns were raised in 1962 over the issues surrounding Ralph Elliott's *Message of Genesis,* Porter Routh said:

> "Some people feel that Southern Baptists are becoming more liberal in theology. If so, we should know it. It seems that the best way to determine that would be to have a committee study the 1925 statement of The Baptist Faith and Message."[76]

This took place during Hobbs's tenure as SBC president. It can easily be said that this was Hobbs's finest hour. The resulting 1963 statement affirmed the convention's biblical roots and rebuilt a consensus that helped advance Southern Baptist work for years, even decades. Yet a similar response failed to develop in the early years of the "inerrancy controversy."

Whether the history of the last two decades would have been different is impossible to say. Hobbs conjectured that they might have been. Regardless, his recognition that Southern Baptist seminaries' primary purpose must be to train leaders for Southern Baptist churches remains right on target. He claimed that "if these leaders are to lead as Southern Baptists, they must be indoctrinated as to those things which Southern Baptists believe and practice . . . [their] reason for being is to prepare future Southern Baptist leaders for a specific task."[77]

Hobbs's biblicism, his sound Christology, his emphasis on salvation by grace through faith, and his unapologetic belief in Christ's sufficient and substitutionary death, Christ's bodily resurrection and imminent return, coupled with belief in the eternal state and the final judgment, provided a healthy framework around which Southern Baptist theology built a strong consensus. We believe a similar framework could again serve Southern Baptists well for years to come, assuming that the normative nature of doctrinal confessions could be understood in a manner more in line with James Leo Garrett than Herschel Hobbs.

We have along the way throughout this chapter noted what we believe to have been weaknesses in Hobbs's thinking—areas such as his views on justification, adoption, union with Christ, sanctification, his overemphasis on individual experience, and his inadequate understanding of doctrinal confessions.[78] But the orthodox framework grounded in Jesus Christ and shaped by Holy Scripture as identified above is a lasting testimony to Hobbs's great legacy, and Southern Baptists would do well to learn from it to build a new and needed convictional consensus for our work together in this new century. As we begin the twenty-first century, we do so with a huge debt of gratitude to a great leader and statesman who so faithfully served the "People of the Book," a Convention that he loved, with a life committed to the teachings of the Book, and moreover to the Lord of the Book. For Herschel H. Hobbs we say, "Thanks be to God."

Bibliography

Books by Hobbs

A Layman's Handbook of Christian Doctrine. Nashville: Broadman, 1974.
Best of the Baptist Hour. Fort Worth: The Radio and Television Commission of the Southern Baptist Convention, 1964.
Christ in You: An Exposition of the Epistle to the Colossians. Evangelical Pulpit Series. Grand Rapids: Baker, 1961.
Cowards or Conquerors. Philadelphia: Judson, 1951.
Exposition of the Gospel of John. Grand Rapids: Baker, 1968.
Exposition of the Gospel of Luke. Grand Rapids: Baker, 1966.
Exposition of the Gospel of Mark. Grand Rapids: Baker, 1970.
Exposition of the Gospel of Matthew. Grand Rapids: Baker, 1965.
First and Second Thessalonians, The Broadman Bible Commentary. Nashville: Broadman Press, 1971.
Fundamentals of Our Faith. Nashville: Broadman Press, 1960.
Galatians: A Verse-by-Verse Study. Waco: Word, 1979.
Getting Acquainted with the Bible. Nashville: Convention Press, 1991.
Herschel H. Hobbs: My Faith and Message. Nashville: Broadman & Holman, 1993.
John: Bible Study Commentary. Grand Rapids: Zondervan, 1968.
Messages on the Resurrection. Grand Rapids: Baker, 1959.
New Men in Christ: Studies in Ephesians. Waco: Word, 1974.
New Testament Evangelism: The Eternal Purpose. Nashville: Convention, 1960.
Romans: A Verse-by-Verse Study. Waco: Word, 1977.
Studies in Hebrews. Nashville: Sunday School Board of the Southern Baptist Convention, 1954.
Studies in Revelation. Nashville: Convention, 1974.
Studying Adult Life and Work Lessons. Nashville: Baptist Sunday School Board, 1968–1993 quarterly.
With E. Y. Mullins. *The Axioms of Religion,* revised. Nashville: Broadman Press, 1978.

The Baptist Faith and Message. Nashville: Convention Press, 1971.
The Cosmic Drama: An Exposition of the Book of Revelation. Waco: Word, 1971.
The Epistles of John. Nashville: Thomas Nelson, 1983.
The Epistles to the Corinthians. Grand Rapids: Baker, 1960.
The Gospel of John: An Invitation to Life. Nashville: Convention Press, 1988.
The Holy Spirit: Believer's Guide. Nashville: Broadman Press, 1967.
The Life and Times of Jesus. Grand Rapids: Zondervan, 1966.
The Origin of All Things: Studies in Genesis. Waco: Word, 1975.
What Baptists Believe. Nashville: Broadman Press, 1964.
Who is This? Nashville: Broadman Press, 1952.
You Are Chosen: The Priesthood of All Believers. San Francisco: Harper & Row, 1990.
George R. Beasley-Murray and Ray Frank Robbins. *Revelation: Three Viewpoints.* Nashville: Broadman Press, 1977.

Articles by Hobbs

"People of the Book: The Baptist Doctrine of the Holy Scripture." *Baptists Why and Why Not.* Edited by Timothy George and Richard Land. Nashville: Broadman & Holman, 1997.
"Reflections on My Ministry." *Southwestern Journal of Theology* 15 (Spring 1973): 70–76.
"Southern Baptists and Confessionalism: A Comparison of the Origins and Contents of the 1925 and 1963 Confessions." *Review and Expositor* 76 (1979): 55–68.
"Theological Erosion of Our Baptist Distinctives" *The Fibers of Our Faith.* Franklin, Tenn.: Providence, 1995.

Dissertations about Hobbs

Baker, James Donald. "An Examination of the Baptist Hour Preaching of Herschel H. Hobbs from 1958–1968." Th.D. dissertation. New Orleans Baptist Theological Seminary, 1972.
Basden, Paul A. "Theologies of Predestination in the Southern Baptist Tradition: A Critical Evaluation." Ph.D. dissertation. Southwestern Baptist Theological Seminary, 1986.
Carroll, Raymond Evans. "Dimensions of Individualism in Southern Baptist Thought." Th.D. dissertation. New Orleans Baptist Theological Seminary, 1995.
Gaines, John Steven. "An Analysis of the Correlation Between Representative Baptist Hour Sermons by Herschel H. Hobbs and Selected Articles of The Baptist Faith and Message." Ph.D. dissertation. Southwestern Baptist Theological Seminary, 1991.
Hopkins, Albert Perry, Jr. "An Analysis of the Theological Method of Herschel H. Hobbs and His Doctrines of Christ and Salvation." Th.D. dissertation. New Orleans Baptist Theological Seminary, 1994.
Turner, Helen Lee. "Fundamentalism in the Southern Baptist Convention: The Crystallization of a Millennialist Vision." Ph.D. dissertation. University of Virginia, 1990.

13
W. A. Criswell

By Paige Patterson

A GREEN CARPET OF AMAZON LUSHNESS, PUNCTUATED BY THE OCCASIONAL blue ribbons of rivers presided over by sun and broken clouds, constituted the totality of the view in September 1964. It was enough. The intellectual curiosity of W. A. Criswell, which extends from the keen observance of Wall Street to the current state of theological reflection, picking up literature, history, biology, music, art, history, and architecture along the way, was peaked by the sight below. This serenity was shattered as the single

233

engine of the Cessna aircraft they were flying suddenly disintegrated in midair in what sounded like machine gun fire. At this point there was almost no hope for a soft landing and little hope for survival. Skillfully, the missionary bush pilot navigated the rapidly descending aircraft into the only small river visible and within range. Miraculously missing trees on both sides of the curving stream, the plane came to a rough but safe halt on a sandbar. Twenty years later when this author sought Criswell's explanation for his survival, the mood turned pensive and theological. Looking as though he were beholding an object so far away that it transcended his world, he replied, "Lad, I do not know. I just do not know. It belongs to the imponderables of Almighty God."[1]

While Criswell is not above marshaling this phrase when he simply prefers not to comment, there is a sense in which the phrase became a summation of all that the far-famed pastor of the First Baptist Church in Dallas, Texas, really believes. He believes in an omnipotent, omniscient Creator who stands both outside and somehow, by choice, within his creation. He is convinced that this wise Creator revealed himself infallibly through the Word of God, leading him to cite Isaiah 40:8 more often than any other single verse.[2] But he also remains confident that this self-disclosure of God, while providing all that we need for faith and practice, was the act of a sovereign God about whose person and acts there remains much incomprehensible mystery.

Inauspicious beginnings can be dated to December 19, 1909, when in Eldorado, Oklahoma, Wallie Amos Criswell and his wife Anna Currie cradled a newborn boy, whom they named simply "W. A." Later Criswell would use Wallie Amos, although no one, including his parents, ever called him anything other than "W. A." His father attempted to farm during the devastating dust-bowl years of drought in the southwestern United States. Losing the family farm because of the weather patterns, Criswell's father reverted to an old trade and opened a barber shop in the Texas panhandle in Texline on the New Mexico border.

Criswell's earliest memories are from Texline. He remembers the poverty of the people, including his own family. A film produced by the Radio and Television Commission of the Southern Baptist Convention, entitled *This I Know*, poignantly focuses on the impact of the life of the small community Baptist church to which his parents belonged. At age ten, he was converted in a weekday morning revival service in which John Hicks from the First Baptist Church of Dalhart was preaching. Even prior to that the boy had a conviction that he would preach. In response to a Baylor University oral history interviewer who asked the origins of this awareness, Criswell replied:

> I have tried to ferret that out and I'm unable to. As far as
> my memory goes back, I had the same conviction that God

wanted me to be a preacher as I have right now, just as far back as I can remember. I cannot remember when I was not going to be a pastor.[3]

The Criswell home was a happy home but in some ways not a home likely to produce a famous preacher. For one thing, neither parent wanted W. A. to be a pastor. Most pastors they knew were subject to harsh criticism and little or no pay. Worse, the two parents did have favorite preachers. Criswell's father was a devoted follower of the flamboyant and unpredictable Fort Worth pastor, J. Frank Norris, while Anna preferred the sedate and statesmanlike George W. Truett and L. R. Scarborough. Criswell says that his parents argued endlessly over which of these were the preachers to follow.[4]

In 1925, W. A. and his mother moved to Amarillo so the boy could attend high school. In 1927, Mrs. Criswell moved once again with her son to Waco, Texas, where he matriculated at Baylor University and took a major in English under a favorite professor, A. J. Armstrong. By the time of his graduation from Baylor in 1931, W. A. had served as pastor of three churches—Devil's Bend in Marlow, Texas; Pecan Grove in Pulltight, Texas; and White Mound Baptist Church in Mound, Texas.

While a student at the Southern Baptist Theological Seminary in Louisville, Kentucky, where he eventually received both the Th.M. and, in 1937, the Ph.D. degrees, Criswell continued to function in student pastorates, including Mount Washington Baptist Church where he met and married Betty Harris, the church pianist. At Southern he knew the famous Greek scholar, A. T. Robertson, but like so many of Criswell's contemporaries, he admired but did not like Robertson. On the other hand, he loved W. Hershey Davis and reduplicated significant portions of Davis's Matthew commentary in his own commentary on that book. Criswell's doctoral dissertation was entitled "The John the Baptist Movement in Relation to the Christian Movement" (1937). Upon graduation a call was extended by the First Baptist Church of Chickasha, Oklahoma, and the young pastor accepted. While in Chickasha, the couple's only child, Mabel Ann, was born, though later the Criswells adopted their own grandson, Chris, who was the only child from Ann's first marriage.

Two important developments transpired during his next pastorate at the First Baptist Church of Muskogee, Oklahoma (1941–44). These two events would powerfully shape both the pastor and eventually his contribution to theology. First, he abandoned topical preaching in favor of book-by-book exposition. This led, in turn, to his embracing premillennialism, though he evidently did not know the word, nor had he had the benefit of study with a premillennial teacher. This new eschatological perspective was destined to loom increasingly large in the development of the pastor's theology.

On July 7, 1944, George W. Truett, pastor at the First Baptist Church of Dallas, Texas, for 47 years, passed to his heavenly home. Truett was the epitome of a statesman-clergyman. His manner was grave, especially following the hunting accident in which Truett accidently discharged his shotgun, killing his friend who was the Dallas chief of police.[5] When he mounted the pulpit, he had the appearance of an avenging angel and the vocal quality of a prophet. He was controlled, awesome, and probably the most admired pastor both inside and outside the Southern Baptist denomination in all of its history. Naturally, it was conceded by most that no one could effectively follow him at First Dallas.

Following an unusual dream, W. A. Criswell was called to succeed the illustrious Truett. Criswell was young, bombastic, loud, sometimes abrasive, and certainly not as polished as in later years. At times Criswell's illustrations could even border on what Truett's generation considered crude. He was also brilliant, confident, determined, and wise enough to honor the memory of Truett at every turn. In fact, every year, on the anniversary of Truett's death, he would, usually to the displeasure of his congregation, preach a sermon about Truett. These were not just sermons but hagiagrapha.[6]

But as Criswell would say, "The lugubrious prognostications" of his inevitable failure at First Dallas proved erroneous. For the next fifty years Criswell would hold court four times weekly, preaching to a church that burgeoned to twenty-six thousand members with more than six thousand regularly in attendance. More than fifty books would come from his pen, and he would travel to the ends of the earth preaching.

During this long pastorate several significant events took place that built on the developments in the Muskogee ministry. First, Criswell announced that he would embark on a journey through the Bible: he would begin in Genesis and, over a period of years, preach straight through to the Apocalypse. The pastor began this series on March 3, 1946, and concluded the series on October 6, 1963.[7] Criswell loves to rehearse how during those years people affiliating with the First Baptist Church did not say that they joined in 1952 or 1961. Rather, the people who joined would cite joining the church in Haggai or being baptized into the membership of the church in Galatians. After 1963, Criswell returned to preach through many of the books more extensively.

Memorable sermons from this period are not difficult to locate. Ask any old-timer at First Baptist about his favorite Criswell sermons, and about the same list will be recited. No one present will ever forget the famous "Wheelbarrow" sermon preached in a series of messages on human problems, this one dealing with matters relating to sex. "Death in Detante" was powerfully influential at a moment of national crisis on August 10, 1975. "Whether We Live or Die" was the message delivered to the Pastors'

Conference of the Southern Baptist Convention in Dallas, Texas, in 1985. This message was vintage Criswell, a devastating attack on theological liberalism delivered to an assembly of more than twenty-five thousand Baptists. But, without a doubt, his most memorable sermon was delivered on December 31, 1961. In response to the senior women of the church who said that they could listen to him preach all night, Criswell said that he would begin at 7:00 P.M. and preach for five hours to usher in the new year. The sermon became known as "The Scarlet Thread Through the Bible," an abbreviated form of which was later published. This author was in attendance that evening. Standing room only gave way to comfortable seating for all by January 1, 1962, but two thousand plus remained all the way through the Apocalypse.

These years were not all glory and no sorrow for W. A. Criswell. There were defeats, as for example when he attempted to lead the church into building senior citizens high-rise apartments. Personal sorrows included his daughter Ann, whose powerful operatic soprano voice and stagemanship positioned her for fame, yet three marriages, two children, and three divorces later, her story remains one of the most sorrowful chapters of his life. Criswell's own mistakes in the handling of personnel matters caused upheaval and sorrow at the time James Draper departed from the staff to become pastor at First Baptist, Euless, Texas. And even noting major contributions made through her eight-hundred-member Sunday school class and its provision annually of about 25 percent of the church budget, Betty Criswell's uncharitable and often selfish attitudes and actions were the cause of endless difficulty. An autobiography *Standing on the Promises,* prepared with the assistance of Mel White, proved to be a major disappointment when White, a few months after publication, revealed himself to be a homosexual.[8] The short pastorate of Joel Gregory, with his alleged affair and subsequent "kiss and tell" book designed apparently to shake the Criswell legend, was a hurtful episode both to Criswell and to the church but more so to Gregory.[9] In the final analysis, however, all of these developments only served to convince Criswell more completely about the mysterious providences of a merciful and loving God. Somehow it all rests "in the imponderables of Almighty God."

Pastoral and Exegetical Theology

The theology of W. A. Criswell is not difficult to assess. But one must note that his theology is distinct from most of the others surveyed in this book—distinct not so much due to its content as to its venue. Criswell wrote only three books during his long ministry.[10] The remainder of his books are the result of tape-recorded sermons that were transcribed and then edited by assistants and last of all approved by himself. The notes in the *Criswell Study Bible* and the *Believer's Study Bible* were prepared by others with the intent of faithfulness to Criswell's views and then approved, changed, or revised by Criswell himself.

Criswell's theology then is not the theology of the cloister—written, contemplated, and rewritten. In fact, not only is his theology sermonic, but also Criswell had a lifelong commitment to preaching without notes.[11] These messages were formulated week by week in the pastor's Swiss Avenue study where every morning was reserved for study and prayer. The sermons grew out of the steamy byways of life, shaped by the needs of the people among whom he moved as shepherd. Delivered under the white-hot theater lights of the Dallas auditorium, Criswell faced not only his own sheep but also the inevitable cast of several hundred curious visitors every Lord's Day morning in addition to a large television audience.

Consequently, Criswell espoused "pastoral theology" and "preaching theology"—exegesis and application of the texts of Scripture that across the years provide a look at Criswell's view of all the major doctrines of the faith. What it may sometimes lack in precision due to its form and forum, it makes up for in passion. What may be missing in organization is replaced by consistency in a preaching ministry of more than fifty years in the same pulpit. Criswell's pulpit theology follows the paradigm of John Chrysostom, C. H. Spurgeon, G. Campbell Morgan, and Donald Gray Barnhouse, whose theologies were beaten out on the anvil of the hearts of the masses over decades.[12] With this in mind, we begin.[13]

Criswell's Doctrine of God

Although the doctrine of God is foundational to Criswell's theology, the subject is, for the most part, Christologically developed. The existence of God is not up for discussion and, to emphasize the point, Criswell spun a yarn.

> A hop-toad and a lizard were watching an express train hurtling by in West Texas. Said the hop-toad: "There are fools who believe somebody made that train. Nonsense! It just happened of itself." Said the lizard: "And there are fools who say the thing is run by a locomotive engineer. Such stupidity! It runs by itself." A sand flea overheard the learned discussion between the two, climbed upon one corner of a railroad spike and said: "Some fools say that there is a man called a president who is at the head of this railroad. Such gross credulity! If there is a president of this railroad, I defy him to come and strike me dead!"

> God ignores the whole senseless travesty with the one comment, "The fool hath said in his heart, There is no God."

Nothing else is added. Nothing else is said. Nothing more in the whole Bible. The atheist believes like a fool.

An atheist never gave an intelligent answer to the vast mystery of the universe. He never gave meaning to a man's life on earth. He denies intelligence, will and personality in creation. He only sees a blind, fortuitous concourse of atoms that created themselves, shaped themselves, and finally produced our minds and souls, without reason, without purpose, without destiny.[14]

Criswell affirms the trinitarian nature of God in orthodox fashion. He suggests that the best analogy is to understand that the Bible sometimes presents man as trichotomous, also a mystery to humans.[15] He further argues the plurality of the godhead based on the use of plural *Elohim* in the Old Testament, as well as numerous Old Testament passages where the Spirit of God and the angel of God are mentioned.[16] In the New Testament, the baptism of Jesus is a point of appeal noting the presence of the Son, the voice of the Father, and the Spirit's descent in the form of a dove.[17]

For Criswell, the manifestation of the Trinity in redemption is crucial to the faith. Criswell wrote:

In my studying I came across one of the most amazing things I have ever found in the Bible. Wherever the three personalities of the Trinity are presented together, and they stand together all through the Bible, without exception it is always in redemptive blessing, in merciful loving-kindness, in salvation, and deliverance.[18]

The consequences of denying the Trinity are pictured as devastating in regard to Jesus, his person, and his ministry.

Let me sum up one other truth. Whenever anyone departs from the revelation of God as a tripersonality, he immediately falls into a barren and sterile faith without comfort and without hope.

That is true with regard to Jesus our Lord. If we deny the Trinity, then Jesus is just another man, and He died as all other men have died and is in a grave somewhere as all other men are in their graves. He could not perfectly represent to us the Father because He is just another man. We have no assurance. He does not hear our prayers. He does not comfort our souls. He does not have any word of grace and salvation. He cannot pardon our sins. He cannot sustain and keep us. He is a man as all other men.[19]

The other aspect of Criswell's doctrine of God that plays prominently in his ministry is the providence of God. In fact, the pastor's confidence in the providence of God is that which enabled him to walk through every difficult moment of his ministry without panic. Church members often spoke to one another about how in the midst of storms Criswell would quietly hunker down and ride out the storm. Once I asked his philosophy on this. He replied that storms were tests allowed by a gracious God to teach us that he is also the Lord of the storms. Understanding was not crucial for Criswell; faithfulness was everything.

Criswell's Doctrine of Revelation and the Bible

The doctrines of revelation and the Bible are the major foci of three distinct volumes and a frequent theme in many more. In 1965, Criswell published *The Bible for Today's World*. Returning to the subject in the midst of increasing controversy in Baptist life, in 1969, he published *Why I Preach the Bible Is Literally True*. Finally, in 1982, during the concluding years of his Dallas ministry, he devoted an entire volume of his doctrinal series to the subject, volume 1 of the *Great Doctrines of the Bible*.

In a sermon from Isaiah, the Texas pastor preached a message called "My Favorite Text." In this study of Isaiah 40:8, Criswell says:

> The reason that Isaiah 40:8 is my favorite verse is because it includes the entire revelation of God. We would not know God without the Book. We would not know Jesus Christ without the Book. We have no assurance of salvation or of heaven without the Book. Our eternal hope lies in the promise, assurance, and revelation of the Lord God written in His book.[20]

As an illustration of this truth, Criswell cites the standards employed at the National Bureau of Standards in Washington and the clock used at the Naval Observatory as unchanging standards by which all other measures are ultimately judged. He concludes:

> His word is fixed and lies before God. The original pattern of God's Word is in glory, and that which we have the Lord wrote out before the foundation of the world was laid.
>
> Thousands of years ago there were thirty-nine books in the Old Testament. There are thirty-nine books in the Old Testament today. In the first Christian centuries there were twenty-seven books in the New Testament. There are twenty-seven books in the New Testament today. They do not change. They are forever settled. They are fixed in heaven.[21]

In fact, God's Word is inerrant. Explaining the Greek term *aphthartos,* the incorruptibility of the Word of God, the author says, "God's Word cannot be corrupted nor be written with error. It cannot be continued with emendations, because God sees to it that any discrepancies in the copies are pointed out, corrected, and removed. 'The grass withereth, the flower fadeth: but the word of our God shall stand for ever.'"[22]

In *The Bible for Today's World*, the pastor introduces his people to the difference between revelation and inspiration, as well as to the various theories of inspiration. Revelation is a reference to the content of what is known, while inspiration refers to the act of transmitting what is made known, keeping that which is known from mistake or error. After discussing various views of inspiration of Scripture, Criswell states his own as being "a dynamic, plenary, verbal, supernatural presentation of the writing of the Holy Book."[23]

For Criswell it was the encounter with the living Word of God that kept him unalterably convinced of the divine nature of the Book. Expounding Hebrews 4:12, he concluded:

> The Word of God is always alive, fresh, and pertinent; it addresses itself to our present hour. If every drop of the Pacific Ocean were to dry up and turn into a dead lake, this Book would still be the fountain of the water of life. If that vast, granite, flint-rock mountain range called the Sierra Nevada should finally turn into heaps of dust, this Book would still be the rock of ages. If the very stars were to grow old and dim and go out, this Book would still be the light of the world. If the time were to come when the very atomic elements of this creation were to melt with fervent heat, this Book would still be witness to the coming of a new heaven and a new earth. This is the immutable, unchanging Word of God. 'Heaven and earth may pass away, but my word will never pass away.' It is quick. It is alive.[24]

Nor was Criswell able to embrace the neo-orthodox claims that the Bible "contained" the Word of God. He insisted that the Bible *is* the Word of God.[25] Neither could he muster much respect for the detractors of the Bible. Inveighing against skeptics, he cited Voltaire and Paine saying:

> Over 200 years ago the skeptic Voltaire said, "Fifty years from now the world will hear no more of the Bible." It is a strange commentary on this prophecy that in the very year the British Museum paid to the Russian government over $500,000 for a copy of a Greek Bible, the ancient Codex Aleph, a first edition of Voltaire's sold on a bookstore counter in Paris for less than eight cents!

Sometimes readers or listeners might even have concluded that Criswell's passion on this subject generated more heat than light, and a few even alleged that he was uncharitable in some declarations. But while his personal demeanor toward even his most vocal critics and detractors was inevitably kind and generous, he viewed the pulpit as a prophetic venue where it was appropriate and even mandatory to thunder with the authority of God. He determined this to be crucial because he genuinely believed that the eternal destinies of millions were at risk if people failed to perceive the truth. Hence Criswell painted liberal critics of the Bible in this way:

> Modern, liberal critics leave behind them a world of jumbled confusion. They tell us that God has revealed Himself but refuse to pin themselves down as to exactly what the revelation is. In fact, upon occasion, we find them glorying in the uncertainty of their preaching because this offers them an opportunity for the exercise of "the leap of faith." The basic thesis of their dialectical theology is that the acts of God in history cannot be detected apart from 'a leap of faith' and the revealed Words of God can never be identified with any words. They avow that divine acts are beyond history and divine words are beyond language. There is a segment of neo-orthodoxy that distinguishes between God's Word and the human expression of the word. The so-called word of God can be recognized only in the area of our experience. This would mean that not even the words of Jesus are valid, that which one feels to be appropriate to Jesus according to the judgment of one's own mind becomes one's own Jesus.[26]

Likewise ministers who sounded an uncertain sound came under similar indictment.

> But to see a minister of the gospel mount the pulpit to find fault with the Word of God and to decry it as a revelation of the truth of heaven is of all things most sad. In our day the Bible is assailed by infidel pseudoscientists, by rash materialists, by cheap secularists, by blaspheming communists, and by all the vice of earth and all the venom of perdition. For the minister to link hands with these enemies of the kingdom of God is unbelievable. If there ever was a time when our wobbling world needed to hear a clamant voice calling it back to the changeless verities of the Word of God, that time is now.[27]

Criswell's Doctrine of Creation

No position was excoriated more often in the preaching ministry of W. A. Criswell than that of Darwinism. To Criswell it appeared that evolution was nothing less than a modern hoax perpetuated on the human family in an effort to get rid of God and theology with him. He saw God as the first cause—everything else as caused. God stood outside his creation in the sense that he was transcendent to and separate from that created order. The grace of God began not in redemption but in Creation.

Grace was the answer to why there was something rather than nothing. Consequently, the mistakes of the evolutionist loomed large to the pastor. Especially was he concerned about the dissemination of evolutionary thought through the schools together with its possible effect on youth. Though he often returned to the theme, his concern for youth prompted a series of sermons, which were ultimately published in 1957 under the title *Did Man Just Happen?* The messages were stenographically transcribed by young people in the chapel choir. As one reads them today, it must be remembered that they were extemporaneously delivered without notes as was Criswell's style. Also science has changed radically since 1957; and truth admitted, some of the science appealed to in this book was of an earlier vintage still, namely from the pastor's university years.

Nevertheless, the sermons demonstrate a remarkably broad grasp of the scientific field, especially for a busy pastor-theologian. Chapters or sermons on biology, embryology, paleontology, geology, anthropology, and the philosophical assumptions of Darwinism are included. Criswell considered biology and embryology to be sciences that were inscrutable to Darwinians, and he thought most anthropology to be simply a hoax.

A description of the Darwinist platform went as follows:

> In my own words, somewhere, somehow a speck of protoplasmic substance came into existence, so small that it could not have been seen by the unaided powers of the eye. And through the generations from that one protoplasmic speck, there developed, there evolved, all the forms of life in the animal world, all the forms of life in the vegetable world. All the forms of life we see today have evolved from that one common speck of substance.[28]

Or again:

> That is no more preposterous and no more insensible than for one to say that out of nothing something came, and that out of something an amoeba came, and out of that amoeba a fish came, and out of that fish an amphibian came, and out of that amphibian a reptile came, and out of that reptile a bird came, and out of that bird a mammal came, and out of that mammal a man came.[29]

The most severe obstacle for evolution was that it was unable to answer ultimate questions such as where did the pristine drop of protoplasm originate? From whence came the primeval fluid to nourish that protoplasm? How did it all get into the vast void of space? Who planned all this? Criswell could only conclude that spontaneous generation had never been seen, could not be produced, and, in fact, is no generation at all.[30]

Only when the subject is geology is the reader in for a bit of a surprise. While Criswell concluded that paleontologists had misinterpreted the record in the rocks, noting that life arose suddenly and in great complexity in the Cambrian age and that no strata anywhere yielded any clearly transitional life forms, he nevertheless shocked many "young earth" creationists by accepting the geologists, estimate of the age of the earth.[31] Accordingly, Criswell had to account for the vast ages posited by the geologists in light of the creation accounts in Genesis. This he did by adopting a form of Catastrophism or a "Gap Theory" of the Genesis 1 narrative.

According to Criswell, there is a gap between Genesis 1:1 and 1:2. That gap encompasses the majority of geological time. The Hebrew word translated "was" in verse 2 is *hayetah* and should be translated "became." Hence, the earth became formless and void. This happened as a result of a conflict in heaven when Lucifer, the anointed cherub, was cast out (Isa. 14 and Ezek. 28). In fury Lucifer ruined creation, necessitating the recreation of the earth, which begins in verse 3. Criswell found support for this theory also in Isaiah 45:18 and Jeremiah 4:23–26, as well as the passages in Isaiah 14 and Ezekiel 28. Editors of both the *Criswell Study Bible* and the *Believer's Study Bible* were able to secure the permission of the pastor to present his view in the study notes of these publications as one of several options. However, this should not be construed as a change in Criswell's own thinking.

Criswell's Christology

Social and psychological circumstances led to a public image of W. A. Criswell that depicted him as focused primarily on the subjects of the Bible and the study of last things. And it is the case that eight of his books are devoted primarily to these two subjects. A case could probably further be made for the accusation of some regarding the issue of the Bible that Criswell preached the crusade in the battle for the Bible, while younger admirers of his position carried it out. But for all of that, the consuming passion of Criswell's life and ministry has been Jesus. The pastor properly discerned that the preexistence, incarnation, life, work, and resurrection of Christ constitutes the central concern for Christianity.

> We have no ultimate answer to the question of Pontius Pilate, "What shall I do then with Jesus which is called Christ?" until we receive Him for all that He said He was and for all that He promised to do. Open the door of your Bible, and you will find that He fits perfectly the three hundred Old Testament promises concerning the coming of that Messiah. Open the door of your home, and you will find that He will sanctify every day, He will enrich every life, He will bless every meal, He will guide

and sustain every holy and worthy decision. Open the door of your heart, bow down before Him, call upon His name, and you will know what it is to have God, Himself, come into your soul. "I bow one knee before thee, O King, my liege lord," said an old hero; "I bow two knees before God, my Saviour alone."

Look up into His face; open the door of your heart; give Him the love and trust and faith of your life; crown Him King and Lord of time and eternity. He will be your all-sufficient, all-adequate Savior.

"What shall I do then with Jesus which is called Christ?" I shall receive Him as Lord and Savior, as the King and Hope of my life in this world and in the world that is to come.[32]

As a matter of fact, Criswell was of the persuasion that there were two great battles in his own era, one regarding the nature and reliability of the Bible and the other the nature and possibility of the virgin birth of Jesus.[33] He describes this scenario as follows:

At the beginning of the age, up in heaven, a volunteer offered to give His life for our iniquities that we might be saved from the judgment of our sins. Hebrews 10 says that a body was prepared in order that God might make an atoning sacrifice for our transgressions. A spirit could never do that. That body, which was necessary to make propitiation for our sins, was framed by the Holy Spirit of God in the womb of the virgin Mary, and God lived in that body. He was incarnate in the framing of that physical shape and form like a man, and He died once for all on the tree. There is no more an offering for sin. He came to make a sacrifice for our sins once for all, and in Him we have redemption, expiation, propitiation, forgiveness, cleansing, and all that God has in store for those who are washed clean and white in the blood of the Lamb. That is the gospel and that is the essence of the Virgin Birth—a body prepared for God in which He made sacrifice and atonement for our sins.[34]

The precise nature of this development was, Criswell confessed, beyond his ability to articulate, but he did venture one effort.

The second great biological miracle of God is this: The Lord's hand reached down and entered into that genetic change of mitosis and did a creative work unparalleled in the history of mankind. Without the spermatozoon He created a body for Christ in which God incarnated Himself to make atonement for our sins and to be our Lord and brother and friend and fellow pilgrim and sympathetic High Priest and Savior and King forever and ever. When I try to say it, it is such a vast, incomparable,

and heavenly truth that I want to apologize to the Lord for saying it so poorly and so stammeringly! But having seen it and read
about it and observed all that Jesus means in this world, then I
understand what I read in the pages of the Bible. This Virgin
Birth, this incarnation of God, becomes so beautifully clear.

It starts in Genesis 3:15, where it says that the seed of the
woman would crush Satan's head. A woman does not have seed.
A man has seed. From the beginning ages rabbis would pour over
that passage. They would never know what it meant until the
story was fulfilled in the birth of our Lord. The seed of the
woman—Jesus, God Incarnate—would bruise Satan's head. That
is what it meant, and we did not know it until thousands of years
later.[35]

Having established the motive and the necessity of the Incarnation,
Criswell then devoted a full chapter of *Great Doctrines of the Bible* to arguing that the man Jesus was in fact the eternal God, the Lord from heaven.
A series of chapters follow under the headings, "Our Lord's Entrance . . .
into Human Flesh," "Into Suffering," "Into the Grave," "Into Resurrection
Life," "Into Heaven," and "Beyond the Veil." In these chapters and elsewhere he argues for the substitutionary atonement of Christ, although
there are also definite elements of what Gustav Aulén would have called
the "Christus Victor" motif or the Classical View of the atonement. In a
sermon from 1 Peter 3:17–22 entitled "Christ in Hades," Criswell pro-
pounds his theology of Christ's *desensus ad inferos*.[36] Admitting that the
passage is one of the most difficult in the Bible, he asserts that during the
three days of bodily interment, Jesus descended into Hades for the purpose
of preaching to the "spirits in prison." In this Criswell takes his cue from
The Apostles' Creed. However, he confesses that he does not know the
purpose of the mission or precisely why the rebellious people of Noah's
generation are singled out.[37]

The resurrection of the Lord was a recurring theme for the Dallas pastor. George W. Truett, in his ministry, had begun pre-Easter services, which
where held in a downtown theater. Criswell continued these through all the
years of his pastorate, eventually moving them to the church auditorium to
accommodate the crowds. Parishioners remember the oft-repeated invitation to business people to "come when you can, leave when you must."
Most came all five days and stayed to the end to hear magnificent messages
on the resurrection. One of the most memorable of those was a sermon on
Job 14:14, "If a Man Die, Shall He Live Again?"[38] In this message Criswell
describes death as the ultimate enemy of mankind and the resurrection of
Jesus as the heart of the Christian faith. In graphic word pictures, the hope
of immortality is described from an assortment of cultures worldwide. But
Criswell concluded that only Jesus was dead and is alive. Similarly, Criswell

made much of the post-resurrection ministry of Christ in his session with the Father and his promised return at the end of the age. This later topic will be discussed below.

Criswell's Soteriology

Criswell's soteriology begins with the promise of the Father to the Son that if the Son would suffer and die for the sins of a fallen race, God would give him a people for a possession.[39] In this Criswell discovers the origin and necessity for the doctrine of election. He stresses repeatedly that election is always and only to salvation.[40] As he evaluates the doctrine of predestination, he concludes that it is an unfathomable mystery. There are, he alleges, two sets of nomenclature in the Bible. One consists of words like *predestination, election, foreknowledge, constancy, sovereignty, omnipotence, omniscience,* and *omnipresence.* The other set speaks of moral freedom, advantage, possibility, contingency, the exercise of volition, freedom of spirit, and freedom of choice. All are a part of the biblical picture of salvation, but no one this side of heaven knows how all those pieces fit together in the soteriological puzzle.[41]

As it relates to man, both repentance and faith are essential to salvation. When these are exercised, God regenerates or generates a new birth for the penitent. While rejecting limited atonement, Criswell accepts the other traditional four points of Calvinism, at least if he defines what each means. A frequent theme in Criswell's preaching was the permanency of salvation. "Once Saved, Always Safe" is the way he entitled his message in the *Great Doctrines* volume.[42]

The necessity for the atonement of Christ as well as for regeneration is brought about by the fall of man into sin. Men are unable to extract themselves from this quagmire of iniquity because they are dead in trespasses and sins, unable to perform any good deed of saving significance. Consequently, either God acts to bring about salvation or else there is no hope.

Criswell's Pneumatology

As a second-year seminarian, this writer dropped by the Swiss Avenue Criswell residence to pick up a promised copy of volume 3 of the pastor's commentary on the Book of Revelation. Instead of handing me one book, he extended two. Laying a hand on the commentary—as his steely eyes met mine and a hint of a smile turned the corners of his mouth—he said, "I think this is right." Moving his hand to a copy of *The Holy Spirit in Today's World,* he continued, "But I know this is right!" Whether Criswell is correct, it is the case that the *Sermons on Revelation* and *The Holy Spirit in Today's World* are the two best volumes in the Criswell collection. This is the case theologically, historically, and exegetically.

The first three chapters of the book on the Holy Spirit are three sermons on the history of the doctrine of the Spirit. Few pulpiteers would attempt to hold the attention of a congregation through three sermons recounting the history of creedal statements, a considerable and, for his own purpose, crucial assessment of Montanism, the history of the debate over the *filioque* clause, and a brief commentary on Reformation and modern interpretation of the Spirit.[43]

The remainder of the work is devoted to the theology and exegesis of the doctrine as Criswell sees it. The Holy Spirit possesses personhood and deity. The various symbols for the Holy Spirit are discussed, such as the dove, the anointing oil, and others. A long discussion focuses on the baptism of the Holy Spirit. Here Criswell takes a rather typically dispensational approach, arguing that only 1 Corinthians 12:13 is definitive on the subject. Thus, the baptism of the Spirit takes place at the moment of conversion when the Holy Spirit (the baptizer) immerses the new believer (the baptizee) into the body of Christ (the element into which the baptizer baptizes the baptizee).[44] Hence there is no "spirit baptism" occurring some time subsequent to salvation, although there may be many fillings of the Spirit.

Several messages are devoted to the gifts of the Spirit. Criswell believes that many are still operative for the church today but takes a cessationist's view of some of the gifts, including tongues. A long section presents the reason behind this conclusion. Included in this is the conviction that women are forbidden to speak in tongues.[45] The study concludes with a chapter on the fruit of the Spirit.

Criswell's Ecclesiology

The doctrine of the church is developed in three major sources—a three-volume exposition of Acts, a small paperback volume called *The Doctrine of the Church,* and volume 3 of the *Great Doctrine* series. For the most part Criswell's ecclesiology is about what one would anticipate from a Baptist pastor. Criswell sees Pentecost as the birthday of the church. By definition the church is the body of Christ, a born-again fellowship of believers who have been baptized. However, Criswell, consistent with his premillennial theology, allows more significance for the universal church than most Baptists would allow.[46]

The church has two offices, pastors and deacons, and two ordinances, baptism and the Lord's Supper. Some of Criswell's most helpful instructions about the ordinances were actually acted out in what was clearly a thoughtful performance of the ordinances themselves. The views he acted out, however, are documented in Criswell's favorite of all his writings,

W. A. *Criswell* 249

Criswell's Guidebook for Pastors.[47] Here he not only provides description of the nature of the ordinances but also instruction regarding how to administer the ordinances. Those who witnessed the pastor's unique handling of the ordinances often learned just from observance. For example, Criswell always insisted that baptism was a burial and should not be roughly administered. As the loved one is laid gently away, the waters should scarcely ripple at all.

One last matter of interest concerns Criswell's ecumenical attitudes, especially as they concerned the Roman Catholic Church. Instinctively suspicious of ecumenical efforts, Criswell, nevertheless, viewed anyone who loved Christ and the Bible as a true brother and sister in Christ. But Catholicism was another matter. In the series on Revelation, in a sermon on "The Reign of the Scarlet Woman," Criswell leaves no doubt that the identity of the scarlet woman is the Roman Catholic Church.

Who invented the Inquisition? Who invented the torture chamber and the rack? Who burned at the stake uncounted thousands and millions of God's servants in the earth? This scarlet whore, dressed in purpose, decked with gold and precious stone and pearls, riding in control of the governments of the world. John "wondered with a great wonder." Who would ever have dreamed that those humble, persecuted, outcast, little *ecclesias,* those little communities of Jesus, would ever rise to be so rich, so bedecked, so merciless and cruel, and so filled with the blood of the martyrs of the Lord? It has been estimated that she has slain more than fifty million of the servants of Jesus Christ.[48]

But the sermons preached in 1964, which clearly identified the Roman Church as the scarlet whore, were subjected to an unexpected event. In 1971, Criswell visited Rome and was invited to meet with Pope Paul VI. The intellectual curiosity, which always motivated the pastor, shifted into high gear. The pope received Criswell cordially, giving him a letter and a beautiful leather bound copy of 1 and 2 Peter. Of this encounter Criswell said:

When Pope Paul VI offered his hand to me did I compromise the faith when I offered my hand back again in love and friendship? When Rabbi Yinon and Rabbi Nathan offered their hands to me did I repudiate my Baptist faith and heritage in offering my hand in love and friendship in return? Just what is it for a man to believe in Christ and to be true to the faith if it is not this, that in all things we are to adorn the doctrine of God our Savior, we are to make it beautiful and attractive, full of love and prayer and warmth.[49]

He concluded:

> What is it to be a Baptist? Is it that I find myself in some cor-
> ner and there I bite and snarl and curse and with all the language
> at my command in vitriolic and acrimonious speech I denounce
> and condemn? Is that what it is to be a Baptist? Or is a Baptist
> somebody who has found the Lord as his Savior and in love,
> prayer, sympathy and intercession seeks to hold up the cross of
> Christ and to invite all men everywhere to find in Him that life
> eternal, that blesses us now and in the world that is come?—"to
> adorn the doctrine of God our Savior."[50]

In all probability Criswell has never changed his mind about the identity of the scarlet woman of Revelation 17. The incident with Paul VI and
its Criswellian commentary certainly indicates a softening of rhetoric, not
to mention an ecumenical spirit, which made it possible for the pastor to
embrace individual Catholics, even if the system itself remained an object
of suspicion.

Criswell's Eschatology

Criswell's thought on end-time events and prophecy occupy the major
content of several volumes. *What to Do Until Jesus Comes Back* was published by Broadman in 1975. The next year the same press published
Welcome Back Jesus. *Expository Sermons on Daniel* in 1976 and *Ezekiel*
in 1987 were concerned principally with prophecy. Volume 8 on eschatology in the *Great Doctrines of the Bible* series appeared in 1984, and one
of his last publications, *Heaven,* coauthored with this writer, appeared in
1991. The *magnum opus,* however, was *Expository Sermons on
Revelation,* which initially appeared in five volumes as he preached the sermons. The first volume appeared in 1962; the last in 1966. In 1969, the
first printing of all five volumes in one appeared. Considering once again
that this is pulpit theology, the volume is a marvel of exegesis, history, philosophy of the end times, and illustration.

Prior to preaching the series on the Apocalypse, Criswell resorted to
two expedients. Having become a convinced premillennialist as a result of
his own study, he, nevertheless, felt unprepared for the venture into the
Apocalypse. Also, he has always had a sixth sense about *kairotic* moments,
and I suspect that he intuitively discerned this to be such a moment. For
one thing, under the influence of Ray Summers, Ray Frank Robbins, and
Herschel Hobbs, the faculties of most Southern Baptist seminaries had been
amillennial for a generation. For another, Truett, in whose shadow Criswell
still lived to some degree, if anything, was postmillennial. In fact, when
Criswell brought to the deacons a statement of faith for the church to
adopt, it was "The Baptist Faith and Message," the official confession of

the Southern Baptist Convention. However, Criswell had revised the article on the Bible explicitly to include inerrancy and the statement on "Last Things" to include a strong premillennial statement and even a less-than-subtle hint of pretribulationism. To this latter change an elderly deacon objected in a public meeting, noting that "George W. Truett could not have signed it." Criswell immediately arose and said in typical Criswellian style, "My sweet deacon is exactly right. When the far-famed Dr. Truett was pastor of our dear church, he could not have signed this statement—*but he can now!*" With that the statement was unanimously approved.

Facing the sermons on Revelation, Criswell decided first on a one-month sabbatical, December of 1961. Next he sought the assistance of J. Dwight Pentecost, professor of theology at Dallas Theological Seminary and author of a massive volume entitled *Things to Come.*[51] Criswell wrote to his congregation:

> In the many years that I attended school (and I went to school twenty-two consecutive years), I never studied the Revelation. I never had a teacher who took time to mention it. It would be impossible for me therefore, to enter into the high privilege of preaching through this glorious and climatic book without first studying it from beginning to end. I shall not be preaching, therefore, after this coming Sunday until the second Sunday in January of the new year. The month in between I shall employ studying this book and getting ready for the long series of sermons that I pray God will help me to deliver from it.[52]

As the sermon series unfolded, it became apparent that Criswell had become even more of a dispensationalist, even to the point of believing that the seven churches addressed in the Apocalypse represented seven eras in the history of the church. The series depended heavily on the work of Seiss.[53] The salient features of Criswell's eschatology can be delineated as follows.

The true church of all the saved is moving along witnessing to Christ during the "times of the Gentiles." The next great event in history will be the rapture of the church, which is imminent.[54] When the glorified Christ is revealed in the heavens, the true church, and all who have died in Christ, will be glorified, judged at the *bema,* and invited to the marriage supper of the Lamb.[55] Meantime back on earth, the world is treated to the reign of the Antichrist and to the Great Tribulation for seven incredible years.[56] Just as it appears that the Jewish nation will be obliterated, Christ returns to the earth and the famous Battle of Armageddon is followed by the Sheep and Goat Judgment to determine who enters into the Millennium.[57] A thousand-year reign of Christ on earth follows during which time Satan is bound. Satan is released at the conclusion of this period only to be vanquished forever to the lake of fire. Then comes the Great White Throne Judgment of all unbelievers, accompanied by the ushering in of the eternal states of heaven and hell.[58]

Criswell's view of heaven and hell is perfectly consistent with his literal hermeneutic. Hell is a tragic, real place originally prepared for Satan and his fallen associates. However, he will be joined by those of the human family who refuse the atoning sacrifice of Christ. On the other hand, the prospect of heaven for believers was always a matter not only of theological commitment but also of much sentimental anticipation. The book on heaven, for example, at Criswell's request, contains just about every hymn on the subject that could be located.[59] That volume contains an interview conducted by Dorothy Patterson, who asked the pastor what he conceived to be the most attractive feature about heaven. He replied:

> The first thing that draws my attention to heaven is just the anticipation of being in the presence of the Lord Jesus, saying something to him, touching him, bowing in his presence, and expressing my love and gratitude for him.
>
> Second I would love to enjoy reunion with those whom I have loved and lost for a while—the precious members of the family that have gone before me and the host of the dear people from my congregation that I have buried in these more than sixty years as an undershepherd. Oh my, what a rendezvous that will be!
>
> Then, of course, what a wonderful prospect it will be to serve the Lord in heaven—to have an assignment from Him and to do it in His love and grace world without end. What a joy and what a prospect![60]

A Critical Evaluation

There are several possible ways to reflect on the impact of a man's life and writings. Substantive and creative thought, influence, and capacity to communicate to the masses are some of the criteria for evaluation. As a substantive thinker and creative theologian, Criswell will not be remembered as a major contributor. Rather, he is a "popularizer" who had the ability to digest the thought of the makers of theology and then relate with his own nuance and illustrative prowess the substantive issues found in other writing theologians. Considering the clarity of his mind, I have no doubt that Criswell could have been a careful "writing theologian" had he elected that course. But while he greatly admired the accomplishments of the academy, he never saw himself—indeed, he could not see himself—in that role. His life mission was to make the great truths of the Bible leap from the pages of the Book he treasured and watch those truths envelope the hearts of his parishoners with eternity-altering force.

To this end of interpreting the biblical message, Criswell kept a wide-margin Bible on his desk. Every book that he received into his ten-thousand-volume library, he carefully numbered with the exception of commentaries. Whenever, in his extensive and broad reading program, he came across something that explained, illuminated, or uniquely applied a given verse or passage, he would enter the number of the book and the page next to the text in the wide-margin Bible.

Consequently, when he came to a passage for preaching, he instantly had a wealth of retrievable information available on the passage.

The rigors of pastoral demands in such a large congregation made it almost impossible for Criswell to "keep up" with the latest developments in theology, biblical studies, and philosophy in the rapidly changing scene of the last half of the twentieth century. But he was curious about it all, dabbled in it as much as he could, and would often surprise an audience with what he had absorbed. A keen sense of logic and incredibly broad general knowledge enabled him to grasp even abstruse matters quickly and assess them with relative ease. Childlike curiosity kept him motivated always to press on.

If objective assessment compels us to conclude that W. A. Criswell is not a careful writing theologian of the academy, we must also acknowledge that through his sermons and books he remains one of the most influential theologians of the present era. The average person never reads a book on the Trinity or on eschatology. He receives his theology almost entirely from the reading of his own Bible, the singing of hymns, and the lessons and sermons of Sunday school teachers and pastors. And this is where Criswell, like his heroes Spurgeon and Chrysostom, excelled. As I noted in another forum, Criswell could "tell the congregation about a perfect periphrastic construction in Greek and have the whole congregation laughing and crying at the same time and garner three professions of faith and sixteen rededications out of an optative mood."[61]

In a sermon's tapestry Criswell would weave together the history of a doctrine, exegete a pivotal text, and apply it to the contemporary milieu in a memorable manner. Those who heard him regularly would admit that consistency, defined as week-by-week excellence, was not his major virtue. But when he was "on," few surpassed him, and for special occasions such as conventions I would argue that he is without peer. Consequently, if judged by his pervasive influence, particularly on the world's largest non-Catholic denomination, an objective assessment would have to evaluate him as one of the most influential theologians of our era.

Through books like *The Holy Spirit for Today's World*, Criswell succeeded in limiting the inroads of the neo-Charismatic movement into Southern Baptist life. He reintroduced a virile premillennialism to Southern Baptists and made the view widely popular again. Criswell's view of the

Bible is that which, after a twenty-year struggle for self-definition, was adopted as the prevailing perspective. Abandonment of topical preaching in favor of verse-by-verse, book-by-book exposition, never succeeded to the same degree but was nonetheless widespread, largely as a result of Criswell's advocacy.

Conclusion

The geographical mileage is not so great between the white-framed Baptist church of Texline, where W. A. Criswell had his earliest experiences of church attendance, and the First Baptist Church of Dallas, Texas, where he served as pastor for more than fifty years. But for the poor barber's son of Texline to become a pastor-theologian of the most famous church of the Baptist denomination, complete a Ph.D. at that denomination's most renowned seminary, pen more than fifty volumes, serve as president of the Southern Baptist Convention, spawn a movement to return the country's largest Protestant denomination to the faith of its fathers, and call that same denomination back to an expository method of preaching is a long journey. Criswell, eighty-nine and in ill health at the writing of this article, still has an alert, curious mind and loves to reminisce about the wonders of God's grace in his own existing life.

Whether in the passing of time the Criswellian penumbra will reach the proportions of his heroes Spurgeon and Chrysostom will have to await the verdict of the years. Regardless of that adjudication, W. A. Criswell will remain as one of the most interesting characters ever to preach from America's pulpits. Because of the sheer volume of publications and the existence of a library of audio and videotapes, he is certain to continue to impact not only Southern Baptists but also all evangelicals in the years that lie ahead. That much Criswell can and will do "until Jesus comes."

Bibliography

Works by Criswell

The Gospel According to Moses. Nashville: Broadman Press, 1950.
Passport to the World. Nashville: Broadman Press, 1951.
These Issues We Must Face. Grand Rapids: Zondervan, 1953.
Did Man Just Happen? Grand Rapids: Zondervan, 1957.
Five Great Questions of the Bible. Grand Rapids: Zondervan, 1958.
Five Great Affirmations of the Bible. Grand Rapids: Zondervan, 1959.
Expository Notes on the Gospel of Matthew. Grand Rapids: Zondervan, 1961.
Expository Sermons on Revelation. Grand Rapids: Zondervan, 1962.
Expository Sermons on Revelation, volume 2. Grand Rapids: Zondervan, 1963.
Expository Sermons on Revelation, volume 3. Grand Rapids: Zondervan, 1964.
Expository Sermons on Revelation, volume 4. Grand Rapids: Zondervan, 1965.

Expository Sermons on Revelation, volume 5. Grand Rapids: Zondervan, 1966.
Our Home in Heaven. Grand Rapids: Zondervan, 1964.
The Bible for Today's World. Grand Rapids: Zondervan, 1965.
The Holy Spirit for Today's World. Grand Rapids: Zondervan, 1966.
In Defense of the Faith. Grand Rapids: Zondervan, 1967.
Why I Preach That the Bible Is Literally True. Nashville: Broadman Press, 1969.
Preaching at the Palace. Grand Rapids: Zondervan, 1969.
Look Up, Brother. Nashville: Broadman Press, 1970.
Expository Sermons on the Book of Daniel, volume 1. Grand Rapids: Zondervan, 1968.
Expository Sermons on the Book of Daniel, volume 2. Grand Rapids: Zondervan, 1970.
Expository Sermons on the Book of Daniel, volume 3. Grand Rapids: Zondervan, 1971.
Expository Sermons on the Book of Daniel, volume 4. Grand Rapids: Zondervan, 1972.
The Scarlet Thread Through the Bible. Nashville: Broadman Press, 1971.
Christ and Contemporary Crises. Dallas: Crescendo, 1972.
The Baptism, Filling and Gifts of the Holy Spirit. Grand Rapids: Zondervan, 1973.
Expository Sermons on Galatians. Grand Rapids: Zondervan, 1973.
Ephesians: An Exposition. Grand Rapids: Zondervan, 1974.
Expository Sermons on the Epistle of James. Grand Rapids: Zondervan, 1975.
Christ the Savior of the World. Dallas: Crescendo, 1975.
What to Do Until Jesus Comes Back. Nashville: Broadman Press, 1975.
Welcome Back Jesus! Nashville: Broadman Press, 1976.
The Compassionate Christ. Dallas: Crescendo, 1976.
Expository Sermons on the Epistles of Peter. Grand Rapids: Zondervan, 1976.
Isaiah: An Exposition. Grand Rapids: Zondervan, 1977.
The Christ of the Cross. Dallas: Crescendo, 1977.
With a Bible in My Hand. Nashville: Broadman Press, 1978.
Acts: An Exposition, volume I. Grand Rapids: Zondervan, 1978.
Acts: An Exposition, volume II. Grand Rapids: Zondervan, 1979.
Acts: An Exposition, volume III. Grand Rapids: Zondervan, 1980.
The Criswell Study Bible. Nashville: Thomas Nelson, 1979.
The Doctrine of the Church. Nashville: Broadman Press, 1980.
Criswell's Guidebook for Pastors. Nashville: Broadman Press, 1980.
Abiding Hope. Grand Rapids: Zondervan, 1981.
Great Doctrines of the Bible, volume I: Bibliology. Grand Rapids: Zondervan, 1982.
Great Doctrines of the Bible, volume II: Theology Proper/Christology. Grand Rapids: Zondervan, 1982.
Great Doctrines of the Bible, volume III: Ecclesiology. Grand Rapids: Zondervan, 1982.
Great Doctrines of the Bible, volume IV: Pneumatology. Grand Rapids: Zondervan, 1984.
Great Doctrines of the Bible, volume V: Soteriology. Grand Rapids: Zondervan, 1985.

Great Doctrines of the Bible, Volume VI: Christian Life/Stewardship. Grand
   Rapids: Zondervan, 1986.
Standing on the Promises. Dallas: Word, 1990.
Heaven. With Paige Patterson. Wheaton: Tyndale, 1991.

Works about Criswell

Allison, Gray M. "The Preaching of W. A. Criswell: A Critical Analysis of Selected
   Messages." Th.D. dissertation, Mid-America Baptist Theological Seminary,
   1990.
Bryson, Harold T. "The Expository Preaching of W. A. Criswell in His Sermons on
   Revelation." Unpublished M.Th. thesis, New Orleans Baptist Theological
   Seminary, 1967.
Charlton, Thomas L., and Rufus B. Spain. Oral Memoirs of W. A. Criswell.
   Religion and Culture Project, Baylor University Program of Oral History.
   Baylor University, 1973.
Diduit, Michael. "Expositor of the Word: An Interview with W. A. Criswell," in
   Preaching 10 (May-June 1995): 15–17.
DuCasse, Robert. "A History of First Baptist Church, Dallas, Texas." Unpublished
   M.Th. thesis, Dallas Theological Seminary, 1964.
Gregory, Joel. *Too Great a Temptation.* Ft. Worth: Summit Group, 1994.
Keith, Billy. *W. A. Criswell.* Old Tappan, N.J.: Fleming H. Revell, 1973.
McBeth, Leon. *The First Baptist Church of Dallas.* Grand Rapids: Zondervan,
   1968.
Roberts, Craig M. W. A. "Criswell's Choice and Use of Illustrations." Unpublished
   M.Th. thesis, Dallas Theological Seminary, 1976.
Rohm, Robert A. *Dr. C: The Vision and Ministry of W. A. Criswell.* Chicago:
   Moody, 1990.
Turner, Helen Lee. "Fundamentalism in the Southern Baptist Convention: The
   Crystallization of a Millenialist Vision." Ph.D. dissertation, University of
   Virginia, 1990.
"Essays in Honor of W. A. Criswell." *Criswell Theological Review* 1 (Spring
   1987).

Of the three biographies, Criswell's autobiography is the best. Rohm's is brief
and plows no new ground. Keith's is sometimes inaccurate. A good biography remains to be written.

14

Frank Stagg

By Robert B. Sloan Jr.

Biography

FRANK STAGG WAS BORN ON HIS GRANDFATHER'S RICE FARM ON OCTOBER 20, 1911, in Acadia Parish, a few miles east of Eunice in southwest Louisiana.[1] Stagg's grandfather, Etienne Stagg, had been reared as a Roman Catholic, but when he and his brother, Adolphe, began reading the Bible, they became convinced Baptists. Adolphe (Frank Stagg's great-uncle) is still remembered by Louisiana Baptists as one of the earliest French preachers of

257

258 THEOLOGIANS OF THE BAPTIST TRADITION

the gospel among the Cajuns of southern Louisiana. The Adolphe Stagg Association in southern Louisiana is not only a memorial to the work of Adolphe Stagg but also an indication of the devout Baptist heritage to which Frank Stagg fell heir.

Stagg's father, Paul, was a Baptist deacon and Sunday school teacher who, though he lived and died as a rice farmer (except for a few years teaching in a one-room schoolhouse), had an educational background in Latin and mathematics. From his father Frank Stagg not only gained a devotional appreciation for the Bible but also learned to be unafraid of the questioning process. At the age of eleven, Frank received Christian baptism and some eight years later experienced a traumatic but decisive call to preach, a decision which he made public in the First Baptist Church at Eunice in 1930, about a year after graduation from high school.

Stagg then entered Louisiana College, where his leadership abilities both on and off campus were often recognized. He was both an outstanding student academically and was deeply involved in various college organizations. He was editor of the *Wildcat,* the college weekly; president of the Athenean Literary Society; and president of the Baptist Student Union of Louisiana in 1933–34. The year before graduation from Louisiana College, Stagg became the quarter-time pastor of the church at Dodson, and on September 10, 1933, he was ordained to the gospel ministry. Upon graduation from Louisiana College in 1934, Stagg gave an additional Sunday to the church in Dodson and also began to serve in two other part-time churches.

On August 19, 1935, Stagg married Evelyn Owen, a brilliant young woman whom he had met during his junior year at Louisiana College. Evelyn Owen Stagg would prove to be in the years ahead a devoted wife and mother to their two sons and one daughter as well as a significant participant in Frank Stagg's academic career, a role that came substantially to the foreground in the Staggs's collaboration on and coauthorship of the 1978 publication *Woman in the World of Jesus.* Evelyn Stagg's contribution to Frank Stagg's academic career was grounded in the Owen family (her three brothers, for example, all served as university professors), and personally nurtured in her own academic pursuits as a student at The Southern Baptist Theological Seminary where she was enrolled in the WMU Training School, having a curriculum identical to that of her husband with the exception of Hebrew and preaching. Stagg graduated from Southern Seminary with the Th.M. in 1938 and the Ph.D. in 1943.

After serving the Highland Baptist Mission in Louisville during his seminary days, Stagg became pastor of First Baptist Church in DeRidder, Louisiana, in 1940. While this was the only full-time pastorate in Stagg's years of ministry, throughout his academic career he struggled with the kinds of pastoral/ethical questions that he wrestled with during his years of pastoral ministry. Making the Bible and Christian theology relevant for the Christian life was and always has been primary to Stagg. During his pastorate in DeRidder, Stagg showed the kind of conscience regarding issues of race and war that would later develop more fully. Stagg's antipathy to racism became strikingly evident in the 1950s with the publication of his commentary on Acts; and with the advent of the Vietnam War in the 1960s, his views on the church, violence, and what he perceived to be the military-industrial complex would further develop.

While Stagg was at DeRidder, a seminary friend, Duke McCall, became president of the Baptist Bible Institute, which was later to become New Orleans Baptist Theological Seminary. McCall urged Stagg to come to New Orleans and fill the post of New Testament professor which, after some hesitation, he did, beginning January 1, 1945. For nearly twenty years Stagg taught New Testament in New Orleans. Those years were not without struggle. His 1955 publication, *The Book of Acts: The Early Struggle for an Unhindered Gospel,* was clearly written with patterns of racial injustice in mind. The social pressure exerted upon those who in the 1950s and 1960s attempted to articulate both the dignity of all persons as creatures made in the image of God and the oneness of all Christians in Jesus Christ may be only a memory to the current generation, but it was very palpable to those brave souls like Frank Stagg who endured the pain and slander of epithets born of hatred and bigotry.

In 1964, while New Orleans Baptist Theological Seminary was still in the throes of controversy and a declining faculty morale, Frank Stagg received an invitation to join the faculty of The Southern Baptist Theological Seminary in Louisville, Kentucky. Apart from the negative factors abiding in the New Orleans situation, there was also the very positive pull to return to Southern and rejoin a college friend and New Orleans colleague, Penrose St. Amant, who was dean of the School of Theology. McCall, who, as president of the Baptist Bible Institute, had originally brought Stagg to New Orleans, was now the president of Southern. Southern, too, had gone through a time of crisis involving the loss of a number of faculty members, and the addition of Stagg was part of the rebuilding process.

Stagg went to Southern as the James Buchanan Harrison Professor of New Testament Interpretation, and until his retirement in 1981, his service as a teacher, preacher, and writer to the Christian world and the Southern Baptist Convention in particular proved nothing short of remarkable. In fact, considering the demands placed upon Baptist professors of religion in terms of classroom hours assigned and the number of students taught, Stagg's academic and professional feats appear herculean by today's standards. In addition to the normal workload of a seminary curriculum, Stagg served on the graduate faculty of Southern Seminary. Furthermore, his literary production, outspoken views, and academic excellence made him much in demand as a conference speaker and preacher. Stagg edited the *Review and Expositor* from 1965 through 1971 and from 1973 to 1975. With all these activities Frank Stagg found still other ways to serve the denomination he loved. Not only did he produce an almost unceasing flow of curriculum materials for denominational publications, but he also worked as a consulting editor for *The Broadman Bible Commentary* and authored volumes on Matthew and Philippians. In 1976, Stagg became senior professor of New Testament Interpretation. After his retirement he and Mrs. Stagg moved to Bay St. Louis, Mississippi, where he continued to enjoy an active role in church and denominational life.

As a teacher Stagg was greatly admired by his students. He was not known as a stimulating lecturer in terms of oratorical and/or charismatic style, but for the attentive student Stagg was always profoundly engaging with respect to course content. His students continue to bear witness to Stagg's academic determination and drive. He never ceased growing and learning. He threw himself wholeheartedly into every new area of research into which his love of the New Testament carried him.

Stagg exerted an enormous influence on Southern Baptist churches throughout the middle part of the twentieth century. Indeed, some would argue that Frank Stagg has been the premier New Testament scholar among Southern Baptists for the middle third of the twentieth century. Certainly the reading, learning, and academic expertise reflected in Stagg's writings serve as strong evidence to that claim. Though Stagg has never been without his theological opponents, almost none would dispute that in Stagg one finds an unusual combination of Christian devotion and academic excellence.

Exposition

Historian, Grammarian, Exegete

Frank Stagg is never better as a scholar than when he is drawing together and summarizing historical, grammatical, or biblical materials. His *New Testament Theology*,[2] for example, is replete with the kind of historical and biblical summary that is most serviceable for the student and minister. In his chapter on the "Plight of Man as Sinner," Stagg summarizes some dozen New Testament terms for *sin*. In his chapter on "Baptism: Origin and Meaning," he summarizes the antecedents of and parallels to Christian baptism with respect to both Jewish proselyte baptism and the baptism of John, then surveys the various New Testament traditions regarding the practice and meaning of baptism. Examples of this sort could easily be multiplied.[3] Another illustration of Stagg's ability to summarize large blocks of material is in his 1962 article on "The Christology of

Matthew." There Stagg offers helpful insight into the structure of Matthew and gives an excellent introductory summary on the importance and functional nature of New Testament Christology. Stagg's gift for summarization is evident in his discussion of the major Christological titles in Matthew such as Son of David, Son of God, Christ, Son of man, and Suffering Servant.[4]

In Stagg's 1966 article, "The Gospel and Biblical Usage," there is further evidence of his ability to draw together various biblical traditions under one theme. First, he presents a brief but fascinating history of the English term *gospel* and then gives a similar survey of the Greek noun *euangelion*. The term is traced through Acts, Mark, Luke, Paul, and Revelation. As is customary, Stagg summarizes the salient points derived from the historical survey and applies the historical and biblical material to Christian living.[5]

"The Holy Spirit in the New Testament," another 1966 article, is a marvelous survey of the function of the Spirit in the Gospels and/or the ministry of Jesus. Using the Book of Acts, Stagg synthesizes extensive amounts of material regarding the gifts of the Spirit, conditions for receiving the Holy Spirit, the Holy Spirit in baptism, the Holy Spirit in glossolalia, the work of the Holy Spirit, and the fruit of the Spirit. Not only has Stagg brought together great amounts of material under various topical headings, but he has assimilated the material according to issues that were particularly relevant for church life in the 1960s. The "charismatic movement" that spread across churches in America brought many instances of division and discord because of the unbiblical practices associated with the movement. Stagg, as always, sought to speak to the needs of the hour.[6]

Stagg shows himself familiar with currents in Lukan scholarship and yet retains readability in his 1967 article, "The Journey Toward Jerusalem in Luke's Gospel." This work is an excellent summary of Luke's so-called "Travel Narrative" (9:51 to 19:27). While providing a fine exposition of this entire midsection of the Gospel of Luke, Stagg does so in a way that is readable but avoids superficiality.[7]

Providing an excellent survey of the various Lord's Supper traditions in the New Testament, Stagg published in 1969 "The Lord's Supper in the New Testament." He shows an uncanny ability, once again, to reflect contemporary scholarship and yet do so in a way that is enormously relevant to the life of the church. Questions related to "open" and "closed" communion have frequently been at issue for Baptists, and Stagg's survey of the biblical traditions with regard to the Lord's Supper does not fail to address such matters. Having taken the reader through the communion traditions in the Pauline literature, Stagg analyzes the relatively similar Markan and Matthean traditions and closes with a brief summary of the tradition in Luke. It must also be noted, however, that Stagg's popular relevance to issues in Baptist life and his capacity for summarization did not render him incapable of advocacy. Stagg is critical of those who (all too commonly in Baptist life) have reduced the meaning of the Supper to "remembrance" alone and have forgotten its other significant dimensions (i.e., covenant, sacrifice, hope, and fellowship). Stagg's writings reflect a recurring focus upon the centrality of *koinonial* fellowship in Christian experience, and therefore, it is not surprising that Stagg spends the greater portion of the article dealing with the divisive forces in Corinth which—in the context of a fellowship meal—were actually destroying the unity of the church.[8]

Virtually all of Frank Stagg's academic output has been published by church-related organs, especially those of the Southern Baptist Convention. The great exception to this is his 1972 article, "The Abused Aorist," which appeared in the *Journal of Biblical Literature,* the professional quarterly of the Society of Biblical Literature. Though Stagg is best known by Southern Baptists for his publications in the *Review and Expositor* and/or through Broadman Press, this brief article on the nature of the aorist tense won Stagg his greatest acclaim in the professional guild of New Testament scholarship. The article is a superb treatment of the function of the aorist tense in New Testament Greek. With humor, incisive analysis, and abundant ancient and contemporary illustration, Stagg burst one of the great myths of modern-day scholarship, commentary, and preaching. The "decisive," "once for all," and/or "punctiliar" nature of the aorist, so often celebrated in sermon and commentary, is little more than scholarly or sermonic nonsense if, according to Stagg, one is arguing that it is the aorist tense *per se* that proves the nature of the action behind it.[9]

Stagg's gift for historical and exegetical summary is also clearly evident in his 1973 publication, *The Holy Spirit Today.* Though Stagg's Trinitarian views and his treatment of the role of demon exorcisms in the Gospels may not find agreement with all, Stagg's summary of New Testament material regarding the work of the Holy Spirit is not only still exegetically and historically rich but extremely relevant in a day of widespread concern over the doctrine of the Spirit. Once again, one may see reflected Stagg's insistence that the fruit of theology be borne out in terms of its relevance for Christian living.[10]

Ralph Herring, Frank Stagg, and others published in 1974 an excellent work, *How to Understand the Bible.* The book is a surprising gold mine of information about the history and interpretation of the Bible. Stagg's gifts as a historian and a popularizer (I do not use the latter term pejoratively) are everywhere in evidence.

New Testament Theologian

No one's theology can be summarized in a few simple propositions, but it is fair to say that some leading concerns are reflected in the writings of

Frank Stagg. In all, it must be maintained that Stagg is, first and foremost, an exegetical theologian. However one may agree or disagree with his theology, his is an attempt to derive a theology from Scripture.

Man as both free and responsible. Stagg's *Polarities of Man's Existence in Biblical Perspective* is a book that was a long time in the making but, in many respects, represents the book that Stagg most wanted to write. As he states in the foreword, the book "is not intended to be a comprehensive review of biblical material on man. Rather, . . . it is concerned primarily with man in certain polar situations, where he is claimed from two sides at once and where he finds his authenic existence in the resulting tension."[11] Stagg's view is that man is neither God nor brute. On the one hand, he is made in the image of God and thus is more than other creatures, and yet, on the other hand, he is not God. Stagg believes that we live "in certain tensions, finding [our] being between what appear to be opposite claims made upon us." For Stagg, man is complex yet holistic, aspective yet not partitive, individual yet part of a community. Man is both being and in need of becoming. He is both free and bound, subject and object, a sinner and a saint, called both to deny and to affirm self, and ultimately "called to a salvation that is absolutely free yet costing everything, as pure gift yet absolute demand."[12]

Stagg does not interpret man in terms of apocalyptic dualism or cosmological oppressors, and certainly not in terms of an inherited Adamic sin. Rather, being a creature made in the image of God, man is part of a universe that, in the nature of the case, involves certain polarities—a kind of existential dialectic—whereby man, living by faith in the tension of these polarities, discovers his authentic self. For Stagg, because man is created free, he is capable both of good and evil; but more than "capable" of evil, man is, even before the "Fall," inclined toward evil. Since man is created inclined toward sin, the Fall is the result and not the cause of this inclination.[13]

Stagg's doctrine of man is deliberately and even polemically articulated in contradistinction to what he would call "Augustinian" presuppositions. In his assertion of the freedom of man, Stagg tends to downplay any theological notions which seem to detract from man's freedom and/or its polarity, his responsibility. Views of man as somehow a participant in Adam's sin are expressly denied by Stagg. In his article, "Adam, Christ, and Us," Stagg's obvious goal is to minimize the role of Adam for biblical theology. He points out the relative infrequency of the appearance of Adam's name in the Bible and gives a lengthy treatment of Romans 5:12, the text which, being commonly misunderstood according to Stagg, forms the basis of the Augustinian theory that mankind has participated in Adam's sin. According to Stagg:

The Augustinian theory of inherited sin opens the way to a transactional view of atonement, by which we got lost and then got
saved without having one thing to do with either, except in a passive and involuntary sense. This is to reduce theology to nonsense, and it is more imposed upon than derived from the
Scriptures. This is Augustinian logic, not biblical theology.[14]

Stagg argues that the key phrase in Romans 5:12 is not, as the Vulgate
reads, "in whom all sinned," but "because all sinned." Instead of referring
mankind's sin to his participation in Adam, Stagg insists that sin involves
the free and voluntary response of every individual.

Stagg's insistence upon man's freedom and individual responsibility is
reflected throughout his writings.[15] Not only is sin not to be regarded as a
result of mankind's participation in Adam, but neither does Stagg accord
any particularly significant role to Satan and/or cosmic oppressors of evil,
these being theological notions which detract from human responsibility.
James 1:13–15 and Romans 1:18 to 3:20 are his primary scriptural models
for understanding the nature of sin, wrath, and human responsibility.[16]
Stagg interprets these passages as having no reference to Adam, Satan, or
apocalyptic/cosmic powers. The blame for sin lies entirely within man and
is a result of his misuse of freedom. For Stagg the gift of authentic freedom
in creation involved not only the potential for both good and evil but also
an "inclination" toward evil, an inclination whose origin the Bible does not
explain but rather assumes by referring to its "activation."[17]

*Salvation as authentic human existence based upon repentance and
faith.* Stagg's anthropology is consistent with his soteriology. Since sin is an
individual problem, not based upon either cosmic oppressors or participation in a fallen order, salvation itself, for Stagg, is not to be seen as a result
of a historical event or a "transactional" atonement.[18] Rather, salvation is
to be grounded in God, based on repentance and trust in the God who has
revealed himself through Jesus Christ. Reflecting the character of God, who
has always been willing to forgive, the work of Christ is thus primarily revelatory. Salvation does not finally depend upon some subsequent event in
salvation history (like the cross or resurrection). Rather, the cross is the culmination and epitome of God's own vulnerability and self-denial as revealed in the person of Jesus Christ.[19] Thus, for Stagg, salvation is
discovered in self-denial, not self-assertion. When man denies himself, he
becomes authentically human. Using a psalm of contrition to illustrate his
doctrine of salvation, Stagg writes:

> It is false to subsume all Scripture under some scheme of
> *Heilsgeschichte.* This is obvious for the Psalms and wisdom liter-
> ature but not less true for much else in Scripture which simply re-
> flects the existence of man in the immediate presence of God,

whether in despair or hope, in fear or faith, in guilt or forgiveness, in rebellion or worship. Psalm 51, for example, is not to be fitted into any transactional "plan of salvation." It is the anguish and faith of a man who believed himself to be addressed directly, and who addressed God directly, with the joy of salvation hanging in the balances, then and there. Salvation as a possibility then and there is grounded on the one side solely in God, with no contingency upon some subsequent transaction in salvation history, and on the other side in the sinner's contrition and openness of faith. It is that direct and simple.[20]

Then, in the following paragraph of the same article, Stagg writes concerning the theology of Jesus and comes to similar conclusions:

When we turn to the Gospels we find Jesus portrayed as bringing God to men and men to God, then and there. God is seen as making Himself knowable to man, and man is called into God's presence and to decision in which he sees his existence as it is and is moved by the presence of God to his existence as it might be. This is salvation. To be saved is to become an authentic human being. It is not to become an angel as in popular thought or divine as with some Gnostics. It is not to become a fraction, either in Gnostic reduction to a bodiless soul nor in secular reduction to a mere animal. It is for the whole man to be made whole (John 7:23) in his total ecological existence in the community of God and man and the world about him.[21]

For Stagg, salvation, like sin, is a matter of human decision. The individually responsible sinner may turn to God in faith and repentance and thus experience salvation, thereby becoming authentically human.

Christ the revealer. Stagg's doctrine of salvation is, in turn, of a piece with his Christology. Opposed to any schema of salvation history which makes salvation dependent on historical events, thereby robbing salvation of its immediacy and its foundation in God alone, Stagg illustrates his doctrine of salvation primarily by appeal to the theology of Jesus. It may be noted that Stagg finds little support for these views in the writings of Paul and thus makes virtually no attempt to ground his soteriology and/or Christology in Paul, except for his views of sin and human responsibility read primarily out of Romans 1:18 to 3:20 (i.e., read so as to minimize the role of Satan and/or other forces outside man's own will).[22]

For Christology, Stagg boldly turns to the Synoptic Gospels, which, though written after Paul, nonetheless reflect what he calls an authentic memory of the theology of Jesus. Stagg's appeal to the "Jesus material" is largely an appeal to selected scenes within the synoptic traditions, but not primarily to the passion and resurrection narratives. For Stagg, certain

Synoptic episodes in the life of Jesus clearly illustrate the immediacy of salvation as a gift of God to all those who come to him in repentance and faith.

Stagg's February 2, 1971, faculty address given in alumni chapel at The Southern Baptist Theological Seminary, later printed in the *Review and Expositor,* clearly sets forth his views; and his 1981 article, "Reassessing the Gospels," is a more detailed attempt to explicate the same basic thesis. Chronologically, the Synoptic Gospels obviously follow the Pauline letters, but Stagg believes that Paul represents something of a departure from the theology of Jesus as reflected in the Gospels, particularly in certain Synoptic episodes. In fact, Stagg suggests that the memory of Jesus contained in these Gospel episodes is retained *in spite of* the theological development in the early church which, though it shaped the Gospel narratives overall, is moving in "another direction" than the theology of Jesus as reflected in the episodes themselves.[23]

Stagg's procedure is the exposition of various synoptic scenes beginning with Mark and moving through Matthew and Luke. The basic point made in each of the episodes adduced is that, without appealing to the contingency of salvation as something to be fulfilled by virtue of a subsequent "transactional" event, Jesus offered salvation immediately to those who would trust. The woman with the hemorrhage of Mark 5:25–34 is told, "Daughter, your faith has healed you; go in peace." To blind Bartimaeus in Mark 10:46–52 Jesus said, "Your faith has healed you." In Stagg's words:

> There is no reflection in the story of any sense of problem as to "soteriology." The man is "saved" then and there simply in response to his cry for mercy. In the perspective of this story, the only ingredients required for salvation are the Savior and a person willing to submit his need to a willing Savior. This salvation occurred before Golgotha, and it is reported with no attention to the sophistications which came to be a preoccupation of a theologizing church.[24]

In Matthew 25:31–46 salvation

> is determined by the criterion of response to such human need as hunger, thirst, alienation, nakedness, sickness, and imprisonment . . . Nothing is said about salvation history. Nothing is said about the fall of Adam or any compensating "atonement." Nothing is said about sacraments or orthodoxy. Salvation is seen in terms of existence (disposition) and relationships.[25]

Stagg's view of salvation, as grounded in the theology of Jesus, is also well illustrated in his treatment of Luke 19:1–10, the story of Zacchaeus.

Luke's story of Jesus and Zacchaeus stands in sharpest contrast to sophisticated rationales as to how God finds a working
plan by which He might save sinners. In the presence of Jesus, a
"collector" became a "distributor;" and in this transformation,
Jesus saw that salvation had come to Zacchaeus: "This day salvation has come to this house" (v. 9). Jesus did not say
"Zacchaeus, I know that you have a problem and I am working
on it; and when I have completed salvation history, I will be able
to forgive your sins and save your soul." Then and there salvation came, the conversion of a man in the presence of Jesus.[26]

Stagg's understanding of the cross is primarily what would be called an
exemplar theory of the atonement. For Stagg, the cross represents the revelation of the divine self-denial which was always at the very heart of God
and thus demands that man find authentic existence as God's creature.[27]

Though Stagg rather dislikes the Nicene language of the three persons
of the Godhead, he strongly affirms Christ as God incarnate. Christ, as
God, is the complete presence and revelation of God, and, especially in his
death on the cross, reflects the very character of God. The cross is thus
"both a particular event at Golgotha" and something that belongs "eternally to the nature of God."[28] The cross reveals the way in which God has
always dealt with man.

The cross is eternal and particular. Its eternality transcends
its particularity at Golgotha and its particularity at Golgotha is
not robbed of its meaning by its eternality. The cross belongs
eternally to the being of God. The cross was in God and in God's
action when in making man He gave up some of His freedom
and power to man, enabling man to accept or reject, trust or dis-
trust, love or hate. The cross was in God's action when the Word
became flesh and lived among us exposed to our understanding
or misunderstanding, love or hate. The cross was in God's action
when at Golgotha he spurned all self-defense and gave Himself to
the fullest. When God created man free, He made it possible for
man to defy Him. When God came in Jesus, He made it possible
for man to crucify Him.[29]

Indeed, for Stagg, one could virtually say that the eternality of the cross
is of more significance than its historical particularity.

Jesus Christ was already the slain Lamb before men nailed
Him to the cross. Redemption is in what He is, not in what was
done to Him. Salvation comes from the unchanging being of
God, not out of some transaction in history, hence salvation is a
possibility whenever man stands open to the presence of God: so

for Abraham, the Psalmist, Zacchaeus, Saul of Tarsus, you, and me.[30]

Christian ethicist: the gift brings demand. Though Frank Stagg was the full-time pastor of only one church, his entire writing and speaking career reflects the concerns of a pastor. The Christian life and the relevance of the Bible and Christian theology for Christian behavior have always been of great importance for him. Indeed, his career can be traced in terms of the great social issues of the times. Stagg was always concerned for the poor. Having grown up in relative poverty and having lived through the Great Depression and two world wars, Stagg never lost the ability to identify with the dispossessed and those who suffer. One need not read far into Stagg's *The Book of Acts: The Early Struggle for an Unhindered Gospel* to realize that racial concerns provided much of the ethical dynamic for that work.[31] One must also note that it was not only racial pride that concerned Stagg, but, in the days following World War II, the sins of national pride also provided impetus for his interpretation of Acts as teaching the universalism of Christianity over against the selfish particularisms of nation and race.[32]

The onset of the Vietnam War also influenced the ethical application of Stagg's theological exegesis. His two lectures at Baylor University on February 22–26, 1975, presented during the Lectures-Workshop on "Civil Religion" as jointly sponsored by the J. M. Dawson Studies in Church and State and the Christian Life Commission of the Baptist General Convention of Texas, declare his opposition to violence in no uncertain terms. As usual, Stagg appeals to the example of Jesus and is convinced thereby that "a part of his radicality was his rejection of violence as a means to revolution."[33]

In that connection the social and theological conservatism of the church's stance toward American military involvement in Vietnam also raised for Stagg important political-ethical questions about the relationship of church and state. In his Baylor lectures Stagg declared that "civil religion" is "any political structure assuming the dimensions of religion, and it is contended that the church *is practicing* civil religion whenever it yields to the state what belongs alone to God."[34] It is clear for Stagg that the Christian owes allegiance to the governing authorities within their own due parameters, but:

> the claim of God must take priority over every other claim . . .
> Man's own personhood is also at stake. One cannot be an au-
> thentic human being if he yields ultimate claim to any other
> human being or human structure . . . The church must disassoci-
> ate itself from all ideologies and crusades of the state.[35]

Questions related to the single person also concerned Stagg as evidenced in his 1977 article, "Biblical Perspectives on the Single Person."[36] Stagg's concern for the role of women and the issue of women's ordination found profound expression in the book he coauthored with his wife, Evelyn, entitled *Woman in the World of Jesus*.[37] This latter work is an outstanding collation of Jewish, Greek, and Roman texts on issues related to women in the ancient world. It proceeds by examining the theology and behavior of Jesus—always critical for Stagg—with respect to women and concludes with an analysis of women in the early church. For Stagg, the theology of Paul, with possibly the lone exception of Galatians 3:28, whereby Paul clearly declares, "There is neither Jew nor Greek, slave nor free, male nor female," is something of a step towards the arbitrary and restrictively regressive application of the gospel to women in the family and in the life of the church. By studying the various household codes reflected in the Pauline literature (including also 1 Pet. 2:13 to 3:7), Stagg became convinced that the theology of Paul represents the beginning of a significant departure from the theology and intention of Jesus with respect to the role of women. The subordinationist outlook of the household codes, in the early church, constitute, for Stagg, cultural "skins" that are not essential to the new wine of the gospel and, thus, may be corrected and/or come under review as necessary.[38]

In the early 1980s Stagg addressed the issue of aging and the role of the elderly in society. His book, *The Bible Speaks on Aging,* is a popular, but responsible, attempt to draw together biblical material relevant to the issues of age and/or the aging process.[39]

Living the Christian life was not a matter to be taken lightly. Stagg's writings are peppered with exhortation, a fact which reflects the moral demand that he insists is inextricably linked to the gracious gift of God. When reading Stagg, one repeatedly encounters his objection to any notion of "forensic" righteousness in the New Testament, especially in the Pauline literature. For Stagg, righteousness is never to be a legal fiction or merely a matter of "perspective" but always a practical and realistic demand imposed on those who dare to name the name of Jesus.

Evaluation

It must always be remembered that an evaluation says as much about the one doing the evaluating as the one being evaluated. Therefore, I offer the following remarks with no attempt whatsoever to hide my own theological preferences. Moreover, it is with the utmost respect for Stagg's historical, grammatical, and exegetical prowess that I offer the following criticisms, and I offer them in the same spirit of openness and theological rigor which Stagg so graciously and vigorously exemplified. One other proviso: though the lines of intellectual continuity are there in Stagg, what follows by way of evaluation is not as true of the early Stagg, the Stagg of *New Testament Theology,* as it is the later Stagg who wrote "Salvation in

Synoptic Tradition," "Reassessing the Gospels," and "The Concept of the Messiah."

I fear that Stagg has ruptured the canon of the New Testament. This rupture is not a literary fissure so much as it is a theological one. It is very clear that Stagg's preference for the theology of Jesus over the theology of Paul finally led him to something of a break with the kerygmatic "cross and resurrection" theology of the apostle and, indeed, the entire New Testament. Stagg's attempt to isolate (i.e., separate) the theology of the historical Jesus from the rest of the New Testament, especially Paul and the overall cross-resurrection context of the Synoptic Gospels themselves, and to prefer that theology to what he would call the "transactional" kind of theology that grounded salvation in historical events, finally destroys the theological unity of the New Testament. Stagg himself has argued that the shape of the New Testament canon is partly a function of theology.[40] But the theological discontinuity envisioned by Stagg between Jesus and Paul does not allow, it seems to me, for the kind of theological consensus historically required to explain the emergence of the New Testament canon. Though he disclaims any return to the new quest for the historical Jesus, Stagg's attempt to separate various Synoptic episodes from the larger cross-resurrection framework of the Gospel narratives and from those episodes, so isolated, to extract a doctrine of salvation has far-reaching implications.

To be sure, Stagg rejects Bultmann's radical, and largely negative, historical conclusions regarding the reliability of the Synoptic Gospels as source material for the theology of Jesus. However, no amount of conservative historical handling of the various episodes can compensate for Stagg's ultimate rejection of the cross-resurrection theological consensus of early Christianity. His efforts to represent Pauline theology as a move away from the theology of Jesus, not only in terms of the domestic codes, but especially in his rejection of the cross and resurrection as the necessary culmination of God's objective saving activity through the person of Jesus Christ, can have only disastrous results for theology.

Of course, Stagg clearly affirms the historical death of Jesus and his bodily resurrection, but that is not the point under discussion here. Stagg drives a wedge between Jesus and Paul that leaves the door open for the kind of canonical/theological reshuffling characteristic of Koester, Robinson, and Pagels.[41] They argue that the Pauline (and/or cross-resurrection) interpretation of the life of Jesus was only one among numerous competing interpretations of the Holy Man, Jesus.

Stagg, of course, clearly affirms the true divinity of Christ and repeatedly maintains that he is the very revelation and presence of God. But the fact still remains that, for Stagg, the Synoptic "memory" of the precross Jesus and/or the theology represented thereby is very different from the kind of cross-resurrection preaching that was characteristic of the apostle

Paul and the earliest communities whose theological concerns shaped the Gospel narratives. It is historical audacity indeed to claim, as Stagg does, that one can detect the authentic "Jesus material" in contradistinction to, and virtually in spite of, the overall theological direction of those who preserved the materials themselves. Indeed, Stagg's critically reconstructed theology of Jesus is apparently not only more primitive (earlier) than, but also to be preferred to, the cross-resurrection theology of the very communities in which (unknowingly?) the Jesus traditions were preserved and embedded in the Gospel narratives.

In the first place, it is difficult to understand how Stagg can justify the extrication of his chosen Synoptic episodes from the larger narrative structure of the Gospels in such a way as to shelter the interpretation of those Synoptic episodes from the overarching point of the Synoptic narratives (i.e., the death and resurrection of Jesus for our salvation). Of course, no one will dispute that the salvation already offered to Zacchaeus (Luke) and the woman with the hemorrhage (Mark) reflects Jesus' own gift of salvation to these two Gospel characters upon the basis of their trust. But surely these episodes, and the many others of like nature cited by Stagg, should not be interpreted in discontinuity with the kerygmatic nature of the Gospels seen as narrative wholes. Such incidences, I would argue, are to be seen as historical and literary anticipations (and/or illustrations) of the way of salvation revealed as itself initially fulfilled in the cross and resurrection of Jesus (I say "initially" because final salvation awaits the return of Christ; Rom. 8:24f.; 1 Pet. 1:3–9).

The salvation given to New Testament characters, prior to the death and resurrection of Jesus, would be of the same proleptic/anticipatory sort as that attributed in the New Testament to Old Testament heroes of faith. The author of Hebrews, for one, certainly makes the salvation of Old Testament saints dependent upon the kerygmatic events (cross-resurrection-exaltation) that have occurred in connection with Jesus (Heb. 11:31). New Testament theology and/or the theological/canonical unity of the New Testament can ill survive the wedge that Stagg has driven between the theology of Jesus and the theology of Paul.

It is also appropriate to note Stagg's rather resounding rejection of the cross as a "transactional" means of salvation. If by "transactional" all Stagg means is some ancient and/or Augustinian belief that the Father must somehow be propitiated or appeased by the Son before salvation can be accomplished, or that the Son had to pay a fee or ransom to the devil, we may all let the criticism stand; but what Stagg ends up doing by his repeated (and pejorative) references to a "transactional" atonement is rather simplistically rejecting virtually every other view of the atonement save a kind of exemplar/repentance model.

Stagg leaves the cross of Christ as little more than revelatory of the character of God. To be sure the cross *does* reveal the nature of the God with whom we have to do (i.e., he is indeed the God of self-sacrifice and suffering). He is the kind of God who is very much unlike the capricious gods of the Greeks and Romans. There is little doubt that the cross of Jesus is both a marvelous and mysterious revelation of the serving, self-giving character of God. Indeed, the New Testament clearly points to the cross of Jesus as having exemplar value (Eph. 4:32 to 5:2); but none of that can dismiss what is also transparently evident in the New Testament: specifically, that the death and resurrection of Jesus actually accomplished something objective for our salvation.

For all of Stagg's affirmations as to the historical particularity of the cross, it becomes clear in the end that the greater value of the cross for Stagg is in its essential eternality (i.e., its revelatory "intensity" as an example of the kind of suffering and self-giving that are at the very heart of God). While one may welcome Stagg's focus upon the revelatory nature of the cross, it is disturbing to note that, for Stagg, the cross and resurrection seem to lack objective and particular redemptive value.

Stagg's appeals over the years to Hebrews 6:6 as a basis for his subjectivizing/departicularizing of the cross ("they crucify *to themselves* the Son of God"), thereby making more palatable what he calls the universality and eternality of the cross, are based upon what appears to be a questionable exegesis of what is a much disputed text.[42] Stagg's views virtually deny the saving value of the death and resurrection of Jesus as events. Indeed, Stagg does insist that salvation is grounded in God and *not* in historical events.[43] In fact, Stagg's attempts to isolate form-critically certain Synoptic scenes from the theologically decisive and literarily dominant cross-resurrection narratives reflect his own tacit admission that the New Testament does characteristically ground salvation in certain events, particularly the historical coming of Jesus and especially his coming as interpreted through his death and resurrection.

Moreover, it is a strange procedure which separates the activity of God from historical events—especially, of course, the historical events of the cross and resurrection. To say that salvation is accomplished by the cross and resurrection does not separate those saving events from their saving function in the eternal purposes of God. I would argue that Stagg has, his own denials notwithstanding, virtually dehistoricized the cross and ultimately dehistoricized salvation. With faith thus separated from specific historical events, salvation becomes (as indeed it does for Stagg) little more than a doctrine of repentance.[44] We are indeed left wondering about the real necessity of the cross.

In a similar vein I would argue that Stagg has deeschatologized large segments of Synoptic theology (especially what he calls "Jesus material") and selected portions of Pauline theology. Stagg's attempt to separate eschatology from apocalyptic is appropriate on a relative basis but cannot stand up absolutely.[45] To speak of the end of history in Jewish eschatology is normally to speak of a catastrophic/apocalyptic day of the Lord. The presence or absence of excessive apocalyptic symbolism or language does not, contrary to Stagg's apparent assumption, eliminate the apocalyptic features of eschatology. His efforts to deapocalpyticize New Testament eschatology are nonetheless consistent with his rejection of "transactional" theology (so construed) and his related attempts to downplay notions of salvation history (though Stagg's own admission, that New Testament theology is eschatological, is, itself, an admission that salvation history is, at least to some extent, both an appropriate and necessary model for doing New Testament theology) and to reduce the role of Satanic and/or cosmic oppressors in the drama of redemption.[46] Indeed, the very language "drama of redemption" is not at all welcome to Stagg.[47] But such efforts will not stand up to the pervasively cross-resurrection kind of theology/eschatology reflected in the New Testament's unapologetically apocalyptic thought world.

As far back as his *New Testament Theology,* Stagg's theological views caused him to minimize the role of Satan and cosmic powers. Stagg prefers to interpret sin on the model of James 1:13–15, and that in a way that does not, it seems to me, see the rather clear-cut allusions to the story of Adam. In this same connection, it may be observed that Stagg's selection of Romans 1:18 to 3:20 as the determinative core for Paul's views of sin and wrath is largely based on Stagg's view that this particular passage in Romans makes no use of apocalyptic language, has no reference to Satan, and none at all to Adam.[48]

In the first instance, I do not think one can read "for the *wrath* of God is *revealed from heaven*" (Rom. 1:18, emphasis added) without seeing the apocalyptic horizon of Paul's thought.[49] Furthermore, given the highly personalistic terminology used to describe "sin" in contradistinction to the sphere of God through Christ, it is hard for this reader of Romans to believe that the single term "sin" in Romans 6 and 7 is not in some respect a reference to cosmic powers of darkness. Romans 7:7–25 cannot, it seems to me, be read apart from either the perception of references to Adam (see especially vv. 8–13) or salvation history (cf. 7:5 with 7:7–25; 7:6 with 8:1ff.).

Apart from Paul, however, I think Stagg's attempt to read the Synoptic Gospels and/or the theology of Jesus apart from Christ's battle with the powers of darkness, as reflected in the demon exorcisms and the preaching tours of the Twelve and seventy, is misguided. The kingdom is manifested in the coming of Jesus and the reign of God inherent in his preaching, his miraculous/eschatological signs of the glorious age to come, and his demon exorcisms. Talk of conquering Satan and/or the defeat of demonic powers may not seem relevant to some moderns, but that has no bearing on the way in which the New Testament and/or the theology of the Synoptics and/or the theology of Jesus is to be historically understood. I, for one, find a great deal of relevance in the New Testament view of principalities and powers who live and work under the aegis of Satan, for nothing short of such cosmic powers of evil can explain the despicable patterns of evil and injustice manifested in the world and against which Stagg so admirably lived, wrote, and preached.

Quite apart from the abiding relevance of such an apocalyptic (New Testament) worldview, it seems historically impossible for a reader of the New Testament to call any theory of the atonement competent which, while trying to be historically descriptive of the theology reflected in the New Testament, does not reckon with Christ's defeat of the powers of darkness in his ministry, death, resurrection, and exaltation. To claim such is not to seek a return to any crude notions of Christ's paying a ransom to Satan, but it is to take seriously the commonly asserted Christian belief— widely reflected in the New Testament—that Christ came to "destroy him who holds the power of death—that is, the devil" (Heb. 2:14).

Stagg's Christology is strong with regard to his affirmation of the divinity of Christ, but his Trinitarian views leave something to be desired.[50] It must first of all be said that Stagg is not always clear in his views on the subject of the Trinity. He certainly sounds like what the historians of doctrine would call a "modalist," though Stagg himself denies this charge.[51] It is abundantly manifest that Stagg dislikes the language of Nicea and, though he speaks of Father, Son, and Spirit, does at times seem to question the tripersonality of God.[52] Concerning passages where Christ prays to the Father, Stagg relegates these to the mystery of the Incarnation[53] and thus leaves this reader both dissatisfied with and puzzled over his views. It must be said, of course, that Stagg's views cannot be called heretical because of his dislike of Nicene language. Indeed, Stagg is to be admired for his attempt to retain terminology that is as fully biblical as possible; but Stagg's views do not, it seems to me, take seriously enough the particularly Trinitarian language of the New Testament, given his hints that specifically *tri*-nitarian (as opposed to *bi*-nitarian or even other numeric models) language is not binding theologically.[54] One gets the feeling that, for Stagg, the difference, for example, between God the Father and God the Son is not a matter of essential distinction within God so much as it is a matter of functional perception on the part of the believer. In that regard there is no necessary or significant theological attachment to "three" in Stagg's discussions of the one God.

Finally, it must be noted that this reader was not always comfortable with Stagg's ethical applications of New Testament materials. Of course, the fact that Stagg consistently endeavored to make the New Testament relevant to Christian living is to be warmly applauded and deeply admired; but I do think that the political agenda of the more liberal side (relatively speaking) of American politics did not receive the kind of dispassionate analysis and criticism that the right wing of American politics in the 1960s and 1970s received. All of us would do well to remember that the gospel can be tied to neither an ideology of the left nor the right.

Though one may not always agree strategically with Frank Stagg's ethical applications of the gospel, there can be little doubt that the New Testament he has so faithfully treasured calls us to a radical discipleship in the world. It is to Frank Stagg's great credit that he has not only courageously chosen to live his own life under the lordship of Jesus Christ, but as a minister/teacher of the gospel, he has also called upon each of us to live in a way that is consistent with our calling in Christ Jesus. However one may disagree with Stagg's theological synthesis, we must all agree that both the confession and the living out of the lordship of Jesus Christ are not only a mandate from the risen Lord himself, but our mission to a lost and dying world.

Bibliography

Works by Stagg

The Bible Speaks on Aging. Nashville: Broadman Press, 1981.
The Book of Acts: The Early Struggle for an Unhindered Gospel. Nashville: Broadman Press, 1955.
The Doctrine of Christ. Nashville: Convention Press, 1984.
Exploring the New Testament. Nashville: Broadman Press, 1961.
Galatians and Romans. Knox Preaching Guides. Edited by John H. Hayes. Atlanta: John Knox Press, 1980.
The Holy Spirit Today. Nashville: Broadman Press, 1973.
The Holy Spirit Today. Rev. ed. Macon, Ga.: Smyth & Helwys, 1995.
New Testament Theology. Nashville: Broadman Press, 1962.
Polarities of Man's Existence in Biblical Perspective. Philadelphia: Westminster Press, 1973.
The Polarities of Existence in Biblical Perspective. Rev. ed. Macon, Ga.: Smyth & Helwys, 1995.
Studies in Luke's Gospel. Nashville: Convention Press, 1967.
Woman in the World of Jesus. With Evelyn Stagg. Philadelphia: Westminster Press, 1978.

Contributions to Other Books

"Adam, Christ, and Us." *New Testament Studies: Essays in Honor of Ray Summers in His Sixty-Fifth Year.* Edited by Huber L. Drumwright and Curtis Vaughan. Waco: Baylor University, 1975.

"Authentic Morality and Militarism." *Proceedings of the 1970 Christian Life Commission Seminar.* Nashville: Christian Life Commission of the SBC, 1970.

"Biblical Perspectives on Women." With Evelyn Stagg. In *Findings of the Consultation on Women in Church-Related Vocations,* edited by Johnni Johnson. Nashville: Southern Baptist Convention, 1978.

"A Continuing Pilgrimage." *What Faith Has Meant to Me.* Edited by Claude A. Frazier. Philadelphia: Westminster Press, 1975.

"Establishing a Text for Luke-Acts." *1977 Seminar Papers, Society of Biblical Literature Book of Reports.* Missoula, Mont.: Scholars Press, 1977.

"Explain the Ending of the Gospel of Mark, Mark 16:17–18." *What Did the Bible Mean?* Edited by Claude A. Frazier. Nashville: Broadman Press, 1971.

"Glossolalia in the New Testament." With Glenn Hinson and Wayne E. Oates. In *Glossolalia: Tongue Speaking in Biblical, Historical, and Psychological Perspective.* Nashville: Abingdon Press, 1967.

"He That Judgeth Me." *More Southern Baptist Preaching.* Edited by H. C. Brown Jr. Nashville: Broadman Press, 1964.

"How I Prepare My Sermons." *More Southern Baptist Preaching.* Edited by H. C. Brown Jr. Nashville: Broadman Press, 1964.

"Matthew." *The Broadman Bible Commentary,* vol. 8. Edited by Clifton J. Allen. Nashville: Broadman Press, 1969.

"Philippians." *The Broadman Bible Commentary,* vol. 11. Edited by Clifton J. Allen. Nashville: Broadman Press, 1971.

"Playing God with Other People's Minds." *Should Preachers Play God?* Edited by Claude A. Frazier. Independence: Independence Press, 1973.

"Preaching from Luke-Acts." *Biblical Preaching: An Expositor's Treasury.* Edited by James W. Cox. Philadelphia: Westminster Press, 1983.

"Preaching from the Sermon on the Mount." *Biblical Preaching: An Expositor's Treasury.* Edited by James W. Cox. Philadelphia: Westminster Press, 1983.

"Rights and Responsibilities in the Teachings of Paul." *Emerging Patterns of Rights and Responsibilities Affecting Church and State.* Washington D.C.: Baptist Joint Committee on Public Affairs, 1969.

"Understanding Call to Ministry." *Formation for Christian Ministry.* Edited by Anne Davis and Wade Rowatt Jr. Louisville: Review and Expositor, 1981.

"What and Where Is the Church?" *What Can You Believe?* Edited by David K. Alexander and C. W. Junker. Nashville: Broadman Press, 1966.

"What Is Truth?" in *Science, Faith and Revelation: An Approach to Christian Philosophy.* Edited by Robert E. Patterson. Nashville: Broadman Press, 1979.

"A Whole Man Made Well." *The Struggle for Meaning,* edited by William Powell Tuck. Valley Forge, Pa.: Judson Press, 1977.

"Women in New Testament Perspective." With Evelyn Stagg. In *Encyclopedia of Southern Baptists,* vol. 4, edited by Lynn Edward May Jr. Nashville: Broadman Press, 1982.

Journal Articles

"The Abused Aorist." *Journal of Biblical Literature* 91 (1972): 222–31.

"An Analysis of the Book of James." *Review and Expositor* 66 (1969): 365–68.

"Biblical Perspectives on the Single Person." *Review and Expositor* 74 (1977): 5–19.

"The Christology of Matthew." *Review and Expositor* 59 (1962): 457–68.

"The Concept of the Messiah: A Baptist Perspective." *Review and Expositor* 84 (1987): 247–57.

"The Domestic Code and Final Appeal: Ephesians 5:21–6:24." *Review and Expositor* 76 (1979): 541–52.

"Eschatology: A Southern Baptist Perspective." *Review and Expositor* 79 (1982): 381–95.

"Exegetical Themes in James 1 and 2." *Review and Expositor* 66 (1969): 391–402.

"The Farewell Discourses: John 13–17." *Review and Expositor* 62 (1965): 459–72.

"Freedom and Moral Responsibility Without License or Legalism." *Review and Expositor* 69 (1972): 483–94.

"The Gospel in Biblical Usage." *Review and Expositor* 63 (1966): 5–13.

"The Great Words of Romans." *Theological Educator* 7 (1976): 94–102.

"The Holy Spirit in the New Testament." *Review and Expositor* 63 (1966): 135–47.

"Interpreting the Book of Revelation." *Review and Expositor* 72 (1975): 331–43.

"Introduction to Colossians." *Theological Educator* 4 (1973): 7–16.

"The Journey Toward Jerusalem in Luke's Gospel." *Review and Expositor* 64 (1967): 499–512.

"The Lord's Supper in the New Testament." *Review and Expositor* 66 (1969): 5–14.

"The Mind in Christ Jesus." *Review and Expositor* 77 (1980): 337–47.

"The Motif of First Corinthians." *Southwestern Journal of Theology* 3 (1960): 15–24.

"The New International Version: New Testament." *Review and Expositor* 76 (1979): 377–85.

"The New Testament Doctrine of the Church." *Theological Educator* 12 (1981): 42–56.

"Orthodoxy and Orthopraxy in the Johannine Epistles." *Review and Expositor* 67 (1970): 423–32.

"The Plight of the Jew and the Gentile in Sin: Romans 1:18–3:20." *Review and Expositor* 73 (1976): 401–13.

"Prophetic Ministry Today." *Review and Expositor* 73 (1976): 179–89.

"The Purpose and Message of Acts." *Review and Expositor* 44 (1947): 3–21.

"Rendering to Caesar What Belongs to Caesar: Christian Engagement with the World." *Journal of Church and State* 18 (1976): 95–113.

"Rendering to God What Belongs to God: Christian Disengagement with the World." *Journal of Church and State* 18 (1976): 217–32.

"Reassessing the Gospels." *Review and Expositor* 78 (1981): 187–203.

"Salvation in Synoptic Tradition." *Review and Expositor* 69 (1972): 355–67.

"Southern Baptist Theology Today: An Interview." *Theological Educator* 3 (1977) 15–36.

"A Teaching Outline for Acts." *Review and Expositor* 71 (1974): 533–36.

"Textual Criticism for Luke-Acts." *Perspectives in Religion Studies* 5 (1978): 152–65.

"The Unhindered Gospel." *Review and Expositor* 71 (1974): 451–62.

Books about Stagg

Andress, Vance Corbet. "A Critical Evaluation of Frank Stagg and His 'Polarities of Existence' with Implications for Pastoral Theology and Caregiving." Ph.D. dissertation, Southwestern Baptist Theological Seminary, 1996.

Carroll, Raymond Evans. "Dimensions of Individualism in Southern Baptist Thought." Th.D. dissertation, New Orleans Baptist Theological Seminary, 1995.

Mills, Watson, E, ed. "Frank Stagg Festschrift." *Perspectives in Religious Studies,* 11 (Winter 1984): 1–108.

15

Carl F. H. Henry

By R. Albert Mohler Jr.

IN AN AGE OF DECLINING THEOLOGICAL VIGOR AND FEW THEOLOGICAL giants, Carl F. H. Henry has emerged as one of the theological luminaries of the twentieth century. His experience as journalist, teacher, theologian, editor, and world spokesman for evangelical Christianity ranks him among the few individuals who can claim to have shaped a major theological movement.

Biography

Born January 22, 1913, to immigrant parents in New York City, Henry's life is in many ways a reflection of America in the early twentieth century. His parents, Karl F. and Joanna (*nee* Vathroder) Heinrich, were both young German immigrants to the United States. The family name was changed to Henry due to the anti-German sentiment occasioned by World War I.

The Henry family lived the lives of a typical immigrant family, with hard-working parents and little luxury. Though his mother was Roman Catholic by family tradition and his father a Lutheran, there was little evidence of religion in the Henry household.[1]

The family later moved to a farm on Long Island, where his father was eventually to purchase a small general goods store. The Henry children grew into adulthood in a spartan but not impoverished setting, and Carl— the eldest of eight children—took a succession of part-time jobs to supplement the family's income.

Public schools provided Henry's early educational experiences, and as a high school student Henry seemed destined for a career in journalism. Graduating in the midst of the Great Depression, he sought and obtained work at *The Islip Press* on Long Island. He quickly became a working reporter and was later to write for the *New York Herald Tribune* and the *New York Daily News*. Just three years after assuming his first newspaper position, Henry became the editor of *The Smithtown Star,* a major weekly paper on Long Island. He was later to cover a large section of Long Island for *The New York Times*.

His newspaper experience put him into contact with a devout Christian woman and, through her, with members of the Oxford Group.[2] At age twenty, with ambitions and success in journalism, Henry was confronted with the claims of the gospel and became a believer.

Perceiving a call from God to a life of vocational Christian service, Henry left his promising newspaper career and enrolled at Wheaton College in the fall of 1935. Henry's experience at Wheaton shaped the course of his later life and thought. He was drawn to Wheaton by its reputation as the "evangelical Harvard" and because he had heard its president, J. Oliver Buswell, speak at a Stony Brook conference on the importance of the rational dimension of faith. At Wheaton, Henry found himself in the bosom of the evangelical movement—and at a very precipitous moment in the development of conservative Christianity in America. Henry was to establish friendships at Wheaton with individuals such as Billy Graham and Harold Lindsell. Most importantly, he was there introduced to Gordon Clark, professor of philosophy, who was to become perhaps the most important intellectual influence on Henry's thought. Clark was a conservative Presbyterian who stressed the inherent rationality of theology and belief in God.[3] By the time of his graduation in August 1938, Henry had determined to pursue graduate study in theology. He considered an invitation to join the Moody Bible College as director of promotion but followed instead his sense that theology was to be his calling.

Wheaton was to introduce Henry to another significant influence on his life, Helga Bender. Married in 1940, they were later to have two children.[4]

Henry remained at Wheaton to complete his M.A. in theology, while engaged in the bachelor of divinity program at Northern Baptist Theological Seminary in nearby Lombard, Illinois. Northern Seminary had been founded as an alternative to the increasingly liberal direction taken by the University of Chicago Divinity School. Henry was to complete the bachelor of divinity and doctor of theology degrees at Northern, completing his work in 1942.[5]

Nine years after his conversion, Henry held a degree from Wheaton and three graduate degrees in theology. The shape of his early thought was already clear, with the battle for the rational and evangelical expression of Christian theism in the forefront. Already a published author, Henry was to release several small volumes on religious thought and theology, which indicate his critical reading of contemporary theology and his call for a vigorous conservative offensive.

Henry began his teaching career at Northern Seminary, teaching theology at his alma mater until 1947, when he was invited to join the faculty of the young Fuller Theological Seminary in Pasadena, California. The seminary was the visionary project of evangelist Charles E. Fuller and Harold J. Ockenga, pastor of Boston's prestigious Park Street Church. Fuller was projected as a great evangelical seminary for the rapidly growing west coast. Henry accepted Ockenga's invitation and moved to Pasadena in 1947. He began his tenure at Fuller while pursuing a Ph.D. in philosophy under personalist philosopher Edgar Brightman at Boston University. At Fuller, Henry was to teach theology and philosophy, with a concentration in apologetics and ethics.

Fuller, though plagued by a difficult birth and an absentee president, made remarkable progress and Henry emerged as a key leader within the faculty.[6] Nevertheless, within a decade of his move to Pasadena, he was to accept an invitation to serve *Christianity Today* as founding editor.

Theological conservatives had long yearned for a flagship vehicle for their evangelical perspective. *Christianity Today* was the brainchild of Billy Graham and Harold J. Ockenga and was intended as an alternative to the more liberal Protestant journal, *The Christian Century*. Henry was the logical choice as editor. With a background in journalism, impeccable academic credentials, and an unquestioned commitment to evangelical orthodoxy, Henry was uniquely poised to lead such an effort. *Christianity*

Today was established with offices in Washington, D.C., and emerged in 1956 with an impressive appearance and solid content.

At the helm of *Christianity Today,* Henry exerted growing leadership over the larger evangelical movement and earned a worldwide reputation for serious engagement with modern thought. Nevertheless, his leadership at *Christianity Today* came to an end in 1967 following a disagreement over the direction of the magazine.[7]

Vacating the editorship at *Christianity Today,* Henry traveled to Cambridge, where he undertook study and research which formed the nucleus of his massive theological project, the six-volume *God, Revelation and Authority.*

Returning to the United States, Henry accepted a teaching post at Eastern Baptist Theological Seminary in Philadelphia. Later he was to serve as lecturer-at-large for World Vision, an evangelical social action agency. He continues to lecture, write, and teach, and has held several visiting professorships. Though formal lectureships have been a part of his experience since the 1940s, the last three decades have been a period of intensive and influential lectures at secular and evangelical universities. He delivered the prestigious Rutherford Lectures at Edinburgh in 1989. In recent years he has taught on a succession of evangelical campuses and to both secular and evangelical audiences.

Exposition

Carl Henry and the Evangelical Movement

The evangelical movement in America is notoriously difficult to define, its precise boundaries and constituencies varied and often blurred. The movement has been most easily identified in terms of specific institutions, agencies, and individuals. The evangelical movement, as it has developed after World War II, has been represented by institutions such as Fuller Seminary, Gordon Conwell Seminary, Trinity Evangelical Divinity School, and World Vision. Publishing houses such as William B. Eerdmans, Baker Book House, and Zondervan release hundreds of evangelical volumes each year. But evangelicalism has been most readily identified by means of individuals. Billy Graham, the world-famous evangelist, has epitomized the evangelistic commitment and orthodox preaching of the gospel. Carl F. H. Henry, however, has represented the intellectual and cognitive defense of evangelical truth so central to the evangelical movement.

The year of Henry's conversion, 1933, was also the year of the release of the Humanist Manifesto, the organized call of the intellectual elite to a humanist agenda. This coincidental timing has not been lost on Henry. This era was also colored by the continuation of the Fundamentalist/Modernist controversy, a battle assumed by most to have been lost by the fundamentalists. Henry's experience at college and seminary put him into contact with those who had decided to separate from the mainline churches, and with those who determined to remain within their denominations as agents of conservative witness.

By the conclusion of his doctoral studies at Northern Seminary, Henry was convinced that the fundamentalist movement would be required to change its anticultural stance if it was to be effective in the twentieth century. His concern that fundamentalism had ignored all social and ethical issues led to the publication of Henry's first epocal work, *The Uneasy Conscience of Modern Fundamentalism*.[8] The volume became a manifesto of a movement later to be known as the "new evangelicalism."

Henry was to become one of the founding fathers of the modern evangelical movement. As defined by these young conservatives, the new evangelicalism would combine a stalwart defense of the orthodox faith, buttressed by solid academic underpinnings, with careful attention to the social application of the gospel message.[9]

The character of this new evangelicalism was to shape Fuller Theological Seminary. Henry, though among the youngest of the founding faculty, was elected dean. His reputation as a premier evangelical thinker and spokesperson was enhanced by his considerable vision and organizational skills. In his decade at Fuller, Henry would write eight books and numerous articles, complete his Ph.D. at Boston University, and emerge as a principal organizer behind such events as the annual Rose Bowl Sunrise Service.[10]

Henry's pivotal leadership at *Christianity Today* solidified his influence among the evangelical leadership. *Christianity Today* represented their hope for a fully respected vehicle for evangelical advance. His editorials and articles, though not lengthy, were known for solid content and indicate the optimism of the movement.[11]

The zenith of Henry's institutional and organizational influence in the evangelical movement was reached in 1966, when he served as chairman of the World Congress on Evangelism in Berlin. This conference, organized by Henry and Billy Graham, was another symbol of evangelical advance.[12] Yet within two years Henry was no longer editor of *Christianity Today,* and the magazine's direction and character was later to undergo significant change.[13]

Henry's role within evangelicalism has been unique and extensive. More than any other evangelical, he has given serious and sustained attention to the issue of evangelical identity and definition. The titles of his books, from *Evangelical Responsibility in Contemporary Theology, Evangelicals at the Brink of Crisis,* and *A Plea for Evangelical Demonstration* to *Evangelicals in Search of Identity* indicate his self-conscious intention to assist in the definition and mobilization of the movement.

The Uneasy Conscience of Modern Fundamentalism established Henry's call for cultural engagement by orthodox Protestants. That same year Ockenga coined the term *new evangelicalism,* and a movement was spawned. Henry differentiated the older conservatism (fundamentalism) from the new (evangelicalism) by a basic distinction in "moods" between the two approaches. Evangelicalism would embody the mood of engagement with broader theological movements and a recognition of the social and cultural dimensions of the gospel.

The new evangelicalism was to be fully orthodox but would cooperate across denominational lines, building a constructive theological movement out of the ruins of a fallen liberalism. The movement would avoid the excessive preoccupation on eschatology, spirit of separatism, and lack of engagement common to fundamentalism. The new evangelicals saw their responsibility in vivid terms, for the fall of the older liberal theologies could presage an even more dangerous theological context.[14]

The new evangelicalism would combine the manifest strengths of the older fundamentalism but would reject its excesses and seek to meet the challenges of modernity as a full intellectual partner.[15]

Though the 1966 World Congress on Evangelism fixed Henry's stature among world evangelicals, it was the eventual publication of the six-volume *God, Revelation and Authority* which established Henry's stature as the primary proponent of an evangelical doctrine of revelation and scriptural authority. The publication of his *magnum opus* also marked Henry's growing sense that American evangelicalism was in grave danger of missing its greatest opportunity for intellectual and cultural influence.[16]

Henry's leadership in the evangelical movement has shifted in his later years from the institutional influence he wielded at Fuller and *Christianity Today* to his current status as senior statesman and acknowledged dean of evangelical theologians. Nevertheless, he has continued an organizational presence through such activities as his cochairmanship of the 1989 "Evangelical Affirmations" conference at Trinity Evangelical Divinity School and his service on the board of Prison Fellowship Ministries.

Henry on Modern Theology

"This generation, with which we die," wrote Henry in 1946, "is a pivot point in world history."[17] This sense of urgency has marked Carl Henry's theological mission from its inception. With much of the world in literal ruins, Henry saw an opportunity to demonstrate the failure of liberal theology to deal with the problems of the age. Theology had reached "the mid-twentieth century impasse" between liberal revisionism and orthodox faith.[18]

Henry identified a "great divide" between evangelical and mediating or liberal systems of thought. Assuming the destruction of schools associated with the older liberalism of Harnack, Ritschl, and Hermann, he aimed his critiques at the "neo-supernaturalist" systems of the neoorthodox theologians and other more contemporary variants of thought.[19]

The basic pattern evident in Henry's critique of mediating systems can be traced to his Boston University dissertation on the Northern Baptist theologian, A. H. Strong. Strong's attempt to forge a mediating system between orthodoxy and liberalism (based in his case upon a personalistic monism) was seen by Henry to end in failure on all fronts. Both conservatives and liberals found the attempted bridge inadequate and untrustworthy. The lesson provided Henry with a model of the failure of mediating systems, especially those based on modern critical philosophy and any post-Kantian epistemology.[20]

Henry's engagement with the theology of Karl Barth reveals his pattern of theological critique. Clearly Barth was the dominant theological presence in postwar Europe, though Rudolph Bultmann's influence was growing swiftly. Henry understood Barth's theological system to be an attempt to mediate between the older liberalism of his teachers and the evangelical heritage of the Reformation. Though not completely unappreciative of Barth's program, Henry was quick to warn his fellow evangelicals against a hasty appropriation of Barth's thought.

Grounded in a Kantian epistemology, Barth's system was therefore based not in a rediscovery of full scriptural authority but in a "neo-supernaturalistic" tradition "which has contributed as much to the theological confusion of our times as it has been a force corrective of some of the weaknesses of liberalism."[21] Henry saw Bultmann as the greater danger but thought Barth to be insufficiently orthodox to stem Bultmann's tide.[22]

The fatal flaw Henry identified in Barth's system centered in the Swiss theologian's insistence on the nonpropositional character of special revelation. This, Henry lamented, led to a doctrine of revelation insufficient to provide a sturdy alternative to Bultmann's program of demythologization. Though Barth was refreshingly orthodox on many doctrinal issues, his system was unable to provide a workable mediation between modernity and theism.[23]

Few movements or theologians escaped Henry's critique. As the neoorthodox schools collapsed, a myriad of variant systems emerged, with the "death of God" movement receiving the most popular attention. Henry considered innovations including the theologies of hope represented by Jurgen Moltmann and Johannes Baptist Metz, the theology of Wolflhart Pannenberg, and the schools of thought associated with liberation and process theologies.[24] Each system was seen by Henry to be based in an inadequate epistemology and thus a faulty doctrine of revelation.[25]

Henry reserved his most forceful theological analyses for those systems which by their compromising nature posed a threat to evangelicalism itself. Thus, though Bultmann was far less orthodox than Barth, it was Barth who represented the greater danger to evangelicals, many of whom found hope in Barth's apparent conservatism. In the same manner he lamented the "hermeneutical relativism" of the narrative theologians and the cultural relativism of Charles H. Kraft as dangerous attractions to the evangelical faithful.[26]

Henry's Theological Method

The Fundamentalist/Modernist controversy set the terms for the theological development of the "new evangelicals." Though issues such as Christology and creation captured popular attention, the evangelicals realized that the most crucial issues were directly related to Scripture and were thus epistemological questions at root. If the modernists' positions evolved from defective understandings of revelation and the resultant lack of commitment to biblical authority, then the evangelicals would have to reestablish an adequate epistemological basis for faith—and commit themselves to Scripture as divine revelation.

A basic divide appeared among the conservatives at this point. Agreed that the epistemological issues were paramount, they differed concerning an appropriate method of integrating faith and reason. This basic divide, between camps later known as evidentialists and presuppositionalists, continues to divide evangelicalism. This cleavage in the conservative camps separates evangelicals who would seek to ground an apologetic approach in arguments from reason and evidence, from those who base their theological thinking in a basic *presupposition* of the authority, truthfulness, and divine inspiration of the Bible.[27]

Henry, while placing himself clearly within the presuppositionalist camp, nevertheless resisted any charge of fideism or irrationality. He saw three rival theological methods, and identified these with the figures of Tertullian, Aquinas, and Augustine. Tertullian, he explained, represented the triumph of irrationality, belief in absurdity (*credo quia absurdum*), while Aquinas ("I know in order to believe") so qualified revelation by his reliance on reason that faith lost its primacy. Augustine, on the other hand, was identified with a *via media* which established the primacy of faith and revelation and constructed a theology based on believing deduction.

The tradition of Tertullian, Henry suggests, was never a prominent option in Western theology until the rise of neoorthodox theology. The evidentialist tradition raised the possibility of a natural theology inferred from general revelation. The Augustinian tradition, on the other hand, identified as well with Anselm, Calvin, and Luther, presents a genuine alternative to an independent natural theology which places reason prior to revelation or to a theology of the absurd, which places faith outside the realm of rational discourse.

Henry's central method was thus deductive, a tradition he rooted in the tradition of the church from its first systematician, Origen. Though evidentialists caricature presuppositionalists as fideists, Henry sought to demonstrate that theology could be based in a prior commitment to revealed truth while remaining open to the questions raised by public reason.[28]

The foundation of Henry's theological system is therefore an affirmation of biblical theism and the authority of Scripture as the inerrant Word of God. Neither axiom is held aloof from reason, but no apology is made for the a priori assertion of the revealed truth.[29]

Though Henry is first and foremost a theologian, he has not produced a systematic theology, choosing instead to concentrate upon the doctrines of revelation, God, and religious authority; the major points of compromise in twentieth-century theology.[30] Glimpses of what his systematic theology would look like are available in his shorter theological writings and within the pages of *God, Revelation and Authority*. What appears is a thoroughly conservative theology in the evangelical tradition yet fully conversant with competing schools of theological thought as well as the worlds of philosophy and science. Yet any review of Henry's theological accomplishment must concentrate on the issues to which Henry dedicated his life and his major writing project.

Revelation

Though God is greater than and ontologically prior to his revelation, Henry begins with revelation as the epistemological starting point for Christian theology. Revelation is, in his words, "the basic epistemological axiom," that is, the foundational principle for any theological investigation—or of any search for truth. As Henry stated:

> Divine revelation is the source of all truth, the truth of
> Christianity included; reason is the instrument for recognizing it;
> Scripture is its verifying principle; logical consistency is a negative
> test for truth and coherence a subordinate test. The task of
> Christian theology is to exhibit the content of biblical revelation
> as an orderly whole.[31]

Thus, the biblical revelation, given by God at his own gracious initiative, is the source from which all theological statements are to be drawn. "Had God insisted on remaining incommunicado," Henry reminds, "we would know nothing whatever about him."[32]

Henry's exposition of the doctrine of revelation stands as an awesome evangelical achievement. His stress on the actuality and trustworthiness of divine revelation serves to remind all evangelicals of the revelatory basis of all theological constructions.

Consistent with his epistemological method, Henry acknowledges the reality of natural revelation but denies it a positive role within his dogmatic system. He affirms "the considerable variety in God's revealing activity"[33] and points to general revelation as part of any evangelical understanding of God's revelatory initiative. General revelation is foundational to understanding human sin and culpability before the divine Creator.[34] Nevertheless, Henry demonstrates that the creature did not move from general revelation to a "natural theology" based upon such revelation but rather to a revolt against the Creator.

His system is based upon an unwavering commitment to divine revelation as found in Scripture, and ultimately in the incarnate Word, as recorded and proclaimed in that Scripture.

The Bible

The theological world, both evangelical and mainline, associates Carl Henry with a fervent and continuing defense of the authority and inerrancy of the Bible. Henry's theological system has given scriptural authority more attention than any other doctrinal issue.

Revelation is, in Henry's words, "rational communication" in "conceptual-verbal form." That is, God has revealed Himself in intelligible concepts, and thus through understandable language. His revelation comes as both act and deed, related in human language. Henry denies any role for revelation through the irrational.[35]

Henry defined the Bible as "the reservoir and conduit of divine truth, the authoritative written record and exposition of God's nature and will."[36] Though modern humans revolt against all authority, Henry articulated a doctrine of inscripturated revelation which allowed for no compromise on the issue of biblical authority. In so doing he set himself against the tide of twentieth-century theology, including neoorthodoxy, narrative theologies, and the contributions of Moltmann and Pannenberg. He also set himself against any compromise within the evangelical camp and set out to refute the criticisms of revisionists such as James Barr.

This defense of biblical authority is tied to Henry's stress upon the validity of propositional revelation. Not all revelation, he asserts, is propositional, but any stance which denies the inherent propositional nature of much of the biblical revelation leads, he suggests, to a loss of biblical truth. A denial of propositional revelation, which Henry associates with neoorthodoxy, devolves into revelation as irrationality; the "Tertullian temptation" to assert faith in the absurd.[37]

Henry has not produced an elaborate theory of biblical inspiration yet steers a middle course between the so-called "dynamic" and "dictation" theories. He affirms the role of the Holy Spirit in both the inspiration and illumination of the text yet allows for a genuine role to be played by the inspired authors of the biblical text.[38] Henry asserts that the evangelical doctrine of biblical inspiration affirms that "the text of Scripture is divinely inspired as an objective deposit of language," thus protecting the verbal character of the revelation; that inspiration "is wholly consistent with the humanity of the prophets and apostles"; that divine inspiration was limited to the chosen biblical authors; that divine inspiration was not limited by the "natural resources" of the authors; that Scripture is inspired as a whole and in its parts; and, in conclusion, that God is understood therefore to be the ultimate author of Scripture.[39]

Biblical inerrancy also serves a role in the evangelical doctrine of Scripture. Henry roots the doctrine within the theological heritage of the church and denies the claim that the concept of inerrancy is a modern (and thus unnecessary) innovation. The term is often misunderstood and has been an issue of messy theological warfare, yet Henry asserts that the concept is vital to any consistent evangelical position.

Inspiration posits the divine authorship of the biblical text. Inerrancy serves to articulate the fact that this divine revelation is therefore free from error and untruth. Inerrancy "affirms a special activity of divine inspiration whereby the Holy Spirit superintended the scriptural writers in communicating the biblical message in ways consistent with their differing personalities, literary styles and cultural background, while safeguarding them from error."[40] Henry's defense of biblical inerrancy is one of the most thorough treatments in the evangelical literature. A reading of Henry's various writings on inerrancy, and especially the relevant sections in *God, Revelation and Authority,* reveals the depth of Henry's passionate commitment to the concept—and indeed to the Word itself—and yet also indicates that Henry is unwilling to allow the Word to become a weapon of theological warfare. He declined to participate in the first meetings of the International Council on Biblical Inerrancy and broke publicly with his former colleague Harold Lindsell by suggesting that inerrancy be a test of evangelical *consistency* rather then *authenticity.*[41]

In other words, *consistent* evangelicalism will maintain biblical inerrancy as a vital corollary. From this point Henry will make no further concessions. He defines *inerrancy* so as to protect its central claims of trustworthiness for the biblical text, while avoiding the excessive claims of modern technical precision or absolute verbal exactitude in New Testament quotations of Old Testament passages made by some proponents of the term. Neither will he claim that a commitment to biblical inerrancy guarantees evangelical orthodoxy on all other points of doctrine.

On the other hand, Henry does suggest that inerrancy implies that the truthfulness of the text extends to scientific and historical matters, as well as ethical and theological teachings. Further, he maintains that inerrancy inheres in the actual words of Scripture; that inerrancy attaches *directly* to the autographs, and only *indirectly* to the copies; and that evangelicals must therefore strive to determine the most accurate text for study.

God

The Scriptures are not an end in themselves but are the self-revelation of the Revealer God. Henry's attention to issues of revelation and biblical authority point toward his massive exposition of the reality, objectivity, and sovereignty of God. The two great divisions within *God, Revelation and Authority* are "God Who Speaks and Shows" and "God Who Stands and Stays." The former established the epistemological basis for the latter, his discussion of the doctrine of God.

In the face of modernity's flight from metaphysics (and the complicity of much modern theology), Henry speaks of the God who *is,* "not a god who *may be,* or a god who *was,* or is yet *to be.*"[42] Modern revisionist renderings of God are thusly denied, along with logical positivism and existentialism.

In summary, Henry affirms the God revealed within the Bible, the Father of Abraham and Isaac and Jacob, and the Lord and Father of Jesus Christ. He affirms the Trinity as a vital biblical teaching and articulates the divine attributes, and his sovereignty, and providence. Furthermore, he maintains the identification of the Creator as none other than the first person of the Trinity.

Refusing to define God by means of analogy, dialectic, or empirical data, Henry bases his treatment of the divine attributes on the biblical revelation. Scripture reveals the simplicity of God as "a living center of activity pervasively characterized by all his distinctive perfections."[43] His treatment of the doctrine defies summary but is a stalwart defense and explication of classical Christian theism based thoroughly in the biblical revelation.

God is seen to be the divine Creator, who created the universe and all within it *ex nihilo* and exercises his providential care and direction over his creation. He defines God in terms of "incomparable love" and unconditioned holiness. He rejects universalism as an implication of this love and provides a brief treatment of divine election.

Jesus Christ is "the personal incarnation of God in the flesh," the climax of revelation, in whom "the source and content of revelation converge and coincide."[44] Henry stresses the preexistence of the Logos, his historical Incarnation and intelligibility, his Incarnation as the focus of prophecy and expectation, and his role as the only divine Mediator between God and humanity. Jesus Christ, crucified, dead, resurrected, and now glorified, was the divine God/Man in his Incarnation; and is now the Lord of the universe at the right hand of the Father.

Ethics

The Uneasy Conscience of Modern Fundamentalism, Henry's epochal volume of 1947, demonstrated his interest in Christian ethics, both personal and social. He was to produce *Christian Personal Ethics,* a work of massive dimensions, and *Aspects of Christian Social Ethics,* a much smaller volume limited by Henry's teaching load and responsibilities at *Christianity Today.* He was also to edit Baker's *Dictionary of Christian Ethics,* a major reference work for evangelicals.[45]

In recent years Henry has emerged as a potent opponent of abortion and a champion of other moral causes. His opportunities for lectures and occasional writings have granted his ethical writings much visibility and considerable influence in the evangelical world.[46]

Evaluation

Carl Henry has emerged as a major influence in twentieth-century theology. His influence, extended through his voluminous writings and public exposure, has shaped the evangelical movement to a degree unmatched by any other evangelical theologian of the period. His staunch defense of classical theism, biblical authority, and the role of the church in society have earned the respect of evangelicals and nonevangelicals alike.

One of his major achievements has been the reestablishment of theology as a vital concern of the Christian community. His theological vigor and force have often laid bare the latent antitheological attitudes among some evangelicals and have reasserted the vital role of theology as a servant of the church.

The evangelical movement has also benefited from Henry's model of aggressive engagement with the broader theological community. Henry has been a master of the theological literature and has addressed variant theological systems with an acknowledged expertise. Yet dialogue alone has never been his goal. As indicated most clearly in his dream for *Christianity Today,* Henry has always been committed to a missionary vision—a truly evangelical vision—of influence in the broader theological community. His mission has been to bring contemporary theology back to a firm commitment to biblical authority.

Evangelicals are in Henry's debt for his effective and thorough restatement of the evangelical doctrine of revelation and biblical authority. Critics have often painted him as a rationalist (or even a Thomist) and have lamented his scholastic approach to epistemological issues.[47] Nevertheless, his achievement in *God, Revelation and Authority* will stand as an encyclopedic *prologomenon* to an evangelical theology.[48]

This function as *prologomenon* (or methological introduction) to a full evangelical theology points to the fact that Henry's theological project has not included a complete systematic theology. As suggested above, this is tied to Henry's reading of contemporary theology and the critical points of theological compromise in the twentieth century. As such, Henry's work reminds evangelicals of the importance of methodological issues as the foundation of any systematic effort. The lack of a systematic expression has left several theological issues untouched or underdeveloped in Henry's system. He has given little attention to the Holy Spirit and, except for his work in personal ethics, to the Christian life and devotion. The most glaring omission in his theological project is the doctrine of the church (ecclesiology).

Henry's pilgrimage mirrors the emergence of the parachurch movement in conservative Protestantism. The evangelical movement itself, while including many within the established churches, was largely a parachurch movement. The momentum and defining characteristics of the movement came from the parachurch institutions which shaped the evangelical consciousness. Henry's biography includes a litany of evangelical parachurch organizations and institutions ranging from Wheaton College and Fuller Seminary to *Christianity Today* and World Vision. Indeed, his conversion experience came by means of a parachurch movement and not through the evangelistic thrust of a local church. In this manner Carl Henry is symbolic of the evangelical movement as a whole.

This raises the important question of Carl Henry as a *Baptist* theologian. Concern for a biblical understanding of baptism led Henry into membership in a Baptist church during his days at Wheaton and Northern Seminary. Upon his call to the ministry he was licensed to preach by the Babylon Baptist Church on Long Island, having been baptized there just ten months earlier. In October 1940, he was called as student pastor of the Humbolt Park Baptist Church in Chicago and was ordained to the ministry there in 1941. The ordination service was performed with the Chicago Baptist Association, affiliated with the Northern Baptist Convention (now the American Baptist Churches).

Henry's involvement with the Northern Convention was marred by his ejection from the convention's annuity program after his move to Fuller Seminary. While at Fuller the Henrys attended a Baptist church, and upon his move to *Christianity Today*, they joined the Capitol Hill Metropolitan Baptist Church in Washington, D.C., an evangelical congregation affiliated with the American Baptist Churches and the Southern Baptist Convention.

These linkages notwithstanding, Henry's most critical involvements have been outside denominational life. Yet he has played a part in theological discussion and debate within both the Northern and Southern conventions. His mission has been to call his fellow Baptists to the high ground of biblical authority, noting that "Baptist distinctives of rebirth, of resolution, of resource are fixed in the confidence that the New Testament revelation is the climax of divine disclosure."[49] Further, Henry chided Baptists for their "theological amnesia" seen in the fact that "Southern Baptists often close their theological history with E. Y. Mullins or W. T. Conner; Northern Baptists with A. H. Strong."[50] He called for a revival of vigorous theology among Baptists as well as an openness to cooperation with other evangelicals in common efforts, for "arbitrarily to equate denominational, and in this case Baptist, affiliation with membership in the body of Christ is obviously theologically naive and increasingly theologically unrealistic."[51]

The 1987 Southern Baptist Pastors' Conference included Henry as a major speaker and honored him for his contributions to theology as a Baptist.[52] In the main, however, Henry is usually identified as an evangelical statesman and theologian.

Numerous honors and accolades have come to Henry. He has served as president of the Evangelical Theological Society and the American Theological Society and has delivered many of the most prestigious lectureships in the world, among them the 1989 Rutherford Lectures at the University of Edinburgh, Scotland.

In 1999 the Southern Baptist Theological Seminary established the Carl F. H. Henry Institute for Evangelical Engagement. The Center is designed to serve as a thinktank for evangelical engagement with the pressing issues of the day. As such, it will be an extension of Henry's own intentional work of engagement.

He has been recognized by evangelicals and nonevangelicals as the premier theological representative of the evangelical movement in the last half of the twentieth century. As E. G. Homrighausen of Princeton Theological Seminary remarked, Henry "has championed evangelical Christianity with clarity of language, comprehensiveness of scholarship, clarity of mind, and vigor of spirit."[53] Baptists and their fellow evangelicals stand in his debt.

Bibliography

Works by Henry

"American Evangelicals and Theological Dialogue." *Christianity Today*, 15 January 1965. 27–29.
"Are We Doomed to Hermeneutical Nihilism?" *Review and Expositor* (1974).
Aspects of Christian Social Ethics. Grand Rapids: William B. Eerdmans, 1963.
"The Authority of the Bible." *The Origin of the Bible*. Wheaton, Ill: Tyndale House, 1992, p. 13–27.
Baker's Dictionary of Christian Ethics. Grand Rapids: Baker Book House, 1973.
Basic Christian Doctrines. Grand Rapids: Baker Book House, 1962.

"Between Barth and Bultmann," *Christianity Today*, 8 May 1961, 24–26.

"The Bible and the Consciousness of Our Age." *Hermeneutics, Inerrancy, and the Bible.* Edited by Earl Rademacher and Robert Preus.

"Biblical Authority and the Social Crisis." *Authority and Interpretation: A Baptist Perspective.* Edited by Duane Garrett and Richard Melick. Grand Rapids: Baker Book House, 1985. 203–20.

"Canonical Theology: An Evangelical Appraisal." *Scottish Bulletin of Evangelical Theology.* 8 (Autumn 1990): 76–108.

Christian Countermoves in a Decadent Culture. Portland, Oreg.: Multnomah Press, 1986.

Christian Faith and Modern Theology: Contemporary Evangelical Thought. New York: Channel Press, 1964.

Christian Personal Ethics. Grand Rapids: William B. Eerdmans, 1957.

"The Christian Pursuit of Higher Education." *Southern Baptist Journal of Theology.* 1 (Fall 1997): 6–18.

Confessions of a Theologian. Waco, Tx.: Word Books, 1986.

Contemporary Evangelical Thought. Grand Rapids: Baker Book House, 1957.

Conversations with Carl Henry: Christianity for Today. Lewiston, N.Y.: The Edwin Mellen Press, 1986.

"The Cultural Relativizing of Revelation." *Trinity Journal* 1 ns (1980): 153–64.

"The Deterioration of Barth's Defenses." *Christianity Today*, 9 October 1964, 16–19.

The Drift of Western Thought. Grand Rapids: William B. Eerdmans, 1951.

"Evangelical." *The New International Dictionary of the Christian Church.* Ed. J. D. Douglas. Exeter: Paternoster Press, 358–59.

Evangelical Affirmations. Grand Rapids: Zondervan, 1990.

Evangelical Responsibility in Contemporary Theology. Grand Rapids: William B. Eerdmans, 1957.

"Evangelicals and Fundamentals." *Christianity Today*, 16 September 1957, 20–21.

Evangelicals at the Brink of Crisis. Waco, Tx.: Word Books, 1967.

Evangelicals in Search of Identity. Waco, Tx.: Word Books, 1976.

"Evangelicals: Out of the Closet but Going Nowhere?" *Christianity Today*, 4 January 1980, 16–22.

"Evangelism and the Sacred Book." *Christianity Today*, 15 October 1956, 22.

Faith at the Frontiers. Chicago: Moody Press, 1969.

Fifty Years of Protestant Theology. Boston: W. A. Wilde, 1950.

Frontiers in Modern Theology. Chicago: Moody Press, 1966.

Fundamentals of the Faith. Grand Rapids: Zondervan, 1969.

"The Genesis of Doctrine: A Review Article." *Journal of the Evangelical Theological Society.* 38 (March 1995): 100–103.

God, Revelation and Authority, six volumes. Waco, Tx.: Word Books, 1976–83. Revised, Wheaton: Crossway, 1999.

The God Who Shows Himself. Waco, Tx.: Word Books, 1966.

Gods of This Age or God of the Ages? R. Albert Mohler Jr., ed. Nashville: Broadman & Holman, 1994.

The Identity of Jesus of Nazareth. Nashville: Broadman Press, 1992.

"Inerrancy and the Bible in Modern Conservative Evangelical Thought." *Introduction to Christian Theology.* Louisville, Ky.: Westminster/John Knox Press, 1998.

"Is it fair? [defends Evangelical theology of universal judgment by God and human guilt]." *Through No Fault of Their Own?* William V. Crockett and James G. Sigountos, eds. Grand Rapids, Mich.: Baker Book House, 1991: 245–55.

Jesus of Nazareth: Savior and Lord. Grand Rapids: Baker Book House, 1966.

"Justification: A Doctrine in Crisis." *Journal of the Evangelical Theological Society.* 38 (March 1995): 57–65.

"Justification by Ignorance: A Neo-Protestant Motif?" *Christianity Today,* 2 January 1970, 10–15.

"Liberation Theology and the Scriptures." *Liberation Theology.* Ronald H. Nash, ed. (Milford, Mich.: Mott Media, 1984, 187–202.

"Narrative Theology: An Evangelical Appraisal." *Trinity Journal.* 8 (1987): 3–19.

"Natural Law and a Nihilistic Culture." *First Things.* 49 (January 1995): 54–60.

"The Nature of Confession: A Review Article." *Journal of the Evangelical Theological Society.* 40 (Spring 1997): 510–11.

Notes on the Doctrine of God. Boston: W. A. Wilde, 1948.

Personal Idealism and Strong's Theology. Wheaton, Ill.: Van Kampen Press, 1951.

A Plea for Evangelical Demonstration. Grand Rapids: Baker Book House, 1971.

"Postmodernism: The New Spectre?" *The Challenge of Postmodernism.* David S. Dockery, ed. Wheaton, Ill.: Bridgeport/Victor, 1995, 34–52.

"The Priority of Divine Revelation: A Review Article." *Journal of the Evangelical Theological Society.* 27 (1984): 77–92.

The Protestant Dilemma: An Analysis of the Current Impasse. Grand Rapids: William B. Eerdmans, 1949.

Quest for Reality: Christianity and the Counter Culture. Waco, Tx.: Word Books, 1973.

"Reflections on the Kingdom of God." *Journal of the Evangelical Theological Society.* 35 (March 1992): 39–49.

Remaking the Modern Mind. Grand Rapids: William B. Eerdmans, 1946.

Revelation and the Bible: Contemporary Evangelical Thought. Grand Rapids: Baker Book House, 1949. (Editor.)

"The Stunted God of Process Theology." *Process Theology.* Ronald H. Nash, ed. Grand Rapids: Baker Book House, 1987, 357–76.

"Theology and Biblical Authority: A Review Article." *Journal of the Evangelical Theological Society.* 19 (1976): 315–23.

Toward a Recovery of Christian Belief. Wheaton, Ill.: Crossway Books, 1991.

Twilight of a Great Civilization: The Drift Toward Neo-Paganism. Westchester, Ill: Crossway Books, 1988.

The Uneasy Conscience of Modern Fundamentalism. Grand Rapids: William B. Eerdmans, 1947.

"The Vagrancy of the American Spirit: [Evangelicals in 1990s]." *Faculty Dialogue: Journal of the Institute for Christian Leadership.* 22 (Fall 1994): 5–18.

"Where Will Evangelicals Cast Their Lot?" *This World.* 18 (1987): 3–11.

"Wintertime in European Theology." *Christianity Today.* 5 December 1960, 12–14.

Works about Henry

Cerillo, Augustus, Jr.; Dempster, Murray W. "Carl F. Henry's Early Apologetic for an Evangelical Social Ethic, 1942–1956." *Journal of the Evangelical Theological Society.* 34 (Spring 1991): 365–79.

Hunsinger, George. "What Can Evangelicals and Postliberals Learn from Each Other: The Carl Henry-Hans Frei Exchange Reconsidered." *The Nature of Confession.* Dennis L. Okholm and Timothy R. Phillips, eds. Downers Grove, Ill.: InterVarstiy Press, 1996, 134–50, 279–83.

Patterson, Bob E. *Carl F. H. Henry.* Makers of the Modern Theological Mind. Waco, Tx.: Word Books, 1986.

Fackre, Gabriel. "Carl F. H. Henry." *A Handbook to Contemporary Theology.* Martin Marty and Dean Peerman, ed.

Mohler, Richard Albert Jr. "Evangelical Theology and Karl Barth: Representative Models of Response." Ph.D. diss., The Southern Baptist Theological Seminary, 1989, 107–34.

Weeks, David L. "Carl F. H. Henry's Moral Arguments for Evangelical Political Activism." *Journal of Church and State.* 40 (Winter 1998): 83–106.

White, James Emery. *What Is Truth? A Comparative Study of the Positions of Cornelius Van Til, Fancis Schaeffer, Carl F. H. Henry, Donald Bloesch, and Millard Erickson.* Nashville: Broadman & Holman, 1994.

16

James Leo Garrett Jr.

By Paul A. Basden

Biography

JAMES LEO GARRETT JR. IS THE MOST RECENT BAPTIST THEOLOGIAN TO WRITE a full-scale work on Christian doctrine. A noted author and speaker, his two-volume *Systematic Theology: Biblical, Historical, and Evangelical* (1990, 1995; 2d ed, 2000, 2001) is the highlight of his half-century career as a Baptist theologian.

Garrett was born on November 25, 1925, in the shadow of Baylor University at Waco, Texas, where his father later taught in the School of Business. Garrett was baptized as a new believer into Seventh and James Baptist Church in Waco in 1935 and was licensed and ordained to the ministry a decade later by First Baptist Church of Waco. After graduating from Baylor in 1945 with a major in English, he enrolled in Southwestern Baptist Theological Seminary to study for the pastorate. While at Southwestern, he pastored three small churches. It was also at Southwestern that he met Myrta Ann Latimer, whom he married on August 31, 1948. To their union were born three sons: James Leo III (b. 1952), Robert Thomas (b. 1954), and Paul Latimer (b. 1958).

Garrett received his B.D. from Southwestern in 1948, his Th.M. from Princeton Theological Seminary in 1949, and his Th.D. from Southwestern in 1954. After two sabbatic leaves, he completed a Ph.D. at Harvard University in 1966.

Garrett began teaching theology at Southwestern in 1949, staying there for a decade. In 1959, he accepted an invitation to move to Louisville, Kentucky, to teach at Southern Baptist Theological Seminary. Southern had just experienced a severe institutional crisis which resulted in the dismissal of numerous professors, particularly in the fields of church history and theology. Garrett remained at Southern until 1973, when Baylor invited him to return to his *alma mater* to direct their program in church and state and to be professor of religion. In 1979, Garrett returned to Southwestern as professor of theology, where he was still teaching in 2001 as distinguished professor of theology emeritus.

For five decades now James Leo Garrett Jr. has taught and written about Baptist theology. Given the size of the schools which he has served, one can only begin to estimate the number of students whom he has influenced to think biblically, historically, and theologically about the Christian faith. Who knows how many young seminarians had their minds broadened in his introductory theology courses or received flashes of inspiration in his famous "after-lecture" discussions, or first encountered the mystery of the Trinity in his beloved patristics elective, or learned to grapple with Luther or Augustine in one of his doctoral seminars? Who knows how many times he invited classes into his home for a meal or recommended former students for church positions or faculty appointments or counseled confused young ministers about their calling or career? He has had an enormous influence on Southern Baptists during the past half century. Beloved by students and fellow professors alike, Garrett is recognized by many of his peers as the most knowledgeable Baptist theologian living today.

Baptist Concerns

While Garrett's first love has always been the systematic and historical formulation of Christian doctrine, he has written extensively on several other important related subjects over the years. His earlier writings reveal a keen interest in many crucial dimensions of the world of theology, especially as these topics relate to the people called Baptists.

Baptist Identity

One of Garrett's chief concerns has been to understand clearly and to state succinctly exactly who Baptists are and what they believe. That is, he has had a passion to discover, uncover, or recover basic Baptist distinctives, those beliefs and practices which form the core of Baptist identity.

In an address he gave in 1995, Garrett summarized a lifetime's reflections on "Major Emphases in Baptist Theology."[1] He followed a simple deductive method that would be clear to his original audience of Eastern Orthodox theologians in Istanbul, Turkey. He first noted the considerable areas of agreement between Baptists and "the wider or worldwide company of Christians."[2] Specifically, he demonstrated that Baptists adhere essentially to the same set of theological tenets as other Christians do in these areas: the Holy Scriptures; the Triune God; creation and providence; humanity and sin; Jesus Christ; the Holy Spirit; redemption; and the last things. Then he focused on those areas where Baptists differ from other Christians, or on "that which is unique to or at least peculiarly emphasized by Baptists."[3] Grouping Baptist distinctives into three overall themes, Garrett first pointed to "congregations gathered around believer's baptism by immersion."[4] Included in this theme are the two practices of congregational polity and believer's baptism. Second, he pointed to religious liberty and church-state separation. Here he highlighted the perennial Baptist concern over the relation of "human conscience in matters of faith with the mandates and powers of civil government."[5] Third, he pointed to the responsibility of all churches and Christians to practice evangelism and missions.

Here we see Garrett dealing with a lifelong question: who are Baptists *vis-a-vis* other Christians? His answer is twofold: they are only one part of the larger body of Christ, holding many beliefs and practices in common with other Christians; but they are an important part of the universal church and bring to other Christian traditions a critical reminder of several crucial biblical emphases that are in danger of being lost or forgotten in the twentieth century. In his own words, "[T]here still exists a *raison d'être* for Baptist Christians."[6]

Garrett also recently tried his hand at defining Southern Baptists *vis-a-vis* other Baptist groups.[7] Based on decades of firsthand observation, he noted seven peculiar characteristics of Southern Baptists. First, he pointed to what he called "the historic coalescing of the regular (Charleston) and the Separate (Sandy Creek) Baptist traditions in the South into a *tertium quid*," which led Southern Baptist worship to express an unusual combination of "order and ardor."[8] Second, he turned to the "race issue" and mentioned not only Southern Baptists' defense of slavery in the nineteenth century but also their continued racial segregation in the South during the twentieth century. He confessed to the sad fact that "no major Baptist body outside the American South ever had for so long a period the albatross of the defense of racism as Southern Baptists."[9] Third, Garrett identified the early acceptance of Landmarkist teachings as the reason for exclusion among so many Southern Baptist churches. Fourth, he stated that the adoption of "the convention method of denominational work instead of the society method"[10] solidified the Southern Baptist Convention. Fifth, he pointed to the obvious by noting that Southern Baptists traditionally have adopted an overtly "Southern" or sectional approach to church life, due to the Southern culture which was so dominant in their origins. Sixth, he claimed that the unifying and organizing center of Southern Baptists functionally has been LifeWay Christian Resources (formerly the Baptist Sunday School Board), which provides churches with normative resources for Christian education, music, discipleship, recreation, and architecture. It became far more than just a publishing house. Seventh, he highlighted a relatively recent phenomenon among Southern Baptists: the "multi-ethnic character of congregations affiliated with the Southern Baptist Convention."[11]

In his conclusion Garrett revealed a deep awareness of the changing character of Southern Baptists. Specifically, the *tertium quid* of "ardor and order" in worship may be reverting back into churches which emphasize one or the other, but no longer both; the old racism has been replaced by a new multiethnicity; Landmarkism continues to lose power and influence; the convention approach to church cooperation is being severely threatened by the denominational controversy begun in 1979; Southernness is yielding to "a national American culture";[12] and LifeWay Christian Resources has less overall influence than in its heyday. In other words, Garrett has identified Southern Baptists as a body of Baptists who are currently undergoing significant revision in their practices and values.

Baptists and Other Christians

Garrett pioneered ecumenism among Southern Baptists. He once wrote: "Baptist Christians tend to be known for their sectarian separatism more than for their cooperation with other Christians and their devotion to Christian unity." Despite that reputation, however, "Baptists have often participated in and even given leadership to expressions of Christian togetherness, cooperation, and unity that transcend denominational lines."[13] Garrett himself was such a participant and leader. His interest in the church universal led him to engage Christians of other traditions in conversation and dialogue. While never relinquishing his Baptist convictions, Garrett has sought to be a Christian first and a Baptist second.

Baptists and Roman Catholics

Garrett has long nurtured a deep interest in Roman Catholicism, the largest Christian denomination in the world. While a young seminary professor, he developed new courses in Roman Catholic theology. In 1965, Garrett attended Vatican Council II in Rome. As guest of the Vatican Secretariat for Promoting Christian Unity, he was present for the final week of the fourth session. The next year he completed his second doctorate, this one at Harvard University, submitting a dissertation which summarized and evaluated American Protestant writings on Roman Catholicism between Vatican Council I and Vatican Council II.

During this time Garrett wrote a monograph entitled *Baptists and Roman Catholicism*.[14] Its thesis is that Baptists have historically adopted one of three "postures toward the Church of Rome."[15] The first is polemical controversy, which itself has assumed several different forms. "The Rebuttalists" have approached Rome as critics, "pointing out theological and ethical errors" in the Mother Church. "The Exposurists" took a more personal approach, "setting forth . . . alleged immoralities or moral abuses" which have dogged the Roman church over the years. "The Successionists" are Baptists who have countered the Roman claim to apostolic succession with their own claim "of a succession of Baptist churches from the New Testament era to today." Finally, "the Church-and-State Writers" have attacked the Roman tendency toward church-state union and defended the Baptist practice of church-state separation, especially in light of American democracy.[16]

The second Baptist posture toward Roman Catholics has been evangelization. This assumes that those who belong to the Church of Rome may not be faithful fellow-Christians who can be trusted but are instead unbelieving non-Christians who need to be converted. The third and final approach has been "dialogue or fraternal discussion and interchange."[17]

In his conclusion Garrett stated his hope for Baptist-Catholic relations:

[We] must at least be open to the possibility that God may yet do wondrous things for the renewal of his people, for the breaking forth of recovered truth from his Word, and for the effectual outreach of the Christian mission to all men in this secularistic, fear-driven age in which Christians must truly be "the light of the world."[18]

Baptists and the Believers' Church

Garrett recognized a deep kinship between Baptists and those ecclesial groups which he referred to as the Believers' Church. He identified the Believers' Church as "that segment of the Protestant Christian heritage which is distinct both from Classical Protestant and from Catholic— Roman, Eastern, Anglican, et al—understandings of the church by its insistence on the indispensability of voluntary churchmanship with its many implications." But by no means did this "imply any denial of true Christian believers in other confessional traditions."[19]

Wanting to explore Baptists' "next of kin," Garrett held a large family reunion in Louisville, June 26–30, 1967. He gathered a group of like-minded scholars, pastors, and laity at Southern Seminary for the first Conference on the Concept of the Believers' Church. The 150 voluntary, nonelected participants represented more than two dozen separate denominations which claimed affiliation with the broader Christian family known as the Believers' Church. They included Baptists of every stripe, Brethren groups, Assemblies of God, Churches of Christ and Disciples of Christ, several Mennonite bodies, and others. Garrett included the thirteen conference addresses in a subsequent book he edited, *The Concept of the Believers' Church*.[20]

Christians within the Believers' Church share several distinctives which derive from their commitment to voluntary church membership. Garrett addressed a number of these distinctives during his lifetime. First, he wrote about regenerate church membership and church discipline. In 1961, he penned an article asserting that "particular congregations of Baptists are supposed to be composed only of those who have given and do continue to give evidence of having been 'begotten' or 'born anew' or 'born from above' by the Holy Spirit."[21] In order to ensure "proper maintenance of the congregational membership,"[22] early Baptists in Philadelphia and Charleston chose to examine candidates for membership in three areas: "doctrinal understanding," "ethical conduct," and "conversion experience."[23] Only if they passed the examination would they be admitted to church membership.

What should a Baptist church do when a person becomes a member but later exhibits a lifestyle that does not show a robust faith but in fact reveals a decided absence of spiritual vitality? Garrett answered that we should return to earlier Baptist precedents, such as the statements on church discipline adopted and used by the Philadelphia Baptist Association and the Charleston Baptist Association. These pioneering Baptists delineated three kinds of church action to be taken against an offending member: verbal rebuke or reproof; temporary suspension from holding office, voting, and the Lord's Supper; and excommunication or exclusion.[24] With a nod of approval, Garrett opined: "What Philadelphia and Charleston conjoined in experience, doctrine, and conduct, let not contemporary Baptists put asunder!"

Garrett went a step further in 1962 when he wrote *Baptist Church Discipline*,[25] which introduced modern Baptists to the *Summary of Church Discipline* adopted in 1773 by the Charleston Association. The opening sentence of the introduction to the monograph revealed his sentiments about the state of Baptist church life: "Baptists in the United States, and Southern Baptists in particular, are giving meager evidence of having today an ordered, disciplined churchmanship."[26] To help correct the problem, he traced the concept of divine discipline and church correction through the Bible and Christian history, ending up at the Charleston document. Confounding those who would equate discipline with mere punishment, he did not finally call for "neo-Pharisaic legalism" when a fellow member stumbled. Rather, he asked for a church discipline which would "be redemptive in purpose and not merely punitive," where "grace and forgiveness" would be the rule and not the exception. In other words, "[t]he restoration of the offending brother must be of equal importance with the purity of the church."[27] Garrett had diagnosed the Baptist malady and prescribed the treatment: a return to the biblical and Baptist distinctives of regenerate membership and church discipline.

Next Garrett turned his attention to a second topic dear to the Believers' Church: the priesthood of all believers. Over the course of more than a dozen years, he wrote three classic articles which traced the doctrine from the New Testament through the fourth century.[28] Convinced that this crucial teaching has suffered greatly from misunderstanding, misapplication, and neglect, he sought to recover its original intent. Of particular concern to him was the Protestant tendency to transmute this concept into nothing more than radical egalitarianism or rugged individualism.[29] Following a careful study of the priesthood in both testaments, he concluded that the biblical meaning of the doctrine "is the offering of 'spiritual sacrifices' such as in worship, witness, stewardship, and service (ministry)."[30] Again Garrett's remedy for problems in the church comes into full view: a return to the Bible and church history for correction.

The third matter Garrett addressed for the Believers' Church was religious liberty. During his tenure at Baylor during the 1970s, he paid more attention to this concern than to any other. Editing *Journal of Church and State* during those years afforded him the opportunity to focus on religious liberty and related subjects on a continual basis. Between 1975 and 1977, he wrote two pairs of editorials on important topics facing Believers' Church groups. The first pair analyzed the First Amendment. Commenting on the "No . . . Establishment" clause, Garrett stated that it "should continue to safeguard excessive entanglement of government and religions without fostering hostility of the former for the latter and so as to give opportunity for those religious expressions to which the 'free exercise' clause more directly speaks."[31] Then reflecting on the "Free Exercise" clause, he wrote: "The freedom of religious beliefs . . . is to be upheld. The freedom to propagate one's religious beliefs . . . must also be protected. . . . But there are limits to 'free exercises'. . . ."[32] In carefully nuanced phrases, he was arguing for an interpretation of the First Amendment which was compatible with full and responsible religious liberty.

The second pair of editorials provided readers with an incisive study of the biblical tension between the Christian and the governing powers. By seeing the dialectical nature of Romans 13:1–7 and Revelation 13, Garrett called Christians to recognize their penultimate allegiance to government and their ultimate allegiance to God. The passage in Romans teaches that Christians should obediently submit to the government because it comes from God and is intended for our good. Therefore to resist it elicits "God's judgment on the resisters," for God exercises divine judgment through the state.[33] But this is not all the New Testament teaches. Revelation 13 reveals that when the government persecutes Christians because of their faith, it is being "authorized and empowered by Satan." A government may indeed ask for or even demand devotion or worship, but that would be nothing short of "blasphemy and/or idolatry, sins against God."[34] By clarifying the relative role of government, Garrett called the church to remember its first love and not to prostitute itself to any other "power" in the world.

Because religious liberty is so precious to those within the Believers' Church, Garrett documented its primary proponents in a lectureship he delivered at Southwestern in 1976. Entitled "Advocates of Religious Toleration and Freedom," these lectures first discussed spokesmen for religious toleration during the fifteenth, sixteenth, and seventeenth centuries, such as Desiderius Erasmus, Balthasar Hubmaier, Menno Simons, and Thomas Helwys, who expanded religious toleration into full religious freedom. Then Garrett discussed spokesmen for full religious liberty from the seventeenth century to the present, paying primary attention to Roger Williams, Baruch de Spinoza, William Penn, John Locke, and the Declaration on Religious Freedom of Vatican Council II. As always, Garrett the historian gathered all of the pertinent information on one of his favorite topics in order to persuade those within the Believers' Church to protect the cherished value and practice of religious freedom.

Baptists and Evangelicals

For Garrett, Baptists have much in common not only with those who identify themselves with the Believers' Church but also with those who describe themselves as Evangelicals. In 1979, Garrett delivered the Carver-Barnes Lectures at Southeastern Baptist Theological Seminary in Wake Forest, North Carolina. The subject was the relationship between Baptists and Evangelicals. During the next two years church historian E. Glenn Hinson, Garrett's former colleague at Southern, addressed the same topic in three sets of lectures. In 1983, Garrett and Hinson published a revised version of these lectures in book form. Baptist theologian James E. Tull provided an introduction and a conclusion.[35]

Intended to be "a fraternal debate" which would "enlighten and strengthen" rather than "divide or disrupt,"[36] this dialogue certainly was very spirited. At times it even got testy. Why? Because Garrett and Hinson approached the topic so differently and reached such opposite conclusions.

Garrett began by asking, "Who are the 'Evangelicals'?" Tracing the word throughout Christian history, he noted that sixteenth-century Protestant reformers used it as a synonym for "Protestant" and "reformed"; eighteenth-century Anglicans used it as a term for the "Low Church" party within their ranks; and recent Latin American Christians have used the term instead of "Protestants."[37] In eighteenth- and nineteenth-century America, *Evangelical* referred to those Christians and churches which were "gospel-oriented and Bible-oriented." Since the 1940s, the word has been used to describe the late twentieth-century descendants of Fundamentalism, seen especially in the National Association of Evangelicals, Inter-Varsity Christian Fellowship, Youth for Christ, the Billy Graham Evangelistic Association, Campus Crusade for Christ, and *Christianity Today.*[38] Garrett finally answered his original question like this: Evangelicals are "the less strict heirs of Fundamentalism" who hold to a handful of theological tenets.[39]

Garrett then proposed another question: "What do Evangelicals believe and practice?" Expanding on his earlier statement, he surmised that Evangelicals are in general agreement on four primary Christian doctrines: "the supremacy of Scripture, the all-sufficiency of the divine-human Jesus Christ, the necessity of the transforming experience of being born anew or justified by grace through faith, and the inner compulsion to share one's faith in Christ with those who do not yet believe."[40]

Finally, Garrett asked the question which formed the heart of the book: "Are Southern Baptists 'Evangelicals'?" Beginning with an examination of Baptist history and doctrine, he identified Southern Baptists as moderately Calvinistic, missionary minded, broadly denominational, conservative theologically, denominationally cooperative but not ecumenical, and proponents of a historical rather than symbolic approach to the Bible. This led Garrett to his thesis: *"Southern Baptists are denominational Evangelicals."*[41] By taking a deductive approach, Garrett was able to conclude that Southern Baptists are Evangelicals because they believe roughly the same major doctrines.

But Hinson took an inductive approach and reached predictably different conclusions. He began by recovering the identity of Southern

Baptists, which he described as "the Baptist tradition."[42] Positing that there is an inevitable tension between "two facets of our Baptist personality"—evangelical and voluntarist—he predicted that "if the two are not held in balance, and integrated in some way, our personality may split."[43] The former leads to evangelism and missions, and when misguided can lead to religious coercion, while the latter supports absolute religious freedom. These impulses tend to be at odds with one another, and Baptists have seldom achieved a long-term healthy balance between the two.

In Hinson's opinion, the SBC controversy of the 1980s revealed the evangelical tendency to coerce those in the minority. As a result, it put the denomination in "grave danger" of forgetting "voluntarist perceptions which stand most at the center of our life together as Baptists, . . . which best represent our *raison d'être* and our contribution to world Christianity and to modern civilization."[44] He contended that Baptists at their best model *"that version of Christianity which places the priority of voluntary and uncoerced faith or response to the Word and Act of God"* over all attempts at theological straightjacketing.[45] In other words, Baptists are voluntarists, while Evangelicals are coercionists. Therefore, "Evangelicalism threatens our most central and basic concerns as Baptists."[46] Hinson could only conclude that Southern Baptists are not basically Evangelicals.

Over a decade later Garrett revisited this issue in a chapter entitled "Are Southern Baptists 'Evangelicals'? A Further Reflection."[47] His differences with Hinson were still pronounced.

Systematic Theology

As stated earlier, Garrett's first love has always been systematic theology, seen through the eyes of Christian history. Therefore it was no surprise when, near the end of his teaching career, he expanded his class notes into book form. The result was his *magnum opus*, a two-volume work with ten sections, eighty-seven chapters, and more than fifteen hundred pages! Entitled *Systematic Theology: Biblical, Historical, and Evangelical*,[48] it treats the major Christian doctrines in classical order: Prolegomena; Revelation and the Bible; God the Holy and Loving Father; the Trinity; Creation, Providence, and Suprahuman Beings; Humankind and Sin; the Person of Jesus Christ; the Work of Jesus Christ; the Holy Spirit; Becoming a Christian and the Christian Life; the Church; and the Last Things.

Major Characteristics

Method

When one begins reading *Systematic Theology*, several things stand out immediately. The first thing one notices is Garrett's method. He is first and foremost a historical theologian. He reviews Christian theology through the lens of Christian history. He brings all of the pertinent historical development of a doctrine to bear upon his final formulation. He makes sure that, on every subject in the theological repertoire, he is in living conversation with those theologians who have provided rich insights in the past. He refuses to write theology in a historical vacuum!

Although Garrett begins his exposition of each doctrine with a review of the germane biblical passages, his strength is not biblical exegesis. Although he occasionally refers to the philosophical framework supporting certain doctrines, his strength is not philosophical reflection either. He is primarily a historical theologian.

Systematic theology stands on three disciplines: biblical exegesis, church history, and philosophy of religion. Exegesis provides interpretation of the primary texts for Christian doctrine found in the Bible. History reveals how doctrine has been understood at seminal times in the past. Philosophy reflects on how the current formulation of doctrine reflects contemporary patterns of thought. No theologian is equally adept in all three areas.

Southern Baptists have produced writing theologians who made their mark by specializing in one of these disciplines and offering a new "window" on theology by virtue of their particular perspective. Garrett's mentor, and perhaps the major influence upon his theology, was W. T. Conner. Conner, a Southwestern legend, was primarily a biblical theologian. His contribution to Baptist theology had more to do with how he interpreted Holy Scripture than anything else. The same can be said for Garrett's fellow teacher at Southern, Dale Moody, who was also a biblical theologian. E. Y. Mullins, on the other hand, is a good example of a theologian whose greatest gift to Baptists came by way of philosophy. His reinterpretation of Baptist thought in terms of philosophical personalism changed the way Baptists looked at theology for decades. Garrett, however, is neither a biblical theologian nor a philosophical theologian. His chief interest is historical: how did each doctrine develop throughout church history? In other words, Garrett is a historical theologian. Historical consciousness is the great gift he gives to Baptists interested in theology. It is the primary contribution of his two-volume work.

Scope

The second thing one notices in *Systematic Theology* is the wide scope of detail. Garrett has done everything in his power to cover each topic in question as thoroughly as possible. He seeks to be exhaustive in his treatment of each doctrine. That explains the intricate organization of each section and chapter, the voluminous number of footnotes throughout the book, and the seemingly endless number of entries in the three indexes at the back of each book. Simply put, his scope is comprehensive.

Result

The third observation one readily makes while reading *Systematic Theology* is its theological conservatism or orthodoxy. Garrett never attempts to write "new theology." He is content to comment on Christian doctrine as it has been given to the church through the Ecumenical Councils and the Protestant Reformers. As a student in one of Garrett's classes in 1980, I once heard him say, "I am an Evangelical, but don't fence me in. Give me some room to kick a little." He follows that prescription well in *Systematic Theology*: his conclusions are by and large what most conservative Evangelicals would identify with, but he always reserves the right to "kick a little"—that is, to think outside the box at times, to color outside of the lines occasionally, to venture outside of the normal way of doing things if the need arises.

Major Contributions

While there is neither need nor space here to review all of the components of Garrett's two-volume work, it is important to mention that he is one of the first systematic theologians to devote a full chapter each to the topics of stewardship, discipleship, and the mission of the church. But the major contributions which he offers to Baptists may be found in his discussions of many of the most controversial subjects in Baptist thought.

Revelation

While appreciating the insights on *general revelation* offered by Karl Barth and Hans Küng, Garrett prefers to follow the interpretation of John Calvin and Emil Brunner. He believes they are "right in stressing that God reveals himself both in creation and in redemption," although he acknowledges that they fail "to provide an adequate answer to the problem as to a revelation that is adequate to condemn but not to save."[49] Surprisingly, Garrett admits the validity of natural theology as a pointer to God, although he is quick to point out that the theistic arguments for God's existence "are not logically demonstrative for all human beings," although they "may be confirmatory and corroborative of Christian faith."[50] Regarding *special revelation,* Garrett is thoroughly Christocentric when he speaks of "the finality of the revelation of Jesus Christ" as the belief that God's revelation in Christ "will not be abandoned, supplemented, or superseded."[51]

The Bible

Garrett's discussion of the Bible is the fullest in many years from a Baptist theologian. He regards *biblical inspiration* as a relevant topic for today's church, yet he warns against an uncritical position that embraces "extremes in respect to the divine and the human associated with the Bible. . . . Neither a 'docetism' nor a mere 'humanitarianism' regarding the Bible can be adequate."[52] Concerning *biblical criticism,* Garrett cautiously accepts the need for historical and scientific analysis of the Bible. But he questions "the assured results of biblical criticism" and encourages "the criticism of criticism."[53]

Garrett saves some of his wisest counsel for the topic of biblical inerrancy, which he calls the *dependability of the Bible.* Steering a precarious route between absolute "errancy" on the one hand and strict "inerrancy" on the other, he concludes that "none of the problems or difficulties connected with specific biblical texts and posed in relation to dependability/trustworthiness/infallibility/inerrancy . . . jeopardizes any basic Christian doctrine unless it should be inerrancy." Then he irenically admonishes "those who engage in theological controversy and warfare over these matters" to remember that they "stand under the mandate of Jesus Christ concerning love for and among his disciples."[54]

Garrett summarizes his views of the Bible with an interesting treatment of *biblical authority.* Although valuing highly the Protestant principle of *sola Scriptura,* he argues that Baptists would do better by affirming *suprema Scriptura.* This safeguards the Bible's role as "the supreme standard or highest ranking channel of religious authority for Christians,"[55] while still allowing Baptists to use their confessions of faith, as well as other historical formulations of doctrine, as legitimate means of understanding Christianity. In what way is the Bible authoritative? First, it is authoritative "primarily as a book of religion or of divine revelation. It is not a textbook on the natural sciences or a record of all ancient history." Second, its authority transcends all cultures, making it applicable in virtually all settings. Third, its authority derives from the authority of God, an insight which can keep modern Christians from falling into the trap of "Bibliolatry." Fourth, its authority depends on its proper interpretation, which centers in Jesus Christ. Finally, it is authoritative "as the Holy Spirit bestows illumination" for the purpose of application and obedience.[56]

God

Garrett begins his discussion of God by identifying the major *attributes of God* as found in Holy Scripture. While admitting limitations in using attributes as the primary way of describing God, he still prefers to follow this method. His approach is indebted to Emil Brunner. He centers all of the divine attributes around the Old Testament idea of holiness and the New Testament emphasis on love. Understanding God's holiness as separateness or transcendence, he states that "[t]he Holy One is the Wholly Other."[57] Then he creatively clusters seven other divine attributes around holiness. They are: eternity, which is "the duration of God's holiness"; changeless- ness, which is the "constancy of God's holiness"; wisdom, which is the "truth of God's holiness"; knowledge, which is the "cognitive reality of God's holiness";[58] power, which is "the strength of God's holiness";[59] jeal- ousy, anger, wrath, which "are the reaction of God's holiness to sin"; and glory, which is "the recognized manifestation of God's holiness as majesty."[60]

Garrett "bridges" from the Old Testament attribute of holiness to the New Testament attribute of love by speaking of God as righteous. He then turns to "the most communicable of all the communicable attributes of God," namely, love.[61] Defining love as both attribute and gift, he claims that the "biblical doctrine of God's *agape* is unique among the world's re- ligions and philosophies."[61] Then he gathers around love five additional classic qualities attributed to God. They are: patience-forbearance, which is "the persistence of God's love"; faithfulness, which is "the reliability of God's love"; mercy-kindness, which is "the deep compassion of God's love"; grace, which is "the free and undeserved condescension of God's love"; and passibility-suffering, which is "the assumed and endured pain of God's love."[62]

In a day when the fatherhood of God has come under frequent attack, Garrett affirms the traditional, orthodox view of *God as heavenly Father.* Radical feminist theology abhors the use of paternal language to describe or address God, calling instead for the feminization of God and for an af- firmation of the motherhood of God. While acknowledging that there "are some biblical texts . . . in which maternal features are ascribed to God,"[64] Garrett emphasizes that we can and should maintain our understanding of God as Father, without falling into the trap of an uncritical paternalism or patriarchialism.[65]

The Trinity

Because of his deep love for early church history and patristic theology, Garrett devotes three chapters to the doctrine of the *Trinity.* No Baptist since A. H. Strong has given so much space to this teaching.[66] Holding firmly to what he calls the "threeness" and the "oneness" in God's myste- rious nature, he rejects an "economic" Trinity and holds out for an "eter- nal, essential, and immanental" Trinity.[67]

Creation

Garrett offers two robust, thoughtful chapters on creation. He interprets Creation as dependent, "not eternal or ultimate"; as an expression of God's free activity, not a necessary action required for divine self-completion; as *ex nihilo,* out of nothing; as originally and essentially good; as "the background and the correlate of redemption"; as historical, but "not in the ordinary sense of recorded history," inasmuch as there were no eyewitnesses there at the beginning; and as "an affirmation or article of faith" rather than a proof offered by either philosophy or science.[68]

Garrett does not dodge the controversial questions related to creation in today's scientific world. Addressing four contemporary issues germane to creation, he adopts the perspective of certain scholars "who, being aware of the differing roles of religion and the sciences, nevertheless see the need for continuing dialogue between the two realms and who seek greater correlation, if not harmonization, wherever legitimate and possible."[69]

First, regarding the *origin of the universe,* he claims that it does not really matter whether one adopts the "big bang" theory or the "steady state" theory or the "oscillating universe" theory, because any of these theories can be harmonized with the Christian faith.

Second, regarding the *age of the earth,* Garrett reviews a dozen theories that seek to reconcile the "confrontation of fossils and faith." Although not stating his preference, he seems to affirm the last one he mentions: Bernard Ramm's "pictorial day theory" or "theory of moderate concordism," which regards Genesis as primarily theological rather than scientific, sees each "day" of Genesis 1 as metaphorical-pictorial rather than literal, and believes that Genesis 1 is "more topical than chronological."[70]

Third, regarding the issue of *creation versus evolution,* he names three views which Christians have held over the years: fiat creation, which argues that God created the world in six literal twenty-four-hour days; theistic evolution, which claims that God initiated creation, then immanently guided it by a *laissez faire* approach through the process of natural evolution; and progressive creation, as advocated by Augustine and Thomas Aquinas, which believes that God not only initiated creation but also directly and actively guided the evolution of new forms of life. Garrett states his preference for the last view.

Fourth, Garrett distances himself from the *"creation science"* movement when he warns readers "against that too facile harmonization of revelation and science, of Genesis and geology, . . . so that legitimate scientific investigation may be hindered or ignored and biblical writings put to uses never intended by their human authors or by God."[71]

Humankind

In his treatment of humans as created in the *image of God,* Garrett gives seven popular answers to the question, "What is the image of God in humankind?" One is the Barthian view that "the image consists of the confrontation or juxtaposition of human beings as male and female, specially in and through marriage, as analogous to the I/Thou nature of the Triune God."[72] Building on the male and female dimensions of the image of God in Genesis 1:27, Garrett devotes an entire chapter to the topic of *Man and*

Woman. His theological understanding of maleness and femaleness has led him to several conclusions: the male-female difference does not fully exhaust the meaning of *imago dei;* the male-female distinction refutes the teaching of androgyny, or the bisexual or nonsexual nature of the first humans; monogamous marriage is God's will for man and woman and is the best setting for raising children; singleness is valid, but not superior or inferior to marriage; conjugal love is a worthy purpose of marriage and, as such, reveals the sinfulness of adultery, homosexuality, and pornography; marriage is temporal, not eternal; and the Bible and Christianity recognize the value and worth and status of women.

Jesus Christ

Starting with a Christology "from below," Garrett explains that *Jesus' humanity* may be clearly seen in his natural human growth, his temptations, his physical exhaustion and hunger and thirst, his pain and suffering, his normal emotions, his limitations of knowledge and power, his individuality, and his dependence on God the Father. Then he draws four important consequences of Jesus' humanity: Jesus' birth was the Incarnation of God; Jesus was one with all humanity; his humanity served as the basis for his saving work; and he is qualified to serve as "a perfect example for humankind."[73]

Although fully human, Jesus is also the sinless son of God, who is the savior of the world and "provides the only effectual salvation for humankind."[74] But how far does this salvation extend when it comes to the unevangelized? Garrett delineates three prominent voices in this dyamic discussion. First is pluralism, advocated by John Hick and others, which claims that salvation can come through numerous and varied religions and saviors—Jesus is by no means the only savior. Second is inclusivism. This view, promoted by Karl Rahner and Clark Pinnock, argues that Jesus was the onological savior of the world (i.e., his death is the only way to salvation), but not the teleological savior of the world (i.e., done dos not have to personally believe in, or even know about, Jesus in order to find salvation in him.) Third is exclusivism, which finds its modern voice in Ronald Nash and R. C. Sproul. It asserts that salvation occurs solely through personal, conscious faith in Jesus Christ. Garrett opts for a modified exclusivism by stating, "It would seem that the church's proclamation should be exclusivist so as not to promise salvation outside the conscious acceptance of Jesus and the gospel but that in God's sovereign freedom he may effectively work outside the boundaries of exclusivism."[75]

Garrett tackles the tough subject of Jesus' *virgin birth* with clarity and force. He first refutes ten common objections to the teaching. Then he formulates his own position in seven theses. First, it was God's chosen means or mode of Incarnation. Second, it is evidence of Jesus' humanity and deity. Third, it was "God's method of transcending original sin or human depravity in the person and life of Jesus."[76] Fourth, the more exact phrase *virginal conception* should replace *virgin birth* as a way of emphasizing the nature of the divine intervention. Fifth, belief in the virginal conception of Jesus is unrelated to the Roman Catholic teachings about the immaculate conception of Mary or the perpetual virginity of Mary. Sixth, this event was historical, not mythical—i.e., Jesus really was "miraculously conceived of the Virgin Mary without a human father."[77] Seventh, belief in this doctrine has plenty of evidence to commend itself as an important aspect of Christian doctrine, but such belief should not become an absolute indicator of Christian conversion.

The Holy Spirit

While Baptists are typically squeamish about the Holy Spirit, Garrett devotes five chapters (almost one hundred pages) to the subject. In his chapter on the Holy Spirit and the Christian, he delineates several important phrases which can be confusing to the uninitiated. The *gift of the Spirit* is common to all Christians—i.e., one receives the Spirit at the new birth. The *baptism by the Spirit* similarly refers to "spiritual rebirth, or Christian conversion, by the Spirit, but apart from any subsequent baptism in or with the Spirit as evidenced by speaking in tongues."[78] *Baptism in or with the Spirit* likewise does not refer to a post-conversion experience of tongues but points to either the Day of Pentecost or the believer's conversion or both. To be *filled with the Spirit* speaks of a continuous or repeated experience of the Spirit's empowerment.

With all of the current talk about revival in the church, it is appropriate for Garrett to address the topic of "the Holy Spirit as Lord, not captive, of the institutional church."[79] This concept of the *Spirit as Lord* of the church does not contradict the idea of Jesus as Head of the church, "for Christ's headship is administered by the Spirit." But the Spirit has a challenging role to play among the people of God on earth: "the Holy Spirit is to rebuke, reform, refine, renew, and redirect the church and thereby deliver the church from the snare of institutionalism or ecclesiasticism."[80] Garrett's prayer is: let the Spirit rule!

Also, given the rapid worldwide growth of Pentecostal and charismatic churches which heavily stress *charismata,* Garrett wisely spends an entire chapter on *spiritual gifts*. The best part of the chapter is his analysis of some popular charismatic "sign gifts," most notably speaking in tongues. While accepting that the gift of tongues is still operable in today's world, Garrett recognizes that the gift's practice has led to many abuses. He encourages "non-tongues-speakers" to "ask tongues-speakers not to elevate this gift above all others . . . or to look upon non-tongues-speakers as inferior or second-class Christians." He also encourages those who do not speak in tongues not to "exclude or disfellowship those who exercise tongues-speaking within the Pauline perimeters." Finally, he gratefully acknowledges Pentecostals and Neo-Pentecostals for their "clear witness to the dynamic agency and the sovereign lordship of the Holy Spirit in today's world."[81]

The Christian Life

Baptists are again debating Calvinism. In several settings and venues, the old arguments for and against predestination and free will are surfacing among Baptists. Garrett helps to illumine the discussion with a chapter on *election*. Facing the controversial questions head-on, he first states that belief in God's "election of the elect" does not require belief in God's "non-election of the nonelect."[82] In other words, election does not imply reprobation. Garrett fails to give his clear opinion about whether election rests on God's "eternal, immutable decrees," but he seems to favor the idea that God's election of humans rests on a conditional decree which does not deny human accountability. On the tough question of the relationship between election and foreknowledge, he seeks a compatibilist *via media* which embraces both divine initiative and human choice. Garrett summarizes his views about election in a 1995 chapel address at Southwestern: "In the intricate interconnectedness of God's sovereign authority, agency, and power and our human responsibility and accountability there needs to be balance."[83]

The Church

Garrett's attention to the controversial question of *women in the church* is found in his treatment of special, or ordained, ministry. He clearly and fairly summarizes the primary biblical arguments for and against the ordination of women as pastors, but he fails to draw his own conclusion.

Eschatology

Garrett follows a traditional approach in tackling the doctrines related to last things. He pays special attention to the interpretation of *hell* as the counterpart of *heaven*. He names two alternatives which are currently vying to replace the view of hell as eternal punishment for all who reject God's revelation in Christ. The first, eschatological universalism, "is the teaching that ultimately or finally all human beings will be restored or reconciled to the favor and fellowship of God so that none will be eternally separated or punished."[84] The second is annihilationism or conditional immortality. It is the claim that "the postmortal punishment of unbelievers or the wicked will consist of their being blotted out of their existence so that they cease to be."[85] After presenting a balanced summary of the pros and cons of each view, he then offers his own conclusion in the form of a sober warning: "Blaise Pascal's wager argument for the existence of God, if applied to eternal punishment, would make its acceptance to be the way of prudence. Any serious contemplation of eternal punishment should be marked by the awesome sense of tragic loss."[86]

Evaluation

To evaluate Garrett's theology, especially his two-volume *magnum opus*, one must ask a handful of crucial questions. First, what is the purpose of *Systematic Theology*? If the purpose is for the author to present a finely honed thesis and then to argue and prove that thesis in every chapter, then Garrett fails to meet that goal. But if his purpose is to let his readers in on an inter-generational discussion of the cardinal truths of Christianity, then he succeeds hands-down. If the purpose is to provide his readers with essaylike opinions on every controversial doctrinal subject, then again Garrett fails. But if his purpose is to provide differing opinions and contrary arguments related to the controversial issues facing the church so that readers can make up their own minds, then he succeeds masterfully. If Garrett's purpose is to simplify theological truth so that uninformed laypersons can easily comprehend great religious themes, then once again he fails. But if his purpose is to lead Evangelicals, especially Baptists, to understand the length and breadth and height and depth of Christian doctrine as it has been formulated for two millennia, then he succeeds beautifully.

Second, what is the long-term value of Garrett's work? Will it assume a place beside the classic Baptist theologies of Dagg, Strong, Mullins, and Conner? It is obviously too early to tell how future generations of Evangelicals and Baptists will respond to Garrett's *Systematic Theology*. But for future theologians who want to see the historical development of virtually every Christian doctrine, from the biblical materials to current debates, Garrett's work will be their best source. This indeed is his greatest contribution to the life of the church and the world of theological education: he has written a virtual reference book on Christian thought, an encyclopedia of theological information for all who seek precise understanding of how the church has addressed doctrinal matters across the last two millennia. What about future readers who will want a systematic theology which offers them brevity or personal opinion or in-depth biblical exposition? They will likely look elsewhere.

Third, how will Garrett be remembered in years to come? I predict that future generations will regard him as a "gentleman theologian" who sought to illuminate theological controversy rather than agitate those with whom he differed. I also think he will be seen as Baptists' finest historical theologian and as one of Southern Baptists' first and most active ecumenists. Finally, I believe he will be remembered as the last Baptist theologian of the twentieth century to grapple with Christian doctrine from a "modern" viewpoint. The future of Baptists theology may well be in the hands of younger postmodern theologians who see life and interpret the Bible and think about doctrine very differently. But Garrett's work will

316 THEOLOGIANS OF THE BAPTIST TRADITION

stand as long as Christians seek to understand Evangelical and Baptist theology as seen through twentieth-century eyes.

Bibliography

Works by Garrett

Are Southern Baptists "Evangelicals"? (coauthored with E. Glenn Hinson and James E. Tull). Macon, Ga.: Mercer University Press, 1983.

Baptist Church Discipline. Nashville: Broadman Press, 1962.

Baptist Relations with Other Christians (editor). Valley Forge, Pa.: Judson Press, 1974.

Baptists and Roman Catholicism. Nashville: Broadman Press, 1965.

The Concept of the Believers' Church (editor). Scottsdale, Pa.: Herald Press, 1970.

Evangelism for Discipleship. Louisville: Private printing, 1964.

Systematic Theology: Biblical, Historical, and Evangelical. Volumes 1 & 2. Grand Rapids: Wm. B. Eerdmans Publishing Co., 1990, 1995. 2d rev. ed, North Richland Hills, Tex.: BIBAL Press, 2000, 2001.

We Baptists. (editor) Study and Research Division, Baptist World Alliance. Franklin, Tenn.: Providence House Publishers, 1999.

17

Millard J. Erickson

By Bradley G. Green

MILLARD ERICKSON HAS EMERGED AS ONE OF THE MOST SIGNIFICANT and prolific Baptist and conservative Evangelical theologians of the last half of the twentieth century and is certainly worthy to be included in a volume dedicated to Baptist theologians. Through a lengthy teaching career and by his publications—perhaps most influentially through his *magnum opus, Christian Theology*—Erickson has secured his place as one of the most significant figures in contemporary Baptist and Evangelical theology.

This essay will introduce the reader to Erickson by means of a brief biographical sketch, a treatment of influences on Erickson, a cursory summary of Erickson's most significant publications, and an exposition of his theology, and will conclude with a brief evaluation of Erickson's strengths and weaknesses as a theologian.

Biography

While Erickson's family roots are in Sweden, he was born on June 24, 1932, in Stanchfield, Minnesota.[1] With his three older siblings, Erickson was raised on a modest farm, where the water was provided via the power of a windmill, and a kerosene lamp provided light for studying. Erickson was converted as a young boy in the Baptist church, which his family had started in their home and where his grandfather was pastor. Having begun formal education in a one-room schoolhouse, Erickson would eventually become valedictorian of his 1949 graduating class at Braham High School.

In the summer before he was to begin studies at Bethel College (St. Paul, Minnesota), Erickson had the opportunity to preach at his church when his pastor suffered a concussion during a softball game. After hearing Erickson, his pastor encouraged him to consider full-time Christian ministry. This pastoral suggestion was affirmed during his freshmen year at Bethel. A significant chapel service at Bethel confirmed that the Lord was indeed calling Erickson to preach, a call to which he soon responded.

After his first year at Bethel, Erickson transferred to the University of Minnesota, where he studied philosophy and earned two minors in psychology and sociology. In 1953, Erickson graduated Phi Beta Kappa. Erickson began his theological studies at Bethel Seminary, where he met Virginia Nepstad, a student at Bethel College, who would become his bride on August 20, 1955. He eventually went to Chicago's Northern Baptist Theological Seminary, where he completed the master of divinity in 1956.

After completing the M.Div. at Northern, Erickson accepted the pastorate of Fairfield Avenue Baptist Church in Chicago in 1957. This multiracial church ordained Erickson to the ministry on March 21 of that same year.

In 1956, Erickson continued his studies at the University of Chicago, earning a master of arts in philosophy in 1958. He then enrolled in the Ph.D. program at Garrett Theological Seminary, a program offered conjointly with Northwestern University (Chicago). Erickson's chief doctoral mentor was William Hordern, a Lutheran and Neo-Orthodox theologian. Two of the Erickson's three daughters were born during Erickson's doctoral studies in Chicago: Kathryn Sue (born February 23, 1959) and Sandra Lynne (born May 1, 1962). Their third child, Sharon Ruth, was born

September 20, 1964. In that year the Erickson family moved to Minneapolis, where Erickson assumed the pastorate of Olivet Baptist Church. During this time Erickson completed his dissertation (finished in 1963, and in 1968 revised and published as *The New Evangelical Theology*), which focused on key figures in American evangelicalism—all of whom were key influences on Erickson's own thought: Edward J. Carnell, Carl F. H. Henry, and Bernard Ramm.

Erickson's career has been constituted by a combination of administrative and teaching capacities. In 1964, he began teaching at Wheaton College as assistant professor of Bible and apologetics and became chairman of the Bible and Religion Department in 1967. In retrospect, it is fitting that Erickson began his teaching at Wheaton, in many ways the intellectual and cultural hub of American Evangelicalism. His future administrative and teaching positions found him in a variety of evangelical institutions.

In 1969, Erickson accepted a position at Bethel Seminary teaching theology. He would spend twenty-three years at Bethel, eventually serving as executive vice president and dean. During his tenure at Bethel, Erickson spent a sabbatical year in Munich, Germany, with Wolfhart Pannenburg in 1976. A number of Evangelicals have been drawn to Pannenburg who, with his passionate arguments for the historicity of the Resurrection and the evidential persuasiveness of the gospel, was a breath of fresh theological air for many. Erickson is appreciative of Pannenburg's theological scholarship, and Erickson's *Christian Theology* is dedicated to Pannenburg (as well as to Bernard Ramm and William E. Hordern).

In 1992, Erickson left Bethel to become research professor of theology at Southwestern Baptist Theological Seminary in Fort Worth, Texas. This unique appointment, with its reduced teaching load, allowed Erickson to devote himself to various writing projects, some of which grew out of the desire to write in-depth treatments of various theological themes treated more briefly in his *Christian Theology* (published initially in three volumes from 1983 to 1985). For example, in the preface to his *The Word Became Flesh: A Contemporary Incarnational Christology* (1991), Erickson writes: "Several years ago, while writing *Christian Theology*, I found I had to resist the temptation to write a book on the topic of each of the chapters. I concluded that I had the agenda for my next sixty books, and I resolved that I would someday attempt to write some of them. The present volume is the first of such efforts."[2] Erickson taught at Southwestern until 1996, when he accepted two appointments to teach theology, one at George W. Truett Theological Seminary in Waco, Texas (Baylor University), and the other at Western Seminary in Portland, Oregon. His reduced teaching responsibilities at both institutions have allowed him to continue producing an impressive number of significant publications.

Survey of Works

This survey of works[3] will offer a cursory look at Erickson's most significant publications.[4] Erickson's dissertation on the theology of such "new evangelicals" as Edward J. Carnell, Carl F. H. Henry, and Bernard Ramm was finished in 1963 and revised and published as *The New Evangelical Theology* in 1968.[5]

In 1973, Erickson edited the first of three volumes of *Readings in Christian Theology*. The first, subtitled *The Living God*, dealt with theological method, how God is known (including the doctrines of revelation and the Bible), and the nature of God. Volume 2, subtitled *Man's Need and God's Gift* (1976), included essays dealing with the doctrines of man, sin, and the person and work of Christ. Volume 3, subtitled *The New Life* (1979), included essays on salvation, the church, and last things. The volumes contain essays by theologians of various persuasions, past and present. Thus, one finds selections from Augustine, Thomas Aquinas, John Calvin, Charles Hodge, Karl Barth, Rudolf Bultmann, John A. T. Robinson, and Carl F. H. Henry, among many others.

In 1974, Erickson published *Relativism in Contemporary Christian Ethics*, which was largely a response to J. A. T. Robinson and especially to Joseph Fletcher and his *Situation Ethics*.[6] Whereas Fletcher denied the value of ethical prescriptions, which are in some sense universally applicable, and argued that "love" was to be applied in all situations, Erickson argued for a "principal" view, in which "objective, normative values" are to be applied to various ethical dilemmas. At the same time, the particular context would shape how that ethical principle is to be applied.[7]

In 1977, Erickson published *Contemporary Options in Eschatology: A Study of the Millennium*.[8] After two initial chapters, which look at the eschatology of Albert Schweitzer, C. H. Dodd, Rudolf Bultmann, and Jürgen Moltmann, Erickson summarizes millennial and tribulational views.

Throughout his career Erickson has published volumes which are more accessible to the lay reader. In 1978, he published *Salvation: God's Amazing Plan*, a book which presents a theology of salvation in easily understandable language. This volume was republished under the title *Does It Matter That I'm Saved?* and includes a study guide and teaching suggestions. Like the rest of the volumes in this *Does It Matter* series, Erickson peppers these popular volumes with helpful personal stories and illustrations. Other volumes in this series consist of the following: *Does It Matter How I Live? Applying Biblical Beliefs to Your Daily Life* (1994; formerly published in 1987 by Harvest Publications as *Responsive Faith*) tries to help Christians understand how to live out what they believe. *Does It Matter What I Believe? What the Bible Teaches and Why We Should Believe It* (1992) is a basic introduction to Christian doctrine.

Does It Matter If God Exists? Understanding Who God Is and What He Does for Us (1996) is an introduction to the doctrine of God and its practical applications.

Perhaps Erickson's most significant single contribution to Christian scholarship is his *Christian Theology*. Originally published in three volumes (1983, 1984, 1985), it was published in one volume in 1986. In 1998, it was revised and republished, the key change being that attention has been given to postmodernism. *Introducing Christian Doctrine*, a "streamlined" version of the larger *Christian Theology* volume, edited by L. Arnold Hustad, was published in 1992. (*Christian Theology* runs 1,302 pages, whereas *Introducing Christian Doctrine* runs 422 pages). *Christian Theology* is the most commonly used theology text in Baptist and Evangelical seminaries and has also been used at non-Evangelical schools as well. *Introducing Christian Doctrine* has also proved itself to be the most popular entry-level text at college and university texts in Christian theology.

In 1991, Erickson published *The Word Became Flesh: A Contemporary Incarnational Christology*. This 660-page volume (which J. I. Packer appropriately calls "workmanlike"[9]) treats the Incarnation in three parts: (1) The Formulation of Incarnational Christology; (2) Problems of Incarnational Christology; (3) The Construction of a Contemporary Incarnational Christology.

During 1993 and 1994, Erickson was research professor of theology at Southwestern Seminary, and these interrelated volumes were published during this time: *The Evangelical Mind and Heart: Perspectives on Theological and Practical Issues* (1993), *Evangelical Interpretation: Perspectives on Hermeneutical Issues* (1993), and *Where Is Theology Going? Issues and Perspectives on the Future of Theology* (1994). All are concerned with the present and future shape of Evangelical theology.

Erickson published his volume on the doctrine of God, *God the Father Almighty: A Contemporary Exploration of the Divine Attributes,* in 1997. The emergence of "free will theism" or "openness view of God" in Evangelical circles was a key impetus behind this volume. Erickson contends for the importance of doctrine today, surveys key theological movements of the day (Pluralism, Process Thought, and Free Will Theism), offers his own contemporary articulation of the attributes of God, and concludes with practical implications of the doctrine of God.

In 1995, Erickson published *God in Three Persons: A Contemporary Interpretation of the Trinity*. The format in this volume is similar to that of his earlier volume on the Incarnation. Erickson (1) surveys the early Christian formulation of the doctrine of the Trinity, (2) surveys key problems related to the doctrine of the Trinity, and (3) offers a contemporary statement of the doctrine of the Trinity.

Another volume that grew out of research opportunities at Southwestern was *How Shall They Be Saved? The Destiny of Those Who Do Not Hear of Jesus* (1996). In this volume Erickson surveys the plethora of work which has recently been written on the question of the destiny of the unevangelized and then offers his own proposal. Of particular interest to Erickson is the openness among some contemporary evangelicals to annihilationism and to various forms of inclusivism.

Erickson teamed up with James L. Heflin to author *Old Wine in New Wineskins: Doctrinal Preaching in a Changing World* (1997). Erickson and Heflin argue that doctrinal preaching is in desperate need today, and they counsel that the step from text to doctrine is an important, but not always easy, step.

Erickson's most recent work has been devoted to contemporary trends in theology such as postconservative and postmodern theology. Erickson is currently working on a major work on postmodernism, but two shorter volumes have appeared in the meantime. *The Evangelical Left: Encountering Postconservative Evangelical Theology* is mainly a critique of four key theologians whom Erickson sees, in a broad sense, as "postconservative": Stanley Grenz, James McClendon, Clark Pinnock, and Bernard Ramm. He critiques these four theologians, positively and negatively, in the areas of theological methodology, doctrine of Scripture, doctrine of God, and doctrine of salvation. Erickson's most recent work, *Postmodernizing the Faith: Evangelical Responses to the Challenge of Postmodernism,* looks at seven theologians, three of which respond negatively, and four positively, to postmodernism (on the negative side: David Wells, Thomas Oden, and Francis Schaeffer; on the positive side: Stanley Grenz, J. Richard Middleton, Brian J. Walsh, and B. Keith Putt).

Finally, a recent work should be mentioned—not *by* Erickson, but *for* him. David S. Dockery has edited *New Dimensions in Evangelical Thought: Essays in Honor of Millard J. Erickson* (1998). This volume features essays by some twenty-five theologians, treating "new dimensions" in biblical theology, historical theology, systematic theology, and applied theology. Contributors include Baptist, Evangelical, and Eastern Orthodox theologians.

Influences

Key influences on Erickson's thought come from his background in his era and place in history as well as particular persons who have helped shape Erickson. Erickson's thought is perhaps best seen against the backdrop of the new Evangelicals that emerged following World War II. Although he is a generation later than such "new Evangelicals" as Edward J. Carnell, Carl F. H. Henry, and Bernard Ramm, Erickson's thought in some ways can be seen as the organic development of the new Evangelicalism. As the new Evangelicals viewed the situation at the end of World War II, fundamentalism had hardened, become reactionary, and was ignoring the social and ethical implications of historic Christianity. While appreciative of fundamentalism's valiant defense of the "fundamentals" against the onslaught of theological liberalism, the new Evangelicals sought to engage the culture, to challenge the strongholds of theological liberalism, and to affirm and live out the social and ethical dimensions of the historic faith.[10]

Erickson's own theological efforts are consistent with the efforts of Henry and Carnell to offer a rational defense and articulation of the Christian faith. But Erickson should not be seen as simply E. J. Carnell (or Carl F. H. Henry or Bernard Ramm) *redidivus*. Erickson did not uncritically accept the agenda of the new Evangelicals, and even in *The New Evangelical Theology* (1968), Erickson suggested what might be possible weaknesses in the movement, and he offered reticent predictions as to how the movement might develop.

Erickson pondered (1) whether the "right and left edges of the movement" would be able to hold together, (2) whether subjective elements in the movement would incline the movement towards neoorthodoxy, and (3) whether the theological methodology of the movement (which stressed rational demonstration of Christian truth claims) was truly distinct from the theological method of liberalism.[11] Nonetheless, Erickson is the most prominent contemporary heir to this general theological movement. His impact on the world of Evangelical theology, particularly in North America, may be no less important than that of such figures. Indeed, William Hordern, Erickson's doctoral mentor from Garrett Evangelical Seminary (Northwestern University), has written concerning Erickson's *Christian Theology,* "His work did for the new evangelical theology what Karl Barth's *Church Dogmatics* did for neo-orthodoxy."[12]

In addition to the general historical background to Erickson's thought, several individuals and their influence on Erickson are worth noting. Erickson's *Christian Theology* is dedicated to three men: Bernard Ramm, William E. Hordern, and Wolfhart Pannenburg. These three men were all Erickson's instructors at different phases of his career.[13] Ramm was Erickson's first theology professor when Erickson was a young seminary student at Bethel Seminary. As Ramm diligently sought to be honest with both genuine science and the teaching of Scripture, Erickson's work evidences a similar desire to engage and understand the relationship between contemporary thought and Christian orthodoxy.

Hordern was Erickson's doctoral mentor at Northwestern, and it is Hordern who distinguished between "transformers" (those who change, and ultimately lose, the essence of Christianity in their efforts at communicating the Christian faith) and "translators" (those who try to communicate the historic essence of the Christian faith in ways that are faithful to historic Christianity). Erickson is certainly a "translator," and virtually all of Erickson's work is shaped by a desire to maintain fidelity to core doctrinal truths while communicating those truths in ways understandable to contemporary audiences.

Erickson spent a sabbatical year with Pannenburg in Germany. Pannenburg's main influence on Erickson appears to have been more in the realm of theological inspiration than in shaping Erickson's particular doctrinal or theological convictions. That is, Erickson was inspired in his own theological endeavors after having spent time with Pannenburg, who modeled religious theological thinking for Erickson.[14]

Theological Content

Preliminary Issues

At the heart of Erickson's theological work is a principle that he saw his doctoral mentor, William Hordern, model. Erickson, following Hordern, suggests that there are two main ways in which one can engage in contemporary theological work. One can either be a *translator* or a *transformer* of "certain basic beliefs" of Christianity.[15] That is, one either (1) affirms that there are certain key doctrines or basic beliefs which must be retained and communicated in each generation (*translators*), or (2) affirms that older doctrines are so thoroughly bound up with a particular culture, worldview, etc., that it is simply *impossible* to restate older doctrines today, and that rather one must offer a significantly different message today (*transformers*). In short, Erickson, a translator, affirms (1) that there really are true and unchanging doctrines at the heart of Christianity, and (2) that these doctrines must be communicated effectively today. This effort to offer a contemporary restatement of doctrine is key to Erickson's theological efforts and is seen particularly in *Christian Theology*, as well as his longer treatments of certain doctrines (e.g., the Incarnation, the doctrine of God, and the doctrine of the Trinity).

Erickson contends that in the task of systematic theology one moves from exegesis to biblical theology to systematic theology.[16] Erickson outlines a nine-step theological method to be generally followed in the task of systematic theology.[17] One collects the biblical materials on the doctrine at hand and seeks to unify the biblical materials (i.e., one is working with the "analogy of faith"—understanding the general meaning of Scripture by interpreting difficult texts in light of more clear texts), and analyzes the meaning of biblical teachings. One then turns to the history of doctrine in order to learn from the past, attempts to identify the essence of the doctrine, and looks to illumination from sources beyond the Bible, such as the sciences. Finally, one seeks to give contemporary expression of the doctrine, seeks to develop/discover a central interpretive motif which can serve as an organizing principle for one's systematic theology (Erickson's motif is the "magnificence of God"), and attempts to stratify the various topics, recognizing which issues are primary, secondary, tertiary, etc.

In light of recent developments in theology which favor a "narrative" approach to the theological task, Erickson's approach to narrative texts in general is worth noting. Erickson contends that when dealing with "didactic" texts and "narrative" texts, didactic texts should be primary in determining theological/doctrinal meaning and that narrative texts should generally be interpreted in light of such didactic texts.[18]

Erickson chooses to treat the traditional *loci* of systematic theology under twelve headings: Studying God, Knowing God, What God Is Like, What God Does, Humanity, Sin, The Person of Christ, The Work of Christ, The Holy Spirit, Salvation, The Church, and The Last Things. It is helpful to draw attention to the way in which Erickson *generally* shapes his treatments of various topics in *Christian Theology,* a style which is particularly seen in his longer treatments of specific doctrines (e.g., incarnational Christology, Trinity, doctrine of God, etc.).[19] First, Erickson begins either by looking at the key scriptural passages touching on an issue (e.g., those texts which speak to the deity of Christ when dealing with Christology)[20] or by offering a brief rationale as to why a certain doctrine is worthy of consideration, and/or why a certain doctrine is difficult to understand today (e.g., with the doctrine of the Holy Spirit).[21]

Second, Erickson will generally survey the key historical issues related to a doctrine (e.g., with the deity of Christology the key heresies are discussed,[22] while with the atonement the key historical theories of the atonement are discussed),[23] and/or key contemporary challenges or issues which pertain to a doctrine (e.g., "functional Christology" is discussed in his Christology section,[24] and the relationship between Christianity and science is treated in the section on creation).[25]

Third, Erickson will offer his own construal of a doctrine, paying particular attention to the biblical witness. This third section will often contain interaction with other key church historical or contemporary construals of a doctrine (e.g., Erickson contends that penal substitution is the central theme of the atonement in Scripture, and that penal substitution best explains and makes sense of competing historical theories of the atonement).[26]

Fourth, after Erickson's construal of a doctrine is proffered, he generally offers implications that flow from a doctrine. These implications are both theoretical and practical in nature (e.g., the doctrine of creation implies an orderly universe, and hence scientific investigation of creation is a worthy endeavor;[27] since the Holy Spirit truly empowers Christians, we should not be deterred or discouraged by our own personal inadequacies).[28]

Revelation and the Bible

After an initial (and rather wide-ranging) discussion of prolegomena in *Christian Theology*, Erickson moves to revelation and the Bible as the source of systematic theology. Erickson affirms the traditional distinction between general and special revelation and argues that there need not be (indeed there must not be) a dichotomy between "prepositional" and "personal" revelation. That is, "revelation is not *either* personal *or* prepositional; it is *both/and*. What God primarily does is to reveal *himself*, but he does so at least in part by telling us something *about* himself."[29]

Erickson affirms that not only were the biblical writers inspired, but all they wrote was inspired as well.[30] After surveying different views of biblical authority, Erickson affirms a nuanced view of inerrancy, which he calls "full inerrancy": "The Bible, when correctly interpreted in light of the level to which culture and the means of communication had developed at the time it was written, and in view of the purposes for which it was given, is fully truthful in all that it affirms."[31] Inerrancy is important (1) *theologically*, since with Scripture we are dealing with what *God* has spoken, and certainly God speaks that which is true[32]; (2) *historically*, since the "church has historically held to the inerrancy of the Bible"[33]; and (3) *epistemologically*, since "if the Bible should prove to be in error in those realms where its claims can be checked, on what possible basis would we logically continue to hold to its dependability in areas where we cannot verify what it says?"[34]

God, the World, and Man

Erickson's doctrine of God is within the main purview of traditional and orthodox doctrines of God.[35] Erickson treats the traditional attributes under the rubrics of the "greatness of God" (often called the "natural attributes") and the "goodness of God" (often called the "moral attributes").[36] Erickson affirms the "attributes of greatness" with slightly new terminology: spirituality, personality, life, infinity (which includes God's omnipresence, timelessness, omniscience, and omnipotence), and constancy (which is essentially God's impassability). Erickson also affirms "attributes of goodness" under somewhat new terminology: moral purity (i.e., holiness, righteousness, justice), integrity (i.e., genuineness, veracity, faithfulness), and love (i.e., benevolence, grace, mercy, persistence). Erickson also stresses the importance of affirming the reality of both God's transcendence and immanence.

In *God the Father Almighty*, Erickson's doctrine of God is worked out after having spent three chapters analyzing the views of Pluralism, Process Thought, and Free Will Theism (i.e., the "openness of God" view).[37] Erickson contends that all three of these movements, while having some positive aspects, are seriously deficient. Erickson contends for God's immutability (with the emphasis being on the "constancy of God's nature");[38]

eternality (Erickson draws a parallel between transcendence/immanence and atemporality/temporally eternal; Erickson suggests that God might be both *atemporal* [God is *transcendent* to and outside of time] and *temporal* [while nonetheless eternal God is *immanent* in time, much like he is immanent within space]);[39] impassability (God's will is impassible; he is never "surprised" by anything outside himself, he does not "feel" all the emotions of his creatures, but God does have an emotional life, "but does not let them control him");[40] omnipotence (God is "able to do all things logically possible, that are consistent with his perfect being");[41] omniscience (God has the "ability to know all things that are the proper objects of his knowledge");[42] simplicity (there is an emphasis on "the unity of [God's] nature, the harmony of his attributes, and the fact that his actions involve the whole of what he is");[43] goodness (God in his being is good, and his actions flow out of his nature);[44] and immanence and transcendence (God is both "in" the world and "above" and "outside" it).[45]

Erickson's view of the providence of God is "moderately Calvinistic" (Erickson's term).[46] Erickson prefers to speak of God's "plan," rather than "decree," but he nonetheless contends that the "plan of God" is "his eternal decision rendering certain all things which shall come to pass."[47] Indeed, Christianity contends "that God has a plan which includes everything that occurs, and that he is now at work carrying out that plan."[48] Erickson is a "compatibilist," in that he contends that God can "render all things certain," *and* human decisions can still legitimately be considered free. To those who would challenge Erickson at this point, Erickson replies with what he considers to be an important distinction: "God renders *certain*, but not *necessary*, the free decisions and actions of the individual." That is, "God brings into being the individual who will freely choose to move his finger to the right rather than an individual who is identical in every respect except that he will choose to move his finger to the left."[49]

After surveying key perspectives on human origins (naturalistic evolution, fiat creationism, deistic evolution, theistic evolution, and progressive creationism), Erickson posits that progressive creationism is most consistent with Scripture and the findings of science.[50] With particular weight given to Paul's soteriological arguments in 1 Corinthians 15:21ff and Romans 5:12ff, Erickson also contends that Adam and Eve are best viewed as historical persons.[51]

Erickson posits that the *imago Dei* is best seen centrally as substantive, rather than primarily as relational or functional: "It refers to something man *is* rather than something he *has* or *does*."[52] Erickson contends that Scripture is unclear as to exactly what constitutes the image, and while it would include things like reason, the image should not be limited to reason.[53]

Erickson holds that Scripture traces the universal sinfulness of man to a historical Adam, and he opts for natural headship (rather than federal headship, or covenant theology), in that we were biologically present in Adam, and thus Adam's sin "was not merely that of one isolated individual, but of the entire human race."[54] All of humanity has received the "entirety of our human nature, both physical and spiritual, material and immaterial . . . from our parents and more distant ancestors by way of descent from the first pair of humans."[55] Regarding children, original sin, and salvation, Erickson contends that just as Christ's righteousness is not imputed to the sinner until that sinner believes, so Adam's sin is not imputed to someone until he or she has voluntarily and consciously embraced one's sin nature. Thus, the infant (or the young child who has not matured to the point of being able to commit a truly sinful act) is not responsible for the sin of Adam until that young person appropriates it personally in his or her life by "accepting" or "approving" one's sin nature.[56]

Christ, Spirit, and Salvation

Erickson affirms both the deity and the humanity of Christ, and he affirms an essentially Chalcedonian Christology which affirms that these two natures are neither radically confused nor radically divided.[57] In the Incarnation Christ took on human nature. Thus Erickson can speak of "kenosis by addition," whereby Christ did not "lose" something by becoming man but rather "added" human nature.[58] Christ did not lose divinity in taking on human nature, and the divine nature is now exercised in consort with human nature, which is how one explains such texts which speak of Jesus' limited knowledge, "lack" of omnipotence, and limited corporeality.[59] Erickson affirms the classical Protestant view of the threefold office of Christ—Prophet, King, and Priest—but reformulates these as *functions* (Erickson's term): Revealer, Ruler, and Reconciler.[60]

Christ's work consists of his "humiliation" (Incarnation, death, descent into Hades) and "exaltation" (Resurrection, Ascension, and session at the Father's right hand, and Second Coming).[61] Key to the work of Christ is the atonement, and Erickson argues for the centrality of penal substitution and satisfaction in his construal of the cross. Other themes such as example, moral influence, governance, and ransom are only truly explained and comprehensible in light of a penal substitute which satisfies God's just nature: "We would contend that it is only on the basis of the substitutionary view that [other theories of the atonement] bear force."[62] For Erickson the question of the extent of the atonement is inextricably linked with one's position on the logical order of God's decrees.[63] That is, "the question is whether God sent Christ to die to provide salvation for all persons [what Erickson calls Sublapsarianism—the "decree to provide salvation sufficient for all" precedes the "decree to save some and reprobate others"], or simply for those whom he had chosen [both Supralapsarianism and Infralapsarianism]."[64] Erickson contends for a "universal" atonement.[65] Since Erickson does affirm unconditional election, he contends that while Christ dies for all, the benefits of the cross are applied only to the elect when they believe.[66]

Erickson affirms that salvation is concerned to some extent with temporal needs, but the key issue is "the eternal spiritual welfare of the individual."[67] He embraces a Calvinistic understanding of election in which God's election is not simply God's foreknowledge of a "future" choice by the individual; rather, God's election of some to salvation is the factor which "renders certain" that the elect will in fact believe.[68] Erickson contends, with Arminianism, that in the "order of salvation" faith precedes regeneration. But, instead of the idea held by many Reformed theologians that regeneration is necessary for one to believe the gospel, Erickson holds that effectual calling is such a persuasive and profound work of God that the elect do in fact respond to this call with faith.[69] Thus, Erickson's *ordo salutis* is: effectual calling, repentance, faith, regeneration.[70] Erickson affirms the judicial nature of justification, that sanctification is the continued work of God in the believer, and that the elect will persevere to the completion of their salvation, which is glorification.[71]

Erickson laments that the Holy Spirit is often seen as the "lower" member of the Trinity and suggests that the study of the Holy Spirit is beset with unique difficulties (e.g., we have less explicit biblical revelation dealing with the Spirit than with the Father and Son, the difficulty of conceptualizing the Holy Spirit, and the servant role of the Holy Spirit in the present era inclines some to see the Holy Spirit as inferior).[72] Erickson affirms the deity and personality of the Holy Spirit, contends that the Holy Spirit is active in both the beginning of the Christian life (in regeneration) and its continuation (in empowering, illuminating, teaching, interceding for, sanctifying, and bestowing gifts upon the believer). Opting for neither a strict cessationist or noncessationist perspective on whether and which spiritual gifts exist today, Erickson points to the important issues of yielding ourselves to the Holy Sprit's reign in our lives and to the fruit of the Spirit.[73]

Church and Last Things

According to Erickson, the church is an undervalued theme in the history of Christian thought. Indeed, "at no point in the history of Christian thought has the doctrine of the church received the direct and complete attention which other doctrines have received."[74] The church is best defined as "the whole body of those who have received new life."[75] While the church is universal it finds expression in local "groupings of believers."[76] The church is not to be equated with the kingdom of God; rather, the church is a particular manifestation of God's rule, or kingdom.[77] The church is indeed the new Israel, but there nonetheless is a "special future" for national Israel.[78] The distinction between the visible and invisible church is legitimate, but every effort should be made to make these two identical.[79] The church began at Pentecost, and the Old Testament people of God—Israel—has now been incorporated into, or included in, the church.[80] While the heart of the church's ministry is the gospel, the church's four main functions are evangelism, edification, worship, and social concern.[81] Erickson opts for congregational church government, believer's baptism by immersion as a public sign of one's faith, and a view of the Lord's Supper where Christ is present in an "influential" (rather than metaphysical) sense, Christ's sacrificial and propitiatory death is commemorated, and the believer focuses on the promise and potential of a closer relationship with Christ.[82]

Erickson affirms that at death people immediately go to either "a place and condition of blessedness" or to "an experience of misery, torment and punishment." Nonetheless, in the future paradise and Hades will be more intense.[83] The one Second Coming[84] will be personal, physical, visible, unexpected, triumphant, and glorious.[85] Christ's Second Coming brings both (1) the resurrection of the dead, in which their bodies receive a transformation or metamorphosis but maintain "some connection" to their original bodies,[86] and (2) the final judgment. Erickson affirms a premillennial and posttribulational return of Christ.[87] Heaven is primarily the presence, and hell the absence, of God.[88] Heaven and hell are both places and states, but primarily states.[89] The final judgment is truly *final,* and eternal punishment is both conscious and everlasting.[90]

Contemporary Trends in Theology

Much of Erickson's recent scholarly efforts have been spent interacting with contemporary trends in theology and how Evangelicals might respond to such trends. Whereas Erickson's treatments of traditional doctrines always include interaction (generally extensive) with contemporary issues and challenges, of particular interest to Erickson at present are the larger currents and shifts in contemporary theology.

In the realm of hermeneutics, Erickson wishes to affirm the importance and possibility of understanding an author's intent, although he suggests speaking of the author's "affirmation" or "assertion," since the latter terms focus properly on the product and not the process of writing. There indeed is meaning in a text that is independent of the hearer, reader, or interpreter. In biblical interpretation, the role of the Holy Spirit as inspirer and coauthor of Scripture must be appreciated.[91]

In general Erickson is rather skeptical regarding such trends as postconservative and postmodern theology. Erickson warns that postconservative Evangelical theology is stretching the label "Evangelical" virtually beyond recognition.[92] Since Erickson contends that eternally true doctrines are at the heart of historic Christianity,[93] he is wary of postconservatives[94] who are hesitant or skeptical about such an affirmation, and who affirm narrative theology over propositional theology. Erickson suggests that for all the eloquent talk of "narrative" theology, postconservatives use narrative mainly only in speaking *about* theology, and that at the end of the day, any theologian who does *theology* will speak in terms of propositions.[95]

Erickson is also fairly skeptical of postmodernism. He suggests that postmodernity can be seen as both an era of time (i.e., that era which simply follows modernism) and as a general ideology.[96] He suggests that in reality there are two types of postmodernism—"hard" and "soft."[97] Erickson wishes to accept the general perspective of "soft" postmodernism, which has wisely rejected logical positivism, behaviorism, and falsely reductionistic scientific approaches to reality.[98] On the other hand, Erickson rejects "hard" postmodernism, which is best represented by deconstructionism and which rejects objectivity and rationality.[99]

Evaluation

Having summarized the major contours of Erickson's thought, we offer a brief evaluation of Erickson's theological work. We mention both the strengths and weaknesses of this and then conclude with a note regarding Erickson's impact and legacy.

Strengths

First, in his teaching[100] and writing Erickson is a model of clarity and fairness. He writes to communicate, not to confuse. In his doctrinal writing, Erickson surveys various views in a fair manner and then offers his construal of a doctrine. For anyone wanting a fair and thorough introduction to systematic theology, one is hard-pressed to better Erickson's *Christian Theology*.[101]

Second, Erickson theologizes out of an impressive understanding of biblical studies, theological studies, philosophy, and broader cultural issues. Erickson's works, particularly his more thorough treatments of a particular doctrine (e.g., his lengthy *The Word Made Flesh*) give evidence of one who is cognizant of current studies in a number of disciplines. In an age of academic specialization, this is certainly an admirable strength.

Third, Erickson is appreciative of the classical Christian tradition, but he does not simply repristinate older conceptions in a slavish way. He is willing to offer a new perspective or construal of a topic when he deems that traditional understandings are inadequate or incomplete, and when he believes that Scripture supports such a move. For example, while affirming the basic intent of Chalcedon, he attempts to articulate a doctrine of the person of Christ without simply repeating the Chalcedonian formula.[102]

Fourth, Erickson is a theologian of the church. In his more academic as well as his more practical work, there is the clear concern that the truth of the Christian faith must be proclaimed to the world, understood by believers, and embraced and lived out in practical ways. This is seen in *Christian Theology* in that most sections end with an "implications" section, which helps the reader understand why these doctrines matter, as well as the fact that Erickson has written numerous works in which difficult doctrinal matters are presented to laypersons in an understandable and practical way.

Fifth, Erickson continues to engage contemporary thought and labors as to how historic Christianity should respond to the plethora of challenges today. Where many scholars are aware of various trends in contemporary theology, Erickson's work reveals that he has taken the time to read primary sources, and his own theologizing is strengthened due to this effort.

Weaknesses

Since Erickson is a contemporary, we have yet to see how history will judge his theological work, and it is harder to see weaknesses at present which will most likely be more apparent to future generations. Nonetheless, while the strengths of Erickson's work are many, we should point out some weaknesses as well.

First, despite the impressiveness of *Christian Theology*, it is difficult at times to see how the "central interpretive motif" of *magnificence of God*, introduced under the eighth step in his proposed theological method,[103] functions in the work. There are times when one wishes that Erickson would draw more theological connections between the various doctrines of Christian theology, and perhaps if this motif had been more explicitly woven throughout the volume such theological connections would have been more pronounced, and the organic nature and unity of Christian truth would have been more "fleshed out" for the reader. A scholar and theologian of Erickson's stature could benefit the church by modeling more thoroughly the organic nature of Christian truth and how the unity of Christian truth is not imposed from the "outside" but flows from a God whose unity is reflected in all of his revelation.[104]

Second, it can be asked whether some of Erickson's attempts at "translating" the Christian faith for the current generation are particularly successful or helpful. While the attempt is to be lauded, some of the efforts may not be effective. For example, while Protestants have traditionally spoken of the Christ as Prophet, King, and Priest, Erickson chooses to speak of Christ as Revealer, Ruler, and Reconciler.[105] While this new terminology seems to communicate the meaning of the older terminology, one must ask if there is a benefit to this terminological shift. In an age where persons (Christian or otherwise) are increasingly ignorant of and unappreciative of the past, would it perhaps be helpful to maintain terms like Prophet, King, and Priest, which help Christians think of Christ in ways which are both biblically grounded and historically rich at the same time?

Finally, it is worthwhile briefly to broach the subject of how Erickson will be viewed in the years to come. Particularly through *Christian Theology* and *Introducing Christian Doctrine*, Erickson has had a widespread impact on the current generation of Evangelical college students and seminarians. His theological scholarship (particularly, again, in *Christian Theology*) has been highly praised by Evangelicals and non-Evangelicals alike. But what of the years to come? Many younger Evangelicals appear particularly anxious to distance themselves from such Evangelical stalwarts and statesmen such as Carl F. H. Henry.[106] But what about Erickson? Will younger evangelicals be anxious to distance themselves from him as well? Perhaps. In both *The Evangelical Left* and *Postmodernizing the Faith*, Erickson suggests that certain Evangelicals are *already* engaged in a theological project which he finds untenable and seriously flawed, and Erickson at least sees *himself* as engaged in a rather different theological project than many of those he is criticizing in these volumes. Erickson, like Henry, is considered by many younger Evangelicals to be a "rationalist" and a "modernist,"[107] and the future Evangelical response to Erickson will depend to a large degree on how Evangelicalism comes to grips with such questions as theological method, in particular the classic theological question of the relation of faith and reason, experience and revelation. But if current trends such as postmodernism and postconservative Evangelical theology dissipate and end up having been little more than the latest fad, Erickson may continue to be viewed as a key exemplar of theological scholarship in our contemporary age.

In closing, Erickson should be praised for his fine scholarship and his pastoral and teaching ministry, through which he has edified the Christian church. His reputation inside and outside of conservative Evangelical circles testifies both to the level of his scholarship and to his genuine Christian spirit. While Erickson's impact on theological students has been immense, particularly due to his writings, we must await coming days to see how Erickson's theological endeavors will be judged by future generations.

Bibliography

Works by Erickson

A Basic Guide to Eschatology: Making Sense of the Millennium. Grand Rapids: Baker Book House, 1998 (formerly published with Baker as *Contemporary Options in Eschatology: A Study of the Millennium* in 1977).

"Absolutes, Moral," "Act Ethics," "Joseph Fletcher," "Norms," "Principles," "Rule Ethics." *Baker's Dictionary of Christian Ethics.* Edited by Carl F. H. Henry. Grand Rapids: Baker Book House, 1973.

"Baptism." In *Nelson's Illustrated Bible Dictionary.* Edited by Herbert Lockyer Sr. Nashville: Thomas Nelson Publishers, 1986.

"Bethel Academy." *Dictionary of Baptists in America.* Edited by Bill J. Leonard. Downers Grove, Ill.: InterVarsity Press, 1994.

"Bethel Seminary." *Dictionary of Baptists in America.* Edited by Bill J. Leonard. Downers Grove, Ill.: InterVarsity Press, 1994.

"Bloesch's Doctrine of Holy Scripture." *Festschrift for Donald Bloesch.* Edited by Elmer Colyer. Downers Grove, Ill.: InterVarsity Press, forthcoming.

"Carl F. H. Henry." *A New Handbook of Christian Theologians.* Edited by Donald W. Musser and Joseph L. Price. Nashville: Abingdon Press, 1996.

Christian Theology. Grand Rapids: Baker Book House, 1986.

"Christology from Above and Christology from Below: A Study in Contrasting Methodologies." *Perspectives on Evangelical Theology.* Edited by Kenneth S. Kantzer and Stanley N. Gundry. Grand Rapids: Baker Book House, 1979.

"Christology from an Evangelical Perspective." *Review and Expositor* 88, 4 (1991): 379–97.

"Christology in America." In *Dictionary of Christianity in America.* Edited by Daniel G. Reid, et al. Downers Grove, Ill.: InterVarsity Press, 1990.

Concise Dictionary of Christian Theology. Grand Rapids: Baker Book House, 1986.

Does It Matter How I Live? Applying Biblical Beliefs to Your Daily Life. Grand Rapids: Baker Book House, 1994 (formerly published with Harvest Publications in 1987).

Does It Matter If God Exists? Understanding Who God Is and What He Does for Us. Grand Rapids: Baker Book House, 1996.

Does It Matter That I'm Saved? What the Bible Teaches about Salvation. Grand Rapids: Baker Book House, 1996.

"Edgren, John Alexis." *Dictionary of Baptists in America.* Edited by Bill J. Leonard. Downers Grove, Ill.: InterVarsity Press, 1994.

"Euthanasia." *Evangelical Dictionary of Theology.* Edited by Walter A. Elwell. Grand Rapids: Baker Book House, 1984.

"Evangelical Christology and Soteriology Today." *Interpretation* 49, 3 (1995): 255–66.

Evangelical Interpretation: Perspectives on Hermeneutical Issues. Grand Rapids: Baker Book House, 1993.

The Evangelical Left: Encountering Postconservative Evangelical Theology. Grand Rapids: Baker Book House, 1997.

The Evangelical Mind and Heart: Perspectives on Theological and Practical Issues. Grand Rapids: Baker Book House, 1993.

"Evangelicalism, USA." *The Blackwell Encyclopedia of Modern Christian Thought*. Edited by Alister A. McGrath. Cambridge, Mass.: Blackwell, 1993.

"The Fate of Those Who Never Hear." *Bibliotheca Sacra* 152, 605 (1995): 3–15.

God in Three Persons: A Contemporary Understanding of the Trinity. Grand Rapids: Baker Book House, 1995.

God the Father Almighty: A Contemporary Exploration of the Divine Attributes. Grand Rapids: Baker Book House, 1998.

"Gordh, Arvid." *Dictionary of Baptists in America*. Edited by Bill J. Leonard. Downers Grove, Ill.: InterVarsity Press, 1994.

How Shall They Be Saved? The Destiny of Those Who Do Not Hear of Jesus. Grand Rapids: Baker Book House, 1996.

"Human Engineering and Christian Ethical Values." *Journal of the American Scientific Affiliation* 30, 1 (1978): 16–20.

"Human Language: Human Vehicle for Divine Truth." *Biblical Hermeneutics: A Comprehensive Introduction to Interpreting Scripture*. Edited by Bruce Corley, Steve Lemke, and Grant Lovejoy. Nashville: Broadman & Holman, 1996.

"Image of God." *Nelson's Illustrated Bible Dictionary*. Edited by Herbert Lockyer Sr. Nashville: Thomas Nelson Publishers, 1986.

"Implications of Biblical Inerrancy for the Christian Mission." *The Proceedings of the Conference on Biblical Inerrancy 1987*. Nashville: Broadman, 1987.

Introducing Christian Doctrine. Edited by L. Arnold Hustad. Grand Rapids: Baker Book House, 1992.

"Is Hell Forever?" *Bibliotheca Sacra* 152, 607 (1995): 259–72.

"Is There Opportunity for Salvation After Death?" *Bibliotheca Sacra* 152, 606 (1995): 131–44.

"Jealousy." *Zondervan's New Pictorial Bible Encyclopedia*. Edited by Merrill E. Tenney. Grand Rapids: Zondervan Publishing House, 1974.

"Joy." *Zondervan's New Pictorial Bible Encyclopedia*. Edited by Merrill E. Tenney. Grand Rapids: Zondervan Publishing House, 1974.

The Living God. Vol. 1, Readings in Christian Theology. Edited by Millard J. Erickson. Grand Rapids: Baker Book House, 1973.

"The Lord's Supper." *People of God: Essays on the Believer's Church*. Edited by Paul Basden and David S. Dockery. Nashville: Broadman Press, 1990.

"Lordship Theology: The Current Controversy." *Southwestern Journal of Theology* 33, 2 (1991): 5–15.

"Man." *Nelson's Illustrated Bible Dictionary*. Edited by Herbert Lockyer Sr. Nashville: Thomas Nelson Publishers, 1986.

Man's Need and God's Gift. Vol. 2, Readings in Christian Theology. Editor. Grand Rapids: Baker Book House, 1976.

"Millennial Views." *Evangelical Dictionary of Theology*. Edited by Walter A. Elwell. Grand Rapids: Baker Book House, 1984.

"Narrative Theology: Translation or Transformation?" *Festschrift: A Tribute to William Hordern.* Edited by Walter Freitag. Saskatoon: University of Saskatchewan Press, 1985.

The New Life. Vol. 3, Readings in Christian Theology. Edited by Millard J. Erickson. Grand Rapids: Baker Book House, 1979.

The New Evangelical Theology. Westwood, N.J.: Fleming H. Revell, 1968; London: Marshall, Morgan and Scott, 1969.

Old Wine in New Wineskins: Doctrinal Preaching in a Changing World. With James L. Hefley. Grand Rapids: Baker Book House, 1997.

"Pannenburg's Use of History as a Solution to the Religious Language Problem." *Journal of the Evangelical Theological Society* 17, 2 (1974): 99–105.

Postmodernizing the Faith: Evangelical Responses to the Challenge of Postmodernism. Grand Rapids: Baker Book House, 1998.

"Presuppositions of Non-evangelical Hermeneutics." *Hermeneutics, Inerrancy and the Bible.* Edited by Earl Radmacher and Robert D. Preus. Grand Rapids: Zondervan Publishing House, 1984.

"Principles, Permanence and Future Divine Judgment: A Case Study in Theological Method." *Journal of the Evangelical Theological Society* 28, 3 (1985): 317–25.

"Problem Areas Related to Biblical Inerrancy." *The Proceedings of the Conference on Biblical Inerrancy 1987.* Nashville: Broadman Press, 1987.

Relativism in Contemporary Ethics. Grand Rapids: Baker Book House, 1974.

"Revelation." *Foundations for Biblical Interpretation: A Complete Library of Tools and Resources.* Edited by David S. Dockery, Kenneth A. Matthews, and Robert B. Sloan. Nashville: Broadman & Holman, 1994.

Salvation: God's Amazing Plan. Wheaton, Ill.: Harvest Publications, 1987.

"Separation." *Evangelical Dictionary of Theology.* Edited by Walter A. Elwell. Grand Rapids: Baker Book House, 1984.

"The State of the Question." *Through No Fault of Their Own.* Edited by William Crockett and James Sigountos. Grand Rapids: Baker Book House, 1990.

"Theories of Atonement in America." *Dictionary of Christianity in America.* Edited by Daniel Reid and others. Downers Grove, Ill.: InterVarsity Press, 1990.

Where Is Theology Going? Issues and Perspectives on the Future of Theology. Grand Rapids: Baker Book House, 1994.

The Word Became Flesh: A Contemporary Incarnational Christology. Grand Rapids: Baker Book House, 1991.

Works about Erickson

Dockery, David S. "Millard J. Erickson." *Baptist Theologians.* Edited by Timothy George and David S. Dockery. Nashville: Broadman Press, 1990.

Dockery, David S., ed. *New Dimensions in Evangelical Thought: Essays in Honor of Millard J. Erickson.* Downers Grove: InterVarsity Press, 1998.

Hustad, L. Arnold. "Bibliographic Essay on the Works of Millard J. Erickson." *New Dimensions in Evangelical Thought: Essays in Honor of Millard J. Erickson*. Downers Grove: InterVarsity Press, 1998.

_____. "Millard J. Erickson." *Handbook of Evangelical Theologians*. Edited by Walter A. Elwell. Grand Rapids: Baker Book House, 1993.

Keylock, Leslie R. "Evangelical Leaders You Should Know: Meet Millard J. Erickson." *Moody Monthly* 87, 10 (1987): 71–73.

White, James Emery. *What Is Truth? A Comparative Study of the Positions of Cornelius Van Til, Francis Schaeffer, Carl F. H. Henry, Donald Bloesch, Millard Erickson*. Nashville: Broadman & Holman, 1994.

18

Looking Back, Looking Ahead

By David S. Dockery

FROM THE BEGINNING BAPTISTS HAVE BEEN A VARIED GROUP WITH A COMPLEX history and no single theological tradition. In this volume we have attempted to provide representatives from a variety of spheres of Baptist life as well as theologians who practiced their art from different perspectives. Yet we have not been able to include many influential thinkers in the preceding chapters. The purpose of this final chapter is, in brief overview fashion, to survey aspects of Baptist theology by looking back as well as looking briefly to the present and the future. As is true for the previous chapters, this concluding chapter will focus primarily on Southern Baptist theology and theologians.

The Beginnings of Baptist Theology

Baptist theology, in common with Baptist churches, can be traced to two common English sources. From English Separatism arose General Baptists who sought asylum in the Netherlands around 1608–1609. One portion of this group, led by John Robinson (1572–1625), became famous as the "Pilgrim Church" that migrated to Plymouth, Massachusetts, in 1620. The other contingent, under the direction of John Smyth (d. 1612), was exiled in Amsterdam. They rejected infant baptism and began *de novo* believer's baptism by affusion. Smyth continued to study the Scriptures and offered new positions on church government and worship, in addition to baptism. These matters were outlined in his major works: *Principles and Inferences Concerning the Visible Church* (1607) and *The Character of the Beast* (1609).[1]

The General Baptist theology was essentially Arminian in soteriological matters, stressing a universal or general atonement, thus the name General

338

Baptists. Smyth's congregation included an independent thinker named Thomas Helwys (1570–1615), who was baptized by Smyth. Smyth attempted to unite the small band of followers with a Mennonite community, but Helwys and other leaders disagreed. Helwys, together with a small contingent, shortly returned to England and organized the first Baptist congregation on English soil at Spitalfields near London in 1612. He eloquently defended the case for religious liberty in his work, *The Mystery of Iniquity* (1612).[2]

In addition to General Baptists, there were also Particular Baptists, influenced by streams of Calvinism. Particular Baptists adhered to a particular understanding of the atonement and originated in Henry Jacob's Independent Church. In 1638, several members from the congregation following the leadership of John Spilsbury, formed the first Particular Baptist church. Over the next few decades this group grew rapidly.[3] They carefully articulated a Calvinistic theology in the First London Confession (1644). A distinctive feature of the Confession called for baptism by single immersion. Soon General Baptists also adopted immersion.[4]

Similar paths were chartered in America, where in 1639, a year after Spilsbury formed the church in London, a Baptist congregation was started at Providence, Rhode Island, by Roger Williams (1603–84). Actually, Williams was only a Baptist for a short time. Yet, due to the assessment of Williams in Isaac Backus's early history of Baptists, Williams's influence as a Baptist and pioneer in the arena of religious liberty looms large. Williams affirmed Baptist positions on Scripture and baptism, at least for a short period, and blazed the trail for the Baptist position on religious liberty with his masterful work, *The Bloody Tenet of Persecution* (1644).[5] Between 1641 and 1646, a more stable Baptist community was established at Newport, Rhode Island, by John Clarke (1609–76). His work, *Ill Newes from New England* (1652), secured the representation of Baptist views in the Charter of Rhode Island (1663), which paved the way for similar expositions in the following century for the colonies.

Back in England, following the Cromwell regime, new confessions of faith were adopted. The Second London Confession (1677), an altered form of the Westminster Confession of Faith, put forth a consistent Calvinistic position, with Baptist views of the Lord's Supper, baptism, and church polity. This statement has served as one of the most influential shaping documents for Baptist theology. The impact of this statement on the Philadelphia and Charleston associations indicates the significance of the confession. In other Baptist circles, the Orthodox Creed (1678) mediated Arminian and Calvinistic positions among General Baptists.[6]

Eighteenth-Century Baptist Theology

The next century saw two negative developments. General Baptists suffered from a deadening Socianianism, and Particular Baptists tended toward a rationalistic hyper-Calvinism.[7] The instrumental leader in the renewal of English General Baptist theology was Dan Taylor (1738–1816) of Yorkshire. In the days of his youth, Taylor was involved in the Wesleyan movement. Later he rejected Wesley's system of discipline and discovered a home among the General Baptists of Halifax. In 1770, Taylor called a special meeting of sympathetic General Baptists from the Midlands and laid the foundation for the New Connection of General Baptists. Central to Taylor's theology was a high Christology, believer's baptism, Arminian soteriology, coupled with evangelistic zeal. He wrote more than forty books or tracts in his development of these themes. Among the most important of his writings were *Fundamentals of Religion in Faith and Practice* (1775) and *The Truth and Inspiration of the Scriptures* (1790). At a time in Baptist history when both General and Particular Baptists faced spiritual and theological decline, Taylor's leadership brought renewal and paved the way for the establishment of the Baptist Union in 1813.[8]

In America great growth took place during the years surrounding the American Revolution. Much of the growth was a by-product of the Great Awakening. The earliest system of Baptist theology in this country was primarily Calvinistic as evidenced in the Philadelphia Confession (1742). Moderating influences developed by the turn of the century, as can be observed in the New Hampshire Confession (1833).

Important contributions arose from a variety of sectors of Baptist life during the period at the end of the eighteenth and the beginning of the nineteenth centuries. Numbered among these were George Leile (ca. 1750–1800), Thomas Baldwin (1753–1825), and William Carey (1761–1834). Leile, the son of Virginia slaves, was baptized in 1773 and was given his freedom by his master in order to employ his several talents and spiritual gifts. He gathered together a group of believers near the Savannah River to begin the first Black Baptist church in America. He became the first Baptist missionary and served in Jamaica, predating Carey's mission by a decade. He reportedly baptized more than five hundred converts in 1791. His ministry significantly advanced the case for the abolition of slavery.[9]

Thomas Baldwin, one of the leading lights among New England Baptists during this time, served as a pastor in Boston and as editor of the *Massachusetts Baptist Missionary Magazine* (1803–24). His theologizing and apologetic work greatly advanced Baptist causes. Among his most important works were *Open Communion Examined* (1789), *Christian Baptism, as Delivered to the Churches* (1812), and *Catechism or Compendium of Christian Doctrine and Practice* (1816).[10]

William Carey led the development of the missionary movement at this time. Built on the theology of Andrew Fuller, this movement maintained a Calvinistic view of theology, including a particular view of the atonement, which was combined with a universal invitation to respond to the gospel message. This combination resulted in a new Baptist missionary theology and the advancement of the world missionary movement. The missionary movement continued through the efforts of Luther Rice (1783–1836) and Adoniram Judson (1788–1850). Rice, a great visionary and administrator, served in India with Judson, and later became a great Baptist statesman.[11] As Baptists moved into the nineteenth century, significant gains were made in the renewal and shape of Baptist theology.

Nineteenth-Century Baptist Theology

Numerous important works were penned during the nineteenth century as Baptist theology matured and developed. John Leland (1754–1841) adeptly defended baptism by immersion, both historically and biblically. He regularly concluded preaching services with an invitation to be baptized. But it was religious liberty that dominated Leland's concerns and contributions.[12] These voluminous writings can be found in *The Writings of John Leland*, edited by L. F. Greene (1845).

Two shining stars during the first half of the nineteenth century were Jesse Mercer (1769–1841) and W. B. Johnson (1782–1862). Mercer, who achieved as pastor, educator, and administrator, was driven by the twofold desire to establish Baptist educational institutions and his prayer for God-sent revival. His major writing contribution, however, was his *History of the Georgia Baptist Association* (1838). Johnson, a Calvinist like Mercer, advanced numerous Baptist causes in the South. His lasting legacy can be found in his formative work on ecclesiology, *A Church of Christ with Her Officers, Laws, Duties, and Form of Government* (1844).

Francis Wayland (1796–1865) ranked as the premier intellect of his day. A pastor in Boston and Providence, he also taught theology at Andover Seminary, Union College, and Brown University. Like Johnson, his major contributions were in the area of ecclesiology, primarily his defense of autonomous congregations in *Notes on the Principles and Practices of Baptist Churches* (1856).

In the middle of the nineteenth century, Landmark theology sprang forth in the South through the controversial James Robinson Graves (1820–93). As editor of *The Tennessee Baptist* for more than forty years, he strategically used the power of the press to advance his unique theological positions. Much of his work was strongly opposed by R. B. C. Howell (1801–68), who had preceded him as editor of the paper and who like Graves had an important influence in shaping the early years of Union

University, the oldest academic institution related to Southern Baptist life.[13] Graves defended the autonomy of the local church and the purity of the church based on an unbroken succession of believer's baptism. He articulated his theology in *Old Landmarkism: What Is It?* (1880). Graves also introduced dispensational theology into Baptist life in his *The Work of Christ in the Covenant of Redemption: Developed in Seven Dispensations* (1883). Graves's ongoing impact on Baptist theology has far surpassed his influence during his life.

Other theologians and shapers of Baptist life who helped form Baptist thought in the nineteenth century are numerous. John Newton Brown (1803–68) contributed a major work on the church titled *The Baptist Church Manual* (1853), which included what has become a standard church covenant for many churches. Richard Fuller (1804–76), who was trained as a lawyer, provided Baptists with a powerful theology of atonement called *The Power of the Cross* (1851). Though a popular preacher to the slave community, he nevertheless has been remembered for his defense of slavery. These wrongheaded views can be found in *Domestic Slavery Considered as a Scriptural Institution* (1845).

The foremost theologian of the day was Alvah Hovey (1820–1903), who served as professor and president of Newton Theological Institute. Strongly influenced by nineteenth-century Evangelicalism, he set forth a high view of biblical inspiration. His Christology was grounded in the norms established by the early church creeds. He provided his generation with a *Manual of Systematic Theology and Christian Ethics* (1877). Also he served as editor of the *American Commentary* series. Another Baptist leader who was both influenced by, as well as a part of, the broad evangelicalism of this time was Adoniram Judson Gordon (1836–95). Primarily he served as a pastor but also as president of the Boston Missionary Training School (later renamed Gordon College). His theological contributions came from his studies and teachings in pneumatology, exemplified in *The Holy Spirit in Missions* (1893).

The Early Years of Southern Baptist Theology

Since 1845, there have doubtless been hundreds of professors and pastors who have influenced the shape of Southern Baptist theology through their lectures, writings, and sermons. Yet for the purposes of this volume, we will focus primarily on major theologians, denominational leaders, and writing pastors, though the influence of popular evangelists, pastors, teachers, and hymn writers has been more formative for shaping Southern Baptists thinking than most of us realize. Let us examine the current variety in Southern Baptist life in light of our more than 150-year tradition.

The first one hundred years were largely shaped by three major theologians: James P. Boyce (1827–88), E. Y. Mullins (1860–1922), and W. T. Conner (1877–1952).[14] From the early years of Boyce to the death of Conner, Southern Baptists witnessed the diminishing influence of Calvinism, the decline of postmillennialism, the rise of revivalism, and an advancement in the understanding of Baptist origins and identity. Also there was during this time the basic introduction into SBC life of such matters as historical criticism, theistic evolution, and experiential apologetics. We could say that Southern Baptist theology moved from a hermeneutic of divine sovereignty with John L. Dagg, J. P. Boyce, and Basil Manly to one of personal revelation and experience with Mullins, and to a lesser degree with Conner. From these changes a growing consensus emerged around the moderate Calvinistic theologies of Mullins and Conner, with additional programmatic, pragmatic, and revivalistic emphases. Shaped by these shifts and concerns, Southern Baptists navigated their way through the first century of their existence.

John L. Dagg

Prior to the establishment of The Southern Baptist Theological Seminary in 1859, Mercer University was a well-known Baptist school with an established department of theology. J. L. Dagg (1794–1884) served as president and professor of theology at Mercer from 1844–1854. During his lifetime Dagg was the most prominent theologian among Southern Baptists. Among his many works was included an article on the "Origin and Authority of the Bible," which was penned in 1853 and was also included in *A Manual of Theology* (1858).[15]

Dagg both led the way for Southern Baptists and mirrored them in almost all areas of theology, including the doctrine of Scripture. His theological contributions were largely isolated from European thinkers of his day, who discussed the nature of revelation in great detail. Dagg did not enter that dialogue. He was quite content with his understanding that the Bible was to be understood as divine revelation.

In his *Manual of Theology,* he explained: "We shall here assume that the Bible is a revelation from God."[16] For Dagg, revelation is information about the Christian religion. He continued, saying: "To us in these last days God speaks in his written word, the Bible, which is the perfect source of religious knowledge and the infallible standard of religious truth."[17]

James P. Boyce and Basil Manly Jr.

James P. Boyce (1827–88) and Basil Manly Jr. (1825–92) formed half of the original faculty of The Southern Baptist Theological Seminary when it opened in 1859. Boyce previously taught at Furman University and Manly was principal of the Female Institute of Richmond, Virginia. Both were equally adept at administrative work, as well as teaching theology. While each made important contributions in several areas, Boyce's major work was his *Abstract of Systematic Theology* (1887) and Manly's primary effort was his *The Bible Doctrine of Inspiration* (1888). Both volumes were the results of their class lectures. The issue of inspiration was not dealt with in detail in Boyce's theology class, because that subject was dealt with in Manly's course on "Biblical Introduction." It is not beyond reason to conclude that Manly's work on Scripture is reflective of Boyce's position on this subject.

Manly's landmark volume was published as a response to the resignation of Old Testament professor, C. H. Toy. Though Manly was an original member of the faculty, he had departed in 1871 to become president of Georgetown College. The fact that he returned following the Toy controversy again confirms Boyce's confidence in Manly's position on the subject of biblical inspiration.

The key to understanding the thought of Boyce and Manly is to recognize their common opposition and response to the work of Toy. Both Boyce and Manly disagreed with Toy's doctrine of Scripture and its practical implications.

Both men built their understanding of Scripture on the work of their Princeton mentors, as well as Alvah Hovey and J. L. Dagg, all of whom affirmed the inspiration and inerrancy of Holy Scripture. J. P. Boyce affirmed the Bible as "infallible."[18] Infallibility for Boyce meant "without error," and nothing in his writings would imply that he distinguished between infallibility and inerrancy.

The most important and informative work on the inspiration and authority of Scripture among Baptists in the nineteenth century was certainly Basil Manly's *The Bible Doctrine of Inspiration* (1888). Manly argued that an uninspired Bible would furnish no infallible standard of thought, no authoritative rule for obedience, and no ground for confidence and everlasting hope.[19] It is important to note the inseparable relationship between inspiration, infallibility, and authority in Manly's work (which diminishes any importance in the change of wording between the term *infallible* in the Second London Confession and the word *authoritative* in the Abstract of Principles). Manly was careful to distinguish inspiration from revelation, which he defined as "that direct divine influence that secures the accurate transference of truth into human language by a speaker or writer, so as to be communicated to another."[20]

While affirming plenary inspiration, Manly carefully refuted any theory of mechanical dictation, because it ignored genuine human authorship. He maintained that every aspect of Scripture is characterized as infallible truth and divine authority. Manly believed that infallibility was the corollary of inspiration. Manly, like Boyce, took seriously the human authorship of the Bible, as well as its divine origin, and balanced this tension more effectively than Dagg while contending for the complete truthfulness of Holy Scripture. Perhaps with less scholarly erudition, but with equally persuasive power, B. H. Carroll (1843–1914) sounded similar concerns in the Southwest.

While Dagg, Boyce, and Manly clearly stand as giants among Southern Baptists, it is impossible to measure how vast and enormous has been the influence of B. H. Carroll on the life and thought of Southern Baptists. Carroll, perhaps more than any other Baptist leader, has served as a model and resource for hundreds of Southern Baptist pastors. Much of the motivation for change in the Southern Baptist Convention over the past two decades reflects Carroll's beliefs that churches, schools, and evangelistic/mission agendas rise or fall according to one's understanding of biblical inspiration.

Moving Toward the Twentieth Century

As the nineteenth century drew to a close, British Baptists found themselves in the midst of a widespread controversy known as the Downgrade Controversy. The struggle involved two leading figures, John Clifford and C. H. Spurgeon. Clifford (1836–1923) advocated forms of biblical criticism and a theological-scientific synergism that was viscously rejected by Spurgeon's supernaturalism. Spurgeon withdrew from the Baptist Union in 1887, and Clifford continued as England's foremost statesman. Not only in the Baptist Union did Clifford exert strategic leadership but also in the Baptist World Alliance at the turn of the century. The issues debated during the Downgrade Controversy set the agenda for ongoing controversies on both sides of the Atlantic in the twentieth century.

During the nineteenth century the consistent Calvinism of the Philadelphia Confession was modified by the growing influence of the more lenient Calvinism of the New Hampshire Confession (1833). In turn, the New Hampshire statement became foundational for the 1925 and 1963 Baptist Faith and Message statements. Such modifications, resulting reactions, and continued diversity have characterized Baptist theology in the twentieth century.

Baptists were not exempt from the inroads of liberalism, as previously indicated and foreshadowed by the Downgrade Controversy. Leading exponents of the liberal trends included: William Newton Clarke (1841–1911), Shailer Mathews (1836–1941), and Harry Emerson Fosdick (1878–1969). A social gospel theology was explicated by Walter Rauschenbusch and a mediating theology, influenced by personal idealism, was brilliantly expounded by A. H. Strong.

Clarke, for almost three decades, taught New Testament and theology at Toronto Baptist Seminary and Colgate Theological Seminary. His many impressive works include *The Use of the Scriptures in Theology* (1905), *Sixty Years with the Bible* (1909), and his classic contribution, *An Outline of Christian Theology* (1909). Clarke developed a semiexistential methodology that centered on Jesus' life and teachings as the revelation of God and the interpreter of human experiences.

Like Clarke, Shailer Mathews inherited a most impressive Baptist heritage. After studying at Newton Theological Institute, Mathews taught briefly at Colby College before beginning his distinguished career at the University of Chicago Divinity School. More than any other twentieth-century Baptist, Mathews embodied liberal ideology. Shaped by German critical approaches to biblical and theological studies, by evolutionary understandings of religious history, and by a basic commitment to a social gospel, Mathews boldly defended modernism. His works on *The Social Teaching of Jesus* (1897) and *The Faith of a Modernist* (1924) expressed Christianity primarily in terms of human need and human freedom. His salient insights challenged traditional theological constructions and established the theological agenda for Baptists in the early years of the twentieth century.

The popular preacher who brought the thought of Clarke and Mathews to a wider audience was the pulpit giant, Harry Emerson Fosdick. Fosdick was a scholar who, at various intervals, taught at Union Theological Seminary for four decades while pastoring three churches in the New York City area. The peak of his popularity came while he served as the eloquent pastor of the Park Avenue Baptist Church (renamed Riverside Church). His challenge to traditional Christianity came in a 1922 sermon, "Shall the Fundamentalists Win?" He popularized liberal Baptist theology in his considerable writings. His thought can be observed in his two most famous works, *Christianity and Progress* (1922) and *The Modern Use of the Bible* (1924).[21]

Reaction to modernist thought came from Baptist fundamentalists especially William Bell Riley (1861–1947), John Franklyn Norris (1877–1952), T. T. Shields (1873–1955), and John R. Rice (1895–1980). By 1926, those who were militant for the fundamentals had failed to expel the modernists from Baptist conventions. They had, for the most part, lost the battles against evolution and historical criticism. The northern fundamentalists created new denominations in order to seek purity apart from the larger bodies they deemed apostate. They formed the General Association of Regular Baptist Churches, the Conservative Baptist Association of America, and the Baptist Bible Fellowship International.[22]

J. Frank Norris carried the banner as the most controversial and sensational of the fundamentalist leaders. Norris studied with B. H. Carroll at

Baylor University and then ambitiously set out to preach regularly at the greatest pulpit in the world. Simultaneously he pastored churches in Fort Worth, Texas, and Detroit, Michigan (1935–52). His primary vehicle of influence and the voice for his fundamentalist theology came through the editorship of *The Fundamentalist* (1909–52). He loathed evolutionary thought and the social gospel. Norris also raised premillennialism to the level of an essential theological belief. He maintained that theology, in all aspects, must be constructed from a literal hermeneutic. His work, *The Gospel of Dynamite* (1933), stressed a theological literalism that included a literal Christ, a literal salvation, a literal hell, and a literal heaven.[23]

T. T. Shields, editor of *The Gospel Witness* (1922–55) and president of Toronto Baptist Seminary (1927–55), joined with Riley and Norris to form the Baptist Bible Union of North America in 1923 and served as the first president of the BBU. A fourth major figure, John R. Rice, helped form the Southwide Baptist Fellowship. Raised a Southern Baptist, a close colleague with J. Frank Norris, Rice founded the *Sword of the Lord* in 1934. This publication became the most widely circulated and most important fundamentalist periodical in America. Through the *Sword of the Lord,* Rice exerted incredible influence, which has been demonstrated through the expanding fundamentalist phenomenon as well as the conservative resurgence that has taken place in the Southern Baptist Convention since 1979.

Two extremely important women who pioneered women's causes and shaped Baptist life and thought were Susan E. C. Griffin (1851–1926) and Helen Barrett Montgomery (1861–1934). Susan Griffin was the first woman to receive ordination among American Baptists (1893) when she and her husband were called as pastors of the Elmira Heights Baptist Church in Elmira Heights, New York. For a decade prior to this call, the couple had served as missionaries in India. A gifted linguist, speaker, and administrator, she effected the union of the women's societies of the Free Baptist General Conference and the Northern Baptist Convention. Montgomery was another key figure in the developing role of women in Baptist life. She prepared numerous Bible study aids, but her most esteemed accomplishment was her *Centenary Translation of the New Testament* (1924). She organized the initial World Day of Prayer. In 1920, in the midst of the Modernist-Fundamentalist controversy, she presided over the national meeting of the Northern Baptist Convention.

Two prominent Baptists who served in the middle of the twentieth century and achieved status in different academic fields were Harold Henry Rowley (1890–1969) and Kenneth Scott Latourette (1894–1968). Rowley, an Old Testament scholar, treated the theological significance of the Old Testament from several perspectives including redemption, election, and worship. He contended that the Bible, the Word of God, was both divine and human and yielded only to the ultimate authority of Jesus Christ, the living Word of God. These views were adequately articulated in *The Relevance of the Bible* (1942), *The Authority of the Bible* (1949), and *The Unity of the Bible* (1953). Rowley, along with H. Wheeler Robinson, advanced the discipline of Old Testament theology among Baptists. Primarily he accomplished this with *The Faith of Israel* (1956) and *The Biblical Doctrine of Election* (1950). He argued persuasively that the Old Testament should be rediscovered and communicated in terms of its abiding significance for the church and Christian theology.

Latourette, a first-class church historian, especially in the area of the history of missions, served as professor of missions at Yale University (1921–53). His most famous work, a seven-volume study of *The History of the Expansion of Christianity* (1937–45), is still a classic, setting high standards for forthcoming Baptist historians. Latourette was a member of the American Baptist Foreign Mission Society for two decades, president of the American Baptist Convention for one term, and an ordained Baptist minister.

Two prophetic preachers whose pulpit theology challenged a generation of Baptist people were Carlyle Marney (1916–78) and Martin Luther King Jr. (1929–68). Marney, born in Harriman, Tennessee, was a prominent Baptist pastor and theologian. He pastored churches in Paducah, Kentucky; Austin, Texas; and Charlotte, North Carolina. The last decade of his ministry shifted Marney's focus to broader ecumenical interests while he served as director of the Interpreter's House, a retreat center for ministers, at Lake Junaluska, North Carolina. His theology and ministry focused on ethical and social concerns. These themes are addressed in *The Structures of Prejudice* (1961), *The Recovery of the Person* (1963), *The Coming Faith* (1970), and *Priests to Each Other* (1974).[24]

Martin Luther King Jr., son of the patriarchal Baptist minister Martin Luther ("Daddy") King Sr., was the leading voice in the civil rights crusade of the 1960s and the foremost advocate of nonviolent strategies for addressing social problems. He pastored churches in Montgomery, Alabama, and Atlanta, Georgia, before being assassinated in Memphis, Tennessee, in 1968. His theology was informed by the writings of Mahatma Gandhi and Walter Rauschenbush. His Ph.D. dissertation focused on the theology of Paul Tillich. King founded the Southern Christian Leadership Conference in 1956, becoming the embodiment of its ideals. He worked with Gardner C. Taylor, a leading black pastor from Brooklyn, New York, to form the Progressive National Baptist Convention in 1961. In 1963, King was named the *Time* magazine Man of the Year. He received the Nobel Peace Prize in 1964, as well as more than three hundred other prestigious awards. The pastor was also a prolific writer. He wrote numerous articles and seven books. Among these, *Stride Toward Freedom* (1958) received the Ainsfield-

Wolf Award. No single Baptist leader has done more to advance economic justice and racial reconciliation.[25]

Southern Baptist Theology in the Twentieth Century

Twentieth-century Southern Baptist theology began with an important compendium of essays titled *Baptists: Why and Why Not,* edited by J. M. Frost in 1900.[26] The opening chapters by J. M. Frost, T. T. Eaton, and F. H. Kerfoot in *Baptists: Why and Why Not* expressed the consensus Baptist position on the Bible. Frost explained in the introduction that the foundation of all the articles in the book was the presupposition that the Bible is inerrant. Perhaps a quotation from Frost, the founding editor and first secretary of the Baptist Sunday School Board, is indicative of this theological consensus: "We accept the Scriptures as an all-sufficient and infallible rule of faith and practice, and insist upon the absolute inerrancy and sole authority of the Word of God."[27] *Baptists: Why and Why Not* set the agenda for the new century. Yet Southern Baptists' two most influential and shaping theologians of the twentieth century were E. Y. Mullins and W. T. Conner.

E. Y. Mullins

E. Y. Mullins (1860–1928) served as the fourth president and professor of theology at The Southern Baptist Theological Seminary from 1899 to 1928. Mullins represents a paradigmatic shift in Southern Baptist theology. Nowhere is this better illustrated than his volume on systematic theology entitled *The Christian Religion in Its Doctrinal Expression* (1917).[28] Not only was his book used as the major textbook at Southern and Southwestern seminaries for decades, but Mullins also powerfully influenced W. T. Conner, who served as professor of theology at Southwestern Seminary for thirty-nine years. Mullins's emphasis on the role of experience and his work on the relationship between science and Scripture paved the way for a new generation of Baptists to raise new questions about the nature and interpretation of Scripture.

Mullins remained very much in the mainstream of conservative Baptist thought during his decades of leadership, while nevertheless engaging wide intellectual interests and contemporary theological formulations. This conservatism became increasingly apparent during his latter years and is especially evident in his handling of the "Fundamentalist-Modernist" debates in the early twentieth century. The release of his final major publication, *Christianity at the Crossroads* (1924),[29] testifies to this shift of emphasis in Mullins's work. E. Y. Mullins moved in a different direction from Boyce, Manly, A. T. Robertson, and the early work of John Sampey (Sampey in his later years seemed to be more willing to embrace the findings of historical criticism and less sure about traditional views of inspiration—at least according to an interpretation offered by W. O. Carver in his oral history of Southern Seminary commissioned by Duke K. McCall).[30] This means that Mullins's ministry, though representing diversity within unity, nevertheless continued the united consensus regarding Scripture that existed in the Southern Baptist Convention during its first seventy-five years.

Mullins's shift may have been more a shift of methodology and context than of content. He was hesitant to equate the Bible with revelation, at least as it has been stated by Manly and Carroll before him. For Mullins, the primary characteristic of the Bible was its authority, not its inspiration or inerrancy. A major shift for Mullins was his insistence that the authority of the Bible was limited to the religious life of the Christian believer, seemingly overemphasizing the characteristic affirmation regarding the Bible's authority in "faith and practice."

Mullins followed A. H. Strong in his affirmation of a dynamic model of inspiration rather than a plenary verbal one, though he quickly commended the plenary view's intent to "preserve and maintain the authority of Scripture as the very Word of God." Mullins argued that the difference between the two approaches was more one of method than of content relating to the Bible. Even though Mullins shifted his methodological understanding of Scripture, he nevertheless emphasized the truthfulness of the Bible. His description of the dynamic theory of inspiration included the affirmation "that men were enabled to declare truth unmixed with error." He rejected any charge of contradictions in the Bible, claiming that Holy Scripture cannot dispute what it is not intended to affirm. The most important shift in the thinking of E. Y. Mullins was his emphasis on experience, which represents both the best of pietism and the experiential emphasis of F. D. E. Schleiermacher. Mullins defended the Bible on the basis of Christian experience both as to what was recorded in Scripture and also what was confirmed by other believers throughout the centuries.

E. Y. Mullins pioneered new ways to theologize in Southern Baptist life, though in essence he seems to restate, in different ways, traditional Southern Baptist tenets. He contended that the Bible is a fully reliable and authoritative guide. Nowhere is his traditional emphases better seen than in his 1923 address to the Southern Baptist Convention on "The Dangers and Duties of This Present Hour," where he concluded that the Bible is "God's revelation of himself and is the sufficient and authoritative guide" for all life.

W. T. Conner

W. T. Conner (1877–1952) carried out the role at Southwestern Seminary which had been played by E. Y. Mullins at Southern Seminary. Conner began his career at Southwestern Seminary in 1910 as professor of theoretical theology. During his career he taught almost everything in the curriculum, but his interest rested primarily in New Testament and systematic theology. Conner's contribution to the matter of biblical interpretation and authority is found in his discussions of the broader subject of revelation contained in his writings on *Revelation and God* (1936)[31] and *Christian Doctrine* (1937).[32] Conner's theology represented a conflation of his mentors: Calvin Goodspeed, B. H. Carroll, A. H. Strong, and E. Y. Mullins. During his tenure, the influence of Carroll waned, and that of Mullins increased; though both shaped his personal theological synthesis.

Conner wrote little on the issue of inspiration. He seemed to have followed Mullins's lead on many of the matters related to the Bible, though unlike Mullins, he did not technically affirm a particular view of the inspiration of the Bible. At this point he followed Carroll's silence. The bottom line for Conner was the authoritative character of Scripture as expressed in his 1918 article in a Southwestern Seminary publication on "The Nature and Authority of the Bible." He maintained: "The only way to realize true freedom is by submission to rightful authority. The Bible then is the medium through which God's authority is made known." Conner unhesitatingly affirmed the fact of the Bible's inspiration and was careful to allow for human agency. In his writing on *Christian Doctrine*, he rightly answered that the Bible is both a divine book and a human book. Conner's work did not discuss either inerrancy or infallibility. Though Conner could be considered a "functional inerrantist," he was less comfortable with the idea of inerrancy than even E. Y. Mullins had been. Yet W. T. Conner did not in any way want to affirm an inspiration only in a partial or limited sense. He did acknowledge that biblical authority is reserved for the spiritual dimensions of life. Conner was ultimately concerned with the function of Scripture in leading men and women toward freedom in Christ.

Conner was open-minded on the relationship of science and the Bible. Yet he adamantly rejected evolution, maintaining that it leaves out God and maintains that without God's creative power or guidance the universe came uncaused out of nothing and has kept on evolving until it produced humanity. One of the first Southern Baptist leaders to endorse evolution was W. L. Poteat, professor and president at Wake Forest College. Poteat wrote widely on this topic, and his words received a strongly negative review from Conner in *The Southwestern Evangel* in May 1925.

While Conner relegated discussions regarding theories of inspiration to theological obscurity, he unhesitatingly confessed the Bible as the product of God's revelation, with redemption its central interest and Jesus Christ as its center and key to its unity. Though Conner would not affirm the term *inerrancy*,[33] he retreated from discussing any errors in the Bible, while emphasizing the Bible's divine origin and absolute authority in all matters spiritual.[34]

Denominational Leadership (1920–1952)

We can conclude this section on the first century of Southern Baptist thought on this subject by highlighting other important contributions to this subject. In a major work published by the Baptist Sunday School Board in 1922 entitled *Fundamentals of the Faith,* William B. Nowlin critiqued historical-critical approaches to the Bible and supported the Scriptures' own self-testimony to its complete inspiration.[35] New Testament scholar, H. E. Dana, defended the historical reliability of the Bible in a 1923 work called the *Authenticity of the Holy Scriptures.*

J. J. Reeve, a professor at Southwestern Seminary, who had previously embraced historical-critical methods and conclusions, contributed an article called "My Experience with Higher Criticism" for *The Fundamentals,* edited by R. A. Torrey and A. C. Dixon (1917).[36] Here he affirmed the absolute truthfulness of Scripture while critiquing the dangers of historical criticism.

The inerrancy of Scripture was popularized by the pulpit oratory of R. G. Lee, who in 1930 penned *The Word of God: Not Broken and Not Bound.*[37] O. C. S. Wallace in *What Baptists Believe* (1934) discussed the need of the Scriptures, the process of writing, and the purpose of the Scriptures.[38] In his conclusion he reaffirmed the 1925 Baptist Faith and Message terminology that the Bible is a "perfect treasure of heavenly instruction." The same year the Sunday School Board also published J. B. Weatherspoon's *The Book We Teach,* in which he maintained the Bible as a book of revelation and sure guidance that is not only a book of Christian faith but of Christian mission and education.[39]

In 1936, J. B. Tidwell, professor at Baylor University, authored *Thinking Straight About the Bible or Is the Bible the Word of God.*[40] In many ways Tidwell's work reflects the consensus viewpoint about the nature of Scripture for the first one hundred years of the SBC's existence, though he had more in common with B. H. Carroll and Basil Manly Jr. than W. T. Conner or E. Y. Mullins. Tidwell identified direct and indirect claims regarding the Bible's inspiration and absolute truthfulness. He then offered fourteen evidences for the complete veracity and divine origin of the Bible.

Yet it must be noted that the syncretistic position of W. O. Carver, the first Southern Seminary faculty member who did not study with J. P. Boyce, the latter positions of J. R. Sampey, and other Southern Baptist scholars, coupled with the openness not only to the new methodology of historical criticism, but in some cases to the conclusions of historical criticism as well, paved the way for shifts in the doctrine of biblical inspiration and authority that impacted theology in the post-World War II era. That being the case, nevertheless, we have seen that a strong consensus existed, represented by scholars, pastors, and denominational leaders. This diverse group affirmed with deep convictions the common heritage regarding the divine origin, the complete truthfulness, and the full authority of the Bible. The historic Southern Baptist position during the first century of its existence was primarily the commonly held conviction that the Bible is the inspired, written, reliable, and authoritative Word of God.

Southern Baptist Theology: Post–World War II

Two historic changes were initiated in the 1950s in Southern Baptist life. The first, and most important for our discussion, was the open practice of historical-critical studies in the curriculums of Baptist seminaries and colleges. The other more wide-ranging shift was the movement to a program-oriented approach to ministry. This shift brought about a generation of leaders committed to programmatic expansion. Nothing typifies this organizational and programmatic growth more than the "Million More in '54" campaign, which resulted in almost 750,000 new Sunday school members in Southern Baptist churches.

With this and other similar successful programs, a movement away from theological commitments to pragmatic ones consciously or unconsciously began to take place. I do not for one minute think it was a malicious attempt to undermine the orthodox theological consensus developed during the convention's first century. The pragmatic outlook was what was central for growing a successful denomination in the post-World War II era. Orthodoxy was understood in terms of "doing the right program" rather than articulating the right belief system. What resulted was not so much a heterodox people but an "a-theological" generation.

When controversies over the nature of Scripture entered the public arena in 1961, 1969, and 1979, the theological understanding necessary to examine and evaluate such issues was lacking.[41] Even men and women who never questioned the reliability of the biblical message or doubted the miraculous claims of the Bible were confused by terms like *inerrancy* and *infallibility*, which we have seen were widely employed in previous generations. The programmatic and pragmatic emphases of the 1950s help us understand how the paradigm shifted in the SBC from the early 1950s to the late 1970s.[42]

Yet even during the 1950s there were ongoing examples that were in basic continuity with the doctrinal affirmations of previous generations. Works such as those by W. R. White, "The Authoritative Criterion" in *Baptist Distinctives* (1950);[43] J. B. Lawrence, "The Word and Words of God" and "The Bible, Our Creed" in *Southern Baptist Home Missions* (1952, 1957),[44] and J. Clyde Turner, "That Wonderful Book" in *Things We Believe* (1956) indicate the ongoing commitments to the trustworthiness and authority of Scripture at this time.[45] Yet things were changing all around.

Theology in the post-Conner/Mullins era introduced an innovative and exciting time in a denomination coming of age. During this period Southern society began to take on a new shape. After World War II the New South started to emerge from its previous isolation. The agricultural economy and culture of the Old South gave way to urban and suburban structures. Populations grew and became more pluralistic, employment trends destabilized, and racial tension soared. Old South values were being visibly disturbed.

Southern Baptists struggled to deal with these challenges, as well as urbanization, growing denominational bureaucracies, territorial expansion, and new emphases in theology, which some identified as "liberal." New tensions were created. New questions were raised in this context. How were people to combine intellectual rigor with personal religious experience?[46] The mid-twentieth century in SBC academic life wrestled with this question, particularly focused on the rise of biblical criticism. The practitioners of this new art sought somehow to combine a form of biblical inspiration with biblical criticism, as publicly evidenced in the debates surrounding the publication of *The Message of Genesis* (1961), by Ralph Elliott, as well as the first volume of *The Broadman Bible Commentary* (1969).[47] Both of these works openly challenged the historical reliability of the Bible.

Many of the public issues dealt with historical matters of the Old Testament, but the influence of form criticism was beginning to be seen on the New Testament as well. Many of these struggles in particular dealt not only with the use of historical criticism but also with the place of Darwinism in the theological arena. Interestingly, E. Y. Mullins, almost a half century earlier, had opened the door, following James Orr and A. H. Strong, in acknowledging some form of theistic evolution. This issue became a major concern for two theological leaders in this period. Both Dale Moody (1915–91) and Eric Rust (1910–91), helped form a new theological paradigm. This paradigm had little use for traditional Calvinistic or popular dispensational systems of thought. Nowhere was the "arminianizing" of the SBC better exemplified than in the writings of Moody and Frank Stagg. Moody's concerns focused on issues of predestination and perseverance, ultimately rejecting both; while Stagg endeavored to redefine the meaning of the cross in terms other than vicarious or substitutionary atonement.[48]

Frank Stagg (1911–), in the eyes of many, was the leading and most influential Southern Baptist theologian during this period, having placed his stamp on two theological institutions: New Orleans Seminary (1945–64) and Southern Baptist Seminary (1964–77). Stagg's commentaries and books, including his major work *New Testament Theology*,[49] all reject the Calvinistic understanding of God's purposes in salvation. Stagg's understanding of the cross of Jesus Christ represents what could be called an exemplary theory of the atonement. For Stagg, the cross represents the revelation of the divine self-denial that was always at the heart of God and thus demands that humans find their authentic existence as God's creatures. In addition to his treatment of the cross, Stagg reinterpreted the concept of atonement, election, and predestination so as to stand diametrically opposed to Calvinism. The only thing God has predetermined, maintained Stagg, is that "whoever is in Christ will be saved."[50]

Though Moody and Stagg greatly influenced the academic theology of the Convention, two popular theological movements held sway in numerous pulpits across the Convention: the "deeper life movement" and "dispensationalism." These two movements merged to bring about unique approaches to the Christian life, eschatology, social ministries, and denominational affiliation. The legendary pastor of the First Baptist Church of Dallas, Texas, W. A. Criswell (1909–) personified this popular grassroots theology. As was to be proven during the decade of the eighties, this group's strength may not have been necessarily its vigorous theological reflection but its numerical predominance.

The SBC thus entered the second half of the twentieth century divided between the progressivism that characterized the moderate leadership in denominational agencies and seminaries and the popular traditionalism in the pulpits. As most major denominational leadership posts were claimed by the progressive or moderate wing of the Convention, the traditionalists or conservatives became defensive and separatistic, focusing on their local churches instead of on the denomination.

The conservatives tended to retreat to a position in opposition to a changing American culture. They saw the American culture of the sixties heading toward an age of insanity. Living in a time of presidential assassination, racial unrest, civil rights protests, rock-and-roll celebrations, "love-ins," "sit-ins," and Vietnam war protests, the traditionalists lambasted these crazy trends and found their own emphasis on a completely truthful Bible to be extremely useful for bringing sense out of this chaos. Nowhere was this better illustrated than in the classic volume by W. A. Criswell published while he was president of the Convention and entitled *Why I Preach That the Bible Is Literally True* (1969).[51] For it was the optimism among conservatives that the "truth" eventually would be victorious, after the craziness of that present age had passed, that spurred them onward. The way to protect the truth in the meantime was through a form of separatism, consistent with either their "deeper life" and/or "dispensational" theology, though they remained somewhat active in the denomination and generally faithful to denominational programs.[52]

The moderates, however, marched into the sixties and seventies seeking to avoid the negative reaction of the traditionalists and hoping to gain respect in the larger cultural context. Further changes in American culture in a post-Watergate and post-Vietnam era created an anti-authoritarian mood among progressives. Thus another shift away from earlier SBC theology can be seen in a movement away from authority. For as W. T. Conner maintained, "If God is not a God of authority, he is not God at all. If God does not reveal himself, religion is impossible. Therefore if God reveals himself to man, it must be in an authoritative way."[53] The new generation of progressive leadership was open to dialogue and interaction with other traditions, while evidencing a renewed concern for social responsibility; contemporary, existential, or reader-oriented hermeneutics; and the ecumenical nature of the church, while basically rejecting all forms of fundamentalism and seeking to embrace mainstream Protestantism, accompanied by the theme that "Baptist means freedom."[54]

During the decade of the seventies the progressive leadership of the denomination moved in directions that forged larger gaps between the moderates and the conservatives. However, two popular heroes, who were greatly admired by both groups, helped both groups to maintain some common ground with each other both within the Convention itself and in the larger sphere of American Christianity. One of these was Herschel Hobbs; the other was Billy Graham. Herschel H. Hobbs (1907–95)[55] has often been called "Mr. Southern Baptist." He preached for eighteen years on the *Baptist Hour,* was president of the Southern Baptist Convention from 1961 to 1963, and chaired the 1963 Committee of the Baptist Faith and Message. Hobbs held to a high view of biblical inspiration, while embracing the classical Arminian interpretation of the doctrine of God, so as to affirm complete divine knowledge of every free human choice, yet in such a way that the choices are not predetermined. In addition to his Arminian tendencies, Hobbs moved away from being a premillennialist without a program toward a thoroughgoing amillennialism. The Arminian and amillennialist position were welcomed by those espousing the progressive perspective.

On the other hand, Billy Graham (1918–),[56] the most well-known international evangelist of our time and a member of the First Baptist Church of Dallas, Texas, proclaimed his simple gospel message to thousands. This message was undergirded by the evangelist's commitment to a completely truthful Bible and augmented by a "deeper life" approach to the Christian life and an apocalyptic dispensational eschatology, both of which were widely accepted and repeated in thousands of churches throughout the SBC. The nation as a whole during this time of unsettling transition was looking for stability and authority. Many were ready to hear the Word of God announced with authority as demonstrated with Graham's now famous words, "the Bible says." Into this vacuum the traditionalists moved, appealing to a fully truthful and authoritative Bible and contending that this was the message needed to address these turbulent times. While the denomination seemingly appeared strong, healthy, and poised for "Bold Mission" endeavors, the conservatives charged that the moderate leadership had moved too far from the popular "orthodox" theology of the grass roots, people, and the heritage of Baptist giants of previous generations. Based on these concerns, the SBC entered the decade of the eighties a very diverse movement with a multifaceted history, faced with its own version of the "modernist-fundamentalist" controversy. Now we turn to these most recent developments.

Southern Baptist conservatives had raised concerns regarding the full truthfulness and trustworthiness of the Bible since the publication of *The Message of Genesis* by Ralph Elliott (1961) and the Broadman Bible Commentary (1969) and the widely circulated article by William Hull entitled "Shall We Call the Bible Infallible?"[57] Southern Baptist conservatives had tended to turn toward northern evangelicals to shape their theology. In particular Francis Schaeffer, Carl F. H. Henry, and J. I. Packer influenced a new generation of Southern Baptists. They also turned to W. A. Criswell's published sermons and his famous work, *Why I Preach That the Bible Is Literally True.*[58]

With the rise of historical criticism, new approaches to biblical interpretation and new ways of describing the Bible's nature were articulated.[59] Many progressives were no longer comfortable describing the Bible in the tradition of B. H. Carroll or Basil Manly. As a matter of fact, the doctrine of inerrancy was virtually absent in academic circles from the mid-twenties to the eighties, usually being relegated to obscurantist thought and falsely equated with a mechanical dictation view of understanding. But now conservatives were calling for a return to Manly's position, though now in a more sophisticated dress enabled by two decades of discussion regarding Scripture in the broader evangelical world, culminating in the Chicago Statements on Biblical Inerrancy (1978) and Biblical Interpretation (1982).[60]

During the seventies and eighties, a number of significant works were penned either challenging or upholding the inerrancy of Scripture. The most important work by conservatives during this time was *Baptists and the Bible* by Russ Bush and Tom Nettles, which attempted to show that biblical inerrancy had been a representative, if not dominant, view in the Baptist tradition.[61] The book met with mixed reviews and was countered by a series of essays edited by Rob James, entitled *The Unfettered Word,* which attempted to show that both the biblical position and historical interpretation in Baptist life differed from the Bush-Nettles proposal.[62]

Moderate Southern Baptists also turned to progressive Evangelicals from Fuller Seminary to help articulate their theological convictions in the 1980s. Some tried to differentiate between infallibility and inerrancy, accepting the former and rejecting the latter. A carefully worded article representing this position was written in the *Review and Expositor* in 1986 by Roy L. Honeycutt, entitled "Biblical Authority: A Treasured Baptist Heritage."[63] Here he rejected inerrancy, suggesting that it was not a position consistent with Baptist tradition, while claiming that the Bible was authoritative and binding in all matters of faith and practice. This reading of Baptist theology followed the proposal of Jack Rogers and Donald McKim in *The Authority and Interpretation of the Bible*.[64] Major theologies during this period by Morris Ashcraft,[65] Dale Moody,[66] and James Leo Garrett[67] tended to follow this distinction with varying degrees, with Moody and Garrett closely following the models of their predecessors Mullins and Conner.

For the next decade more heat than light was generated by both sides; though steadily the inerrancy position gained a hearing. Many thought inerrancy to be only a political position, but conservatives building on works of peripherally related or former Southern Baptists like Clark Pinnock's *A New Reformation and Biblical Revelation*[68] and Carl F. H. Henry's six-volume set, *God, Revelation and Authority*[69] pressed on to reestablish the doctrinal consensus of previous generations. Also very helpful was the three-volume work of Millard Erickson, *Christian Theology*.[70]

A Southern Baptist consensus had been reached by the 1990s, reflective of earlier Baptist theologians.[71] This consensus position affirms that revelation is both personal and propositional. While emphasizing propositional revelation, it notes that conservatives are careful to maintain that Scripture's literary diversity is more than a historic accident or decorative device; it is a vehicle for imaginative thought and creative expression about things difficult to grasp. Commands, promises, parables, analogy, metaphor, symbol, and poetry cannot be forced into propositional form without loss. This recognition of literary diversity brings a healthy realization of the human aspect in Scripture, thus balancing the divine-human authorship of the Bible.

This position also maintains that the Bible attests to its own inspiration, which can be characterized as plenary and concursive. While affirming verbal inspiration, there is an awareness of contemporary linguistic theory that suggests that meaning is at the sentence level and beyond.

Based on a plenary view on inspiration of Scripture, this view maintains the inerrancy of Scripture and stresses that what the Bible affirms is completely true. Such a position attempts to be sensitive to the diversity and development in the Bible, recognizing different literary genres while seeking to determine the original meaning of Scripture. Harmonization is accepted as a legitimate means of handling the diversity in the biblical text but not at the expense of running roughshod over the context and forcing the Bible to say what it does not say. Because the Bible is a divine-human book, the interpretive tools of literary and historical criticism can be employed with care and faith-oriented presuppositions.

Recent Developments

Systematic theology has seen major renewal in the closing years of the twentieth century. In addition to Millard Erickson, Wayne Grudem and Stan Grenz have penned major works on theology. Grudem follows a Reformed Baptist perspective. Grenz's work is characterized by an openness to narrative theology as he seeks to interact with postmodern issues. Among Southern Baptists pride of place must go to James Leo Garrett Jr. He has taught at Southwestern Seminary, Southern Seminary, and Baylor University. Garrett is well-known for his work on W. T. Conner, ecclesiology, evangelicalism, and the Believers' Church movement. An accomplished historian and theologian, Garrett's two-volume work, *Systematic Theology*, will surely be a standard for years to come. James McClendon has written a multivolume narrative theology from a baptistic perspective. Other multivolume sets include Bruce Demarest and Gordon Lewis, *Integrative Theology*.

Philosophical theology has been greatly enhanced by the prolific production of John Newport, longtime professor of theology and philosophy at Southwestern Seminary. Among dozens of books, his crowning achievements are *Life's Ultimate Questions* (1989) and *The New Age Movement and the Biblical Worldview* (1998). Aesthetic theology, a developing field of theology within Baptist circles, has been pioneered by William Hendricks. Hendricks, a brilliant and creative mind who has taught at Golden Gate Seminary, Southwestern Seminary, and Southern Baptist Seminary, has broken new ground in the field of theology and the arts. Hendricks's creativity has been demonstrated in his *A Theology for Children* and *A Theology for Aging*. Two biblical theologians, Wayne E. Ward and E. Earle Ellis, have attained international acclaim for their work in New Testament theology. Ward, an eclectic thinker, has popularized biblical theology with his dynamic pulpit presence. Ellis, a front-rank Evangelical scholar, has authored numerous articles and commentaries, in addition to his outstanding volume on Pauline theology.

Future Agendas

A paradigm shift has taken place among Southern Baptists regarding the doctrine of Scripture, a shift demonstrating considerable continuity with the views that Boyce, Manly, and Carroll maintained in the early years of the SBC, though reflecting distance and discontinuity from the progressive positions adopted and advocated in the 1960s and 1970s. While there are several nuanced approaches to Scripture in the SBC, which we have discussed in several other places, generally it can be observed that the majority of Southern Baptists believe the Bible is God's truthful, written Word. Likewise, they believe it can and should be trusted in all matters. Scriptural authority has now been heartily affirmed, but it must continue to be carefully clarified since the issue is still often misunderstood and misrepresented by progressives, moderates, and even many traditionalists as well.

In coming days discussions will continue regarding the doctrine of God, the doctrine of the church, and worship styles.[72] Southern Baptists have differed over the question of divine sovereignty, election, and the place of human response in salvation.[73] The last decade has seen a renewed emphasis in Calvinistic thinking. This emphasis is likely to continue and perhaps expand in the twenty-first century. Theology in the coming century must become more sensitive to and interactive with global and intercultural concerns.

New insights, groundbreaking works, and the art and practice of contextualizing theology are taking place in Africa, Asia, parts of Europe, and the Third World. The development of these important contributions will help assure that our theologizing is focused on missiological and ecclesiological concerns. We have learned that theologians are not free to think anything, go anywhere, or be anything we like. Future directions must be grounded in Scripture, connected to the church, in touch with missiological issues, and shaped by a doxological emphasis focused on the glory of God.[74]

Theological education must not lose touch with the churches. Baptist theologians must work hard to bring the church and academy together again as colaborers for the cause of Christ. Baptist theologians can help churches enable and educate leaders and enhance worship to bring about spiritual renewal in the church and in our world. Christ-followers, as a result, can grow in obedience to the command of our Lord, who has commissioned the church to evangelize, disciple, baptize, and teach. The same Lord who two thousand years ago commissioned us still calls us to teach and equip his people for service and move them to maturity and unity.

Hopefully, this volume will help us all to realize the multifaceted nature of Baptist theology and will enable us to recover the best from the past history of Baptist theologians. Building on this foundation, we can work to unlock the potential for creative and edifying theological work among Baptists in years ahead.

Notes

Chapter 1, "The Future of Baptist Theology," by Timothy George

1. Will D. Campbell, *The Glad River* (New York: Holt, Rinehart and Winston, 1982), 107.

2. Timothy George and David S. Dockery, eds., *Baptist Theologians* (Nashville: Broadman Press, 1990), 13.

3. William L. Lumpkin, ed., *Baptist Confessions of Faith* (Valley Forge: Judson Press, 1959), 244.

4. Michael Watts, *The Dissenters* (Oxford: Clarendon Press, 1978), 83.

5. Henry Sacheverell, *The Perils of False Brethren* (London, 1709), 36.

6. David Benedict, *Fifty Years Among the Baptists* (New York: Sheldon and Co., 1860), 93–94.

7. Francis Wayland, *The Principles and Practices of Baptist Churches* (London: J. Heaton and Son, 1861), 15–16.

8. See George H. Shiver, ed., *American Religious Heretics* (Nashville: Abingdon, 1966), 56–88.

9. James M. Frost, ed., *Baptist Why and Why Not* (Nashville: Sunday School Board, 1900).

10. See the classic statement by James P. Boyce in his "Three Changes in Theological Institutions," in Timothy George, ed., *James Petigru Boyce: Selected Writings* (Nashville: Broadman Press, 1989), 48–59.

11. Thus by the end of his life in 1921 A. H. Strong, a moderate throughout his career, had sided with the Fundamentalists in their dispute with Modernism. Lamenting "some common theological trends of our time," Strong warned: "Under the influence of Ritschl and his Kantian relativism, many of our teachers and preachers have swung off into a practical denial of Christ's deity and of His atonement. We seem upon the verge of a second Unitarian defection, that will break up churches and compel secessions, in a worse manner than did that of Channing and Ware a century ago. American Christianity recovered from that disaster only by vigorously asserting the authority of Christ and the inspiration of the Scriptures. . . . Without a revival of this faith our churches will become secularized, mission enterprise will die out, and the candlestick will be removed out of its place as it was with the seven churches of Asia, and as it has been with the apostate churches of New England." *Systematic Theology* (Valley Forge, Pa.: Judson Press, 1907), ix.

12. H. Leon McBeth, *The Baptist Heritage* (Nashville: Broadman Press, 1987), 68.

13. W. L. Lumpkin, ed., *Baptist Confessions of Faith* (Valley Forge: Judson Press, 1959), 326.

14. David Benedict, *A General History of the Baptist Denomination in America* (Boston: Lincoln and Edmands, 1813), 2:456.

15. George, ed., *Boyce*, 33.

16. Quoted, Thomas J. Nettles, *By His Grace and for His Glory* (Grand Rapids: Baker, 1986), 50.

361

17. James B. Taylor, *Memoir of Rev. Luther Rice, One of the First American Missionaries to the East* (Baltimore: Armstrong and Berry, 1840), 332–33.

18.See Timothy George, "The Reformed Doctrine of Believers Baptism," *Interpretation* 47 (1993): 242–54.

Chapter 2, "John Gill," by Timothy George

1. Augustus M. Toplady in the "Memoir of the Life, Labours, and Character of the Reverend and Learned John Gill, D.D.," printed in the 1830 London edition of Gill's *A Body of Doctrinal and Practical Divinity*, xxxiv. This memoir, including Toplady's eulogy, first appeared as an introductory preface to a two-volume *Collection of Sermons and Tracts* of Gill published in 1773. John Rippon drew on this source in gathering his more definitive account of Gill's life: *A Brief Memoir . . . of the late Rev. John Gill* (London, 1838). The Rippon memoir was originally drafted in 1800.

2. Quoted, Thomas J. Nettles, *By His Grace and for His Glory* (Grand Rapids: Baker, 1986), 75.

3. In 1719 Gill became the third pastor of the Baptist congregation meeting at Goat Yard, Horsleydown in Southwark, succeeding Benjamin Stinton, who had served this church for fifteen years, and the venerable Benjamin Keach, who had founded it in 1672. In turn, Gill was succeeded by his biographer, John Rippon, who served the church for a period of sixty-three years, from 1773 to 1836. In 1854 Charles Haddon Spurgeon became pastor of this congregation, which under Gill's ministry (1757) had relocated to Carter Lane, Tooley Street, near London Bridge.

4. Walter Wilson, *The History and Antiquities of Dissenting Church and Meeting Houses in London, Westminster, and Southwark* (London: n.p., 1810), 4:221.

5. Henry C. Vedder, *A Short History of the Baptists* (Valley Forge, Pa.: Judson Press, 1907), 241. H. Leon McBeth, *The Baptist Heritage* (Nashville: Broadman Press, 1987), gives a somewhat more objective account of Gill, recognizing him as "the most eminent Particular Baptist of his age." He too, however, alleges that Gill's theology "brought the kiss of death to Particular Baptists," 176–78. Nettles, *By His Grace*, 73-107, has reviewed the historiography on Gill and challenged many of the misrepresentations of him.

6. Olinthus Gregory and Joseph Belcher, eds., *The Works of the Rev. Robert Hall* (New York: Harper & Bros., 1854), 3:82.

7. This sketch draws on the two memoirs cited in note 1, as well as the following studies: William Cathcart, "John Gill," *The Baptist Encyclopedia*, I (1881): 452–54; B. R. White, "John Gill in London, 1719–1729: A Biographical Fragment," *Baptist Quarterly* 22 (1967): 72–91; O. C. Robison, "The Legacy of John Gill," *Baptist Quarterly* 24 (1971): 111–25. There are also two unpublished Ph.D. dissertations on Gill, both submitted to the University of Edinburgh: R. E. Seymour, "John Gill—Baptist Theologian" (1954); and Curt Daniel, "Hyper-Calvinism and John Gill" (1983).

8. Rippon, *Memoir*, 4. This saying was later paraphrased by his parishioners, who frequently remarked, "As surely as Dr. Gill is in his study."

9. Gill, *Sermons and Tracts*, 1:ix. Gill later commented on this text, recalling the effect the words must have had on him as a young man, as well as on Adam in the Garden of Eden. They were, he says, a summons to appear before "the Judge of all, and answer for his conduct; it was in vain for him to secrete himself, he must and should appear, the force of which words he felt, and therefore was obliged to surrender himself." *Gill's Commentary* (Grand Rapids: Baker Book House, 1980; London: William Hill, 1852-54), 1:20–21.

10. White, "Gill in London," 76.

11. Ibid., 75.

12. Ibid.

13. Ibid., 79.

14. Ibid., 81–88. The second division centered on Thomas Crosby, Gill's erstwhile supporter and a strong-willed deacon in the church. Apparently, Crosby's mother-in-law, Susannah Keach, who was also the widow of the church's founding pastor, had spoken critically of Elizabeth Gill, who had taken a longer than expected time to recover from a miscarriage in 1720. White has suggested that Gill may have been pleased to be rid of Crosby and his meddlesome relatives who left with him since their exit freed the church of "the foremost living exponents of the Keach-Stinton tradition."

15. Charles H. Spurgeon, *The Metropolitan Tabernacle, Its History and Work* (London: n.p., 1876), 40.

16. Rippon, "Memoir," in *Commentary*, 1:xx. The diploma refers to Gill as "praeclaros in Sacrio Literis, Linguis Orientalibus et Antiquitatibus Judaicis progressus fecisse." Gill's most technical work in this field was his *Dissertation concerning the Antiquity of the Hebrew Language, Letters, Vowel Points and Accents,* published in 1767.

17. Cathcart, "Gill," 1:453.

18. Gill, *Body,* xxxvi.

19. Ibid., xxxv.

20. Gill, *Commentary,* 1:xxix.

21. *Calvini Opera,* 4:55: "Neque tamen a gratuita iustitiae imputatione separetur realis (ut loquar) vitae sanctitas." Seymour's claim that Gill so emphasized the doctrine of salvation by sovereign grace that he failed to exhort his people to good works is not borne out by a close examination of his sermons. See his "Gill—Baptist Theologian," 297–98. Gill frequently applied the moral law to Christians and in 1756 published a sermon on *The Law Established by the Gospel.*

22. John Gill. *Attendance in Places of Religious Worship* (London: n.p., 1757), 43–44.

23. Thomas Craner, *A Grain of Gratitude* (London: n.p., 1771), 31–32.

24. Rippon, "Memoir," in *Commentary,* xxxiii.

25. Samuel Stennett, *The Victorious Christian Receiving the Crown* (London, 1771), 32–33.

26. Gill's letter tendering his resignation, along with the church's reply, are found in the Church Record Book, which is housed at the Metropolitan Tabernacle in London. Portions of both letters are reproduced in Seymour, "Gill—Baptist Theologian," 305–06.

27. Gill, *Sermons and Tracts,* 3:569.

28. Stennett, *Victorious Christian,* 48.

29. David M. Thompson, ed., *Nonconformity in the Nineteenth Century* (London: Routledge and Kegan Paul, 1972), 1.

30. Gilbert Burnet, *The History of My Own Times* (Oxford, 1833), IV, Bk. Vl, 550.

31. Michael R. Watts, *The Dissenters* (Oxford: Clarendon Press, 1978), 1:264.

32. John Gill, *The Watchman's Answer* (Oxford: Clarendon Press, 1978), 1:264.

33. Quoted, Roland N. Stromberg, *Religious Liberalism in Eighteenth Century England* (London: n.p., 1965), 1.

34. "A Declaration of the Faith and Practice of the Church of Christ at Horsleydown under the Pastoral Care of Mr. John Gill," in *Commentary,* 1:xi. This confession, which displaced the earlier articles of faith adopted under Benjamin Keach in 1697, became a model for other Particular Baptist church covenants and confessions. See Robison, "Legacy," 113–15.

35. Gill, *Body,* 25.

36. Ibid., 13.

37. Ibid., 12.

38. Ibid., 20.

39. Ibid., 21. A helpful analysis of Gill's doctrine of Scripture is found in L. Russ Bush and Tom J. Nettles, *Baptists and the Bible* (Chicago: Moody Press, 1980), 101–09.

40. W. L. Lumpkin, ed., *Baptist Confessions of Faith* (Valley Forge, Pa.: Judson Press, 1959), 326.

41. Ibid., 295.

42. Raymond Brown, *The English Baptists of the Eighteenth Century* (London: Baptist Historical Society, 1986), 23.

43. Gill, *Body,* 138.

44. Ibid., 140.

45. Ibid., 128.

46. W. T. Whitley, ed., *Minutes of the General Assembly of General Baptists* (London: n.p., 1909–10), 1:43.

47. Gill, *Body,* xli.

48. Gill, *Sermons and Tracts,* 3:555. This quotation is from Gill's *Dissertation Concerning the Eternal Sonship of Christ,* published in 1773. This treatise is a veritable catena of citations from theologians throughout the history of doctrine that Gill adduces in support of this "fundamental doctrine of the Christian religion." Gill felt so strongly about the eternal generation of the Son that in 1768 he led his church to withdraw fellowship from one of its members, a certain James Harmon, who had long opposed it. See Seymour, "Gill—Baptist Theologian," 89.

49. The Canons of Dort are printed in Philip Schaff, *Creeds of Christendom* (New York: Harper and Bros., 1877), 3:550–97.

50. Quoted, Alan R F. Sell, *The Great Debate: Calvinism, Arminianism and Salvation* (Grand Rapids: Baker Book House, 1983), 82.

51. John Gill, *The Cause of God and Truth* (Grand Rapids: Baker Book House, 1980), iii.

52. Ibid., 220.

53. Gill, *The Declaration of Faith and Practice, is* given in full in Seymour J. Price, "Dr. John Gill's Confession of 1729," *Baptist Quarterly* 4 (1928): 366–71. This excerpt is quoted in Sell, *Debate,* 80.

54. Quoted, J. Sears McGee, *The Godly Man in Stuart England* (New Haven: Yale University Press, 1976), 1.

55. Gill, *Body,* 201, 503.

56. John Gill, *The Doctrine of God's Everlasting Love to His Elect, and Their Eternal Union with Christ* (London: n.p., 1752), 40.

57. Lumpkin, *Confessions,* 266. There is a striking parallel between Gill's doctrine of eternal justification and Karl Barth's understanding of "the covenant as the presupposition of reconciliation." Barth writes, "Jesus Christ alone is the content of the eternal will of God, the eternal covenant between God and man. He is this as the Word of God to us and the work of God for us, and therefore in a way quite different from and not to be compared with anything we may become as hearers of this Word and those for whose sake this work is done." *Church Dogmatics* 4:1 (Edinburgh: T. & T. Clark, 1956), 54.

58. Quoted, Sell, *Debate,* 79.

59. Gill, *Commentary,* 1:xxviii–xxix.

60. Peter Toon, *The Emergence of Hyper-Calvinism in English Nonconformity, 1689–1765* (London: The Oliver Tree, 1967), 70–89.

61. Gill, *Sermons and Tracts,* 2:81.

62. G. F. Nuttall, "Northamptonshire and *The Modern Question,*" *Journal of Theological Studies* 16 (1965): 110.

63. Quoted, Brown, *Baptists,* 76.

64. Nettles, *By His Grace,* 101–102. Cf. *Commentary,* 5:101.

65. Gill, *Cause,* 164.

66. John Gill, *The Doctrine of the Cherubim Opened and Explained. A Sermon at the Ordination of the Reverend Mr. John Davis at Waltham-Abbey* (London: n.p., 1754), 36. Quoted, Robison, "Legacy," 118.

67. Ibid., 117.

68. See Nettles, *By His Grace*, 73–130. See also the very helpful study of E. P. Clipsham, "Andrew Fuller and Fullerism: A Study in Evangelical Calvinism," *Baptist Quarterly* 20 (1963): 99–114.

69. *The Complete Works of the Rev. Andrew Fuller*, ed. Joseph Belcher (Philadelphia: American Baptist Publication Society, 1845), 2:422.

70. Ibid. In 1830 W. T. Brantley wrote an article entitled "Gill and Fuller" in which he acknowledged the importance of both for Baptist theology, while also recognizing the nuanced differences between them. "Both were ardent and honest in their attachment to the doctrines of grace, firmly persuaded of the humbling facts of human impotence and guilt, animated with the most blessed affections towards the blessed Jesus, as an all-sufficient Saviour in whom believers are complete in righteousness and salvation. To both we are greatly indebted." *Columbian Star and Christian Index* 2 (Jan. 16, 1830):39–40.

71. This fact, along with other details of Gill's funeral, are given in Horton Davies, *Worship and Theology in England, 1690–1850* (Princeton, N.J.: Princeton University Press, 1961), 136.

72. John Fellows, *An Elegy on the Death of the Rev. John Gill* (London: n.p., 1771), 16.

73. Gill, *Body*, xxxii.

74. Charles Haddon Spurgeon, *Autobiography* (London: Passmore and Alabaster, 1900), 4:261–62.

75. John Gill, A *Sermon Occasioned by the Death of Elizabeth Gill* (London: n.p., 1738), 37–41, also 4.

76. Quoted, E. J. Carnell, *The Case for Orthodox Theology* (London: Marshall, Morgan and Scott, 1961), 14.

Chapter 3, "Andrew Fuller," by Phil Roberts

1. Quoted from the anonymous work "Carmen Flebile: or an Ode to the Memory of the late Reverend Andrew Fuller of Kettering, Who Departed this Life, Much and Justly Lamented, May 7, 1815" (London: n.p., 1815).

2. Andrew Fuller, *Andrew Fuller* (London: n.p., 1882), 11.

3. Andrew Fuller, *The Gospel Its Own Witness, with a Life of the Author by Thomas Nelson* (Edinburgh: n.p., 1830), xlv–xlvi.

4. Andrew Fuller, *The Complete Works of the Rev. Andrew Fuller: with a Memoir of His Life by Andrew Gunton Fuller*, ed. Joseph Belcher, 3d ed. in three vols. (reprinted by Sprinkle Publications, Harrisonburg, Va., 1988), 1:2. Hereafter Fuller, *Complete Works*.

5. Ibid., 3

6. John Ryland, *The Work of Faith, the Labour of Love, and the Patience of Hope, illustrated in the Life and Death of the Rev. Andrew Fuller*, 2d ed. (London: n.p., 1818), 18.

7. Fuller, *Complete Works*, 1:5.

8. Ibid.

9. Ibid., 1:6.

10. Andrew Fuller, personal correspondence to Dr. Stuart, Liverpool, February 1815. Fuller Correspondence—Angus Library, Regent's Park College, Oxford, England.

11. William Newman, in *Reflections on the Fall of a Great Man. A Sermon Occasioned by the Death of the Rev. Andrew Fuller* (London: n.p., 1815), wrote that the work of the mission was "always in his head, always in his heart, always in his hands," 13.

12. J. W. Morris, *Memoirs of the Life and Writings of the Rev. Andrew Fuller* (London: n.p., 1826), 90.

13. Ibid.

14. Ibid., 49.

15. For examples of his evangelistic preaching see his *Works* in 3 vols., Sprinkle edition— 1:236–37, 265–66, 298–300, 421, 444, 453, and 471–72.

16. See Gilbert Laws, *Andrew Fuller, Pastor, Theologian, Ropeholder* (London: n.p., 1942), 96. Fuller felt that there should be no distinctive titles among Christian brethren.

17. Newman, *Reflections*, 21.

18. See, for instance, his "Letters on Systematic Divinity," *Works*—Sprinkle edition 1:684–711.

19. The *GWAA* (Northampton: n.p., 1785), 111.

20. See Button's *Remarks on a Treatise*, 1785, 15–19, 76ff, 87ff., 94ff.

21. Fuller, *A Defense of a Treatise Entitled The GWAA*, 15.

22. Ibid., 87.

23. Dan Taylor, *Observations on the Rev. Andrew Fuller's late Pamphlet, entitled The Gospel of Christ Worthy of All Acceptation, in Nine letters to a Friend* (London: n. p., 1786), 49.

24. Ibid., 57.

25. Fuller, *Complete Works*, 1:459–83.

26. Ibid., 1:483–511.

27. Booth, *Glad Tidings* (London: n.p., 1796), 2.

28. Fuller, *Works*, Sprinkle edition 2:407.

29. Ibid., 3:776–79.

30. Ibid., 3:561–646.

31. Ibid., 3: 808–09.

32. Ibid., 1:667–69.

33. See Geoffrey Rowell, "The Origins and History of Universalist Societies in Britain, 1750–1850," *Journal of Ecclesiastical History* (1971): 39–55.

34. Fuller, *Works*, Sprinkle edition, 2:301–04.

35. Ibid., 304.

36. His anti-Deistic and Socinian polemics included *The Calvinistic and Socinian Systems Compared* (1793), *Socinianism Indefensible* (1797), *The Gospel Its Own Witness* (1799). They will not be considered here as they were not primarily theological treatises but attempts to demonstrate the ethical superiority of Calvinism versus Socinianism and Deism.

37. F. H. Foster, *A Genetic History of the New England Theology* (Chicago: n.p., 1907), 114 *ff.*, 199 *ff.* See also Joseph A. Conforti, *Samuel Hopkins and the New Divinity Movement* (Grand Rapids: Wm. B. Eerdmans, 1981), 159–74.

38. This was the view expounded in Crisp's *Christ Alone Exalted*, first published in 1643 and republished in 1691, under the aegis of Hanserd Knollys. It was reissued in 1755 by John Gill. Fuller identified this view as "Crispianism," *Works* (1818), 2:449–51.

39. Fuller, *The Gospel Worthy* (1801) in *Works* (1841), 1:170–71.

40. Ibid., 317.

41. Fuller, *Works*, Sprinkle edition, 2:81.

42. See as well the collection of his "Essays, Letters, etc., on Ecclesiastical Policy" in volume 3 of the Sprinkle edition of his works. He expressed opinion, there of everything from the state of dissenting discipline to his thoughts on singing and the use of instrumental music in Christian worship.

43. Personal correspondence housed at the Angus Library, Regent's Park College, Oxford University. See the letter to Carey dated April 18, 1799.

44. Ibid., and *Works* (1841), 470.

45. Fuller, *Works*, Sprinkle edition, 1:699.

46. See his article on "Creeds and Subscriptions," Ibid., 3:449–51.

47. Ibid., 487. For additional perspective see 3:335, 487, 490. Fuller always advocated that theological disagreement, however, must be handled only in an attitude of Christian love.

Chapter 4, "John L. Dagg," by Mark E. Dever

1. E. Y. Mullins, "A Southern Baptist Theologian," *The Baptist Argus* 7 (May 7, 1903): 1.

2. Other than in brief articles, Dagg has never been the subject of a published biography. His life must be pieced together from his sketchy autobiography, correspondence, and dissertations written on some aspect of his theology.

3. The Baptist church at Alexandria, Virginia, was interested in him in 1822, but he declined to consider the matter. First Baptist of Richmond, then the largest Baptist congregation in the nation, extended a call to Dagg in December 1824, which he also declined.

4. Dagg was an officer in the Philadelphia Baptist Missionary Society (1825–27) and one of the founders of the Pennsylvania Baptist Missionary Society (forerunner of the Pennsylvania Baptist Convention). Dagg also served on the board of managers of the Triennial Convention (1826–36), as a vice president of the Triennial Convention (1838–45), on the board of directors of the American Baptist Home Missionary Society (1832–36), as vice president of the American and Foreign Bible Society (1837–43), and as president, vice president, and other positions of the Baptist General Tract Society (1824–43). He also served as the host pastor for the 1829 Triennial Convention.

5. Dagg, "Mercer University," *The Christian Index* (August 8, 1844), 3.

6. Dagg's close friend, Basil Manly, Sr., had suggested Dagg for the presidency of Mercer after Manly himself declined the appointment. Dagg had earlier turned down an offer of the Chair of Theology at the Howard Institute in Birmingham. At Mercer Dagg not only served as professor and president but also as the only officer of the institution ever to serve on the board of trustees (1848–55).

7. While a student at Mercer, W. L. Kilpatrick was asked what he thought of President Dagg. Referring to Dagg's physical infirmities, Kilpatrick replied, "He can neither read nor write, he can neither walk nor talk, but he is a very good President," B. D. Ragsdale, *Story of Georgia Baptists* (Atlanta: Foote and Davies Co., 1932), 1:101.

8. After moving to Georgia, Dagg became active in the Georgia Baptist Convention. He served on the Executive Committee (1844–55). Dagg was one of ten people appointed to meet on April 28, 1845, in Providence, Rhode Island, to arrange for the dissolution of the American Baptist Home Missions Society. One month later, while attending the organizational meeting for the Southern Baptist Convention, Dagg was appointed as one of the vice presidents of the new Domestic Missions Board of the Southern Convention. He also was appointed to the committee to draw up the constitution for the new convention. Dagg again attended the Southern Baptist Convention in 1849. His activities there included chairing a committee on the China mission, delivering its report to the Convention, and addressing the Convention as a corresponding messenger from the American Sunday School Union.

9. Laudatory reviews were published in Baptist papers and magazines across the nation. See *The Southern Baptist* 12 (Sept. 29, 1857): 2; *Western Recorder* 24 (Oct. 7, 1857): 154; *Mississippi Baptist* 1 (Oct. 8, 1957): 2; *The Commission* 2 (Jan. 1858): 223; *The Baptist Family Magazine* 1 (Oct. 1857): 310; *The Religious Herald* 26 (Oct. 1, 1857): 2. C. D. Mallary's review in *The Christian Index* even suggested that "this would be a good Book to have read in our churches—especially those that are not regularly supplied with preaching. The volume could be easily divided into about 25 portions of from 12 to 18 pages—each portion supplying rich matter for a Sabbath day's meditation." Mallary, *The Christian Index* 36 (Oct. 14, 1857): 162–63. Although he strenuously disagreed with Dagg's ecclesiology, J. M. Pendleton assigned Dagg's *Manual of Theology* as his textbook at Union College in Tennessee (1857–61). James P. Boyce made some use of Dagg's *Manual of Theology* during the first two years of The Southern Baptist Theological Seminary's existence.

10. J. B. Jeter, R. H. Mell, E. T. Winkler, J. B. Gambrell, and J. P. Boyce were requested to assist Dagg and to take the task on themselves if he was unable. There is no record of the results of this request of the Convention. It is interesting to note that Whitsitt's colleague, Boyce, chairman of the faculty at the seminary, and president of the Convention that year, currently had a catechism in print.

11. Considering the widespread use of his *Manual of Theology* throughout the rest of the nineteenth century and his many students, listeners, and friends, Dagg's influence has certainly

been underestimated. An aspect of Dagg's life that has been completely overlooked is the influence that he exerted beyond his own person, not merely through his preaching, teaching, writing, and denominational service, but also through his family. His son, John L. Dagg, served as pastor of the Baptist church at Milledgeville, Georgia (1847–1851); editor of the Georgia Baptist paper, *The Christian Index* (1851–1857); clerk of the Georgia Baptist Convention (1855); pastor of the Cuthbert Baptist Church (1857–1866); professor (1857–1866) and president (1861–1866) of Cuthbert Female College in Cuthbert, Georgia; and president of Bethel Female College, Hopkinsville, Kentucky (1866–1872). Dagg's stepson by his second wife's first marriage was Noah K. Davis. Since Davis's father died when he was only a few months old, Dagg was the only father that Davis ever knew. Davis graduated from Mercer in 1849. He served as president of Bethel College in Russellville, Kentucky (and in that capacity actively opposed Boyce's idea to move the seminary to Louisville). He later became widely celebrated as professor of Moral Philosophy at the University of Virginia. (In this capacity, Davis delivered one of the first series of Gay Lectures at The Southern Baptist Theological Seminary in 1901.) Dagg's daughter Elizabeth married S. G. Hillyer, a prominent Baptist minister in Georgia who served successively as professor of Belles Lettres and Theology and as president of Mercer University. Another daughter of Dagg's, Mary Jane, married Rollin D. Mallary, son of the well-known Georgia Baptist, C. D. Mallary. R. D. Mallary graduated from Mercer in 1851, and served as president of Southwestern Baptist College, Cuthbert, Georgia; Shorter College, Rome, Georgia; and Shelby Female College, Shelby, North Carolina.

12. Dagg, *Manual of Theology*, v.

13. Ibid., 13.

14. Ibid., 21. Dagg held the prevalent notion of an inerrant Scripture—". . . the Scriptures were originally penned under the unerring guidance of the Holy Spirit," 24.

15. Dagg, *Theology*, 110.

16. That this was not universally taught among evangelical Baptists of the time is evidenced by the sermons of President Francis Wayland of Brown University. Wayland dismissed the issue of the historicity of the Fall narrative as unimportant. Francis Wayland, *University Sermons* (Boston: Gould, Kendall and Lincoln, 1849), 87–88. Cf. Dagg, *Theology*, 144.

17. John L. Dagg, *Autobiography of Rev. John L. Dagg, D.D.* (Rome, Ga.: J. F. Shanklin, Printer, 1886), 8.

18. Dagg, *Theology*, 152.

19. "In our natural state we are totally depraved. No inclination to holiness exists in the carnal heart; and no holy act can be performed, or service to God rendered, until the heart is changed. This change, it is the office of the Holy Spirit to effect." Dagg, *Theology*, 277.

20. Dagg, *Theology*, 152.

21. Ibid., 213.

22. Ibid.

23. Ibid., 246.

24. Ibid., 253–57.

25. Ibid., 258.

26. Dagg has a careful discussion of that faith which precedes regeneration, and that living faith which can only be the result of regeneration in *Theology*, 279–85.

27. Ibid., 309.

28. Dagg's discussion of this doctrine is a good model of a sensitive pastoral discussion, appropriate for a committed church member. See Dagg, *Theology*, 309–23.

29. Ibid., 324. Dagg cites Ephesians 5:25–27; Titus 2:14; John 10:11; Revelation 1:5–6; Acts 20:28; Hebrews 10:14; Isaiah 53:5, 11. As strange as this doctrine may sound to many evangelicals today, Dagg held what had clearly been considered the biblical position among Southern Baptists and Presbyterians throughout most of the eighteenth and nineteenth centuries.

30. Ibid., 345.

31. Ibid., 364.

32. John L. Dagg, *A Treatise on Church Order* (Charleston: Southern Baptist Publication Society, 1858), 12.

33. Ibid., 71.

34. Ibid., 97–99.

35. Ibid., 88.

36. Dagg's *Treatise on Church Order* has lengthy treatments of specific arguments used by Landmarkers to deny that "church" has a universal reference in Matthew 16:18 and Ephesians 1:22; 3:21 (Dagg, *Church Order*, 100–21). Dagg's willingness to quote human authorities in his *A Treatise on Church Order* suggests that Dagg realized he was dealing with issues less clearly taught by Scripture and less central to the gospel.

37. Dagg, *Church Order*, 124.

38. Ibid., 143.

39. Therefore, Dagg insisted (at some length) on baptism by immersion even in cold climates. See Dagg, *Church Order*, 308–12.

40. Ibid., 70.

41. Ibid., 174.

42. Ibid., 257.

43. Ibid., 301–302

44. Ibid., 209.

45. Ibid., 218.

46. Ibid., 238.

47. Ibid., 248.

48. Dagg, *Theology*, iii.

49. Ibid., iv.

50. John L. Dagg, *Elements of Moral Science* (New York: Sheldon and Co., 1859), 170.

51. Cf. E. Brooks Holifield, *The Gentlemen Theologians* (Durham, N.C.: Duke University Press, 1978), 153.

52. Dagg's treatment of theology, though, provides unusually clear, simple explanations of many biblical doctrines in ways that show much pastoral sensitivity to the questions often asked by church members.

Chapter 5, "James Petigru Boyce," by Timothy George

1. The standard life of Boyce remains John A. Broadus, *Memoir of James Petigru Boyce* (New York: A. C. Armstrong and Son, 1893). Other studies include Lansing Burrows, "James Petigru Boyce," *Review and Expositor* 4 (1907): 173–89; Z. T. Cody, "James Petigru Boyce," *Review and Expositor* 24 (1927): 129–66; David M. Ramsay, "James Petigru Boyce—God's Gentleman," *Review and Expositor* 21 (1924): 129–45. A. J. Holt's unpublished address, "Christ the Builder, Boyce the Builder," (1923) is on file in the Boyce Centennial Library of The Southern Baptist Theological Seminary, Louisville, Kentucky. Other biographical details may be gleaned from the "Boyce Family File" and "Story Recollections of Dr. Boyce" by his daughter Elizabeth F. Boyce, both on deposit in the Boyce Centennial Library. Some of the material in this chapter has been adapted from the Founder's Day address, "'Soli Deo Gloria!' The Life and Legacy of James Petigru Boyce," delivered by Timothy George in the alumni chapel of Southern Seminary on February 2, 1988. It appears as the opening chapter in Timothy George, ed., *James Petigru Boyce: Selected Writings* (Nashville: Broadman Press, 1989), 14–27.

2. Broadus, *Memoir*, 54.

3. E. Brooks Holifield, *The Gentlemen Theologians* (Durham: Duke University Press, 1978), 218.

4. Broadus, *Memoir*, 17.

5. Ibid., 51.

6. Ibid.

7. Letter of W. O. Carver to Robert Soileau, January 20, 1954.

8. Basil Manly Sr. was pastor of the First Baptist Church of Charleston from 1826 until 1837. He was succeeded by W. T. Brantly, Sr. (1837–44) and N. M. Crawford (1845–47). All of these men were staunch Calvinists, however much they may have nuanced their adherence to that position in slightly different ways. On this point see Walter Wiley Richards, "A Study of the Influence of Princeton Theology upon the Theology of James Petigru Boyce and His Followers with Special Reference to the Works of Charles Hodge" (Th.D. diss., New Orleans Baptist Theological Seminary, 1964).

9. Broadus, *Memoir,* 88.

10. Ibid., 120.

11. George, *Boyce,* 20. The complete text of "Three Changes in Theological Institutions" is given in this volume on pp. 30–59.

12. Ibid., 50.

13. Ibid., 56.

14. Ibid., 51–52. Thomas J. Nettles, "Creedalism, Confessionalism, and the Baptist Faith and Message," *The Unfettered Word,* ed. Robison B. James (Waco: Word Books, 1987), 138–54, has shown how deeply rooted in Southern Baptist history is the appeal to clear confessional guidelines. For example, he quotes B. H. Carroll, who declared, "The modern cry, 'Less creed and more liberty,' is a degeneration from the vertebrate to the jellyfish, and means less unity and less morality, and it means more heresy. . . . It is a positive and very hurtful sin to magnify liberty at the expense of doctrine." Ibid., 148. Walter B. Shurden, on the other hand, has interpreted the growing confessional consciousness in Southern Baptist life as a threat to traditional Baptist freedoms. See his "The Problem of Authority in the Southern Baptist Convention," *Review and Expositor* 75 (1978): 219–33.

15. See Danny M. West, "The Origin and Function of the Southern Baptist Theological Seminary's 'Abstract of Principles,'" Th.M. thesis, The Southern Baptist Theological Seminary, 1983.

16. Robert Lynn, Southern Seminary Founder's Day Address (1982). Quoted, George, *Boyce,* 20.

17. Letter of John A. Broadus to James R Boyce, December 5, 1862.

18. Broadus, *Memoir,* 200.

19. Ibid., 310.

20. Ibid., 265. Another student, A. W. Middleton from Mississippi, proved less tractable. One of his fellow students recalled his classroom controversy with Boyce: "Not infrequently would Middleton raise a breeze in the lecture room when Dr. Boyce held forth from the professorial chair in Systematic Theology. He could not endure the perpendicular 'Calvinism' inculcated therefrom. . . . Boyce was no stranger to the fiery zeal for dogma which usually inheres in men whose minds and hearts are thoroughly inbred with this school of theology. He did not take very patiently the dissent which the good brother from Mississippi sometimes ventured to express quite emphatically." A. J. Dickinson, "Parrotic Theology," *The Seminary Magazine,* 1 (1888): 74.

21. George, *Boyce,* 49.

22. Ibid.

23. David Benedict, *A General History of the Baptist Denomination in America* (Boston: Lincoln and Edmands, 1813), 2:456. Compare also the statement of Francis Wayland written in 1861: "The theological tenets of the Baptists, both in England and America, may be briefly stated as follows: they are emphatically the doctrines of the Reformation, and they have been held with singular unanimity and consistency." Francis Wayland, *The Principles and Practices of Baptist Churches* (London: J. Heaton and Son, 1861), 16.

24. H. A. Tupper, ed., *Two Hundred Years of the First Baptist Church of South Carolina* (Baltimore: R. H. Woodward and Co., 1889), 85.

25. Tom J. Nettles, ed., *Baptist Catechisms* (n.p., 1983), 232.

26. Cf. Mark E. Dever, "Representative Aspects of the Theologies of John L. Dagg and James R Boyce: Reformed Theology and Southern Baptists" (Th.M. thesis, The Southern Baptist Theological Seminary, 1987), 53–72. B. B. Warfield criticized Boyce for his attribution of the imputation of sin to both the natural and federal headship of Adam. See his review of Boyce's *Abstract of Theology* in *Presbyterian Review* 10 (1889): 502–3.

27. James R Boyce, *Abstract of Systematic Theology* (Philadelphia: American Baptist Publication Society, 1887), 246.

28. Ibid., 317. While Boyce criticized Andrew Fuller's presentation of the atonement as providing merely a means for redemption, rather than actual reconciliation, he too spoke of a universal reference of the atonement in a way not entirely dissimilar from Fuller. On this inconsistency in his thought, see Dever, "Representative Aspects," 92–102, and Thomas J. Nettles, *By His Grace and for His Glory* (Grand Rapids: Baker Book House, 1986), 201–202.

29. *The Seminary Magazine,* 1 (1888): 29–31.

30. Boyce, *Abstract,* "Preface," viii.

31. James B. Taylor, *Memoir of Rev. Luther Rice, One of the First American Missionaries to the East* (Baltimore: Armstrong and Berry, 1840), 332–33.

32. George, *Boyce,* 45.

33. On the curriculum of Southern Seminary, see William A. Mueller, *A History of Southern Baptist Theological Seminary* (Nashville: Broadman Press, 1959), 112–18. E. Glenn Hinson acknowledges the conservative biblical orientation of the seminary's founding fathers while frankly admitting "that our theology would not agree with theirs." See his "Between Two Worlds: Southern Seminary, Southern Baptists, and American Theological Education," *Baptist History and Heritage* 20 (1985): 28–35.

34. Boyce, *Abstract,* "Preface," vii.

35. Nettles, *Catechisms,* 230.

36. Boyce, *Abstract,* 48.

37. Dwight A. Moody, "Doctrines of Inspiration in the Southern Baptist Theological Tradition" (Ph.D. diss., The Southern Baptist Theological Seminary, 1982), 77.

38. Boyce, *Abstract,* 173.

39. Ibid., 190–94. On Boyce's efforts to harmonize scriptural truth with contemporary scientific evidence, see L. Russ Bush and Tom J. Nettles, *Baptists and the Bible* (Chicago: Moody Press, 1980), 203–11.

40. Ibid., 226. Edgar V. McKnight, "A. T. Robertson: The Evangelical Middle Is Biblical 'High Ground,'" *The Unfettered Word,* ed. Robison B. James (Waco: Word Books, 1987), 96, cites as evidence to the contrary an 1883 sermon by Broadus as well as a statement from his commentary on Matthew that one should be "cautious in theorizing as to verbal inspiration." In the sermon, Broadus distinguishes truth in substance from truth in statement, but he assumes that the scriptural writings are true—"thoroughly true," as he puts it—in both areas. The caution against theorizing is simply a good Reformed principle: theology must not give way to "vain speculation," but stay within the limits of revelation alone. Broadus's comments concerning the harmonizing of synoptic questions and the loose citation of scriptural sources are fully compatible with a nuanced doctrine of inerrancy as set forth, for example, in the Chicago Statement on Biblical Inerrancy (1978).

41. A. T. Robertson, *The Life and Letters of John A. Broadus* (Philadelphia: American Baptist Publication Society, 1901), 434.

42. C. H. Toy, *The Claims of Biblical Interpretation on Baptists* (New York: Lange and Hillman, 1869), 13.

43. Robertson, *Broadus,* 301.

44. Quoted, Bush and Nettles, *Baptists,* 233.

45. Taylor, *Memoir,* 263–64.

46. On the Toy Controversy, see Mueller, *History,* 135–42; Billy G. Hurt, "Crawford Howell Toy: Interpreter of the Old Testament" (Th.D. diss., The Southern Baptist Theological

372 Theologians of the Baptist Tradition

Seminary, 1965); Pope A. Duncan, "Crawford Howell Toy: Heresy at Louisville," *American Religious Heretics,* ed. George H. Shriver (Nashville: Abingdon Press, 1966), 56–88.

47. George, *Boyce,* 23.

48. Ibid.

49. J. P. Boyce, "The Doctrine of the Suffering of Christ," *The Baptist Quarterly* 4 (1870): 386.

50. J. P. Boyce, "Two Objections to the Seminary," *The Western Recorder,* June 20, 1874.

51. Compare the following letter of James P. Boyce to John A. Broadus: "I am anxious for Williams to go to Mississippi. If they should treat him badly I shall be sorry on his account and their's, but it will help us. Soul liberty is worth more than alien immersion, even with Landmarkers." Quoted, Mueller, *History,* 105.

52. See Mark E. Matheson, "Religious Knowledge in the Theologies of John Leadley Dagg and James Petigru Boyce: With Special Reference to the Influence of Common Sense Realism" (Ph.D. diss., Southwestern Baptist Theological Seminary, 1984), 192–209, especially page 191, n. 105.

53. David M. Ramsay, "Boyce and Broadus, Founders of the Southern Baptist Theological Seminary," 4.

Chapter 6, "The Broadus-Robertson Tradition," by David S. Dockery

1. A. T. Robertson, "Broadus as Scholar and Preacher," *The Minister and His Greek New Testament* (1923; Nashville: Broadman, reprint 1977), 118.

2. A. T. Robertson, *Life and Letters of John A. Broadus* (Philadelphia: American Baptist Publication Society, 1901), x.

3. Ibid., 33–34.

4. W. J. McGlothlin, "John Albert Broadus," *Review and Expositor* 27 (April 1930), 147.

5. Robertson, *Life and Letters,* 35.

6. Ibid.

7. The story of the providential founding of The Southern Baptist Theological Seminary and the details of Broadus's significant role in the founding as I have described can be found in William Mueller, *A History of The Southern Baptist Theological Seminary* (Nashville: Broadman, 1959); and Roy L. Honeycutt, "Heritage Creating Hope: The Pilgrimage of The Southern Baptist Theological Seminary," *Review and Expositor* 81 (Fall 1984), 367–91.

8. Robertson, *Life and Letters,* 197.

9. See R. Albert Mohler, "Classic Texts Deserve Valued Spot in the Preacher's Bookshelf," *Preaching* (March-April, 1989), 33–34.

10. James W. Cox, "On the Preparation and Delivery of Sermons: A Book Review," *Review and Expositor* 81 (Fall, 1984), 464–66; idem., "The Pulpit and Southern," *Review and Expositor,* 82 (Winter, 1985), 77–78.

11. See Steve Reagles, "The Century After the 1889 Yale Lectures: A Reflection on Broadus's Homiletical Thought," *Preaching* (November-December, 1989), 32–36; also see A. T. Robertson, "Broadus the Preacher," *Methodist Quarterly Review* 69 (April, 1920), 152. E. C. Dargan, Broadus's successor in teaching homiletics at Southern Seminary, attempted to incorporate portions of the Yale lectures in a revised edition of *On the Preparation and Delivery of Sermons.*

12. Most of the material in this section can be found in Robertson, *Life and Letters.* The concluding quote is from *Life and Letters,* 431. Also see Bernard R. DeRemer, "The Life of John Albert Broadus," *Christianity Today* (April 13, 1962), 22–23; E. Y. Mullins, "One Hundred Years: A Retrospect," *Review and Expositor* 24 (April, 1927), 129–31; and Claude W. Duke, "Memorial Address of Dr. John A. Broadus," *Review and Expositor* 24 (April, 1927), 167–76.

13. See Everett Gill, *A. T. Robertson: A Biography* (New York: Macmillan, 1943), 198.

14. See David S. Dockery, compiler, *The Best of A. T. Robertson* (Nashville: Broadman & Holman, 1996).

15. In fact it was Robertson's expanded translation of the New Testament. See Everett Gill, *A. T. Robertson: A Biography* (New York: Macmillan, 1943).

16. Frank H. Leavell, "Archibald Thomas Robertson: An Interview for Students," *The Baptist Student* 10 (May, 1932), 3.

17. Gill, *A. T. Robertson*, 28.

18. Ibid., 42.

19. Ibid., 57. Robertson noted in his journal that an advantage of seminary life in Louisville was the added opportunity to hear great preachers and lecturers who would come to the city. In addition to Moody, he particularly mentioned: Sam Jones, Henry Ward Beecher, Edward Judson, Joseph Cook, Will Carleton, Justin McCarthy, P. S. Henson, George W. Lorimer, Phillips Brooks, Joseph Parker, Arthur O'Conner, Sir Thomas Grattan Esmond, DeWitt Talmage, Francis Murphy, J. William Jones, and James G. Blaine.

20. Gill, *A. T. Robertson*, 65.

21. Ibid., 67.

22. Ibid.

23. Ibid., 198.

24. Edgar McKnight, "A Baptist Scholar," Founder's Day Address, The Southern Baptist Theological Seminary, February 4, 1986, p. 6.

25. William A. Mueller, *A History of the Southern Baptist Theological Seminary, 1859–1959* (Nashville: Broadman, 1959), 124.

26. See the Southern Seminary faculty's letter to their fellow Southern Baptists in Mueller, *A History*, 162–64.

27. Ibid., 164.

28. McKnight, "A Baptist Scholar," 3.

29. For an account of the Toy controversy, see Mueller, *History of The Southern Baptist Theological Seminary*.

30. See John A. Broadus, *Commentary on the Gospel of Matthew* (Philadelphia: American Baptist Publication Society, 1886), 58.

31. See David S. Dockery, *Christian Scripture: An Evangelical Perspective on Inspiration, Authority and Interpretation* (Nashville: Broadman & Holman, 1995), 177–99.

32. Robertson, *Life and Letters*, 430.

33. Broadus, *Paramount and Permanent Authority of the Bible*, 1–2.

34. Ibid., 3.

35. Ibid., 5.

36. Ibid., 8.

37. Ibid., 13.

38. John A. Broadus, *Three Questions as to the Bible* (Philadelphia: American Baptist Publication Society, 1883), 9.

39. Ibid., 34.

40. *Gospel of Matthew*, x–ix.

41. E.g., the manner he dealt with the variations in the genealogies in Matthew and Luke; see *Gospel of Matthew*, 6–7.

42. In one sense the New American Commentary is not new, for it represents the continuation of a heritage rich in biblical and theological exposition. The title of this forty-volume set points to the continuity of this series with an important commentary project published at the end of the nineteenth century called An American Commentary, edited by Alvah Hovey. The older series included, among other significant contributions, the outstanding volume on Matthew by John A. Broadus, from whom the publisher of the new series, Broadman Press, partly derives its name. Broadman Press was named for John A. *Broad*us (Broad) and Basil *Man*ly, Jr. (Man). See The New American Commentary, David S. Dockery and E. Ray Clendenen, general editors (Nashville: Broadman, 1991–).

374 Theologians of the Baptist Tradition

43. See the preface of A. T. Robertson, *A Harmony of the Gospels in the Revised Version* (New York: Doran, 1903); also the comments by Martin Marty, *Pilgrims in Their Own Land* (New York: Penguin, 1984), 304.

44. Roger Finke and Rodney Starke, *The Churching of America, 1776–1990—Winners and Losers in Our Religious Economy* (New Brunswick, N.J.: Rutgers University Press, 1992), 1790; also A. H. Newman, *A History of Baptist Churches in the United States* (New York: Scribner, 1915), 1518.

45. These unpublished notes are housed in the James P. Boyce Library on the campus of The Southern Baptist Theological seminary. I am indebted to Greg Thornbury for his research help at this point in particular, and for his help with other aspects of this chapter.

46. Gill, *A. T. Robertson*, 184.

47. Mueller, *A History*, 206.

48. A. T. Robertson, "Is the Virgin Birth Credible Today?" *The Watchman-Examiner* (Nov. 18, 1920), 1168.

49. Gill, *A. T. Robertson*, 239.

50. Portions of this work previously appeared in David S. Dockery, "John A. Broadus" in *Evangelical Biblical Interpreters*, ed. Walter A. Elwell (Grand Rapids: Baker, 1999) and David S. Dockery, editor and compiler, *The Best of A. T. Robertson* (Nashville: Broadman & Holman, 1999), and are used here with permission.

Chapter 7, "Charles Haddon Spurgeon," by Lewis A. Drummond

A large portion of this chapter was taken from Lewis A. Drummond, *Charles Spurgeon* (Grand Rapids: Kregel, 1990). Full bibliographical material can be found in this volume. The vast majority of quotations in this chapter are from Spurgeon's own sermons and autobiography. It is therefore not necessary that all these be noted as they have been published numerous times by various publishers for over a century and appear in the author's biography.

1. W. Y. Fullerton, *C. H. Spurgeon* (London: Williams and Norgate, 1920), 30–31.

2. C. Kruppa, A. *Preacher's Progress* (unpublished Ph.D. thesis).

3. Melton Mason, Jr., *The Theology of Charles Haddon Spurgeon* (unpublished Ph.D. thesis), 155.

4. Ibid., 156.

5. Preached at Exeter Hall, April 1855.

Chapter 8, "Augustus Hopkins Strong," by Gregory Alan Thornbury

1. A brief account of Cornelius Woelfkin's life and participation in the Fundamentalist-Modernist controversy is given by David O. Beale in *In Pursuit of Purity: American Fundamentalism Since 1850* (Greenville, S.C.: Unusual Publications, 1986), 205. An autobiographical account of Cornelius Woelfkin's "conversion" to modernism can be found in *The Baptist,* 15 October 1921.

2. Paul M. Minus, *Walter Rauschenbusch: American Reformer* (New York: MacMillan Publishing Co., 1988), 100.

3. Augustus Hopkins Strong, *Autobiography of Augustus Hopkins Strong,* Crerar Douglas, ed. (Valley Forge, Pa.: Judson Press, 1981), 19.

4. E. Y. Mullins, "The Theological Trend," *Review and Expositor* 2 (1905): 506–21.

5. J. L. Neve, *A History of Christian Thought,* vol. 2 (Philadelphia: Fortress Press, 1946), 288–89.

6. Clark H. Pinnock, "Overcoming Misgivings About Evangelical Inclusivism," *The Southern Baptist Journal of Theology* 2, no. 2 (Summer 1998): 33.

7. Richard Sewall, as cited in Strong, Autobiography of Augustus Hopkins Strong, 19.

8. Strong recounts his father's encounter with Finney in *Autobiography,* 33: "He [Alvah] sought the great evangelist at his room in the hotel. Mr. Finney bade him be seated by the door until he had finished a letter. At length my father, then a young man of twenty-one, perceived

a towering form approaching him and heard a searching voice: 'Well, what is it?' Father stammered out that he thought he ought to be a Christian, but that he could not *feel*. Mr. Finney reached down for the iron poker that lay beside the stove and raised it fiercely as if he would beat out my father's brains. Father naturally dodged, whereupon the great evangelist simply said, 'Ah, you feel *now*, don't you?' and returned to his writing. Father went away indignant at such a reception. But then he began to reflect. He concluded that Mr. Finney meant to teach him a lesson. If he was afraid of a poker, he had far greater reason to be afraid of hell. He soon had feeling enough."

9. Strong, *Autobiography*, 58.

10. Augustus Hopkins Strong, *What Shall I Believe?* (New York: Fleming H. Revell Company, 1922), 87.

11. Strong, *Autobiography*, 86.

12. For a detailed consideration of Robinson's life and ministry, see Ezekiel Gilman Robinson, *Ezekiel Gilman Robinson: An Autobiography* (Boston: Silver, Burdett and Company, 1986).

13. Strong, *Autobiography*, 120.

14. Ibid., 113.

15. Ibid., 113–15.

16. Ibid., 115.

17. Ibid., 184.

18. Despite Strong's proclivity for academic enterprises, he always cherished opportunities for preaching and honored the work of the pastor. He confessed: "I profess that the greatest enjoyment of existence, the very acme and honor of dignity, is to stand before a company of your fellow beings bound to the judgment seat of Christ and proclaim to them the message of divine love and mercy. One single experience in which you forget yourself in the word of God and are so taken possession of by God's Spirit that you hold your audience in the hollow of your hand and do with them what you will is worth all the struggles and trials and humiliations of the Christian ministry" [Ibid., 119–20].

19. Ibid., 203.

20. Augustus Hopkins Strong, *Address at the Dedication of Rockefeller Hall, May 19, 1880* (Rochester: Press of E. R. Andrews, 1880), 10–11.

21. Ibid., 11.

22. Ibid., 26–27.

23. Ron Chernow, *Titan: The Life of John D. Rockefeller, Sr.* (New York: Random House, 1998), 307.

24. For a detailed consideration of this issue, see Grant Wacker, *Augustus Hopkins Strong and the Dilemma of Historical Consciousness* (Macon, Ga.: Mercer University Press, 1985).

25. Augustus Hopkins Strong, *A Tour of the Missions* (Philadelphia: The Griffith Rowland Press, 1918).

26. Minus, *Rauschenbusch*, 100.

27. Augustus Hopkins Strong, "Confessions of Our Faith," *The Watchman-Examiner*, 7 July 1921.

28. Augustus Hopkins Strong, *Systematic Theology*, 8th ed. (Philadelphia: The Judson Press, 1907).

29. Strong, *Christ in Creation and Ethical Monism*, 476–77.

30. Strong, *Christ in Creation*, 106.

31. Wacker, *Strong and Historical Consciousness*, 11.

32. George M. Marsden, *Fundamentalism and American Culture: The Shaping of Twentieth Century Evangelicalism: 1870–1925* (New York: Oxford University Press, 1990), 14.

33. Thomas Reid, *Lectures on Natural Theology (1780)*, trans. Elmer Duncan (Washington, D.C.: The University Press of America, 1981).

34. William R. Eakin, "Reid: First Principles and Reason in the Lectures on Natural Theology," in Thomas Reid, *Lectures on Natural Theology*, xxx.

35. Reid, *Lectures on Natural Theology*, 2.

36. Strong, *Autobiography*, 102.

37. Ibid.

38. Ibid.

39. Augustus Hopkins Strong, "Ezekiel Gilman Robinson as a Theologian," in *Ezekiel Gilman Robinson: An Autobiography*, ed. E. H. Johnson (Boston: Silver, Burdett, and Company, 1896), 168.

40. Augustus Hopkins Strong, *Lectures on Theology* (Rochester, N.Y.: Press of E. R. Andrews, 1876).

41. Augustus Hopkins Strong, *Philosophy and Religion* (New York: A. C. Armstrong and Son, 1888), 86. Strong acknowledges that through sin, men have dimmed their knowledge of God, but that it remains real. Even God's attributes can be known, if imperfectly, through this natural theology. Strong thus leaves considerable material upon which a natural theology may be constructed.

42. Ibid.

43. Ibid., 3.

44. Carl F. H. Henry, *Personal Idealism and Strong's Theology* (Wheaton, Ill.: Van Kampen Press, 1951), 55. Henry's commentary on Strong's thought as it relates to monism is unsurpassed in its lucidity and accuracy. For a detailed explanation of the contours of Strong's philosophical and theological pilgrimage, chapters 2 and 3 of Henry's work are indispensable.

45. As Henry remarks, "All departments of modern thought—including physics, literature, theology, and philosophy—were all moving toward monism. Monism was therefore the 'ruling idea' of the times, and it was essential that the Christian movement have the right attitude toward it. [Strong] confessed that he had 'come to believe this universal tendency toward monism . . . a mighty movement of the Spirit of God . . . preparing for the way of reconciliation of diverse creeds and parties by disclosing their hidden ground of unity.'" *Personal Idealism and Strong's Theology*, 106–07.

46. Strong, *Systematic Theology*, 90.

47. Ibid., vii.

48. Ibid., 109.

49. Strong, *Christ in Creation*, 47.

50. Strong, *Autobiography*, 102–03.

51. For more information on Strong's position on this issue, see *Systematic Theology*, 117–33, and "The Miracle at Cana. With an Attempt at a Philosophy of Miracles," delivered at the Second Conference, held at Mathewson Street Methodist Episcopal Church, 11 November 1903 (Rochester, N.Y.: The American Baptist Historical Society).

52. Casper Wistar Hodge Jr., Review of *Systematic Theology* (1907, vols. 1–2) by Augustus Hopkins Strong. *Princeton Theological Review* 6 (1908): 335–41.

53. Strong, *Philosophy and Religion*, 45.

54. Strong, *Christ in Creation*, 11.

55. Ibid., 74–75.

56. Strong, *Systematic Theology*, 472.

57. Strong, *What Shall I Believe?* 85.

58. Ibid., 86–87.

59. Ibid., 91.

60. *Lectures on Theology*, 52–53.

61. Ibid., 54.

62. Strong, *Philosophy and Religion*, 151.

63. Ibid., 153–54.

64. Strong, *Systematic Theology*, 226.

65. Strong, *Christ in Creation*, 126.

66. Augustus Hopkins Strong, "Address Before the Minister's Conference, Rochester, Oct. 2, 1893, Rockefeller Hall" (Rochester, N.Y.: Strong Manuscript Collection, American Baptist Historical Society), 2.

67. Ibid., 3.

68. Ibid.

69. Ibid., 4.

70. Strong, *Systematic Theology,* 211.

71. Strong, *Christ in Creation,* 126.

72. Strong, *What Shall I Believe?* 64–65.

73. Ibid., 65.

74. Ibid., 67.

75. Ibid., 83.

76. Strong, *Systematic Theology,* 843.

77. Millard Erickson, *The Evangelical Left* (Grand Rapids: Baker Book House, 1997), 112.

78. Henry, *Personal Idealism and Strong's Theology,* 11.

Chapter 9, "Benajah Harvey Carroll," by James Spivey

1. J. M. Carroll, "B. H. Carroll," in *Dr. B. H. Carroll, the Colossus of the North,* ed. J. W. Crowder (Fort Worth: By the editor, 1946), 13. Hereafter *Colossus.*

2. B. H. Carroll, "My Infidelity and What Became of It," in *Sermons and Life Sketch of B. H. Carroll, D.D.,* ed. J. B. Cranfill (Philadelphia: American Baptist Publication Society, 1895), 13–17.

3. Ibid., 14–15.

4. Ibid., 15.

5. Jeff D. Ray, *B. H. Carroll* (Nashville: The Baptist Sunday School Board of the SBC, 1927), 15; W. W. Barnes, "Biography of B. H. Carroll," in Index of the Carroll Collection, Roberts Library, Southwestern Baptist Theological Seminary. Most sources say Carroll never earned a university degree. Ray and Barnes note that Baylor granted him the B.A. in absentia without requiring him to sit examinations.

6. The B. H. Carroll Personal Memorandum Book, 1, file 158 and miscellaneous files 157 and 167 of the Carroll Collection; M. V. Smith, "B. H. Carroll, Pastor of First Baptist Church, Waco," *Texas Baptist Herald,* 25 July 1878, 2; Robert A. Baker, *Tell the Generations Following* (Nashville: Broadman Press, 1983), 59, 105–06; Carroll, in *Colossus,* 13; Wilson L. Stewart, "Ecclesia: The Motif of B. H. Carroll's Theology" (Th.D. diss., Southwestern Baptist Theological Seminary, 1959), 5; Keith L. Cogburn, "B. H. Carroll and Controversy: A Study of His Leadership Among Texas Baptists, 1871–1899" (M.A. diss., Baylor University, 1983), 7; Civil Minutes of the District Clerk, Burleson County, Caldwell, Texas; and the correspondence file of Dr. Leon McBeth of Southwestern Baptist Theological Seminary. The marriage license was issued December 11, 1861, to Carroll and O[phelia] A. Crunk, daughter of Nicolas S. Crunk. Harvey allowed his brother to bring suit for him in his absence, and the charges against Ophelia were confirmed November 9, 1863 (see Civil Minutes, Book C, 277). Two days later, she married B. D. Evans (see Burleson County Marriage Records, ii: 100).

7. Carroll, "Infidelity," in *Sermons,* 17.

8. Carroll, in *Colossus,* 48.

9. Baker, 60.

10. Ray, 31.

11. Carroll, "Infidelity," in *Sermons,* 21.

12. Ibid., 22–23.

13. Baker, 63.

14. Dove Church Minutes (FBC, Caldwell) show he was to be licensed on the fourth Sunday (27th) of May and ordained on the fourth Sunday (15th) of November.

15. Ray, 46. Eventually they had nine children. Hassie, Ellen, Hallie, and Jimmie died in infancy. Guy Sears died in early adulthood. B. H. Jr. became a U.S. consular official. Charles taught at the New Orleans Baptist Theological Seminary. Kate was a missionary in Brazil. Louise was the wife of a New Mexico rancher.

16. Cogburn, 16–24; Ray, 120. A similar incident occurred ten years later when Carroll defeated a Disciples opponent named Dr. Wilmeth.

17. Barnes, "Biography."

18. George W. Truett, "B. H. Carroll, the Titanic Champion of the Truth," in *Colossus,* 90.

19. J. B. Cranfill, "The Passing of B. H. Carroll," in *Colossus,* 105.

20. Ray, 74–75, 84–87.

21. Frank E. Burkhalter, *A World-Visioned Church* (Nashville: Broadman Press, 1946), 127–31.

22. Baker, 70–75.

23. Ray, 77.

24. Cogburn, 35–52. See B. H. Carroll, "Temperance Resolutions of *The First Baptist Church of Waco, Texas,* in 'Defending the Faith,'" 113–43.

25. B. H. Carroll, "The Sunday Opening Question," in "Defending the Faith and Practice of Baptists," ed. J. W. Crowder, Roberts Library, Southwestern Baptist Theological Seminary (typewritten manuscript, 1957), 265–69, gives the ministers' resolutions.

26. Cogburn, 110.

27. George W. McDaniel, "B. H. Carroll, the Colossal Christian," in *Colossus,* 160.

28. Pat M. Neff, "B. H. Carroll, the Champion of a Great Cause," in *Colossus,* 138.

29. L. R. Scarborough, "B. H. Carroll, a Kingdom-Builder," in *Colossus,* 127–29.

30. Robert A. Baker, *The Blossoming Desert, a Concise History of Texas Baptists* (Waco: Word Books, 1970), 134–52. The BGCT consolidated the Baptist General Association with the Baptist State, the East Texas Baptist, the North Texas Baptist Missionary, and the Central Texas Baptist Conventions. Baker, *Generations,* 76, 78–79.

31. Baker, *Generations,* 82–83; Ray, 101–02; Cranfill, *Sermons,* xi. For his sermon on this see B. H. Carroll, "The Indwelling Spirit of God," in *Saved to Serve,* comp. J. W. Crowder and ed. J. B. Cranfill (Dallas: By the editor, 1941), 175–91.

32. Carroll Collection, File 208–1, Letter to B. H. Carroll, August 24, 1896.

33. Ray, 97–101. Robert A. Baker, *The Southern Baptist Convention and Its People, 1607–1972* (Nashville: Broadman Press, 1974), 292–93. For his Chattanooga address (May 14), see B. H. Carroll, "Evangelism," in "Biblical Addresses," comp. J. W. Crowder, Roberts Library, Southwestern Seminary (typewritten manuscript, 1958), 226–44.

34. Cogburn, 54–73.

35. For an account of Crawfordism in one association, see B. H. Carroll, "Concerning Grayson County Association (September 30, 1897)," in "Defending the Faith," 339–51.

36. Baker, *Generations,* 81–83; *Southern Baptist Convention,* 278–82; Cogburn, 98–129.

37. B. H. Carroll, "Back to the Realm of Discussion (May 27, 1897)," in "Defending the Faith," 326.

38. Cogburn, 74–97. See also Charles B. Bugg, "The Whitsitt Controversy: A Study in Denominational Conflict" (Th.D. diss., The Southern Baptist Theological Seminary, 1972), and Rosalie Beck, "The Whitsitt Controversy: A Denomination in Crisis" (Ph.D. diss., Baylor University, 1984).

39. B. H. Carroll, "Co-operation (1896)," in "Defending the Faith," 297–98.

40. B. H. Carroll, "The Real Issue in Whitsitt Case," *Texas Baptist Standard,* 5 (August 1897).

41. J. B. Cranfill, "The Passing of B. H. Carroll," in *Colossus,* 106.

42. J. B. Gambrell, "The Home-Going of President Carroll, an Appreciation," in *Colossus,* 101.

43. P. E. Burroughs, "Benajah Harvey Carroll," in *Ten Men from Baylor*, ed. J. M. Price (Kansas City: Central Seminary Press, 1945), 65.

44. Baker, *Generations*, 78; Cogburn, 26–27, 33. Carroll was also a member of the Central Baptist Education Commission of Texas, created to facilitate unification of Baylor and Waco Universities. His reasons for leaving the commission are given in B. H. Carroll, "Withdrawal from the Commission," in "Defending the Faith," 210–19.

45. Ray, 134; Barnes, "Biography."

46. Carroll Collections, File 14, Letter of Resignation (December 31, 1898).

47. Baker, *Generations*, 97–105; Ray, 107–14, 127–28. They had one son, Francis Harrison, who became a journalist in Los Angeles.

48. B. H. Carroll, "A Chair of Fire" (July 2, 1908), in "Our Seminary or the Southwestern Baptist Theological Seminary, Fort Worth, Texas," Roberts Library, Southwestern Baptist Theological Seminary (typewritten manuscript, 1957), 307.

49. Baker, *Generations*, 111–59.

50. W. W. Barnes, *The Southern Baptist Convention, 1845–1953* (Nashville: Broadman Press, 1954), 209.

51. B. H. Carroll, "Baptist Church Polity and Articles of Faith," comp. J. W. Crowder, Roberts Library, Southwestern Baptist Theological Seminary (typewritten manuscript, 1957), 38, 95; Carroll Collection, File 73, "Safeguards of the Seminary," *Baptist Standard*, June 13, 1910.

52. Stewart, 55–60.

53. B. H. Carroll, *Inspiration of the Bible*, ed. J. B. Cranfill (New York: Fleming H. Revell Co., 1930), 121–22.

54. Ibid., 25.

55. B. H. Carroll, *Saved to Serve*, comp. J. W. Crowder and ed. J. B. Cranfill (Dallas: Helms Printing Co., 1941), 16.

56. B. H. Carroll, *An Interpretation of the English Bible*, ed. J. B. Cranfill and J. W. Crowder (Nashville: Broadman Press, 1947), 1:9.

57. Carroll, *Inspiration*, 84.

58. Ibid., 54.

59. Carroll, *Inspiration*, 26–27; Ray, 75.

60. Carroll, *Saved to Serve*, 35.

61. B. H. Carroll, *Baptists and Their Doctrines*, comp. J. B. Cranfill (New York: Fleming H. Revell Co., 1913), 9–10.

62. Carroll, "Biblical Addresses," 175.

63. B. H. Carroll, *Opening of the Course in the English Bible* (Waco: Kellner Printing Co., 1902), 2, 11–12; B. H. Carroll, *Jesus the Christ*, comp. J. W. Crowder and ed. J. B. Cranfill (Nashville: Baird-Ward Press, 1937), 99; J. Dee Cates, "B. H. Carroll: The Man and His Ethics" (Th.D. diss., Southwestern Baptist Theological Seminary, 1962), 190.

64. Carroll, "Baptist Church Polity," 35–38, 82–93.

65. Carroll, "Biblical Addresses," 167–68; B. H. Carroll, *Ambitious Dreams of Youth*, ed. J. B. Cranfill (Dallas: Helms Printing Co., 1939), 136.

66. Carroll, "Baptist Church Polity," 112–23.

67. Carroll, "Defending the Faith," 292–94.

68. Carroll, *Interpretation*, 1 :66, 156–57; B. H. Carroll, "Memorial, Meetings and Miscellanies," comp. J. W. Crowder; Roberts Library, Southwestern Baptist Theological Seminary (typewritten manuscript, n.d.), 75; B. H. Carroll, *Courses in the English Bible: Lectures 111 and 1F Creations, with Questions on Four Lectures* (Waco: Kellner Printing Co., n.d.), 25.

69. Carroll, *Interpretation*, 1:61–62, 79; 12:195.

70. B. H. Carroll, *Christ and His Church*, comp. J. W. Crowder and ed. J. B. Cranfill (Nashville: Broadman Press, 1940), 189.

71. B. H. Carroll, *The Providence of God,* comp. J. W. Crowder and ed. J. B. Cranfill (Dallas: Helms Printing Co., 1940), 21–24.

72. Carroll, *Saved to Serve,* 149.

73. Ibid., 249–50, 159–60.

74. Carroll, *Providence,* 17–29; Carroll, *Saved to Serve,* 152.

75. Carroll, "Baptist Church Polity," 130–31; Stewart, 44, 104.

76. Stewart, 44–45.

77. Carroll, "Baptist Church Polity," 120, 143–44.

78. B. H. Carroll, *The Holy Spirit,* ed. J. B. Cranfill (Grand Rapids, Mich.: Zondervan, 1939), 17, 20, 31, 40–45, 57–59, 76–79.

79. Carroll, *Inspiration,* 32.

80. B. H. Carroll, *Christian Education and Some Social Problems,* ed. J. W. Crowder (Fort Worth: By the editor, 1948), 14.

81. Carroll, "Biblical Addresses," 38–39; Cates, 98.

82. Carroll, *Ambitious Dreams,* 59; Carroll, *Interpretation,* 1 :63.

83. B. H. Carroll, *Southwestern Journal of Theology* 5 (October 1921); Carroll, "Defending the Faith," 80–81; Carroll, *Interpretation,* 1:105–106.

84. Carroll, *Southwestern Journal,* vol. 5; Carroll, "Baptist Church Polity," 126; Carroll, *Interpretation,* 1:81.

85. Carroll, *Interpretation,* 12:70; Carroll, *Christian Education,* 16–17.

86. Carroll, *Interpretation,* 1:117–19; 14:125; Carroll, "Baptist Church Polity," 185; Carroll, "Biblical Addresses," 38–39. Carroll uses the doctrine of total depravity as further proof against the theory of evolution.

87. Carroll, "Baptist Church Polity," 128–32, 156–57, 184; Carroll, *Interpretation,* 1:84, 136.

88. B. H. Carroll, *The Day of the Lord,* comp. J. W. Crowder and ed. J. B. Cranfill (Nashville: Broadman Press, 1936), 93, 96.

89. Carroll, "Biblical Addresses," 31–32; B. H. Carroll, *Ecclesia—the Church* (Louisville: Baptist Book Concern, 1903), 13–14.

90. Carroll, *Interpretation,* 3:37.

91. B. H. Carroll, *The River of Life and Other Sermons,* ed. J. B. Cranfill (Nashville: The Sunday School Board of the Southern Baptist Convention, 1928), 68–79.

92. Carroll, "Baptist Church Polity," 129.

93. Carroll, *Ambitious Dreams,* 69.

94. Carroll, *Interpretation,* 15:78–79; 16:206–07.

95. B. H. Carroll, *The Faith That Saves,* comp. J. W. Crowder and ed. J. B. Cranfill (Dallas: Helms Printing Co., 1939), 164. B. H. Carroll, *Evangelistic Sermons,* comp. J. B. Cranfill (New York: Fleming H. Revell Co., 1913), 74; Carroll, *Interpretation,* 2:310; 3:58; 4:122.

96. Carroll, *Interpretation,* 2:338–39; 11:393; 15:220.

97. Carroll, *Interpretation,* 11:395; 16:298, Carroll, *Evangelistic Sermons,* 62.

98. Carroll, "Defending the Faith," 83; Carroll, *Interpretation,* 14:92, 127.

99. Carroll, "Baptist Church Polity," 155. But he also understood justification in the sense of Christians' works justifying their faith. See Carroll, *Interpretation,* 13:29–30.

100. Carroll, "Defending the Faith," 86.

101. Carroll, "Baptist Church Polity," 161.

102. Carroll, *Interpretation,* 14:245; Carroll, "Baptist Church Polity," 156, 159.

103. Carroll, *Interpretation,* 15:78.

104. Carroll, "Baptist Church Polity," 188.

105. Carroll, "Baptist Church Polity," 181–83, 205; Carroll, "Biblical Addresses," 26–28; Carroll, *Interpretation,* 10:285–88.

106. Cogburn, 55–56, 66–67; Cates 65–66; Carroll, "Questions on Saving Faith and Assurance" and "Martin on Prayer," in "Defending the Faith," 92–102.

107. Carroll, "Baptist Church Polity," 209.

108. Ibid., 202–03, 208.

109. Ibid., 205.

110. Carroll, "Biblical Addresses," 39–40; Carroll, "Baptist Church Polity," 206–08.

111. Carroll, *The Providence of God,* 191.

112. Carroll, "Defending the Faith," 2–38.

113. Carroll, *Interpretation,* 13:140, 151. Carroll admitted that in a sense Christians are already sanctified as God sees them as complete in Christ.

114. Carroll, "Baptist Church Polity," 153–56.

115. Ibid., 5–20; B. H. Carroll, "Distinctive Baptist Principles: A Sermon Before the Pastors' Conference at Dallas, November 4, 1903," 9–14.

116. Carroll, "Biblical Addresses," 58–60.

117. Carroll, *The River of Life,* 136; Carroll, *Saved to Serve,* 39.

118. Carroll, "Distinctive Baptist Principles," 14–15.

119. Carroll, "Baptist Church Polity," 8.

120. B. H. Carroll, "Memorials, Meetings and Miscellanies," comp. J. W. Crowder, Roberts Library, Southwestern Baptist Theological Seminary (typewritten manuscript, n.d.), 194; B. H. Carroll, *The Supper and Suffering of Our Lord,* ed. J. W. Crowder (Fort Worth: Seminary Hill Press, 1947), 42.

121. Carroll, "Baptist Church Polity," 84, 267–68, 274; B. H. Carroll, *Baptism: Its Law, Its Administrator, Its Subject, Its Form, Its Design* (Waco: Baptist Standard Press Print, 1893).

122. Carroll, *The Supper and Sufferings,* 39; Carroll, *Baptist Church Polity,* 276, 345; Stewart, 137; B. H. Carroll, *Communion, from a Bible Standpoint: A Sermon* (Dallas: "Texas Baptist" Book and Job Printing House, 1876).

123. Cates, 197–98; Carroll, "Baptist Church Polity," 51–80.

124. Stewart, 138–39.

125. Carroll, "Baptist Church Polity," 2–4.

126. Baker, *Generations,* 94; Carroll, *Baptists and Their Doctrines,* 84; Carroll, "Distinctive Baptist Principles," 5.

127. For Carroll's explanation of this doctrine, see Carroll, "Biblical Addresses," 57–102; Carroll, *Interpretation,* vol. 17; and Carroll, *The Day of the Lord.* For studies, see Stewart, 146–68; and Tom L. Watson, "The Eschatology of B. H. Carroll" (M.Th. thesis, Southwestern Baptist Theological Seminary, 1960).

128. Carroll Collection, File 583, "New Testament English, Fall Term, 1912–1913," 2, 12; Carroll, "Biblical Addresses," 87–97; Carroll, *The Day of the Lord,* 177–78.

129. Carroll, "Biblical Addresses," 88–92; Carroll, *Interpretation,* 11:219; 17:274–75. Carroll believed the Jews would again become a nation and that most of them would be converted, but he did not identify this political nation as the "New Israel."

130. B. H. Carroll, *Jesus the Christ* (Nashville: Baird-Ward Press, 1937), 28.

131. Ray Summers, *The Life Beyond* (Nashville: Broadman Press, 1959), 124; Carroll, *The River of Life,* 148.

132. Carroll, *The Day of the Lord,* 177–78.

133. Carroll, *Interpretation,* 11:281.

134. Gambrell, "The Home-Going," in *Colossus,* 103.

135. B. H. Carroll, *The Theology of the Bible* (Fort Worth: Southwestern Baptist Theological Seminary, n.d.), 2; Carroll, *Inspiration,* 32.

136. Carroll, "Defending the Faith," 2–38, 92–102; Carroll, "Baptist Church Polity," 191.

137. Carroll, *Baptists and Their Doctrines,* 94–95.

138. Carroll, *The Holy Spirit,* 43.

139. Carroll Collection, File 583, Lecture Notes, 12.

140. Carroll, *Saved to Serve,* 22–24; Baker, *Generations,* 96–97; see Carroll, "The Death of Spurgeon," in *Sermons,* 24–44.

141. H. Leon McBeth, *The Baptist Heritage: Four Centuries of Baptist Witness* (Nashville: Broadman Press, 1987), 624–25; Baker, *Generations,* 500; Carroll Collection, File 76, "The Constitution of the Southern Baptist Convention and the Illinois Messengers." Later, Throgmorton served as a trustee of Southwestern Baptist Theological Seminary (1916, 1929).

142. Carroll, *Interpretation,* 1:135–36; 14–124.

143. Carroll, "Baptist Church Polity," 139, 167, 176, 214, 216; Carroll, "Defending the Faith," 80, 98–99; Stewart, 126.

144. Carroll, *Interpretation,* 15:86–92.

145. Carroll, *Interpretation,* 17:273.

146. Carroll, "Baptist Church Polity," 208.

147. Ibid., 156, 159, 163–64, 219–21; Carroll, "Defending the Faith," 93–94.

148. Ibid., 200; Ibid., 80.

149. Crowder, *Colossus,* 181.

150. Carroll, *Baptists and Their Doctrines,* 47.

151. W. T. Conner, *Southwestern Evangel,* December 1925, 6.

152. Carroll, *Saved to Serve,* 35.

Chapter 10, "E. Y. Mullins," by Fisher Humphreys

1. Gaines S. Dobbins, "Edgar Young Mullins," *Encyclopedia of Southern Baptists* (Nashville: Broadman Press, 1958), 2:930. Except where otherwise indicated, biographical information about Mullins has been taken from this article.

2. Isla May Mullins, *Edgar Young Mullins* (Nashville: The Sunday School Board of the Southern Baptist Convention, 1929), 9.

3. William E. Ellis, *A Man of Books and a Man of the People* (Macon, Ga.: Mercer University Press, 1985), 2. Ellis points out that S. G. Mullins owned four slaves in 1860.

4. Mullins, *Edgar Young Mullins,* 10. Isla May Mullins says the family moved when Edgar was eight years old. William E. Ellis (p. 4) says they began the move on November 16, 1869.

5. Isla May Mullins, "Dr. Mullins as a Student," *The Review and Expositor* (April 1929): 142.

6. Mullins, *Edgar Young Mullins,* 15.

7. Ellis, *A Man of Books and a Man of the People,* 40.

8. Jerry M. Stubblefield, "The Ecumenical Impact of E. Y. Mullins," *Journal of Ecumenical Studies* (Spring 1980): 99.

9. Louie D. Newton, "Baptist World Alliance," *Encyclopedia of Southern Baptists* (Nashville: Broadman Press, 1958), 1:130.

10. See, for example, Russell H. Dilday Jr., "E. Y. Mullins: The Bible's Authority Is a Living Transforming Reality," *The Unfettered Word,* ed. Robison B. James (Waco: Word Books, 1987), 109.

11. W. O. Carver, "Edgar Young Mullins—Leader and Builder," *The Review and Expositor* (April 1929): 128.

12. See the newspaper article appended to the biography by Isla May Mullins, *Edgar Young Mullins,* 214.

13. Bill Clark Thomas, "Edgar Young Mullins: A Baptist Exponent of Theological Restatement" (Ph.D. diss., The Southern Baptist Theological Seminary, 1963), 91.

14. E. Y. Mullins, *The Christian Religion in Its Doctrinal Expression* (Valley Forge, Pa.: Judson Press, 1917), vii.

15. E. Y. Mullins, *The Axioms of Religion* (Philadelphia: American Baptist Publication Society, 1908), 14.

16. "Moderation, indeed, remains a hallmark of Mullins' system of doctrine." Sydney E. Ahlstrom, "Theology in America: A Historical Survey," *Religion in American Life,* vol. I, ed.

James Ward Smith and A. Leland Jamison, *The Shaping of American Religion* (Princeton: Princeton University Press, 1961), 306.

17. Dilday, "E. Y. Mullins: The Bible's Authority Is a Living Transforming Reality," 114.

18. Ellis, *A Man of Books and a Man of the People*, 218. Ellis is writing specifically of the evolution controversy and generally about the Fundamentalist-Modernist controversy. See also 221–22.

19. The Whitsitt controversy antedates his presidency and is traced by Gaines Dobbins to an encyclopedia article by Whitsitt, that appeared in 1886. See Gaines S. Dobbins, "William Heth Whitsitt," *Encyclopedia of Southern Baptists*, 2: 1896.

20. E. Y. Mullins, *Why Is Christianity True?* (Philadelphia: The Judson Press, 1905), 354. It is not clear whether Mullins wrote this book before or after he returned to Louisville. Ellis (*A Man of Books and a Man of the People*, 74) and others report that he wrote it in response to a request that came after he arrived in Louisville. However, the book itself contains evidence that he wrote it before the close of the nineteenth century; see 376, where he refers to the nineteenth century as "the present century."

21. Ahlstrom, "Theology in America: A Historical Survey," 303–04.

22. Mullins, *The Christian Religion in Its Doctrinal Expression*, 425.

23. William A. Mueller, *A History of Southern Baptist Theological Seminary* (Nashville: Broadman Press, 1959), 113.

24. Robert Wood Lynn, "Notes toward a History: Theological Encyclopedia and the Evolution of Protestant Seminary Curriculum, 1808–1869," *Theological Education* (Spring 1981): 118–44.

25. The Faculty of the Southern Baptist Theological Seminary, *Edgar Young Mullins: A Study in Christian Character* (Louisville: n.p., n.d.), 5. Bill Clark Thomas listed twelve books by Mullins in his bibliography. Mullins was a prolific writer; the list of all his writings given by Thomas is forty-three pages long! See Thomas, "Edgar Young Mullins: A Baptist Exponent of Theological Restatement," 412–54.

26. The phrases are book titles by C. S. Lewis, J. B. Phillips, and John Stott, respectively.

27. Mullins, *The Axioms of Religion*, 59, 73.

28. Ibid., 79.

29. Ibid., 90.

30. Ibid., 92.

31. Ibid., 94.

32. Ibid., 127.

33. Ibid., 134.

34. Ibid., 147.

35. Ibid., 150.

36. Ibid., 185.

37. Ibid., 187.

38. Ibid., 194.

39. Ibid., 197.

40. Ibid., 201.

41. Ibid., 208–209.

42. Ibid., 210.

43. Ibid., 232.

44. Ibid., 307.

45. Martin E. Marty, "Baptistification Takes Over," *Christianity Today*, 2 September 1983, 33–36.

46. E. Y. Mullins, *Baptist Beliefs* (Valley Forge, Pa.: Judson Press, 1925; reprint of 1912 edition, published by Baptist World Publishing Co.), 5–6.

47. William L. Lumpkin, *Baptist Confessions of Faith* (Philadelphia: Judson Press, 1959), 391–98.

48. E. Y. Mullins, *Freedom and Authority in Religion* (Philadelphia: The Griffith & Rowland Press, 1913), 128.

49. Ibid., 257.

50. Ibid., 288.

51. Ibid., 402–03.

52. Ibid., 394.

53. Mullins, *The Christian Religion in Its Doctrinal Expression,* 18.

54. Ibid., 135–3.

55. Ibid., 141.

56. Ibid., 142.

57. Ibid., 211.

58. Ibid., 252.

59. Ibid., 323–24.

60. Ibid., 437.

61. Ibid., 503. Mullins's only two children died very young.

62. E. Y. Mullins, *Christianity at the Cross Roads* (Nashville: The Sunday School Board of the Southern Baptist Convention, 1924), 67.

63. Ibid., 97.

64. Ibid., 149.

65. Ibid., 163.

66. Ibid., 185.

67. Ibid., 233–34.

68. Mullins seems to have realized this sometime after the publication of *The Axioms of Religion* (1908); in *The Christian Religion in its Doctrinal Expression* he wrote, "Christianity emphasizes duties rather than rights," 427.

Chapter 11, "Walter Thomas Conner," by James Leo Garrett Jr.

1. Much of this section has been taken with some modification from James Leo Garrett Jr., "The Theology of Walter Thomas Conner" (Th.D. diss., Southwestern Baptist Theological Seminary, 1954), 1–23.

2. *Who's Who in America* (Chicago: A. N. Marquis Co., 1950), 26:547; Stewart A. Newman, *W. T. Conner: Theologian of the Southwest* (Nashville: Broadman Press, 1964), 19–20.

3. W. T. Conner, "Trip to Arkansas, January 1948," unpublished manuscript now deposited in the library of Southeastern Baptist Theological Seminary, Wake Forest, N.C., 1. Copy in A. Webb Roberts Library, Southwestern Baptist Theological Seminary, Fort Worth, Tex.

4. Newman, *W. T. Conner,* 19.

5. Ibid.

6. Ibid.; W. T. Conner, "Autobiographical Sketch," *Southwestern Men and Messages,* ed. J. M. Price (Kansas City, Kan.: Central Seminary Press, 1948), 41.

7. Conner, "Trip to Arkansas," 5.

8. Conner, "Autobiographical Sketch," 41.

9. Conner, "Trip to Arkansas," 6; Newman, *W. T. Conner,* 19–20.

10. Conner, "Autobiographical Sketch," 41.

11. W. T. Conner, "My Religious Experiences," unpublished manuscript now deposited in the library of Southeastern Baptist Theological Seminary, Wake Forest, N.C., 1. Copy in A. Webb Roberts Library, Southwestern Baptist Theological Seminary, Fort Worth, Tex.

12. Ibid., 2.

13. Ibid., 3–4.

14. Conner, "Autobiographical Sketch," 41.

15. L. R. Scarborough, *A Modern School of the Prophets* (Nashville: Broadman Press, 1939), 190; Newman, *W. T. Conner,* 29, based on the minutes of Harmony Baptist Church, Caps, Texas.

16. Conner, "Autobiographical Sketch," 41.

17. Conner, "My Religious Experiences," 5–6.

18. Conner, "Autobiographical Sketch," 41.

19. Conner, "My Religious Experiences," 7.

20. Conner, "Autobiographical Sketch," 41.

21. Ibid.

22. Scarborough, *A Modern School of the Prophets,* 190.

23. Conner, "Autobiographical Sketch," 42.

24. Conner, "My Religious Experiences," 12.

25. Conner, "Autobiographical Sketch," 41–42.

26. Conner, "My Religious Experiences," 10–11.

27. Conner, "Autobiographical Sketch," 42.

28. John S. Ramond, comp., *Among Southern Baptists* (Shreveport, La.: author, 1936), 1:106.

29. Conner, "My Religious Experiences," 14.

30. Conner, "Autobiographical Sketch," 42.

31. Conner, "My Religious Experiences," 14–15.

32. Conner, "Autobiographical Sketch," 42–43.

33. W. T. Conner, "Some Outstanding Men That I Have Known," unpublished manuscript now deposited in the library of Southeastern Baptist Theological Seminary, Wake Forest, N.C., 10–15. Copy in A. Webb Roberts Library, Southwestern Baptist Theological Seminary, Fort Worth, Tex.

34. Conner, "Autobiographical Sketch," 43.

35. *Second Annual Catalogue of the Southwestern Baptist Theological Seminary, 1908–1909,* 18.

36. Hugh R. Peterson, registrar, Southern Baptist Theological Seminary, to James Leo Garrett Jr., 28 September 1953.

37. Conner, "Autobiographical Sketch," 43.

38. Peterson to Garrett.

39. For the documentation, see Garrett, "The Theology of Walter Thomas Conner," 12–13.

40. Ibid., 13–14.

41. "Connerisms," *The Southwestern News* 10 (November 1952): 6.

42. Frank K. Means, "Advocate of Missions," *The Commission* 15 (September 1952): 242.

43. W. T. Conner, "Theological Education," *Fourth Baptist World Congress: Record of Proceedings,* ed. W. T. Whitley (London: Kingsgate Press, 1928), 286–91.

44. John W. Cobb to James Leo Garrett Jr., 17 September 1953.

45. Charles W. Koller to James Leo Garrett Jr., 18 September 1953.

46. Based on the author's conversations with Mrs. W. T. Conner, 1953.

47. W. T. Conner, "Here and There," unpublished reflections, 18 December 1931—31 December 1939, deposited in the library of Southeastern Baptist Theological Seminary, Wake Forest, N.C. Copy in A. Webb Roberts Library, Southwestern Baptist Theological Seminary, Fort Worth, Tex.

48. Newman, *W. T. Conner,* 143.

49. See Garrett, "The Theology of Walter Thomas Conner," 24–132.

50. John S. Tanner, S. P. Brooks, B. H. Carroll, A. H. Newman, and Calvin Goodspeed.

51. A. H. Strong, Walter Rauschenbusch, W. A. Stevens, and H. C. Mabie.

52. E. Y. Mullins and W. O. Carver.

53. George B. Foster, Shailer Mathews, and Gerald B. Smith.

54. Especially Landmarkism.

55. L. R. Scarborough, J. Frank Norris, Charles B. Williams, H. E. Dana, W. W. Barnes, et al.

56. James Denney, P. T. Forsyth, H. R. Mackintosh, A. B. Davidson, James Orr, James Moffatt, et al.

57. A. T. Robertson, John B. Champion, T. P. Stafford, E. C. Dargan, et al.

58. George B. Stevens, B. B. Warfield, J. Gresham Machen, James H. Snowden, Newman Smyth, E. Stanley Jones, E. F. Scott, James M. Campbell, A. C. Knudson, Nels F. S. Ferré, et al.

59. William James, Borden P. Bowne, et al.

60. John Baillie, A. E. Garvie, R. Newton Flew, Sydney Cave, et al.

61. Karl Barth, Emil Brunner, Gustav Aulén, et al.

62. Augustine of Hippo, John Calvin, et al.

63. George Barker Stevens, The Theology of the New Testament (New York: Charles Scribner's Sons, 1899).

64. Henry Clay Sheldon, New Testament Theology (New York: Macmillan, 1922).

65. For a fuller treatment, see Garrett, "The Theology of Walter Thomas Conner," 294–319.

66. The Teachings of Mrs. Eddy. Conner had written articles about Christian Science prior to 1926.

67. The Teachings of "Pastor" Russell. Conner's monograph, though written during the presidency of Joseph F. Rutherford, was directed against the teachings of Charles Taze Russell.

68. For a fuller treatment, see Garrett, "The Theology of Walter Thomas Conner," 133–81.

69. W. T. Conner, The Gospel of Redemption (Nashville: Broadman Press, 1945), ix.

70. James William McClendon, Pacemakers of Christian Thought (Nashville: Broadman Press, 1962), 54.

71. For documentation and a fuller treatment, see Garrett, "The Theology of Walter Thomas Conner," 182–205.

72. W. T. Conner, Revelation and God: An Introduction to Christian Doctrine (Nashville: Broadman Press, 1936), 212.

73. Arthur Lynn Allen, "A Comparative Study of the Person of Christ in Selected Baptist Theologians: Augustus H. Strong, William N. Clarke, Edgar Y. Mullins, and Walter T. Conner" (Th.D. diss., New Orleans Baptist Theological Seminary, 1979), chapter 6.

74. For documentation and a fuller treatment, see Garrett, "The Theology of Walter Thomas Conner," 205–34.

75. Ibid., 234–41.

76. Paul Abbott Basden, "Theologies of Predestination in the Southern Baptist Tradition: A Critical Evaluation" (Ph.D. diss., Southwestern Baptist Theological Seminary, 1986), 173, 208–29.

77. See Walter D. Draughon III, "A Critical Evaluation of the Diminishing Influence of Calvinism on the Doctrine of Atonement in Representative Southern Baptist Theologians: James Petigru Boyce, Edgar Young Mullins, Walter Thomas Conner, and Dale Moody," (Ph.D. diss., Southwestern Baptist Theological Seminary, 1987), chapter 3.

78. For documentation and a fuller treatment, see Garrett, "The Theology of Walter Thomas Conner," 241–57.

79. Robert Keith Parks, "A Biblical Evaluation of the Doctrine of Justification in Recent American Baptist Theology: With Special Reference to A. H. Strong, E. Y. Mullins, and W. T. Conner" (Th.D. diss., Southwestern Baptist Theological Seminary, 1954), 147–57, 188–89, has contended that Conner went too far in abandoning the values of the forensic view.

80. Clark Richard Youngblood, "The Question of Apostasy in Southern Baptist Thought Since 1900: A Critical Evaluation" (Ph.D. diss., The Southern Baptist Theological Seminary, 1979), chapter 2.

81. For documentation and a fuller treatment, see Garrett, "The Theology of Walter Thomas Conner," 257–76.

82. Ibid., 277–93.

83. Conner's deliberate decision not to write for scholars and not to include detailed documentation may be considered by some to be a basic weakness.

84. See Garrett, "The Theology of Walter Thomas Conner," 320–26.

85. Holmes Rolston, Review of W. T. Conner, "The Gospel of Redemption," *Interpretation* 1 (October 1947): 527–28.

86. James Leo Garrett Jr., "W. T. Conner: Contemporary Theologian," *Southwestern Journal of Theology* 25 (Spring 1983): 59–60.

87. H. N. Wieman and B. E. Meland, *American Philosophies of Religion* (Chicago: Willett, Clark, and Co., 1936), 61–76.

Chapter 12, "Herschel H. Hobbs," by David S. Dockery

1. Herschel H. Hobbs, *My Faith and Message* (Nashville: Broadman & Holman, 1993), 1–4.

2. Ibid., 11.

3. See Stanton Nash, "Operation Baptist Biography Data Form for Living Persons," Hobbs Collection, Southern Baptist Historical Commission Archives, 4.

4. Hobbs, *My Faith and Message,* 17–63.

5. Ibid., 25.

6. Ibid.

7. Ibid.

8. During his years at the seminary, Hobbs developed strong friendships and created a wide-ranging network that would serve him well throughout his life. Many of these relationships grew out of his involvement in a "secret supper club" called *Dodeka,* the Greek word for twelve. Each year twelve couples were invited to join this exclusive group. Herschel and Frances were received as members during their first year at the seminary (see Hobbs, *My Faith and Message,* 63). Important friendships with W. A. Criswell and others were birthed during this time. Hobbs was the first guest preacher Criswell invited after he was called to the pastorate of the First Baptist Church, Dallas, Tex. Hobbs also drove the "getaway car" at the wedding of W. A. and Betty Criswell.

9. See Hobbs's personal recollections of these days in the foreword to *The Best of A. T. Robertson,* compiled by David S. Dockery and edited by Timothy and Denise George (Nashville: Broadman & Holman, 1996), xi–xv. Of all the professors at Southern, Hershey Davis was the most influential in Hobbs's life. He said, "Robertson had an accumulative mind. . . . Davis had an incisive mind. He was more like Alexander the Great cutting the Gordion Knot; he cut right through and went to the hearts of the thing" (Hobbs, *My Faith and Message,* 76).

10. Hobbs, *My Faith and Message,* 61, 74. Hobbs said: "In my judgment Dr. E. Y. Mullins was the greatest theologian Southern Baptists have ever had. He died in 1928 so I never knew him. . . . Next to Mullins I would place Dr. W. T. Conner of Southwestern Baptist Theological Seminary. . . . When they spoke, Southern Baptists listened" (Hobbs, *My Faith and Message,* 74).

11. The dedication to the revised edition reads: "Dedicated to Edgar Young Mullins, whom I never knew personally but who through his books has been my teacher through the years."

12. One of his earliest trustee appointments was to the board of New Orleans Baptist Seminary. He recounted his fondness for John Jeter Hurt Sr., president of Union University in Jackson, Tennessee. "Though many years separated us in age, he and I were kindred souls. He liked to recite Baptist history, and I liked to listen to it. Often at night during trustee meetings

he and I would get to ourselves in the corner of the motel lobby for such sessions" (Hobbs, *My Faith and Message*, 63).

13. See John Steven Gaines, "An Analysis of the Correlation between Representative Baptist Hour Sermons by Herschel H. Hobbs and Selected Articles of The Baptist Faith and Message" (Ph.D. diss., Southwestern Baptist Theological Seminary, 1991).

14. Herschel H. Hobbs, "Reflections on My Ministry," *Southwestern Journal of Theology* 15 (Spring 1973), 76. In another place he replied similarly, "I have been asked many times what I consider my greatest privilege of service in the Southern Baptist Convention has been. My answer is the privilege of being chairman of the committee which drew up the 1963 statement of 'The Baptist Faith and Message.' A close second would be writing *Studying Adult Life and Work Lessons* for more than twenty-five years." The consensus he helped build for Southern Baptists following the Elliott controversy in 1963 evidenced his impressive leadership skills.

15. Hobbs said about C. B. Arendall, who preceded him as pastor at Dauphin Way in Mobile, "He taught me how to work, and he taught me how to retire" (*My Faith and Message*, 130).

16. Hobbs, *My Faith and Message*, 216. Like his mentor, A. T. Robertson, Hobbs wrote every work in longhand.

17. Walter B. Shurden, "In Defense of the SBC: The Moderate Response to Fundamentalism," *The Theological Educator* 30 (1985) 13; likewise see Shurden, "The Pastor as Denominational Theologian," *Baptist History and Heritage* (July 1980): 21.

18. See Herschel H. Hobbs, *A Layman's Handbook of Christian Doctrine* (Nashville: Broadman, 1974), 2–3.

19. Herschel H. Hobbs, *What Baptists Believe* (Nashville: Broadman, 1964), 8.

20. Ibid.

21. See the preface in Herschel H. Hobbs, *Fundamentals of Our Faith* (Nashville: Broadman, 1960).

22. See Hobbs, *My Faith and Message*, 27.

23. James Leo Garrett, *Systematic Theology*, 2 vols. (Grand Rapids: Eerdmans, 1990–95), 1:5; see Herschel Hobbs, "Southern Baptists and Confessionalism: A Comparison of the Origins and Contents of the 1925 and 1963 Confessions," *Review and Expositor* 76 (1979): 55–68.

24. See Herschel H. Hobbs, *The Baptist Faith and Message* (Nashville: Convention, 1971), 20–21.

25. Herschel H. Hobbs, *Getting Acquainted with the Bible* (Nashville: Convention, 1991), 10–11.

26. Hobbs, *Baptist Faith and Message*, 23. In my opinion Hobbs misunderstood the dictation theory and the verbal plenary theory, unfortunately blurring them and failing to distinguish this key matter regarding the doctrine of biblical inspiration. See David S. Dockery, *Christian Scripture* (Nashville: Broadman & Holman, 1995).

27. Herschel H. Hobbs, "People of the Book: The Baptist Doctrine of the Holy Scripture," *Baptists Why and Why Not Revisited*, edited by Timothy George and Richard Land (Nashville: Broadman & Holman, 1997), 12–16.

28. Ibid., 16, 18.

29. Ibid., 14. In this sense he is both an heir to and continuation of the Broadus-Robertson tradition.

30. That Hobbs was always a thoroughgoing biblicist is unquestioned. Yet there were nuances that could be detected in his emphases along the way. In *Fundamentals of Our Faith* (1960), the first chapter contends that the doctrine of Scripture is foundational to others. In this book the order of the initial chapters was the Bible, God, Jesus Christ, and the Holy Spirit. The order of the initial chapters in *What Baptists Believe* (1964) was God, Jesus Christ, the Holy Spirit, and the Bible. One wonders if the Elliott controversy (1961–62) or discussion regarding these important matters during the writing of "The Baptist Faith and Message"

(1963) influenced the shift. Following the Genesis controversy (1970) related to the release of volume 1 in the *Broadman Commentary*, Hobbs seemingly adopted a position similar to an "inerrancy of purpose" or infallibility, which he later stated differently. In 1971, in his commentary on *The Baptist Faith and Message*, he wrote: "What is the infallibility of the Bible? It is infallible as a book of religion. While Southern Baptists hold to the inerrancy of the Scriptures, their infallibility rests upon the fact that they do what they are designed to do" (p. 29). At the 1980 convention in St. Louis, Hobbs's warning that a commitment to inerrancy was a form of creedalism was not well received by the messengers. In 1981, at the convention in Los Angeles, Hobbs, as chairman of the 1963 Baptist Faith and Message Committee, was asked to explain the meaning of the phrase, "truth without any mixture of error for its matter." He explained, based on the Greek construction of 2 Timothy 3:16, "all Scripture is given by inspiration of God," that it "means every single part of the whole is God breathed. And a God of truth does not breathe error." (See Leon McBeth, *A Sourcebook for Baptist Heritage* [Nashville: Broadman, 1990], 527; also Bill Leonard, *God's Last and Only Hope* [Grand Rapids: Eerdmans, 1990], 52–53; and Jesse C. Fletcher, *The Southern Baptist Convention* [Nashville: Broadman & Holman, 1995], 268). In his chapter on "People of the Book" in *Baptists Why and Why Not Revisited*, Hobbs affirms that the Bible is inspired, truthful, inerrant, and authoritative in all areas, including not only matters of religion but areas such as science and history as well.

31. It was my privilege to discuss many of these things with Dr. Hobbs on several occasions including a lengthy private conversation at the Baptist Sunday School Board in the fall of 1995, just weeks before his death.

32. Hobbs, "People of the Book," 22.

33. Hobbs, *Fundamentals of Our Faith*, 25.

34. Hobbs, *Baptist Faith and Message*, 34, citing Mullins, *The Christian Religion in Its Doctrinal Expression* (Philadelphia: Judson, 1917), 214–15.

35. Ibid., 36–37.

36. Ibid., 38.

37. Herschel H. Hobbs, *The Origin of All Things: Studies in Genesis* (Waco: Word, 1975).

38. Hobbs, *Fundamentals of Our Faith*, 28.

39. Hobbs, *The Baptist Faith and Message*, 39.

40. Ibid.

41. Hobbs, *Fundamentals of Our Faith*, 42.

42. Herschel H. Hobbs, *An Exposition of the Gospel of John* (Grand Rapids: Baker, 1968), 25–27.

43. See Herschel H. Hobbs, *Who Is This?* (Nashville: Broadman, 1952); also Herschel H. Hobbs, *The Life and Times of Jesus* (Grand Rapids: Zondervan, 1966).

44. Hobbs, *Who Is This?*, 104–05.

45. Hobbs, *What Baptists Believe*, 40–41.

46. Hobbs, *Baptist Faith and Message*, 43.

47. Hobbs, *Fundamentals of Our Faith*, 49–50. A very fine and more complete summary of Hobbs's Christology can be found in Albert Perry Hopkins Jr., "An Analysis of the Theological Method of Herschel H. Hobbs and His Doctrines of Christ and Salvation" (Th.D. diss., New Orleans Baptist Seminary, 1994).

48. Hobbs, *Baptist Faith and Message*, 46–47.

49. Ibid., 61.

50. Ibid., 62.

51. Gaines, "An Analysis of the Correlation between Representative Baptist Hour Sermons by Herschel H. Hobbs on Selected Articles of *The Baptist Faith and Message*," 159.

52. Hobbs, *Getting Acquainted with the Bible*, 159.

53. See Paul A. Basden, "Theologies of Predestination in the Southern Baptist Tradition: A Critical Evaluation" (Ph.D. diss., Southwestern Baptist Theological Seminary, 1986); idem., "Predestination" in *Has Our Theology Changed? Southern Baptist Thought Since 1845*

390 THEOLOGIANS OF THE BAPTIST TRADITION

(Nashville: Broadman & Holman, 1994), 62–65. While Boyce gave too little emphasis to matters of individual experience and freedom of the will, Hobbs gave too much.

54. Hobbs, *The Baptist Faith and Message*, 52–54.

55. Hobbs, *Fundamentals of Our Faith*, 91–93.

56. Herschel H. Hobbs and E. Y. Mullins, *The Axioms of Religion* (Nashville: Broadman, 1978), 70–72.

57. Ibid., 71.

58. Hobbs, *Fundamentals of Our Faith*, 106; also see Hobbs, *Studies in Hebrews* (Nashville: Sunday School Board of the Southern Baptist Convention, 1954), 52–59; idem., *What Baptists Believe* (Nashville: Broadman, 1964), 103–04; idem., *A Layman's Handbook of Christian Doctrine* (Nashville: Broadman, 1974), 130. See James Leo Garrett's discussion of these matters in vol. 2 of his *Systematic Theology*.

59. Hobbs, *Studies in Hebrews*, 55.

60. Hobbs, *What Baptists Believe*, 94.

61. Hobbs, *Handbook of Christian Doctrine*, 39–40.

62. Ibid., 128.

63. See Raymond E. Carroll, "Dimensions of Individualism in Southern Baptist Thought" (Th.D. diss., New Orleans Baptist Theological Seminary, 1995), 127–48.

64. An example of how Hobbs confused these issues is found in *Fundamentals of Our Faith*, 106–07. For Hobbs, regeneration and adoption are how one is brought into the family of God, deemphasizing the legal aspect of adoption and merging both metaphors into union with God. Regeneration, he said, "declares the sinner righteous as though he had never sinned." In reality this is justification, not regeneration.

65. We have previously discussed Hobbs's unique understanding of sanctification in the section on the Holy Spirit.

66. Hobbs, *The Baptist Faith and Message*, 75.

67. Hobbs, *My Faith and Message*, 243–44.

68. See Hobbs, *The Axioms of Religion* and Hobbs, *You Are Chosen*. In each the competency of the soul is given priority of attention. Timothy George counters Hobbs's understanding, contending that the priesthood of all believers is not to be equated with "soul competency," "religious liberty," "modern individualism," or "theological minimalism" and as "a part of the doctrine of the church" "has more to do with the Christian's service than with his status." See George, "The Priesthood of All Believers," *The People of God: Essays on the Believers' Church*, edited by Paul A. Basden and David S. Dockery (Nashville: Broadman, 1991), 85–92; also see Garrett, *Systematic Theology*, 2:562–63.

69. Hobbs, *The Baptist Faith and Message*, 80–82.

70. See Herschel Hobbs, *The Cosmic Drama: Studies in Revelation* (Waco: Word, 1971).

71. See Helen Lee Turner, "Fundamentalism in the Southern Baptist Convention: The Crystallization of a Millennialist Vision" (Ph.D. diss., University of Virginia, 1990).

72. The words "one of a kind" are taken from Harold Bennett's foreword to Hobbs's autobiography, *My Faith and Message*.

73. Hobbs, *The Baptist Faith and Message*, 102–103.

74. Hobbs, *My Faith and Message*, 252.

75. Ibid.

76. Ibid., 236.

77. Ibid., 250–52. Hobbs lamented that Baptist seminary students in the 1960s and 1970s knew more about German theologians than they knew about Mullins and Conner.

78. I offer these observations not only out of conviction from biblical exegesis/theology and Baptist tradition, but out of great respect for Hobbs's leadership and appreciation for his friendship and support for me during the latter years of his life.

Chapter 13, "W. A. Criswell," by Paige Patterson

1. See Paige Patterson, "The Imponderables of God," *The Criswell Theological Review,* 1 (Spring 1987): 237–53. Pages 255–67 of the same issue contain a superb bibliographical article by Lamar Copper entitled "The Literary Contributions of W. A. Criswell.". See this appended bibliography.

2. Isaiah 40:8, "The grass withers, the flowers fade, but the word of our God stands forever" (NKJV).

3. Thomas L. Charlton and Rufus B. Spain, *Oral Memoirs of W. A. Criswell,* Religion and Culture Project, Baylor University Program of Oral History (Baylor University, 1973), 18.

4. Ibid.

5. Some claimed that Truett never smiled again, but my father, T. A. Patterson, who knew him well, denies this.

6. In private Criswell also praised Truett, whom he genuinely admired. But he would also point out that the church in Truett's last years had quiesced to a shell and noted that Truett's preaching was topical, repetitive, and predictable. In these early years he struggled monumentally with the influence of Mrs. Truett's Sunday school class, a mistake Criswell would strangely duplicate in the closing years of his own ministry.

7. Harold T. Bryson, "The Expository Preaching of W. A. Criswell in His Sermons on Revelation." Unpublished Master of Theology Thesis, New Orleans Baptist Theological Seminary, 1967, 20.

8. W. A. Criswell, *Standing on the Promises* (Dallas: Word Publishing, 1990).

9. Joel C. Gregory, *Too Great a Temptation* (Ft. Worth: Summit Group, 1994). This volume poorly masquerades the bitterness of its author. The account is sometimes accurate but almost wholly false. By this I mean that Gregory rehearsed incidents that did happen but conveniently omitted context, motive, aftermath, and, most critically, his own turpitude. Nevertheless, the book is a fabulous, though unintentional, testimony to the dangers of embarking on a "career" in the ministry with wrong motives.

10. These were *Passport to the World* (Nashville: Broadman Press, 1951) written with Duke McCall; *Look Up, Brother* (Nashville: Broadman Press, 1970); and *Criswell's Guidebook for Pastors* (Nashville: Broadman Press, 1980).

11. W. A. Criswell, *Criswell's Guidebook for Pastors* (Nashville: Broadman Press, 1980), 50–52.

12. In the first edition of this volume, the chapter on W. A. Criswell was prepared by L. Russell Bush III. This superb chapter should also be consulted for a slightly different perspective.

13. In the introduction to volume 1 of Criswell's *Great Doctrines of the Bible* (Grand Rapids: Zondervan Publishing House, 1982), the present author summarized Criswell's preaching theology.

> This volume contains no ivory-tower theology. The research has been as thorough as if the author wished to present an erudite, multi-volume *Magnum Opus.* Then the research was laid before the One whose eyes are like a "flame of fire" until cold insights were warmed into white-hot convictions of the soul in prayer before God.
>
> Then, twice each Lord's Day morning, Dr. W. A. Criswell approached the sacred desk in the auditorium of the First Baptist Church in Dallas, Texas, where he has served as pastor for thirty-six years. Three thousand people, a standing-room-only crowd, lined the holy place in the heart of one of America's great cities, and listened intently as the investigations, experiences, and convictions of a fifty-year ministry resounded throughout the sanctuary.
>
> Nor were these concepts laboriously deposited in the minds of hearers gathered for the purpose of curing the most hopeless insomniac. Those of us who attended each Sunday went like "empty pitchers to a full fountain." We listened to profound truths depicted in picturesque language, cogently illustrated, and delivered with the fiery

oratorical excellence that has characterized our pastor from his youth. We laughed, wept, confessed, expressed thanksgiving, and marched out to engage the enemy.

14. W. A. Criswell, *In Defense of the Faith* (Grand Rapids: Zondervan Publishing House, 1967), 18–19.

15. W. A. Criswell, *Great Doctrines of the Bible,* vol. 2 (Grand Rapids: Zondervan Publishing House, 1982), 68.

16. Ibid., 70–71.

17. W. A. Criswell, *Expository Notes on the Gospel of Matthew* (Grand Rapids: Zondervan Publishing House, 1961), 22.

18. Criswell, *Great Doctrines of the Bible,* vol. 2, 74.

19. Ibid., 76.

20. W. A. Criswell, *Isaiah* (Grand Rapids: Zondervan Publishing House, 1977), 182.

21. Ibid., 183.

22. Ibid., 184–85.

23. W. A Criswell, *The Bible for Today's World* (Grand Rapids: Zondervan Publishing House, 1965), 49.

24. W. A. Criswell, *Great Doctrines of the Bible,* vol. 1 (Grand Rapids: Zondervan Publishing House, 1982), 76–77.

25. W. A. Criswell, *Why I Preach That the Bible Is Literally True* (Nashville: Broadman Press, 1969), 66.

26. Ibid., 151.

27. Ibid.

28. W. A. Criswell, *Did Man Just Happen?* (Grand Rapids: Zondervan Publishing House, 1957), 12–13.

29. Ibid., 24.

30. Ibid., 16–17.

31. Ibid., 62–73.

32. W. A. Criswell, *Five Great Questions of the Bible* (Grand Rapids: Zondervan Publishing House, 1976), 36–37.

33. Criswell, *Great Doctrines of the Bible,* vol. 2, 79.

34. Ibid., 84.

35. Ibid., 85.

36. Ibid., 136–47. Typical of Criswell's playfulness, curiosity, and unreported lack of dogmatism about difficult passages was the incident involving this author while I was preaching through 1 Peter on Wednesday nights at First Baptist Dallas. Since I disagreed with the pastor about the "spirits in prison," I asked him to preach that passage the next Wednesday, explaining that I did not think it wise to use his pulpit to propound an alternative view. With a playful and somewhat alarming twinkle in his eye, Criswell said, "No lad, you preach it like you see it, and I'll be your most eager listener." The next Wednesday evening Criswell arrived, Greek Testament, yellow pads, and pen in hand and to my horror announced, "The young theologian says he is going to teach the pastor a thing or two tonight. I'll take notes, and then we'll have a discussion."

37. W. A. Criswell, *Expository Sermons on the Epistles of Peter* (Grand Rapids: Zondervan Publishing House, 1976), 76ff.

38. Criswell, *Five Great Questions of the Bible,* 20ff.

39. W. A. Criswell, *Great Doctrines of the Bible,* vol. 5 (Grand Rapids: Zondervan Publishing House, 1985), 139.

40. Ibid., 140.

41. Ibid., 124–25.

42. Ibid., 115ff.

43. W. A. Criswell, *The Holy Spirit in Today's World* (Grand Rapids: Zondervan Publishing House, 1966), 13ff.

44. Ibid., 93ff.

45. Ibid., 119ff. See especially pp. 167ff. See also W. A. Criswell, *The Baptism, Filling and Gifts of the Holy Spirit* (Grand Rapids: Zondervan Publishing House, 1973).

46. W. A. Criswell, *Great Doctrines of the Bible,* vol. 3 (Grand Rapids: Zondervan Publishing House, 1983), 18.

47. Criswell, *Criswell's Guidebook for Pastors,* 199–214.

48. W. A. Criswell, *Expository Sermons on Revelation,* vol. 4 (Grand Rapids: Zondervan Publishing House, 1969), 186.

49. James E. Towns, *The Social Conscience of W. A. Criswell* (Dallas: Crescendo Publications, 1977), 74.

50. Ibid., 75.

51. J. Dwight Pentecost, *Things to Come* (Findlay, Ohio: Dunham Press, 1958).

52. Bryson, "Expository Preaching," 21.

53. J. A. Seiss, *The Apocalypse* (Grand Rapids: Zondervan Publishing House, 1962).

54. W. A. Criswell, *Expository Sermons on Revelation,* vol. 3, 13ff.

55. W. A. Criswell, *Great Doctrines of the Bible,* vol. 8 (Grand Rapids: Zondervan Publishing House, 1989), 20ff.

56. W. A. Criswell, *Expository Sermons on the Book of Daniel,* vol. 4 (Grand Rapids: Zondervan Publishing House, 1976), 71ff.

57. Criswell, *Matthew,* 139ff.

58. Criswell, *Expository Sermons on Revelation,* vol. 5, 83ff.

59. W. A. Criswell and Paige Patterson, *Heaven* (Tyndale House Publishers, 1991), 233ff.

60. Ibid., 101–102.

61. Paige Patterson, "What Athens Has to do with Jerusalem: How to Tighten Greek and Hebrew Requirements and Triple Your M.Div. Enrollment at the Same Time." A paper presented to the Evangelical Theological Society in Orlando, Florida, 20 November 1998.

Chapter 14, "Frank Stagg," by Robert Sloan

1. For extensive biographical information, see Malcolm Tolbert, "Frank Stagg: Teaching Prophet," *Perspectives on the New Testament: Essays in Honor of Frank Stagg,* ed. Charles H. Talbert (Macon, Ga.: Mercer University Press, 1985), 1–16. It will be evident to those familiar with Tolbert's excellent piece that I have been greatly helped by his work in this biographical section; see also Penrose St. Amant, "A Continuing Pilgrimage: A Biographical Sketch of Frank Stagg," *The Theological Educator* 8 (Fall 1977): 37–49; Ann Evory, ed., *Contemporary Authors,* New Revision Series, vol. I (Detroit: Gale Research Co., 1981), s.v. "Stagg, Frank," 623; Frank Stagg, "A Continuing Pilgrimage," *What Faith Has Meant to Me,* ed. Claude A. Frazier (Philadelphia: Westminster Press, 1975), 146–56.

2. Frank Stagg, *New Testament Theology* (Nashville: Broadman Press, 1962).

3. See, for example, the very helpful survey of biblical terms and theological ideas in chapter 4, "The Doctrine of Salvation," ibid., 80–121.

4. Frank Stagg, "The Christology of Matthew," *Review and Expositor* 59 (October 1962): 457–68.

5. Frank Stagg, "The Gospel in Biblical Usage," *Review and Expositor* 63 (Winter 1966): 5–13.

6. Frank Stagg, "The Holy Spirit in the New Testament," *Review and Expositor* 63 (Spring 1966): 135–47.

7. Frank Stagg, "The Journey Toward Jerusalem in Luke's Gospel," *Review and Expositor* 64 (Fall 1967): 499–512.

8. Frank Stagg, "The Lord's Supper in the New Testament," *Review and Expositor* 66 (Winter 1969): 5–26.

9. Frank Stagg, "The Abused Aorist," *Journal of Biblical Literature* 91 (June 1973): 222–31.

10. Frank Stagg, *The Holy Spirit Today* (Nashville: Broadman Press, 1973), passim.

394 THEOLOGIANS OF THE BAPTIST TRADITION

11. Frank Stagg, *Polarities of Man's Existence in Biblical Perspective* (Philadelphia: Westminster Press, 1973), 11.

12. Ibid., 16.

13. Ibid., 10; cf. Frank Stagg, *New Testament Theology* (Nashville: Broadman Press, 1962), 20.

14. Frank Stagg, "Adam, Christ, and Us," *New Testament Studies: Essays in Honor of Ray Summers in His Sixty-Fifth Year,* ed. Huber L. Drumwright and Curtis Vaughn (Waco: Baylor University Press, 1975), 125.

15. See Frank Stagg, "Salvation in Synoptic Tradition," *Review and Expositor* 69 (Summer 1972): 355–367; Frank Stagg, "The Great Words of Romans," *The Theological Educator* 7 (Fall 1976): 94–102; Frank Stagg, "The Mind in Christ Jesus: Philippians 1:27–2: 18," *Review and Expositor* 77 (Summer 1980): 337–47; Frank Stagg, "Reassessing the Gospels," *Review and Expositor* 78 (Spring 1981): 187–203; Frank Stagg, "Eschatology: A Southern Baptist Perspective," *Review and Expositor* 79 (Summer 1982): 381–95; Frank Stagg, "The Concept of the Messiah: A Baptist Perspective," *Review and Expositor* 84 (Spring 1987): 247–58.

16. For James 1:13–15 see, for example, Frank Stagg, "Exegetical Themes in James 1 and 2," *Review and Expositor* 66 (Fall 1969): 391–402; for Romans 1:18 to 3:20 see Frank Stagg, "The Plight of Jew and Gentile in Sin: Romans 1:18–3:20," *Review and Expositor* 73 (Fall 1976): 401–13; Stagg, "The Great Words of Romans," 94–102; and Stagg, *New Testament Theology,* 21 ff.

17. Stagg, "Salvation in Synoptic Tradition," 359.

18. Stagg's soteriology is most evident in "Salvation in Synoptic Tradition," passim; and "Reassessing the Gospels," passim.

19. Stagg, "The Concept of Messiah: A Baptist Perspective," 257.

20. Stagg, "Salvation in Synoptic Tradition," 358.

21. Ibid.

22. This by no means indicates that Stagg utterly ignores Paul; but he does clearly prefer to ground his theology in the Gospels. See Frank Stagg, "Southern Baptist Theology Today," *The Theological Educator* 8 (Fall 1977): 35.

23. Stagg, "Reassessing the Gospels," 189.

24. Ibid., 192–93.

25. Ibid., 194f.

26. Ibid., 197.

27. See Stagg, "The Mind in Christ Jesus," passim; "Southern Baptist Theology Today," 36; and "The Concept of Messiah," 257.

28. Stagg, "Salvation in Synoptic Tradition," 366f.

29. Ibid., 367.

30. Ibid.

31. Frank Stagg, *The Book of Acts: Early Struggle for an Unhindered Gospel* (Nashville: Broadman Press, 1955), viii, 123f, 186.

32. Ibid., 18.

33. Frank Stagg, "Rendering to Caesar What Belongs to Caesar: Christian Engagement with the World," *Journal of Church and State* 18 (1976): 101.

34. Frank Stagg, "Rendering to God What Belongs to God: Christian Disengagement from the World," *Journal of Church and State* 18 (1976): 217.

35. Ibid.

36. Frank Stagg, "Biblical Perspectives on the Single Person," 5–19.

37. Frank Stagg and Evelyn Stagg, *Woman in the World of Jesus* (Philadelphia: Westminster Press, 1973).

38. Cf. Frank Stagg, "The Domestic Code and Final Appeal: Ephesians 5:21–6:24," *Review and Expositor* 76 (Fall 1979): 543f.

39. Frank Stagg, *The Bible Speaks on Aging* (Nashville: Broadman Press, 1981).

40. Ralph Herring, Frank Stagg, et al., *How to Understand the Bible* (Nashville: Broadman Press, 1974), 132.

41. See an excellent summary and theological evaluation of these views in Raymond Brown's 1986 Presidential Address delivered at the Forty-first General Meeting of *Studiorum Novi Testamenti Societas,* printed in *New Testament Studies* 33 (1987): 321–43.

42. I read Hebrews 6:6 not as an actual reference to the subjective recrucifixion of Christ on the part of those who turned away from him but as a hypothetical reference to something which cannot in fact happen; indeed, no other author in all the New Testament makes it more clear than the author of Hebrews that Christ has suffered but once and indeed cannot die again.

43. Stagg, "Salvation in Synoptic Tradition," 357; Stagg, "Reassessing the Gospels," 192f.

44. Ibid.

45. Stagg, "Eschatology," 382.

46. Ibid., 385.

47. Stagg, "The Mind in Christ Jesus," 340–43.

48. Stagg, *New Testament Theology,* 21; Staff, "The Plight of Jew and Gentile," 402f.; Stagg, "Adam, Christ, and Us," passim.

49. Calvin Schoonhoven, *The Wrath of Heaven* (Grand Rapids, Mich.: Eerdmans, 1966), 17ff.; for compelling arguments that Paul cannot be understood apart from the apocalyptic texture and core of his thought cf. J. Christaan Beker, *Paul the Apostle* (Philadelphia: Fortress Press, 1980).

50. Stagg, "Reassessing the Gospels," 190; Stagg, "Southern Baptist Theology Today," 23–28; Stagg, "The Concept of Messiah," 252–54; Stagg, *The Doctrine of Christ* (Nashville: Convention Press, 1984), 90–99.

51. Frank Stagg, *The Holy Spirit Today* (Nashville: Broadman Press, 1973), 17–19.

52. Stagg, "Southern Baptist Theology Today," 26; Stagg, *The Doctrine of Christ,* 91–95; cf. Stagg, "Matthew," in The Broadman Bible Commentary, ed. Clifton J. Allen, vol. 8 (Nashville: Broadman Press, 1969), 252ff.; Stagg, "The Concept of Messiah," 254.

53. Stagg, "The Christology of Matthew," 461; Stagg, *The Doctrine of Christ,* 99.

54. See note 52.

Chapter 15, "Carl F. H. Henry," by R. Albert Mohler Jr.

1. As Henry recalled: "In respect to church participation we were Christmas and Easter Christians. My father was Lutheran by family heritage and my mother Roman Catholic. But we had no family prayers, no grace at table, no Bible in our home." See Carl F. H. Henry, *Confessions of a Theologian: An Autobiography* (Waco: Word Books, 1986), 17–18.

2. The Oxford Group was an evangelistic and devotional movement founded by Frank Buchman. The Group's emphasis on personal spiritual direction caused a considerable degree of controversy among evangelicals. Though members of the group were instrumental in his conversion, Henry was never to join the movement.

3. Clark's tenure at Wheaton came to an end when his Calvinism became an issue of controversy in the evangelistically charged community of the college and its supporters. He was later to teach at Butler University in Indianapolis and Covenant College in Tennessee.

4. Born to the Henrys were Paul Brentwood (1942) and Carol Jennifer (1944). Both children followed their parents in academic training. Carol was to become a musician, and Paul, who taught political science at Calvin College for some years, was later elected to the U. S. House of Representatives, holding the Grand Rapids seat once held by Gerald R. Ford.

5. Henry identified his mentors at Northern Seminary as Peder Stiasen, Julius R. Mantey, Ernest E. Smith, Faris D. Whitesell, William Emmett Powers, William Fouts, and J. N. D. Rodeheaver. In roughly the same period he was also to study at Indiana University under W. Harry Jellema and Henry Veitch. Jellema, a Calvinist, was to influence Henry and be honored

as one of "three men of Athens" to whom Henry dedicated his first foray in theology, *Remaking the Modern Mind.* The other two so honored were Gordon Clark and Cornelius Van Til.

6. The history and development of Fuller Seminary is well documented by George M. Marsden in *Reforming Fundamentalism: Fuller Seminary and the New Evangelicalism* (Grand Rapids, Mich.: Eerdmans, 1987). Marsden's history is a model of interpretive historiography and provides critical insights into the development of American evangelicalism as seen through the history of one of its primary institutions. The critical role played by Carl F. H. Henry in Fuller's early struggles is documented by Marsden.

7. See Henry, *Confessions of a Theologian,* 141–302.

8. Carl F. H. Henry, *The Uneasy Conscience of Modern Fundamentalism* (Grand Rapids, Mich.: Eerdmans, 1947). Henry lamented the loss of evangelical social concern and compared the fundamentalist movement to the priest and Levite in the parable of the good Samaritan, "by-passing suffering humanity." He called for a "New Reformation" to correct this failure in fundamentalism. Nevertheless, this prescription, matched with the lack of separatism among the "new evangelicals," brought on an eventual break with the older fundamentalist movement. See Farley R Butler, "Billy Graham and the End of Evangelical Unity" (Ph.D. diss., University of Florida, 1976).

9. Others among the "new evangelicals" were Bernard Ramm, Edward John Carnell, Harold J. Ockenga, and Vernon Grounds. The exact origin of the term *new evangelical* is unclear, though it is generally attributed to Ockenga and linked to his 1947 convocation address at Fuller Seminary. See Harold J. Ockenga, "From Fundamentalism, Through New Evangelicalism, to Evangelicalism," *Evangelical Roots,* ed. Kenneth S. Kantzer (Nashville: Thomas Nelson, 1978), 35–48. Though Henry evidently did not coin the term, its popularization and conceptualization were largely due to his efforts. See especially Carl F. H. Henry, "The Vigor of the New Evangelicalism," *Christian Life and Times,* January 1948, 30–32; March 1948, 35–38, 85; April 1948, 32–35, 65–69.

10. Henry's experience at Fuller was mixed. Though fully in agreement with the vision of its founding, he was aware of a lack of consensus among the faculty concerning its future direction.

11. A review of *Christianity Today* under Henry's leadership reveals his commitment to evangelical orthodoxy paired with a missionary zeal to reach beyond the evangelical movement.

12. For Henry's evaluation of the congress, see his *Evangelicals at the Brink of Crisis: Significance of the World Congress on Evangelism* (Waco: Word Books, 1967). Henry's optimism was tempered by concerns that evangelicalism would miss a critical opportunity for influence and extension. He wrote of the event as indicative of evangelicalism's "new prominence," as well as "a brink of decision."

13. Under Henry's editorship the magazine was directed toward a readership of trained pastors and therefore dealt with a wide array of theological issues. The magazine is now marketed to a general readership and has lost much of its intellectual content.

14. As Henry commented: "The masses are craving an *authoritative word*—not the discredited probability of the modernist mood. But the downfall of liberalism need not be the rise of evangelicalism; rather, it may be the forerunner of a secularism even worse than that of recent decades." See *Christian Life,* April 1948, 69.

15. Though liberalism was understood to be the foe, the evangelicals, and Henry among them, rejected the tendency of the fundamentalists to reduce theology "to simple cliches, without much thought of their profounder systematic implications." See Carl F. H. Henry, *Evangelical Responsibility in Contemporary Theology* (Grand Rapids, Mich.: Eerdmans, 1957), 33. Over twenty years later, Henry responded to James Barr: "American evangelicals have for a generation distinguished between what is desirable and what is undesirable in fundamentalism. We did not have to wait until 1977 [the publication of Barr's *Fundamentalism*] and Barr to realize that fundamentalist preaching is often exegetically shallow, that

fundamentalism uncritically elevated certain prudish traditions to scriptural status, that not infrequently its spokesmen argue that historical criticism 'inevitably' tears apart the whole fabric of faith, and that many fundamentalists tend to appropriate selected bits of nonevangelical scholarship rather than to initiate creative studies, so that serious students all too often turn to mediating scholars for productive challenge." See Carl F. H. Henry, "Those Incomprehensible British Fundamentalists," *Christianity Today*, 2 June 1978.

16. This growing sense of a missed opportunity is evident throughout Henry's later writings and can be traced to his indictment of evangelicalism's failure to fulfill the promise of the Berlin Congress. In the 1970s and 1980s, Henry released a steady stream of jeremiads intended to invigorate the evangelical movement in both its theological commitments and its engagement with alternative theological systems. See, for example, Carl F. H. Henry, *Evangelicals in Search of Identity* (Waco: Word Books, 1976); *A Plea for Evangelical Demonstration* (Grand Rapids, Mich.: Baker Book House, 1971); and "The Evangelical Prospect in America," the concluding chapter to his *Confessions of a Theologian*, 381–407. See also the series of interviews with Henry published as *Conversations with Carl Henry: Christianity for Today* (Lewiston, N.Y.: Edwin Mellen Press, 1986).

17. Carl F. H. Henry, *Remaking the Modern Mind* (Grand Rapids, Mich.: Eerdmans, 1946), 19.

18. Carl F. H. Henry, *The Protestant Dilemma: An Analysis of the Current Impasse in Theology* (Grand Rapids, Mich.: Eerdmans, 1948).

19. Carl F. H. Henry, *Fifty Years of Protestant Theology* (Boston: W. A. Wilde, 1950); *The Drift of Western Thought* (Grand Rapids, Mich.: Eerdmans, 1951); *Notes on the Doctrine of God* (Boston: W. A. Wilde, 1948).

20. See Carl F. H. Henry, *Personal Idealism and Strong's Theology* (Wheaton, Ill.: Van Kampen Press, 1951). Though this pattern of thought is evident in Henry's earliest writings, its basis is most clearly seen in this study, the published version of his Boston University dissertation under Edgar S. Brightman.

21. Henry, *Fifty Years*, 37.

22. Carl F. H. Henry, "Between Barth and Bultmann," *Christianity Today*, 8 May 1961, 24–26; "The Deterioration of Barth's Defenses," *Christianity Today*, 9 October 1964, 16–19; "The Pale Ghost of Barth," *Christianity Today*, 12 February 1971, 40–43; "Wintertime in European Theology," *Christianity Today*, 5 December 1960, 12–14.

23. For a thorough analysis of Henry's interaction with Karl Barth, see Richard Albert Mohler Jr., "Evangelical Theology and Karl Barth: Representative Models of Response" (Ph.D. diss., The Southern Baptist Theological Seminary, 1989), 107–34.

24. Carl F. H. Henry, "The Stunted God of Process Theology," *Process Theology*, ed. Ronald H. Nash (Grand Rapids, Mich.: Baker Book House, 1987), 357–76; "Liberation Theology and the Scriptures," *Liberation Theology*, ed. Ronald H. Nash (Milford, Mich.: Mott Media, 1984), 187–202.

25. His responses to alternative theological systems take many forms, among them the following: Carl F. H. Henry, "Narrative Theology: An Evangelical Appraisal," *Trinity Journal* 8 (1987): 3019; "Theology and Biblical Authority: A Review Article," *Journal of the Evangelical Theological Society* 19 (1976): 315–23 (a response to David Kelsey, *The Uses of Scripture in Recent Theology*); "The Priority of Divine Revelation: A Review Article," *Journal of the Evangelical Theological Society* 27 (1984): 77–92 (a response to Avery Dulles, *Models of Revelation*); "The Cultural Relativizing of Revelation," *Trinity Journal* 1 ns (1980): 153–64 (a response to Charles Kraft, *Christianity in Culture*).

26. Henry, "Narrative Theology" and "The Cultural Relativizing of Revelation." See also the interesting exchange between Henry and Mark Ellingsen. Ellingsen, a mainline Protestant, called for a dialogue and eventual merging of the evangelical and mainline movements based in a form of narrative theology. See Mark Ellingsen, *The Evangelical Movement: Growth, Impact, Controversy, Dialog (GRA)* (Minneapolis: Augsburg Publishing House, 1988), and Henry's response in "Where Will Evangelicals Cast Their Lot?" *This World* 18 (1987): 3–11.

27. This controversy is, of course, as old as Christian theology itself, but is of particular importance among the evangelicals. The most ardent and influential presuppositionalist of the twentieth century was Cornelius Van Til, who influenced generations of evangelicals with his unyielding rejection of evidentialist apologetics. The evidentialist tradition has also been a major influence in the evangelical movement, with neo-Thomists such as Norman Geisler and Reformed figures such as John Gerstner influencing large segments of conservative Protestantism.

28. See Henry, *GRA*, 1:181–87. See also his Rutherford Lecture, "Presuppositionalism and Theological Method."

29. Henry states: "Evidentialists who disparage the primacy of faith do no special service to evangelical theology. The fact is, that to affirm the priority of faith need not mean, as all presuppositionalists are charged with holding, that truth rests on faith alone *apart from, instead of,* or *over against* reason. The emphasis that faith precedes reason in establishing certain basic truths does not require that reason and evidence are not irrelevant to authentic faith" ("Presuppositionalism and Theological Method," 4).

30. During his doctoral studies at Northern Baptist Seminary, Henry and his fellow graduate students had announced their intention to produce a systematic theology which would replace the work of A. H. Strong in Baptist seminaries.

31. Henry, *GRA*, 1:215.

32. Ibid., 2:18.

33. Ibid., 79.

34. "Anyone who denies this doctrine places himself not only in unmistakable contradiction to the Bible and to the great theological traditions of Christendom that flow from its teaching, but also against the living God's disclosure in cosmic reality and in mankind to which Scripture testifies (Rom. 1:19–21)" (Henry, *GRA*, 2:83–84). Further, "Since human beings are culpable sinners because of revolt against light, to deny general revelation would destroy the basis of moral and spiritual accountability" (Henry, *GRA*, 2:85).

35. In so doing Henry places himself against certain strands of neoorthodoxy, modern language philosophy, and analytic philosophy, though he shows himself thoroughly conversant with these positions. See Henry, *GRA*, 3 and 4.

36. Henry, *GRA*, 4:7.

37. As Henry demonstrates, any denial of propositional truth requires a *propositional* denial. See his treatment of this issue in *GRA*, 3:455–81.

38. Note that Henry criticizes the Chicago Statement on Biblical Inerrancy (1978) which "strenuously disavows dictation, but unfortunately in some passages suggests divine causation of each and every word choice." See *GRA*, 4:141.

39. Ibid., 129–61.

40. Ibid., 166–67.

41. See Carl F. H. Henry, *Conversations with Carl Henry: Christianity for Today* (Lewiston, N.Y.: Edwin Mellen Press, 1986), esp. 23–30. Henry's careful distinction at this point should not be missed. While claiming inerrancy as a critical component of an evangelical doctrine of Scripture, Henry nevertheless recognized that inerrancy is not the *first* claim to be made for the biblical text. An affirmation of inerrancy should not, in his mind, be the *sine qua non* of evangelical identity. It is critical enough to function as a test of evangelical *consistency* but cannot alone bear the weight of a test of evangelical *authenticity*. To allow this would be to identify critical allies in the fight for biblical authority as nonevangelicals. As Henry asserts: "I think it highly unfortunate that the *primary* thing that should now be said about men like F. F. Bruce and [G. C.] Berkouwer, men who have made significant contributions to the conservative position—even though we might have hoped for somewhat more from them—is that they are not authentic evangelicals because of their position at this one point." See *Conversations,* 24.

42. Henry, *GRA*, 5:21.

43. Ibid., 130.

44. Ibid., 3:9.

45. Carl F. H. Henry, *Christian Personal Ethics* (Grand Rapids, Mich.: Eerdmans, 1956); *Aspects of Christian Social Ethics* (Grand Rapids: Eerdmans, 1964); and ed., *Dictionary of Christian Ethics* (Grand Rapids, Mich.: Baker Book House).

46. See the collections of lectures, sermons, etc. in Carl F. H. Henry, *The Christian Mindset in a Secular Society* (Portland, Oreg.: Multnomah Press, 1978); *Christian Countermoves in a Decadent Culture* (Portland, Oreg.: Multnomah Press, 1986); and *Twilight of a Great Civilization: The Drift Toward Neo-Paganism* (Westchester, Ill.: Crossway Books, 1988).

47. Note, for example, the assessment offered by William Abraham of Southern Methodist University. Abraham, who represents the Wesleyan tradition within evangelicalism, charged that *God, Revelation and Authority is* "over three thousand pages of turgid scholasticism." See William Abraham, *The Coming Great Revival* (San Francisco: Harper and Row, 1984), 37. This statement indicates something of the great divide between those who define evangelicalism primarily by a set of theological commitments and those who point instead to an evangelical faith experience and concern for personal holiness. To be fair, Henry has evidenced a concern for both dimensions but has given the cognitive dimension primary attention in his writings.

48. Thomas Reginald McNeal's doctoral dissertation at Southwestern Seminary identified Henry as a Thomist and termed his theological method "apologetic presuppositionalism." As he stated: "The thesis of this dissertation is that Henry's apologetic presuppositionalism represents a rationalistic theological methodology dominated by the priority of reason over faith." See Thomas Reginald McNeal, "A Critical Analysis of the Doctrine of God in the Theology of Carl F. H. Henry." (Ph.D. diss., Southwestern Baptist Theological Seminary, 1986), 1. Yet Henry has always stressed that revelation is *prior* to both reason and faith, even as he has championed the role of reason and rationality in human thought. Henry has provided a key to understanding this issue through his models of Tertullian, Thomas Aquinas, and Augustine, with Augustine representing Henry's own position of reason working upon divine revelation. Henry may be *rationalistic,* if by this we indicate his reliance upon reason as an instrument of understanding; but he is not a *rationalist,* if by this he is thought to place reason prior to revelation. As Henry stated: "To be sure, evangelicals need not tremble and take to the hills whenever others charge us with rationalism, since not every meaning of the term is objectionable; those who glory in the irrational, superrational, or subrational ought to be challenged head-on" (Henry, *GRA* 3:480).

49. Carl F. H. Henry, "Twenty Years a Baptist," *Foundations,* 47.

50. Ibid., 53.

51. Ibid., 54. He continued: "Our century is surrounded and crowded, rather, by the insistent problem: in thought and in practice does the quantitative and qualitative value ascribed to the Word, incarnate and written, produce both a Christian and a Baptist? The turmoil over Baptist distinctives, within Baptist distractions, yields ambiguous Baptist directives."

52. Nelson Price, 1987 president of the Pastors' Conference, presented Henry a plaque celebrating his influence and claiming his identity as a Southern Baptist. Henry has also served as a visiting professor at The Southern Baptist Theological Seminary and has delivered lectureship at New Orleans Baptist Seminary and Southeastern Baptist Theological Seminary, among others.

53. E. G. Homrighausen, Review of a *Plea for Evangelical Demonstration* by Carl F. H. Henry, *Princeton Seminary Bulletin* 65 (July 1972): 96.

Chapter 16, "James Leo Garrett Jr.," by Paul A. Basden

1. James L. Garrett Jr., "Major Emphases in Baptist Theology," *Southwestern Journal of Theology* 37 (Summer 1995): 36–46. See also "Who Are the Baptists?" *The Baylor Line* 47 (June 1985): 11–15.

2. "Major Emphases in Baptist Theology," 37.

3. Ibid.

4. Ibid., 44.

5. Ibid., 45.

6. James L. Garrett Jr., ed., *Baptist Relations with Other Christians* (Valley Forge, Pa.: Judson Press, 1974), 195. This was a volume of Baptist World Alliance study commission papers. Garrett's long-term responsibilities with the BWA began in 1968.

7. *Baptist History and Heritage* 31 (October 1996): 6–16.

8. Ibid., 7.

9. Ibid., 9.

10. Ibid., 10.

11. Ibid., 12.

12. Ibid., 13.

13. Ibid., 11.

14. James L. Garrett Jr., *Baptists and Roman Catholicism*, (Nashville: Broadman Press, 1965).

15. Ibid., 7.

16. Ibid., 7–27.

17. Ibid., 35.

18. Ibid., 45.

19. Ibid., 5.

20. James L. Garrett Jr., *The Concept of the Believers' Church* (Scottsdale, Pa.: Herald Press, 1969). For more insights on Garrett's ecumenism, see William L. Pitts, "The Relation of Baptists to Other Churches," in *The People of God: Essays on the Believers' Church*, ed. Paul A. Basden and David S. Dockery (Nashville: Broadman Press, 1991), 235–50. This book was a *festschrift* for Garrett.

21. James Leo Garrett Jr., "Seeking a Regenerate Church Membership," *Southwestern Journal of Theology* 3 (April 1961): 25.

22. Ibid., 27.

23. Ibid., 29.

24. Ibid., 30.

25. James Leo Garrett Jr., *Baptist Church Discipline*, (Nashville: Broadman Press, 1962).

26. Ibid., 1.

27. Ibid., 25.

28. James L. Garrett Jr., "The Biblical Doctrine of the Priesthood of the People of God," *New Testament Studies: Essays in Honor of Ray Summers in His Sixty-Fifth Year*, ed. Huber L. Drumwright and Curtis Vaughan (Waco, Tx.: Markham Press Fund of Baylor University Press, 1975), 137–49; "The Pre-Cyprianic Doctrine of the Priesthood of All Christians," *Continuity and Discontinuity in Church History: Essays Presented to George Hunston Williams on the Occasion of His 65th Birthday*, ed. Forrester Church and Timothy George, Studies in the History of Christian Thought, vol. 19 (Leiden: E.J. Brill, 1979), 45–61; and "The Priesthood of All Christians: From Cyprian to John Chrysostom," *Southwestern Journal of Theology* 30 (Spring 1988): 22–33.

29. "The Biblical Doctrine of the Priesthood of the People of God," 137.

30. Ibid., 149.

31. James L. Garrett Jr., "The 'No . . . Establishment' Clause of the First Amendment: Retrospect and Prospect," *Journal of Church and State* 17 (Winter 1975): 13.

32. James L. Garrett Jr., "The 'Free Exercise' Clause of the First Amendment: Retrospect and Prospect," *Journal of Church and State* 17 (Autumn 1975): 397.

33. James L. Garrett Jr., "The Dialectic of Romans 13:1–7 and Revelation 13: Part 1," *Journal of Church and State* 18 (Autumn 1976): 441.

34. James L. Garrett Jr., "The Dialectic of Romans 13:1–7 and Revelation 13: Part 2," *Journal of Church and State* 19 (Winter 1977): 20.

35. James Leo Garrett Jr., E. Glenn Hinson, and James E. Tull, *Are Southern Baptists "Evangelicals"?* (Macon, Ga.: Mercer University Press, 1983), vii–viii.

36. Ibid., vii.

37. Ibid., 35–43.

38. Ibid., 43–45.

39. Ibid., 62–63.

40. Ibid.

41. Ibid., 126 (italics his).

42. Ibid., 140.

43. Ibid., 147.

44. Ibid., 165.

45. Ibid., 173 (italics his).

46. Ibid., 182.

47. James L. Garrett Jr., "Are Southern Baptists 'Evangelicals'? A Further Reflection," *Southern Baptists and American Evangelicals: The Conversation Continues*, ed. David S. Dockery (Nashville: Broadman and Holman, 1993), 218–23.

48. James L. Garrett Jr., *Systematic Theology: Biblical, Historical, and Evangelical* (Grand Rapids: Eerdmans, 1990, 1995).

49. Ibid., 1:53.

50. Ibid., 1:90–91.

51. Ibid., 1:105.

52. Ibid., 1:121.

53. Ibid., 1:142.

54. Ibid., 1:167.

55. Ibid., 1:181.

56. Ibid., 1:181–82. On Garrett's doctrine of the Bible, see Dwight A. Moody, "The Bible," *Has Our Theology Changed? Southern Baptist Thought since 1845*, ed. Paul A. Basden (Nashville: Broadman & Holman, 1994), 7–40.

57. Garrett, *Systematic Theology*, 1:209.

58. Ibid., 2d ed., 1:264. In this context Garrett opines on the "openness of God" movement which, standing as an opposing view to traditional omniscience, suggests that God learned the future as humans help to create it. He warns evangelicals "not to place undue limits on God's knowledge because of the limits on our human understanding of the issue. We can be open to the view of middle knowledge as a potentially helpful *via media* between extremes" (ibid., 257).

59. Ibid., 1st ed., 1:228.

60. Ibid., 1:235.

61. Ibid., 1:239.

62. Ibid., 1:251.

63. "Christians can seek to 'de-patriarchalize' the language and concept of God as Father and yet to preserve the abidingly valid dimensions of divine fatherhood." *Systematic Theology*, 2d ed., 1:303.

64. Ibid., 1st ed., 1:261.

65. In his *Systematic Theology* (Philadelphia: Judson Press, 1907), Strong devotes 49 pages to the subject of God as Trinity. Garrett's 27 pages on the Trinity surpasses the page count in the standard systematic theologies written by Mullins, Conner, Moody, and even Erickson.

66. Garrett, *Systematic Theology*, 1:283.

67. Ibid., 1:298–301.

68. Ibid., 1:311.

69. Ibid., 1:314.

70. Ibid., 1:319.

71. Ibid., 1:400.

72. Garrett, *Systematic Theology,* 2d ed., 1:661.

73. Ibid., 663.

74. *Systematic Theology,* 1st ed., 1:543.

75. Ibid., 543.

76. Ibid., 1:595.

77. Ibid., 1:596.

78. Ibid., 2:167–68.

79. Ibid., 2:190.

80. Ibid., 2:192.

81. Ibid., 2:214–15.

82. Ibid., 2:443,447.

83. "Should Southern Baptists Adopt the Synod of Dort?" *Baptists Today,* 26 June 1997, 18–19.

84. Garrett, *Systematic Theology,* 2:793.

85. Ibid., 799.

86. Ibid., 807.

Chapter 17, "Millard J. Erickson," by Bradley G. Green

1. Much of the biographical information has been gleaned from personal conversations with Erickson, as well as from David S. Dockery's chapter on Erickson in the first edition of *Baptist Theologians,* ed. David S. Dockery and Timothy George (Nashville: Broadman Press, 1990).

2. Millard J. Erickson, *The Word Became Flesh: A Contemporary Incarnational Christology* (Grand Rapids: Baker Book House, 1991), 7.

3. Erickson has published more since the first edition of *Baptist Theologians* (1990), than in the entire rest of his career. His scholarly production in the last ten years is truly impressive.

4. A complete bibliography of Erickson's work is provided in *New Dimensions in Evangelical Thought: Essays in Honor of Millard J. Erickson,* ed. David S. Dockery (Downers Grove: InterVarsity Press, 1998), 451–55.

5. Millard J. Erickson, *The New Evangelical Theology* (Westwood, N.J.: Fleming H. Revell, 1968; London: Marshall, Morgan and Scott, 1969).

6. Joseph Fletcher, *Situation Ethics* (Philadelphia: Westminster Press, 1966).

7. After spending 127 pages critiquing relativistic ethics, Erickson offers his own contribution in the final chapter.

8. Baker republished this volume as *A Basic Guide to Eschatology: Making Sense of the Millennium* (1998). I am working from this recent edition for this essay.

9. From the endorsement on back cover of book.

10. See Erickson, *The New Evangelical Theology,* 13–45.

11. Ibid., 225–27. It is intriguing to note that Erickson's concerns and reflections in that early volume were rather insightful. Evangelicalism has indeed struggled with what constitutes the appropriate boundaries of Evangelicalism, and many Evangelicals (including Erickson's first professor of theology, Bernard Ramm) have moved from a traditionally conservative Evangelical position toward neoorthodoxy. Indeed, Erickson's recent work (specifically *The Evangelical Left* and *Postmodernizing the Faith*) engages virtually the identical concerns as raised in *The New Evangelical Theology.*

12. William Hordern, "Tribute to Millard J. Erickson," *New Dimensions in Evangelical Thought: Essays in Honor of Millard J. Erickson,* ed. David S. Dockery (Downers Grove, Ill.: InterVarsity Press, 1998), 14.

13. The relationship with Pannenburg is of course different, since Erickson's "student" relationship with Pannenburg took place during Erickson's 1976 sabbatical.

14. In personal conversation with Erickson, he noted that he probably could have learned more information by staying at home and reading through Pannenburg's corpus. However, he remarked that simply seeing how Pannenburg's theological mind worked through an issue was invaluable for his own theological thinking.

15. Erickson, *Christian Theology*, 112ff.; idem, *The Word Became Flesh*, 13. For Hordern's own articulation of this basic paradigm, see his "Introduction," *New Directions in Theology Today*, vol. 1 (Philadelphia: Westminster, 1966).

16. Erickson, *Christian Theology*, 66.

17. Ibid., 66–79.

18. Ibid., 68–69.

19. We here for the most part look at Erickson's format as found in *Christian Theology*. We note that while Erickson does not always follow *chronologically* the points we have listed, he nonetheless does generally follow *thematically* the points we are discussing here.

20. Erickson *Christian Theology*, 684–93.

21. Ibid., 846–48.

22. Ibid., 693–98.

23. Ibid., 783–800.

24. Ibid., 698–703.

25. Ibid., 378–84.

26. Ibid.

27. Ibid., 386.

28. Ibid., 882.

29. Ibid., 196.

30. Ibid., 214–20.

31. Ibid., 233–34.

32. Ibid., 225.

33. Ibid.

34. Ibid., 227.

35. Since the last edition of *Baptist Theologians* (pp. 265–344), we now, in addition to the sections of *Christian Theology* devoted to the doctrine of God, can turn to Erickson's *God the Father Almighty* to see Erickson's more complete doctrine of God.

36. Erickson, *Christian Theology*, 265–300.

37. Erickson devotes one chapter each (chapters 2–4) to Pluralism, Process Thought, and Free Will Theism. In personal communication with Erickson, he has commented that the emergence of these types of trends in contemporary theology motivated him to write *God the Father Almighty*.

38. Erickson, *God the Father Almighty*, 107.

39. Ibid., 127f. Erickson offers the analogy between (1) transcendence/immanence and (2) atemporal timelessness/temporal eternality somewhat tentatively, suggesting that this *might* be the case.

40. Ibid., chapter 7 (quote from p. 150).

41. Ibid., 171.

42. Ibid., 173.

43. Ibid., 216.

44. Ibid., 237.

45. Ibid., 239–58.

46. Ibid., 356–62. It is worth noting that while on the doctrine of providence the adjective *modified* (in "modified Calvinism"), is perhaps overstated; in terms of soteriology Erickson's Calvinism is genuinely "modified." That is, Erickson's view of God's providence and foreordination, to this writer, yields little ground to options which would limit in any way God's foreordination of all things. On the other hand, in relation to the atonement and salvation, Erickson affirms a general atonement (the benefits of which the Holy Spirit efficaciously applies to the elect), and contends, with Arminianism, that faith precedes regeneration

(contra the traditionally Reformed view that God regenerates a sinner logically "before" faith). Clark Pinnock considers Erickson's Calvinism to be "very diluted," and states that on the atonement "Erickson is treading on Arminian ground." See Pinnock's review of all three volumes of *Christian Theology,* "Erickson's Three-Volume *Magnum Opus,*" *TSF Bulletin* (Jan-Feb 1986): 29–30.

47. Erickson, *Christian Theology,* 346.

48. Ibid., 345.

49. Ibid., 358, footnote 11.

50. Ibid., 477–84.

51. Ibid., 474–77.

52. Ibid., 513.

53. Ibid., 512–15.

54. Ibid., 636.

55. Ibid., 637.

56. Ibid., 638–39.

57. In *The Word Became Flesh,* 10, Erickson writes: "In a sense, this volume is an attempt to do for our time what the Chalcedonian statement did for its time."

58. Erickson *Christian Theology,* 555.

59. Ibid., 555–61.

60. Ibid., 762–69.

61. Ibid., 769–79.

62. Ibid., 819.

63. Ibid., 826.

64. Ibid. We ask the question here and not in the critique section below (since this question is over a particular point of doctrine rather than broad tendencies in Erickson's thought and writing) whether this emphasis on the decrees is helpful. I have been reading Erickson for years, and this construal of the extent of the atonement continues to puzzle me. No matter where one lands on the order of the decrees, the atonement took place *in time,* and the question of the extent of the atonement (which is probably more helpfully construed as a question regarding the *nature* of the atonement—an emphasis which is perhaps not emphasized enough in Erickson's treatment) has to do not simply with God's intention in eternity but with what was happening on the cross *in time* when Christ died. It seems to this writer that Erickson's emphasis on the decrees diverts attention from the crucial issue of Christ's work in time, indeed, from what God was doing in Christ's work on the cross in time.

65. Ibid., 832–35.

66. Ibid., 835, 930ff.

67. Ibid., 905.

68. Ibid., 924–27.

69. Erickson here does not want to be accused of teaching that faith is somehow initiated solely by the unbeliever. Thus, effectual calling serves in Erickson's theology much like regeneration serves in traditional Reformed construals of the order of salvation and of the nature of faith.

70. Erickson, *Christian Theology,* 929–46.

71. Ibid., 947–1,002.

72. Ibid., 845–88.

73. Ibid., 881–82.

74. Ibid., 1,026.

75. Ibid., 1,034.

76. Ibid.

77. Ibid., 1,042.

78. Ibid., 1,043.

79. Ibid., 1,048.

80. Ibid., 1,048–49.

81. Ibid., 1,051–67.

82. Ibid., 1,121–23.

83. Ibid., 1,183.

84. That is, Erickson (*Christian Theology,* 1,190–92), contra many dispensationalists, affirms that the Second Coming is one event and should not be construed in terms of an initial "coming for" the saints and a later "coming with" the saints.

85. Ibid., 1,185–92.

86. Ibid., 1,194–1,200. Erickson suggests that whereas Christ's exaltation took multiple steps (Resurrection, followed by Ascension, which produced a second substantive change in Christ's state), believers are transformed to their glorious state in the one event of the future resurrection (1, 199).

87. Ibid., 1,205–1,224.

88. Ibid., 1,234.

89. Ibid., 1,231–32.

90. Ibid., 1,234–40. See Erickson, *How Shall They Be Saved?* (217–32), where Erickson argues against annihilationism, and for conscious and everlasting punishment for unbelievers. Also see Erickson, *The Evangelical Mind and Heart,* (129–52), where Erickson also argues for conscious and everlasting punishment, rejects arguments for salvation by implicit faith (as elicited by general revelation), and postmortem evangelism.

91. Erickson, *Evangelical Interpretation,* 11–54.

92. Erickson, *The Evangelical Left,* 145–47.

93. Ibid., 43–45.

94. Erickson focuses on four key figures as "postconservative evangelicals": Stanley Grenz, James McClendon, Clark Pinnock, and Bernard Ramm. In this essay I use the terms "postconservatives" or "postconservative Evangelicals" as Erickson does, to refer to this general group or movement.

95. Ibid., 43–44, 56–59.

96. Erickson, *Postmodernizing the Faith,* 13. To those who would balk at the idea that postmodernism is an ideology and who would contend that postmodernism is essentially *anti*-ideological, it should be noted that Erickson is aware of the diverse ways of viewing and defining postmodernism. Here he is simply noting that any worthwhile discussion of postmodernism cannot simply treat it as an era of time but must pay attention to the various ideas, thoughts, philosophies, etc., which in general fall under the (often bewildering) rubric of "postmodernism."

97. Ibid., 19–20. Erickson's affirmation of the strengths of "soft" postmodernism should not be misconstrued to mean that Erickson sees something terribly profound in "soft" postmodernism. Erickson *also* contends that the strengths of "soft" postmodernism (the rejection of logical positivism, behaviorism, and falsely reductionistic scientific approaches to reality) are not unique to "soft" postmodernism and can be found in such theologians as Carl F. H. Henry (who by most "postconservatives" is considered to be a paradigmatically *modern* theologian). See Erickson, *Postmodernizing the Faith,* 151–57.

98. Ibid., 19.

99. Ibid. As noted above, Erickson is working on a more complete response to postmodernism. *Postmodernizing the Faith* and to a lesser extent *The Evangelical Left* are preliminary works which nonetheless show the general contour of Erickson's thought, but his forthcoming larger work will more fully respond to this current trend.

100. This writer has been fortunate enough to be a student of Erickson's. Anyone who has been a student of Erickson can attest to his talents and gifts as a gifted communicator and teacher.

101. This writer has a friend who used a different systematic theology text in seminary, but when it came time for understanding the material and mastering theological content for exams, he and others were quick to study Erickson! Erickson's *Christian Theology* is one of

the few texts written by a conservative Evangelical that has been used outside of conservative Evangelical circles. See Hordern, "Tribute to Millard J. Erickson," 15.

102. This is most thoroughly seen in *The Word Made Flesh,* especially 531–77.

103. Erickson, *Christian Theology,* 77–78.

104. It should be noted that Erickson draws a number of these theological connections throughout *Christian Theology,* especially in the "implications" section which concludes many chapters of *Christian Theology.* However, it would have been more helpful if his central motif could have been used more to help weave these theological connections throughout the text.

105. Erickson, *Christian Theology,* 762–69.

106. It is striking how often younger Evangelicals wish to distance themselves from persons such as Carl F. H. Henry. This can be seen in any number of works, for example: Stanley J. Grenz and Roger Olson, *Twentieth-Century Theology* (Downers Grove: InterVarsity Press, 1992), devote an entire chapter to Henry, where the overall impression is a negative one.

107. Again, even a brief perusal of contemporary theological literature will expose one to the rage against "rationalism" and "modernity." Perhaps the key problem is that rarely is there a distinction made between (1) *rationalism* (i.e., when the use of reason is lifted to a point above faith or is treated as an autonomous tool or reality to be used without regard or in defiance of revelation and other ways of knowing) and (2) being *rational* (i.e., using one's reason to attempt to understand, penetrate, or order reality). The charge of "rationalism" is often sloppily made, and the term should be carefully defined when levied as a criticism.

Chapter 18, "Looking Back, Looking Ahead," by David S. Dockery

1. H. Leon McBeth, *The Baptist Heritage* (Nashville: Broadman, 1987), 30; cf. Timothy George, *John Robinson and the English Separatist Tradition* (Macon, Ga.: Mercer, 1982).

2. McBeth, *Baptist Heritage,* 32–39.

3. Ibid., 39–44.

4. Ibid., 44–48.

5. Cf. Edmund S. Morgan, *Roger Williams: The Church and State* (New York: Harcourt, Brace and World, 1967).

6. Cf. William L. Lumpkin, *Baptist Confessions of Faith* (Valley Forge, Pa: Judson, 1959).

7. Cf. James Leo Garrett Jr., "History of Baptist Theology," *Encyclopedia of Southern Baptists* (4 vols., Nashville: Broadman, 1958–82), 2:1412–13. On the point of "hyper-Calvinism," see the discussion in Thomas J. Nettles, *By His Grace and for His Glory* (Grand Rapids: Baker, 1986) and Curt Daniel, "Hyper-Calvinism and John Gill," Ph.D. diss., University of Edinburgh, 1983.

8. McBeth, *The Baptist Heritage,* 154; also cf. William H. Brackney, "Dan Taylor," *The Baptists* (New York: Greenwood, 1988), 271–72.

9. Cf. E. A. Holmes, "George Leile: Negro Slavery's Prophet of Deliverance," *Foundations* 9 (1966), 333–45.

10. Cf. N. A. Baxter, "Thomas Baldwin: Boston Baptist Preacher," *The Chronicle* 19 (1956): 28–35.

11. Cf. H. W. Thompson, *Luther Rice: Believer in Tomorrow* (Nashville: Broadman, 1983).

12. Edwin S. Gaustad, "The Backus-Leland Tradition," *Foundations* 2 (1959), 131–52; also cf. Brad Creed, "John Leland: American Prophet of Religious Individualism," Ph.D. diss., Southwestern Baptist Theological Seminary, 1986.

13. Cf. Homer L. Grice and R. Paul Caudill, "Graves-Howell Controversy," *Encyclopedia of Southern Baptists,* 1:580–85; also see James E. Tull, *Shapers of Baptist Thought* (Valley Forge, Pa.: Judson, 1972), 129–51.

14. See the fuller treatment of J. P. Boyce by Timothy George, E. Y. Mullins by Fisher Humphreys, and W. T. Conner by James Leo Garrett in this volume.

15. See Mark Dever, "John L. Dagg," in this volume.

16. J. L. Dagg, *A Manual of Theology* (Charleston, S.C.: Southern Baptist Publications Society, 1858), 21.

17. Ibid.

18. J. P. Boyce, *Abstract of Systematic Theology* (Philadelphia: American Baptist Publication Society, 1887), 137.

19. Basil Manly Jr., *The Bible Doctrine of Inspiration* (New York: A. C. Armstrong and Sons, 1888), 15.

20. Ibid., 37.

21. McBeth, *The Baptist Heritage*, 596–600; cf. R. V. Pierard, "Theological Liberalism," *Evangelical Dictionary of Theology* (Grand Rapids: Baker, 1984), 633–35.

22. Cf. George W. Dollar, *A History of Fundamentalism in America* (Greenville, S.C.: Bob James University Press, 1973); George M. Marsden, *Fundamentalism and American Culture* (New York: Oxford, 1980); and C. Allyn Russell, *Voices of Fundamentalism* (Philadelphia: Westminster, 1976).

23. Bobby D. Compton, "J. Frank Norris and Southern Baptists," *Review and Expositor* 79 (1982): 63–84.

24. See John J. Carey, *Carlyle Marney: A Pilgrim's Progress* (Macon, Ga.: Mercer University Press, 1985).

25. See James M. Washington, ed., *A Testament of Hope: The Essential Writings of Martin Luther King Jr.* (San Francisco: Harper & Row, 1986).

26. J. M. Frost, ed., *Baptists: Why and Why Not* (Nashville: Baptist Sunday School Board, 1900).

27. Ibid., 12.

28. E. Y. Mullins, *The Christian Religion in Its Doctrinal Expression* (Philadelphia: Judson, 1917).

29. E. Y. Mullins, *Christianity at the Crossroads* (Nashville: Baptist Sunday School Board, 1924).

30. This material is located in the James P. Boyce Library at Southern Baptist Theological Seminary, Louisville, Kentucky.

31. W. T. Conner, *Revelation and God* (Nashville: Broadman, 1936).

32. W. T. Conner, *Christian Doctrine* (Nashville: Broadman, 1937).

33. See his review of *Fundamentals of Christianity* by F. C. Patton in *The Southwestern Evangel* 10 (May 1926): 45.

34. I am largely dependent for the understanding of Conner's works on James Leo Garrett Jr., "Theology of Walter Thomas Conner" (Th.D. diss., Southwestern Baptist Theological Seminary, 1954). Also see L. Russ Bush and Tom J. Nettles, *Baptists and the Bible* (Chicago: Moody, 1980).

35. W. B. Nowlin, *Fundamentals of the Faith* (Nashville: Baptist Sunday School Board, 1922).

36. J. J. Reeve, "My Experience with Higher Criticism," *The Fundamentals,* eds. R. A. Torrey and A. C. Dixon (1917; Grand Rapids: Baker, 1980).

37. R. G. Lee, *The Word of God: Not Broken and Not Bound* (Orlando: Christ for the World, 1930).

38. O. C. S. Wallace, *What Baptists Believe* (Nashville: Baptist Sunday School Board, 1934).

39. J. B. Weatherspoon, *The Book We Teach* (Nashville: Baptist Sunday School Board, 1934).

40. J. B. Tidwell, *Thinking Straight about the Bible or Is the Bible the Word of God* (Nashville: Broadman Press, 1936).

41. The 1961 controversy was over Ralph Elliott's *Message of Genesis* (Nashville: Broadman, 1961). The 1969 controversy focused on volume one of *The Broadman Bible Commentary* (Nashville: Broadman, 1969). The 1979 Southern Baptist Convention initiated

the conservative resurgence in the SBC and has been referred to as the "inerrancy controversy." See the response in Ralph H. Elliott, *The "Genesis Controversy" and Continuity in Southern Baptist Chaos* (Macon, Ga.: Mercer, 1993).

42. This is not to find fault with the programmatic emphases in themselves, for they helped to create the strong church programs that gave identity to Southern Baptists as a people and provided a framework for effective outreach.

43. W. R. White, "The Authoritative Criterion," *Baptist Distinctives* (Nashville: Convention Press, 1950).

44. J. B. Lawrence, "The Word and Words of God," *Southern Baptist Home Missions* (Nashville: Convention Press, 1952); idem, "The Bible, Our Creed," Southern Baptist Home Missions (Nashville: Convention Press, 1957).

45. J. Clyde Turner, "That Wonderful Book," *Things We Believe* (Nashville: Convention Press, 1956).

46. I have profited from the social analysis in James Spivey, "The Millennium," *Has Our Theology Changed,* ed. Paul A. Basden (Nashville: Broadman & Holman, 1994), 230–62.

47. The controversy surrounding *The Broadman Bible Commentary,* edited by Clifton J. Allen, should not detract from the recognition that Southern Baptists had now produced a major work of biblical scholarship that provided exegetical help for many pastors, students, and Bible teachers. The contributions of Roy Lee Honeycutt, Frank Stagg, William Hull, Jack MacGorman, Marvin Tate, and Ray Summers were of especially high quality, though their critical conclusions at times detracted from their overall positive contributions.

48. See the penetrating analysis of Stagg's theology in Robert Sloan, "Frank Stagg," *Baptist Theologians,* 496–517.

49. See Frank Stagg, *New Testament Theology* (Nashville: Broadman, 1962).

50. Ibid., 88; see the discussion in Paul A. Basden, "Predestination," *Has Our Theology Changed?* 62–65.

51. W. A. Criswell, *Why I Preach That the Bible Is Literally True* (Nashville: Broadman, 1969).

52. See Helen Lee Turner, "Fundamentalism in the Southern Baptist Convention: The Crystallization of a Millennialist Vision" (Ph.D. diss., University of Virginia, 1990).

53. See Conner, *Revelation and God.*

54. See Walter B. Shurden, *The Struggle for the Soul of the SBC* (Macon, Ga.: Mercer, 1992).

55. See Herschel Hobbs, *My Faith and Message* (Nashville: Broadman, 1993).

56. See J. D. Woodbridge, "William (Billy) Graham," *Dictionary of Baptists in America,* ed. Bill Leonard (Downers Grove: InterVarsity, 1994), 135–37.

57. See William Hull, "Shall We Call the Bible Infallible?" *The Baptist Program* (1970).

58. In addition to Schaeffer, Henry, and Packer, the early works of Clark Pinnock and Harold Lindsell's *Battle for the Bible* (Grand Rapids: Zondervan, 1976) were significantly influential. See the discussions in David S. Dockery, ed., *Southern Baptists and American Evangelicals* (Nashville: Broadman & Holman, 1991).

59. The use of historical criticism in and of itself can be very positive. However, some methodological approaches initially carried with them antisupernatural biases that resulted in denying the veracity of Holy Scripture. Such was the case with the *Message of Genesis.* Positive employment of critical approaches can be found in David A. Black and David S. Dockery, *New Testament Criticism and Interpretation* (Grand Rapids: Zondervan, 1991).

60. Both statements were produced and signed by more than one hundred Evangelical scholars. The product of the 1978 conference can be found in the volume edited by Norman Geisler, *Inerrancy* (Grand Rapids: Zondervan, 1979). The second conference resulted in the work edited by Earl Radmacher and Robert Preuss, *Hermeneutics, Inerrancy, and the Bible* (Grand Rapids: Zondervan, 1984). Southern Baptists who signed the "Inerrancy" (1978) statement included L. Russ Bush, Larry Walker, and L. Paige Patterson. Southern Baptists who signed the "Interpretation" (1982) statement included Bush, Walker, and David S. Dockery.

61. L. Russ Bush and Tom J. Nettles, *Baptists and the Bible* (Chicago: Moody, 1980).

62. See James, *Unfettered Word.*

63. See Roy L. Honeycutt, "Biblical Authority: A Treasured Baptist Heritage," *Review and Expositor* 83 (1986): 605–22.

64. See Jack Rogers and Donald K. McKim, *The Authority and Interpretation of the Bible* (San Francisco: Harper and Row, 1981).

65. Morris Ashcraft, *Christian Faith and Beliefs* (Nashville: Broadman, 1984).

66. Dale Moody, *The Word of Truth* (Grand Rapids: Eerdmans, 1981). Moody tended to equate inerrancy with a mechanical dictation view of inspiration and thus rejected the term *inerrancy.* He did, however, later give his affirmation to the 1978 Chicago Statement and its careful nuances.

67. See James Leo Garrett Jr., *Systematic Theology: Biblical, Historical, and Evangelical* (Grand Rapids: Eerdmans, 1990). Garrett follows Conner in not affirming a particular model of inspiration. He has, however, in this volume offered full and significant treatment on the doctrine of Scripture not before offered by a Southern Baptist systematic theologian. His conclusions are a sound, balanced, and evangelical synthesis of the works of W. T. Conner, A. H. Strong, and Millard J. Erickson. He confesses the truthworthiness of the Bible (p. 161) and maintains its full divine inspiration. He says, "The greatest single need with respect to the doctrine of inspiration is for balance between divine agency and human involvement" (p. 110). For a fine analysis of Garrett's work, see Paul Basden's chapter in this volume.

68. See Clark Pinnock, *A New Reformation* (Tigerville, S.C.: Jewel, 1968); idem, *Biblical Revelation* (Chicago: Moody, 1971).

69. See Carl F. H. Henry, *God, Revelation and Authority*, 6 vols. (Waco: Word, 1976–83). This magisterial set has been re-released by Crossway in 1998.

70. See Millard J. Erickson, *Christian Theology* (Grand Rapids: Baker, revised 1998).

71. For example, see David S. Dockery, *Christian Scripture* (Nashville: Broadman & Holman, 1995). Perhaps the most important indicator of this new consensus is the publication of the New American Commentary, eds. David S. Dockery and E. Ray Clendenen (Nashville: Broadman & Holman, 1991–).

72. See the discussions in *Baptists Why and Why Not Revisited,* edited by Timothy George and Richard Land (Nashville: Broadman & Holman, 1996). Also see the helpful articles and agenda setting discussions in the initial issues of *Southern Baptist Journal of Theology.* In addition see the 5–6 February 1998 Day-Higginbotham Lectures at Southwestern Baptist Seminary, "To God Be the Glory: Baptist Worship Then and Now," by David S. Dockery.

73. A very helpful balanced confession of faith was released in June 1999 called "The Gospel of Jesus Christ: An Evangelical Celebration." This statement can be very helpful for pulling together diverse perspectives by focusing on the common beliefs on essential matters. Several Southern Baptist leaders initially supported this statement, including the editors of this volume. In addition to those who formally signed the statement, the shaping of Southern Baptist theology in the next century will be influenced by Craig Blaising, Bruce Ware, R. Albert Mohler, Danny Akin, Stan Norman, Greg Thornbury, Brad Green, Chip Conyers, Alan Day, and Jim Patterson among many other fine young Christian thinkers who will lead through their teaching and publications.

74. Particularly important in this regard has been the work of Baptist pastor, John Piper. Also see future agenda issues in David S. Dockery, ed., *New Dimensions in Evangelical Thought* (Downers Grove: InterVarsity, 1998).

Name Index

410

Index by Cindy Meredith and Kathy Bragg